Money in Historical Perspective

A National Bureau
of Economic Research
Monograph

Money in Historical Perspective

Anna J. Schwartz

with an Introduction by
Michael D. Bordo and
Milton Friedman

 The University of Chicago Press

Chicago and London

ANNA J. SCHWARTZ is research associate emerita with the
National Bureau of Economic Research. MICHAEL D. BORDO is
professor of economics at the University of South Carolina and a
research associate at the National Bureau of Economic Research.
MILTON FRIEDMAN is a senior research fellow at the Hoover
Institution.

The University of Chicago Press, Chicago 60637
The University of Chicago Press, Ltd., London

Library of Congress Cataloging-in-Publication Data
Schwartz, Anna Jacobson.
  Money in historical perspective.

  (A National Bureau of Economic Research monograph)
  "These articles were presented to Anna at a
conference held in her honor in New York City on
October 6, 1987"—Pref.
  "Publications of Anna J. Schwartz"—P.
  Bibliography: p.
  Includes index.
  1. Money—United States—History. 2. Money—
Great Britain—History. 3. Monetary policy—History.
4. Gold standard—History. I. Title. II. Series.
HG538.S354   1987   332.4′9   87-5973
ISBN 0-226-74228-8

Relation of the Directors to the
Work and Publications of the
National Bureau of Economic Research

1. The object of the National Bureau of Economic Research is to ascertain and to present to the public important economic facts and their interpretation in a scientific and impartial manner. The Board of Directors is charged with the responsibility of ensuring that the work of the National Bureau is carried on in strict conformity with this object.

2. The President of the National Bureau shall submit to the Board of Directors, or to its Executive Committee, for their formal adoption all specific proposals for research to be instituted.

3. No research report shall be published by the National Bureau until the President has sent each member of the Board a notice that a manuscript is recommended for publication and that in the President's opinion it is suitable for publication in accordance with the principles of the National Bureau. Such notification will include an abstract or summary of the manuscript's content and a response form for use by those Directors who desire a copy of the manuscript for review. Each manuscript shall contain a summary drawing attention to the nature and treatment of the problem studied, the character of the data and their utilization in the report, and the main conclusions reached.

4. For each manuscript so submitted, a special committee of the Directors (including Directors Emeriti) shall be appointed by majority agreement of the President and Vice Presidents (or by the Executive Committee in case of inability to decide on the part of the President and Vice Presidents), consisting of three Directors selected as nearly as may be one from each general division of the Board. The names of the special manuscript committee shall be stated to each Director when notice of the proposed publication is submitted to him. It shall be the duty of each member of the special manuscript committee to read the manuscript. If each member of the manuscript committee signifies his approval within thirty days of the transmittal of the manuscript, the report may be published. If at the end of that period any member of the manuscript committee withholds his approval, the President shall then notify each member of the Board, requesting approval or disapproval of publication, and thirty days additional shall be granted for this purpose. The manuscript shall then not be published unless at least a majority of the entire Board who shall have voted on the proposal within the time fixed for the receipt of votes shall have approved.

5. No manuscript may be published, though approved by each member of the special manuscript committee, until forty-five days have elapsed from the transmittal of the report in manuscript form. The interval is allowed for the receipt of any memorandum of dissent or reservation, together with a brief statement of his reasons, that any member may wish to express; and such memorandum of dissent or reservation shall be published with the manuscript if he so desires. Publication does not, however, imply that each member of the Board has read the manuscript, or that either members of the Board in general or the special committee have passed on its validity in every detail.

6. Publications of the National Bureau issued for informational purposes concerning the work of the Bureau and its staff, or issued to inform the public of activities of Bureau staff, and volumes issued as a result of various conferences involving the National Bureau shall contain a specific disclaimer noting that such publication has not passed through the normal review procedures required in this resolution. The Executive Committee of the Board is charged with review of all such publications from time to time to ensure that they do not take on the character of formal research reports of the National Bureau, requiring formal Board approval.

7. Unless otherwise determined by the Board or exempted by the terms of paragraph 6, a copy of this resolution shall be printed in each National Bureau publication.

(Resolution adopted October 25, 1926, as revised through September 30, 1974)

Contents

Preface

It is a pleasure to issue this collection of articles by Anna Jacobson Schwartz. For more than five decades, Anna has contributed to our understanding of the economy. Her studies of monetary policy, banking, and the gold standard have added significantly to our knowledge of these important topics. It is indeed fortunate for NBER that she has been associated with us since 1941.

These articles were presented to Anna at a conference held in her honor in New York City on October 6, 1987. They maintain the high level of scholarship all Bureau publications hope to achieve. In one important respect, however, some of these articles depart from the Bureau's firm tradition of avoiding policy recommendations. Other NBER publications must confine themselves to analyzing the effects of policies and strictly eschew recommending one course of action over another. Some of the papers in this volume were originally written for other purposes and do take policy positions. Rather than omit any of these papers, we decided instead to make an exception to the Bureau's rule.

I would like to thank Michael D. Bordo and Milton Friedman for selecting these articles and for organizing the conference honoring Anna. Without their initiative and hard work, this volume would not have been published. Mark Fitz-Patrick of NBER gave valuable guidance in preparing the manuscript and able research assistance was provided by Ivan Marcotte. I would also like to thank the Alex C. Walker Educational and Charitable Foundation and the Earhart Foundation for their generous financial support of the conference and the publication.

Martin Feldstein

Acknowledgments

The author and the University of Chicago Press wish to thank the original publishers of the essays in this volume for permission to reprint them and to thank Michael Bordo, Phillip Cagan, and Milton Friedman for permission to reprint the essays that they coauthored.

Chapter 1. "The Beginning of Competitive Banking in Philadelphia, 1782–1809," *Journal of Political Economy* (October 1947): 417–431. Copyright 1947 by The University of Chicago. Reprinted by permission of The University of Chicago Press.

Chapter 2. "Money and Business Cycles," by Milton Friedman and Anna J. Schwartz, *Review of Economics and Statistics* (February 1963): supplement, 32–64. Copyright 1963 by the President and Fellows of Harvard College. Reprinted by permission of Elsevier Science Publishers B. V. (North-Holland).

Chapter 3. "Secular Price Change In Historical Perspective," *Journal of Money, Credit, and Banking* (February 1973): part II, 243–269. Copyright 1973 by Ohio State University Press. Reprinted by permission of the Ohio State University Press. All rights reserved.

Chapter 4. "Understanding 1929–1933," in *The Great Depression Revisited,* ed. Karl Brunner (Boston: Martinus Nijhoff), 5–48. Copyright 1981 by University of Rochester Center for Research in Government Policy and Business. Reprinted by permission of Kluwer-Nijhoff Publishing.

Chapter 5. "A Century of British Market Interest Rates, 1874–1975" The Henry Thornton Lecture (January 1981). Reprinted by permission of The City University, Centre for Banking and International Finance.

Chapter 6. "Why Money Matters," *Lloyds Bank Review* (October 1969): 1–16. Reprinted by permission of *Lloyds Bank Review.*

Chapter 7. "How Feasible Is a Flexible Monetary Policy," by Phillip Cagan and Anna J. Schwartz, in *Capitalism and Freedom: Problems and Prospects,* ed. R. T. Selden (Charlottesville: University of Virginia Press). Copyright 1975 by The University of Virginia. Reprinted by permission of the University of Virginia Press.

Chapter 8. "Has the Growth of Money Substitutes Hindered Monetary Policy?" by Phillip Cagan and Anna J. Schwartz, *Journal of Money, Credit, and Banking* (May 1975), 137–159. Copyright 1975 by Ohio State University Press. Reprinted by permission of the Ohio State University Press. All rights reserved.

Chapter 9. "Clark Warburton: Pioneer Monetarist," by Michael D. Bordo and Anna J. Schwartz, *Journal of Monetary Economics* (January 1979): 43–65. Copyright 1979 by North-Holland Publishing Company. Reprinted by permission of Elsevier Science Publishers B. V. (North-Holland).

Chapter 10. "The Importance of Stable Money: Theory and Evidence," by Michael D. Bordo and Anna J. Schwartz, *The Cato Journal* 3 (May 1983): 63–82. Copyright 1983 by the Cato Institute. Reprinted by permission of *The Cato Journal.*

Chapter 11. "Real and Pseudo-Financial Crises," in *Financial Crises and the World Banking System,* ed. Forrest Capie and Geoffrey E. Wood (New York: Macmillan, 1986), 1:11–31. Copyright 1986 by Forrest Capie and Geoffrey E. Wood. Reprinted by permission of Forrest Capie and Geoffrey E. Wood.

Chapter 12. "Has Government Any Role in Money?" by Milton Friedman and Anna J. Schwartz, *Journal of Monetary Economics* (January 1986): 37–62. Copyright 1986 by Elsevier Science Publishers B. V. (North-Holland). Reprinted by permission of Elsevier Science Publishers B. V. (North-Holland).

Chapter 13. "Reflections on the Gold Commission *Report,*" *Journal of Money, Credit, and Banking* (November 1982): part 1, 538–551. Copyright 1982 by Ohio State University Press. Reprinted by permission of the Ohio State University Press. All rights reserved.

Chapter 14. "Postwar Institutional Evolution of the International Monetary System," in *The International Transmission of Inflation,* ed. Michael R. Darby, James R. Lothian, et al. 1983, 2:14–45. Copyright 1983 by the University of Chicago. Reprinted by permission of the University of Chicago Press.

Chapter 15. "Alternative Monetary Regimes: The Gold Standard," in *Alternative Monetary Regimes,* ed. C. Campbell and W. Dougan, 1986. Copyright 1986 by Johns Hopkins University. Reprinted by permission of the Johns Hopkins University Press.

Chapter 16. "Lessons of the Gold Standard Era and the Bretton Woods System for the Prospects of an International Monetary System Constitution." Presented at the July 1986 meeting of the Western Economic Association, San Francisco.

Introduction

Michael D. Bordo and Milton Friedman

Background

Our collaboration with Anna Jacobson Schwartz has been a rare and wonderful experience—spanning more than three decades for Friedman, over a decade for Bordo.

As an economic historian and monetary economist, Anna is dedicated to accuracy, precision, and thoroughness—qualities present even in the earliest of her papers reprinted in this volume, a fascinating account of the beginning of competitive banking in Philadelphia (Chapter 1). That dedication, repeatedly demonstrated during the course of our collaboration, has guaranteed a solid scholarly foundation for our joint publications.

As a friend and colleague, Anna is a thoughtful, considerate, uniformly helpful, and warm human being with firm principles and wide-ranging tolerance—as demonstrated by the remarkable fact that we cannot recall any episode involving acrimony in our many years of collaboration. Disagreement, frank criticism, discussion, strongly held views, yes; acrimony, personal recrimination, pettiness, never. That has been the common experience of the several persons of widely different temperaments and personalities who have been privileged to collaborate with her closely at one time or another.

Born Anna Jacobson on November 11, 1915, in New York City, Anna received a B.A. from Barnard College in 1934, an M.A. and Ph.D.

Michael D. Bordo is professor of economics at the College of Business Administration, University of South Carolina, and a research associate of the National Bureau of Economic Research.

Milton Friedman is a Senior Research Fellow at the Hoover Institution on War, Revolution and Peace, Stanford University.

from Columbia University in 1936 and 1964, respectively. Married to Isaac Schwartz in 1936, she did not let her marriage, or the loving care she and Isaac lavished on their four children, all now grown and living independently, interfere with the pursuit of a demanding professional career, devoted primarily to research, though with occasional forays into teaching (at Brooklyn College 1952, Baruch College 1959–60, Hunter College 1967–68, and New York University 1969–70).

A year at the U.S. Department of Agriculture in 1936 was followed by five years at Columbia University's Social Science Research Council, where she collaborated with A. D. Gayer and W. W. Rostow on a study of *The Growth and Fluctuation of the British Economy, 1790–1850,* published in 1953 in two volumes under that title. Although the study has become something of a classic in British economic history, and was republished in a second edition in 1975, Anna's later work led her to revise her views on the role of monetary forces in British economic history, as she explains in a new preface to the second edition. Anna's interest in and profound understanding of British institutions and British economic history have continued ever since. Two examples are the papers on secular price change and on British interest rates that are reprinted in Chapters 3 and 5 of this book. So also, on a larger scale, is her contribution to *Monetary Trends in the United States and the United Kingdom,* authored jointly with Friedman (1982).

In 1941, Anna joined the National Bureau of Economic Research and has remained with the bureau ever since, becoming an emeritus research associate in 1985.

In 1981–82, Anna performed a major public service when she served as staff director of the U.S. Gold Commission, in which capacity she wrote volume 1 of the Report of the Gold Commission. Once again, her scientific and personal qualities stood her in good stead.Despite the controversy surrounding the role of gold, and the highly political nature of the commission, Anna was able to work effectively and congenially with all the members of the commission to gain their respect and trust and to produce a report that will long serve as an invaluable source document for anyone interested in the gold standard. Her interest in the gold standard also led to an NBER conference that she helped to organize in 1982, and her "Introduction" to the resulting volume, *A Retrospective on the Classical Gold Standard, 1921–1931* (1984).

Anna has served at various times as a member of the Board of Editors of the *American Economic Review,* the *Journal of Money, Credit, and Banking,* and the *Journal of Monetary Economics.* She has been a regular participant in the Carnegie Rochester Conference Series on Public Policy and is a founding member of the Shadow Open Market

Committee. She is currently an Honorary Visiting Professor at the City University, London Business School, and will be president of the Western Economic Association in 1987–88.

Scholarly Work

Anna's major scholarly contributions are contained in the impressive body of work that she has written in collaboration with others: the book authored jointly with Gayer and Rostow; the series of books and articles that developed out of her long collaboration with Friedman on the National Bureau of Economic Research's money and business cycle project; her participation with Michael Darby, James Lothian, and others on a bureau study of the international transmission of inflation; her collaboration with Phillip Cagan on two articles on monetary policy; and a series of articles jointly authored with Bordo. (Appendix 1 contains a complete bibliography of her writings.)

Anna's contributions to these publications, as well as to those that she has authored alone or jointly with still other collaborators, are in four related areas: economic statistics, particularly monetary statistics; economic history, particularly monetary history; monetary theory and policy; and international monetary arrangements.

Statistics

The meticulous care she has expended on constructing basic statistical series is exemplified in the British share price index and commodity price index developed in the Gayer-Rostow study; in the monthly estimates of currency holdings in the United States from 1917 to 1944, published jointly with Emma Oliver (1947); in monthly estimates of gross dividends and interest payments by all corporations in the United States in the nineteenth century (1960); and, above all, in the massive collection of monetary and economic statistics for the United States and the United Kingdom contained in three Friedman-Schwartz books (*Monetary History of the United States* [1963], *Monetary Statistics of the United States* [1970], and *Monetary Trends in the United States and the United Kingdom* [1982]). Most of these series have by now become the common stock in trade of economists and historians.

Economic History

A characteristic feature of Anna's work on economic history is its strong quantitative base. Never a compiler of statistical data for its own sake, she has sought to test her interpretations of historical episodes not only with qualitative data but also, whenever possible, with numerical data. The interweaving of descriptive history, economic analysis, and quantitative evidence is characteristic of all her historical work, whether in the early Gayer-Rostow-Schwartz book on British history, the later Friedman-Schwartz *Monetary History,* or the articles reprinted here in Part I.

In the process, she has helped to construct a sound factual and analytical base for later students of related topics.

Monetary Policy

The historical evidence linking economic instability to erratic monetary growth, in turn largely a product of discretionary monetary management, has persuaded Anna of the importance of stable money and of the case for a constant money growth rule. As a consequence, she has devoted much attention in the past two decades to the study of monetary policy in the United States and other countries.

As a founding member of the Shadow Open Market Committee, organized by Allan Meltzer and Karl Brunner in 1971, Anna has been engaged in continuous critical evaluation of the Federal Reserve's performance.

This aspect of her work is reflected in Part II of this book, which reprints seven articles published over a seventeen-year span, dealing with a variety of basic issues of monetary policy.

International Monetary Arrangements

Anna's interest in international monetary arrangements began with her collaboration with Michael Darby, James Lothian, and others on a study of the international transmission of inflation, leading, as noted earlier, to her organizing with Bordo a conference on the Gold Standard, and culminating in her role as staff director of the U.S. Gold Commission. Her contribution to the Darby-Lothian study assessing postwar international monetary arrangements is reprinted in Part III as Chapter 14. Her reflections on the Gold Commission Report are summarized in Chapter 13. The final two articles reprinted in Part III provide a wide-ranging survey of the historical development of the gold standard (Chapter 15), and of the lessons that can be drawn from current policy from past attempts at constructing international monetary constitutions (Chapter 16).

Conclusion

These brief comments only scratch the surface of a body of work, impressive alike for its scope, its quality, and its adherence to the highest standards of scholarly care and objectivity. The reader who dips further into this collection of essays will enjoy contact with a subtle mind of wide learning and rare judgment. Unfortunately, he or she will not be able to share our experience of close collaboration with a modest, unassuming, remarkable human being.

Michael D. Bordo
Milton Friedman

I   Money and Banking in Historical Perspective

1 The Beginning of Competitive Banking in Philadelphia, 1782–1809

> Two capital banks operating in one city . . . might, perhaps, act in opposition to each other and, of course, destroy each other.—Pelatiah Webster (1786).

The founders of commercial banking in this country doubted seriously that several banks in one community could get along together, especially that the initial bank could survive if one more intruded upon its domain. They reasoned that each new bank would embarrass the established institutions by drawing on their specie reserves to build up its own. A corollary of this argument for monopolistic banking was that each newcomer must of necessity reduce the profits of the others.

But in Philadelphia, the home of the country's first bank, it was demonstrated—as one rival after another opened its doors in the face of the opposition of older institutions—that competition did not impede their growth. Yet no sooner did a bank win friendly recognition from its elders than it fell prey to the same fear of newcomers. In New York and Baltimore (and possibly also in Boston),[1] as in Philadelphia, a new institution was looked upon as a threat to the security of intrenched banking interests. Only after considerable experience did the banks learn how to minimize the impact of the immediate repercussions of the establishment of another bank, and also how to conduct themselves in their relations with it. This experience, its effects lightened by an expanding demand for bank accommodations and fortuitous accretions to their specie holdings, made the banks generally realize that a competitor's advent did not necessarily mean their eclipse.

1.1

In May 1781, when the Continental Congress approved the establishment of the Bank of North America, it recommended that, for the duration of the war, no other banking institution be chartered by any state. There was nothing, however, in the charter granted the Bank of

North America in March 1782, to suggest that it had been accorded an exclusive right to banking in Pennsylvania either during or after the war. Yet, for a decade after the war ended, the bank was able to preserve its monopolistic position in both Philadelphia and the state.[2]

Early in 1784 the Bank of North America was faced with the prospect of a rival. The first two years of its existence had been extremely profitable; it paid $8\frac{3}{4}$ percent on its shares in 1782 and $14\frac{1}{2}$ percent in 1783.[3] This handsome return in itself was sufficient inducement for others to engage in banking, but there was another motive. The closed character of the ownership of the bank's stock and its board membership gave rise to an opposition group among the merchants. Quaker businessmen in Philadelphia were excluded from bank proprietorship and claimed that the directors' partiality to insiders prevented them from obtaining bank loans.

Their demands evidently compelled the Bank of North America to issue more shares. Meeting on January 12, 1784, stockholders agreed to sell one thousand additional shares at $500 each (although the par value of the original shares was $400) and to treat the new and the old shares as equal.[4] If we can judge by what Thomas Willing, the president of the bank, wrote William Bingham, his son-in-law, before the stockholders' meeting, the subscription was intended only for outsiders during the first six months: ". . . you'll be excluded as well as myself from any more shares before the 1st Aug. next . . . unless you get some other person to act for you in the Matter."[5] But when the sale of the new shares started, they were offered to stockholders as well as to the general public.

The terms of the proposed increase in the bank's capital did not cancel plans, announced nine days after the stockholders' meeting, for a new institution, to be known as the Bank of Pennsylvania. Shares were priced at 400 Spanish milled dollars. On February 5, when seven hundred shares had been subscribed and apparently paid for,[6] the holders elected a board of directors, composed mainly of Quaker merchants whom the opposition press satirically dubbed "rigid Presbyterians," "unshaken Quakers," and "furious Tories."[7] On February 10 the subscribers applied to the Assembly for a charter, and the petition was favorably received by the committee to which the matter was referred. When the legislature tabled a request of February 26 by the Bank of North America to be heard in opposition to the new charter, and two days later appointed a committee to bring in a bill,[8] the bank hastily called a stockholders' meeting for March 1.

The meeting passed a resolution increasing the amount of the new subscription from one thousand to four thousand shares and reducing the price to $400. Those who had subscribed to five hundred shares at $500 per share were to be refunded the difference. In a statement to the public—signed by Willing; James Wilson, counsel; Thomas

FitzSimons and Gouverneur Morris, stockholders—the original advance in the price of the shares was defended. It was claimed that the price was now reduced not out of private considerations but in the public interest, since a new bank would injure commerce.[9]

The bank's revised stock offer appeased the discontented merchants who had planned forming a rival institution. On March 16, when the bill creating the Bank of Pennsylvania was reached, its directors obtained leave to withdraw their application for a charter.[10] The general subscription to the Bank of North America was so well received that by the end of March its capital, though less than half of the possible $2 million, had more than doubled. One hundred and thirty new stockholders subscribed six hundred shares; the rest were taken by old stockholders or those who had subscribed before March 1.[11]

The Bank of North America's anxiety about the scheme to establish another bank cannot be explained simply in terms of the supposed effects that sharing the market would have on its profits, although that apprehension was undoubtedly at the root of its opposition. It also feared for its specie holdings. Subscribers to the proposed Bank of Pennsylvania could pay for their shares with specie in general circulation or with Bank of North America notes. Most of them had chosen the latter. As its notes were at once presented for redemption, the Bank of North America was drained of gold and silver. William Seton, the cashier of the proposed Bank of New York, who was visiting in Philadelphia, wrote to Alexander Hamilton on March 27: "Gold and silver had been extracted in such amounts that discounting was stopped, and for this fortnight past not any business had been done at the bank this way. . . . Therefore, for the safety of the community at large, it became absolutely necessary to drop the idea of a new bank, and to join hand in hand to relieve the old bank from the shock it has received."[12]

Hamilton, who had originally favored the incorporation of the Bank of Pennsylvania, now saw the competition in a different light. He wrote Gouverneur Morris: "I had no doubt that it was against the interests of the proprietors; but, on a superficial view, I perceived benefits to the community, which, on a more close inspection, I found were not real."[13] Robert Morris, concluding that there was not enough capital in the country to support several banks, wrote Jefferson on April 8, 1784: "The establishment of so many banks, instead of aiding credits and facilitating operations, will for some time to come have a contrary effect, and it is not without great difficulty that they will each collect a capital sufficient to support its own operations. The struggle to get such capital places these institutions in a degree of opposition to each other injurious to them all."[14]

At the time Morris was writing, exports of specie exceeded imports, owing to an unfavorable balance of trade and the payment of the claims of English creditors for debts contracted before the war.[15] The consequent tightening of the specie supply seemed to confirm his gloomy foreboding that the creation of a new bank would lead to disaster. But he knew, as he indicated two years later, that the flow of specie from this country would soon be reversed.[16] When the balance of international payments shifted in our favor, gold and silver were bound to become more generally available. Morris' argument against a new bank had at best only temporary cogency.

A real fallacy was his assumption that a new bank could obtain specie for its reserve only from the vaults of the preexisting institution. He ignored the fact that only a fraction of the country's specie was held by the Bank of North America; that if a rival drew on its reserve, it could hope that is holdings would be replenished by deposits of gold and silver in the public's possession.[17]

Had the Bank of Pennsylvania's capital consisted entirely of Bank of North America notes and had there been no transfer to it of specie held by the public in strong boxes, the Bank of North America might indeed have suffered by the redistribution of its holdings.[18] But if we assume that the credit supply would have been more rationally distributed when two banks instead of one were in operation, the community might have benefited from the opening of a second bank even if it added no specie to the amount already in vault and the total credit supply remained unchanged.

The proposition against competitive banking generally, as stated by Morris, seems indefensible. Specie kept in strong boxes would have found its way to the new bank, presumably just as it did to the older bank when it increased its capital. If enough capital could not be scraped together for two banks, as Morris asserted, it is difficult to understand how the subscription of the older bank was doubled.[19]

In short, the crux of the Bank of North America's opposition to a potential competitor was concern over its specie holdings, but, had its relations with the Bank of Pennsylvania been amicable, an agreement would have been reached at the outset concerning the acceptance of each other's notes. And the run on the Bank of North America for specie, described by Seton, might have been avoided.

1.2

During the decade 1784–93 the Bank of North America modified its attitude. On its own initiative it established good relations with out-of-state banks and submitted, willingly or unwillingly, to the authority of the Bank of the United States. And when the legislature chartered a second bank in 1793, the Bank of North America discovered that its operations were not crippled.

At the same time that it was resisting local bank competition, it was encouraging the founding of banks outside Pennsylvania. To help Boston merchants who proposed opening the Bank of Massachusetts, Willing in January 1784 described his experience in running his bank. In March, Seton went to Philadelphia bearing a letter of introduction from Hamilton to FitzSimons, requesting his advice concerning the operation of a bank.[20]

Th...... the management of the Bank of North America looked ...... nk in Philadelphia as an interloper, it tolerated banks ...... even admitting that they might be useful: first, be...... to a bank in Boston or New York were not likely ...... delphia bank notes that would recoil on the issuer; ...... d operate within their own local markets, with...... for and supply of loans in Philadelphia; third, ... Bank of North America customers who had ...... to make in their vicinity.[21] In contrast to its ...... wcomer in Philadelphia, the Bank of North America ...... th banks in other cities were exemplary.

...... th course of the organization of the Bank of the United ...... 1791 afforded other evidence of how harmoniously the situ...... might have been managed in Philadelphia in 1784. By opening the subscription books for the national bank, the Bank of North America surprised the skeptics who expected it to be antagonistic; Willing was one of the commissioners.[22] Philadelphians subscribed heavily; some even were disappointed, so keen was the demand for shares.[23] There must have been repercussions on the specie holdings of the Bank of North America, but when Willing was chosen to head the national bank, it became obvious that a *modus vivendi* would be found.[24] The Bank of the United States opened on December 12, 1791. On February 6, 1792, the Bank of North America adopted a resolution providing for a daily exchange of notes with it and on March 23 one providing for the appointment monthly of a committee of three to consult with a similar committee from the Bank of the United States, "for the purpose of communicating freely upon the business of both, as well to prevent improper interference with each other as to promote the accommodation of the citizens."[25]

The attitude of an elder sister institution toward a newcomer in the local banking field was of crucial importance. Its opposition to the proposed Bank of Pennsylvania in 1784 had caused a crisis in the Bank of North America's affairs. But, because the state bank cooperated, all went smoothly when the first Bank of the United States was organized.[26] Yet it lost some local business as well as the accounts of the federal government, which had been exceedingly profitable. The services the Bank of the United States rendered the merchant business order were acknowledged to be more important than any possible loss its competition might entail.[27]

Whether Bank of North America stockholders suffered is problematical. The bank paid 13½ percent in 1791, 12½ percent in 1792, 12 percent for the next six years, and never less than 9 percent as long as the first Bank of the United States was in existence.[28] However, in July 1792, after an exceedingly good year, the dividend committee of the Bank of North America recommended a payment at a lower rate than the bank's financial situation warranted. Taking for granted that the competition of the new bank would lower profits, it warned that another dividend at a high rate might raise false hopes which would have to be dashed. But the committee had an ulterior motive in urging a low rate: "Another probable consequence of two successive high dividends deserves consideration; would it not be likely to induce others to engage in a business that yielded so large a profit, and if the Legislature of the State had an advantageous offer made to them, would they not be likely to grant another charter?"[29] Preventing the creation of a new bank meant holding the legislature as well as the commercial elements in the community at bay.

At this time a Treasury surplus challenged the attention of Pennsylvania state authorities. After the entire public debt had been liquidated from the proceeds of sales of public lands and paid-up back taxes, a tidy sum remained unappropriated. The high dividends paid on bank stock attracted notice in political quarters. Governor Mifflin on August 13, 1792, proposed to subscribe, on behalf of the commonwealth, to a substantial quantity of Bank of North America stock.[30] On January 29, 1793, the stockholders agreed to admit the state on terms to be set by a committee to be appointed to confer with the governor.[31] Its offer seems to have been a $750,000 subscription at the rate of $400 for each share, half to be borrowed from the bank.[32]

The negotiations were unsuccessful. Merchants, perhaps because they were dissatisfied with their accommodation at the Bank of North America and the Bank of the United States, seized on the political circumstance of the state's search for an investment for its surplus to promote a bank.[33] The state struck a bargain with the new institution, the Bank of Pennsylvania, which it incorporated for twenty years on March 30 and used thereafter as its fiscal agent. To the bank's authorized capital of $3 million the governor subscribed $1 million on behalf of the state, paying part with public stock of the federal government owned by the state at the value fixed by the legislature; part in specie; and the rest with the proceeds of a $250,000 loan from the bank.[34]

Possibly in deference to the view that a competitor would impair the profitability of the Bank of North America, the Bank of Pennsylvania's charter stipulated that two thousand shares at $400 each should be set aside for Bank of North America stockholders, if they decided to re-

linquish their charter within three months after it was granted. The Bank of North America turned down this suggestion; evidently a year and a half's profitable operation alongside the Bank of the United States had changed its views on competitive banking.[35] It had no cause to regret the decision to retain its identity. "It appears . . . that establishment of the Bank of Pennsylvania hath not *upon the whole* lessened the business, but hath increased it in several departments," reported a committee appointed by the directors of the Bank of North America to examine the possibility of reducing the staff.[36]

There is no evidence that the Bank of North America and the Bank of Pennsylvania did not get on well. The Bank of the United States also established friendly relations with the new bank, including it in the arrangement for the daily settlement and exchange of notes. A joint committee of the three banks, meeting on March 2, 1797, adopted the rule that "after March 31, all bills made payable at sight or on demand must be paid on the same day they are presented" and agreed that no bank would discount a note from which the qualifications "without defalcation" or "without set-off" were omitted. Joint action was proposed in June when the Bank of North America appointed a committee to meet with committees which the Bank of the United States and the Bank of Pennsylvania might appoint "to attend to the bill depending before the House of Representatives of the United States for levying a stamp duty and to report their opinion thereon." Committees from the three banks conferred again in May 1799 on "the prevailing distress of the mercantile interests of this city."[37]

The older institutions probably could not risk harassing a rival with which the state was identified; moreover, they were no doubt learning that mutual trust was a *sine qua non* of a successful banking community. The regularization of interbank relations was a prerequisite to the expansion of credit merchants required for the carrying trade. Mercantile houses combining importing and exporting multiplied as the Napoleonic wars, until the embargo period, opened business opportunities for Americans. The shipment of colonial produce to the several belligerent mother-countries—as well as its purchase for their own account in the French, Spanish, and Dutch colonies—engaged the energies of a growing merchant class. American firms also imported European manufactures, especially British, and the manufactures and produce of the East Indies and China for re-export to the West Indies, the Spanish colonies in South America, and Europe. They got the British products on longterm credits but—in order to purchase ships and domestic produce and also to speculate in land and securities—had to borrow from American banks.[38]

Without an effective banking community, ambitious businessmen during the Napoleonic era would not have been able to go so far as they did. Interbank claims were inevitable; and the merchant business order could not thrive unless banks trusted one another. City banks, not only in Philadelphia but also in other coastal cities where merchants organized banks to further their business interests, had to accept and adapt themselves to competitive banking. Their compliance was reluctant. Despite the experience afforded by the formation of the Bank of the United States and the Bank of Pennsylvania, "Civis" noted in the *Aurora General Advertiser* on December 21, 1801: "On the propriety of establishing a banking house there exist various sentiments; without at present hazarding an opinion upon it, I can venture to say, that the banks now in this city will not approve the establishment. From this quarter there will presumably proceed the greatest opposition."

1.3

When the Philadelphia Bank began operations as an unincorporated association in September 1803, the wisdom its predecessors had acquired in interbank relations was put to the test. Merchants who had gone into business for themselves after the start of the Napoleonic wars, and who claimed that they were being unfairly treated by the banks, had a prominent share in the new institution's organization. Designed to appeal to men of smaller means than those who had invested in the older banks and were their customers, its shares were priced at $100. The strength of investors' demands may be gauged from the ease with which the new bank accumulated capital. By December 31, 1803, $1 million was fully paid in.[39]

To avoid antagonizing other banks in the city the Philadelphia Bank received and paid out their notes along with its own. Yet the other banks refused to reciprocate.[40] On September 21 the board of directors of the Philadelphia Bank resolved: "That so long as the Banks of the United States, Pennsylvania, and North America continue to refuse the notes of this Bank, that the Cashier apply every day to the said Banks for Specie in exchange for such of their notes as may be on hand in this Bank."[41] This retaliation brought to heel all except the Bank of Pennsylvania, which continued prey to the fears that had exercised the Bank of North America a decade earlier. "Anti-Monopoly" wrote: "That the Pennsylvania Bank is opposed to the policy and prosperity of Pennsylvania is obvious—for though they have refused the paper of the Philadelphia Bank, the Banks of Boston, Hartford, New York, Baltimore, Delaware, and Alexandria accept them—and their acceptance was voluntary. Jealousy and the spirit of monopoly of the Pennsylvania Bank opposes the credit of citizens of Philadelphia."[42] Before its quarters offered suitable protection, the Philadelphia Bank had placed a box of money for safekeeping in the Bank of Pennsylvania. As a rebuke to the latter it now moved the box to the Bank of the United States and ordered Bank of Pennsylvania notes to be presented for redemption immediately upon their receipt.

In this atmosphere of uncertain acceptance by the local banking fraternity, the Philadelphia Bank applied to the legislature for a charter on December 13.[43] This action put the state in a dilemma: as a stockholder in the Bank of Pennsylvania, its interests presumably coincided with those of the private investors in the bank, but as arbiter of the public welfare, it had to consider the views of the promotors of the Philadelphia Bank. These conflicted with the ambitions of Bank of Pennsylvania stockholders. The contradictions implicit in the state's position were stated in a resolution read in the House at a later date:

> Whereas, the intimate connexion and union of pecuniary interests between a government and great monied institutions, tends to create an influence, partial to the latter and highly injurious to the former. It being the duty of government to consult the general will and provide for the good of all, embarrassments must frequently be thrown in the way of the performance of this duty, when the government is coupled in interest with institutions whose rights are founded in monopoly, and whose prosperity depends on the exclusion and suppression of similar institutions. The government in such cases becomes identified with these establishments, and the means of promoting and extending commerce, manufactures and agriculture equally over the whole state for the general good are too often lost sight of by this dangerous and unnatural union.[44]

In resolution of these conflicting interests a committee appointed by the Philadelphia Bank's stockholders made various proposals to compensate the state for the charter: to pay $15,000 outright for a ten-year charter or $20,000 for a fourteen-year charter. For a fourteen-year charter it offered alternative terms: The bank would agree to lend the state $100,000 for three years, without interest, "on condition that if the legislature should, at any time hereafter, impose a tax on banks, that the interest so remitted should be considered as a set off against any tax which the legislature might be disposed to lay on this institution." Finally, it suggested that the legislature authorize a $500,000 subscription to its stock, payable in Bank of Pennsylvania stock held by the state, at par, on the transfer of which the Philadelphia Bank would pay by June 1804 $125,000 in specie as a premium.[45]

The House committee, under the chairmanship of Adcock, to which the Bank of Philadelphia's petition was referred, favored the fourth proposal because it contained the largest spot-cash offer and did not impair the state's equity in the banking business. Although the committee was unwilling to express an opinion regarding the ultimate effects of the "multiplication of Banks" on the general public interest, it approved the petition for incorporation.[46]

On December 17, the day after Adcock's committee reported, six Bank of Pennsylvania directors (including Matthew Carey) appointed by the legislature sent a letter to both houses requesting that nothing be done about chartering a new bank until a memorial then being prepared was laid before them. They asserted that another bank in Philadelphia would "materially injure the property of the state in the Bank of Pennsylvania, and the interest of the community at large. We also believe there are no terms on which a charter could be granted, that would compensate the state for the injury it would sustain thereby."[47] The memorial duly submitted by the Bank of Pennsylvania on December 29 stated: "Immense injuries must inevitably arise to the institution and the state, should the legislature incorporate the said bank."[48]

The House had postponed a second reading of the Adcock report but, when the Bank of Pennsylvania submitted its protest, referred both the report and it to a new committee, for which Maclay was spokesman.[49] Aware of the pressure the Bank of Pennsylvania was bringing to bear on the legislature, the Philadelphia Bank revised its four proposals with a view to making them more attractive.[50]

The Maclay committee reported on January 20 against the incorporation of the Philadelphia Bank. It argued that more banks would mean smaller profits for all and hence reduce the value of the state's investment in the Bank of Pennsylvania. No premium which the Philadelphia Bank might pay for a charter could offset this loss. The committee, furthermore, was skeptical of the bank's ability to live up to its proposals and doubted the accuracy of its valuation of the various premiums: "Banks already chartered . . . are fully competent to the business of the state and . . . [their] protection, more especially of that one where the property of the state is lodged, is of more utility . . . than the chartering of new ones."[51]

Having disposed of the Philadelphia Bank's application, the Maclay committee indorsed a measure proposed by the Bank of Pennsylvania. If the state would extend its charter for fourteen years beyond 1813 (the expiration date under the act of incorporation), the Bank of Pennsylvania would pay the state $200,000 in specie or bank notes.[52] During this time (*a*) no other bank (except the Bank of North America) should be chartered by the state; (*b*) no incorporated association with more than ten members in Philadelphia or within the state of Pennsylvania should be permitted to carry on banking or issue notes; (*c*) stockholders should be personally liable for the debts of an unincorporated company; (*d*) the Bank of Pennsylvania should not be subject to taxation.

The House took no immediate action on the Maclay report. In the Senate a resolution was introduced on January 24 to discharge the committee appointed December 13 to consider the Philadelphia Bank's petition.[53] The chances for a charter looked slim. The stockholders of the Philadelphia Bank, however, again memorialized the House, presenting three rejoinders to the Maclay report: (a) the paid-in capital proved that the bank was fully capable of carrying out any proposals it had made; (b) as its specie holdings equaled its circulation, the bank was in a sound condition; (c) the bank's proposals had been misunderstood; it was ready to pay into the state treasury $145,000, $154,000, $152,000, or $400,667, depending upon which of the four proposals was accepted. The stockholders had some additional bait with which to tempt the state: "As banks must necessarily increase with our growing population and industry; we are willing should the legislature wish that at the end of every four years the state may subscribe two hundred thousand dollars to the Philadelphia bank at par, and dispose of the same, for the sole emolument of the commonwealth."[54]

On January 27 the House, in committee of the whole, reported against the Maclay resolution and recommended that a committee bring in a bill of incorporation for ten years under the terms of the bank's first proposal. The report was adopted fifty to thirty-five, and on January 31 a bill was introduced and read the first time.[55]

In the form in which it was reported with amendments by the committee of the whole and ultimately adopted, the bill required the Philadelphia Bank to pay a cash gratuity of $135,000 to the state for a ten-year charter; the state was privileged to subscribe $300,000 by paying that sum in 6 percent stock of the United States (but if the bank should fail, the United States stock was to be retransferred to the state); the state had the right to subscribe an additional $200,000 at par at the end of four years and a like sum at the end of eight years; and, whenever required by the governor, the bank was obligated to lend the commonwealth $100,000 at 5 per cent for any period not exceeding ten years.

When the second reading of the bill was reached in the House, the Bank of Pennsylvania approached the legislature with an offer of a $100,000 interest-free loan for one year, to be repaid in 6 percent stock of the United States, at par, provided the Philadelphia Bank was not granted a charter before the next session of the Assembly. Postponement was urged to give the Assembly time to make inquiries concerning the injury already done the Bank of Pennsylvania, which would be aggravated by the incorporation of a new bank, and to permit the representatives to consult their constituents.[56]

The Bank of Pennsylvania's efforts to block the bill in the House were fruitless; the bill progressed through its second reading uneventfully and was finally passed by a vote of forty-five to thirty-five.[57]

The Senate ordered a second reading of the House bill for February 21. Residents of Lancaster borough and county presented a petition expressing regret that the bill had passed the House: "Reflecting on the extensive interest which the state holds in the Bank of Pennsylvania, they cannot too seriously consider the probable baneful effects of an additional chartered Bank at this period, on the fiscal concerns of the state and on the banking system.''[58] The next day a petition by Lancaster residents favoring the chartering of the Philadelphia Bank was read. A letter from the Bank of Pennsylvania to the legislature confirmed the offer made ten days earlier of an interest-free loan for a year and, in addition, proposed another scheme to reward the state if the bill to incorporate the Philadelphia Bank was postponed. Though the Bank of Pennsylvania calculated the monetary value of its new offer to be $440,000,[59] the legislature was apparently no more pleased than it had been with the offer embodied in the bill chartering the Philadelphia Bank; perhaps not so much, since the Bank of Pennsylvania attached many conditions.[60] Despite attempts to amend the House bill, the Senate passed it without change by a vote of thirteen to ten.[61] The legislature thus supported an expanding and competitive banking system, which existing institutions perforce had to accept.

1.4

Once the Philadelphia Bank had been incorporated, opposition to the creation of rivals steadily dwindled. Even while it lasted, the existing institutions did not try to tie the hands of a new bank by obstructive tactics.[62] Committees appointed by each bank conferred upon subjects of common interest; e.g., they fixed the values at which foreign coins would be taken after September 1804. And by cooperative action the banks made possible the multiple expansion of credit on a given specie base.

The argument that additional competition would diminish profits was once again advanced in 1807–8 when the fourth bank, the Farmers' and Mechanics', appeared on the scene. Unlike the older banks, which had been organized by merchants predominantly, the Farmers' and Mechanics' Bank was founded by a mixed group—merchants, manufacturers, and mechanics.[63] The older banks appealed to the selfish interest of the commonwealth itself in their profits in the hope that it would deny the new bank a charter. The emptiness of the argument became obvious when business expanded—there was enough for all. Thus in approving one of seven offers to remunerate the state, together with the Farmers' and Mechanics' Bank's petition for incorporation, the House committee on banks remarked in 1808 that the Bank of Pennsylvania was not injured by the Philadelphia Bank, nor was either of them affected by the operation of the Farmers' and Mechanics' Bank as an unincorporated association.[64] Moreover, the business drawn to banks of adjoining states did not reduce their profits.

The offer of monetary inducements for the granting of a charter, which began as a voluntary solicitation of the legislature, came to be looked upon as a necessary accompaniment of a petition for incorporation. The committee reported that, since the petitioners sought a charter for profit-making purposes, the state had a right to require a payment for the privileges it conferred.

The rationale of a competitive banking system was also elaborated.

The banking system, being once introduced, (its) evils, if they have any real existence, will probably find their most effectual remedy in the rivalship which an increase of the number of banks to a proper extent is calculated to create. . . . An extravagant emission of bank paper will be prevented by the fear of being called upon for specie, and partiality in the distribution of loans, destroyed by the anxiety each will feel to secure to itself the best customers. And if (which no former experience seems to warrant) there was real ground to apprehend that a bank might, by extending or withholding accommodations, acquire a power over the conduct and independence of individuals, the danger would, perhaps, be best counteracted by a fair competition, depriving the several institutions of the ability to command custom, and obliging them to merit and attract it by their conduct.[65]

The incorporation of the Farmers' and Mechanics' Bank by the Act of March 16, 1809, heralded the coming of a decade of unlimited increase in the number of Pennsylvania banks.

1.5

Between 1784 and 1809 Philadelphia banks moderated their resistance to competition. The oldest successfully opposed the formation of any state-chartered rival during the first ten years of its existence but managed to adjust itself to the conditions created by the opening of the national bank in 1791 and, two years later, of a bank in which the state was the largest stockholder. It discovered that it could prosper despite, or perhaps with the help of, the newcomers. Opposition to the charter of additional banks did not, however, cease. In 1803–4 it was led by the state-supported bank. But expanding trade proved too strong; by 1809 the restrictive drive had collapsed.

The privilege of banking was not to be confined to one or two large institutions. A competitive unit-banking system seemed more desirable both to businessmen and the state. New bank incorporation provided them with profitable investment outlets. The state, moreover, favored a unit-banking system because the grant of a charter served as an opportunity to secure a payment for the valuable right conferred. Dissatisfaction on the part of groups of businessmen with the loan policies of existing institutions also encouraged the formation of rival banks.

Increments to the country's specie supply, which the carrying trade yielded, reduced the tensions of bank competition that Robert Morris and Hamilton had pictured.[66] A new bank was a source of specie deposits, which extended the basis of loans for the whole system, not a threat. The issue of monopoly or competition in commercial banking became extinct.

Notes

1. I am not sure that, in Boston, the initial bank or banks actively opposed the addition of members to the banking community. N. S. B. Gras comments: "From time to time other banks were established in Boston (in addition to the Boston branch of the first Bank of the United States), but apparently they rarely or never received from the Old Massachusetts anything but a doubtful welcome and hard terms" (*The Massachusetts First National Bank of Boston, 1784–1934* [Cambridge: Harvard University Press, 1937], p. 37). I have not, however, found any explicit references to the problems of the adjustment of the first Boston bank or banks to newcomers. See Edwin A. Stone, *A Century of Boston Banking* (Boston: Rockwell & Churchill, 1894), pp. 8–12.

2. James Wilson, *Considerations on the Bank of North America* (Philadelphia: Hall & Sellers, 1785), p. 4; *Pennsylvania Statutes, Laws Passed 1781– 82*, chap. ix.

3. Lawrence Lewis, Jr., *A History of the Bank of North America* (Philadelphia: Lippincott, 1882), p. 152.

4. Bank of North America stock was closely held in 1783 by wartime associates of Robert Morris—largely non-Quaker businessmen related by marriage to the Willing family—and non-Pennsylvanian capitalists. The directors were well-born and wealthy, with common religious, social, and business interests (R. A. East, *Business Enterprise in the American Revolutionary Era* [New York: Columbia University Press, 1938], p. 290). "It is notorious," Gouverneur Morris, a bank supporter, wrote, "that if the directors had not been under compulsion, they would not have extended the subscription beyond the first four hundred thousand dollars" (Jared Sparks, *Life of Gouverneur Morris* [Boston: Gray & Bowen, 1832], III, 462). *Pennsylvania Gazette,* January 21, 1784, reported the stockholders' meeting on January 12, 1784.

5. Willing to Bingham, November 29, 1783, "Provincial Delegates," V, 17, in the Historical Society of Pennsylvania.

6. *Pennsylvania Gazette,* January 21, 1784; *Freeman's Journal,* February 11, 1784.

7. Quoted from the *New York Journal,* March 18, 1784, by East (*op. cit.,* p. 291, n. 24).

8. *Journal of the Assembly,* VIII, 54, 123–24, 156–57.

Incorporation was not at this time a statutory requirement for banks in Pennsylvania. Why, then, did the promoters of the Bank of Pennsylvania seek a charter? We may conjecture that they sought to place the proposed new institution on the same footing as the Bank of North America with respect, for example, to its expectancy of unlimited life and its capacity for suing and being sued and for holding and transmitting property.

The strenuous efforts of the Bank of North America to defend its charter against revision by the unfriendly legislature of 1784–86 and to regain it upon its repeal in September, 1785, indicate the value placed on legal incorporation. See Matthew Carey, *Debates and Proceedings of the General Assembly of Pennsylvania, on the Memorials Praying a Repeal or Suspension of the Law Annulling the Charter of the Bank* (Philadelphia: Seddon & Pritchard, 1786), *passim.*

Oscar Handlin and Mary F. Handlin have shown ("Origins of the American Corporation," *Journal of Economic History,* V, 1–23) that, at its origin in Massachusetts, the business corporation was not characterized by the attributes it later acquired: unique economic efficiency, limited liability, and perpetual freedom from state interference. They argue that the corporation was conceived as an agency of government, designed to serve a social function for the state, and therefore was used in the organization of business activities determined by the community, not the enterprising capitalist—e.g., turnpikes, not trade; banks, not land speculations. The applicability of this interesting thesis to the use of the corporate form in Pennsylvania requires special study.

9. *Pennsylvania Gazette,* March 3, 1784.

10. *Journal of the Assembly,* VIII, 186.

11. Directors' Minutes, March 1, 1792, "Bank of North America Papers" in the Historical Society of Pennsylvania.

12. J. C. Hamilton, ed., *The Works of Alexander Hamilton* (New York: J. C. Trow, 1850–51), I, 417.

13. Hamilton to FitzSimons, March 21, 1784; to Morris, April 4, 1784, *Hamilton,* I, 416, 418. The switch in Hamilton's views may be judged from a letter he wrote William Seton under date of January 18, 1791, regarding a projected rival to the Bank of New York. " 'Tis impossible but that three great banks in one city must raise such a mass of artificial credit as must endanger everyone of them, and do harm in every view." He was sure that the combined force of the Bank of New York and the Bank of the United States branch would "remove the excrescence which has just appeared."

It seems strange that a man with Hamilton's aggressive business instincts should have assumed that businessmen would go to a new bank for additional credit for speculative purposes only. Such a view could more easily be ascribed to Jefferson.

14. Jared Sparks, ed., *The Diplomatic Correspondence of the American Revolution* (Boston: Nathan Hall and Gray & Bowen, 1830), XII, 485.

15. Pelatiah Webster, *Political Essays* (Philadelphia: Joseph Cruikshank, 1791), p. 267, n. 448.

16. Carey, *op. cit.,* pp. 82 and 89.

17. Pelatiah Webster estimated the country's specie stock in 1780 to be $10 million. There were large accessions from 1780 until some time in 1783, due to expenditures by foreign troops, the French loans, and the profitable trade with the Spanish Islands. See *Political Essays,* p. 267 n.

Brissot de Warville wrote of Pennsylvania: "It was from their farms that the American and French armies were principally supplied during the last war; it was from their produce that came those millions of dollars brought from the Havanna after the year 1780—millions which laid the foundation of the Bank of North America, and supported the American army till the peace" (*New Travels in the United States of America Performed in 1788* [London: Jordan, 1792], p. 336). See also W. G. Sumner, *The Financier and the Finances of the American Revolution* (New York: Dodd, Mead, 1892), I, 99–100.

When the bank was opened, the United States subscribed $254,000 in specie; other stockholders, $70,000; but it is not clear how this amount was paid. Thomas Paine refers to a transfer of subscriptions from the Pennsylvania Bank of 1780—which functioned for a year and a half apparently as a government purchasing agency rather than as a bank—to the Bank of North America. Individual subscriptions to the latter institution may have consisted of bills of exchange, drawn on the Ministers of the United States in Europe in favor of the directors of the Pennsylvania Bank—not of specie. See Carey, *op. cit.*, p. 48; M. D. Conway, *The Writings of Thomas Paine* (New York: Putnam, 1894–96), II, 153; W. M. Gouge, *A Short History of Paper Money and Banking in the United States* (Philadelphia: T. W. Ustick, 1833). pp. 34–35.

At the end of 1793, the first date for which a figure exists, the Bank of North America held $462,000 in coin and specie. End-of-year figures for 1794–1810 were considerably lower, ranging from $102,000 to $312,000. See "Bank of North America Papers."

18. The effect would, however, have been mitigated (if we take for granted that Bank of North America loans did not exhaust the demand) by the possibility of further expansion of bank credit on the given specie base. Erick Bollmann (*Paragraphs on Banks* [Philadelphia: C. & A. Conrad, 1811], p. 38) pointed out, on the other hand, that two banks doing the same amount of business formerly done by one might require larger specie holdings than a single bank: "The most favorable situation of a bank therefore would be to be the only one in the country and to have for customers all the merchants in it, because then all payments would be made in checks on the same bank and the call for notes would be extremely limited. . . . As banks increase the custom naturally divides, which tends, as we have seen, to cause an issue of more paper and though this operates both ways, putting one bank as often in possession of the paper of the other banks as its own is held by them—yet it admits of fluctuation and prudence will require to be prepared with a greater quantity of specie."

19. The new capital was doubtless only partly paid in specie. But Morris did not decry the enlargement of the bank's capital.

20. Willing's letter, dated January 6, 1784, to "Messrs. Wm. Phillips, Isaac Smith, Jona. Mason, Thos. Russell, J. Lowell, S. Higginson of Boston" ("Bank of North America Papers"). See Hamilton to FitzSimons, March 21, 1784. *Hamilton,* I, 416.

21. On April 14, 1794, for example, the president of the Bank of North America was requested to arrange with the Bank of New York a mutual credit of $40,000 "for the accommodation of the respective customers of both banks in remitting moneys between New York and Philadelphia" (Directors' Minutes, Bank of North America).

22. *General Advertiser,* June 24, 30, 1791. Pelatiah Webster was outraged by Willing's promotion of a rival institution (*To the Stockholders of the Bank of North America by a Citizen of Philadelphia* [Philadelphia: Joseph Crukshank, 1791]), *passim.*

23. Hamilton had discussed converting the Bank of North America into a national bank (*Report on a National Bank . . . Treasury Department, December 13, 1790* [60th Cong., 1st sess., Senate Doc. 379]) as an alternative to forming the Bank of the United States. The Bank of North America showed no interest in Hamilton's suggestion. See Fisher Ames to Hamilton, July 31, 1791, *Hamilton,* V, 473.

Bingham may have planted the proposals concerning conversion of the state into a national bank. See J. O. Wettereau, "Letters from Two Busi-

ness Men to Alexander Hamilton on Federal Fiscal Policy, Nov. 1789,"
Journal of Economic and Business History, III, 681–82. Bingham was
uneasy lest the price of his Bank of North America shares decline if a
national bank entered the field. See M. L. Brown, "William Bingham,
Eighteenth Century Magnate," *Pennsylvania Magazine of History and Biography*, LI, 405.

24. Only one-quarter of the private subscription ($8,000,000) to the stock of
the Bank of the United States had to be paid in specie; the rest was paid in
stock of the United States. To pay for its subscription ($2,000,000), the United
States borrowed from the bank.

An unsigned article ("On Banks," *Gazette of the United States*, March 10,
1792) repeated the orthodox fears respecting bank competition. "A new bank
produces no new deposits of specie. There is not a dollar more money added
to the circulation. A new bank divides the deposits of specie and of course
diminishes the advantages of credit. For it is manifest that two banks with
small capitals will do less than one bank with both capitals. Besides the ordinary
banking risks, each institution is in danger from the others." For the opposite
view see Russell, "On Banking Companies in the United States," *American
Museum*, XII (September 1792), 144–45.

25. Directors' Minutes, Bank of North America.

26. There is, nevertheless, some evidence that in the beginning interbank
relations were strained. Hamilton wrote Seton, August 17, 1792: "Large
payments into the Bank of North America on account of the State of
Pennsylvania subscriptions to canals, etc., and large calls upon the Bank
of the United States for the service of government, joined to liberal
discounts, had produced a considerable balance in favor of the Bank of
North America which rendered it expedient to draw a sum of specie from
New York, not to leave the National Bank in any degree in the power
of the Bank of North America, which once manifested a very mischievous
disposition, that was afterwards repaid by acts of kindness and generosity"
(*Hamilton*, V, 521).

27. The Bank of North America's operations declined considerably between
1791 and 1792, according to year-end reports. But the rate of dividends was
relatively unaffected. In 1792 the par value of the bank's outstanding stock
was only $742,800, compared with $946,800 seven years before. The difference
represented stock bought in at one time or another. See Directors' Minutes,
March 1, 1792.

	1791	1792
	($000's)	
Discounts	2,557	1,771
Circulation	1,000	531
Deposits	1,293	953

28. Lewis, *op. cit.*, p. 152.

29. Directors' Minutes, Bank of North America, July 2, 1792.

30. An Act of April 10, 1792 (*Pennsylvania Statutes: Laws Passed 1791–92*,
chap. lxxvi), empowered the governor to apply certain moneys "in the pro-
curing of shares in the Bank of North America for the use of this Commonwealth, provided the same may be obtainable at par."

31. *Senate Journal 1792–93*, pp. 90–91; Stockholders' Minutes.

32. *Senate Journal 1792–93*, pp. 180–81; Anthony Morris (a director of the
Bank of North America, 1800–1808) made this proposal in a bill he read in the

Senate after moving to postpone the House bill incorporating the Bank of Pennsylvania.

33. While the older banks financed principally merchants engaged in foreign trade, the customers of the Bank of Pennsylvania were described as chiefly retail shopkeepers. See Henry Adams, *The Writings of Albert Gallatin* (Philadelphia: Lippincott, 1879), I, 80. Thomas Leiper, the tobacconist, was dissatisfied with the accommodation he received at the Bank of the United States and transferred his business to the Bank of Pennsylvania, of which he became a director. Cf. a speech by James Lloyd, United States Senator from Massachusetts, *Annals of Congress*, XXII (11th Cong., 3d sess., Senate), 165.

34. *House Journal 1792–93*, pp. 142, 156–57; *Pennsylvania Statutes: Laws Passed 1792–93: Act of March 30, 1793*, chap. xxix, sec. xi; *Senate Journal 1793–94*, p. 44.

A select committee of the Senate noted in 1809: "The object of the legislature in the establishment of this bank was to promote the regular, permanent and successful operation of· the finances of the state, so as to be productive of benefit to trade and industry in general" (*Senate Journal 1809–10*), p. 67. Henry Adams quotes Gallatin: "The apprehension that this (the surplus) would be squandered by the Legislature was the principal inducement for chartering the Bank of Pennsylvania" (*The Life of Albert Gallatin* [New York: Peter Smith, 1943], p. 86). *Gazette of the United States* (March 9, 1793) published the following rhyme of opposition:

> "ANOTHER BANK
> "The State, in cash 'tis said abounds,
> To th' amount of many thousand pounds;
> Snug in the banks the treasure lies—
> A sure defence should dangers rise;
> For while 'tis hid from public view,
> It mocks the grasping, scheming crew;
> But cunning now exerts its springs,
> To give the dormant eagles wings;
> Hence a new banking plan is form'd,
> And soon the bolted vaults are storm'd,
> On paper plumes they mount the air,
> And fly—the Lord alone knows where;
> Meantime the Sharks of speculation,
> Laugh at the sages of the Nation!"

35. Stockholders' Minutes, Bank of North America, May 28, 1793; *Senate Journal 1809–10*, pp. 67–80. In Baltimore in 1795 a proposal to establish a new bank was also coupled with a clause providing for the consolidation of the Bank of Maryland with the new institution, if both parties consented. The clause was not accepted, and the Bank of Baltimore was chartered as an entirely separate institution. See A. C. Bryan, *History of State Banking in Maryland* (Baltimore: Johns Hopkins Press, 1899), pp. 20–21.

36. Directors' Minutes, June 2, 1794.

37. J. T. Holdsworth, *The First Bank of the United States* (Washington: Government Printing Office, 1910), p. 41; Directors' Minutes, Bank of North America, March 2, June 26, 1797; May 16, 1799.

38. Adam Seybert, *Statistical Annals* (Philadelphia: T. Dobson & Son, 1818), p. 60; "Minutes of Evidence . . . respecting the Orders in Council," *Parliamentary Papers, 1808*, X, No. 119, 2, 3, 9, 15, 35, 48, 143; Alexander Baring

Ashburton, *An Inquiry into the Causes and Consequences of the Orders in Council* (2d ed.; London: J. M. Richardson, 1808), p. 62.

39. *House Journal 1803–4*, p. 258; Stephen N. Winslow, *Biographies of Successful Philadelphia Merchants* (Philadelphia: James K. Simon, 1864), pp. 167–69; Abraham Ritter, *Philadelphia and Her Merchants* (Philadelphia, 1860), pp. 49, 70; *Observations on the Principles and Operation of Banking with Strictures on the Opposition to the Bank of Philadelphia by Anti-Monopoly* (Philadelphia, 1804).

40. Joel Cook, *The Philadelphia National Bank: A Century's Record, 1803–1903, by a Stockholder* (Philadelphia: W. H. Fell, 1903), p. 23.

An analogous situation developed in New York. For fifteen years the Bank of New York had no rival. When the Manhattan Company was incorporated, ostensibly to supply water to the City of New York but in reality to carry on a banking business, the directors of the Bank of New York at a special meeting on August 22, 1799, resolved not to accept its notes. The resolution was rescinded on April 15, 1800. See H. W. Domett, *A History of the Bank of New York* (New York: G. P. Putnam's Sons, 1884), pp. 57–58. The Bank of New York must have learned that an aggressor was no more immune to attack than its victim.

41. Cook, *op. cit.*, p. 30.

42. *Observations* . . . , p. 15. Because street money rates declined as bank loans increased, the author claimed that usurers were among the most violent opponents of the new bank.

43. In Baltimore the atmosphere was similarly hostile to the formation of the third city bank. The application of the Union Bank for a charter from Maryland in 1804 was bitterly opposed by the Bank of Maryland and the Bank of Baltimore. Bryan, *op. cit.*, pp. 23–24.

44. *House Journal 1812–13*, p. 193. The resolution, which was defeated, proposed either to sell the state's stockholdings in incorporated banks, the receipts to be lent to the federal government, or to transfer the stock to it on terms agreed upon.

45. *House Journal 1803–4*, pp. 67–68.

46. *Ibid.*, pp. 66–67.

47. *Ibid.*, pp. 83–84; *Senate Journal 1803–4*, pp. 52–53.

48. *Ibid.*, p. 71.

49. William Maclay, who served as United States senator from Pennsylvania, 1789–91, was Jeffersonian in outlook before the party came into existence. The Hamiltonian system was exceedingly distasteful to him, but his efforts to curb it were unsuccessful. A quotation from his diary, dated January 1, 1791, reveals his views on banks. "This day the Bank [of the United States] bill reported. It is totally in vain to oppose this bill. The only useful part I can act is to try to make it of some benefit to the public, which reaps none from the existing banks" (E. S. Maclay, ed., *The Journal of Maclay* [New York: A. & C. Boni, 1927], p. 353).

50. It added two supplements to each proposal: (*a*) to permit the state to subscribe $300,000, paying in at par 6 percent stock of the United States, then selling at a discount; (*b*) to lend the state not over $100,000, whenever required, for the term of its charter, at not more than 5 percent interest. It advanced the premium it was prepared to give under the fourth proposal (for an exchange of $500,000 of Philadelphia Bank stock for Bank of Pennsylvania stock) from $125,000 to $166,666.67 and guaranteed to pay within six months $100,000 above the par value of the Philadelphia Bank stock the state would thus acquire,

if the legislature should pass a law within one year relinquishing the stock. Moreover, it suggested that the state have the right to appoint directors in proportion to its stockholdings. See *House Journal 1803–4*, pp. 257–58; *Senate Journal 1803–4*, p. 273. (The state owned thirteen twenty-thirds of Bank of Pennsylvania stock but had power to appoint only six twenty-fifths of the directors. When the Philadelphia Bank was finally incorporated, the state owned three-thirteenths of its stock and was represented by three-elevenths of the directors.)

51. *House Journal 1803–4*, p. 252.

52. *Ibid.*, pp. 260–61. A bill embodying the measure proposed by the Bank of Pennsylvania was printed, without authority, to accompany the Maclay report, and distributed in handbills to members; see *ibid.*, pp. 348–52. This minor scandal was, however, suppressed.

53. *Senate Journal 1803–4*, p. 168.

54. *House Journal 1803–4*, pp. 285–87.

55. *Ibid.*, pp. 298–300, 304–5, 319.

56. *Ibid.*, p. 379; *Senate Journal 1803–4*, pp. 250–51.

57. *House Journal 1803–4*, pp. 387–88, 392, 396.

58. *Senate Journal 1803–4*, pp. 249, 257, 269–70.

59. *Ibid.*, pp. 272–74. The Bank of Pennsylvania would give the state and permit it to subscribe $200,000 at par. The state would make a profit of $120,000 by taking advantage of its right to subscribe a further sum of $300,000, in exchange for 6 percent United States stock at par. At the end of one year, if the state wanted to sell the stock, the bank would purchase it at a 40 percent increase in price. At the end of five years the state would also receive $120,000, the estimated excess of payments over par from the sale of $300,000 of unsubscribed stock.

60. With one addition, the conditions were the same as those the Maclay committee had reported and indorsed. The bank now further demanded the return of $200,000 of the state's stock, at par, should the legislature grant another charter for a bank before 1827; see *ibid.*, p. 274.

61. *Ibid.*, pp. 277–84, 287–89.

62. The notes of the private bank which Stephen Girard founded in Philadelphia in May, 1812, with a capital of $1,200,000, were at first refused by some banks, but opposition collapsed early in 1813. The chartered banks were possibly indignant that Girard had ceased paying out their notes, as had been his practice until his own were printed. Nonacceptance of his notes had a basis in law, as the Act of March 19, 1810, prohibited the issue of bank notes by unincorporated Pennsylvania banks. Government agents evidently did not initially accept them, but to Girard's subscription, exceeding $5 million, to the United States loan of 1813, there was a proviso that the private bank be placed on the same footing as chartered banks in Philadelphia. David Lenox, a trustee of Girard's bank, who was elected president of the Philadelphia Bank in January, 1813, is said to have been instrumental in arranging to have Girard's notes honored by the chartered bank. See Stephen Simpson, *Biography of Stephen Girard* (Philadelphia, 1832), p. 114; K. L. Brown, "Stephen Girard's Bank," *Pennsylvania Magazine of History and Biography*, LXVI, 36–42; Cook, *op. cit.*, pp. 55, 58.

63. From then on banks were controlled by and offered accommodation to others besides merchants in foreign trade. See *General Advertiser*, February 11, 12, 16, 1807, and February 3, 1808; James Robinson, *The Philadephia Directory for 1807*.

64. *House Journal 1807–8,* I, 194–95. The chairman of this committee was John Sergeant, whose legal talents were early enlisted in support of banks and commercial interests.

65. *Ibid.,* p. 197.

66. C. J. Bullock, J. H. Williams, and R. S. Tucker, "The Balance of Trade of the United States," *Review of Economic Statistics* (1919), I, 215–17.

2   Money and Business Cycles

Milton Friedman and Anna J. Schwartz

The subject assigned for this session covers too broad an area to be given even a fairly cursory treatment in a single paper. Accordingly, we have chosen to concentrate on the part of it that relates to monetary factors in economic fluctuations. We shall still further narrow the scope of the paper by interpreting "monetary factors" to mean the role of the stock of money and of changes in the stock—thereby casting the "credit" market as one of the supporting players rather than a star performer—and by intrepreting "economic fluctuations" to mean business cycles, or even more exactly, the reference cycles studied and chronicled by the National Bureau.

The topic so interpreted has been rather out of fashion for the past few decades. Before the Great Depression, it was widely accepted that the business cycle was a monetary phenomenon, "a dance of the dollar," as Irving Fisher graphically described it in the title of a famous article.[1] Different versions of monetary theories of the business cycle abounded, though some of these were really "credit" theories misnamed, since they gave little role to changes in the money stock except as an incident in the alteration of credit conditions; and there was nothing like agreement on the details of any one theory. Yet it is probably true that most economists gave the money stock and changes in it an important, if not a central, role in whatever particular theory of the cycle they were inclined to accept. That emphasis was greatly strengthened by the course of economic events in the twenties. The high degree of economic stability then achieved was widely regarded as a consequence of the effectiveness of the monetary policies followed by the only recently created Federal Reserve System and hence as evidence that monetary factors were indeed a central factor in the cycle.

The Great Depression radically changed economic attitudes. The failure of the Federal Reserve System to stem the depression was widely interpreted—wrongly as we have elsewhere argued[2] and elaborate below—to mean that monetary factors were not critical, that "real" factors were the key to economic fluctuations. Investment—which had always had a prominent place in business cycle theories—received new emphasis as a result of the Keynesian revolution, so much so that Paul Samuelson, in the best selling textbook in the country, could assert confidently, "All modern economists are agreed that the important factor in causing income and employment to fluctuate is investment."[3] Investment was the motive force, its effects spread through time and amplified by the "multiplier," and itself partly or largely a result of the "accelerator." Money, if it entered at all, played a purely passive role.

Recently, a revival of interest in money has been sparked less by concern with business cycles than with concern about inflation. Easy money policies were accompanied by inflation; and inflation was nowhere stemmed without a more or less deliberate limitation of growth of the money stock. But once interest was aroused, it naturally extended to the cycle as well as to inflation. In the United States, indeed, there has been something of a repetition of the 1920s. A high degree of economic stability has been accompanied by a large measure of talk about an active monetary policy, and the monetary authorities have often been given credit for playing an important role in promoting stability. As the experience of the twenties suggests, this fair-weather source of support for the importance of money is a weak reed.

Examining the present state of our understanding about the role of money in the business cycle, we shall first present some facts that seem reasonably well established about the cyclical behavior of money and related magnitudes and then speculate about some plausible interpretations of these facts. The facts we present are drawn largely from our own unpublished work done under the auspices of the National Bureau of Economic Research and associated unpublished work by Phillip Cagan.

2.1 Some Facts about the Cyclical Behavior of Money

2.1.1 Cyclical Pattern of the Money Stock

The outstanding cyclical fact about the stock of money is that it has tended to rise during both cyclical expansions and cyclical contractions. This is clear from figure 2.1 which plots (1) the stock of money from 1867 to 1960, with money defined as including currency plus adjusted deposits in commercial banks (both demand and time) held by the nonbanking public (i.e., excluding both balances of the federal government and of banks); and (2) from 1914 on, a narrower total which excludes time deposits. From 1867 to 1907, our data are at annual or

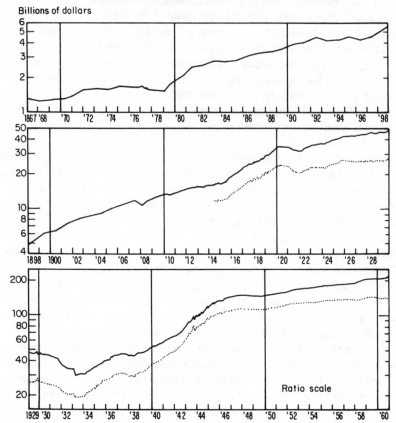

Figure 2.1   Money stock including commercial bank time deposits, 1867–1960, and currency plus demand deposits adjusted, 1914–60. *Source:* Friedman and Schwartz, *A Monetary History of the United States, 1867–1960* (Princeton, N.J.: Princeton University Press, for the National Bureau of Economic Research, 1963a), table A-1, cols. 7 and 8. These are seasonally adjusted figures, dates as of end of month, 1867–1946; for 1947–60, currency plus demand deposits adjusted is an average of daily figures, and commercial bank time deposits, a 2-month moving average of last-Wednesday-of-month figures, for a month centered at mid-month.

semiannual dates; from 1907 on, monthly. The only major exceptions since 1867 to the tendency of the money stock to rise during both cyclical expansions and cyclical contractions occurred in the years listed in the following tabulation, which gives also the percentage decline during each exception.

Years of Exception	Percentage Decline
1873–79	4.9
1892–94	5.8
1907–08	3.7
1920–21	5.1
1929–33	35.2
1937–38	2.4

In addition, there were two minor exceptions since the end of World War II,

1948–49	1.4
1959–60	1.1

The major exceptions clearly did not fall in a random subset of years. Each corresponds with an economic contraction that was major as judged by other indicators; in the period covered, there was no other economic contraction more severe than any in the list; and there appears to be a considerable gap between the severity of those contractions and of the remainder, with the possible exception of the contraction of 1882–85 which might be regarded as a somewhat borderline case.

For mild depression cycles, therefore, the cycle does not show up as a rise and a fall. Figure 2.2 gives the average reference-cycle patterns for mild and deep depression cycles since 1867, excluding only war cycles. (Patterns are given separately for the period before and after 1907, because the availability of monthly data after 1907 permits the construction of a more detailed pattern—a nine-point instead of a five-point pattern.) The patterns for mild depression cycles rise almost in a straight line, though there is some indication of a slower rate of growth from mid-expansion to mid-contraction than during the rest of the cycle (especially in the nine-point pattern for monthly data). In its cyclical behavior, the money stock is like other series with a sharp upward trend—such as population, the total stock of houses, the number of miles of railroad track in operation in the pre-1914 period, the amount of electrical energy produced. In all of these, the cycle shows up not in an absolute rise and fall but in different rates of rise.

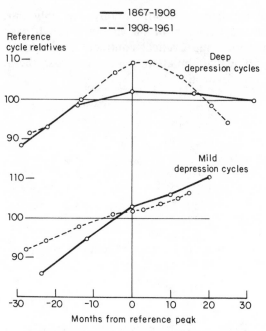

Figure 2.2   Money stock: average reference-cycle patterns for mild and deep depression cycles, 1867–1961. War cycles, not shown, are 1914–19 and 1938–45. Deep depression cycles are 1870–79, 1891–94, 1904–8, 1919–21, 1917–33, and 1933–38. All others are mild depression cycles. *Source:* For method of deriving reference cycle relatives for the 9-point pattern, see A. F. Burns and W. C. Mitchell, *Measuring Business Cycles* (Cambridge, Mass.: National Bureau of Economic Research, 1946), pp. 160–70; we used a variant of the National Bureau's standard technique for annual series (pp. 197–202) for the 5-point pattern.

For deep depression cycles, the cyclical pattern is nearer the stereotype of a rise during expansion and a fall during contraction. From these patterns, it would be easy to conclude that the two groups of cycles distinguished are members of different species with respect to the behavior of the stock of money.

2.1.2 Cyclical Pattern of the Rate of Change in the Money Stock

Because the strong upward trend of the stock of money tends to dominate its cyclical behavior, it is desirable to eliminate the effect of the trend in order to reveal the cyclical behavior more clearly. There are various ways of doing this.[4] The method we have used is to take logarithmic first differences of the money stock, which is equivalent to using the percentage rate of change from one time unit to the next.

Figure 2.3 plots the resulting series. It is clear that this device effectively eliminates trend. It is clear also that, as first differencing usually does, it produces a highly jagged series with a sawtooth appearance. The reason is that independent errors of measurement in the original stock series introduce negative serial correlation into first differences.

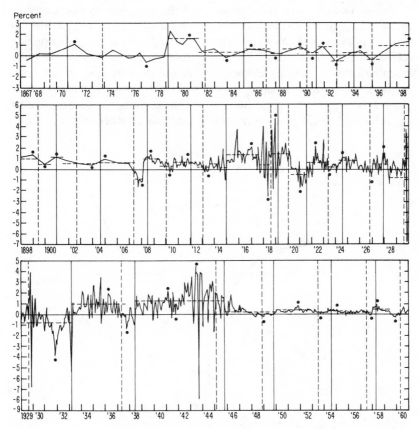

Figure 2.3   Month-to-month rate of change in U.S. money stock, 1867–1960. Solid vertical lines represent reference cycle troughs; broken lines, peaks. Dots represent peaks and troughs of specific cycles. The horizontal broken lines represent high and low steps in the rate of change. *Source:* In the annual or semi-annual segment, 1867–1907, the change in natural logarithm from one date to the next in the data underlying figure 2.1 was divided by the number of months intervening, and the quotient was plotted at the middle of the month halfway between. In the monthly segment, 1907–60, the month-to-month change in natural logarithm was plotted in the middle of the second month. Reference dates are from the National Bureau (see table 2.1).

But despite these short-term irregularities, the series shows clearly marked cyclical fluctuations corresponding to reference cycles.

Figure 2.4 gives the reference cycle patterns for this series. They show a clear cyclical pattern with the mild and deep depression cycles distinguished, this time primarily by their amplitude, so that they now look more like different members of the same species. The peak rate of change occurs early in expansion and the trough early in recession. Indeed these occur so early as to suggest the possibility of interpreting the rate of change series as inverted, i.e., as generally declining during reference expansion and rising during reference contraction. We have examined this possibility elsewhere.[5] A full presentation of our tests is not feasible in this paper; it will suffice to note that they rather decisively support treating the rate of change series as conforming to the reference cycle positively with a long lead, rather than inversely

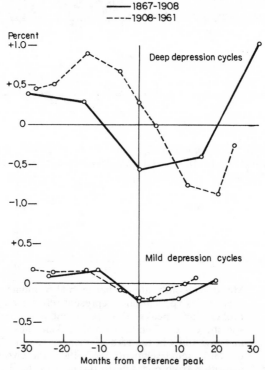

Figure 2.4   Rate of change in money stock: average reference-cycle patterns for mild and deep depression cycles, 1867–1961. War cycles, not shown, are 1914–19 and 1938–45. Deep depression cycles are 1870–79, 1891–94, 1904–8, 1919–21, 1927–33, and 1933–38. All others are mild depression cycles. *Source:* see n. 5.

with a somewhat shorter lag. Though we have not analyzed in as much detail the narrower total of currency plus adjusted demand deposits, its cylical pattern since 1914 is very similar in general form to the pattern of the broader total.

2.1.3   Cyclical Timing of the Rate of Change in the Money Stock

Evidence on cyclical timing derived from a comparison of turning points is clearly not available from the stock of money series, because it has so few turning points. For the rate-of-change series, we have dated turning points in two ways: (1) We have sought to approximate the series by a step function, with successively high and low steps, because at times the series gives the impression of dropping suddenly from one level to a decidedly lower level, or of rising from one level to a decidedly higher level. The horizontal broken lines in figure 2.3 indicate the steps we have used. We call the date at which a high step ends, the date of a step peak, the date at which a low step ends, the date of a step trough. (2) We have applied the usual National Bureau specific cycle dating procedure to the rate-of-change series, and have designated specific cycle peaks and troughs. They are marked by black dots in figure 2.3.

Table 2.1 gives the step and specific cycle peaks and troughs we have selected, the dates of the reference cycle turns with which we have matched them, and the indicated lead ($-$) or lag ($+$) at the corresponding turn.[6] Clearly, leads predominate, and clearly also, there is much variability.

Table 2.2 gives the average lead and the standard deviations of the leads for mild depression cycles, deep depression cycles, all nonwar cycles and all cycles, for both step dates and specific cycle dates. For step dates, the average lead for all cycles is 7 months at the peak and 4 months at the trough; for specific cycle dates, the average lead is 18 months at the peak and 12 months at the trough; for step dates, the standard deviation of the lead is 6 months at troughs and 8 months at peaks; for specific cycle dates, the standard deviation of the lead is 6 months at troughs and 7 months at peaks.

Estimation of timing relations by a comparison of turning points seems inefficient, because it uses so little of the information contained in the series. Therefore, we have experimented extensively with other devices, in particular, cross-correlograms and cross-spectral analysis. While these devices, particularly cross-spectral analysis, offer great promise for the future, as yet we have no substantive results worth reporting.

We have tested to determine whether there is any secular trend in the leads or lags; whether the pre-1914 timing, before the establishment of the Federal Reserve System, differs from the post-1914 timing

Table 2.1 Timing of Specific Cycle and of Step Troughs and Peaks in the Rate of Change in the Money Stock Compared with Timing of Business Cycles

| | Troughs | | | | Peaks | | | | |
| | Date of: | | Lead(−) or Lag(+) in Months at Reference Trough of: | | | Date of: | | Lead(−) or Lag(+) in Months at Reference Peak of: | |
Step Trough	Specific Cycle Trough	Matched Reference Trough	Step Trough	Specific Cycle Trough	Step Peak	Specific Cycle Peak	Matched Reference Peak	Step Peak	Specific Cycle Peak
				Semi-annual and Annual Data					
2/79	5/77	3/79	−1	−22	2/72	7/71	10/73	−20	−27
6/85	12/83	5/85	+1	−17	8/81	5/81	3/82	−7	−10
6/88	12/87	4/88	+2	−4	6/87	12/85	3/87	+3	−15
6/91	12/90	5/91	+1	−5	6/90	12/89	7/90	−1	−7
6/93	12/92	6/94	−12	−18	6/92	12/91	1/93	−7	−13
6/96	12/95	6/97	−12	−18	6/95	12/94	12/95	−6	−12
6/00	12/99	12/00	−6	−12	6/99	12/98	6/99	0	−6
6/04	12/03	8/04	−2	−8	6/01	12/00	9/02	−15	−21
					6/07	12/04	5/07	+1	−29

Monthly Data

2/08	1/08	6/08	−4	−5	6/09	10/08	1/10	−7	−15
8/10	4/10	1/12	−17	−21	6/12	10/11	1/13	−7	−15
7/13					5/14				
12/14	6/13	12/14	0	−18	7/17	12/16	8/18	−13	−20
5/18	5/18	3/19	−10	−10	3/20	12/18	1/20	+2	−13
7/21	1/21	7/21	0	−6	5/23	4/22	5/23	0	−13
3/24	6/23	7/24	−4	−13	9/25	7/24	10/26	−13	−27
12/26	12/26	11/27	−11	−11	4/28	11/27	8/29	−16	−21
4/33	10/31	3/33	+1	−17	7/36	4/36	5/37	−10	−13
5/38	10/37	6/38	−1	−8		2/41	2/45	+8	−20
	10/41				10/45	6/43	11/48		
10/45	10/45	10/45							
1/50	1/49	10/49	+3	−9	12/52	11/51	7/53	−7	−20
4/54	9/53	8/54	−4	−11	9/55	2/55	7/57	−22	−29
1/58	12/57	4/58	−3	−4	5/59	6/58	5/60	−12	−23
6/60	12/59	2/61	−8	−14					

Source: Figure 2.3. Step peaks and step troughs are last months of alternate steps shown here.

Note: Reference dates through April 1958 are shown in *Business Cycle Indicators*, Geoffrey H. Moore, ed., Princeton University Press for NBER, 1961, vol. 1, p. 670; subsequent dates are from an unpublished National Bureau table. For timing comparisons, both the rate of change series and the steps made from it are treated as well conforming, because of the nearly 1-to-1 correspondence between their turning points and reference cycle turning points, and because the money stock series from which both were derived has moderately high conformity indexes (100 for expansions, −43 for contractions, −71 for trough-to-trough full cycles, +50 for peak-to-peak full cycles, +61 for full cycles both ways). Matching of step and specific cycle turns with reference turns follows Burns and Mitchell, *Meaning of Business Cycles*, NBER, 1949, pp. 115–28. Earlier versions of this table were based on data now superseded.

Table 2.2   Average Timing of Specific Cycle and of Step Peaks and Troughs in the Rate of Change in the Money Stock and Standard Deviation of Lead or Lag, by Period and Type of Cycle

Period	Number of Observations				Mean Lead (−) or Lag (+) in Months				Standard Deviation of Lead or Lag in Months			
	Step Analysis		Specific Cycle Analysis		Step Analysis		Specific Cycle Analysis		Step Analysis		Specific Cycle Analysis	
	Trough	Peak	Trough	Peak	Trough	Peak	Trough	Peak	Trough	Peak	Trough	Peak
					All Cycles							
1870–1908	8	9	8	9	−3.6	−5.8	−13.0	−15.6	5.7	7.7	6.7	8.3
1908–1960	13	12	13	12	−4.5	−8.1	−11.3	−19.1	5.7	8.3	5.2	5.5
1870–1960	21	21	21	21	−4.1	−7.1	−12.0	−17.6	5.6	7.9	5.7	6.9
					War Cycles							
1908–1960	1	2	1	2	−10.0	−2.5	−10.0	−20.0	—	14.8	—	0
					Deep Depression Cycles							
1870–1908	2	3	2	3	−6.5	−8.7	−20.0	−23.0	7.8	10.6	2.8	8.7
1908–1960	4	3	4	3	−1.0	−8.0	−9.0	−15.7	2.2	9.2	5.5	4.6
1870–1960	6	6	6	6	−2.8	−8.3	−12.7	−19.3	4.8	8.9	7.2	7.4
					Mild Depression Cycles							
1870–1908	6	6	6	6	−2.7	−4.3	−10.7	−11.8	5.4	6.4	6.0	5.6
1908–1960	8	7	8	7	−5.5	−9.7	−12.6	−20.3	6.3	6.9	5.3	6.3
1870–1960	14	13	14	13	−4.3	−7.2	−11.8	−16.4	5.9	7.0	5.5	7.2

Source: Table 2.1. To avoid duplication, each cycle is represented only by its peak and terminal trough. War, deep depression, and mild depression cycles are grouped as in figure 2.2.

whether timing during mild depression cycles differs from timing during deep depression cycles; and whether there is any relation between the length of the lead and the amplitude of the subsequent or prior cyclical phase. Our results so far are negative: none of these criteria appears to be associated with a statistically significant difference in timing.

2.1.4   Amplitude of Movements in the Rate of Change in the Money Stock

1. The subdivision between mild and severe depression cycles in figure 2.4 corresponds to a sharp difference in the amplitude of reference cycles in the rate of change. This result suggests that the amplitude of the changes in the rate of change in the money stock is related to the severity of cyclical movements in general business, even though the timing of the changes in the rate of change in the money stock is not.

2. One way in which we have investigated this relation further is to correlate the ranking of the amplitudes of cyclical movements in the rate of change with the ranking of the amplitudes of the corresponding cyclical movements in general business, as measured by two different indicators: one, bank clearings to 1919 and bank debits thereafter; the other, an index computed by Geoffrey H. Moore. The correlations, summarized in table 2.3, are throughout positive—for expansions alone, for contractions alone, and for full cycles, for the period before 1908 and for the period since, as well as for the whole period.

The correlations between the rate of change measure and the Moore index are sufficiently high so that, even with the small number of observations on which they are based, they could hardly have arisen from chance. There is a less close connection between the clearings-debits figures and the rate of change, especially in expansions. The Moore index is adjusted for trend and reflects primarily changes in physical units. Likewise, the shift from the total stock of money to the rate of change is, as noted earlier, equivalent to adjusting for trend; in addition, it involves a change from a measure expressed in nominal units—dollars—to a measure expressed in relative units—per cent— and as a flow—per month. The amplitude of clearings-debits, however, is not adjusted for intracycle trend, and clearings-debits are, in their original form, in dollars. It would be interesting to know whether the adjustment for trend, or the different weight given to financial and physical transactions, is primarily responsible for the closer connection of the Moore index than of clearings-debits to the rate of change.

The table as a whole leaves little doubt that there is a fairly close connection between the magnitude of monetary changes during the course of cycles, and the magnitude of the associated cyclical movement in business. The relation is by no means perfect for the measures

Table 2.3 **Rank Difference Correlation Between Change in Rate of Change in Money Stock and Change in Two Indicators of General Business, 1879–1961, Excluding War Cycles and 1945–49**

| Specific Cycles in Rate of Change in Money Stock Correlated with: | Rank Difference Correlation of Amplitudes | | | |
| | NBER Reference | | NBER Reference Full Cycle | |
	Expansion	Contraction	Trough-to-Trough	Peak-to-Peak
Annual and semiannual data		1879–1907 (8 pairs)		1882–1908 (7 pairs)
Reference cycles in clearings-debits	.36	.64	.43	.68
Specific cycles in Moore index	.76	.85	.76	.79
Monthly data		1907–1960 (10 pairs)		1908–1960 (10 pairs)
Reference cycles in clearings-debits	.30	.54	.37	.57
Specific cycles in Moore index	.82	.58	.75	.81
Whole-period data		1879–1961 (18 pairs)		1882–1960 (17 pairs)
Reference cycles in clearings-debits	.27	.64	.41	.62
Specific cycles in Moore index	.77	.70	.78	.77

Source: Rate of change in money stock: Figures underlying figure 2.3 were analyzed for specific cycles, as in Burns and Mitchell, *Measuring Business Cycles,* pp. 115–141; matching of peaks and troughs with reference turns follows table 2.1.

Clearings-debits: Bank clearings outside New York City, monthly, 1879–1919; bank debits outside New York City, monthly, 1919–61. 1879–1942: Seasonally adjusted from *Historical Statistics of the United States, 1789–1945,* Bureau of the Census, 1949, pp. 324–325, 337–388. 1943–61: Board of Governors of the Federal Reserve System, Division of Bank Operations, mimeographed table "Bank Debits and Rates of Turnover" (C. 5, Revised Series, 1943–52), December 23, 1953; thereafter *Federal Reserve Bulletin,* adjusted for seasonal variation by NBER. Reference cycle analysis follows Burns and Mitchell, pp. 160–170.

Moore index: Unpublished memorandum by Geoffrey H. Moore, extending table in *ibid.,* p. 403, and revising and updating table in *Business Cycle Indicators,* G. H. Moore, ed., vol. I, p. 104. An average of three trend adjusted indexes of business activity—A. T. & T., Persons-Barrons, and Ayres—each of which was analyzed for specific cycles, suppressing specific cycle turns not corresponding to reference cycle turns.

Note: In our full study we have used three measures of the amplitude of the change in money, each both in total and as a rate per month, measuring the change in cycle relatives between reference dates, between step dates, and between specific cycle peaks and troughs in the rate of change. To simplify our presentation here, we restrict the comparison to the total change in amplitude between peaks and troughs in the rate of change.

War cycles 1914–19 and 1938–45 are omitted because of their special characteristics. The 1945–49 cycle is omitted because the expansion is skipped by the rate of change

Table 2.3   (continued)

series (see table 2.1). No tied ranks correction is used in getting correlation coefficients. "Amplitude" of rate of change in money stock is expressed in units of the data as plotted in figure 2.3 above. For expansions, it is the change in stages I–V of the specific cycle; for contractions, the change in stages V–IX of the specific cycle. For clearings-debits the reference cycle amplitude (stages I–V–IX), expressed in reference-cycle relatives, was used. For the Moore index, specific cycle amplitudes only are available, but they have a one-to-one correspondence with reference cycles. For full cycles, trough-to-trough, the change from V to IX was subtracted from the change from I to V to obtain the total rise and fall used in the correlations; for full cycles, peak-to-peak, the change from I to V was subtracted from the change from V to IX.

we use. But we have no way of knowing from this evidence alone to what extent the discrepancies reflect the inadequacies of our indexes of economic change, the statistical errors in our money series, or a basic lack of connection between monetary and economic changes.

3. To get further evidence, we have investigated this relation in a different way using annual data. For the period from 1869 to 1960, we have annual estimates of net national product, and also, of course, annual estimates of the stock of money. For this period, we have computed logarithmic first differences (i.e., year-to-year percentage changes) of both series. We have then computed moving standard deviations (comparable to moving averages) from these rates of change involving 3, 4, 5, and 6 terms. To illustrate: for the 3-term moving standard deviation, we took the initial three rates of change (1869–70, 1870–71, 1871–72), computed their standard deviation by the usual statistical formula,[7] and dated the result as of 1870–71; then dropped the initial year and added a year, computed the standard deviation for the resulting triplet of rates of change (1870–71, 1871–72, 1872–73), and dated the results as of 1871–72; and so on.

These moving standard deviations are a measure of the variability of the rates of change—in the one case, of money; in the other case, of income. If such a computation were made for a strictly periodic series, say, a sine wave of fixed period and fixed amplitude, and if the length of the moving standard deviation were the same as the period of the sine wave (or an integral multiple of it), then the computed moving standard deviation would be constant over time, and its value would be equal to $\sqrt{1/2}$ times the amplitude of the sine wave.[8] If the length of the moving standard deviation were shorter than the period of the sine wave, the computed moving standard deviation would fluctuate over time, its value never exceeding the value just cited. The same proposition holds if the length of the moving standard deviation is longer than the period of the sine wave but not an integral multiple of it, though it is perhaps obvious that, as the moving standard deviation is lengthened, the standard deviation will approach the constant value noted above, since the fractional cycle becomes less and less important compared to the whole cycles included in the computation of the standard deviation.

It follows from these considerations that, for our purpose, which is to see how the amplitude of the cycles in the rate of change in the money stock is related to the amplitude of business cycles, we want to use a number of terms equal to the length of the cycle in which we are interested. This explains why we have used 3, 4, 5, and 6 terms, for the reference cycle since 1867 has averaged four years in length but has occasionally been shorter or longer. As it happens, the results are not very different for different numbers of terms, so we present a chart for only the 4-term results, though we give some numerical data for all.

One more point before turning to the results. Net national product, which we are using as an index of general business and whose fluctuations we are interpreting as a measure of the amplitude of business cycles, has a sharp upward trend, though a less steep one than the money stock has, so that it typically declines absolutely during contractions. If we were to take a moving standard deviation of its absolute values, or their logarithms, the result would overestimate cyclical variability because of the intracycle trend, and the overestimate would vary over time as the intracycle trend did. Accordingly, to eliminate the effect of the intracycle trend from our measure of variability, we have used logarithmic first differences for net national product as well. This procedure is of the same class and for the same purpose as the National Bureau's standard technique of estimating full cycle amplitudes by subtracting the change during contraction from the change during expansion. However, the use of first differences can also be taken to mean that what we are calling the amplitude of business cycles refers to a construct rather different from the National Bureau's standard reference cycle; it refers to a cycle in the rate of change in aggregates rather than in the level of aggregates. As is well known, for a sine wave, the rate of change series has the same amplitude and pattern as the original series but differs in phase, its peaks and troughs coming one-quarter of a cycle earlier or three-quarters of a cycle later than the peaks and troughs of the original series.

Aside from removing the effect of intracycle trend, another advantage of using the first differences of net national product is that the results would be almost identical for total net national product and net national product per capita. Since population has grown at a steady rate over periods of 3 to 6 years, the use of per capita data would affect only the moving average of the rates of change but not the moving standard deviation.

Figure 2.5 plots the 4-term moving standard deviations for money and net national product. It should be noted that since we have used natural logarithms, the vertical scale can be interpreted directly in terms of percentage points. For example, a value of .100 means that the

Natural logarithms

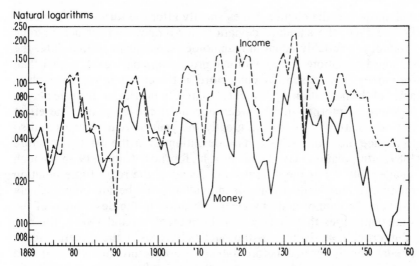

Figure 2.5   Moving standard deviation of annual rates of change in money,
1869–1958, and in income, 1871–1958, 4-term series. *Source:*
Money figures described in source for figure 2.1 are annual
averages centered on June 30. Income figures are annual
estimates of net national product, beginning 1869, from worksheets underlying Simon Kuznets, *Capital in the American
Economy: Its Formation and Financing* (Princeton, N.J.:
Princeton University Press for NBER, 1961). For computation of moving standard deviation, see subsections 3 of this
section, and n. 7.

standard deviation is equal to an annual rate of growth of 10 percentage
points.[9] The scale on the chart is logarithmic. The reason is that, since
the standard error of the estimated standard deviation is proportional
to the (true) standard deviation, the standard error of the logarithm of
the standard deviation is roughly a constant, regardless of the size of
the (true) standard deviation. Hence the logarithmic scale makes sampling fluctuations appear the same size throughout.

It is clear from the chart that there is a close relation between the
variability of money and of net national product: the two curves parallel
one another with a high degree of fidelity, especially when it is borne
in mind that standard deviations based on only four observations (three
degrees of freedom) are subject to a good deal of sampling variation,[10]
that the net national product and money series are, so far as we know,
wholly independent in their statistical construction, and that both are
subject to an appreciable margin of error.

At first glance, it appears from figure 2.5 that income has become
more variable relative to money over the period covered. Unless we
are mistaken, this is a statistical artifact. A closer look at the chart

will show that the change comes shortly after the turn of the century. Before 1900, the standard deviations for money and for net national product are roughly equal in magnitude; subsequent to that date, the standard deviations for net national product are noticeably higher than for money. The reason, we conjecture, is the changing statistical character of the net national product estimates, in particular, the role played in them by interpolation between decennial census years. The effect of interpolation is to smooth greatly the year-to-year changes and so to reduce the estimated standard deviations. For the estimates before 1889, interpolation played a major role; for those from 1919 on, a much smaller role.[11] For the intermediate decades, the role of interpolation relative to independent data for individual years became successively smaller. We cannot find any clear indication in the description of the statistical series that there was a sharp break around 1900 in the role of interpolation. However, the data behave as if there were such a break. For the period before 1900, we conjecture that the standard deviations appreciably understate the variability of income. For the subsequent period, it is much harder to make a comparable judgment. The statistical errors of estimation tend to raise the computed standard deviation; interpolation tends to lower it.

For money, the degree of interpolation in the annual estimates is small throughout (interpolation plays a much larger role in our monthly estimates). Hence the standard deviations for money are probably overestimates of the "true" standard deviations, thanks to the errors of estimation. However, because of the character of the basic data, such errors are probably appreciably smaller than for net national product.

Aside from the shift in the level of the standard deviations for net national product, the most striking feature of the chart is what appear to be fairly regular cyclical fluctuations, of about 8 to 15 years in length, in the standard deviations of both money and net national product; these are the counterparts of the long swings that have received much attention. However, a warning is in order about any such interpretation of these results. The moving standard deviations for successive years are highly correlated because they have three out of four items in common. As is well known, a moving average applied to a series of random terms will produce a series that seems to move systematically; and the moving standard deviation is a moving average and so has the same effect. For our purposes, what is important is the parallelism of the two series plotted in figure 2.5, not the character of their common fluctuations.

Table 2.4 presents numerical evidence for all four lengths of moving standard deviations we have computed. Because of the break in the net national product data, the results are given separately for the period before and after 1899. We used 1899 as the dividing point because it is

Table 2.4   **Moving Standard Deviations of Annual Rates of Change in Money and Net National Product: Means, Standard Deviations, and Correlation Coefficients for Different Numbers of Terms**

Period	Number of Terms in Moving Standard Deviations	Mean Standard Deviation (Natural Logarithms)		Standard Deviation of Standard Deviation		Correlation Coefficient between Standard Deviations of Money and NNP						
						Money Leading NNP by: (Years)			Synchronous	NNP Leading Money by: (Years)		
		M	NNP	M	NNP	3	2	1		1	2	3
1869–1898	3	.049	.065	.022	.039	.293	.535	.616	.476	.114	−.011	−.099
	4	.052	.067	.023	.033	.364	.648	.718	.540	.263	−.049	−.163
	5	.054	.068	.022	.029	.378	.672	.717	.657	.431	.044	−.252
	6	.057	.069	.021	.027	.398	.583	.755	.759	.543	.144	−.069
1899–1960	3	.039	.081	.028	.408	.003	.113	.345	.670	.589	.248	.036
	4	.044	.089	.029	.046	.135	.243	.456	.814	.721	.472	.263
	5	.048	.095	.029	.046	.216	.385	.608	.840	.821	.637	.435
	6	.051	.100	.029	.044	.272	.481	.672	.870	.841	.707	.518
1869–1960	3	.042	.076	.027	.046	.001	.141	.349	.591	.429	.149	−.026
	4	.047	.081	.027	.044	.111	.242	.425	.687	.561	.311	.133
	5	.050	.085	.027	.043	.172	.348	.534	.721	.665	.465	.266
	6	.053	.089	.027	.042	.220	.404	.581	.748	.690	.536	.360

Source: Same as for figure 2.5.

a census year. The results for the separate periods are more meaningful than the results for the period as a whole.

This table reinforces the visual evidence of figure 2.5 and adds to it a number of important points. One is that the correlation is generally highest when the standard deviations are compared synchronously; it is generally lowered if standard deviations for money are compared with either later or earlier standard deviations for NNP though, for the earlier period, the correlation is highest when money leads one year for three of the four lengths of moving standard deviations. If there be any lead or lag for the later period, it is presumably less than a year in length. The slightly higher correlations for the later period for NNP leading by a year than for money leading by a year may reflect a lead of NNP by a fraction of a year. A second point added by the table is that the standard deviation for net national product for the period after 1899 is roughly double the standard deviation for money.[12] As a first approximation, therefore, the amplitude of cyclical fluctuations in income is twice that in money.

The correlations rise steadily as the number of terms in the moving standard deviations is increased. The rise presumably reflects the smoothing of the standard deviations introduced by the larger number of degrees of freedom and hence the reduction in the role of chance fluctuations. Calculations not summarized in the table indicate that the peak synchronous correlation is reached for seven terms. The fact that the mean standard deviations rise is less easily explained, since these should average the largest for a period equal to the average length of a cycle. The explanation is presumably the existence of the longer waves. We conjecture that the mean standard deviation would continue to rise as terms are added and reach a maximum at something like 10 to 15 terms.

To summarize these results: They strongly reinforce the evidence from the earlier comparison of reference cycle amplitudes. There is unquestionably a close relation between the variability of the stock of money and the variability of income. This relation has persisted over some nine decades and appears no different at the end of that period than at the beginning, if allowance is made for the changing characteristics of the statistical raw materials.

2.1.5 Cyclical Behavior of Velocity

1. The ratio of income to the stock of money, which is to say, the income velocity of money, has been rising in the post–World War II period. However, over the whole of the more than nine decades our data cover, it has declined sharply, from 4.6 at the outset of the period to 1.7 at the end. As a result, velocity has frequently declined during

both expansions and contractions in general business. When that has not been the case, velocity has conformed positively to the cycle, rising during expansions and falling during contractions. When it has been, the cyclical effect has shown up in a slower rate of decline in expansion than in contraction. The average cyclical patterns of velocity, for mild depression and deep depression cycles (excluding war cycles), are given in figure 2.6.

2. In an earlier article,[13] it was demonstrated that this cyclical pattern of velocity could be largely though not wholly accounted for by supposing that the amount of money demanded in real terms is linked, not to current measured income and current measured prices, but to longer-term concepts of permanent income and permanent prices. By this interpretation, the amount of money demanded rises during the expansion phase of a cycle in greater proportion than permanent income, as suggested by the secular results. However, measured income rises in still greater proportion, so that measured income rises relative to the stock of money, and conversely during a contraction. While this interpretation does not rule out the possibility that changing interest

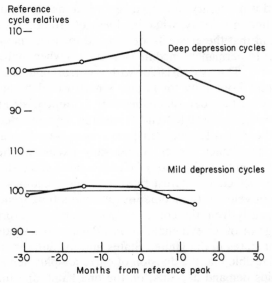

Figure 2.6   Income velocity: average reference cycle patterns for mild and deep depression cycles, 1870–1958. War cycles, not shown, are 1914–19 and 1938–46. Deep depression cycles are 1870–78, 1891–1904, 1904–8, 1919–21, 1927–32, and 1932–38. All others are mild depression cycles. These dates differ from those shown in figures 2.2 and 2.4 because they are annual instead of monthly.

rates over the cycle play a role in the cyclical behavior of velocity, it assigns them a less important role than it assigns to the discrepancy between measured and permanent concepts.

3. This interpretation has been criticized as assigning much too small a role to interest rates. Henry A. Latané, in particular, has argued that the whole of the movement of velocity, both over longer periods and over the cycle, can be accounted for by changes in interest rates, higher interest rates leading to economy in the use of money and so to higher velocities, and conversely.[14] His analysis covers a shorter period than ours does (1909–58).

4. There is no necessary contradiction between these two interpretations, the appearance of contradiction arising primarily from our definition of money as the sum of currency plus all adjusted deposits in commercial banks, and Latané's definition of money as the sum of currency plus adjusted demand deposits alone.

a. Time deposits in commercial banks appear to have a substantially higher income elasticity of demand than currency or demand deposits have, so that the income elasticity of money by our use of the term is doubtless higher than it is by Latané's use of the term. This can explain why we find it necessary to introduce an income effect to explain the secular decline in velocity, while he does not. To put this point differently, we find that the elasticity of demand for (real) money balances with respect to permanent income is about 1.8 when money is defined as we define it. This is consistent with a corresponding elasticity not much different from unity for Latané's narrower definition, provided the elasticity for time deposits is between 2.5 and 3.5.[15] Furthermore, since there is a considerable trend element in the movement of interest rates over the period Latané's analysis covers—as, of course, there is in income for a much longer period—any excess of the "correct" elasticity over unity could readily be confounded in the statistical analysis with the effects of interest rates. Our own readiness to attribute the decline in velocity to income, despite the strong trend in income, derives primarily from the consistency of such an interpretation with a wide range of other evidence, in particular, cross-section evidence for different states in the United States and for different countries.

b. It is plausible that the division of currency plus deposits between currency plus demand deposits, on the one hand, and time deposits, on the other, is sensitive to rates of interest, since the differential between interest paid on time deposits and interest paid on demand deposits (which can be and for long periods has been negative) and on currency (typically zero) can be expected to widen as interest rates rise—and conversely. Hence a rise in interest rates might be expected to lead to an increase in commercial bank time deposits relative to commercial bank demand deposits plus currency—and conversely. It follows that the interest elasticity of demand can be expected to be greater in absolute value for currency plus demand deposits, than for currency plus demand deposits plus time deposits in commercial banks.

c. The two preceding points have especial importance for the longer-term movements in velocity. For the cyclical behavior of velocity, the distinction between measured and permanent income can be combined with either demand function, and will help to explain the cyclical behavior of velocity.

Needless to say, neither definition of money can be said to be "the" correct definition. Just where the line is drawn between those temporary abodes of purchasing power we choose to term "money" and those we term "near-monies," or "liquid assets," or what not, is largely arbitrary. We have found it convenient to draw the line where we do largely because that enables us to use a single concept for the whole of our period, since the distinction between commercial bank demand and time deposits did not acquire its current significance—or indeed have much significance at all—until after 1914. In the course of using it, we have found it to have some other advantages.[16] In addition, even for the period since 1914, it is by no means clear that demand deposits as recorded correspond fully with the economic construct Latané wishes to measure, namely, deposits subject to check. The lower reserves required against time deposits have given banks an incentive to classify as large a fraction of deposits as time deposits as possible. There is some evidence that, particularly during the 1920s, banks managed so to classify some deposits that were in effect demand deposits. A full understanding of the behavior of money in business cycles requires an analysis of the components of the money stock, however defined, and of near-monies as well, so, despite our reservations about the meaning of some of his data, we welcome Latané's analysis as a valuable complement to ours.

5. A basically more important question is the extent to which velocity can be regarded as passively reflecting independent changes in its numerator and denominator. This is the presumption implicit in the cycle theories, popular these past few decades, that have regarded investment as the dominant cycle-producing factor. These theories implicitly take for granted that an expansion of investment will produce an expansion in income regardless of what happens to the money stock. In their most extreme form, these theories imply that the magnitude of the expansion in income is independent of the size of any concurrent change in the money stock. If the money stock does not rise, then velocity will simply rise to fill the gap; if the money stock does rise, velocity will not rise as much or may even fall. The most rigorous explicit theoretical formulation of this position is in terms of either a "liquidity trap"—an infinitely elastic liquidity preference function at a finite interest rate—

or a completely inelastic demand schedule for investment—a zero response of spending to a change in the rate of interest. Though few
economists would explicitly maintain that either the one or the other
prevails currently, or has prevailed during most of our past history,
many would accept the logically equivalent assertions that the rate of
cyclical expansion or contraction can be regarded as fairly rigidly determined by the rise or fall in investment or autonomous expenditure,
that the link is far more crucial than any link with the contemporary
behavior of the money stock, and can be reversed, if at all, only by a
very atypical behavior of the money stock. Some relevant empirical
evidence on this issue is summarized in the subsection below on the
relative roles of money and investment.

2.1.6   Cyclical Behavior of Proximate Determinants of the
Money Stock

1. Changes in the stock of money can, arithmetically, be attributed
to changes in three proximate determinants, each under the immediate
control of a different class of economic actors:

a. High-powered money, consisting of currency held by the public,
plus currency held in bank vaults, plus deposits of banks at Federal
Reserve Banks. This total is either a consequence of international payment flows and associated gold movements, or of Treasury or Federal
Reserve policy.

b. The division of the public's money holdings between currency
and deposits, which can be summarized by any one of a number of
ratios—of currency to the money stock; of currency to deposits; or of
deposits to currency. This division is in the first instance determined
by the public, the holders of money, though, of course, the public's
decision is affected by the terms offered by banks for deposits.

c. The relation between deposits and the amount of high-powered
money held by banks, which can be termed their reserves. This relation
can be summarized by either the ratio of reserves to deposits or its
reciprocal, the ratio of deposits to reserves. This ratio is in the first
instance determined by banks though, of course, their decision is affected by legal requirements imposed by the government, by the terms
they must offer to obtain deposits, and by the returns they can receive
on the alternative assets they acquire.

Given the two ratios, a rise in high-powered money implies a proportional rise in the stock of money. Given the amount of high-powered
money and the deposit-reserve ratio, a rise in the deposit-currency
ratio implies a rise in the stock of money, because it means that less
high-powered money is required to meet the currency demands of the
public and more is available for bank reserves to be multiplied by the

deposit-reserve ratio. Similarly, given the amount of high-powered money and the deposit-currency ratio, a rise in the deposit-reserve ratio implies a rise in the stock of money, because it means that each dollar of high-powered money held by banks gives rise to a larger number of dollars of deposits.

2. Phillip Cagan has analyzed in detail the contribution of changes in each of these three proximate determinants to the cyclical fluctuations in the rate of change in the money stock.[17] He finds that the deposit-currency ratio was the most important single contributor. Throughout the period from 1877 to 1954, it accounted on the average for roughly half the cyclical fluctuations in the rate of change in the money stock. Though this fraction varied from cycle to cycle, it did not change in any consistent secular fashion and was not markedly different for severe and mild movements. The main deviation in its contribution occurred at times of money panics in which it often played a dominant role.

Changes in high-powered money were as large in amplitude as changes in the deposit-reserve ratio but much less regular in timing. Changes in the deposit-reserve ratio were regular in timing but relatively small in amplitude.

3. Cagan finds that the main impact of the Federal Reserve System has been on the relative importance of changes in high-powered money and in the deposit-reserve ratio. By providing banks with an alternative source of liquidity, the Reserve System intensified a tendency for banks to trim any excess of reserves over legal requirements—a tendency fostered in earlier decades by the Treasury's assumption of enlarged money market responsibilities. The result was a reduction in the amplitude of cyclical movements in the reserve ratio after 1914. However, this was more than offset by an increase in the amplitude of cyclical movements in high-powered money.

4. The deposit-currency ratio had a rising long-term trend to 1929, declined substantially thereafter until the end of World War II, and has since been rising. Relative to these longer-term movements, the deposit-currency ratio tended to rise during the early part of expansions, at first at an increasing rate; to reach a peak near mid-expansion; then to decline to mid-contraction; and then to start rising. Cagan shows that these movements played an important part in accounting for the tendency of the rate of change in the money stock to reach its peak around mid-expansion and its trough around mid-contraction. He attributes the timing of movements in the deposit-currency ratio to divergent cyclical patterns in the velocity of currency and deposits.

5. The deposit-reserve ratio rose during most of the period covered, except for its sharp decline during the later 1930s. Relative to trend,

it tended to rise during expansions, reaching its peak before the reference peak, and tended to decline during contractions, reaching its trough before the reference trough.

6. These patterns bespeak a rather complex feedback mechanism whereby changes in business activity react on the stock of money. This feedback mechanism has not yet been worked out in the detail that would be desirable.

2.1.7   Relative Roles of Money and Investment in the Cycle

In an extensive statistical study using standard correlation techniques rather than the National Bureau's cycle analysis, one of us in collaboration with David Meiselman investigated the relative stability of monetary velocity and the investment multiplier.[18] Both the stock of money and the level of autonomous expenditures are positively related to consumption and to income over both short and long spans of years. However, it turns out that the correlation is generally much higher for money than for autonomous expenditures. Moreover, the partial correlation between money and consumption, holding autonomous expenditures constant, is roughly the same as the simple correlation, whereas the partial correlation between autonomous expenditures and consumption, holding the stock of money constant, is on the average roughly zero, being sometimes positive, sometimes negative. Similar results were obtained for year-to-year and quarter-to-quarter changes in the stock of money, autonomous expenditures, and consumption.

Additional evidence is provided by correlations between the variability of annual changes in money and in consumption, on the one hand, and between the variability of annual changes in investment and in consumption, on the other. Because there are occasional negative figures for net capital formation, we used gross capital formation as the measure of investment and computed first differences of logarithms and moving standard deviations of the first differences, as in table 2.4, for money, consumption, and investment. The synchronous correlation coefficients we obtained are consistently higher, both for the period as a whole and for the period since 1899, for money-consumption variability than they are for investment-consumption variability. These are exactly the same results as in the Friedman and Meiselman study, although derived by a wholly different procedure. For the full period, the correlation coefficient for money-investment variability is slightly lower than for investment-consumption variability; for the period since 1899, slightly higher. In addition, the partial correlation between money-consumption variability, holding investment variability constant, is significantly higher than the partial correlation between investment-consumption variability, holding money variability constant; for the period since 1899, the partial correlation between money-investment variability, holding consumption constant, is significantly higher than the partial correlation between investment-consumption variability, holding money constant, although for the whole period, the former is lower. Essentially the same results were obtained for the simple and partial correlations with leads and lags.[19]

These results are striking because they contradict so sharply the widespread presumption among economists that investment (or, more generally, autonomous expenditures) is the prime mover in cyclical fluctuations, transmitting its influence to the rest of income via a multiplier effect on consumption. So far as these results go, they suggest that, *for a given stock of money,* there is no systematic relation at all between autonomous expenditures and consumption—in experience, the multiplier effect on consumption is as likely to be negative as positive.[20] These results may of course be misleading, because some crucial variables have been neglected, or because the definition used for autonomous expenditures is inappropriate, or for some other reason. But they tend to be supported by preliminary results for other countries, and we know of no contrary evidence for the United States. The widespread presumption to the contrary that unquestionably does exist, whether it be right or wrong, does not rest, so far as we can see, on any coherent, organized body of empirical evidence.[21]

2.2 Some Plausible Interpretations of the Factual Evidence

The stock of money displays a consistent cyclical behavior which is closely related to the cyclical behavior of the economy at large. This much the factual evidence summarized above puts beyond reasonable doubt.

That evidence alone is much less decisive about the direction of influence. Is the cyclical behavior of money primarily a reflection of the cyclical behavior of the economy at large, or does it play an important independent part in accounting for the cyclical behavior of the economy? It might be, so far as we know, that one could marshal a similar body of evidence demonstrating that the production of dressmakers' pins has displayed over the past nine decades a regular cyclical pattern; that the pin pattern reaches a peak well before the reference peak and a trough well before the reference trough; that its amplitude is highly correlated with the amplitude of the movements in general business. It might even be demonstrated that the simple correlation between the production of pins and consumption is higher than the simple correlation between autonomous expenditures and consumption; that the partial correlation between pins and consumption—holding autonomous expenditures constant—is as high as the simple correlation; and that the correlation between consumption and autonomous expenditures—holding the production of pins constant—is on the average zero. We do not, of course, know that these statements are valid for pins and, indeed, rather doubt that they are but, even if they were demonstrated beyond a shadow of doubt, they would persuade neither us nor our readers to adopt a pin theory of business cycles.

If the only decisive statistical evidence for money were comparable to the items just cited for pins, it would correspondingly not justify the acceptance of a monetary theory of business cycles. At the same time, it is worth noting that, even then, the monetary theory and the pin theory would by no means be on all fours. Most economists would be willing to dismiss out of hand the pin theory even on such evidence; most economists would take seriously the monetary theory even on much less evidence, which is not by any means the same as saying that they would be persuaded by the evidence. Whence the difference? Primarily, the difference is that we have other kinds of evidence. We know that while pins are widely used and occasionally of critical importance, taken as a whole, they are a minor, if not trifling, item in the economy. We expect the effect to be in rough proportion to the cause, though this is by no means always the case—a rock can start a landslide. We can readily conceive of an economy operating without pins yet experiencing cycles like those of history; we can readily conceive of large autonomous changes occurring in the production of pins, but we cannot readily conceive of any channels through which such autonomous changes could have wide-reaching effects on the rest of the economy. Men who have thought about and studied these matters have never been led to suggest the pin industry as a prime mover in the cyclical process. In all these respects, the monetary theory is on a wholly different footing. We know that money is a pervasive element in the economy; that the stock of money is sizable compared with other aggregate economic magnitudes; that fluctuations of the kind we call business cycles have apparently occurred only in an economy in which "economic activities are . . . carried on mainly by making and spending money."[22] We not only can conceive of the money stock's being subject to large autonomous changes, but we can also readily conceive of channels through which such changes could have far-reaching effects on the rest of the economy. Men who have thought about and studied these matters have been led to give money a critical role in their theories.

One more preliminary observation. The key question at issue is not whether the direction of influence is wholly from money to business or wholly from business to money; it is whether the influence running from money to business is significant, in the sense that it can account for a substantial fraction of the fluctuations in economic activity. If the answer is affirmative, then one can speak of a monetary theory of business cycles or—more precisely—of the need to assign money an important role in a full theory of business cycles. The reflex influence of business on money, the existence of which is not in doubt in light of the factual evidence summarized above, would then become part of the partly self-generating mechanism whereby monetary disturbances are transmitted. On the other hand, if the influence from money to business is minor, one could speak of a cyclical theory of monetary fluctuations but not of a monetary theory of business cycles. To illustrate again with pins: Changes in business conditions doubtless affect the production of pins, and no doubt there is some feedback effect of changes in the production of pins on general business. But, whereas the first effect may well be large relative to the total fluctuations in pin production, the feedback effect is almost certainly trivial relative to the fluctuations in business. Hence we are ready to accept a business cycle theory of pin production but not a pin theory of business cycles.

The factual evidence summarized above goes beyond the list of items we conjectured for pins and contains some bits that are relevant to the key question at issue. The most important is the fact that the relation between money and business has remained largely unchanged over a period that has seen substantial changes in the arrangements determining the quantity of money. During part of the' period, the United States was on an effective gold standard, during part, on an inconvertible paper standard with floating exchange rates, during part, on a managed paper standard with fixed exchange rates. The commercial banking system changed its role and scope greatly. The government arrangements for monetary control altered, the Federal Reserve System replacing the Treasury as the formal center of control. And the criteria of control adopted by the monetary authorities altered. If the predominant direction of influence had been from business to money, these changes might have been expected to alter the relation between business changes and monetary changes, but the relation has apparently remained much the same in both timing and amplitude.[23] Yet this evidence is by no means decisive. As noted above, Cagan shows that the public's decisions about the proportion in which it divides its money balances between currency and deposits is an important link in the feedback mechanism whereby changes in business affect the stock of money. The changes in monetary arrangements have affected greatly the trends in the deposit-currency ratio but appear not to have affected its cyclical behavior. Hence this part of the supply mechanism has been roughly constant and has played a roughly constant role over the whole period.

In our view, the most convincing evidence supporting the idea that money plays an important independent part is not the evidence summarized in the first part of this paper but evidence of a rather different kind—that garnered from study of the historical circumstances underlying the changes that occurred in the stock of money.[24] This evidence is much more clear cut for major movements than for minor.

2.2.1   Major Economic Fluctuations

Major movements in U.S. history include the deep depressions used here to distinguish deep from mild depression cycles in our classification of historical reference cycles (see fig. 2.2 for the classification); the substantial inflations which have occurred primarily during wartime; and a few long-continued movements in one direction, such as the generally rising level of money income and prices from 1896 to 1913. With respect to these events, the historical record justifies two important generalizations.

1. There is a one-to-one relation between monetary changes and changes in money income and prices. Changes in money income and prices have, in every case, been accompanied by a change in the rate of growth of the money stock, in the same direction and of appreciable magnitude, and there are no comparable disturbances in the rate of growth of the money stock unaccompanied by changes in money income and prices.

2. The changes in the stock of money cannot consistently be explained by the contemporary changes in money income and prices. The changes in the stock of money can generally be attributed to specific historical circumstances that are not in turn attributable to contemporary changes in money income and prices. Hence, if the consistent relation between money and income is not pure coincidence, it must reflect an influence running from money to business.

Inflationary Episodes

The second generalization requires little more than its statement to be recognized as true for the inflationary episodes. During periods of U.S. engagement in wars, the increased rate of growth of the money stock stemmed from use of the printing press, in more or less subtle ways, to help finance government military expenditures. During our neutrality in World War I from 1914 to early 1917, it had its origin in use by the Allies of their gold reserves to finance war purchases here. During those war years, the reflex influence of the rising tide of business on the stock of money was in the opposite direction to the actual movement in the money stock, since business expansion of itself tended to produce a worsening in the balance of payments and hence an outflow of gold or a decreased inflow.

The situation is equally clear from 1896 to 1913. The rise in the stock of money reflected predominantly an increase in the U.S. gold stock, which was part of a worldwide growth of the gold stock emanating from the discovery of new mines and improvements in techniques of extracting gold from low-grade ore. The domestic expansion alone would have made for gold outflows. The feedback was therefore counter to the main current.[25]

For the wartime episodes, the evidence is equally consistent with a different theory, that the independent force was a major shift in government spending propensities; that the shift in spending propensities would have had the same effect on income and prices if it had been financed wholly by borrowing from the public at large with an unchanged money stock, rather than being financed in part by the use of monetary reserves (as it was in the early years of World War I) or by government creation of money (as in the other war years); that it was not financed wholly by borrowing because resort in part to use of monetary reserves and the printing press was politically easier and perhaps financially cheaper.

Evidence from the study by Friedman and Meiselman (discussed in subsection 2.1.7 above on the relative roles of money and investment) rather decisively contradicts this alternative explanation. In any event, the alternative explanation will not hold for the 1896–1913 inflation, since there was no obvious independent shift of major magnitude in spending propensities. The only immediate factor producing such a shift that comes to mind is the income earned from gold production. However, although the increase in the stock of gold over that period was large compared to the gold stock at the start and was capable of producing large increases in the stock of money via a multiplicative effect on other kinds of money, the gold stock itself was a small fraction of the total money stock, and the increase in the money stock only a fraction of the increase in money income. Hence, the value of gold production was a small fraction indeed of the increase in income.[26] The increased gold production could hardly have produced the observed increase of money income through any spending multiplier effect. But any effect it might have had must have been through its effect on the stock of money.

Deep Depressions

For deep depressions, the historical evidence justifying our second generalization is as clear as for the inflationary episodes, though less well known and hence less self-evident. A summary statement of the proximate source of the change in the money stock will in most instances enable the reader to judge for himself the extent to which the decline in the stock of money can be explained by the contemporary change in money, income, and prices.

1875–78: Political pressure for resumption led to a decline in high-powered money, and the banking crisis in 1873 and subsequent bank failures to a shift by the public from deposits to currency and to a fall in the deposit-reserve ratio.

1892–94: Agitation for silver and destabilizing movements in Treasury cash produced fears of imminent abandonment of the gold standard by the United States and thereby an outflow of capital which trenched on gold stocks. Those effects were intensified by the banking panic of 1893, which produced a sharp decline, first in the deposit-currency ratio and then in the deposit-reserve ratio.

1907–8: The banking panic of 1907 led to a sharp decline in the deposit-currency ratio and a protective attempt by banks to raise their own reserve balances, and so to a subsequent fall in the deposit-reserve ratio.

1920–21: Sharp rises in Federal Reserve discount rates in January 1920 and again in June 1920 produced, with some lag, a sharp contraction in Federal Reserve credit outstanding, and thereby in high-powered money and the money stock.

1929–33: An initial mild decline in the money stock from 1929 to 1930, accompanying a decline in Federal Reserve credit outstanding, was converted into a sharp decline by a wave of bank failures beginning in late 1930. Those failures produced (1) widespread attempts by the public to convert deposits into currency and hence a decline in the deposit-currency ratio, and (2) a scramble for liquidity by the banks and hence a decline in the deposit-reserve ratio. The decline in the money stock was intensified after September 1931 by deflationary actions on the part of the Federal Reserve System, in response to England's departure from gold, which led to still further bank failures and even sharper declines in the deposit ratios. Yet the Federal Reserve at all times had power to prevent the decline in the money stock or to increase it to any desired degree, by providing enough high-powered money to satisfy the banks' desire for liquidity, and almost surely without any serious threat to the gold standard.

1937–38: The doubling of legal reserve requirements in a series of steps, effective in 1936 and early 1937, accompanied by Treasury sterilization of gold purchases led to a halt in the growth of high-powered money and attempts by banks to restore their reserves in excess of requirements. The decline in the money stock reflected largely the resultant decline in the deposit-reserve ratio.

A shift in the deposit-currency ratio and the accompanying bank crises played an important role in four of these six episodes. This ratio, as we have seen, has a systematic cyclical pattern which can be regarded as a feedback effect of business on money. However, in each of those episodes, the shift in the deposit-currency ratio represented a sharp departure from the typical cyclical response and, in at least two

(1875–78 and 1892–94), represented a subsequent reaction to an initial monetary disturbance that had no such close link with contemporary changes in money income and prices. Moreover, in two episodes (1920–21 and 1937–38), neither a shift in the deposit-currency ratio nor bank failures played any role. And such a shift has played no important role in any of the large expansions in the stock of money. A fractional reserve banking structure susceptible to runs is an institutional feature that renders the stock of money sensitive to autonomous deflationary changes; hence runs may frequently play an important role in sharp declines. This feature, however, is clearly not essential for a large economic change to be accompanied by a large monetary change in the same direction.

The 1907–8 episode is a particularly nice example of the intermixture of autonomous monetary disturbances and a feedback. The failure of the Knickerbocker Trust Company in the fall of 1907 converted what had been a mild decline in the money stock as a result of gold exports and a consequent decline in high-powered money into a severe decline as a result of bank runs and a consequent decline in the deposit-currency ratio. The accompanying sharp rise in short-term interest rates and a premium on currency produced a large gold inflow. The accompanying sharp intensification in the business decline worked in the same direction by its effect on the balance of international payments. Since the runs were prevented from producing widespread bank failures through the concerted suspension by banks of convertibility of deposits into currency, these feedback effects fairly promptly reversed the money decline and, along with the reversal, the business decline came to an end.

Conclusions for Major Movements

The factors that produced the changes in the stock of money are autonomous only in the sense of not being directly attributable to the contemporary cyclical changes in money income and prices. In a broader context, each of course has its origins and its explanation, and some are connected fairly clearly with longer-term economic developments. There can be no doubt, for example, that the silver agitation was intensified by prior declining agricultural prices, or that the financial boom in the early 1900s encouraged financial activities which laid the basis for Knickerbocker Trust's failure, or that the worldwide declining price trend of the 1870s and 1880s encouraged exploration for gold and improvement of refining techniques.

The narrower sense is, however, important for our purpose. The question at issue is whether the one-to-one relation between monetary change and major economic change can be explained by a relation running from economic change to money, as a one-to-one relation between changes in pin production and in economic activity could be explained if it existed. Such an explanation would require that the changes in money be connected rather rigidly with either the contemporary changes in economic conditions or more basic factors that could account alike for the course of economic events and for the changes in the stock of money. The demonstration that the major changes in the stock of money have been attributable to a variety of sources, many of which are connected directly neither with contemporary business developments nor with earlier business developments—which themselves can be regarded as determining the contemporary course of business—therefore contradicts any such explanation of the one-to-one relation between economic change and monetary change.

There seems to us, accordingly, to be an extraordinarily strong case for the propositions that (1) appreciable changes in the rate of growth of the stock of money are a necessary and sufficient condition for appreciable changes in the rate of growth of money income; and that (2) this is true both for long secular changes and also for changes over periods roughly the length of business cycles. To go beyond the evidence and discussion thus far presented: our survey of experience leads us to conjecture that the longer-period changes in money income produced by a changed secular rate of growth of the money stock are reflected mainly in different price behavior rather than in different rates of growth of output; whereas the shorter-period changes in the rate of growth of the money stock are capable of exerting a sizable influence on the rate of growth of output as well.

These propositions offer a single, straightforward interpretation of all the historical episodes involving appreciable changes in the rate of monetary growth that we know about in any detail.[27] We know of no other single suggested interpretation that is at all satisfactory and have been able to construct none for ourselves. The character of the U.S. banking system—in particular, for most of its history, the vulnerability of the system to runs on banks—can come close to explaining why sizable declines in money income, however produced, should generally be accompanied by sizable declines in the stock of money; but this explanation does not hold even for all declines, and it is largely irrelevant for the rises. Autonomous increases in government spending propensities plus the irresistible political attraction of the printing press could come close to providing a single explanation for wartime inflations, accounting for the coincidence of rising incomes and rising stock of money without any necessary influence running from money to income; but this explanation cannot account for peacetime inflations, in which the growth of the money stock has reflected a rise in specie rather than in government-issued money; and it is not even a satisfactory explanation for the wartime episodes, since price rises in different wartime episodes seem more closely related to the concurrent changes in the stock of money than to the changes in government expenditure.[28]

It is perhaps worth emphasizing and repeating that any alternative interpretation must meet two tests: it must explain why the major movements in income occurred when they did, and also it must explain why such major movements should have been uniformly accompanied by corresponding movements in the rate of growth of the money stock. The monetary interpretation explains both at the same time. It leaves open the reasons for the change in the rate of growth of the money stock and, indeed, at this point is highly eclectic, taking account of the fact that historically there have been many different reasons.

We have emphasized the difficulty of meeting the second test. But even the first alone is hard to meet except by an explanation which asserts that different factors may from time to time produce large movements in income, and that these factors may operate through diverse channels—which is essentially to plead utter ignorance. We have cited several times the apparently widespread belief in investment as the prime mover. The alternative explanation for times of war, suggested above, is a special application of this theory, with investment broadened to mean "autonomous expenditures" and government spending included in the same category. But even for the first test alone, we find it hard to accept this theory as a valid general explanation: can a drastic collapse in autonomous investment explain equally 1873–79, 1892–94, 1920–21, 1929–33, 1937–38? Capital formation at the end of the seventies was apparently one and one-half times its level at the beginning and seems not to have slumped seriously at any time during the decade, judging by the rough indications given by Kuznets's figures.[29] The 1890s saw some decline, but the following decade was marked by a vigorous and sustained rise. The 1920–21 episode was destined to be followed by a construction and investment boom. If the experience of 1920–21 is to be interpreted as a result of an investment collapse, that decline must have been a consequence of the decline in government expenditures and the subsequent collapse of inventory speculation before fixed capital expenditures had developed to take their place. But why, then, did the sharp decline in government expenditures after World War II not produce a subsequent economic collapse? Emphasis on inventory speculation involves a highly episodic interpretation, since it characterizes few of the other episodes. Surely, one cannot adduce that in World War I, slow using up of investment opportunities—often implicitly or explicitly called on to explain why, from time to time, there is allegedly a collapse of investment or a position of stagnation—was responsible for the 1920–21 recession. This is an equally implausible explanation for 1937–38 and, as already implied, for earlier episodes as well.

Of course, in most or all of these contractions, the incentive to invest and the actual amount spent on investment declined. The question at issue, however, is whether the decline was a consequence of the contemporary economic collapse—triggered, we would say, by monetary changes—or the ultimate working out of autonomous elements of weakness in the demand for investment that themselves triggered the contraction.

Even if all these episodes of contraction can somehow be interpreted as reflecting an autonomous decline in investment, is a sharp increase in investment opportunities a satisfactory explanation for the worldwide 1897–1913 rise in money income? If money is not a critical link but only a passive accompaniment of change, how is it that China escaped the early years of the Great Depression? We would say thanks to being on a silver standard and hence having a floating exchange rate vis-à-vis gold currencies, whereas all countries linked to gold were enmeshed in the depression. And how is it that China had the most severe contraction of all in the years from 1933 to 1936, when our silver purchase program drained silver from China and caused a sharp decline in its money stock, whereas the rest of the world was in a period of business expansion? And we could extend this list of embarrassing questions without difficulty.

We feel as if we are belaboring the obvious and we apologize to any reader who shares that feeling. Yet repeated experience has led us to believe that it is necessary to do so in order to make clear how strong is the case for the monetary explanation of major movements in money income.

Of course, it is one thing to assert that monetary changes are the key to major movements in money income; it is quite a different thing to know in any detail what is the mechanism that links monetary change to economic change; how the influence of the one is transmitted to the other; what sectors of the economy will be affected first; what the time pattern of the impacts will be, and so on. We have great confidence in the first assertion. We have little confidence in our knowledge of the transmission mechanism, except in such broad and vague terms as to constitute little more than an impressionistic representation rather than an engineering blueprint. Indeed, this is the challenge our evidence poses: to pin down the transmission mechanism in specific enough detail so that we can hope to make reasonably accurate predictions of the course of a wide variety of economic variables on the basis of information about monetary disturbances. In the section below on the relation between variations in income and money, we outline one part of the transmission mechanism which can account for the greater amplitude of variation in income than in money and on which we have some empirical evidence; in the last section, we sketch in a much more tentative way the major channels through which monetary fluctuations might be able to account for economic fluctuations, both the major movements we have so far been considering, and the minor movements to which we now turn.

2.2.2 Minor Economic Fluctuations

The case for a monetary explanation is not nearly so strong for the minor U.S. economic fluctuations that we have classified as mild depression cycles as the case is for the major economic fluctuations. Clearly, the view that monetary change is important does not preclude the existence of other factors that affect the course of business or that account for the quasirhythmical character of business fluctuations. We have no doubt that other factors play a role. Indeed, if the evidence we had were solely for the minor movements, it seems to us most unlikely that we could rule out—or even assign a probability much lower than 50 percent to—the possibility that the close relation between money and business reflected primarily the influence of business on money.

If we are inclined to assign a probability much lower than 50 percent, it is primarily because the evidence for minor movements does not stand alone. If money plays an independent role in major movements, is it likely to be almost passive in minor movements? The minor movements can be interpreted as less virulent members of the same species as the major movements. Is not a common explanation for both more appealing than separate explanations, especially when there is no well-tested alternative separate explanation?

A fully satisfactory explanation of the minor movements would require an explicit and rigorously stated theory, which could take the form of a series of simultaneous differential equations describing the reaction mechanism of the economy, together with a specification of the joint distribution function of the random disturbances impinging on it, and a specification of the systematic disturbances that could be introduced into it. Our belief that money plays an important role in minor movements is equivalent to asserting that some of these differential equations would contain the stock of money as a variable; that disturbances in the stock of money are among the random or systematic disturbances impinging on the system; and that these disturbances alone would be capable of generating a path for such major economic variables as money income, prices, output, and the like, comparable to the path they actually follow during mild depression cycles.

One factor that has doubtless contributed to skepticism about a monetary theory is the fact, documented above, that fluctuations in income are wider in relative amplitude than fluctuations in the stock of money. We have seen that income velocity varies positively over the cycle, which means that income varies more widely than money. We have seen also that the standard deviation of year-to-year percentage changes in income tends to be roughly double the standard deviation of year-to-year changes in the stock of money. How is it that such small changes in money can produce so much larger changes in income? Why should marginal velocity be systematically higher than average velocity?

While we are far from having a rigorous and comprehensive theory to answer this and related questions, in the next section we outline one element of such a theory which can, in our view, explain the difference in amplitude; and on pages 64–70 we outline even more broadly a tentative transmission mechanism.

2.2.3 Relation between Amplitude of Cyclical Variations in Income and Money

One of us has elsewhere suggested that holders of money can be regarded as adjusting the nominal amount they demand to their views of their long-run income status—itself a measure of their wealth—of the long-run level of prices, and of the returns on alternative assets.[30] Let us neglect for the time being the effect of returns on other assets, as well as still other possible variables, so that we can write the relationship for the community as

$$(1) \qquad\qquad M_d = P_p f(y_p),$$

where M_d is nominal amount of money per capita, P_p is permanent prices, and y_p is permanent aggregate real income per capita.[31] The capital letters here and later refer to magnitudes in nominal terms or current prices, the lower-case letters to magnitudes in real terms or constant prices.

Let us suppose further that estimates of per capita permanent income and permanent prices are compounded of two elements: (1) an expected average annual rate of change to allow for secular trend at a rate of, say, a_y for income and a_P for prices; (2) a weighted arithmetic or geometric average of past per capita incomes and prices adjusted for such a trend.

For the present, we shall assume that a_y and a_P are both zero, or alternatively that the actual past record is replaced by the past record adjusted for trends of a_y and a_P in magnitude. At the present level of discussion, this assumption involves no loss of generality, since the only effect of nonzero values of a_y and a_P is to add secular trends without affecting cyclical fluctuations. On a more sophisticated level, it would make a difference, since both a_y and a_P might be variables in the demand function for money, the former since future prospects might modify present demand for money, the latter since it would affect the returns on some alternative assets.

We can then write:

(2) $$P_p(T) = F[P(t); t < T]$$

(3) $$y_p(T) = G[y(t); t < T],$$

where $P(t)$ and $y(t)$ are measured prices and measured real income per capita at time t, and the functions are to be interpreted as saying that permanent prices and income are functions of the past history of measured income or prices. If we consider discrete data, say, annual data, we can approximate equations 2 and 3 by either

(2a) $$P_p(T) = \sum_{i=0}^{\infty} w_i' P(T - i) = w_0' P(T) + (1 - w_0') P_p(T - 1),$$

(3a) $$y_p(T) = \sum_{i=0}^{\infty} w_i' y(T - i) = w_0' y(t) + (1 - w_0') y_p(T - 1),$$

where

$$\Sigma\, w_i' = 1;$$

or by

(2b) $$\log P_p(T) = \sum_{i=0}^{\infty} w_i \log P(T - i)$$
$$= w_0 \log P(T) + (1 - w_0) \log P_p(T - 1),$$

(3b) $$\log y_p(T) = \sum_{i=0}^{\infty} w_i \log y(T - i)$$
$$= w_0 \log y(T) + (1 - w_0) \log y_p(T - 1)$$

where

$$\Sigma\, w_i = 1.$$

Note that, in both cases, we have assumed that the same weights are used for income and prices.

Suppose the community is regarded as always being on its demand curve for money. Then an increase in the stock of money will require an increase in permanent income or prices or both sufficient to make the community satisfied with the new stock of money, and these increases can be brought about only by increases in measured income or prices or both. To illustrate: Suppose, for simplicity, real measured income and real permanent income remain unchanged. Then from equation 1, a 1 percent change in M will require a 1 percent change in P_p. But from equation 2a or 2b, a 1 percent change in P_p will require that $P(T)$ rise by more than 1 percent or by $1/w_0'$ *percent for equation 2a and* $1/w_0$ *percent for equation 2b. But* w_0' *and* w_0 are less than unity.

Hence, the percentage rise in measured prices and income will be larger than the percentage rise in money.

To be more specific and to allow for changes in both prices and income, let us replace equation 1 by a special form we have found to work rather well empirically:

(4) $$\frac{M}{P_p} = \gamma(y_p)^\delta,$$

where γ and δ are numerical constants (or, more generally, functions of omitted variables, such as returns on other assets), all the variables are at time T, and we have dropped the subscript d from M because of our assumption that the amount demanded is always equal to the amount supplied. In logarithmic form, (4) is

(4a) $$\log M(T) = \log \gamma + \log P_p(T) + \delta \log y_p(T).$$

Substitute (2b) and (3b) into (4a), giving

(5) $$\log M(T) = \log \gamma + w_0 (1 - \delta) \log P(T) + \delta w_0 \log Y(T)$$
$$+ (1 - w_0) [\log P_p(T - 1) + \delta \log y_p(T - 1)],$$

where

$$\log Y(T) = \log y(T) + \log P(T),$$

i.e., $Y(T)$ = measured income per capita. Replace the final bracket in (5) by its equivalent from (4a) for $T - 1$, namely, [$\log M(T - 1) - \log \gamma$], and then solve (5) for $\log Y(T)$. This gives

(6) $$\log Y(T) = \frac{1}{\delta w_0} \{\log M(T) - \log \gamma$$
$$- w_0(1 - \delta) \log P(T) - (1 - w_0)$$
$$[\log M(T - 1) - \log \gamma]\}.$$

Differentiate equation 6 with respect to $\log M(T)$, allowing for the fact that $P(T)$ will change along with $Y(T)$. This gives

(7) $$\frac{d \log Y(T)}{d \log M(T)} = \frac{1}{\delta w_0} \left[1 - w_0 (1 - \delta) \frac{d \log P(T)}{d \log Y(T)} \times \frac{d \log Y(T)}{d \log M(T)} \right].$$

Solve for $d \log Y(T)/d \log M(T)$ to get

(8) $$\frac{d \log Y(T)}{d \log M(T)} = \frac{1}{w_0[\delta + (1 - \delta) \eta]},$$

where η is the elasticity of the measured price level with respect to measured income, and can be expected to be between zero and unity for cyclical fluctuations (i.e., both prices and output can be expected to move in the same direction as money income). We may designate $d \log Y(T)/d \log M(T)$ the money multiplier, analogous to the investment multiplier, though it should be noted that the analogy is somewhat incomplete. The money multiplier gives the ratio of the *percentage* change in income to the *percentage* change in the money stock.[32] To get the number of dollars of income change per dollar change in the stock of money, it is necessary to multiply the money multiplier by the income velocity of money.

It so happens that our earlier work furnishes empirical estimates for the United States of all the quantities entering into the right-hand side of equation 8. Hence, we can construct an estimate of the elasticity of money income with respect to the money stock. These estimates are as follows:[33]

$$w_0 = 0.33$$
$$\delta = 1.81$$
$$\eta = 0.20$$

Inserting these figures in equation 8 gives

(9) $$\text{Estimate } \frac{d \log Y(T)}{d \log M(T)} = 1.84$$

This estimate is certainly remarkably close to the estimate, based on table 2.4, of the ratio of the variability of income to the variability of money. It will be recalled that we there found this ratio to be almost exactly 2.0. So far as we can see, these two numbers are estimates of the same theoretical construct.[34] Yet, statistically, they are almost completely independent. The estimate in equation 9 comes from the following sources: w_0 is based on a study of the consumption function which used no data on money whatsoever; δ is based on a correlation between average cycle bases of money and estimated permanent income; and η is based on the ratio of per month cyclical amplitudes computed from average cycle patterns of money income and prices. Hence, so far as we can see, no one of these items uses in any way the intracyclical movements of money. Yet the estimate of 2.0 based on table 2.4 has in its denominator the average standard deviation of sets, containing 3, 4, 5, or 6 years, of year-to-year percentage changes in the stock of money. The close agreement of two estimates, statistically so independent, certainly strongly suggests that the theoretical structure which produced them deserves further exploration.[35]

In such further exploration it would be desirable to generalize this analysis in a number of respects. (1) η should not be treated as a numerical constant. One would expect it to be different at different stages of the cycle and under different circumstances. Under conditions of full employment and inflation, it would be unity or close to it, which—given that δ is greater than unity—would make the money multiplier a maximum of $1/w_0$, or with our estimate of w_0, 3. At the other extreme, if there were extensive unemployment, η might be close to zero (though it is by no means clear that this has been true in experience), which would make the money multiplier a minimum of $1/w_0\eta$, or with our estimates, 1.67. More generally, η plays an important role not only in any theory along the general lines we have been sketching but also in income-expenditure theories.[36] It deserves much more systematic study than it has received. (2) The demand equation 4 should be expanded to include interest rates and perhaps the rate of change in prices. Though our studies suggest that these are far less important than income in affecting the demand for money, interest rates do have a statistically significant effect and, since they have a fairly regular cyclical pattern, should be included in a cyclical analysis. (3) The effect of expected trends in prices and income should be allowed for explicitly and not simply neglected, as we have done. (4) For cycle analysis, the demand equations should be estimated on a quarterly rather than annual basis. (5) In generalizing to a quarterly basis, it will no longer be satisfactory to suppose that actual and desired money balances are always equal. It will be desirable to allow instead for a discrepancy between these two totals, which the holders of balances seek to eliminate at a rate depending on the size of the discrepancy. This will introduce past money balances into the estimated demand equation not only as a proxy for prior permanent incomes but also as a determinant of the discrepancies in the process of being corrected. In addition, it will permit lag patterns other than the simple exponential kind we have used.

2.3   A Tentative Sketch of the Mechanism Transmitting Monetary Changes

However consistent may be the relation between monetary change and economic change, and however strong the evidence for the autonomy of the monetary changes, we shall not be persuaded that the monetary changes are the source of the economic changes unless we can specify in some detail the mechanism that connects the one with the other. Though our knowledge is at the moment too meager to enable us to do this at all precisely, it may be worth sketching very broadly some of the possible lines of connection, first, in order to provide a plausible rationalization of our empirical findings; second, to show that a monetary theory of cyclical fluctuations can accommodate a wide variety of other empirical findings about cyclical regularities; and third, to stimulate others to elaborate the theory and render it more specific.

Let us start by defining an Elysian state of moving equilibrium in which real income per capita, the stock of money, and the price level are all changing at constant annual rates. The relation between these rates depends on whether real income is rising or falling, whether wealth is remaining constant as a ratio to income or is rising or falling relative to income, on the behavior of relative rates of return on different forms of wealth, and on the wealth elasticity of demand for money. To simplify, let us suppose that all interest rates in real terms (i.e., adjusted for the rate of change in prices) and also the ratio of wealth to income are constant, so that the wealth elasticity of demand for money can be approximated by the elasticity of demand for money with respect to permanent income. If real income is rising at the rate of a_y per year, the stock of money demanded will then be rising at the rate of δa_y per year, where δ is the income elasticity of demand for money, and prices will be rising at the rate of $a_P = a_M - \delta a_y$, where a_M is the rate of rise in the nominal stock of money per capita. For example, if income per capita is rising at 2 percent per year, the stock of money at 4 percent a year, and δ is 3/2, then prices would be rising at 1 percent a year.[37] If δ and a_y were to be the same, and the stock of money were to rise at, say, 10 percent a year, prices would be rising at the rate of 7 percent a year; if the stock of money were to be declining at 10 percent a year, prices would be falling at the rate of 13 percent a year.[38]

Let us now suppose that an unexpected rise to a new level occurs in the rate of change in the money stock, and it remains there indefinitely—a single shock, as it were, displacing the time path of the money stock. In tracing the hypothetical effects of the higher rate of growth of the money stock, there will be some difference in detail depending on the source of the increase—whether from gold discoveries, or central bank open-market purchases, or government expenditures financed by fiat money, or a rise in the deposit-currency ratio, or a rise in the deposit-reserve ratio. To be definite, therefore, let us suppose it comes from an increased rate of open-market purchases by a central bank.

Although the initial sellers of the securities purchased by the central bank were willing sellers, this does not mean that they want to hold the proceeds in money indefinitely. The bank offered them a good price, so they sold; they added to their money balances as a temporary step in rearranging their portfolios. If the seller was a commercial bank, it now has larger reserves than it has regarded before as sufficient and will seek to expand its investments and its loans at a greater rate than before. If the seller was not a commercial bank, he is not likely even temporarily to want to hold the proceeds in currency but will deposit them in a commercial bank, thereby, in our fractional reserve system, adding to the bank's reserves relative to its deposits. In either case, therefore, in our system, commercial banks become more liquid. In the second case, in addition, the nonbank seller has a higher ratio of money in his portfolio than he has had hitherto.

Both the nonbank seller and commercial banks will therefore seek to readjust their portfolios, the only difference being that the commercial banks will in the process create more money, thereby transmitting the increase in high-powered money to the total money stock. The interposition of the commercial bank in the process means that the increase in the rate of growth of the money stock, which initially was less than in high-powered money, will for a time be greater. So we have here already a mechanism working for some overshooting.

It seems plausible that both nonbank and bank holders of redundant balances will turn first to securities comparable to those they have sold, say, fixed-interest coupon, low-risk obligations. But as they seek to purchase these they will tend to bid up the prices of those issues. Hence they, and also other holders not involved in the initial central bank open-market transactions, will look farther afield: the banks, to their loans; the nonbank holders, to other categories of securities—higher-risk fixed-coupon obligations, equities, real property, and so forth.

As the process continues, the initial impacts are diffused in several respects: first, the range of assets affected widens; second, potential creators of assets now more in demand are induced to react to the better terms on which they can be sold, including business enterprises wishing to engage in capital expansion, house builders or prospective homeowners, consumers who are potential purchasers of durable consumer goods—and so on and on; third, the initially redundant money balances concentrated in the hands of those first affected by the open-market purchases become spread throughout the economy.

As the prices of financial assets are bid up, they become expensive relative to nonfinancial assets, so there is an incentive for individuals and enterprises to seek to bring their actual portfolios into accord with desired portfolios by acquiring nonfinancial assets. This, in turn, tends to make existing nonfinancial assets expensive relative to newly constructed nonfinancial assets. At the same time, the general rise in the price level of nonfinancial assets tends to raise wealth relative to income, and to make the direct acquisition of current services cheaper relative to the purchase of sources of services. These effects raise demand curves for current productive services, both for producing new capital goods and for purchasing current services. The monetary stimulus is, in this way, spread from the financial markets to the markets for goods and services.

Two points need emphasis at this stage. The first is that the terms "financial markets," "assets," "investment," "rates of interest" and "portfolio" must, in order to be consistent with the existing empirical evidence, be interpreted much more broadly than they often are. It has been common to restrict attention to a small class of marketable financial securities and the real capital it finances, to regard "the" rate of interest as the market yield on such securities, and the "investment" which is affected by changes in the rate of interest as solely or mainly the items classified as "capital formation" in national income accounts. Some of the empirical results summarized earlier are inconsistent with this view.[39] To rationalize the results, it is necessary to take a much broader view, to regard the relevant portfolios as containing a much wider range of assets, including not only government and private fixed-interest and equity securities traded on major financial markets, but also a host of other assets, even going so far as to include consumer durable goods, consumer inventories of clothing and the like and, maybe also, such human capital as skills acquired through training, and the like. Similarly, it is necessary to make "rate of interest" an equally broad construct, covering explicit or implicit rates on the whole spectrum of assets.[40]

The second point is to note how readily these tentative lines on our sketch accommodate some of the documented regularities of business cycles. The cyclical counterpart to our assumed initial shock is the rise in the rate of growth of the money stock that generally occurs early in contraction. On the basis of the sketch so far, we should expect it to have its first impact on the financial markets, and there, first on bonds, and only later on equities, and only still later on actual flows of payments for real resources. This is of course the actual pattern. The financial markets tend to revive well before the trough. Historically, railroad bond prices have risen very early in the process. Equity markets start to recover later but still generally before the business trough. Actual expenditures on purchases of goods and services rise still later. The consistent tendency for orders to lead actual purchases would of course be expected on this theory, but it would follow simply from the mechanics of the production process. Hence it gives no definite support to this or any other theory. It is simply a stage in the way any impulse, however generated, will be transmitted. The tendency for the prices of financial assets to rise early in the pattern is quite a different matter. If the initial impulse were generated by an autonomous increase in spending on final goods and services, it would be plausible to expect the timing to be the reverse of what it actually is. Of course, on the theory being sketched, the precise timing will depend on the source of the initial monetary impulse. However, under the banking structure of the United States and other financially developed countries, whatever the initial impulse, commercial banks will play a key role in transforming it into an increased rate of growth in the money stock, and this will impose a large measure of uniformity on the outcome.

One other feature of cyclical experience that our sketch may be able to rationalize and that is worthy of special note is the behavior of the deposit-currency ratio. The initial monetary impulse is concentrated among holders of financial assets and is then diffused to the rest of the community. But this means, as we have noted, that the redundant balances are initially in the hands of asset holders with a high ratio of deposits to currency. As the redundant balances are diffused, they spread to more nearly a representative group in the population. Consistently with this sequence, the ratio of deposits to currency starts to rise early in contraction, not very far removed in time from the trough in the rate of rise in the money stock; the deposit-currency ratio continues to rise during the rest of contraction and early expansion but then reaches a peak around mid-expansion, and falls. The turning point, on this sketch, reflects the point at which the net tide of redundant balances has shifted from the financial community to the rest of the community.

To return to our sketch, we had reached the stage at which the demand for the services of factors of production was rising, which means, of course, a rise in money incomes. This will tend to be partly reflected in a rise of the prices of resources and of final goods; at the same time, the prices of nonfinancial assets will already have been rising as demand shifted to them from financial assets. These price rises themselves tend to correct portfolios by making the real value of monetary assets less than they otherwise would be. The result is to reduce the relative redundancy of monetary assets, which sets the stage for a rise in the structure of interest rates in place of the prior decline. The exact sequence of rises in prices, whether it affects first prices of final products, and only later prices of factors and so shifts profit margins— and so on—depends on the structure of the product and factor markets. Like the relation between new orders and production, this is part of the transmission mechanism common to all theories and tells little or nothing about the generating impulse. This does not mean it is unimportant. On the contrary, it may well determine the sequence of events once the stage is reached at which income is rising, as well as the time duration of subsequent reactions.

However, the important point for our purposes is very different. It is that the process we have described will tend to overshoot the mark; it will not simply produce a smooth movement to the new path consistent with the new rate of growth of the money stock assumed to prevail. There are two classes of reasons embodied in our analysis that explain why the process will overshoot. One, and in our view the more basic theoretically, has to do with the demand for money. At the higher rate of price rise that is the new ultimate equilibrium, the amount of money demanded will be less in real terms than it was initially, relative to wealth and hence income. But this means that, in the process of going from the initial to the new equilibrium, prices must rise at a faster rate than their ultimate rate. Hence the rate of price rise must overshoot. This effect is reinforced by that embodied in the subsection "Conclusions for Major Movements." In the initial stages of the process, money holders overestimate the extent of monetary redundancy, since they evaluate money stocks at unduly low levels of prices; they are slow, that is, to revise their estimates of permanent prices upward, hence they initially seek more radical readjustments in their portfolios than will ultimately turn out to be required. (If this analysis is applied to a cyclical process rather than to our special case of a shift from one moving equilibrium to another, a second element from that part of the section would also enter to produce overshooting—a slow revision of estimates of permanent real income.) The second class of reasons for overshooting has to do with feedback effects through the monetary mechanism. Two of these have already been mentioned. First, the effect of the initial assumed shock is to cause a greater rate of rise in high-powered money than in the money stock as a whole. But since there is nothing about the shock that will permanently alter the ratio of money to high-powered money, it follows that the money stock must for a time grow faster than ultimately in order to catch up. Second, there is reason for the deposit-currency ratio to rise in the initial stages of the process above its long-run equilibrium level. In addition to these two classes of reasons for overshooting, which derive from the specifically monetary elements in our sketch, there may of course be those arising from the other elements of the transmission mechanism common to almost any theory.

The tendency to overshoot means that the dynamic process of transition from one equilibrium path to another involves a cyclical adjustment process. Presumably, these cyclical adjustments will be damped, though no merely verbal exposition can suffice to assure that the particular mechanism described will have that property. Presumably also, the extent of overshooting will not be negligible relative to the disturbance, though again no merely verbal exposition can suffice to assure that the mechanism described will have that property.

The passage from this analysis of a single displacement of the rate of growth of money to a monetary theory of partly self-generating cyclical fluctuations is direct and has in large part been embodied in the preceding statement. It may be worth noting, however, that it would be rather more plausible to suppose a shock to take the form of an unusually high or low rate of growth of the stock of money for some time, with a reversion to a previous level rather than a shift to a permanently new level. Such a shock is equivalent to two shocks of the kind we have been considering—but shocks in opposite directions. Hence the shock itself gives rise to a cyclical movement in addition to the cyclical adjustment to each shock separately. The fact that in the cycle there is never that complete adjustment to the existing state of affairs that is present in the assumed initial Elysian state of moving equilibrium is of no decisive importance. It merely means that one state of incomplete adjustment succeeds another and that successive widenings and narrowings of discrepancies between actual and desired portfolios replace the introduction of a discrepancy and the correction of it. As noted parenthetically earlier, of somewhat more moment are the fluctuations in real income and employment over the cycle, which introduce an important reason for overshooting.

The central element in the transmission mechanism, as we have outlined it, is the concept of cyclical fluctuations as the outcome of balance sheet adjustments, as the effects on flows of adjustments between desired and actual stocks. It is this interconnection of stocks and flows that stretches the effect of shocks out in time, produces a diffusion over different economic categories, and gives rise to cyclical reaction mechanisms. The stocks serve as buffers or shock absorbers of initial changes in rates of flow, by expanding or contracting from their "normal" or "natural" or "desired" state, and then slowly alter other flows as holders try to regain that state.

In this stock-flow view, money is a stock in a portfolio of assets, like the stocks of financial assets, or houses, or buildings, or inventories, or people, or skills. It yields a flow of services as these other assets do; it is also subject to increase or decrease through inflows and outflows, also as the other assets are. It is because our thinking has increasingly moved in this direction that it has become natural to us to regard the rate of change in the stock of money as comparable to income flows and to regard changes in the rate of change as a generating force in producing cyclical fluctuations in economic activity.

2.4 Summary

The statistical evidence on the role of money in business cycles assembled in the first section demonstrates beyond any reasonable doubt that the stock of money displays a systematic cyclical behavior. The rate of change in the money stock regularly reaches a peak before the reference peak and a trough before the reference trough, though the lead is rather variable. The amplitude of the cyclical movement in money is closely correlated with the amplitude of the cyclical movement in general business and is about half as large as the amplitude of cyclical movements in money income. The most important single determinant, from the supply side, of the cyclical pattern of money is the cyclical pattern in the division of the public's money holdings between currency and deposits. The stock of money is much more closely and systematically related to income over business cycles than is investment or autonomous expenditures.

In the second section we suggested plausible interpretations of these facts, pointing out that the close relation tells nothing directly about whether the cyclical changes in money are simply a consequence of the changes in income or are in large measure the source of those changes. For major movements in income, we concluded that there is an extremely strong case for the proposition that sizable changes in the rate of change in the money stock are a necessary and sufficient condition for sizable changes in the rate of change in money income. For minor movements, we concluded that, while the evidence was far less strong, it is plausible to suppose that changes in the stock of money played an important independent role, though certainly the evidence for these minor movements does not rule out other interpretations. In the subsection, "Conclusions for Major Movements," we formalized one element of a theory designed to account for the observed tendency of cyclical fluctuations in income to be wider in amplitude than cyclical fluctuations in money are. The theory, plus earlier empirical work, yielded an independent statistical estimate of what we call the money multiplier, or the ratio of the percentage change in income to the associated percentage change in the stock of money. The independent estimate was 1.84; the directly observed ratio 2.0. This agreement does not reflect any common statistical origin of the two estimates. It therefore suggests that further elaboration of the theory might be well worthwhile.

Finally, in the last section, we sketched in broad strokes the kind of transmission mechanism that could explain how monetary changes can produce cyclical fluctuations in income, and that is consistent with our knowledge of economic interrelationships. The final picture that might ultimately develop out of this sketch could be of a partly self-generating cyclical mechanism. Disturbances in the rate of change in the money stock set in train a cyclical adjustment mechanism including a feedback in the rate of change in money itself. Additional disturbances from time to time would prevent the fluctuations from dying out. The mechanism emphasizes the reciprocal adjustment of stocks to flows, with money playing a key role as a component of the stock of assets. We emphasize that this sketch is exceedingly tentative and, of course, not preclusive. The mechanism outlined can be combined with other adjustment mechanisms.

Notes

1. "The Business Cycle Largely a 'Dance of the Dollar,' " *Journal of the American Statistical Association,* December 1923, pp. 1024–1028.

2. See our "A Monetary History of the United States, 1867–1960," Princeton University Press for NBER, 1963a, Chapter 7.

3. *Economics,* 3d ed., 1955, p. 224.

4. See the discussion of this problem in Milton Friedman, "The Lag in Effect of Monetary Policy," *Journal of Political Economy,* October 1961, pp. 453–454.

5. See our forthcoming "Trends and Cycles in the Stock of Money in the United States, 1867–1960."

The patterns in figure 2.4 differ in construction from the reference patterns for the stock of money in figure 2.2. The rate of change series, being the percentage change from month to month, is already in a form that is independent of units of measure. In addition, the rate of change in the money stock can be zero or negative as well as positive, and hence its average value for a given cycle can hardly serve as a base for computing reference cycle relatives. For these reasons, the basic data, instead of being expressed as relatives to the average for a cycle, are expressed as deviations from the average for a cycle (as in A. F. Burns and W. C. Mitchell, *Measuring Business Cycles,* New York, NBER, 1946, pp. 137–138). This is why the base lines in figure 2.4 are labeled 0 instead of 100 as in figure 2.2, and the scale is in terms of deviations rather than of relatives.

Because of a discontinuity in the underlying money figures in early 1933, we have estimated stage IX for the 1927–33 cycle and stage I for the 1933–38 cycle from the average value for January, April, and May 1933, instead of for February, March, and April. Restricted deposits before the banking holiday are counted in full in the recorded money stock. However, after the holiday both restricted and unrestricted deposits in unlicensed banks are excluded completely from the recorded money stock. That shift in treatment is the major factor behind the sharp decline in the recorded figures in March 1933 (see our "A Monetary History of the United States, 1867–1960," Chapter 8, section 1).

6. Though our money series starts in 1867, the first reference turn with which we have matched a specific cycle turn is the peak in October 1873. Hence we do not match the reference trough of December 1867, peak of June 1869, and trough of December 1870. The absence of a specific cycle turn to match with the December 1867 trough may simply result from the fact that our series does not go far enough back in time—a possibility suggested by the long average lead at troughs. For the other two reference turns, we conjecture that the annual data for successive Januarys—all we have for that period—may conceal by their crudeness turns that monthly data would reveal. This conjecture seems especially plausible because of the unusual brevity of the expansion phase, only 18 months, followed by a contraction of equal length.

7. That is, estimate of s.d. $= \sqrt{\dfrac{\Sigma(x - \bar{x})^2}{n - 1}}$, where x is the observation, $\bar{x}$,

the mean, and n the number of items in the group, in this example, 3.

8. Let the sine wave be $A\sin\dfrac{2\pi}{m}t$, where t is time. Then m is the period of the wave and A the amplitude, the wave fluctuating from $+A$ to $-A$.

9. Let $p(t)$ be the continuous rate of growth from year t to year $t + 1$, so that

$$X_{t+1} = X_t\, e\rho(t),$$

where X_t and X_{t+1} are successive annual observations. Then $\log_e X_{t+1} - \log_e X_t = \rho(t)$.

Note also that

$$\log_e X_{t+1} - \log_e X_t = \log_e \left(1 + \frac{X_{t+1} - X_t}{X_t} \right).$$

But $\log_e (1 + k)$ is approximately equal to k for small k. Hence the first difference is approximately equal to

$$\frac{X_{t+1} - X_t}{X_t}.$$

10. A more precise statement for these data is hard to arrive at, since successive first differences are not statistically independent.

11. See Simon Kuznets, *National Product since 1869,* New York, NBER, 1946, pp. 90 ff. These considerations have the obvious implication that net national product estimates are untrustworthy as a source of evidence on secular changes in the amplitude of business cycles.

12. The same reason that recommends a logarithmic scale for figure 2.5 also suggests an advantage in making computations like those in table 2.4 from the logarithms of the moving standard deviations. We have done so for the period from 1899 through 1960. The correlation results are quite similar. The synchronous results are .600, .797, .837, and .880 for 3, 4, 5, and 6 periods, respectively.

The ratio of the geometric mean of the standard deviation of NNP to the geometric mean of the standard deviation of money is 2.31, 2.25, 2.19, 2.13, for 3, 4, 5, and 6 periods, respectively. This method of estimation therefore suggests that income is roughly 2¼ times as variable as money.

13. Friedman, *The Demand for Money: Some Theoretical and Empirical Results,* New York, NBER, 1959, Occasional Paper 68, reprinted from *Journal of Political Economy,* August 1959, pp. 327–351.

14. "Cash Balances and the Interest Rate—a Pragmatic Approach," *Review of Economics and Statistics,* Nov. 1954, pp. 456–460; also "Income Velocity and Interest Rates—a Pragmatic Approach," *Employment, Growth, and Price Levels,* Joint Economic Committee, Hearings, part 10, 86th Cong., 1st sess., pp. 3435–3443 (reprinted with minor changes in *Review of Economics and Statistics,* Nov. 1960, pp. 445–449); and see Allan H. Meltzer, "The Demand for Money: The Evidence from the Time Series," presented at the Dec. 1961 meeting of the Econometric Society.

15. The elasticity of a total is a weighted average of the elasticities of the components, the weights being the ratio of each component to the total. Over the period from 1914 to 1960, commercial bank time deposits have varied from 19 to 44 percent of money as we define it.

16. Still another bit of evidence on which of the two definitions of money is to be preferred is available. We computed correlations like those in table 2.4 for the period 1915–60 between the variability of the narrower definition and the variability of net national product, and also between the variability of our broader definition and the variability of net national product. The broader definition has almost always a somewhat higher correlation coefficient. the synchronous results for standard deviations of varying terms are shown in the following tabulation, giving correlation coefficients between synchronous standard deviations of annual rates of change in money—defined narrowly and broadly—and in net national product, for different number of terms.

Definition of Money	3-Term	4-Term	5-Term	6-Term	7-Term	8-Term	9-Term
M_1	.592	.833	.865	.909	.937	.931	.912
M_2	.596	.785	.842	.883	.907	.899	.874

M_1 = Currency held by the public, plus demand deposits adjusted, plus commercial bank time deposits.

M_2 = Currency held by the public, plus demand deposits adjusted.

17. See his forthcoming monograph, "Determinants and Effects of Changes in the U.S. Money Stock, 1875–1955," a National Bureau study.

18. Milton Friedman and David Meiselman, "The Relative Stability of Monetary Velocity and the Investment Multiplier in the United States, 1897–1958," in *Stabilization Policies* (in press, 1963), pp. 165–268, Prentice-Hall for the Commission on Money and Credit.

19. The synchronous simple and partial correlation coefficients for the moving 4-term standard deviations of the first differences of logarithms are shown in the following tabulation for the full period and the period since 1899.

	Simple Correlations			Partial Correlations		
Period	r_{CM}	r_{CI}	r_{IM}	$r_{CM.I}$	$r_{CI.M}$	$r_{IM.C}$
1871–1958	.749	.404	.330	.713	.252	.044
1899–1958	.811	.600	.677	.687	.120	.406

C = Consumption
M = Money stock
I = Gross capital formation

If net capital formation is used as the measure of investment, first differences of absolute values must be obtained. We calculated the standard deviation of those first differences, and the logarithm of the standard deviation, and then correlated the logarithms as above. There is a trend element in these calculations that it would be desirable to eliminate but, even so, the correlation coefficients are similar to those described for the standard deviation of first differences of logarithms.

20. The investment multiplier is generally defined as the ratio of a change in *income* rather than in consumption to the change in autonomous expenditures to which the change in income is attributed. In these terms, the conclusion is that the multiplier is as likely in practice to be less than unity as greater than unity.

21. It is well established that (1) investment expenditures have a wider cyclical amplitude than consumption expenditures have relative to their mean value; (2) orders and other series reflecting investment decisions, as contrasted with expenditures, display a consistent tendency to lead cyclical turns; (3) there is a high correlation between consumption and income.

None of these is very strong evidence for the multiplier effect of investment on consumption, which is the point at issue. Item 1 simply means that investment is a more variable component of income than consumption is; it says nothing about whether both fluctuate in response to common influences, investment influencing consumption, or consumption influencing investment. Note that a strict multiplier model has no implications about whether autonomous or induced expenditures should show wider absolute fluctuations. Absolute fluctuations in induced expenditures would presumably be wider or narrower as the usual multiplier is greater or less than 2.

Item 2 has more significance and has some suggestive value. However, it may simply mean that decisions are affected early by whatever also affects spending later on (see page 64 below). Item 3 is entirely irrelevant. Consumption is a major component of income, as both are measured. For multiplier effects, what is important is the effect of investment on consumption. See M. Friedman and G. S. Becker, "A Statistical Illusion in Judging Keynesian Models," *Journal of Political Economy,* Feb. 1957, pp. 64–75.

22. Wesley C. Mitchell, *Business Cycles: The Problem and Its Setting,* New York, NBER, 1927, Chapter 2 and p. 62.

23. See also comments in Friedman, "The Lag in Effect of Monetary Policy," pp. 449–450.

24. For the United States, since the end of the Civil War, see our volume, *A Monetary History of the United States, 1867–1960.*

25. This point is discussed in more detail in Cagan's forthcoming "Determinants and Effects of Changes in the U.S. Money Stock, 1875–1955."

26. For the United States from 1896 to 1913, the value of the gold stock increased by roughly $1.4 billion or by about $80 million a year; net national product increased from about $11 billion in 1896 to $34 billion in 1913 or at the rate of about $1,300 million a year.

27. Though we have summarized here and have, ourselves, investigated in detail only the U.S. experience since 1867, this statement is deliberately worded so as to cover a wider range of experience. For example, it is consistent with the hyperinflations studied by Cagan ("The Monetary Dynamics of Hyperinflation," *Studies in the Quantity Theory of Money,* M. Friedman, ed., University of Chicago Press, 1956, pp. 25–117); with U.S. experience during the 1830s and 1840s studied by George Macesich ("Monetary Disturbances in the United States, 1834–45," unpublished Ph.D. thesis, University of Chicago, June 1958); with U.S. experience during the Revolutionary War, the War of 1812, and the Civil War; with Chilean experience, as studied by John Deaver ("The Chilean Inflation and the Demand for Money," unpublished Ph.D. thesis, University of Chicago, 1961); with the price revolution in the sixteenth century, as studied by Earl J. Hamilton (*American Treasure and the Price Revolution in Spain, 1501–1650,* Harvard University Press, 1934).

28. See Friedman, "Price, Income, and Monetary Changes in Three Wartime Periods," *American Economic Review,* May 1952, pp. 612–625.

29. Kuznets, *Capital in the American Economy: Its Formation and Financing,* Princeton for NBER, 1961, p. 572.

30. Friedman, *The Demand for Money.*

31. We call to the reader's attention the difference in this notation from that in *The Demand for Money.* M_d and y_p here refer to per capita money and income, whereas in the earlier paper they were used to refer to aggregate money and income. The shift was prompted by the desire to simplify the expressions that follow. The same shift is made for all variables referring to money and income. The remaining symbols all have the same meaning here as in *ibid.*

32. Because of the assumption that a_y and a_P are zero, or alternatively that the actual past record is replaced by the past record adjusted for trend, what is here called a change in the money stock is logically equivalent to a change in the money stock relative to its trend, or to a change in the rate of change.

33. From Friedman, *The Demand for Money.* (1) A value of $\beta = 0.4$ implies a weight for the first year of 0.33; (2) the value of δ is from equation 9 of *ibid.*; (3) the value of η is derived from table 1 of *ibid.* by dividing the entry for "implicit price deflator" in column (3) by the entry for "money income" in the same column.

With respect to (1), it should be noted that permanent income and prices were computed in *ibid.* by equations 2a and 3a rather than 2b and 3b. We have nonetheless taken the resulting value of w'_0 *in our present notation as an estimate of w_0.* This is correct as a first approximation, but in further work it would probably be better to work directly with equations 2b and 3b.

With respect to (3), the number used is for aggregate money income, not per capita. However, since the number is the difference between the per month rates of rise during expansion and contraction, and since population shows little response to cycles, the per capita figures would be lower by roughly the same amount for expansion and for contraction, and hence the difference would be unaffected.

34. One way to see this is to consider the problem of estimating directly the magnitude of the money multiplier from data on actual year-to-year changes in the logarithms of income and money. The first step would be to express the first differences as deviations from some mean values, designed to be the empirical counterparts of our theoretical constructs: $a_y + a_p$ = the expected rate of change in money (permanent) income; and $a_p + \delta a_y$ = the rate of change in the stock of money that would be consistent with a rate of change of a_y in real income and a_p in prices. That is, if money income, prices, and the stock of money all changed at exactly these rates, all expectations would be realized and there would be no disturbances to set the money multiplier, as we have defined it, to work. This first step is accomplished in our moving standard deviation analysis by computing, first, moving averages, and then expressing the observed first differences as deviations from the relevant average. Call these deviations from means, $\Delta' \log Y$ and $\Delta' \log M$.

The second step would be to estimate the mean ratio of $\Delta' \log Y$ to $\Delta' \log M$. But it would be undesirable to do this by averaging the ratio of the one to the other, since either might on occasion be close to zero (i.e., the variance of the ratio is in principle infinite). It would be better to estimate a value of, say, K in

$$\Delta' \log Y = K \Delta' \log M.$$

But as a statistical matter, there is no particular reason to prefer the estimate obtained by regressing $\Delta' \log Y$ on $\Delta' \log M$ to the estimate obtained by regressing $\Delta' \log M$ on $\Delta' \log Y$. In its rigid form the money multiplier analysis would imply perfect correlation, so the two regressions would be the same except for statistical errors of estimate. The "correct" regression then depends on the magnitude of errors in $\Delta' \log Y$ and $\Delta' \log M$. As is well known, the two simple regression coefficients give upper and lower bounds to any estimates obtained by treating both variables as subject to error. The geometric mean of these two bounding estimates is precisely the ratio of the standard deviation of $\Delta' \log Y$ to the standard deviation of $\Delta' \log M$.

35. We have used the estimates of w_0, δ, and η above because they are available in published form. We have been experimenting further with estimating demand equations using annual data instead of cycle bases, and estimating w_0 internally from the money correlations themselves, rather than externally. This work is still tentative but one set of results may be cited, because they are at the moment the most divergent from those given above.

For the years 1885–1960, one estimate of w_0 is 0.22 and of δ is 2.27. Inserting these along with $\eta = 0.20$ into equation 8 gives an estimate of the money multiplier of 2.25, or on the other side of the estimate of 2.0 from table 2.4. Interestingly enough, this estimate is very close to the ratio, formed from the geometric means of the computed standard deviations, which ranges from 2.13 to 2.31 for different numbers of terms (see footnote 12).

36. See Friedman and Meiselman, "The Relative Stability of Monetary Velocity."

37. These are roughly the actual values of a_y, a_P, and a_M over the 90 years 1870–1960 in the U.S. They yield a rather smaller value of δ (1.5) than we estimate by multiple regression techniques (roughly 1.8).

38. It may seem strange that a 1 percentage point difference in the rate of change of the stock of money produces precisely a 1 percentage point difference in the rate of change of prices regardless of the magnitude of the rate of change of money. Will there not, it is tempting to say, be a flight from money as the rate of change in prices and hence the cost of holding money rises? The answer is that we are comparing states of equilibrium, not the transition from one state to another. In a world in which prices are rising at 7 percent a year, the stock of money will be smaller relative to income (i.e., velocity will be higher) than it would in a world in which prices are falling at 13 percent a year. But, in both, velocity will be *changing* only in response to the change in real income, which is by assumption the same in the two worlds. Of course, it is possible that δ is different at different levels of cost of holding money; but that would be an effect of a rather subtler kind.

39. In particular, those in Friedman and Meiselman, "The Relative Stability of Monetary Velocity."

40. See *ibid.* for a fuller discussion of these points.

3   Secular Price Change in Historical Perspective

The phenomenon of sustained commodity price rises that has characterized both industrial and less developed economies in the past three decades is only the most recent such episode in the long historical record of secular price changes. This suggests that price history merits some investigation for the light it may throw on contemporary price experience.

Before we can hope to interpret the record of history, we need some provisional model to focus our attention on the few variables that might conceivably explain secular price changes. We can then test the model by the historical record. If the inferences drawn from the model do not conflict with the record, the model will survive to the next test.

The key variable that I associate with secular price movements is the ratio of the money stock to real output, a rise in the ratio matching secular price inflation, a decline matching secular price deflation. This by itself does not tell us whether the ratio is changing because of influences from the side of money or from the side of output. On a priori grounds, however, a wider possible range of variation may be expected in the numerator than in the denominator of the ratio. At any moment in time, given resources and technology determine real output. Over time, real output will grow, apart from cyclical disturbances and wars (in earlier centuries, also plagues), but sudden, abrupt discontinuities in level are unlikely. On the other hand, by various devices the money stock can be augmented or reduced very sharply in a brief time span, and the historical record provides rich evidence on the use of such devices.

A positive link between changes in the money stock per unit of output and secular price movements does not imply a simple proportional relationship between changes in the money stock and changes in the price level.[1] In addition, once a price movement establishes itself, it tends to be reinforced by its effect on expectations, rising prices leading to a rise in velocity, falling prices to a fall in velocity. Finally, although commodity price movements bear the initial impact of a secular change in money stock per unit of output, the impact then spreads to factor prices and to interest rates, as cooperating agents of production come to anticipate inflation or deflation. Thus, money wages tend to rise faster and interest rates tend to be higher during periods of secular price rise than of price fall.

Ideally, one would need data on money supply, real output, commodity prices, money wages, and interest rates to test the model. Clearly, a full set of such data is unavailable except for recent decades for most countries. I propose, therefore, on the basis of admittedly unsatisfactory data the further back in time one goes, first, to sketch what evidence there is for past episodes of price change, in the process commenting on alternative models that have been suggested, and second, to draw some conclusions from this evidence.

The episodes I shall comment on cover a time span of $2\frac{1}{2}$ millenia, so I cannot pretend to give more than a very superficial account of material drawn from writings of specialized scholars of the past with rather different interests from mine. Chronologically the episodes may be divided into four periods: (1) from antiquity through the fourth century of the Christian era; (2) from the fifth through the fifteenth centuries—the Middle Ages; (3) from the sixteenth century to the Napoleonic Wars; (4) from the nineteenth century through the early 1930s.

3.1 Antiquity

Three developments of Graeco-Roman times are relevant to this survey. One is the contrast between Greek and Roman monetary arrangements. The second is the monetary experience of the Hellenistic world following Alexander the Great's conquest of the Persians (330 B.C.). The third is the monetary crisis at the beginning of the 4th century A.D. in the Roman Empire.

a. From the fifth century B.C., Athenian silver coins of uniform fineness and weight became the prevailing standard not only among other Greek city-states but also among Attic trading partners in Asia Minor. Athens did not tamper with her coinage even when the state treasury was bare and when military needs were urgent. Rome, on the other hand, even when its monetary system was far less advanced than that of Greece, had a history of debasement. In the two centuries before the Punic Wars, it debased its copper coinage. During the next two centuries, when silver was introduced, it debased both silver and copper coinage and added an increasing amount of alloys to the dwindling amount of fine metals. Gold coins came into use at the beginning of the Empire in 30 B.C. For the next four hundred years, debasements were again the rule (Glotz 1926, pp. 230–37; Louis 1927, pp. 80–84, 207–8, 313–18).

Why Greek and Roman practice should have been so different I cannot say. There is evidence of persistent inflation under the Empire, but I cannot report that price stability characterized Classical Greece. The reason is that, though there are numerous relative price statistics, with one exception to which I shall refer in a moment, I do not know of reliable documentation of price level changes. The other bit of evidence related to the contrast in monetary arrangements between Greece and Rome is that interest rates on "normal" loans, comparable to modern personal loans, declined in Greece from 16 percent in 550 to 6 percent in 250 B.C., and then remained stable to 50 B.C.; whereas in the Roman Empire, they rose from 4 percent in A.D. 50 to over 12 percent by A.D. 250 (Homer 1963, p. 64; Louis 1927, pp. 317–18). There were clearly influences other than monetary arrangements affecting the levels of interest rates, but the contrasting trends in interest rates under the two regimes are in line with a dominant monetary effect.

b. The one case of a documented price level change in the annals of ancient Greece occurred as a consequence of Alexander the Great's conquest of the Persian kingdom (330 B.C.) Immense hoards of Persian gold were introduced by him into the Greek economy, transforming a silver into a predominantly gold standard. Prices and wages increased not only in Greece but also throughout the Hellenistic empire, as gold coinage was diffused through trade in markets from India and Egypt to Western Mediterranean lands. There is some reason to believe that prices were more unstable during the aftermath of Alexander's conquests than in earlier or following centuries of antiquity (Michell 1946; Heichelheim 1935, pp. 1–2).

c. The Emperor Diocletian in A.D. 296 tried to reform the chaotic state of the Roman currency by introducing full-weight gold and silver coins and a new bronze coin. This action might have been expected to stabilize prices but an overwhelming increase in the money stock supervened. Two alternative explanations have been advanced to account for the sources of the increase. One is that it occurred in the supply of precious metals from three sources: from (1) Diocletian's conquests in the East; (2) temple treasures that were dishoarded with the decline of paganism; and (3) private stocks transferred under compulsion to the imperial account. The last source would have contributed a net increase only if the Emperor coined metal transferred to his account that was not previously used in private transactions. This explanation has been rejected as unsubstantiated and replaced by one stressing that prices were fixed not in silver or in gold but in bronze (or copper). The source of the increase in the money stock, on this view, was the manufacture of copper coins. In any event, a pronounced price inflation followed, which Diocletian attempted to repress by issuing in A.D. 301 an Edict on Maximum Prices. Of price ceilings covering 900 commodities, 130 grades of labor, and various freight rates, the sections of the Edict in existence list maximum prices for 100 articles and wages ranging from a common laborer's to a lawyer's, the penalty for exceeding the maximum being death for both buyer and seller. The system of price control was a failure. Numerous death penalties, disturbances in the labor market, and the disappearance of new output from the product market characterized the period until A.D. 305 that the price edict was in effect. In that year Diocletian abdicated (Mattingly 1928, pp. 217, 222–27, 232–34; Michell 1947, pp. 1–3; West 1951, pp. 300–301; Jones 1953).

3.2 The Middle Ages

For almost a thousand years there are no statistics for either commodity prices or interest rates. Following the sack of Rome in 410, Western Europe was held by barbarian kingdoms. Barter transactions became common in domestic trade, while international trade declined. In the East, the Byzantine Empire, the successor of the Asiatic portion of the Roman Empire, revived the Classical Greek tradition of an intrinsically stable and uniform coinage, in this case, of gold. Its coinage became accepted in international trade. Not until the eighth century was the monopoly of Byzantine coins in international use broken. Then a new Moslem Arabic coin, the symbol of Arabic ascendance in Asia Minor, North Africa, and Spain, gained wide acceptability. In later medieval Europe, a variety of silver coins, issued by ecclesiastics, feudal lords, and kings—often debased—was in local use. By the thirteenth century, with the expansion of trade, Italian merchant republics began to coin gold, the coin of Florence in particular becoming the favored means of international payment. Later in the century, gold coinage was established in France and, in the fourteenth century, also in England, Flanders, Castile and Aragon, and Germany (Spufford 1965, pp. 576–602).

Fragmentary price quotations, available for a few English and French commodities, indicate that prices were higher at the end than at the beginning of the thirteenth century. Even if it could be established that the movement is not a statistical artifact, the explanation of the rise would remain to be determined. Coinage, population, and output all increased over the century. Of these factors, presumably only the increase in coinage would be expected to raise the general level of prices. Interest rate quotations are too sporadic to suggest any trend.

For the fourteenth century, price history is less scanty. The effect on prices of repeated changes in the silver coinage in France has been compared with that of relative stability of the silver coinage in England. The advantage of such an international comparison is that it enables one to treat as ceteris paribus contemporary nonmonetary factors, such as wars, famine, plague, and institutional changes, which can be shown to have had common effects on both countries, and to concentrate on the effects of monetary factors. Over the century, French kings ordered thirty-two changes in the maximum number of livres—the French unit of account until the Revolution—struck from a standard silver mark, the maximum number ranging from 2.9 to 125 livres per mark. The changes alternated between restorations and debasements of the metallic content of the coin. In the fourteenth century, by contrast, English alterations of silver money were relatively few and limited in size. If for each year, a comparison is made between the maximum price of wheat quoted in each country (actually, prices in the vicinity of Oxfordshire and in Chartres and Paris), on the assumption that it was the maximum that was paid in the most debased money, the movements of the French and English series, each expressed in the monetary units in which they existed, with no reference to the metal content of the unit of account, are usually diverse. However, when the prices in each country are expressed in money of constant metallic value and the units made comparable between the two, the movements of the two series are similar enough to suggest that French prices fully adjusted to alterations of the coinage, whether there was peace or war, famine or plenty, military success or failure (Miskimin 1963, pp. 37–38, 47, 82).

The comparative analysis is of particular interest, in view of difficulty in reconciling money supply and price estimates in the case of alterations of English coinage in the sixteenth century. Before turning to that episode, let me summarize the evidence on price and wage trends at the close of the Middle Ages in France, England, and three Spanish provinces that were then independent kingdoms (table 3.1). A price rise in the third quarter of the fourteenth century was the result of a sharp decline in population and output, due to the spread of bubonic plague through Europe, while the supply of money was increasing. The sources of that increase included the discovery of gold in Silesia and Hungary; an increase in trade with goldmining countries of northwestern Africa; debasement of, and a rise in money of account values assigned to, existing coinage. In the final quarter of the fourteenth century the trend of prices was declining, though Navarre is an exception; the price rise there is attributable to deliberate monetary expansion that offset a decline in prices quoted in gold. Elsewhere, the decline in prices reflected the resumption of vigorous population growth, and an increase in output, with no significant change in the money supply. The downward pressures on the price level were exacerbated in the

Table 3.1   Comparison of Rates of Change in Prices and Money Wages in Selected Countries at the Close of the Middle Ages (in Money of Account, Percent Per Year)

Series and Period	England (1)	France (2)	Aragon (3)	Navarre (4)	Valencia (5)
Prices:					
1326–50 to 1351–75	1.2	1.9	3.6	2.4	
1351–75 to 1376–1400	−1.0	−0.9	−1.0	2.1	
1376–1400 to 1476–1500	0	0	0		−0.1
Money wages:					
1326–50 to 1351–75	1.3	1.9		2.4	
1351–75 to 1376–1400	0.1	−0.5		3.1	
1376–1400 to 1476–1500	0.2	0.4	0		

Source: (by column):

(1) Phelps Brown and Sheila Hopkins, 1956, pp. 311–12. Prices refer to a "composite unit of consumables"; wages refer to builders' wages in Southern England. Quarter-century averages were computed from annual figures for prices and real wages. Annual figures for the latter are lacking in some cases. Money wages were computed by multiplying real wages by the price indexes.

(2) Phelps Brown and Sheila Hopkins, 1957, p. 305. Original source is Viscomte d'Avenel (*Histoire Economique de la Propriété, des Salaires, des Denrées, et de Tous Prix en Général,* Paris, 1894–1926, Vols. I–VII), on the basis of whose collection, index numbers were constructed by Georg Wiebe, *Zur Geschichte der Preisrevolution des XVI and XVII Jahrhunderts,* Leipzig, 1895. Prices refer to composite unit of consumables; wages refer to builders' wages.

(3–5) Hamilton, 1936a, pp. 59, 105, 162 (prices), 74, 115, 183 (wages). Quarter-century averages were computed from annual figures. For Aragon, a single annual figure is available for the first two quarter-centuries, with occasional gaps thereafter in the price series. Wages are reported beginning the last quinquennial of the 14th century. For Navarre, index numbers for prices are limited to only three, and for wages are limited to only one annual figure for the first quarter-century. The series for prices ends in 1445, for wages, in 1450. For Valencia, prices and wages are available beginning in the last decade of the 14th century.

Note: Rate of change is the difference between the natural logarithms of the average values of index numbers of the terminal and initial periods divided by the time interval between their mid-points.

fifteenth century by the spread of the money economy and specie flows to the Far East in payment for spices and luxury goods, yet general price stability characterized the period. Debasements and the marking-up of existing coinage apparently offset the deflationary forces (Hamilton 1936a, pp. 124–28, 193–204).

Money wages also rose as the Black Death struck, and continued to rise or decline less than prices over the next century and a quarter. Again, it is difficult to determine a trend in interest rates from the available quotations.

3.3   From the Sixteenth to the Close of the Eighteenth Century

For the English experiment in the sixteenth century with alterations of the coinage, estimates of the money supply and the price level are available. From May 1542 to mid-1551, Henry VIII and his successor, Edward VI, ordered progressive increases in the value assigned to fine gold and silver in the money of account. They reduced the weight of coins, increased the proportion of alloy in them, or else placed a higher value on existing coin with no change in their physical character. Private individuals and the government had an incentive to remint existing coins so long as their face value before deduction of seignorage was less than the price in newly minted coin which the Mint paid to a tender of their weight in fine silver. On government account, there was also an incentive to remint whenever seignorage charges exceeded the costs of reminting. In addition, there was appreciable monetization of plate and ornament the government obtained from suppressed religious orders (Gould 1970, pp. 71–86). In less than a decade, the estimates of English money supply more than doubled, while estimates of prices less than doubled (table 3.2).

In August 1551, Edward VI called down the silver coinage, and the money supply estimates show nearly a 50 percent decline. No comparable change is registered in the annual price statistics. In the next nine years, the money supply increased by one-third. Then in 1560 Queen Elizabeth called down the base silver coinage, and the money supply estimates show an 18 percent decline. The price estimates, however, reflect neither the growth nor the abrupt contraction revealed by the money supply estimates.

This is the one episode I have come across for which the price data do not seem to reflect the behavior of money stock per unit of output. Perhaps the price statistics are at fault, perhaps the money stock estimates. Perhaps velocity responses to debasement or restoration of

Table 3.2   **Estimates of English Money Supply and Prices, 1542–62 (in Money of Account)**

Date		Money Supply (Thousand £s) (1)	Prices (1451–75 = 100) (2)
	1542	848	172
April	1546	1188	248
early	1549	1755	214
early	1551	2022	
July	1551	2171	285
August	1551	1188	
Pre-calling down	1560	1581	265
Post-calling down	1560	1295	266
	1562	1391	

Source (by column): (1) Gould 1970, pp. 81–82; (2) same as for table 1, col. (1), prices.

the currency produced offsetting effects. Did debasement encourage increased holding of existing coinage and a reduction in goods purchases, and did restoration encourage the opposite tendency? However, until one or another of these explanations is tested and found satisfactory, this episode must be regarded as a contradiction to the basic hypothesis.

It has been suggested that debasements and coinage restorations should not be regarded as capricious actions taken by governments for revenue reasons, but instead as possibly stabilizing if debasements were instituted during periods when prices would otherwise have declined and restorations when prices would otherwise have risen. At the time the Great Debasement of 1546–51 began, prices in England had been rising at an annual rate of 1.3 percent per year since the turn of the century, although prices during the decade of the 1530s were relatively stable. Pursuing this line, one could argue that the intention of debasement was to insure the continuance of rising prices and of coinage restoration to slow the rate of price rise; hence both were stabilizing.

The episode of the Great Debasement in England occurred during the course of a price rise that marked the sixteenth and early seventeenth century in Europe, known as the Price Revolution. Compared with modern experience, the annual rates of price rise in various countries over this time span hardly seem to warrant such a designation. The price statistics, however, are often not expressed in terms of current coinage but are reduced to a silver basis, to facilitate comparison among countries. After correcting for the varying premium on silver, the price statistics show more modest rates of rise then would be the case if they were expressed in current coinage. For France, rates of change in prices expressed in money of account can be compared with the corresponding rates when prices are expressed in silver. For England, a similar comparison may be less reliable because the underlying indexes are not the same. In any event, table 3.3 shows both sets of results.

For Spain, for which the most detailed price statistics on a silver basis are available, and the country where the Price Revolution first occurred, the continuously compounded rate of rise from the first decade of the sixteenth to the first decade of the seventeenth century is 1.2 percent. For other European countries, for which statistics are less complete, the comparable annual rates of price rise are 1.0 (France and England) and 0.8 (Saxony). Expressed in money of account, the price rises for France and England are converted to 2.1 and 1.7 percent per year, respectively. Money wage rates also rose during the sixteenth century, on a silver basis in Spain, at 1.1 percent per year through the closing decade (at 1.3 percent if the following decade is included); in terms of current coinage in France and England, at 1.1 percent per

Table 3.3   **Comparison of Rates of Change in Prices and Money Wages in Selected Countries during the Price Revolution (Percent per Year)**

| | Prices | | Money Wages | |
| | in | in Money | in | in Money |
Country and Period	Silver	of Account	Silver	of Account
Spain:				
1. 1501–10 to 1601–10	1.2		1.3	
France:				
2. 1501–25 to 1576–1600	1.0	2.1	0.3	1.1
England:				
3. 1501–10 to 1593–1602	1.0	1.7	0.3	0.8
4. 1501–10 to 1581–90		1.5		1.4
Saxony:				
5. 1476–1500 to 1591–99	0.8			

Source (by line): ll. 1–3 and 5, prices and money wages in silver, from Hamilton 1929, pp. 352 (England) and 353 (France); Hamilton 1934, pp. 271 and 403 (Spain) and 209 (Saxony). The original source of the English figures is Thorold Rogers (*A History of Agriculture and Prices in England, Oxford,* 1882–87, Vols. III–VI), on the basis of whose collection Georg Wiebe (see table 1, col. 1) constructed index numbers. 1. 2, prices and money wages in money of account, same as for Table 2.1, col. 2. ll. 3–4, prices and money wages in money of account, same as for table 2.1, col. 1.

Note: Same as for table 2.1.

year in the former, 1.4 percent in the latter through the ninth decade of the sixteenth century, following which money wages were essentially unchanged. Such interest rate quotations as exist suggest a sharp rise in their level during the course of the century.

Let me digress from price history for a bit to discuss the two broad explanations of the Price Revolution that have coexisted from the time its impact was first recognized by contemporaries. One explanation traced the price rise to an initial increase beginning in the last quarter of the fifteenth century in European silver output, which was dwarfed in the next century by an influx first of gold and later of silver from the Spanish possessions in the New World (Nef 1941, pp. 585–86; Hamilton 1934, pp. 293–302). By 1660, the close of the period of Spanish imports, the European stock of gold had nearly doubled, and the stock of silver had increased three and two-fifths times (Brenner 1961).[2]

The precious metals that reached Spain first were dispersed to other European countries by unfavorable trade balances in Spain, due to the earlier impact of the increase in money supply on its prices, and by military expenditures and administrative expenses incurred in maintaining the Spanish empire. Hence the widespread scope of the Price Revolution. The extent of the price rise in individual countries varied with the size of specie inflows, the amount diverted to nonmonetary uses, the relative growth of output, and the spread of the money economy.

The second explanation traced the price rise to nonmonetary factors. The Spanish price rise in the sixteenth century was ascribed to an expansion of European demand for Spanish wool and other products, the cessation of the price rise in the seventeenth century to ruinous taxation, agricultural decay, depopulation, and malfeasance of businessmen (Hamilton 1929).

Several economic historians have seized on the second type of explanation. One objection they have raised against the monetary explanation is that it has to be shown that the increase in Spain's stock of metals actually was dispersed through Europe, as asserted. The basis for this objection is the absence of a rise after the middle of the sixteenth century in figures for the quantity of woollen cloth exports from the port of London, the argument being that if there were an outflow of specie from Spain, England should have had a favorable balance of trade. However, the woollen cloth exports are quantity figures, for which no export prices are available; the port of London was evidently declining, while other ports were rising in importance; and, finally, no value figures exist for imports; so no balance of trade data can be cited in support of the challenge. A second objection is that prices were rising before American treasure could have had an appreciable effect. The rise in European silver output beginning in the last quarter of the fifteenth century, to which reference has been made, disposes of this point. A third objection is that if there were an increase in the money supply, the increase in volume of trade should have offset it. The answer is that the increase in the money supply was far greater than the increase in output. A fourth objection is that if the increase in the money supply produced the price change, why were there not similar effects on prices of all commodities and services. The question indeed is turned around: since some prices rose sharply, others rose less markedly, and still other prices fell, how could monetary increase possibly be a common explanation for the diversity? The preceding objection is grouped with a final one, namely, demographic changes can account for the differential price changes without invoking monetary factors at all (Brenner 1961, 1962; Gould 1964; Hammarström 1957).

The theory of a causal relation between population and prices distinguishes between agriculture and industrial prices. Given an increase in population and inelastic agricultural supply and demand, two consequences are deduced: (1) food prices rise sharply; (2) the increase in the labor force finds industrial employment, so industrial output rises, but as residual income left to wage-earners after providing themselves with food is limited, demand for industrial output is weak. Consequently, prices of agricultural goods with inelastic demand and supply rise more sharply than prices of elastic industrial goods. Accordingly, periods of secular population increase can be linked with periods of rising prices, periods of declining population with periods of stable or falling prices.

The difficulty with this analysis is that it cannot explain why industrial prices rise at all during periods of population increase; under the stated conditions, they should fall. Moreover, although it is alleged that in periods of declining population, supplies of food were plentiful and cheaper because marginal lands were abandoned, the theory cannot account for the rise in prices in the third quarter of the fourteenth century that accompanied the decline in population at the time of the Black Death.

In any case, changes in relative prices tell us nothing about changes in the aggregate. Economic historians frequently display a bias against aggregates, in part, possibly, because aggregate data are lacking for past centuries. A charge they level against monetary analysis is that it deals only with aggregates. In addition, as noted, they allege that a monetary explanation to be valid implies a similar monetary effect on all prices. This is true but it does not follow that all prices will therefore move in unison. The common monetary effect has superimposed on it forces that affect relative prices. For particular commodities, the factors affecting relative prices may be far more important than the common monetary effect. However, the price of commodity X, for example, can double with respect to commodity Y by the absolute price of X doubling and the price of Y staying the same, or by the absolute price of X staying the same and the price of Y halving, or by any of an infinite number of other combinations. No amount of information on the factors affecting the relative prices of X and Y can explain which of these alternatives will occur. That is the role of aggregate analysis.

To resume the description of the course of prices in the seventeenth century, Spanish prices reached a peak in the first decade of the seventeenth century, while English and French prices continued to rise until the middle of the century, in the French case with an interruption in the upward movement from 1600 to 1625. Up to 1650 a composite price index for all of Spain is available; thereafter only separate regional indexes exist (see table 3.4). The different behavior of Valencian and Castilian prices in the second half of the seventeenth century is of some interest. Prices in Valencia were declining from mid-century on, but they rose steeply in New Castile until 1680 and then reversed movement to the end of the century. The difference reflects the independent monetary system in Valencia, where the money of account was virtually constant in terms of silver during the period, while Castilian money was progressively debased and overissue of fractional coins drove the

Table 3.4   Comparison of Rates of Changes in Prices and Money Wages and Nominal Interest Rates, in Selected Countries during the 17th and 18th Centuries

Country and Period	Prices		Money Wages		Yields on Long-Term Government Securities (Percent per Year per Year)
	in Silver	in Money of Account	in Silver	in Money of Account	
	(Percent per Year)				
Spain:					
1. 1601–10 to 1641–50	−0.1		0.3		
Valencia:					
2. 1651–55 to 1686–90		−0.8			
3. 1701–05 to 1721–25		−0.2			
4. 1721–25 to 1746–50		0.4			
5. 1751–55 to 1786–90		0.7			
New Castile:					
6. 1656–60 to 1676–80		2.0			
7. 1676–80 to 1696–1700		−2.3			
8. 1701–05 to 1721–25		−0.4			
9. 1721–25 to 1746–50		0.3		0.4[a]	
10. 1756–60 to 1786–90		1.0		0.3	

Table 3.4 (continued)

Country and Period	Prices in Silver	Prices in Money of Account	Money Wages in Silver	Money Wages in Money of Account	Yields on Long-Term Government Securities (Percent per Year per Year)
		(Percent per Year)			
England:					
11. 1593–1602 to 1643–52	0.6	0.6	0.7		
12. 1643–52 to 1693–1702	0	0	0.6		
13. 1593–1602 to 1710–19		0.3		0.5	
14. 1693–1702 to 1731–40		−0.5			
15. 1731–40 to 1781–90		0.8			0.3
16. 1710–19 to 1781–90		0.3		0.4	
France:					
17. 1576–1600 to 1601–25	−1.1	−0.7	0	0.2	
18. 1601–25 to 1626–50	1.0	1.6	0.5	0.8	
19. 1626–50 to 1676–1700	−0.1	0	0	0.5	
American Colonies:					
20. 1726–50 to 1751–75		1.2			

Source (by line): l. 1, same as for table 3.3, line 1. ll. 2–5, Hamilton 1947, pp. 121, 141, 157 (prices). Only fragmentary wage figures are given (p. 211). ll. 6–10, same as for lines 2–5, except money wage figures are given, beginning 1737 (p. 208). ll. 11–16, prices and money wages, same as for table 3.3, lines 1 and 3–4; line 15, yields, Homer 1963, pp. 161–62. ll. 17–19, same as for table 3.3, lines 1–2.1. 20, Warren and Pearson 1932, pp. 7–8.

Note: Same as for table 3.1.

ᵃ1737–40 to 1746–50.

precious metals out of circulation. The premium on silver in Castile quintupled between 1650 and 1680, when the inflation was abruptly halted (Hamilton 1947, pp. 27–32, 1121). The military, political, and economic decline of Spain during the seventeenth century is apparently not unrelated to the monetary disorders in Castile. In the eighteenth century, Spanish prices moved downward moderately until 1725, and the rose at a rate of under 1 percent per year until the closing decade. From 1650 to 1740, English prices moved within a narrow range, alternately rising and falling at rates well under 1 percent per year until the half-century before the outbreak of the Napoleonic Wars, when they rose at 8 percent per year.

Although it did not involve a secular change in the price level, let me interject a comment here on the British recoinage toward the end of the seventeenth century. Two kinds of silver coin were then in use, hammered ones minted before 1663 and milled ones introduced thereafter. Hammered coins differed in weight when issued, were easily clipped, and wore down in use. The milled coins were more uniform when issued, resisted clipping because of the raised and grooved rim, and did not show wear. By the early 1690s, the contrast between the condition of the two kinds of coin eroded confidence in the clipped and worn ones. In the second half of 1695, the efforts of holders of these coins to exchange them for gold guineas and commodities led to a rise in the sterling value of the guineas from twenty-one to thirty shillings, and an increase in the monthly prices of a sample of nonagricultural commodities at an annual rate of 23 percent. The price rise was also a response to a 19 percent increase in the money supply in 1695 as coinage of gold guineas increased.

Finally, in December, 1695, the government took action. It demonetized all clipped and worn silver coins as of February 1696, after which the Mint would accept them by weight only. The recall of the silver coinage to the Mint in 1696, without provision for prompt reissue of coin of standard weight and fineness, led to an abrupt reduction in the money supply in the first half of 1696. This effect was offset to some extent by the dishoarding of standard weight coins and by note issues of the Bank of England which suspended specie payments; money substitutes, for which there are no estimates, were also pressed into use. The monthly price data, in any event, declined at a 12 percent annual rate in the first half of 1696, reflecting not only the contraction in the money supply but also the unloading of stocks of commodities accumulated earlier. Thereafter, as the new coinage was disbursed by the Mint, the money supply grew slowly, reaching the same level in mid-1698 as in mid-1694. Since the monthly price data end in April 1697, we cannot trace the price change for the parallel period, but prices are rising at the time the series ends (Horsefield 1960; Letwin 1964; Ashton 1960).[3]

The French price series, which ends in 1700, follows a roughly similar course to that of the English series. One exception occurred in the eighteenth century, during the years 1716–20, when John Law's experiment with banknote issues slightly more than doubled the volume of French currency. Commodity prices exhibited a similar rise, though money wages rose only 60 percent. This episode may be observed in the monthly data for Paris, but not for London, Madrid, or Philadelphia (Hamilton 1936b, pp. 62–70). Wholesale prices in the American Colonies apparently increased from 1726–50 to 1751–75 at an annual rate of 1.2 percent per year.

For the European countries, rates of change in money wages are shown for available dates and matching price changes are given (table 3.4). Money wages sometimes rose faster than prices, sometimes slower. Depending on the initial and terminal dates chosen, the pattern shifts, but in general the wage data show movements paralleling commodity prices. The trend of the spotty interest rate data in the seventeenth century is downward. Beginning 1727 yields on long-term British government securities are available. They are remarkably similar in movement to British commodity price changes (Homer 1963, pp. 161–62).

Our statistical information regarding the monetary experience of the American colonies is sketchy, so it is difficult to determine the extent to which it conforms to the money-output-price relationship I have been describing. From 1720 to 1774, discontinuous annual estimates of the outstanding value of bills of public credit and Treasury notes are available with better coverage for five of the colonies than for seven others. Matching price data for each colony are unavailable. Exchange rates on London are, however, known for each of the five colonies. The depreciation of exchange rates varied from 12 to 13 percent in New York and in Virginia, to 27 percent in Pennsylvania, 330 percent in Boston, and 1340 percent in Rhode Island. The outstanding value of bills of public credit issued does not closely match exchange rate movements, although in general the New England colonies issued far more than did the Middle Atlantic colonies and Virginia. However, bills of credit were only one form of paper money then in use. Estimates of loan bank issues and of private bills of exchange plus such specie as there was would need to be included to form some judgment of how serious the disparity is between total nominal money issues and the real values of those issues expressed as sterling at current exchange rates (U.S. Bureau of the Census 1960; Weiss 1970).

Since the focus here is secular price change, I omit discussion of the two short-term episodes at the conclusion of this subperiod: the $8\frac{1}{2}$ percent *per month* average rate of rise in prices during the American Revolution, ending in the discontinuation in use of continental currency; and the 10 percent per month average rate of rise in prices in France during the revolutionary era, ending in the discontinuation in use of assignats (Bezanson 1951, pp. 93, 343; Harris 1930, pp. 106, 108).

One important change in the eighteenth century was the proliferation of forms in which money was held and used. In England, silver and gold coin were supplemented by note issues of the Bank of England, London private banks, and, after 1750, country banks, as well as by inland bills of exchange created by individual borrowers or lenders. In Holland, where the Bank of Amsterdam was founded at the beginning of the seventeenth century, paper money became well known. In Spain, its use became familiar in the last quarter of the eighteenth century. In France, lingering distrust created by John Law's ill-fated banknote issues effectively ended further public willingness to hold money in any form but coin until the Revolution.

The eighteenth century was punctuated by brief periods of peace between prolonged wars involving at one time or another all the leading countries. Though wars in modern experience are associated with price increases as monetary authorities finance government expenditures to prosecute their military involvements, in the eighteenth century before the Napoleonic Wars no consistent relationship between wars and prices is observed. The Bank of England, for example, curtailed loans on private account when it increased them on government account (Ashton 1959, p. 65). In Spain, outflows of specie and blockades against imports from Spanish America occurred during wartime, and except when paper money issues were introduced, prices did not rise. During peacetime, inflows of specie and paper money issues matched periods of price rise (Hamilton 1947, p. 217).

For the eighteenth century, as for the Price Revolution, European population change has been invoked by some economic historians as the causal factor producing the rough stability of prices until the middle of the century, and the rise thereafter, with differential effects on agricultural and industrial prices. Change in rate of population growth, however, is not consistently related to change in secular price movements in the nineteenth and twentieth centuries, the final historical evidence that I want to consider (Grauman 1968, pp. 378–79).

3.4   From the Napoleonic Wars to the Twentieth Century

Table 3.5 shows annual average rates of price change for the series available for selected countries for each of six secular episodes in the period from 1790 to the early 1930s. Wage and interest rate data are included where possible. Three periods of secular price rise alternate with three periods of secular price decline.

In the extensive literature devoted to these episodes, four main explanations have been advanced: explanations stressing (1) monetary factors, (2) cost-push and cost-pull factors, (3) a long-wave mechanism,

Table 3.5 Six Episodes of Secular Price Change, Four Countries, 1790–1934

Episode: General Chronology:	1. Inflation 1790–1815	2. Deflation 1815–50	3. Inflation 1850–73	4. Deflation 1873–96	5. Inflation 1896–1920	6. Deflation 1920–34
	Annual Average Rate of Change (Prices and Money Wages in Percent per Year; Interest Rates in Percent per Year)					
Great Britain:						
Prices	2.8	−2.2	0.9	−1.7	4.7	−4.1
Money wages	2.9	−0.6	1.9	−0.1	5.2	−3.8
Interest rates	0.09	−0.05	0.01	−0.04	0.13	−0.16
U.S.:						
Prices	3.3	−2.3	5.3	−1.8	4.2	−3.9
Money wages				−0.3	5.0	−2.2
Interest rates				−0.13	0.09	−0.09
Germany:						
Prices	3.2	−1.9	1.9	−0.8	11.0	−1.2
Money wages				−0.2		−0.3
Interest rates		−0.06	0.02	−0.04	0.24	−0.27
France:						
Prices		−1.0	1.2	−2.5	8.2	−8.4
Interest rates		−0.10	0.07	−0.10	0.10	−0.25

Note: Rates of change are from initial to terminal values assuming continuous compounding.

Sources:

Great Britain—Prices: 1790–1813; 1813–50 (Gayer, Rostow and Schwartz index of domestic and imported commodities, from Mitchell and Deane 1962, p. 470); 1873–96; 1896–1920; 1920–34 (through 1913, an approximation of retail prices, furnished by Phyllis Deane; thereafter, 1914–18, Ministry of Labour cost-of-living index; 1919–34, Ministry of Labour retail price index). Wages: 1790–1810; 1810–45 (from Mitchell and Deane 1962, p. 343, Part A, Great Britain); 1850–74 (*ibid.*, Part B); 1874–95; 1895–1920; 1920–34 (wage rates from Phelps Brown and Sheila Hopkins, 1950, pp. 276, 281—1914–20 shifted to level of 1895–1914). Interest rates: 1792–1812; 1812–52; 1852–74; 1874–97; 1897–1920; 1920–35 (yield on Consols, from Homer 1963, pp. 162, 195–197, 409).

United States—Prices: 1791–1814; 1814–49; 1849–65 (from Warren and Pearson 1932, pp. 8–9); 1869–96; 1896–1920; 1920–33 (price deflator implicit in unpublished annual net national product estimates of Robert Gallman, 1869–1909, thereafter ot Simon Kuznets). Wages: 1869–95; 1895–1920; 1920–33 (wage rates, from Phelps Brown and Sheila Hopkins, 1950, pp. 277, 282—1914–20 shifted to level of 1895–1914). Interest rates: 1869–99; 1899–1921; 1921–34 (through 1899, railroad bond yields, adjusted to level of following segment, which is the basic yield on 30-year corporate bonds, from Homer 1963, pp. 310, 316, 374).

Germany—Prices: 1792–94 to 1807–09; 1807–09 to 1848–50 (wholesale prices from Jacobs and Richter 1935, pp. 82–83); 1850–74; 1874–95 (price deflator implicit in net national product, from Hoffmann 1965, pp. 825–828); 1896–1920; 1924–31 (cost-of-living index, from Bry 1960, pp. 325–327). Wages: 1873 to 1894–95; 1925–33 (Phelps Brown and Margaret Browne 1968, pp. 436–438). Interest rates: 1818–52; 1852–73; 1873–96; 1896–1924; 1924–33 (yield on Prussian State 4s or 3½s; Bavarian 3½s; computed average of bond yields; high-grade bond yields, from Homer 1963, pp. 259–260, 260–261, 461).

France—Prices: 1820–51; 1851–73; 1873–96; 1896–1920; 1926–34 (wholesale prices, from Jacobs and Richter 1935, pp. 34–35). Interest rates: 1816–52; 1853–73; 1873–97; 1897–1920; 1925–34 (yield on 5% or 3% French government rentes, from Homer 1963, pp. 222–223, 426–427).

and (4) rates of economic growth. I shall summarize each approach and then discuss objections raised against each.

1. In each pair of episodes the monetary explanation notes the following factors:

a. Wartime expansion of note issues in England, especially after the Bank of England suspended specie payments in 1797, followed by contraction of paper money issues, especially after England resolved to return to the gold standard at the prewar parity in 1821. The return to gold was coupled with a decline in the output of precious metals in Latin America; and accompanied by growth in output and population.

b. Gold discoveries in the United States and Australia, 1848–51, increased world gold output over the following decade and a half at an annual rate of 8 percent. The gold producing countries distributed the output among their trading partners, thus leading to faster monetary growth in those countries. Monetary expansion was greatly increased in the United States during the Civil War when specie payments were suspended, and in France and Germany during the Franco-Prussian War. This episode was succeeded by a 1 percent per year decline in the rate of growth of world gold output, 1873–87, at a time when the gold standard was adopted by several countries, the United States resumed specie payments, and silver was demonetized. An expansion of world gold output during the following decade was accompanied by rapid growth in population and output (Warren 1933, p. 97).

c. An increase of about 4.5 percent per year in world gold output, 1896–1914, permitted faster growth of money supply. To finance World War I, the belligerent countries stepped up monetary growth further. Prices collapsed in 1920 or 1921 as extraordinary wartime rates of growth of money ceased, except in Austria, Germany, Hungary, Poland, and Russia, where hyperinflations intervened. Thereafter, the progressive contraction of the U.S. money supply, 1929–32, and the collapse of the U.S. banking system produced a sharp price decline. The U.S. contraction ensured a worldwide decline in prices because of the links forged by fixed rates of exchange under the gold exchange standard to which most countries adhered in 1929.

2. The cost-push or cost-pull explanation stresses demand and supply conditions in individual markets. Rises in costs are associated with poor harvests, obstructions in supply conditions—including wartime blockades—increases in foreign exchange, insurance, freight, and interest costs. Declines in costs are associated with good harvests, improved transportation facilities, discovery of new foreign sources of supply, technological improvements, and reduced foreign exchange, insurance, and interest costs.

The cost-push explanation was advanced with special emphasis on the price rise from 1896 to 1910 at a session on the causes of the inflation at the December 1910 annual meeting of the American Economic Association. J. Laurence Laughlin argued that since the increase in the supply of gold had just been offset by the increase in demand for gold, and since the supply of credit was determined by the demand, factors other than an increase in money supply must have been responsible for the price rise. The factors he cited included the Dingley Tariff of 1897, higher tax rates, agricultural conditions, speculation, general extravagance—"new wealth makes a liberal spender" (Laughlin 1911, p. 36)—and, finally, two factors with a very modern ring: wages and unionism, and monopolies and trusts. A year and a half earlier, in the *Journal of Political Economy,* Laughlin had argued that "the pressure of labor unions" had been "an influence independent of prices" which acted to raise the rate of wages, and that once a high rate of wages had been granted, it was not easy for employers to force a reduction. His proof was "the after-effects of the recent panic of 1907" (Laughlin 1909, pp. 267, 269). As for monopolies and trusts, Laughlin stated, "As every economist knows, in the conditions under which many industries are today organized, expenses of production have no direct relation to prices. In such conditions, there is a field in which the policy of charging 'what the traffic will bear' prevails; and this includes industries that are not public utilities" (Laughlin 1911, p. 35). (A companion paper at this session was delivered by Irving Fisher, who responded gallantly, "I find myself unable to agree with most of the positions taken by Professor Laughlin in his able paper.")[4]

3. The long-wave explanation, in Schumpeter's version, stresses the role of new techniques, as, for example, in the manufacture of textiles and iron in the Industrial Revolution of the first pair of episodes, the introduction of railways in the second pair, and innovations utilizing electric power and chemistry in the third pair. Prices rise in the upward phase of a long wave, corresponding to the introduction of innovations by pioneering entrepreneurs, because credit is expanded and the demand for goods increases while the output of the innovations is not yet fully realized. Prices fall during the downward phase of a long wave, corresponding to the period when hordes of followers imitate the innovators, and the cost-reducing effects of the innovations are realized in increased output. Profits and interest rates are high during the upward phase and low during the downward phase. Since variation in the output of commodities is determined by the long-wave process, unless the behavior of the money supply were exactly compensatory, price movements are generally determined by output movements (Schumpeter 1939).

4. The explanation stressing economic growth compares rates of growth of world industrial capacity and the output of primary products since 1815. When industrial capacity grows faster than the output of

primary products, the prices of primary products rise absolutely and relatively to industrial wages. The rise in wholesale prices of raw materials raises prices "fixed" for final products, which induces wage earners to press for rises in money wages. Other incomes rise in turn, causing further rises in costs and prices. The risk of raising prices is smaller for sellers at such a time when competitors are also raising their prices and customers' expectations of price increases justify them. It is granted that monetary restriction could stop prices from rising, but in fact, it is asserted, in the past, monetary restriction has taken place only enough to raise the long-term rate of interest gradually as the upward price trend has gone on. All these reactions to a rise in wholesale prices are in the reverse directions when wholesale prices fall. Long-period price declines have not been due to shortage of money, it is asserted, although presumably monetary expansion could stop prices from falling (Brown and Ozga 1955).

Let me now examine in turn the objections that have been raised against each of these explanations. Three have been raised against the monetary explanation.

1. One objection to the monetary explanation was based on erroneous British money supply statistics, particularly from about 1875 to 1913, which purported to show a relatively constant rate of growth of the series, unaffected by variations in gold production. Improved statistics indicate that the growth rate of the British money supply was decidedly lower from 1873 to 1895 than from 1851 to 1873 and from 1895 to 1913, and the same seems to be true of money growth rates of other countries with defective banking statistics (Higonnet 1957, pp. 350–354).

2. Another objection judged the fall in interest rates during periods of secular price decline to be an embarrassment to the monetary explanation, implying that no distinction need be made between nominal and real interest rates. Once the distinction is made, however, declining interest rates can be interpreted as a reflection of declining prices. Insofar as changes in the purchasing power of money are anticipated, bond prices will tend to be higher and nominal yields lower when commodity prices are falling than when they are rising, the increase in the real value of the principal constituting a return in addition to the nominal interest paid. Since anticipations usually lag the actual fall in prices, interest rates will usually fall together with commodity prices as they adjust to the price fall. The Gibson Paradox, in short, is an implication of rather than an embarrassment to the monetary explanation of secular price movements.

It has been suggested that the paradox disappears if the assumption is made that movements in the price level are inversely related to the change in money supply. A rise in prices would imply "(other things being equal) an extension of the demand for monetary balances, and higher rates of interest" (Brown and Browne 1968, p. 108); a decline in prices would imply a contraction of the demand for monetary balances, and a lower rate of interest. In my view, the willingness to "allow the possibility that the rise of the price level may come about without an antecedent increase in the stock of money" reflects both error regarding the movements of the money stock and commitment to the belief that changes in money supply influence interest rates only, and that the channel of influence is only through a negative liquidity effect.

3. A final objection is that the monetary explanation cannot incorporate cost changes. The argument is essentially a statement of the view that prices rise when money costs rise and prices fall when money costs fall. Thus, this objection to the monetary explanation ties in with the cost approach to secular price change, so I shall discuss it in the more general context of that view.

The monetary explanation, it must be said at the outset, incorporates all supply influences in the output variable to which the growth in the money supply is related. The effects of reduced real costs are allowed for in the monetary explanation in the increase in output which cost reduction has achieved, or in the decrease in output which real cost increases entail, under given demand conditions.

What the cost explanation, on the other hand, fails to show is, first, where the autonomous increase in cost comes from. Fundamentally, it begs the question. Of course, if costs rise more than productivity, so will prices in general. But what produces the rise in cost? Here the explanation is generally ad hoc, relying on different factors in different circumstances,[5] and typically confusing effects on relative costs with effects on absolute costs. Moreover, even if this basic defect is overlooked, and we suppose an autonomous rise in nominal costs, the cost explanation must then show how the increase in money costs increased either money supply or velocity or both or how a decrease in money costs decreased either money supply or velocity or both. It has failed to do so. With respect to the relationship between costs and money supply we can set aside the political argument that is advanced in respect of post–World War II conditions, namely, that the existence of a full-employment policy enforces growth in the money supply to validate cost increases that would otherwise lead to unemployment. This political argument obviously has no relevance to the world of the nineteenth and first third of the twentieth century. An alternative argument to the effect that changing costs affected the demand for working capital, on the surface, seems more plausible. It implies that demand for bank loans determined the rate of growth of money.

On this issue, we have some evidence in Cagan's study of the U.S. money supply. If banks were the channel through which secular changes in the rate of growth of the money supply were produced, we should expect to find the usable reserve ratio—Cagan's term for total minus required reserve ratio—rising during secular periods of price decline, when presumably the demand for bank loans would have been weak, and declining during secular periods of price rise, when presumably the demand for bank loans would have been strong. We do not observe such movements in the data. The usable reserve ratio declined during the period of secular price decline to 1895, declined further during the following period of secular price rise to 1920, and during the succeeding period of price decline also declined through 1929. So the U.S. reserve ratio gives no confirmation to the argument that demand for loans determined the money supply. More basically, Cagan has shown that the major source of secular changes in the U.S. money supply has been changes in high-powered money, not changes in the reserve ratio (Cagan 1965, pp. 280–286).

It has been asserted that there need be no "preliminary permissive or causal movement on the side of money" (Brown and Browne 1968, p. 156) for the general level of prices to change. "The general level of prices can rise . . . if particular price rises originating in the balance of supply and demand for particular products or factors of production are passed on, and compensated, by rises of other prices and money incomes. Recent years of full employment have shown how a tacit conspiracy to do this can be formed and perpetuate itself when once each man who takes part in it comes to believe that the others are in it too" (Brown and Browne 1968, p. 108). This is a modern example of the confusion between relative and absolute costs discussed earlier.

However, the modern version of the fallacy is buttressed by a more sophisticated argument, namely, that with no change in the money stock, a rise in costs or prices will force interest rates up, since the demand for nominal money rises; the rise in interest rates will then push up velocity; a decline in costs or prices will pull interest rates down, since the demand for nominal money falls; the decline in interest rates will then pull down velocity. But this raises two problems: first, the standard problem of what causes *absolute* costs to rise or fall; and, second, how this effect, even if it occurred, could be more than a once-for-all effect. For inflation to continue, velocity must continue to rise. As already stated, the monetary explanation implies such a pattern, following an increase in the rate of monetary growth, because of the effect of inflation on nominal interest rates. However, the cost-inflation explanation must produce the result with no change in the money stock. On the cost-inflation view, there is no reason why price rises and falls should be correlated at all with rates of monetary growth; they should rather be correlated with velocity. In fact, the correlations are decidedly higher with rates of monetary growth per unit of output than with velocity. Indeed, the theoretically expected relation between velocity and rate of price change, while it can be detected in the data by sophisticated statistical analysis, is generally hidden to the naked eye. For example, velocity declined in the United States during both secular price declines and secular price rises in the period from 1869 to 1932. Finally, secular velocity changes, at least through 1929 in the United States, did not parallel closely similar swings in interest rates.

The cost-push cost-pull argument amounts to an assertion that there is no common element affecting the price level. The price level is only the collection of prices determined in individual markets. A rise in an individual price has an inflationary effect, with no force producing offsetting changes if one relative prices increases. Relative price changes accordingly are identical with price level changes.

No better response to this approach can be cited than one Irving Fisher gave sixty years ago (Fisher 1911a):

> The legitimacy of separating the study of price levels from that of [individual] prices will be clearly recognized, when it is seen that individual prices cannot be fully determined by supply and demand, money cost of production, etc., without surreptitiously introducing the price level itself. We can scarcely overemphasize the fact that the "supply and demand" or the "cost of production" of goods in terms of money do not and cannot completely determine prices. Each phrase, fully expressed, already implies *money*. There is always hidden somewhere the assumption of a general price level.

> . . . In elementary textbooks much emphasis is laid on the fact that "demand" and "supply" are incomplete designations and to give them meaning it is necessary to add to each the phrase "at a price." But emphasis also needs to be laid on the fact that "demand at a price" and "supply at a price" are *still* incomplete designations, and that to give them meaning it is necessary to add "at a price level." The demand for sugar is not only relative to the price of sugar, but also to the general level of other things. . . . The price of sugar in dollars depends partly on sugar and partly on dollars, that is, on what dollars will buy—that is, on the price level. . . . We have more need to study the price level preparatory to a study of the price of sugar than to study the price of sugar preparatory to a study of the price level.

> . . . The terms "demand" and "supply," used in reference to particular prices, have no significance whatever in explaining a rise or fall of price *levels*. In considering the influence affecting individual prices we say that an increase in supply lowers prices, but an increase in demand raises them. But in considering the influences affecting price *levels* we enter upon an entirely different set of concepts, and must not confuse the proposition that an increase in the *trade* tends

to lower the price *level,* with the proposition that an increase in supply tends to lower an individual price.

I now turn to the Schumpeter long-wave interpretation of secular price changes. This is not the occasion to review the detailed challenges to the validity of the whole long-wave conception, so I shall limit myself to two comments. Long-run price behavior of individual commodities and services may be adequately explained by an innovation process such as Schumpeter describes, but it is hard to believe that the impact of innovation limited to a few pioneering entrepreneurs can be as decisive a factor for the economy as a whole as Schumpeter's thesis requires in the long-wave upswing. It is also hard to believe that pioneering entrepreneurs would emerge in all Western countries at approximately the same time. This is not to deny that the long-wave conception may have some merit in ascribing increased output in the downswing to the widespread adoption of new techniques, but at best the explanation is incomplete and partial.

More important, this explanation would call for change in the rate of monetary growth of a smaller order of magnitude than of either changes in the rates of price rise and output growth. But the facts are the other way around. Variability in monetary growth is of far larger order of magnitude than variability in rates of price rise and output growth.[6]

Finally, with respect to the hypothesis that secular price changes came about through disparities between the world growth rates of industrial capacity and output of primary products, the only evidence presented in support of the conception is a chart for 1872–1951 of a world (less Russia) pig iron output—to indicate industrial capacity—expressed as a ratio to an index of world output of eight primary products. Although the results are described as "not inconsistent with our account of the origin of the wholesale price level" (Brown and Ozga 1955, p. 13), I do not observe a downward trend that is supposed to characterize the period 1872–94, one of three subperiods the chart is supposed to substantiate (data for the years 1946–51 can hardly be considered a fourth secular subperiod). At a minimum, parallel data on prices and output for industrial and primary products would be required, and some evidence as well on leads and lags to give substance to the hypothesis. Even so, it would still be necessary to show that the assumptions the hypothesis makes relating to monetary behavior are valid.

There are no doubt models other than those I have discussed in the literature on secular price movements of the nineteenth and twentieth centuries, but I hope I have said enough to indicate the variety that exists. It is time now to state the conclusions that I draw from the historical record.

3.5 Conclusions from the Historical Evidence

I draw ten conclusions from the historical record:

1. Episodes of rising prices have alternated with episodes of declining prices, apparently for as long as money has been used as a medium of exchange.[7]

2. Until the eighteenth century, the sources of monetary expansion and contraction were the output of precious metals and debasement or restoration of the coinage. These sources have since been supplemented or supplanted by paper money issues of banknotes or deposit currency. All forms of money issue have been subject to governmental control.

3. Before the era of twentieth-century central banking, governments tended to be passive in relation to long-term changes in world precious metal output and the changing rate of accrual to their national stocks. In earlier centuries, debasements and restorations of coinage seem to have been determined mainly by fiscal needs, although this does not explain why the Greek practice was so different in this respect from that of the Romans, or why England engaged in little debasement in the fourteenth century while France engaged in much, and in a following century why England debased and France did not. On some occasions such measures may have offset the retardation or acceleration of the growth of precious metals, but there are only limited data to confirm this suggestion. Since the eighteenth century, deliberate large-scale increases in paper money issues have usually been associated with war financing, but John Law's experiment is an exception. Deliberate contraction of paper money issues has been associated with postwar return to the gold standard at a prewar parity, or a decision to call a halt to a postwar inflation, as in the United States in 1920.

4. Long-run price changes consistently parallel the monetary changes, with one exception for England in the sixteenth century.

5. With the exception of war and immediate postwar periods; in earlier centuries, plagues; and the economic disaster of 1929–32, output has apparently grown during both periods of secular price rise and fall.

6. Discrepancies between movements of the ratio of the money stock to real output and price movements reflect long-run changes in the public's demand for money balances. U.S. and British data suggest that the long-run movement until World War II trended upward. Such a trend would accentuate price declines and moderate prices rises.

7. In recent centuries, the price episodes occurred at approximately the same dates in numerous countries. The mechanism for the diffusion of an episode was the mutual adjustment of price levels between countries by international trade and the redistribution of the world stock of monetary reserves. This was the case under both the gold standard before 1914, when the quantity of money in each country was a de-

pendent variable, which had to adjust to produce a level of prices relative to prices abroad consistent with balance of payments equilibrium, and in the period after the war, when monetary authorities had more leeway with respect to control of the quantity of money. In both cases, a change in the quantity of money was the mechanism whereby prices in one country were kept in line with prices abroad. Changes in the quantity of money in any one country were produced by changes in that country's prices relative to foreign prices. Changes in the quantity of money then produced changes in the country's absolute price level.

8. Over the centuries it has been alleged that factors other than the ratio of money stock to output have caused secular price movements. These factors have ranged from changing population growth to changes in costs of production to the presence or absence of speculation. If each price episode were a response to a constellation of factors other than money, it would then be necessary to show how that constellation produced either a change in money stock or in velocity associated with an individual price episode. No one has done so.

9. Costs of production are prices that are subject to change by the same monetary influences as are prices of final goods. Prices of factors that did not change in unison with commodity prices would indicate a defect in the market for labor or capital, lack of foresight that would lead to an effective wage below the marginal product of labor, or too low an interest rate to leave borrower-lender relations unaffected when prices are rising and the opposite when prices are falling. The existence of a temporary lag is conceivable in cases where arrangements are contractual or customary, but contracts were renegotiated and custom changed, so presumably prices of factors eventually responded. The rise in wages and interest rates during price upswings and their fall during price downswings were not the causes of the price movements but reflections of the same forces that produced the price movements.

Particularly with respect to secular price movements from the sixteenth to the twentieth centuries, the literature of economics contains many analyses contending that wages lagged behind prices, swelling business profits during inflations and inflicting business losses during periods of declining prices. As Kessel and Alchian (1960) have shown, this is an untested hypothesis. If it were true, it would be difficult to reconcile with the cost-push, cost-pull hypothesis.

Were there autonomous forces raising wages and prices? Increasingly strong unions and increasingly strong monopolies in the process of raising their wages and prices to levels consistent with their newly acquired monopoly power can push their relative wages and prices up, and if there is a lag in the adjustment of other absolute prices, for a time this can produce a rise in the absolute price level without a monetary stimulus—though not without unemployment. The attribution in 1909 of the U.S. price rise after 1897 to the effect of unions and trusts suggests that the pre–World War I economy was viewed by some contemporaries in much the same light as the post–World War II economy is viewed by some contemporaries now. The difficulty posed by this explanation is that, if used to account for the secular price rise, it cannot then account for the sharp reversal in the price movement in 1920. Union membership constituted 3.5 percent of all nonagricultural employees in 1897, 9.9 percent in 1909 (when Laughlin wrote), and peaked at 19.6 percent in 1921, a year *after* the wholesale price index had declined 37 percent and the consumer price index had declined 11 percent (Troy 1965, p. 2). Similarly, monopoly power was evidently growing during the first decade of the century; no data suggest that it subsequently disintegrated. The absurd conclusion the explanation compels is that strong unions and monopolies chose to lower wages and prices drastically in 1920.

10. The role of price expectations as an autonomous factor lowering or raising interest rates, reducing or adding to wage demands in past secular price movements, is difficult to establish. However, some preliminary results of a study of monetary trends that Professor Friedman and I have been engaged in suggest that in the form in which we express our variables, past price change is a good index of expectations about current price behavior. The higher the index, the larger the fraction of current monetary expansion that is absorbed by prices. Similarly, we find that over periods longer than a cycle, a higher rate of monetary change is associated with a higher level of nominal interest rates. This relationship is a reflection of a relationship between price expectations and the level of interest rates.

Having completed this summary of what I believe the historical record teaches us, I want finally to give some indication that the lessons of the past are not irrelevant to the present. Rates of change in money stock (currency plus demand deposits), per unit of output, and rates of change in prices in forty countries over the period 1952–69 are plotted as a scatter diagram in figure 3.1.[8] Each dot plots the rate of change in prices over the 17-year period against the rate of change in the quantity of money per unit of output over the same period. There are 40 dots for 40 countries. The diagonal lines across the chart is the line on which a 12 percent change in prices is associated with a 12 percent change in the quantity of money, a 10 percent change in one with a 10 percent change in the other, and so on. The points are closely scattered along such a diagonal line. At the top of the chart are the countries that have had about a 30 percent increase in the quantity of money per unit of output and they have had about a 30 percent change in prices. At the bottom are the countries that have had a small rate

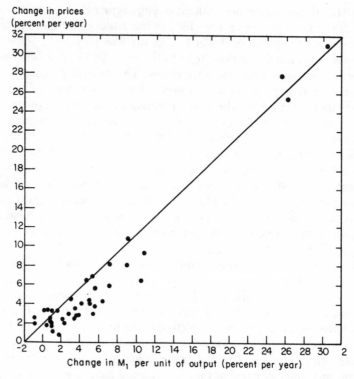

Figure 3.1   Rate of change in prices and in M_1 per unit of output forty countries, 1952–69.

of change in money per unit of output and a small rate of change in prices. In the post–World War II world, there has been an extremely close long-term relationship between the rate of change in prices and in money per unit of output. Adjusted R^2 is .942. The scatter suggests to me that the key to understanding secular price change now as in the past is the behavior of money stock per unit of output. A fitting conclusion to this look backward, I therefore believe, is George Santayana's remark, "Those who cannot remember the past are condemned to repeat it."

Notes

1. If the income elasticity of the demand for money is greater than unity, obviously there will be no perfect one-to-one correspondence between changes

in the ratio of money to output and prices. I regard Paul Trescott's comments on this score as a refinement of, rather than a challenge to, the broad-brush picture I have drawn. The first-order effect I have examined seems to me to have high explanatory power. Trescott's comment introduces a second-order effect. A similar statement applies to his reference to the presence of a lagged influence of money on prices, which I in no way dispute.

2. Judged by modern monetary experience, these growth rates of the gold and silver stock are modest. For example, the U.S. money supply multiplied 157-fold in the period 1867–1960 or at an annual rate of 5.4 percent. Debasement, of course, and later, paper money issues permitted faster growth of national money stocks than of their metallic constituent. The estimates of the English money stock in 1562 (table ? above) and 1697 (see n. 3, below) indicate that during the period it multiplied 15.5-fold or at an annual rate of 2 percent. Prices rose .8 percent per year over the comparable period. After allowance for the rate of price rise, in the absence of the underlying estimates, we cannot say how the annual rate of monetary growth was divided among the rate of population growth, per capita output, and the growth in per capita holdings of money.

3. I find less of a problem with this episode than does Horsefield, the author of the money supply estimates. He distorted the relationship between the money and price figures because of the way he chose to summarize them. His half-yearly estimates of the volume of coin and bank notes in circulation are for end of June and end of December. The price indexes are for the first week of each month. In my comments, I compared the movements from, say, end of June to end of December in the money estimates and from the first week in July to the first week in January prices. Horsefield averaged June and December, December and June of the money estimates, and related the percentage change from the first to the second average to the percentage change in the six-month averages of the price data. As a result, for example, a decline of 36 percent in his original December 1695 to June 1696 money estimates and a rise of 9 percent from June 1696 to December 1696 appear as a decline of 16 percent in the first half of 1696 and a decline of 19 percent in the second half of 1696.

Money Supply Estimates[a]

Year	End of Month	£m. (1)	% Change (2)	Col. 1 as Averaged by Horsefield (3)	% Change Col. 3 (4)	Horsefield's Date for Col. 4 (5)
1695	June	25.3				
				25.9		
	Dec.	26.5	19			
				21.7	−16	Jan.–June, 1696
1696	June	16.9	−36			
				17.7	−19	July–Dec., 1696
	Dec.	18.5	9			
				19.5	10	Jan.–June, 1697
	June	20.5	11			

[a]Horsefield (1960), p. 14.

Index of Nonagricultural Prices[b]

First Week of Month		1695 = 100 (1)	% Change at Annual Rate, Col. 1 (2)	Six Month Averages		% Change (5)
				Period (3)	Level (4)	
1695	July	98.3		July–Dec.	97.1	
1696	Jan.	109.6	23	Jan.–June	103.2	7
	July	102.7	−12	July–Dec.	110.4	7
1697	Jan.	105.0	4	Jan.–June	102.4	−7

[b]Horsefield (1960), pp. 18, 252. Underlying data from *A Collection for Improvement of Husbandry and Trade,* edited by John Hougton, 1692–1702.

The failure of the money supply changes so derived to match the price changes led Horsefield to invoke changes in velocity as a factor that must have been important. Without denying that velocity changes may well have played a role, I believe that Horsefield would have had less difficulty in analyzing the episode had he used his estimates directly. Ashton (1960) observed that the decline in the money supply in Horsefield's estimate for June 1696 is exaggerated because of his failure to take account of sound silver coin that returned to circulation that year when only standard weight coins became acceptable. Letwin (1964) prepared alternative Dec. 31 estimates of the money supply, 1694–98, that he regarded as consistent with the price movements of those years.

I am indebted to Martin Bronfenbrenner for suggesting that comment be included in this paper on the 1696 English recoinage as well as on American colonial monetary experience, which is discussed in the text.

4. Irving Fisher's paper was based on chapter 12 of *The Purchasing Power of Money,* a forthcoming publication at the time of the AEA meeting (Fisher 1911b). He concluded that the increase in M, which was due in turn to an increase in gold production, was the chief cause of the rise in prices, 1896–1909. The increase in V' was next in importance to the increase in M as a cause of the rise in prices. He attributed the rise in V' to the concentration of population in cities. Almost equal in importance to the rise in V' was the increase in the ratio of M' to M, which Fisher attributed to the "opening up of the South" and the change in the banking law favoring small banks (Fisher 1911a, pp. 44–45).

5. Lance Davis' comments constitute a rejection of the approach of this paper. I leave it to the reader to decide whether a common explanation of the episodes in terms of the change in money stock per unit of output or an ad hoc explanation of each episode has greater intellectual appeal.

6. This finding is drawn from a study of monetary trends in the United States and the United Kingdom since 1880 (see Friedman and Schwartz 1963a).

7. The widespread belief in the historical law of rising prices is apparently based on five major inflations in the past seven centuries: (1) the Price Revolution of the sixteenth and early seventeenth centuries; (2) the inflation in the half century before the Napoleonic Wars; inflations during (3) the Napoleonic Wars; (4) World War I; and (5) World War II. Only the first two inflations and the last one permanently shifted the price level upward. If these are excluded from the historical record, a bet on a rise in prices ten years hence starting every year beginning 1275 would be wrong more times than it would be right. It may, of course, be the case that the world has changed since World War II, so that in every year since a bet on a rise in the price level over a ten-year

span would be right, but then the argument would be that rather than an extrapolation from the past, future price experience will differ from the long historical record. For an illuminating discussion of the evidence, see Lipsey (1960a).

8. James Lothian kindly provided me with a printout of annual data for the forty countries through 1966, and I updated the figures to 1969, except for two countries (Brazil and the Dominican Republic) for which the period ends in 1968 and three (Iceland, Peru, and Uruguay) for which the period ends in 1967. The money and price figures come from *International Financial Statistics Supplement*, 1971. Money is defined as currency plus demand deposits held by the public. Prices are cost-of-living indexes on a 1963 base. Income data are from U.N., *Yearbook of National Account Statistics*, 1970, table 179, and U.N., *Monthly Bulletin of Statistics*, Oct. 1971, table 61, except for Sweden, which were derived from Sweden, *The Swedish Economy: Revised National Budget, 1971.2*, p. 590. Income figures are net national income except for Brazil (net national product) and Nicaragua, Sweden, and Uruguay (gross domestic product).

On the printout I obtained from Lothian money was defined as the sum of "Money" and "Quasi-Money" (commercial and mutual savings-bank time deposits, postal savings deposits, and savings and loan shares where they existed)—as shown in *International Financial Statistics*. Adjusted R^2 for the observations based on this definition of money for the period Lothian covered was .877.

4   Understanding 1929–1933

Nearly half a century after August 1929 the debate has resumed about what produced the unusual length and extreme severity of the ensuing 43-month contraction. No new facts about that business contraction have become available that have led to revision of earlier judgments. Rather, new hands have imposed new, or reimposed old, patterns on the known facts. So we must ask whether the new hands do explain the known facts better than did earlier investigators or whether their explanations must be rejected because they do not fit the full set of known facts.

In the '30s, '40s, and '50s, the prevailing explanation of 1929–33 was essentially modeled on Keynesian income-expenditure lines. A collapse in investment as a result of earlier overinvestment, the stock market crash, and the subsequent revision of expectations induced through the multiplier process a steep decline in output and employment. The collapse in investment was consistent with a procyclical movement in interest rates and velocity. The revision of expectations in turn set off a demand for liquidity that could not be met. The attempt to meet it, however, forced widespread liquidation of bank loans with a resultant decline in the value of private claims and debts, leading to the failure of nonfinancial corporations, to bank insolvency, and to runs on banks. Try as the Federal Reserve System might, its easy money policies—

For the Granger causality tests and the preparation of tables 4.1 and 4.2 I am indebted to Thomas J. Sargent. Milton Friedman, who read the first draft of this paper, suggested that I include the Granger test results and the chart of the inverse of the price level. I have also restructured the paper on his advice. My indebtedness to him in a more general sense should be obvious. I have also benefited from comments by Arthur E. Gandolfi and James R. Lothian. R. A. Gordon gave me detailed comments, which I acknowledge, as I also do the views expressed by the discussant, Peter H. Lindert. I am grateful to Linda Dunn for preparing the figures and tables other than 4.1 and 4.2.

110

as evidenced by the decline in short-term interest rates until the summer of 1931—did not stabilize the economy.

In the Keynesian story, the quantity of money as such played no important part in the explanation of 1929–33. The story was faithful to the prevailing belief that the importance of money can be measured by the behavior of interest rates, and since econometric tests that included an interest rate revealed no significant effect of the variable, that seemed to dispose of the need to consider the behavior of money.

Fifteen years ago when Milton Friedman and I reviewed the facts about 1929–33, we did, of course, have at hand a new monthly series on the quantity of money outstanding. Earlier estimates by Currie (1935) and Warburton (1945), however, had measured the extent of the decline in the quantity of money over the contraction, so we did not discover the fact of sharp decline. What we did illuminate was the process by which the decline in the quantity of money was produced. This shed a new light on the course of the contraction. There were distinct stages of the contraction—it was not all of one piece.[1] The stages we noted included: (1) The period prior to the first banking panic—that is, August 1929 to October 1930. This period encompassed the stock market crash in October 1929, to which the Federal Reserve responded by a short-lived increase in the quantity of money. Subsequently, an earlier decline in the quantity of money was resumed, but there was no attempt by banks to liquidate loans or by depositors to shift from deposits to currency. During this interval, the contraction would have been defined as severe relative to earlier ones. (2) The first banking panic, covering the final quarter of 1930, when the real economy markedly worsened. (3) The first quarter of 1931, when signs of revival were nipped upon the onset of a second banking crisis in March 1931. (4) The last half of 1931, when the response of the Federal Reserve to Britain's departure from gold was accompanied by another outbreak of banking panic and a substantial deepening of the real decline that persisted through the first quarter of 1932. (5) The second quarter of 1932, when the Federal Reserve undertook open-market purchases, following which there was a widespread revival in the real economy in the summer and fall. (6) The final six months of the contraction, when problems with the banks spread, the real economy turned downward again, and the contraction ended with a collapse of financial markets.

Thus, after the 1929 peak in business, five negative shocks in turn destabilized the economy: the stock market crash and four episodes of banking panic—in the final quarter of 1930, from March to June 1931; from August to the end of the year (the response to the currency crisis abroad); and a final outbreak of panic in the last quarter of 1932, culminating in the Bank Holiday of March 1933. There was at least one positive shock—the open-market purchases of March–July 1932—and possibly a second, if we count the short-lived open-market purchase following the stock market crash. In our analysis, we distinguished the contraction in general from the banking and liquidity crises that punctuated its course. Our main theme was that the effect of whatever economic forces produced the contraction was magnified by the unprecedented decline in the quantity of money resulting from the banking crises. Our ancillary judgment was that the Federal Reserve System could have prevented the monetary consequences of the banking crises but failed to do so.

Two published studies by Kindleberger (1973) and Temin (1976) have recently challenged the interpretation of 1929–33 in *A Monetary History,* and an unpublished study by Abramovitz incidentally also offers a dissenting opinion.

Kindleberger's focus is on the world economic system in the interwar period. He attributes an important role, in propagating the world depression, to rising stocks and falling prices of world primary products after 1925 and to maladjustments inherited from World War I.[2] He believes that the contraction in the United States was initiated by a decline in housing—that it started as a mild contraction and was transformed into a depression by the stock market crash. In his view, during the initial phase of the depression, money was abundant and cheap, but the spread between interest rates on high-grade and low-grade assets proves that an increase in the quantity of money by itself would not have been helpful, that "one also had to improve credit-worthiness by improving the outlook" (p. 138). He traces the intensification of the depression to repercussions of the initial world contraction on the economies of the countries producing primary products, not to developments in the United States, and emphasizes the halt in international lending to peripheral countries. Given their limited gold and foreign exchange reserves, they were forced to sell their primary products for whatever they would bring. Tariff increases and quota restrictions by the industrial countries exacerbated the problems of the primary-producing countries and reduced world trade. On his reading, falling security prices and commodity prices, for which Kindleberger assigns no special responsibility to the United States, made banking systems everywhere vulnerable and led to the financial crisis of 1931. He argues that the open-market purchases by the Federal Reserve in 1932 did little to relieve the squeeze on the economy outside financial markets and that only two means were available to achieve world recovery: (1) simultaneous programs of government spending in all countries, and (2) simultaneous devaluations to create gold profits that would be available for spending. Conspicuous by its absence is any discussion of monetary expansion and the liberation of monetary policy made possible by floating exchange rates in the 1930s, a regime Kindleberger deplores.

Peter Temin's story about the contraction concentrates on the United States during the period beginning with the stock market crash through the end of 1930. It seems that it was not a disturbance in investment behavior but an unexplained decline in consumption and a decline in exports as a result of world agricultural depression that produced a decline in U.S. income. This set off a decline in the demand for money to which the supply of money passively adjusted. Action by the Federal Reserve to meet the demand for increased currency holdings, as depositors attempted to convert deposits into currency in the several rounds of bank runs that characterized the contraction, or to provide increased reserves to banks would not, in his view, have prevented a decline in the quantity of money. Had there been no endogenous bank failures that served to reduce the quantity of money, the deposit-reserve ratio would have declined in response to the fall in short-term interest rates, and the decline in the quantity of money would simply have occurred through a different route. Temin does not deny that action by the Federal Reserve to restrict monetary growth may have played a role in initiating the economic downturn in 1929. What he disputes is whether the Federal Reserve engaged in such restrictive monetary action subsequently, until the Federal Reserve's sharp rises in discount rates in response to gold outflows in September 1931 when Britain abandoned gold. I defer until a later point the specific points on which he challenges *A Monetary History*.

Abramovitz's perspective is much broader than cyclical developments in 1929–33. In his unpublished study, he attempts to introduce the behavior of money into his analysis of U.S. long swings, which hitherto had concentrated on their real aspects. The usual model of long swings views waves in real income as an interaction between real expenditures on the one hand and growth of stocks of labor and capital on the other, each explained by real variables. In his current work, Abramovitz finds that nominal income growth parallels real income growth and proceeds to partition the swings in nominal income growth into its monetary elements—money-stock growth and velocity change— and, in turn, money-stock growth into its components. He proposes a model in which nominal income growth and its handmaiden, money-stock growth, are governed by the growth rate of the sum of current merchandise exports and net capital imports. U.S. factors affecting immigration, internal migration, railroad profits, the demand for urban buildings, territorial settlement, and other real matters, on this view, were important through their effects on the growth of merchandise exports and net capital imports. He then applies this hypothesis to the long swing centering on 1929–33 and suggests that the great declines in merchandise exports both after World War I and after 1929 limited the scope for Federal Reserve action. He regards the great declines of nominal income as inevitable, short of implausibly drastic accelerations in the creation of Federal Reserve credit or in the high-powered money multiplier sufficiently large to offset the declines in the sum of merchandise exports and capital movements.[3]

Underlying these three reevaluations of old facts is the view that income changes dominated money changes during the interwar period. A test of that view is now possible and is presented in the first section. I consider the appropriate measure of monetary stringency in the second section. The reciprocal of the price level in the interwar period counters what Temin regards as the decisive evidence on the price of money as measured by short-term interest rates.[4] I then comment in section 4.3 on the decline-in-spending explanations, including Temin's version, and in section 4.4 on the explanations stressing international factors, referring not only to Kindleberger and Abramovitz but also to recent work on the Great Depression by Haberler, Meltzer, and Brunner and Meltzer, among others. I conclude in section 4.5 with some summary observations about cyclical experience with particular reference to 1929–33. In an appendix, I take up explicit criticisms of the explanation offered in *A Monetary History.*

4.1 Money and Income: A Test of Causality

The three reevaluations of the interwar years implicitly or explicitly regard the direction of change between income and money as running from income to money. Temin says his purpose is to discriminate between the "spending hypothesis" and the "money hypothesis," with which he identifies *A Monetary History,* as an explanation of 1929–33. As he states the money hypothesis, for Friedman and Schwartz (1963*a*):

> Either changes in the stock of money caused income to change, or vice versa. The resolution was equally simple. The stock of money was determined by a variety of forces independent of the level of income . . . and the direction of causation therefore must be from money to income, not the other way. (P. 14)

Temin cites as the source of this passage our article on "Money and Business Cycles." Let me therefore quote from it:

> The key question at issue is not whether the direction of influence is wholly from money to business or wholly from business to money; it is whether the influence running from money to business is significant, in the sense that it can account for a substantial fraction of the fluctuations in economic activity. If the answer is affirmative, then one can speak of a monetary theory of business cycles or—

more precisely—of the need to assign money an important role in a full theory of business cycles. The reflex influence of business on money, the existence of which is not in doubt in light of the factual evidence summarized above, would then become part of the partly self-generating mechanism whereby monetary disturbances are transmitted. . . . As noted above, Cagan shows that the public's decisions about the proportion in which it divides its money balances between currency and deposits is an important link in the feedback mechanism whereby changes in business affect the stock of money. (1963b, pp. 49–50)

Whatever our view was, it clearly cannot be described as one-way causation. Since we wrote, there have been important advances in the statistical analysis of the interdependence between two series. One test of the existence and direction of causality between two series in the sense of Granger (1969) is reported here.[5] According to Granger, "We say that Y_t is *causing* X_t if we are better able to predict X_t using all available [past] information than if the information apart from [past] Y_t had been used" (p. 428). The statistical test of this formulation, using the method of least squares, is to estimate the linear regression of X_t on lagged X's and lagged Y's as

(1) $$X_t = \sum_{j=1}^{m} \hat{\alpha}_j X_{t-j} + \sum_{j=1}^{n} \hat{\beta}_j Y_{t-j},$$

where the $\hat{\alpha}_j$'s and $\hat{\beta}_j$'s are least-squares estimates. On the null hypothesis that Y does *not* cause X, the parent parameters $j, j = 1, \ldots, n$, equal zero. The null hypothesis, with current income on the left-hand side (X_t) and money on the right-hand side (Y), is that income is not *caused* by money, in which case the Y variable (money) will have zero coefficients. Alternatively, with current money on the left-hand side (X_t), the null hypothesis is that money is not caused by income, in which case the Y variable (income) will have zero coefficients.

For money, the variable I used was monthly M_2. The choice of an income variable for the interwar years is limited. The monthly personal-income series first becomes available beginning 1929. A proxy for income—bank debits to deposit accounts at 140 centers excluding New York City—is available for the period beginning 1919.[6] The equations fitted, including a constant, a residual term, a trend term, and alternatives with and without seasonal dummies, were the following:

(2) $$\text{MO\^NSUP}_t = \sum_{j=1}^{m} \hat{a}_j \ \text{MONSUP}_{t-j} + \sum_{j=1}^{n} \hat{b} \ \text{PERINC}_{t-j},$$

(3) $$\text{MO\^NSUP}_t = \sum_{j=1}^{m} \hat{a}_j \ \text{MONSUP}_{t-j} + \sum_{j=1}^{n} \hat{c} \ \text{BKDED}_{t-j},$$

(4) $\hat{\text{PERINC}}_t = \sum_{j=1}^{m} \hat{a}_j \text{ PERINC}_{t-j} + \sum_{j=1}^{n} \hat{K} \text{ MONSUP}_{t-j},$

(5) $\hat{\text{BKDED}}_t = \sum_{j=1}^{m} \hat{a}_j \text{ BKDED}_{t-j} + \sum_{j=1}^{n} \hat{m} \text{ MONSUP}_{t-j}.$

Table 4.1, covering the shorter period beginning 1929, with personal income as the income variable, and table 4.2, covering the longer period beginning 1919, with bank debits to deposit accounts as the income variable, report the probability of obtaining a value of F greater than that actually obtained if the null hypothesis is valid [Prob $(F > f)$]. If this probability is low, it indicates that the null hypothesis is implausible and can be rejected. Over the shorter period, one cannot reject exo-

Table 4.1   Granger Causality Test Results, 1929–39

Reg. No.	X_t	Y_t	Prob $(F > f)$		F-Statistic	NOBS	Lags (min)
(1)	MONSUP	PERINCN	0.8851	~	$F(24,47)$	108	(24,24)
(2)	PERINC	MONSUP	0.3767		$F(24,47)$	108	(24,24)
(3)	MONSUP	PERINCN	0.8027	~	$F(18,65)$	114	(18,18)
(4)	PERINC	MONSUP	0.3971		$F(18,65)$	114	(18,18)
(5)	*MONSUP	PERINCS	0.6334	~	$F(24,58)$	108	(24,24)
(6)	*PERINCS	MONSUP	0.3488		$F(24,58)$	108	(24,24)
(7)	*MONSUP	PERINCS	0.7685	~	$F(18,76)$	114	(18,18)
(8)	*PERINCS	MONSUP	0.5034		$F(18,76)$	114	(18,18)
(9)	MONSUP2	PERINCN	0.9850	~	$F(24,47)$	108	(24,24)
(10)	PERINCN	MONSUP2	0.2501		$F(24,47)$	108	(24,24)
(11)	MONSUP2	PERINCN	0.7807	~	$F(18,65)$	114	(18,18)
(12)	PERINCN	MONSUP2	0.0771		$F(18,65)$	114	(18,18)
(13)	*MONSUP2	PERINCS	0.6130	~	$F(24,58)$	108	(24,24)
(14)	*PERINCS	MONSUP2	0.6508		$F(24,58)$	108	(24,24)
(15)	*MONSUP2	PERINCS	0.8030	~	$F(18,76)$	114	(18,18)
(16)	*PERINCS	MONSUP2	0.2760		$F(18,76)$	114	(18,18)

Sources: MONSUP = M_2, from Friedman and Schwartz 1970, table 1, col. 9. MONSUP2 = M_2, as above, adjusted for exclusion of deposits in unlicensed banks, March 1933–May 1935, by applying the ratio of licensed and unlicensed bank to licensed bank deposits (Friedman and Schwartz 1963a, table 15, cols. 4, 2). PERINC = Personal income, OBE from Moore 1961, 2: 139.

Note: All regressions include a constant and linear trend, and regressions (5)–(8) and (13)–(16) (shown with asterisk), seasonal dummies also. Regressions are of the form

$$X_t = \sum_{i=1}^{m} \alpha_i X_{t-i} + \sum_{i=1}^{n} \beta_i Y_{t-1} + \text{residual.}$$

Table reports marginal significance level of F-statistic pertinent for testing null hypothesis $\beta_1 = \beta_2 = \ldots = \beta_n = 0$, which is the null hypothesis "Y fails to Granger-cause X." Where f is the calculated value of the pertinent F-statistic, the marginal significance level is defined as prob $[F > f]$ under the null hypothesis.

Table 4.2   **Granger Causality Test Results, 1919–39**

Reg. No.	X_t	Y_t	$(F > f)$		F- Statistic	NOBS	Lags (min)
(1)	MONSUP	BKDED	0.2685	~	$F(36,131)$	216	(36,36)
(2)	BKDED	MONSUP	0.0007		$F(36,131)$	216	(36,36)
(3)	MONSUP	BKDED	0.4401	~	$F(24,167)$	228	(24,24)
(4)	BKDED	MONSUP	0.0008	~	$F(24,167)$	228	(24,24)
(5)	*MONSUP	BKDEDS	0.2410	~	$F(18,185)$	234	(18,18)
(6)	*BKDEDS	MONSUP	0.00003	~	$F(18,185)$	234	(18,18)
(7)	MONSUP2	BKDED	0.7318	~	$F(36,131)$	216	(36,36)
(8)	BKDED	MONSUP2	0.0031	~	$F(36,131)$	216	(36,36)
(9)	MONSUP2	BKDED	0.9634	~	$F(24,167)$	228	(24,24)
(10)	BKDED	MONSUP2	0.0011	~	$F(24,167)$	228	(24,24)
(11)	*MONSUP2	BKDEDS	0.7854	~	$F(18,185)$	234	(18,18)
(12)	*BKDEDS	MONSUP2	0.0002	~	$F(18,185)$	234	(18,18)

Source: BKDED = Bank debits to deposit accounts, except interbank accounts, 140 centers (excluding New York City), from U.S. Board of Governors of the Federal Reserve System 1943, pp. 236–37.

Note: See note to table 4.1. Here, regressions (5)–(6) and (11)–(12) (shown with asterisks) include seasonal dummies.

geneity in either direction, though the probability of exceeding the observed f is, with one exception [(13), (14)], uniformly lower for those equations testing the influence of money on income than for those testing the reverse relation.

For the longer period, the situation is very different: not one of six regressions yields any evidence that income had a significant influence on money—the lowest of the probabilities associated with the observed f is 0.24, which means that in at least one time in four, chance alone would yield as strong an influence of income on money as that observed. In sharp contrast, every one of the six regressions testing the influence of money on income yields a far stronger relation than could be expected by chance if money really had no influence on income. The least-favorable regression yields a probability of 0.003 for the computed f, which means that a relation this strong would occur by chance less than 3 times in 1,000.

So far as these results go, then, for the interwar years as a whole, they clearly support unidirectional causality running from money to income. The reverse hypothesis that Temin, Kindleberger, and Abramovitz appear to embrace receives no support at all. For the shorter period, the results are not inconsistent with the passage I quoted above from "Money and Business Cycles"—mutual interdependence of money and income, with money the senior partner; but neither do they give it much support. Perhaps the only conclusion they support is that eight years[7] is too short a period to give very much evidence on direction of causation, given the large random element in the month-to-month movements of both money and personal income.[8]

4.2   Measuring Monetary Stringency

Temin has revived the Keynesian view that the importance of money can be measured by the behavior of interest rates. In Keynesian analyses, the measure of monetary stringency is a rise in interest rates. The interest rate is regarded as "the price of money." In quantity theory analyses, the price of money is $1/P$, the inverse of the price level. In the former case, stringency is reflected in credit markets. In the latter case, money is an asset, actual and desired holdings of which are adjusted through prices, so that stringency is reflected in a rise in the reciprocal of prices.

Figure 4.1 plots the reciprocal of the U.S. wholesale price index, monthly, 1919–39. It is of some interest that every monetary event of significance during these two decades is mirrored in the movements of the price of money. Moreover, the reaction of prices to each monetary event is either observed in the coincident month or within five months of the event. The monetary events in the three deep contraction phases of the interwar period—1920–21, 1929–33, and 1937–38— are marked by vertical lines on the figure and identified by number above it. Table

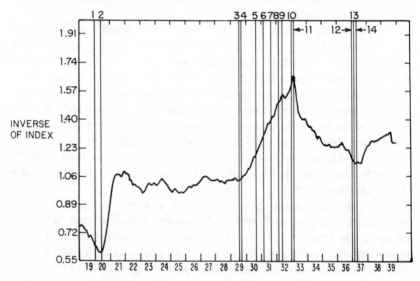

Fig. 4.1   Inverse of U.S. wholesale price index, 1919–29 (1926 = 1.0).
To identify the numbered monetary events on the figure, see table 4.3. *Source:* U.S. Bureau of the Census 1949, p. 344.

4.3 shows the lag in months in the price response to the monetary events listed.[9]

Figure 4.1 refutes the allegation that Temin makes that there is no evidence of monetary stringency in 1930 and 1931 before Britain abandoned gold. I might also have entered dates of monetary events between 1921 and 1929 but refrained from doing so, because during this period the Reserve System attempted to anticipate business movements, so the monetary events and the reaction of the price of money could be regarded as the common result of movements in autonomous spending or whatever third other force produces the cycle. For the three deep contractions of the interwar years, however, the Federal Reserve took policy steps that cannot be regarded as necessary consequences of contemporary changes in business activity. The restrictive actions were followed, with brief lags, by sharp declines in the quantity of money and sharp rises in the inverse of the price level. The one important expansive action—the 1932 open-market purchases—was followed three months later by an end to large monthly declines in the quantity of money, and four months later by the largest decline in the inverse of the price level during the whole 1929–33 period.

Table 4.3   **Monetary Events Reflected in Inverse of U.S. Wholesale Price Index in Three Interwar Deep Cyclical Contractions**

Cyclical Contraction			Date of Monetary Event	Lag (in months) of Initial Response of $1/P$
1920–21	1.	1/20	Rise in discount rate	+5
	2(a).	6/20	Final rise in discount rate	
	(b).	6/20	Peak in M_2	+1
1929–33	3.	8/29	Rise in discount rate	+1
	4.	10/29	Stock market crash	0
	5.	10/30	Onset of first banking crisis	0
	6.	3/31	Onset of second banking crisis	+1
	7.	9/31	Britain leaves gold	0
	8.	3/32	Onset of open-market purchases	+4
	9.	6/32	Last of large monthly declines in M_2	+1
	10.	1/33	Final banking crisis	+1
	11.	3/33	Bank Holiday	0
1937–38	12.	1/37	Announcement of final rise in reserve requirements	+4
	13.	3/37	Peak in M_2	+2
	14.	5/37	Effective date of final rise in reserve requirements	0[a]

[a] +5 for date of onset of rapid rise in 1/P.

As it happens, we had never before made this particular use of the inverse of the price level, yet we had earlier dated the numbered monetary events, so this comparison is fresh and unbiased evidence. Frankly, we were surprised at how uniform the connection was.

4.3 Decline in Spending

I now turn to the detailed profile of the 1929–33 contraction provided by different investigators. Temin himself (1976) has reviewed critically earlier versions of what he terms the "spending hypothesis," the class of explanations that account for the severity of the Great Contraction by the collapse of one or another category of expenditure. Temin finds that the data do not support a fall in autonomous investment—the leading candidate in the Keynesian approach.

Temin reviews[10] the versions of the spending hypothesis associated with the names of Alvin Hansen, R. A. Gordon, Joseph Schumpeter, Thomas Wilson, and Keynes himself and econometric models of the interwar period constructed by Ben Bolch and John Pilgrim, Lawrence Klein, Jan Tinbergen, and John B. Kirkwood. He concludes that all of these versions are unacceptable because they rest on untested assumptions. He also reviews the long-swing or Kuznets cycle hypothesis. He asserts that it assumes that only a large shock—presumably, World War I—could have produced a large cycle in income. He then dismisses it because it cannot explain why the World War I shock did not generate a downturn until a decade later. He leaves open the possibility, but is half-hearted in offering it, that the stock market crash and the fall in construction might have been the channels through which a mild downturn was converted into a severe one.

In part, then, Temin provides a critique of both Kindleberger's and Abramovitz's approaches to 1929–33. His own version of the spending hypothesis, however, turns out to be equally vulnerable. According to him, two unexplained developments in 1930 changed the nature of the downturn. The minor one was a decline of approximately $1 billion in constant prices in American exports as a result of "the deepening world agricultural depression" and "European troubles independent of the United States. Events outside the United States therefore exerted a deflationary impact within this country" (p. 68).

The major unexplained development, according to Temin, was an autonomous fall in consumption in 1930 (see table 4.4). He specifically rejects an explanation of the fall in consumption as reflecting the effect on wealth of the stock market crash, on the ground that the wealth effect was too small. In this sense he regards the fall as autonomous and unexplained.

Temin's conclusion that there was such a fall in consumption is based on regressions of total and nondurable nominal consumption spending

Table 4.4 Changes in Macroeconomic Variables in Three Periods

	1920	1921	Change (in Percent or Percentage Points)	1929	1930	Change (in Percent or Percentage Points)	1937	1938	Change (in Percent or Percentage Points)
GNP, current prices (billion $)	91.5	69.6	− 23.9	103.1	90.4	− 12.3	90.4	84.7	− 6.3
constant (1958) prices	140.0	127.8	− 8.7	203.6	183.5	− 9.9	203.2	192.9	− 5.1
Personal consumption expenditures				139.6	130.4	− 6.6	143.1	140.2	− 2.0
Gross private domestic investment				36.9	28.0	− 24.1	24.5	19.4	− 20.8
Net exports of goods and services				1.5	1.4	− 6.7	− .7	1.9	+ 371.4
Government purchases of goods and services				22.0	24.3	+ 9.5	30.8	33.9	+ 10.1
Implicit price index (1958 = 100)	65.4	54.5	− 16.7	50.6	49.3	− 2.6	44.5	43.9	− 1.3
Unemployment rate	5.2	11.7	+ 6.5	3.2	8.7	+ 5.5	14.3	19.0	+ 4.7
							(9.2)	(12.5)	(+ 3.3)

	1919	1921	Change (in Percent or Percentage Points)	1928	1930	Change (in Percent or Percentage Points)	1936	1938	Change (in Percent or Percentage Points)
GNP, current prices (billion $)	84.0	69.6	− 17.1	97.0	90.4	− 6.8	82.5	84.7	+ 2.7
constant (1958) prices	146.4	127.8	− 12.7	190.9	183.5	− 3.9	193.0	192.9	− 0.1
Implicit price index (1958 = 100)	57.4	54.5	− 5.1	50.8	49.3	− 3.0	42.7	43.9	+ 2.8
Unemployment rate	1.4	11.7	+ 10.3	4.2	8.7	+ 4.5	16.9	19.0	+ 2.1
							(10.1)	(12.5)	(+ 2.4)

Sources: U.S. Bureau of the Census 1975, series F-1, F-3, F-5, F-48, F-53, F-63, F-66, D-86. Figures in parentheses are Darby's (1976) estimates of unemployment rate.

on nominal current disposable income and nominal wealth for the period 1919–41. Actual consumption expenditures were above the level predicted by these regressions for 1921 and 1938 but below the predicted level for 1930. Hence Temin concludes that 1930 was unusual since consumption expenditures declined by more than would have been predicted from the associated decline in income and from the behavior of consumption expenditures in the other interwar major contraction years.[11]

Temin also compares yearly first differences in residuals from his regressions for 1921, 1930, and 1938 on the ground that a movement from a high positive to a low positive residual indicates a deflationary effect on the autonomous component of consumption. The year-to-year changes in residuals based on the regression were $6.1 billion in 1921, – $1.43 billion in 1930, and $1.81 billion in 1938. He then averages the changes in residuals for 1921 and 1938, subtracts the change in residuals in 1930, and concludes:

> On the assumption that the [average] overprediction of decline in consumption shown for 1921 and 1938 is the norm for this function in depression years, the predicted decline in consumption was $5 billion too low in 1930. (P. 72)

This is his current price estimate of the autonomous fall in consumption between 1929 and 1930, two-thirds of the total fall. In constant prices, the estimate is $3 billion of the actual fall in real consumption expenditures of $4.3 billion. Thus, according to Temin, before the onset of the October 1930 runs on banks, the economy was set on a course of deep contraction by the combined autonomous fall of $1 billion in exports and $3 billion in consumption expenditures.

Questions immediately arise with regard to these estimates. With respect to exports, the obvious question is whether the decline in U.S. exports was attributable to events abroad independent of the U.S. cyclical contraction. I shall deal with this question when I turn to explanations stressing international factors.

Temin's estimate of the autonomous decline in consumption expenditures raises questions of an entirely different order. In the first place, the consumption functions he fits are so crude by standards of the present state of the art that it is hard to take them seriously. Second, his assertion that the positive residuals he observes for 1921 and 1938 from this questionable regression are the norm for interwar contractions is strictly an obiter dictum. He gives no basis for regarding 1921 and 1938 as in some unspecified sense "normal" contraction years. But unless this is granted, he has no basis for regarding his small negative residual for 1930 as abnormal.

Thomas Mayer (1978a) in a recent paper has reestimated Temin's equations for the interwar years and has found larger negative residuals in other years of the period. Why did the negative residual in 1930 cause a deep contraction but the larger negative residual in 1925, for example, not cause one? This is ad hoc economics without qualification.

Gandolfi and Lothian (1977), in a review of Temin's book, fit a more sophisticated consumption function for the longer period 1899–1941. They regressed the log of real per capita total consumption on the log of real per capita permanent income and the log of transitory income, defined as the difference between the logs of measured and permanent income. The inclusion of the transitory income variable is designed to reduce the effect of purchase of durable goods, as opposed to their flow of services, as a component of total consumption expenditures. Since purchases of durable goods are more cyclical than their service flows, they are more dependent on transitory than on permanent income. For the sake of comparison with Temin's results, Gandolfi and Lothian also examined year-to-year changes in residuals as well as their levels. They found 1930 far from unique. Of the five severe contractions other than 1930 (1894, 1896, 1908, 1921, and 1938), only 1921 had a very large positive residual. Overprediction of the fall in consumption expenditures, then, is hardly a normal feature of deep contractions. The negative value for 1930 is not abnormal by comparison with all years, not simply deep contraction years. Of 41 changes in residuals, 14 are positive, 27 negative, of which 15 are larger than 1930. Of all 41 changes, 25 are larger in absolute value, 15 smaller. Why is it that these 15 did not produce a violent reaction in economic activity, while the 1930 shift did?

Temin combines his hypothesis that there was an autonomous decline in (nominal and real) spending relative to output with the hypothesis that the demand for (nominal) money was falling more rapidly than the quantity of money during 1930 and the first three quarters of 1931. The decline in the quantity of money itself he regards as a movement along a stable supply-of-money function in response to a downward shift in the demand function. For logical rigor, this statement needs to be supplemented by a more precise specification of the arguments of the demand and supply functions—changes in which would equate quantity demanded with quantity supplied.

For the demand for nominal money, Temin would presumably include as arguments the price level (or, the inverse of the price level), real income, and interest rates. Assume, now, with Temin that for fixed values of the arguments, the nominal quantity of money demanded fell relative to the quantity supplied. To eliminate the putative excess supply of money (that is, make money holders willing to hold it), prices would have to rise—but they fell, which exacerbated the excess supply; real income likewise would have to rise, but it fell, again exacerbating the excess supply. The one remaining possibility is that interest rates would have had to fall, which they did. As a formal matter of monetary theory, then, Temin treats the whole process as an autonomous *decline* in liquidity preference reinforced by declines in prices and in real income produced by other (spending) equations in the system, and wholly countered by lower interest rates—in other words, a large-scale shift of flow demand from goods to securities, and of stock demand from money to securities. But then, why no stock market boom? As Allan Meltzer (1976) points out, perhaps the temporary rally in the market in the spring of 1930 is consistent with Temin's construction; so also, of course, is the decline in interest rates in 1930, but hardly anything else is. Indeed, put this way, the notion of a sharp *decline* in liquidity preference is hard to square with a severe contraction accompanied by increasing industrial bankruptcies and unprecedented failures of banks.

With respect to the supply function, under the gold standard in effect in 1930 and 1931, both declining prices and declining real income would be expected to produce a gold inflow (which they did) and thereby increase the nominal quantity of money. Here too, therefore, Temin must treat the decline in interest rates as a sufficiently powerful force reducing the nominal quantity of money to have overcome the opposite influences of the other two variables. And apparently he does, since he argues that in the absence of bank failures the same decline in the quantity of money would have occurred through a decline in deposit-reserve ratios.

Temin presents no independent evidence of such great sensitivity of either demand for or supply of money to interest rates as would be required for his explanation. The general conclusion of most studies is that quantity of money supplied is largely insensitive to the interest rate (see Cagan 1965; Fand 1967; Rasche 1972) and that the quantity of money demanded is only moderately sensitive to the interest rate, displaying an elasticity a good deal less than unity with respect to long-term rates.

The various versions of the spending hypothesis—one of which attributes the Great Contraction to an autonomous decline in investment, another to an autonomous decline in housing, a third to an autonomous decline in consumption and exports—cast doubt on the value for cyclical analysis of the Keynesian distinction among investment, consumption, and net exports. The authors of the various versions write as if the cycle is necessarily propagated by the component of GNP that first reaches a peak or that is most volatile. Is this more than the most vulgar post hoc–propter hoc reasoning? If not, where is the evidence? The particular category of expenditure that first reaches a peak may not be the trigger of the downturn but the first to respond to a common influence on all expenditures, and similarly the variability of housing or investment or of exports is not an indicator of causal dominance, as Temin, for example, assumes in analyzing the German national product in constant prices, 1924–29 (p. 156).

One other general comment needs to be made about Keynesian models. It is difficult to understand how the experience of 1929–33 could have spawned the notion of the need for the replacement of the classical assumption of a price-adjustment by a quantity-adjustment system of movement toward equilibrium. One key aspect of the contraction was that the decline in nominal income was divided almost equally between a fall in quantities and in prices. Real income fell by more then one-third, implicit prices by more than one-quarter. Why quantities changed as they did in response to price changes should be the goal of analysis. A model in real terms to explain a contraction in which price declines were so prominent is bound to serve imperfectly the cause of historical understanding.[12]

Finally, no decline-in-spending model has ever been able to explain the detailed development of the contraction.

4.4 International Explanations

The main problem with Kindleberger's account of the world in depression is his assumption that, because the contraction was worldwide in scope once it got under way, it therefore did not originate in the United States. The U.S. share in world trade, world capital and financial markets, and the world's stock of gold has been sufficiently large since World War I to give the United States the capacity to initiate worldwide movements and not merely to react to them. Of course, once having initiated a worldwide disturbance, it would in turn be subject to reflex influences.

From 1923 on, the Federal Reserve sterilized much of the gold inflow into the United States, preventing the kind of expansionary effect on the stock of money and thence on prices that would have occurred under the prewar gold standard. Instead, the system sought, and to a large measure achieved, stable economic growth with falling wholesale prices. This achievement was largely at the expense of economic stability in Great Britain and the peripheral countries tied to sterling. Britain's return to gold in 1925 at a parity that overvalued sterling would have caused less difficulty for Britain if prices in the United States had risen instead of falling thereafter.

Similarly, any problems of agricultural depression in the peripheral countries before 1929 were not independent of U.S. policy. For the contraction itself, the record is equally clear. The stock market boom, which is said to have drained funds from the rest of the world, and the stock market crash occurred in the United States. The downward movement in the U.S. money stock, including the sequence of bank failures, was not the consequence of influences from abroad. The gold inflow into the United States (during the first two years of the contraction) to which reference will be made below is further evidence that other countries were being forced to adapt to the U.S. monetary policies rather than the reverse. The decline in U.S. lending abroad and the protectionist Smoot-Hawley Tariff Act were clearly U.S. actions that destabilized the world financial system.[13]

The United States was no pitiful, helpless giant on whom the rest of the world inflicted the Great Contraction. It is true that when the pound and other currencies were cut loose from gold in 1931, the U.S. trade balance was adversely affected and speculative pressure on the dollar developed. These devaluations, however, were themselves the reflex consequences of the U.S. contraction, and even so, their subsequent effects were not crippling, given the size of the U.S. economy.

This point is also relevant to both Temin's assumption that the decline in U.S. exports was independent of U.S. actions and to Abramovitz's analysis. Temin never alludes to the monetary standard of fixed exchange rates that enforced a worldwide decline in income and prices after 1929.[14] The central role of the United States in the worldwide scope of the contraction is attested to by the balance of payments.[15] If the decline in income in the rest of the world was being transmitted to the United States, we should have observed a balance-of-payments deficit in the United States, leading to a gold outflow. However, the U.S. gold stock rose by nearly $200 million from the annual average of 1929 to that of 1930. From August 1929 to August 1931, the gold stock rose by over $600 million. The gold inflow strongly suggests that any decline in U.S. exports to the rest of the world was attributable to the effects on the rest of the world of contraction here.

Likewise, Abramovitz, by assuming that there were forces making for a major decline in the dollar value of U.S. exports independently of U.S. monetary actions, is able to conclude that there was a significant constraint on the power of the Federal Reserve to sustain the growth of the money stock. In fact, however, there were no such forces. The gold inflows contradict the assumption that the initiating force was a serious decline in the dollar value of our export market independent of what was happening in the United States. The other exogenous factor for Abramovitz's analysis—net capital imports—is also an item that was crucially determined by events within the United States. In the 1930s the decline in U.S. capital exports may have been exogenous in the sense that the state of the capital market abroad and the prospective yields on investment in various foreign countries discouraged capital exports. But equally the volume of saving available for capital export relative to the volume of investment demand at home were important endogenous elements. Internal developments in the United States enormously affected U.S. capital exports.

Is the monetary approach to the balance of payments helpful in understanding 1929–33? The theory asserts that the active element in the balance-of-payments adjustment process is the equalization of the quantity of money demanded with the quantity of money supplied. Flows of specie are interpreted as responses to changes in demand for or domestic supply of money in various countries. A reduction in the public's demand for goods and securities leads to reduced imports and expanded exports on the goods side and to higher interest rates and capital imports on the securities side. The current account or the capital account or both move into surplus. Although the law of one price has frequently been associated with the monetary approach, some adherents allow for significant slippage between the rate of change of domestic prices and of world prices. Similarly, some adherents also accommodate interest rate differentials between domestic and foreign assets in their versions of the monetary approach.

Are the gold flows and price movements, 1929–33, consistent with the monetary approach to the balance of payments? As already noted, from August 1929 to August 1931, there was a gold inflow of $600 million. An increase in the demand for money in the United States relative to other countries, or a decrease in the supply of money in the United States relative to other countries, or any combination would be required by the monetary approach to account for the inflow. Such a change in the relative demand or supply of money would be manifested in a decline in U.S. wholesale prices relative to those in the rest of the world—either along with the inflow or as an intermediate step in producing the inflow. If changes in wholesale prices shown in table 4.5 for various countries are reliable, the 1929–31 decline in U.S. prices was steeper than in France and Germany, but not in the other countries. From the time Britain cut the pound loose from gold in September 1931 until July 1932, the United States had a gold outflow of $1 billion, absorbed principally by France, Belgium, Switzerland, and the Netherlands. The outflow would be interpreted as a relative increase in the demand for or decrease in the supply of money in those countries. The data on wholesale prices in the United States and France confirm an only slightly steeper rate of price decline in France than in the United States during this interval. The return flow of gold to the United States until the climactic weeks before the Bank Holiday in March 1933 restored the U.S. gold stock so that it was only $80 million lower than at the cyclical peak in business in 1929. Again, a relative increase in the demand for money in the United States and a steeper rate of price decline in the United States than abroad would be consistent with the inflow. This seems to be the case from September 1932 to February 1933.

It does not seem to me that the discussion of the international setting of 1929–33 as set forth in *A Monetary History* requires modification.

Table 4.5   **Percentage Changes in Wholesale Prices at Annual Rates for Various Countries, 1929–33**

From	To		U.S.	France	Japan	Canada	U.K.	Germany	Italy
						Annual Rates of Change			
Aug. 1929	Mar. 1933		–13.1	–11.9	– 5.8	–11.8	– 9.2	–11.6	–12.3
Aug. 1929	Sept. 1930		–12.2	– 6.7	–22.3	–16.0	–14.9	–10.8	–14.1
Sept. 1930	Sept. 1931		–17.0	–16.2	–13.6	–16.9	–15.2	–12.3	–16.2
Sept. 1931	June 1932		–13.0	–14.3	– 3.0	– 6.5	– 1.5	–16.2	– 9.5
June 1932	Sept. 1932		+ 6.5	–11.5	+53.7	– 3.1	+16.0	– 4.6	+ 4.0
Sept. 1932	Feb. 1933		–17.6	– 5.3	+16.8	– 8.5	– 7.6	–10.0	–11.5

Sources: U.S.: U.S. Bureau of the Census, 1949, p. 344. France: Librarie de Recueil Sirey 1937, table 11. Japan, Canada, U.K., Germany, Italy: League of Nations 1929–33, table 10. The U.K. index was constructed by the Board of Trade; the Italian index is labeled "Bachi."

Countries within the British orbit along with Britain were depressed during the '20s while the rest of the world prospered, partly thanks to U.S. capital exports. When the U.S. capital flow declined in 1928 and virtually ceased in the succeeding years, the economic position of the formerly recipient countries deteriorated. The gold exchange standard made the international financial system vulnerable. Given the attachment to fixed exchange rates, there was no way for other countries to insulate themselves from the effects of U.S. contraction. Deflation in the United States forced an adjustment on the rest of the world reflected partly in the gold inflows to the United States, partly in internal deflation necessary to avoid or reduce further gold flows. We exported deflation and depression to the rest of the world. Even though deflation abroad then reacted unfavorably on the United States, much leeway still remained for U.S. policy.

4.5   Understanding 1929–33

For Temin, 1929–33 was characterized by the absence of two equilibrating factors: a decline in real wages and a strong real-balance effect. Real wages in manufacturing, as the quotient of nominal wages divided by wholesale prices, were higher on both hourly and weekly bases in 1930, 1931, and 1932, and also on an hourly basis in 1933. Real wages in manufacturing, as the quotient of nominal wages divided by consumer prices, were higher on an hourly basis in every year except 1932 but lower in every year on a weekly basis. From the hourly wholesale price deflated series, Temin concludes that the marginal physical productivity of labor rose as employment fell, which is consistent with the classical theory of factor substitution: lowering the wage rate further might have avoided unemployment. The weekly consumer price deflated series shows, however, that this was a vain hope, since lower wages decreased the level of demand. He adds that if the real hourly wage series deflated by consumer prices is more accurate than the wholesale price deflated series, then no part of the classical theory is accurate.

I do not believe, however, that we can gain an understanding of 1929–33 by assigning a central role to real wages. Further, by dismissing the evidence of the hourly wholesale price deflated series, Temin fails to see a link between it and the aborted recoveries that Mitchell and Burns (1936) noted in 1930, 1931, and 1932.

The second equilibrating factor that Temin alleges was absent in 1929–33 was a strong real-balance effect. He defines that effect, however, as relating to the stock of money or the stock of money plus other financial assets. Yet the proper measure of the real-balance effect is the effect of the change in the net indebtedness of the government sector—that is, the sum of noninterest- and interest-bearing government liabilities. The nominal value of currency plus government debt increased 27 percent from 1929 to 1933; the real value increased 62 percent. This may be described as a strong increase in real balances, whatever the strength of the effect on spending for consumption.

In Temin's account, an unexplained change in spending set the economy on its downward slide. No monetary change could stop the downward slide. An increase in the supply of money would not help, since the public had an excess supply of money. Things could get worse, as they did, when in September 1931 the Federal Reserve for the first time since 1929 in his view exerted a deflationary effect on the economy. Temin's analytical structure is a throwback to the Keynesian position of the quarter century after 1933. It has no theoretical explanation of the price level. It makes no distinction between nominal and real magnitudes. It presumes that no evidence exists on the relation of monetary change to income change. It ignores recent theoretical developments.

The period 1929–33 began as a cyclical contraction much like others, this time in response to the immoderate concern of the Federal Reserve Board about speculation in the stock market. Application of the theory of stock values as affected by expectations of the growth of earnings now suggests, as Irving Fisher believed, that marked overvaluation of stocks was not general (Sirkin 1975). Had high employment and economic growth continued, prices in the stock market could have been maintained. In the event, restriction of the growth of money from 1928 on produced a peak in business and some months later the stock market crash. A temporary increase in the money stock in October 1929 eased the effect of the shock of the crash. This may account for the increase in output recorded in early 1930 as a lagged effect of monetary growth.

The economy was thus subjected to two sharp shocks: the initial restrictive money growth and then the collapse of stock prices. Still, what followed suggests an adjustment that moved the economy toward equilibrium, but not for long. It is not hard to explain why an unanticipated decline in aggregate demand will lead employers to hire fewer workers at each real wage rate as perceived by them and will lead workers to refuse offers of work at lower nominal wages on the basis of unchanged anticipations. Along rational-expectations lines, however, employers and workers will in time revise their anticipations in accordance with the change in opportunities. If the Federal Reserve had maintained the initial moderate rate of decline in the money stock, presumably the economy after a time would have adjusted to this condition. But this is not what happened. The screw was tightened again and again, until 1932, and unanticipated change in each case required a new period of adjustment. To add to the problem, leading government officials and industrialists exhorted employers to maintain wage rates and share employment, which must have contributed to shorter average work weeks and higher layoffs.

Still, one must acknowledge the resilience of the economy after the first shocks in 1929 and the first banking crisis at the end of 1930. In early 1931, some industries with relatively smaller price declines revived. Again, the adjustment was aborted by a second round of banking failures, subsequently compounded by the Federal Reserve's reaction to gold losses, in the autumn of 1931. The favorable shock in April 1932, when the Federal Reserve System finally began an open-market purchase program in response to congressional pressure, produced a positive reaction in the economy. Prices began to move upward and output increased. The adjustment was short-lived. The purchase program ended in early August, and the political campaign spawned rumors about the condition of banks the Reconstruction Finance Corporation (RFC) had aided. The consequence was a series of runs that ended with the shutdown of all banks as the new administration took office. The economy was at its lowest ebb. Yet vigorous growth was not precluded during the expansion phase that followed.

A far more satisfactory explanation of 1929–33 than Temin's is, therefore, that a series of negative shocks, monetary in origin, reduced real output and the demand for labor and shifted the demand for securities to short-term instruments and high-grade, long-term securities. Destroy a banking system, and the real economy will grind to a halt. There are no unexplained changes in spending that serve as deus ex machina. The presence of equilibrating forces is attested to by the interludes during the course of the contraction when real output increased. The behavior of the economy was determined by public policies. Different policies would have resulted in different behavior.

Appendix
Dissents from the Views in a Monetary History

Temin rejects the account in *A Monetary History* of the way an initial mild decline in the money stock from 1929 to 1930, accompanying a decline in Federal Reserve credit outstanding, was converted into a sharp decline by a wave of bank failures beginning in late 1930. I shall discuss in turn five items in Temin's catalog of dissent: (1) the money-stock identity, (2) the behavior of high-powered money, (3) the behavior of interest rates, (4) the price of deflation and the behavior of real money balances, (5) the role of bank failures; and I will comment finally

(6) on his and others' approaches to monetary policy during the contraction.

4.A.1 The Money-Stock Identity

In *A Monetary History*, we used an identity that relates money broadly defined to three proximate determinants: high-powered money, the deposit-reserve ratio, and the deposit-currency ratio. The three proximate determinants reflect, respectively, the behavior of the monetary authorities (in the United States, the Treasury and the Federal Reserve System), the commercial banks, and the public. The monetary authorities provide high-powered money—the sum of reserves and currency—that the banks and public divide between themselves in light of the factors influencing the two sets of ratios. The deposit-reserve ratio is affected by legal reserve requirements, banks' expectations of currency movements into and out of their vaults, and interest rates. The deposit-currency ratio is affected by interest rates, income, and the public's preference for holding coin and currency. The ratios clearly reflect demand factors that interact with the supply of high-powered money. The argument of *A Monetary History*, as already noted, is that the Federal Reserve System through its control of the issue of high-powered money can offset any undesired change by the other actors in some short run, and hence the system plays a dominant role in the control of the quantity of money.

Temin believes he has isolated a fatal error in *A Monetary History*, because the identity suggests to him that the stock of money is determined by supply factors alone, instead of being joined with a demand equation to determine equilibrium supply in the market for money. Temin writes:

> Consider the stock of bonds. The size of the stock is the product of past decisions about corporate and government finance. It is fixed at any moment of time by these previous supply decisions. If the demand for bonds shifts, it will not change the number of bonds in existence immediately; it will change their price. In the short run, therefore, the quantity of bonds is determined by the supply, and the price is determined by the demand. In the longer run, the price will be a function of both the supply and demand working through a recursive relationship. Friedman and Schwartz employed the short-run part of this argument; they appear to have rejected the long-run part. (P. 18)

According to Temin, we treat changes in the demand for money as affecting only the price of money, meaning the interest rate, and not quantity, the equilibrium stock of money. This is standard Keynesian doctrine, in which the price of money is defined as the interest rate rather than the reciprocal of the price level.

The problem with Temin's analysis, as with much Keynesian analysis, is the assumption that the price level is predetermined and the resulting failure to treat the price level as a variable that helps to equate nominal demand for money with the nominal supply of money or, alternatively, to enable any level of real balances demanded to be attained for any level of nominal balances. Temin's failure to recognize the importance of the distinction between nominal and real magnitudes leads him to stress instead the distinction between long run and short run, but this distinction is not highly relevant to the determination of the stock of money. Undoubtedly, different forces exert different influences on the behavioral patterns underlying the proximate determinants in the short and long run. But in both runs, it is the behavioral patterns underlying the proximate determinants that determine the size of the nominal quantity of money outstanding. The demand forces emanating from the public that affect the nominal quantity of money are those that have to do with the forms among which they choose to distribute their nominal (or real) assets—the fraction they choose to hold in real assets, securities of various kinds, bank deposits of various kinds, and high-powered money. These demand forces interact with the supply conditions of high-powered money, and of various forms of deposits or securities, to determine the nominal quantity of money. The demand for real money balances interacts with the nominal quantity of money to determine the price level. Of course, this is an oversimplified statement. A more sophisticated statement would assert that all of these variables are determined simultaneously and that some of the variables that enter into the demand for real money balances may also enter into the functions that determine the distribution of the total balance sheet among various forms of assets. But the important point is fully brought out by the simplified picture: to leave price expectations out of the picture in the short run from 1929 on is to leave out a major part of the picture—both for monetary analysis and for income analysis. As the public adjusts discrepancies between its actual real money balances and desired real money balances, nominal income is altered and the breakdown into prices and output is determined.

Temin alleges that the supply of money in our specification is "determined by forces independent of income and interest rates" (p. 19). Yet we specifically note that the deposit ratios are functions of the interest rate, among other variables (contrary to Temin's discussion, which suggests that we do not include it) and that the deposit-currency ratio is a function also of income. He is right that we regard banking panics as "far and away the most important single determinant" (p. 20) of the ratios, not only in the early 1930s, but also during other panic episodes. How do we know this? By studying the pattern of behavior in these ratios during panic episodes. The early 1930s do not stand alone. We have evidence on the behavior of the ratios in all the post–Civil War panics in the United States. They tell a uniform story of a shift from deposits to currency by the public once the economy is engulfed in panic and of a belated attempt by banks to increase reserves relative to their deposits once the panic subsided.

We have evidence also from Canadian experience in 1929–33. The percentage fall in Canadian nominal income over these years was about the same as in U.S. nominal income, yet the percentage fall in the Canadian stock of money was considerably smaller. The reason is that Canada was spared the ordeal of bank failures. There was no shift from deposits to currency in Canada comparable to that in the United States, and so there was no effect from this proximate determinant in producing a decline in the stock of money. There was no decline in the "quality" of deposits comparable to that in the United States because of a loss of confidence in banks, and hence there was less of a decline in the demand for real money balances in Canada. That is why a smaller decline in the quantity of money was consistent with almost the same decline in income and prices. The sharp decline in Canadian income and prices occurred because Canada kept its exchange rate with the United States fixed until September 1931 and then maintained its exchange rate at a new level involving a smaller depreciation than that undergone by the pound sterling. For Canada, it is entirely appropriate to regard the quantity of money as adapting in large measure to movement in income and prices, rather than as an exogenous force. It was the tail. The United States was the dog.

4.A.2 The Behavior of High-Powered Money

The decline in the quantity of money from August 1929 to October 1930, before the first banking panic, did not result from any weakness of the private economy. The decline was entirely the result of a decline in Federal Reserve credit outstanding. There were no problems with the banking structure, no attempted liquidation of loans by banks, no attempt by depositors to shift from deposits to currency that contributed to reducing the quantity of money. In fact, the banks were reducing reserves relative to deposits, and the public was increasing its deposits relative to currency—enough to offset half the decline in Federal Reserve credit.

Temin counters that a decrease in bank discounts at the Fed, in response to the decline in market interest rates, and not any failure of the Fed, was responsible for the decline in Federal Reserve credit outstanding. Bank borrowings declined from a peak of $1,096 million in July 1929 to $189 million by September 1930. Total bank reserves fell about $40 million. Temin does not allude to the punitive attitude of the system toward member bank borrowing, hence bypasses the reason there was little incentive for them to increase rediscounting, absent any panic, when the Reserve Banks lowered discount rates— "dramatically," according to him (p. 21)—and he takes the absolute amount of discounting to be "low."[16]

In fact, the discount rate was not reduced uniformly at all Reserve Banks. By mid-1930, New York had reduced its rate in six steps from 6 to 2.5 percent, while at other Reserve Banks the rate had gone from 5 to 4 and 3.5 percent. By the end of 1930, the New York rate stood at 2 percent, the rates at two other banks at 3 percent, and at the remaining nine at 3.5 percent. The discount rate fell less than the commercial paper rate even in New York; a lot less, in other districts. The spread between the commercial paper rate and the discount rate at New York was a shade lower in 1930 than in 1929; at other Reserve Banks, much lower. Of course, under the lash of runs by the public, the banks did increase their borrowings—from $189 million in September 1930 to $338 million in December. But this increase in Reserve Bank credit outstanding was smaller than the increase in the public's currency holdings.

Temin's general Keynesian tendency to treat interest rates as the crucial monetary variable leads him astray in evaluating both the role of the Fed and our views about its responsibility. For example, he writes that the Federal Reserve "could have offset changes in interest rates by changing the discount rate, and it could have avoided the banking panics by changing its procedures" (p. 20). That is not our view. We put major emphasis, not on discount rate changes or on "procedures," but on Federal Reserve control of high-powered money, or bank reserves, through open-market operations.

From our view, the crucial question is whether the Federal Reserve was powerless to engage in open-market purchases to restore the level of its credit outstanding, given that, until the first banking panic, the banks, for whatever reason, were not willing to come to the discount window. Temin's discussion of the system's behavior is ambiguous, to say the least:

> No one disputes that the Fed has the power to undertake open-market operations. And most people agree that these actions have effects on the economy. But very few of the monetary changes in the early 1930's were the results of conscious decisions to undertake open-market operations. Friedman and Schwartz argued that the decline in the stock of money in 1930 was the result of a fall in discounts at the Fed in response to a fall in market rates not fully duplicated by the discount rate, and that the fall in 1931 was due to a decline in

the two deposit ratios produced by the banking crises. These events are not the same as open-market purchases. (P. 25)

These events clearly are the opposite of open-market purchases, which would have increased Reserve credit outstanding and high-powered money. They are precisely the kind of events that conventional central-bank wisdom would regard as requiring open-market purchases in order to offset their effects. Temin objects that we imply that "all changes in the stock of money were the results of actions by the Federal Reserve" (p. 25). They are the results of actions or inactions by the Federal Reserve. In 1930 before the panic condition developed at the end of the year, the Federal Reserve could have readily reversed the decline in Federal Reserve credit outstanding. Temin evades the central issue of why they did not do so.

Temin makes much of the fact that high-powered money on an annual average continued to increase except in 1930. Hence, he argues, there was no restraint on the supply of money. High-powered money grew after the first banking crisis, not because member bank reserves were expanding, but because the public's currency holdings began to climb in the usual shift of its preferences toward currency as an aftermath of the banking crisis. By August 1931, the public's currency holdings had increased by $583 million over its holdings in October 1930, but high-powered money was only $558 million higher. High-powered money growth, barely adequate to meet the public's growing distrust of bank deposits, had contractionary effects on the reserve position of the banking system—hardly impressive evidence of monetary ease.

4.A.3 The Behavior of Interest Rates

According to Temin, the money hypothesis fails its most important test because there is no evidence in interest rates of monetary stringency at the end of 1930 as the result of bank failures. Temin has not examined the data for earlier panics, but it is true that short-term rates in those episodes did rise during the weeks of panic, and we do not observe a comparable rise during the weeks of the first banking crisis in the last quarter of 1930 or of the second banking crisis from March to June 1931.[17] The failure of short-term rates to rise, however, is not necessarily inconsistent with the presence of monetary stringency—both because monetary stringency might be reflected in prices rather than in interest rates and because other factors were simultaneously impinging on short-term rates. In particular, the failure of short-term rates to rise may have reflected, first, declines in the 1920s in the supply of short-term instruments issued by both private borrowers and the government and, second, the special role of the commercial banks as demanders of these short-term instruments. There are two markets to consider, the commercial paper market and the market for short-term government securities.

The commercial paper market today is a different market from the one that existed in the 1920s through the Great Contraction.[18] In today's market, the finance companies are the dominant borrowers. In the 1920s, corporate enterprises in textiles, foodstuffs, metals, and leather were the main borrowers. There was a dramatic decline in the market from 1924 to 1933, interrupted by a brief expansion from the stock market crash to April 1930. Outstandings fell from a peak of $925 million in October 1924 to a low of $265 million in September 1929, largely because firms that had formerly borrowed in the commercial paper market found it more advantageous to float stocks and bonds. The stock market crash and the reduction in commercial paper rates relative to bank lending rates led to a rise in outstandings in April 1930 to $553 million. Thereafter, the volume declined to $358 million in December 1930 and $275 million in August 1931.

Currently, nonfinancial corporations are the main holders of commercial paper. In the 1920s through the Great Contraction, the banks were virtually the sole buyers of commercial paper, with country banks the mainstay of the market. From the member bank call date of December 31, 1930, through the September 29, 1931, call date, member bank holdings of commercial paper ranged from 102 to 141 percent of the reported total amount outstanding, the excess over the reported amount outstanding rising steadily over the interval covered. The explanation for the excess is that the banks purchased paper from dealers other than those reporting to the Federal Reserve Bank of New York and is one indication of the strength of member bank demand for commercial paper.

The chief advantage of commercial paper to member banks apart from its yield was its eligibility for rediscount at the Reserve Banks. This advantage gained in importance during a panic, so that, from the demand side, a panic, rather than putting pressure on commercial paper rates, to some extent relieved the pressure. Instead of selling commercial paper, banks increased borrowings using commercial paper as collateral to meet depositors' demand for currency. As we have seen, bills discounted rose in the last quarter of 1930 and again in June 1931, the culmination of the second banking panic. With limited supply and persistent demand, the failure of commercial paper rates to rise during the panic in no way contradicts the money hypothesis.

With respect to the government securities market, the reduction of the public debt, dating from 1919, continued through December 1930. This constituted an increase in the supply of loanable funds, thereby reducing the interest rate that would clear the market at any given price level. The increase in the public debt was small through August 1931, so the influence on the supply of loanable funds and hence on the upward pressure on interest rates from this source must likewise have been small (see table 4.A.1).

As is true for later years also, we lack adequate data on the maturity distribution of the debt, 1929–31. Treasury bills—first issued in December 1929—and certificates of indebtedness had a maturity of less than one year when issued; Treasury notes, of three to five years; and bonds, of more than five years. When purchased or held, however, the remaining maturity might be quite different from the original maturity. So the distribution of security holdings among the indicated categories is only a rough index of their distribution by maturity.

Of the reduced total of the public debt, through December 1930, less than 10 percent of member bank holdings were in less than one-year maturities when issued; four-fifths were in long-term bonds (see table 4.A.2). Their holdings amounted to less than one-quarter of the bills and certificates outside the Federal Reserve from the October 1929 call date through the June 1930 call date, rose to three-tenths at the September 1930 call date when the first banking panic had not yet erupted, and then to three-eighths by the call date in December after the Bank of United States had been suspended. In 1931, the composition of member bank holdings of government securities shifted toward the short-term when issued, probably reflecting a shift in the composition

Table 4.A.1   **U.S. Federal Government Interest-bearing Debt Outstanding, Various Months, 1929–31 (in Millions of Dollars)**

Situation as of Last Day of:	Bonds	Treasury Notes	Certificates of Indebtedness	Treasury Bills	Total
June 1929	12,124	2,254	1,640	—	16,018
Aug. 1929	12,126	2,781	1,620	—	16,527
Oct. 1929	12,115	2,649	1,658	—	16,422
Dec. 1929	12,110	2,513	1,306	100	16,029
Mar. 1930	12,112	2,570	1,385	56	16,123
June 1930	12,112	2,390	1,264	156	15,922
Sept. 1930	12,113	2,345	1,247	120	15,825
Oct. 1930	12,113	2,345	1,247	223	15,928
Nov. 1930	12,113	2,343	1,247	230	15,933
Dec. 1930	12,113	2,342	1,192	128	15,775
Mar. 1931	12,709	1,129	2,228	214	16,280
June 1931	13,531	621	1,924	445	16,520
Aug. 1931	13,536	644	1,883	523	16,586
Sept. 1931	14,336	644	1,545	524	17,049
Dec. 1931	14,298	795	1,860	576	17,529

Source: U.S. Treasury Department 1929–31.

Table 4.A.2 Chief Kinds of U.S. Government Direct Obligations Held by Member Banks, Member Bank Call Dates, 1929–31

| | Member Bank Holdings (Millions of Dollars) | | | | Percent of Total Member Bank Holdings in: | | | Holdings as Percent of Total Amounts Outside FR Banks | | | |
	Total (1)	Bills and Certificates (2)	Notes (3)	Bonds (4)	Bills and Certificates (5)	Notes (6)	Bonds (7)	Total (8)	Bills and Certificates (9)	Notes (10)	Bonds (11)
1929											
June 29	4,155	446	704	3,005	10.8	16.9	72.3	26.3	28.8	32.6	24.8
Oct. 4	4,022	365	665	2,992	9.1	16.5	74.4	25.0	24.0	26.5	24.8
Dec. 31	3,863	249	520	3,094	6.4	13.5	80.1	24.9	21.0	22.6	25.7
1930											
Mar. 27	4,085	273	524	3,288	6.7	12.8	80.5	26.3	23.4	21.9	27.5
June 30	4,061	259	463	3,340	6.4	11.4	82.2	26.5	22.6	21.0	27.9
Sept. 24	4,095	334	418	3,343	8.2	10.2	81.6	26.9	30.7	19.4	27.9
Dec. 31	4,125	369	485	3,271	8.9	11.8	79.3	27.4	37.6	22.9	27.4
1931											
Mar. 25	5,002	899	332	3,771	18.0	6.6	75.4	31.9	42.2	30.1	30.3
June 30	5,343	901	403	4,039	16.9	7.5	75.6	33.7	44.5	67.8	30.5
Sept. 29	5,564	914	371	4,279	16.4	6.7	76.9	34.1	54.2	60.5	30.5
Dec. 31	5,319	679	441	4,199	12.8	8.3	78.9	31.8	33.7	57.9	30.1

Sources, by columns: (1): Sum of cols. (2)–(4). (2)–(4). (2)–(4): U.S. Board of Governors of the Federal Reserve System 1943, p. 77. (8): Holdings of the Federal Reserve Banks were deducted from the total of the three kinds of debt outstanding (ibid., pp. 332, 343, 375, 509–10); col. (1) was expressed as a percentage of the difference. (9)–(11): Procedure similar to that for col. (8), except that no breakdown of Federal Reserve holdings was available except at Dec. 31; the percentage distribution of the three kinds of debt was assumed the same at other dates in each year as on the following Dec. 31.

of outstandings, but also reinforcing the growing concentration of bank demand on these issues, already manifested in December 1930. Bank holdings of short-term governments were more than 50 percent of outstandings in September 1931, and 60 percent of outstanding medium-term governments.

Mayer (1978*b*) asks whether one would not expect "the demand for other assets to decline, and hence their yields to rise" (p. 140) when bank failures reduced the money supply. But the short-term assets for which we have yield information, primarily commercial paper and short-term governments, are not those for which demand declined. The banks dominated these markets, and with good reason. After the experience of two banking panics, the remaining banks chose to acquire assets with assured convertibility into cash sums at need and at short notice.

Short-term governments did not experience the unremitting declines in rates that characterized the commercial paper market in 1930. Continuous monthly data are available only for the yields on three- to six-month Treasury notes and certificates (see figure 4.A.1). (There were only five issues of Treasury bills that year, so there are quotations only on new offerings.) As the chart in figure 4.A.1 shows, small increases in yields occurred during three months in 1930—5 basis points in April, 27 in September, and 8 in December, the month the Bank of United States failed.

Given these conditions in both the commercial paper and short-term government markets until Britain cut loose from gold on September 21, 1931, why did the commercial paper rate rise from 2 percent, during the week ending October 3, to 4.13, during the week ending November 14, after which it continued an uninterrupted decline to the week ending with the Bank Holiday—its low point during the contraction of 1.38 percent? Why did the average rate on new issues of Treasury bills, which reached a low of 0.485 percent in July 1931, rise steadily thereafter to 3.253 percent in December 1931? Outstandings of commercial paper continued to decline to the end of the year, but outstanding Treasury bills rose somewhat. It is clear from the pattern of short-term rates of private instruments that the rate rise followed the increase in the discount rate at New York on October 9, from 1.5 to 2.5 percent, and on October 16, to 3.5 percent. In this instance, the Federal Reserve led the market. In the discount rate reductions from November 1929 to May 1931, it followed the market. In the short-term government market, an added factor contributing to the rise in interest rates may have been the increase in Treasury notes.

Bills discounted had been rising from July 1931, when discounts averaged $169 million, to $282 million in September. They then rose to $614 million in October, peaking at $848 million in February 1932.

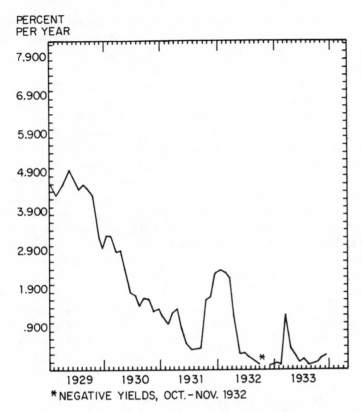

PERCENT
PER YEAR

Fig. 4.A.1   Yields on three- to six-month treasury notes and certificates, 1919–33. *Source:* U.S. Board of Governors of the Federal Reserve System 1943, p. 460.

In addition to the increase in their indebtedness, member banks lost $74 million in reserves between July and September 1930 and a further $426 million between September 1931 and February 1932.

Interest rate behavior is not, then, inconsistent with monetary stringency both before and after September 1931. The pattern of short-term interest rate declines before September 1931 reflected firm demand by commercial banks for commercial paper and short-term government securities and a generally declining supply of these instruments. When the Federal Reserve increased discount rates sharply in October 1931, it led market rates, pulling them up, whereas its earlier discount rate reductions followed market rate declines.

Temin, however, is right in arguing that short-term interest rates are the ones to examine because they most nearly resemble holding-period yields. For long-term rates, only yields to maturity are available, although investors make plans on the basis of holding-period yields. Temin therefore regards long-term rates as unsuitable for analysis because they are complicated for the years 1928–31 by the growing risk of default for some bonds and the rising price of risk.

In *A Monetary History,* we noted that while both long- and short-term interest rates had been declining before the first banking crisis, a widening spread began to emerge, synchronous with the first crisis, between yields to maturity on lower-grade corporate bonds and on government bonds as yields on corporate bonds rose sharply and yields on government bonds continued to fall. Temin says "this suggestion will not stand up" (p. 105) because bond prices began to fall well before the panic, and only the prices of lower-grade bonds fell; the prices of high-grade corporate and government bonds stayed roughly constant.

The point of Temin's insistence that the value of bank portfolios declined well before the bank panic of 1930 is that the price decline of bonds was not a result of the liquidity scramble but rather a cause. He argues that bonds were being moved from one quality class to another so that movements in the Baa rate do not show the change in the price of banks' portfolios. The price decline in any actual bond portfolio in the 1930s was the result of both the decline in the price of a given quality class and the decline in the quality ratings of the bonds in the portfolio. The yields on the fixed sample of bonds that Temin constructed for December and June dates 1928–31 rise continuously and far exceed the yields on Baa bonds.

No one disputes that bond prices were depressed in 1928 and 1929 while the boom in equities was in full swing. Temin's assertion that yields on high-grade corporate and on government bonds thereafter were constant is hard to assess. Yields on high-grade corporate bonds fell from December 1929 through October 1930, from 4.67 to 4.42. At the end of 1930, during the months of panic, they rose to 4.52. They then resumed a decline to 4.36 in July 1931. Yields to maturity on government bonds fell from 3.43 in January 1930 to 3.19 in November 1930, then rose to 3.30 in February 1931, falling thereafter until June, when the yield was 3.13. These small changes are consistent with monetary stringency before the first banking panic—given the steady decline in commodity prices, so that real rates rose appreciably; and the upward movements and subsequent declines at the end of 1930 are consistent with an intensification of monetary stringency during the panic.

In any event, the relative constancy of high-grade yields does not contradict the argument that the sale of low-grade bonds was induced by a scramble for liquidity. Temin counters that banks were net sellers of bonds in 1931 because "they perceived the risk more quickly or because they were more risk averse than individuals. The fact that they

sold while individuals bought is not evidence of a liquidity scramble''
(p. 106 n.). This ignores the effect that dumping securities, for whatever motives, by some banks produced on the values of the investment
portfolios of other banks. As for money and income, there is no reason
to expect a one-way relation. The reflex influence of bond sales in
setting off other bond sales is the essence of a liquidity crisis that Temin
fails to recognize.

4.A.4   Price Deflation and the Behavior of Real Balances

Temin argues that the distinction between nominal interest rates and
real interest rates can be neglected. To begin with, he doubts that
anyone apart from professional economists makes such a distinction.
Further, even if the distinction were made, it would not salvage the
monetary explanation. If high real interest rates dominated all other
explanations of 1929–33, he asks, why do we not observe a similar
effect in 1920–21 with a greater deflation and the same institutional
constraint that nominal interest rates cannot be negative? There were
indeed high real rates in 1920–21, but their effect was not prolonged
by banking panic effects on the money stock.

The final major indication for Temin that monetary causes cannot
account for the severity of the economic decline is that real balances
did not decline. Because prices fell so rapidly, the stock of real money
balances did not fall from 1929 to 1931; hence, in his view there could
not have been any deflationary effect from the decrease in the nominal
stock of money. He asks:

> Why . . . should the level of real expenditures and hence of em-
> ployment have been lower in, say, 1931 than in 1929 since the real
> stock of money was larger by all of the measures shown in Table 23?
> (P. 142)

For Temin, there is no contradiction between his assertion that the
demand (i.e., demand function) for nominal balances declined while
real balances (i.e., quantity of real balances held) were constant or
increased. Real money balances are a statistical construct that he examines merely because quantity theorists consider it important. If he
thought it represented the basic monetary total demanded, he would
have had to explain why a decline in the demand for money did not
produce a rise in prices, for a fixed nominal stock, to produce a decline
in real money balances.

If one regards real money balances as the basic monetary total demanded, there is no evidence that the demand function declined. Gandolfi and Lothian (1976) have shown that the function that predicts
actual real money balances for 1900–1929 predicts actual real money

balances during the Great Contraction with no loss in predictive power. The demand for real money balances is conventionally defined as related positively to real income and negatively to the rate of interest. Hence the movement of real balances over the cycle depends on the relative movements of the determinants. There is no evidence of a leftward shift in the demand curve during the Great Contraction. The rise in real money balances to 1931 and similarly the decline from 1931 to 1933 were due to changes in the determinants of the demand. There were movements along the demand function, not a shift in the function, as Temin would have it.

Gandolfi and Lothian have also challenged Temin's assumption that a fall in the nominal quantity of money accompanied by a corresponding fall in prices should leave real output unchanged, since real balances remain constant. In this case, Temin fails to note a distinction between anticipated and unanticipated price change. Suppose output depends on the price of output relative to expected price of inputs. An unanticipated fall in all prices, given imperfect information on input prices, will be perceived by producers as a relative fall in output prices. Temin ignores a growing literature on the supply effect of unanticipated price changes on real output change. Hence his assertion that the behavior of real balances is inconsistent with a monetary explanation of the contraction is untenable.

4.A.5 The Role of Bank Failures

As indicated earlier, Temin's explanation of the role of bank failures is that they served as the channel through which the supply of money adjusted to the falling demand. He alleges that the banking panic of October 1930 was induced by the decline in agricultural income and in the prices of relatively risky long-term securities presumably held by banks and, in particular, that the failure of the Bank of United States in the course of that panic did not precipitate a liquidity crisis. In *A Monetary History* we devoted a section to the question of the origin of bank failures during the contraction. Did the failures arise primarily because of imprudent financial practices of the 1920s? Or were they the product of developments of the early 1930s?

> Whatever may have been true of the initial bank failures in the first banking crisis, any ex ante deterioration in the quality of loans and investments in the later twenties or simply the acquisition of low-quality loans and investments in that period, even if no different in quality than in earlier periods, was a minor factor in the subsequent bank failures. As we have seen, the banking system as a whole was in a position to meet the demands of depositors for currency only by a multiple contraction of deposits, hence of assets. Under such

circumstances, any runs on banks for whatever reason became to some extent self-justifying, whatever the quality of assets held by banks. Banks had to dump their assets on the market which inevitably forced a decline in the market value of those assets and hence of the remaining assets they held. The impairment in the market value of assets held by banks, particularly in their bond portfolios, was the most important source of impairment of capital leading to bank suspensions, rather than the default of specific loans or of specific bond issues. (P. 355)

So even if we were to concede that all the banks that failed in the first banking panic beginning October 1930 were bad banks that deserved to fail, this series of failures would have provoked difficulties for other good banks, the market value of whose assets would have been affected by the dumping of assets by the failing banks. Such failures could well have promoted panic among all depositors. In a panic the public is mired in doubts that institutions are as sound as they are said to be.

I believe that the concession to Temin about the first banking crisis is not supported by the evidence, however. Good banks went down in that panic. His allegation that the Bank of United States failed because of fraudulent practices of its officers will not be sustained by an impartial examination of the record of the bank. The charge of fraud tells you something about the temper of the times, not the facts of the case.

Moreover, the panic of October 1930 does not stand alone in the U.S. monetary history if we look back this time, not forward to the succeeding banking crises from 1931 to 1933. Cagan (1965) noted in his study, to which Temin does not refer, that panics in U.S. monetary history appeared in the early stages of cyclical contraction and therefore themselves could not have been the major cause of the contractions. He concluded that panics made ordinary business contractions severe when they led to a substantial decline in the rate of monetary growth and not otherwise. "Substantial decline in this rate, by itself, and with no panic, could and has produced severe business contraction" (p. 267).

4.A.6 Monetary Policy

I turn finally to the issue of monetary policy during the Great Contraction. In *A Monetary History* we argued that alternative policies were available that the Federal Reserve System could have pursued and that would have made the contraction less severe. Temin refuses to be drawn into a discussion of alternative policies. "The question posed" in his book "is not whether some alternative policy would have worked, but rather what happened to make such a corrective policy desirable" (p. 7). Nevertheless, he has himself referred to alternative policies, himself conducted a counterfactual "thought experiment," as he labeled our section on alternative policies. It is counterfactual for Temin to state that, had there been no bank failures, the quantity of money would have been reduced to the same extent by a rise in the reserve-deposit ratio rather than the rise in the currency-deposit ratio that actually occurred. And this counterfactual assertion is refuted by Cagan's study. Temin assumes that the reserve-deposit ratio would have risen as a result of the decline in interest rates in the absence of bank failures. Cagan finds little interest elasticity in this ratio and concludes that the larger part of the change in the ratio was related to panics. A lagged reaction to a panic on the part of banks was to raise the ratio of their reserves to their deposit liabilities.

But to turn to the main question: We do have some evidence for 1930–31 on what alternative policies would have accomplished. We know that when the Federal Reserve System finally undertook open-market purchases of $1 billion between April and August 1932, the money stock grew at a 1.75 percent annual rate of rise from September 1932 until January 1933 compared with the preceding 14 percent annual rate of decline. We know that industrial production rose 14 percent in the second half of 1932 after sharp earlier declines and that commodity prices rose in the second and third quarters of 1932 after declining in the two preceding years. Temin counters that we merely assume that the change in the quantity of money changes the level of income and do not disprove the possibility of reverse causation. Can he really mean that the Federal Reserve undertook the open-market purchases in 1932 as a passive response to an increased demand for money that was a result of rising output and prices that lagged the change in monetary policy? There is evidence also on what alternative policies would have accomplished if we turn to the system's open-market purchases in 1924 and 1927. The omission of discussion of these policy measures in Temin's book reflects his assumption that money is passive. Supply simply adjusts to the demand. This is a real-bills vision with a vengeance.

In *A Monetary History* we found a contrast between the policy actions of the Federal Reserve in 1924 and 1927 on the one hand and 1930–33 on the other. Elmus Wicker (1966) denies such a contrast, arguing that international considerations accounted for the open-market purchases in the '20s and that international considerations were unimportant in 1930–33. In his view, the Federal Reserve never accepted domestic economic stability as a goal of monetary policy. Brunner and Meltzer (1968) also deny the contrast, arguing that in all three contractions, if market rates, particularly short-term rates, fell, policy was regarded as expansive, and if market rates rose, policy was regarded as contractionary. In the earlier contractions, gold inflows and a decline in the demand for currency and bank loans produced a decline in interest rates accompanied by an increase in high-powered money. As a result, money supply rose and the economy recovered. In 1929–30, gold inflows and declines in the demand for currency and bank loans also produced a decline in interest rates, but high-powered money and the money supply fell. Hence the economy continued to deteriorate. But, as Brunner and Meltzer document, nearly all of the members of the Open Market Committee regarded monetary policy as easy.

We regard Wicker's view as untenable. If the Federal Reserve did not accept domestic economic stability as a goal of monetary policy, why did the system allocate resources to improving the data on economic activity, why did the staff prepare detailed studies on the state of the domestic economy in preparation for open-market committee meetings, why did the system claim credit for domestic prosperity when it occurred? There is without doubt some merit to the Brunner-Meltzer analysis, yet it cannot be accepted as a complete description of the situation. After all, the governor and the chief economists on the staff of the New York Federal Reserve Bank all recognized that the decline in interest rates was not equivalent to monetary ease; they urged, and with some support from others in and outside the system, extensive open-market purchases at various times in 1930, 1931, and 1932 and were not dissuaded from doing so by the decline in interest rates. And these were the people who, so long as Benjamin Strong was alive, effectively dominated Federal Reserve policy. Hence, we continue to believe that had Strong lived or had he been succeeded by someone of similar views and equal personal force, the same monetary growth policies followed in 1924 and 1927 would have been followed in 1930, hence the decline in high-powered money either would not have occurred or would have been promptly reversed, and the economy would have been spared its prolonged ordeal.

Notes

1. In their study of production during the business-cycle contraction of 1929–33, W. C. Mitchell and A. F. Burns (1936) noted:

The long decline was interrupted by three partial and abortive revivals. Of these, the first, in the early months of 1930, was brief and restricted mainly to automobiles, steel, and heavy construction. The second, in the first half of 1931, had wider scope, lasted longer, and went further. It was especially pronounced in the textile, rubber tire, shoe, and leather industries. The revival in the summer and autumn of 1932 was fairly general, as is indicated by the preceding discussion of the "double bottom" in the terminal trough of this cycle. In some industries one of these abortive revivals lasted long enough and went far enough to produce an "extra" specific cycle during the depression. (P. 18)

2. Haberler (1976, pp. 22–23) notes that the Majority Report of the Gold Delegation of the Financial Committee of the League of Nations in 1932 also attributed the depression to maladjustments caused by the war, but Gustav Cassel in a Memorandum of Dissent disputed the importance of maladjustments and stressed instead monetary phenomena—the undervaluation of the French franc, the overvaluation of the pound, the cessation of U.S. capital exports, and the U.S. depression. Maladjustments were also the explanation of the Great Depression advanced in later studies issued by the Royal Institute of International Affairs (Arndt 1944) and the United Nations Economic Commission for Europe (Svenillson 1954).

3. Abramovitz, in private correspondence with me, has called to my attention qualifications to this statement in his paper. He notes that since the "small-country" model in that paper was designed to apply to long swings, it was inappropriate for use within a single business-cycle contraction and, in any event, could not apply in full force to the United States. On the basis of a subsequent paper (1977), in which he analyzed models of a "large country" and a "small country," Abramovitz believes efforts by the Federal Reserve to sustain the growth of the U.S. money supply in 1930–31, unaccompanied by similar actions by leading European countries, would not have been adequate to prevent the massive decline in income that in fact occurred.

4. See the appendix for a demonstration that Temin's interpretation of interest rate movements as showing no monetary stringency in 1930 and 1931 is contradicted by evidence on the supply of and demand for the relevant money-market instruments during that period.

5. Christopher Sims (1972) introduced a sophisticated alternative test of Granger causality between a pair of variables by running two regressions, with each as dependent variable and both leading and lagged values of the other as independent variables.

6. George Garvy (1959, pp. 71–73) has shown that bank debits to deposit accounts at these centers is a good proxy for nominal income. Peter Lindert (1981) objects to this conclusion since Garvy (p. 87) also reports a lack of perfect conformity of cyclical movements in debits with interwar NBER reference dates (debits lag the turns in January 1920 and July 1921 and skip turns in October 1926 and November 1927). Nonetheless, Moore (1961, vol. 1, chap. 5) includes debits in his list of coincident indicators for that period. Gordon and Wilcox (1981), using quarterly GNP estimates, obtained results similar to those in table 4.2.

7. Eight years because of the need to include lagged values.

8. One other approach to determine unidirectional relationship that some investigators have reported involves cross-correlations of the innovations in X and Y processes derived from Box-Jenkins procedures. Christopher Sims (1977a) has criticized that approach as biased "for any null hypothesis except the null hypothesis of no relation between the series." The defect in testing whether "x causes v," he points out, in a formulation

(1) $y = a(L)y + b(L)c(L)x + v,$

"with a, b, and c, as polynomials in positive powers of the lag operator, L, and v uncorrelated with past values of y or x," is as follows:

The null hypothesis "x does not cause y" is represented by $b(L) = 0$. Whether or not a, b, and c are linear in the problem's parameters, maximum likelihood will be, for stationary x, y, asymptotically equivalent to choosing *a, b,* and *c* to minimize the sum of squares of *v* in the sample period. With any fixed *c*, an asymptotically valid test of the null hypothesis can be obtained by estimating *a* and *b jointly* by maximum likelihood or nonlinear least squares, then applying standard test statistics. Though this is not a difficult procedure, [the criticized author] instead chooses *c* as a filter which makes *c(L)x* serially uncorrelated, and chooses *a* as a filter which makes *a(L)y* serially uncorrelated, then *holding a and c fixed,* estimates *b*. But this amounts to testing the significance of *b* by first estimating the regression (1) with *b* set to zero, then testing for the contribution of *b* to the regression by examining correlations between the *residuals* of this first-stage equation and the omitted variables of the form *c(L)x*. Anyone versed in the theory of least-squares regression will recognize this as involving a bias in favor of the null hypothesis, except in the special case when the omitted variables are uncorrelated with the included variables. (P. 24)

9. Contrary to Temin (1981), the monetary events listed in the tabulation are, in the main, not "changes in the quantity of money" or "changes in [market] interest rates." They are events, like a change in the Federal Reserve discount rate or an episode of bank runs or Britain's departure from gold or the 1932 open-market purchase program, that are newsworthy and attract attention. They have immediate announcement effects. Moreover, a quick adjustment of prices does not preclude a long distributed lag adjustment. A partial adjustment that shows up quickly is not equivalent to the full adjustment of prices.

10. In a journal article that postdates Temin's review, Barber (1978) traces the origins of the Great Depression to demographic factors that he links to a decline in the residential construction market in the United States and to "a markedly unfavourable influence on the capital spending plans of business firms throughout the developed world" (p. 453).

Annual growth in standardized nonfarm households declined from 3 percent per year to under 2 percent per year from 1924 to 1932. This is supposed to have triggered the decline in U.S. residential construction. Yet the annual growth in standardized nonfarm households from the early 1950s to 1970 was lower than growth of households in any year from 1924 to 1932. Barber attempts to rationalize this inconsistency by citing the availability of mortgage finance since World War II. In that case, the demand for housing is not dependent on demographic factors exclusively.

Similarly, a rapid decline in the rate of population growth after World War I in developed countries, which was accompanied by a lower rate of labor-force growth in the United States and Germany, need not have had the consequence he assumes on capital spending. What evidence is there that firms throughout the world were aware of this demographic trend?

Essentially, Barber fails to establish a connection between his empirical evidence on the decline in population and disequilibrium in the steady-state growth model he presents and a model that would explain recessions. Disequilibrium in a steady-state sense does not explain why the peak in capital spending occurred in 1929 rather than 1928 or 1930.

11. Temin tries to determine (1976, p. 64) from the components of real GNP whether 1930 was a more depressed year than 1921 or 1938. Table 4.4, based on Commerce annual estimates of GNP in current and 1958 prices, the GNP implicit price deflator, and the unemployment rate, is an alternative to Temin's table which shows percentage changes in Kendrick's annual GNP estimates

in 1929 prices, the consumption and investment expenditures components of GNP, and merchandise exports deflated by wholesale prices. For the Commerce estimates, the components of GNP are available only since 1929. The first part of table 4.4, following Temin, relates the changes in the year following the peak in 1920, 1929, and 1937, to the magnitudes of the peak year. The bottom half of the table relates the changes in the year following those peaks to the year preceding the peaks on the ground that the 1929 magnitudes were not typical of the interwar years. One may ask whether 1920 or 1937 was any more typical. In any event, such comparisons between consecutive or nearly consecutive annual figures are subject to substantial error because of possible differences in patterns within the base year and the comparison year. For example, a cyclical peak in December preceded by a rapid rise during the year might be accompanied by a zero year-to-year change, despite a severe recession.

For whatever such comparisons may be worth, the real income decline was somewhat greater in 1930 than in 1921, the rise in unemployment was smaller, and the price decline was much smaller. In all of these respects, 1938 was much the mildest of the three contraction years. Over a two-year span, the results show the 1930 change to be even milder relative to 1921. Of course, 1930 was a contraction year from beginning to end, whereas in 1921 a trough was reached in July, and in 1938, in June. In addition, Temin's use of gross merchandise exports as if that were an independent component of GNP is misleading. The variable normally examined in the national income accounts is net export of goods and services. The change in the variable from 1929 to 1930 is one-third the magnitude of the change Temin reports for gross merchandise exports.

What sets 1930 apart from both 1921 and 1938 is that a banking panic that changed the monetary character of the contraction occurred in the last quarter of the year. In 1921 there were many bank suspensions—triple the number in 1920, for a total of 505 banks with deposits of $172 million. In 1930, there were 1,350 bank suspensions, with deposits of $837 million. In 1938, post-FDIC, suspensions are negligible, 54 banks with $10 million in deposits. Despite the increase in bank suspensions in 1921, there were no runs on banks. That is what distinguishes 1930 from 1921–there was panic in 1930 but not in 1921. Bank suspensions in 1921 were perceived by the public as special problems of agricultural and rural areas but not as affecting confidence in banks generally.

12. On the role of real wages, see section 4.5 of this paper.

13. The fall in prices made the Smoot-Hawley tariff level even higher than it otherwise would have been since specific duties are automatically raised with a declining price level (Haberler 1976, p. 34, n. 65). Meltzer (1976, pp. 459–60) assigns a large role to the Smoot-Hawley tariff and subsequent tariff retaliation by many countries in exacerbating the 1929–33 contraction. The effect of the tariffs was to impede the price-specie flow mechanism and the adjustment of the U.S. and the world economy. Absent the tariff, U.S. prices would have fallen relative to those abroad and led to an increase in foreign demand and net exports.

The protectionist policy that influential British economists in 1930 advised the British government to adopt played a role there parallel to that of the Smoot-Hawley tariff in the United States. In his memoir about the "golden age" of the great British economists, Colin Clark (1977) discusses a "might-have-been":

It is now unmistakably clear that what Britain, being still a power strong enough to give a lead to the world, should have done in 1930–31, irrespective of whether or not other countries so acted, would have been to have preserved Free Trade, accompanied by an expansionist demand policy, and allowing the exchange rate to move freely in response to market pressures. It is now universally agreed that the exchange rate had been overvalued on the return to the Gold Standard in 1925, and a reduction would, in any case have been required. (Though he had protested strongly against the overvaluation in 1925, Keynes himself was not recommending devaluation in 1930–31—the only prominent men to recommend the policy were R. G. Hawtrey, the Treasury's economic adviser, and Ernest Bevin.) Once the exchange rate had been freed, a strongly expansionist policy would have been possible. The preservation of free trade would have allowed the benefits of this expansion to flow to other countries and also, a matter of equal importance, would have set the right example, and spread economic expansion more widely over the world. (P. 90)

Clark's "might-have-been" applied a fortiori to the case of the United States.

14. In *A Monetary History,* we noted that since China was on a silver standard, it was hardly affected internally, 1929–31, by the worldwide economic contraction. Choudri and Kochin (1977) provide similar evidence for Spain for those years. Spain then had flexible exchange rates and a reasonably stable monetary policy.

15. Allan Meltzer (1976) traces the start of the contraction to "economic policies in the United States and other countries operating under the rules of the interwar gold standard" (p. 457). In his view, a relative decline in prices in the United States, as in 1928–29, under the price-specie flow mechanism can induce a recession abroad. He attempts to account for subsequent U.S. price change by relating anticipated price change at the start of the year to the average rate of monetary growth in the preceding three years relative to the rate of monetary expansion in the most recent year, with acceleration from the maintained average having much the larger effect under the gold standard. He regards his predicted rates of U.S. price change for 1930–31 and 1933 as not substantially different from actual price change. For 1932, when the predicted rate was only half the actual rate of price decline, he concludes the decline cannot be explained by the price-specie flow mechanism and the expected response to monetary contraction.

16. The percentage of eligible paper offered for rediscount rejected by the Reserve Banks of New York, Dallas, Philadelphia, and St. Louis (of those reporting such figures) was higher in 1930 than in 1929, possible evidence that acceptability standards were higher despite the decline in discount rates. Of course, member banks had the option of borrowing against their 15-day promissory notes secured by government obligations. See Beckhart, Smith, and Brown (1932).

17. Minor increases in yields on short- and long-term governments and on municipals are reported for December 1930 and March-April 1931.

Brunner and Meltzer (1968) interpret the persistent decline in short-term interest rates despite currency drains and bank failures as the result of adventitious factors offsetting the effects on short-term market rates that would otherwise have been observed. They cite an inflow of gold—mostly from South America and Japan—in the last quarter of 1930 (p. 343).

18. On the change in the character of the commercial paper market since the 1920s, see Selden (1963). The commercial paper market during the 1920s is discussed in Beckhart (1932).

5 A Century of British Market Interest Rates, 1874–1975

5.1 Introduction

Henry Thornton left a spare account—best described by the Latin phrase, *multum in parvo,* much in little—of his thoughts about the British monetary system during the Napoleonic era. That spare account is an incredibly rich source both of the elements of monetary theory and of instruction on the proper conduct of monetary policy. Any one of a dozen different insights recorded in Thornton's work could serve as the subject of this lecture. He understood:

the fallacy of the real-bills doctrine,

the distinction between the first-round and ultimate effects of monetary change,

the lag in effect of monetary change,

the problem market participants faced in distinguishing relative from general price changes,

the distinction between internal and external gold drains,

the factors influencing the foreign exchanges including the role of purchasing power parity,

how to bring inflation under control,

the relation of the Bank of England to other English banks,

types of effects of monetary disturbances on interest rates,

the distinction between the market rate and the natural rate of interest and between nominal and real rates of interest.

From this impressive list of ideas, I have chosen as my point of departure what Henry Thornton had to say about nominal and real interest rates. I shall then turn to a review of the behavior of market interest rates in Britain in the century from 1874 to 1975, with some reference also to the differences between the British and American record. The historical material is drawn from a study, now nearing completion, of monetary trends in the United States and the United Kingdom, on which I have collaborated with Professor Milton Friedman.

Henry Thornton was among the first to call attention to the distinction between the nominal and real rate of interest. He explained the difference by the anticipated rate of inflation. On this view, when inflation comes to be anticipated, lenders demand and borrowers are willing to pay higher interest rates to compensate for the expected decline in the purchasing power of the principal of and interest on the loan. The nominal interest rate is then a sum of the real rate of interest and the expected percentage change in the price level. The Usury Laws in force when Thornton lived made the permitted maximum interest rate in Britain 5%. To describe the price anticipations effect on interest rates, Thornton had to cite a case other than an English one. He wrote:

> Accordingly, in countries in which the currency was in a rapid course of depreciation, supposing that there were no usury laws, the current rate of interest was often . . . proportionably augmented. Thus, for example, at Petersburgh, at this time [1811], the current interest was 20 or 25 per cent, which he conceived to be partly compensation for an expected increase of the depreciation of the currency.

Much later in the nineteenth century, Irving Fisher expressed the same idea, which he subsequently elaborated in mathematical form. The question I propose to examine is the extent to which Thornton's and later Irving Fisher's views are confirmed by the empirical behavior of interest rates in Britain during the century from 1874 to 1975. I shall first report on the behavior of average nominal yields on three categories of assets: short-term nominal assets, long-term nominal assets, and physical assets, specifically, the short-term rate on three-month bankers' bills; the long-term rate on consols; and a proxy yield on physical assets, namely, the rate of change of nominal income. I shall then discuss the behavior of average real yields on these categories of assets. Finally, I shall discuss the relation between nominal interest rates and the rate of price change.

In the study from which this evidence is drawn, we express the data as an average over a business expansion from cyclical trough to cyclical peak or a business contraction from cyclical peak to cyclical trough, sometimes referred to as half-cycles. In all, there are thirty-five such half-cycles for Britain during the period we cover. I shall also report the averages over peacetime half-cycles and over various subperiods.

5.2 Average Nominal Yields

Over the century the several average nominal yields display a relation consistent with expectations. The short-term yield averaged 3.5%, the long-term yield 4.2%, the difference of 77 basis points presumably reflecting a liquidity premium which studies of the term structure of interest rates have shown to exist.

The proxy for the nominal yield on physical assets is nearly identical with the nominal yield on long-term assets, as if arbitrage operated to equate the yields over the century. The equality does not, however, hold for subperiods, and the difference between nominal yields on nominal assets and on physical assets turns out to be a sensitive index of economic conditions.

A comparison of nominal yields in the United States with those in Britain over the period as a whole shows US yields to be about one-half of one percentage point higher. However, the yields for the two countries are not directly comparable because of changes in the exchange rate. The price of the pound in dollars at the end of our period was lower than at the beginning, the rate of decline averaging 0.9% per year. Hence, a hypothetical long-lived Englishman who had purchased US assets at the beginning of the period, held them throughout the period, and converted them back to pounds at the end of the period would have earned in pounds 0.9 percentage points more than the nominal US yields. Alternatively, an American who did the same with British assets would have earned in dollars 0.9 percentage points less the nominal British yields. The difference between the yields in the two countries in comparable terms is therefore roughly 1.4 percentage points rather than one-half of one percentage point. This difference is consistent with the net outflow of capital from Britain to the United States for much of the period, offset not by a private return flow induced by interest rate differentials but by UK government repatriation of capital during World Wars I and II.

5.3 Ex-Post Real Yields

We calculate the *ex-post* real yield by subtracting the rate of change of prices from the nominal yield for all three categories of assets. Henry Thornton's description of the relationship between nominal and *ex-post* real yields is apt:

> . . . if, for example, a man borrowed of the Bank £1000 in 1800, and paid it back in 1810, having obtained it by means of successive loans through that period, he paid back that which had become worth less by 20 or 30 per cent than it was worth when he first received it. He would have paid an interest of £50 per annum for the use of this

money; but if from this interest were deducted the £20 or £30 per annum, which he had gained by the fall in the value of money, he would find that he had borrowed at 2 or 3 per cent, and not at 5 per cent, as he appeared to do.

The relation among the *ex-post* real yields on our three categories of assets over the century we cover is the same as the relation among the nominal yields. However, as between the United States and Britain, the real yields are directly comparable. No further adjustment for exchange rate changes is required because all yields are, as it were, expressed in the prices, and hence exchange rate, of a given base date, in this study, 1929.

The real yield, that is the excess of the nominal yield over the average rate of inflation, averaged about 1¼% for Britain, about 3% for the United States. The reason the US yield exceeded the UK yield more for real than for nominal yields is that British prices rose on the average more rapidly than American prices, a difference that was reflected in the average behavior of the exchange rate.

5.4   Yields in Peace-Time Cyclical Phases

When war-time phases are excluded from the averages, it is no longer true that the proxy measure of the yield on physical assets approximates the yield on long-term nominal assets. It is decidedly lower than yields on either short- or long-term nominal assets. The excluded war-time phases are inflationary phases, when yields on physical assets have tended to be higher than yields on nominal assets. In addition, governmental policy of holding down interest rates on nominal assets in World War II also contributed to the change in the differential return on nominal and physical assets in war and nonwar phases.

The assets that differ most in real yields between peace-time and all phases, however, are nominal, not physical, assets. The proxy for the nominal return on physical assets is higher for all phases than for peace-time phases by only a trifle less than the differential rate of inflation, so that the real return on physical assets is only slightly lower for all phases than for peace-time phases only. By contrast, the nominal return on nominal assets is about the same for all phases as for peace-time phases, so that the real return is appreciably less for all phases. The war-time periods highlight a point to which I shall revert in discussing other periods, namely yields on nominal assets for the most part behave as if price changes were unanticipated.

We distinguish between nominal yields on nominal assets and nominal yields on physical assets. There is no comparable explicit distinction in Henry Thornton's writings, but he does make the distinction implicitly. The man who borrowed £1000 in 1800 used the proceeds, he tells us, "by investing his money either in land or in successive commercial undertakings . . . and then finally selling his land or his commodities in the year 1810." At the sale, the man "would find the produce amount[ed] to £200 or £300 above the £1000 which he had borrowed," that is by the extent of the price rise over the decade, as estimated by Thornton.

The point of the distinction is that nominal yields on nominal assets are contracted in advance, reflecting anticipated price changes, but not unanticipated price changes. The borrower of the £1000 knew in advance that he would have to pay £50 a year in interest. The *ex-post* real yield on the loan reflected in full the unanticipated price change. The real yield on the £1000 loan made at 5% was only 2 or 3% because of unanticipated inflation.

For physical assets, on the other hand, neither the nominal nor the real yield, as measured, is contracted in advance. The investor in land or in successive commercial undertakings did not know in advance what either the nominal or real yield would be at the time of sale. What is clear from Thornton's example is the reflection in the sale price of the estimated rate of price rise in Britain from 1800 to 1810. There is, as it were, a measure of automatic indexing of yields on physical assets.

Reflecting this difference in the characteristics of nominal assets and physical assets, nominal yields on nominal assets are consistently less variable than the real yields on nominal assets, whereas the reverse is true for yields on physical assets. The real yield on physical assets tends to be less variable than the nominal yield.

5.5   Yields during Sub-Periods

We subdivide the century we cover into sub-periods, by separating the pre–World War I period into the period before 1896, when prices were generally falling, and the subsequent period, when prices were generally rising, separating out the war periods, and treating the interwar period as one unit, because of the paucity of phase observations, even though the behavior of prices varied greatly during the nearly two decades covered. On the average, however, the interwar period was certainly a period of falling prices. The postwar period requires no subdivision. It clearly is a period of generally rising prices.

We therefore have two periods of generally falling prices (before 1896, and interwar), two war-time periods of rising prices, and two peace-time periods of rising prices (1896–1914, post–World War II). Using the division into periods, we can supplement the conclusions for the period as a whole with respect to, first, the differences between Britain and the United States; second, the effect of price experience on the differential between the yields on nominal and on physical assets. We confine the comparisons for the subperiods to the short rate and the proxy yield on physical assets, omitting long rates.

5.6 US–UK Differential Yields

If the differential of the short rate as between the United States and Britain is examined over the six subperiods, it shows a steady decline from period to period, with a particularly sharp decline from the pre-1896 to the 1896 to World War I period. In the pre-1896 period, the short rate was 2.5 percentage points higher in the United States than in Britain. In the post–World War II period, the short rate was 1.5 percentage points lower in the United States than in Britain.

Different factors played a role in different sub-periods in contributing to the decline in the differential yield. The most interesting episode in the decline of the differential occurred in the pre-1896 period, when the differential averaged one percentage point higher than in the subsequent period to World War I. A substantial increase in the degree of financial sophistication in the United States relative to that in Britain as between the two pre–World War I periods could have produced a decline in the market rate of interest on nominal assets like commercial paper that was traded in active US financial markets. However, a detailed examination of the US–UK differential year by year contradicts this interpretation. There was no gradual reduction in the differential such as might be expected from a gradual growth in financial sophistication. The differential rather shows an abrupt drop from one level from 1874 though 1896, to another level from 1897 to 1914, with sizable year-to-year fluctuations about those levels. The extreme values for 1893 and 1896 suggest an explanation for the drop in level. The extreme value in 1893 reflects the banking panic of that year in the United States, which led after July to a restriction of cash payments by banks and to a market premium on currency, which was equivalent to a depreciation of the US dollar vis-à-vis the British pound. The 1896 extreme value of the US–UK differential reflects the capital flight of that year produced by William Jennings Bryan's nomination for president, exacerbating fears that the United States would abandon the gold standard. In both cases, fear of devaluation was a deterrent to the flow of British short-term capital to the US market except at a substantial premium. The election of William McKinley in 1896 changed the outlook. It made US adherence to the gold standard secure for the time being and the subsequent flood of gold from South Africa, Alaska, and Colorado removed all doubts.

The fear that the United States would abandon the gold standard was equivalent to a fear that the United States would inflate at a faster rate than Britain or deflate at a slower rate. The fear of inflation also animated the opponents of free silver, the endemic political issue of the pre-1896 period. The paradoxical effect was to produce deflation— or more rapid deflation than would otherwise have occurred. The paradox shows up to the full in interest rates. Before 1896, US prices were falling at a 1 percentage point per year faster rate than in Britain. That alone should have produced an appreciation of the US dollar by 1% a year and a 1 percentage point *lower* interest rate. But the fear of inflation more than countered the fact of deflation; kept the currency in danger of being devalued; and made interest rates in the United States 1 percentage point higher relative to those in Britain than they were after the fear was resolved.

The contrast between fact and belief continued after 1896. In the subsequent eighteen years, prices rose in the United States by something over 1 percentage point more per year than in Britain. The fact of inflation by itself should have produced a depreciation of the US dollar and a 1 percentage point higher interest rate in the United States. But the altered attitudes and the elimination of the silver issue meant that the exchange value of the dollar was never threatened and US interest rates, while higher than in Britain, were 1 percentage point less so than they were before 1896. The facts would have justified a 2 percentage point rise in the differential US–UK rate on nominal assets from before to after 1896. The beliefs about inflation produced a 1 percentage point decline!

There was a further 1 percentage point decline in the differential on nominal assets in the United States over that in Britain from the average of the two pre–World War I periods to the interwar period. That decline is matched by a decline of 1 percentage point in the differential real yield on physical assets over the corresponding period, which may be regarded as largely accounting for the decline in the differential on nominal assets.

The final decline of 2 percentage points in the US–UK differential from the interwar to the postwar period corresponds to the 2.4 percentage point decline in the rate of price rise in the United States relative to that in Britain. This differential rate of price decline was reflected in the depreciation of the British pound relative to the US dollar.

To summarize: the decline in the US–UK differential for the nominal short rate from before to after 1896 reflects the resolution of fears that the United States would inflate and the US dollar would be devalued; the further decline from pre–World War I to the interwar period reflects a decline in the real yield on physical capital in the United States relative to that in Britain; and the further decline from the interwar period to the post–World War II period reflects greater inflation in Britain than in the United States and an accompanying depreciation of the pound.

5.7 Differential Yields on Nominal vs. Physical Assets

If in each subperiod arbitrage had worked as well as it did for the period as a whole, the yields on nominal and physical assets would be equal or differ by a constant reflecting the average preference for physical versus nominal assets or the reverse. For peace-time periods, however, as I indicated earlier, the equality did not hold, so arbitrage clearly did not work as well in each subperiod as in the period as a whole.

In the two periods of falling prices, the yield on nominal assets was decidedly higher for both countries than our proxy for the yield on physical assets. Deflation was not anticipated. Lenders did well. Borrowers did poorly. Since in the main, entrepreneurs borrow in nominal terms to acquire physical assets, *rentiers* did well, entrepreneurs badly, which would seem to support the widely believed generalization that a period of unanticipated deflation is adverse to enterprise and growth. That generalization is belied, however, for the pre-1896 period of falling prices in both Britain and the United States, since real output grew at the rate of 2.2% and 3.3% per year in each country, respectively.

With the exception of Britain from 1897 to World War I, during periods of inflation our proxy for the yield on physical assets was higher than the yield on nominal assets. Apparently inflation too was not anticipated. Entrepreneurs did well, *rentiers* did poorly; capital was transferred from savers to borrowers, which would seem to support the widely believed generalization that unanticipated inflation is favorable to enterprise and growth. Yet that generalization is also belied for the 1897–World War I period of rising prices in both Britain and the United States, since real growth was greater during the pre-1896 period of falling prices than during the post-1896 period of rising prices. But the public perception at the time was clearly the reverse. Alfred Marshall referred to this phenomenon in 1886, when he wrote, "I think there is much less difference than is generally supposed between the net benefits of rising and falling prices."

Henry Thornton was aware that holders of physical assets appeared to do better than holders of nominal assets during an inflation. He observed:

> It was true, that men did not generally perceive, that, during a fall in the price of money [the value of money], they borrowed at this advantageous rate of interest; they felt, however, the advantage of being borrowers. The temptation to borrow operated on their minds,

as he believed, in the following manner: . . . they balanced their books once a year, and, on estimating the value of those commodities in which they had invested their borrowed money, they found that value to be continually increasing, so that there was an apparent profit over and above the natural and ordinary profit on mercantile transactions.

One way to examine the effect of the rate of price change on the difference between the yields on nominal and physical assets is to array the subperiods by the rate of price change, disregarding both chronology and country. If the price change had been fully anticipated, and the real yield had been independent of the rate of price change, the nominal yields on nominal assets would rise as the rate of price change increased, and the real yields on physical assets would stay constant. In fact, the nominal yields fluctuated about a roughly constant level, so that the effect of inflation produced a sharp decline in the real yield on nominal assets as the rate of price change increased. The hypothetical pattern of yields for a fully anticipated inflation came close to being realized for physical assets. Their nominal yield rose with inflation and their real yield fluctuated about a more or less constant level. However, this pattern does not reflect anticipations so much as the physical character of the assets and their real yields.

For nominal assets, investors fix rates in nominal terms and contract for a period ahead; prescience is therefore required if these rates are to reflect future price behavior. For physical assets, investors may fix no rates, and certainly not in nominal terms, and generally make no contracts about either real or nominal yields for a period ahead. The yield is generated out of the economic activity in which the asset is employed. It requires no prescience for the nominal yield on physical assets to reflect current price behavior, only that the physical asset participate along with other assets in the nominal income and spending flows.

The excess of the yield on physical assets over that on nominal assets is sharply negative for deflation, sharply positive for inflation. If inflations were fully anticipated, the differences between yields on physical and nominal assets might be expected to be roughly a constant, reflecting any preference among asset holders for one category or other of assets. For peacetime periods, there is no indication of such constancy. If inflation were wholly unanticipated, and there were no preference for one or the other category of assets, *ex-post,* the nominal yield on physical assets would reflect the actual rate of inflation, whereas the *ex-ante* nominal yield on nominal assets would not. This seems to describe the facts, with some indication that there was a 1 percentage point preference for physical over nominal assets, that is a willingness to accept that much less in yield in order to hold a physical rather than a nominal asset.

This description of the pattern that would be produced by wholly unanticipated inflations does not apply accurately to both US war-time episodes and especially World War I for Britain. There appears to be rough constancy in these three episodes in the excess of the yield on physical assets over that on nominal assets, as if they corresponded to anticipated inflations. But interpreting these episodes in this way implies a very great preference—about 8 percentage points—for nominal assets during war-time periods over physical assets—which seems most implausible. Possibly the war-time estimates are an aberration rather than an indication of correct anticipation of war-time inflation.

These results are inconsistent with the hypothesis that the *ex-ante* nominal yields on nominal assets incorporate correctly anticipated rates of inflation—which merely confirms what has long been known, that the public has not in fact been able over long periods, at least, until possibly very recently, to make correct anticipations of inflation. We can, however, examine the observations within the subperiods to determine whether there is evidence of a gradual recognition of and adjustment to inflation or deflation.

5.8   Relations between Yields on Nominal and Physical Assets

Our proxy for the real return on physical assets varied in the six subperiods, ranging for Britain from −2.6 to +2.2% per year, but the variation was far less than for the *ex-post* real yield on nominal assets, which ranged from −10.8 to +4.8% per year. Moreover, one extreme item accounts for most of the British range for our proxy for the real return on physical assets. Omitting World War I leaves five observations, ranging from 1.3 to 2.2% per year. No remotely comparable reduction in the range can be achieved for the real yield on nominal assets by omitting the most discrepant observation.

We can adopt Irving Fisher's view that the *ex-post* real return on physical assets can be taken to be roughly constant on the average over time—though at a higher level in the United States than in Britain. Then the wide variation among subperiods in the difference between the returns on nominal and physical assets reflects primarily the failure of nominal yields on nominal assets to adjust to the actual rate of inflation. As a result, *ex-post* real returns on nominal assets vary widely. The implication of rough constancy of real returns on physical assets is that the variation in *ex-post* real returns on nominal assets reflects primarily unanticipated changes in inflation.

In Irving Fisher's analysis, nominal yields adjust not to the actual rate of inflation but to the anticipated rate of inflation, which in turn adjusts to actual inflation after a considerable lag. In line with his analysis, we would expect to find that, shortly after a change from, say, falling to rising prices, the yield on physical assets would exceed substantially the yield on nominal assets, reflecting the incorporation in the yield on nominal assets of the lagged anticipations of falling prices. As prices continued to rise, the differential would decline and approach the equilibrium difference, reflecting (inversely) any general preference for physical over nominal assets (or conversely).

For the pre–World War I period, there is evidence of a response by nominal yields to price anticipations. During the pre-1896 period of falling prices, the nominal short-term yield fell as if it were adjusting to anticipations of deflation. During the subsequent period of rising prices, the nominal short-term yield rose as if it were adjusting to anticipations of inflation. This pattern is not visible in the US data. Since the British financial market before 1914 was more sophisticated than the US market, it is not implausible that yields were more responsive to anticipations of price change in Britain.

The only other subperiod that shows evidence of a response by nominal yields to price anticipations is the post–World War II period. The nominal short-term yield rises steadily throughout the period; the *ex-post* real yield on nominal assets rises sharply in the early part of the period and then fluctuates about a more or less constant trend; and our proxy for the real yield on physical assets shows no steady trend.

5.9 Nominal Yields and Rates of Change of Prices

These results led us to examine more closely the relation between nominal yields on short-term nominal assets and the rate of change of prices. A chart reveals an apparent connection for two widely separated periods: the period before World War I, and the period after 1970.

One feature of the relationship is the much wider variability of price change than of the rate of interest. This may reflect greater measurement error in the series on price change than in the series on interest rates, but a more plausible explanation is economic: the wider variation in prices reflects the existence of monetary and other disturbances that were random and could not be readily anticipated. In the relatively stable decades before World War I, in Britain, it was possible to identify the tides through the much smaller waves; in the post-1970 decade, variability was great, but attributable to policy, not change.

If the short-term rate and the rate of price change are correlated for phases of our individual sub-periods, the only significant correlation is for the post–World War II period. The indication that there may have been a change in the relation between interest rates and the rate of change of prices in the 1970s made it desirable to exploit data for shorter time units than cyclical phases. We plotted beginning in 1915 monthly averages of the rate of change—averaged over six-month intervals to reduce extreme variability—of the cost-of-living index, which the retail price index superseded in 1956, against the monthly three-month bankers' bill series. There is evident a lack of any short-term systematic relation between interest rates and the recorded rate of price change, and much wider short-period fluctuations in price change than in interest rates. There is a drastic reduction in the variability of recorded price change in Britain after the mid-1950s, presumably reflecting the comprehensive statistical revision of the price index in 1956. It may well be that a large part of the recorded fluctuations in prices before this date consisted of measurement error. Hence, the possibility cannot be ruled out that the statistical noise in the recorded price series drowns out a systematic relation between interest rates and the "true" rate of price change.

The UK monthly results from 1956 to the early 1970s rather argue against this conclusion. Despite the lesser amplitude of price fluctuations, this period, like earlier periods, shows essentially no relation between the rate on three-month bankers' bills and the rate of price change.

The monthly figures also reveal that the rate on three-month bankers' bills was often sticky, calling into question the extent to which the rate was truly market determined. The problem is by no means limited to the commercial bill market. Other short-term rates are also sticky. With the introduction of Competition and Credit Control in May 1971, the three-month bankers' bill rate for some years exhibited a reduction in rigidity. In the past few years, that is less evident.

One further feature of the relation deserves mention. The current rate on three-month bankers' bills since 1965 has been more highly correlated with the six-month price change average six months in the future than with the current six-month average. Interest rates apparently are forecasting price change over the next half year. This would suggest that lenders and borrowers have become better able to protect themselves against price changes than they were earlier in the postwar period.

The explanation may be that market participants have belatedly recognized the drastic change in the character of the monetary system from a largely specie standard to a fiduciary standard. The change altered the information relevant to predicting the future course of prices. There is less short-term but more long-term variability in rates of inflation and much higher levels of inflation than had been experienced in peace-time over the past century. As a result, market participants have a greater incentive to seek to allow for future price movements.

In Britain, the indication that interest rates and price change move symmetrically has lasted for a brief period only. The apparent shift may prove temporary. Whether it does, or whether it is carried farther, may well depend on whether future rates of inflation remain as high and as variable as in the past decade (or even higher and more variable) or whether rates of inflation return to earlier peacetime levels.

5.10 Conclusion

Two themes of this lecture—the relation between yields on nominal and on physical assets, and the relation between rates of change of prices and interest rates in Britain over the past century—examine empirically an idea that Henry Thornton presented in his speech on 7 May 1811, in the debate in the House of Commons on the Report of the Bullion Committee. He observed that nominal interest rates were relatively high when prices were rising because lenders and borrowers anticipated price movements and allowed for them in the interest rates they charged or paid.

The empirical evidence suggests that for much of the past century an effect in this direction has been very much damped. In recent years, however, nominal interest rates have begun to track the rate of price change more closely than at any earlier time in the century from 1874. Nominal rates of interest have become more variable than real rates of interest, as Irving Fisher believed them to be, and nominal returns on nominal assets have become as variable as nominal returns on physical assets. The shift to a fiduciary monetary standard in the postwar period and the increased long-term variability of prices that ensued have driven lenders and borrowers to seek to predict price changes more accurately, and to adjust the terms of lending and borrowing accordingly.

II Monetary Policy

6   Why Money Matters

August this year marks the tenth anniversary of the publication of the celebrated *Radcliffe Report,* which enshrined what had come to be conventional wisdom during the preceding quarter of a century, namely, that monetary policy is unimportant. According to the Radcliffe Committee, the Bank of England can exercise no effective control of the money supply. However, this is of no consequence since the money supply does not play a critical rôle in the economy. What really matters (para. 397) is "the liquidity position of financial institutions and of firms and people desiring to spend on real resources."

Since the 1950s, the testing of hypotheses against the facts has increasingly characterized both government and academic economic studies. Yet, the views expressed in the *Report* were not accompanied by any analysis of the actual behavior of the supply of money or the demand for money in the United Kingdom. Indeed, the *Radcliffe Report* does not contain any series at all on the quantity of money. At the time, there was little empirical research on the influence of money that could provide the basis for challenging the Committee's conclusions. Today, the situation is very different. Extensive historical and statistical investigations have been conducted into the role of money in the United States. These investigations give no support to the views expressed in the *Radcliffe Report.* In the United Kingdom, too, as in the United States, the evidence is that the quantity of money has a significant influence on the level of economic activity.

The next four sections of this article summarize studies bearing on some of the issues posed by the *Radcliffe Report:* Can the central bank control the quantity of money? Is there a direct relationship between changes in the quantity of money and changes in income? What is the link between monetary change and income change? What is the link between monetary change and financial markets? Most of this relates to the United States, but in a final section some preliminary results are presented of a study of British monetary experience since 1880.

6.1   Can the Central Bank Control the Quantity of Money?

For the United States, the answer to this question is clearly "yes." Commercial banks, the public and the central bank all affect the quantity of money available to be held, but the central bank can dominate the other two. Three factors largely determine the supply of money:

(1) "High-powered money" (sometimes called the monetary base) is provided in amounts determined by the central bank, to serve as "required" and "excess" reserves of the commercial banks and as coin and currency holdings of the public. "Required" reserves relate to the legal minima that the banks have to maintain against demand and time deposits, while "excess" reserves are the amount by which actual reserves exceed required.

(2) The ratio of deposits to reserves is determined by the banks in light of their legal (or customary) reserve requirements, expectations of currency flows and interest rates. Given existing financial conditions, an increase in reserves will induce banks to acquire earning assets, thus increasing their deposits and restoring the desired ratio of deposits to reserves.

(3) The ratio of deposits to currency is determined by the public in light of interest rates, income and its preferences for holding coin and currency.

In the United States, growth in high-powered money has dominated the long-term growth of the quantity of money, the deposit ratios playing a more important role in cyclical changes in the money stock. But, even then, their behavior does not negate the central bank's control of the quantity of money over short periods because it can take action, if it wishes, to offset the behavior of the ratios.

An examination of the circumstances surrounding the major changes in the quantity of money in the United States over the past century reinforces this evidence of the close correlation between high-powered money and the quantity of money over short periods. These major changes in the quantity of money have been largely independent of contemporary changes in business conditions and, since 1914, have clearly been the result of decisions by the Federal Reserve System.

Some economists have argued that central bank control of high-powered money does not confer control over the total quantity of money. They regard an open-market purchase of a certain class of securities by the central bank as having its full effect when some holders of the securities are induced to sell them. But this is only the initial reaction of the sellers. They sold the securities not to add to their money holdings but as a step toward rearranging their portfolios in light of changed opportunities. The money they receive is a "temporary abode" of the proceeds from the sale, pending the purchase of other items. Money is serving its usual function of separating the act of sale from the act of purchase. Evidence shows that, by this process, the change in high-powered money will be translated by the reactions of banks and the public into a prompt and predictable change in the quantity of money.

6.1.1

The central bank's ability to control the quantity of money does not, of course, mean that changes in it are necessarily the immediate objective of monetary policy. The bank may have other objectives, e.g., maintenance of fixed exchange rates or of fixed prices of Treasury securities. In such cases, the quantity of money must be whatever is consistent with these alternative objectives. In the United States, current policy, for example, aims at keeping certain short-term interest rates within a range specified every three weeks at the Federal Open Market Committee meeting. The Committee instructs the manager of the trading desk at the Federal Reserve Bank of New York to conduct open-market operations that will keep specified interest rates within the indicated range. If this produces too rapid a growth of bank credit, the manager is instructed to allow rates to rise above the range. If it produces too slow a growth, he is instructed to allow them to fall below the range. However, when the Treasury is attempting to issue coupon securities, maintaining prices of Treasury securities within a fairly narrow range may take precedence over maintaining specified limits on the rate of growth of bank credit. In that event, current policy operates to raise the flow of reserves and, hence, the growth rate of the quantity of money above the desired rate in the absence of Treasury financing. As a result, there are periodic reactions by the Federal Reserve System to the cumulative effects of special regard on its part for the Treasury. These periodic reactions involve contraction of the flow of reserves and of the rate of growth of money—as during the last three quarters of 1966, and since the end of 1968.

On balance, while the Federal Reserve can control the quantity of money if it chooses to do so, over the past decade control has been exercised at best fitfully. Most of the time the growth rate has been inadvertent, a side effect rather than the direct objective of monetary policy.

Much the same conclusion apparently applies to Britain. The Bank of England can control the quantity of money if it chooses to do so. However, it has, in general, at least until recently, chosen to supply whatever quantity of money is necessary to stabilize the prices of the public debt at those interest rates it considers desirable.

An empirical analysis of what determines Britain's money stock, corresponding to that for the U.S. money stock, does not yet exist. One reason is probably the difficulty of assembling detailed data for all commercial banks even yearly, let alone at more frequent intervals. Yet, such an analysis is clearly needed to supplement the theoretical analyses that have demonstrated the shortcomings of the assertion in the *Radcliffe Report* that the Bank of England cannot control the quantity of money.

6.2   Changes in Quantity of Money and in Income

Two dramatic episodes in the United States have recently focused public attention on the relation between changes in the quantity of money and subsequent changes in incomes, which are, of course, the combination of movements in output and in prices.

One episode was in 1966. From April 1966 to January 1967 monetary policy was contractionary: the quantity of money was not permitted to grow, following a year in which it had expanded at the rate of 6 percent. Over the same nine months, fiscal policy was highly expansionary: the federal government's (high-employment) budget[1] shifted from balance to an $11 billions deficit at an annual rate, the deficit then remaining above that level for the rest of 1967. Yet, during the nine months from October 1966 to July 1967 there was a sharp slowdown in both production and prices. Production, which had risen 9.6 percent the preceding year, actually fell 2.6 percent at an annual rate, while consumer prices, which were up 3.7 percent in the preceding year, continued to rise, but at the lower annual rate of 2.4 percent. This episode, like many historical predecessors, suggests that within a few quarters after the onset of a reduction in the monetary growth rate, output will contract and the rate of price rise diminish, despite a highly expansionary fiscal policy.

The second episode began at the end of 1968, when the growth rate of the quantity of money, which had been at the annual rate of 6.8 percent during the preceding 23 months, was reduced to roughly 3 percent at an annual rate. In 1968, while monetary policy was highly expansionary, fiscal policy turned highly contractionary: the federal government's (high-employment) budget, seasonally adjusted, shifted from $16 billions deficit at an annual rate in the second quarter to a small surplus at the end of the year, with the size of the surplus estimated to rise by $5 billions in the first half of 1969. Economists who disregard the quantity of money anticipated a reduction in output and prices after the middle of 1968. None having occurred, they then forecast a slow-down in the first half of 1969 and an improvement in economic activity in the second half. In contrast, economists who stress the importance of changes in the quantity of money anticipated no contraction of economic activity in 1968 or the first half of 1969 and forecast, if anything, a slow-down of economic activity in the second half of 1969. At mid-year, the forecast of the former group of economists had not been confirmed. This episode, again like many historical predecessors, suggests that the effects of a high monetary growth rate will persist for several quarters after it is reversed in raising the level of output and the rate of price rise, despite a highly contractionary fiscal policy.

6.2.1

Apart from these dramatic episodes, many systematic findings support a close association between changes in the quantity of money and those in money income. For the United States, the correlation between year-to-year changes in the quantity of money and those in income for the 94 years from 1870 to 1963 is quite close. The corresponding result for the United Kingdom for the year-to-year percentage changes for 77 years between 1881 and 1967, omitting war years, is, in fact, slightly better.[2] Quarter-to-quarter changes in the U.S. money stock are most closely associated with changes in income when they precede the latter by two quarters. In principle, this association might be considerably misleading: the changes in money and in consumption might be common consequences of associated changes in "autonomous" investment expenditure, investment expenditure, that is, determined independently of current business activity. In practice, this possibility turns out not to be true. A number of statistical studies indicate that money has an influence of its own and not merely as a disguised reflection of such expenditures, whose influence is generally less strong and less consistent than that of money.

6.2.2

A recent study by the Federal Reserve Bank of St. Louis has further documented the close association between changes in money and in income. A statistical test of the relative power of fiscal actions and monetary actions to predict quarterly changes in gross national product from the first quarter of 1952 through the second quarter of 1968 yielded results which indicated that the response of economic activity to monetary actions, compared with that of fiscal actions, is larger, more predictable and faster. Measures of fiscal action tested included federal government (high-employment) receipts and expenditures and the differences between them. The conclusion of the study regarding fiscal actions was that "either the commonly used measures of fiscal influence do not correctly indicate the degree and direction of such influence, or there was no measurable net fiscal influence on total spending in the test period." Measures of monetary action tested included the monetary base and the quantity of money narrowly defined to include coin and currency and current accounts held by the public, and defined more broadly to include also commercial bank deposit (time) accounts. The conclusion regarding monetary actions was that there was a strong relationship between economic activity and measures of monetary action.

Another set of studies has examined a different aspect of the relation between money and economic activity. These studies compare the cyclical patterns of the rate of change in the quantity of money and of general economic activity. Over the past century in the United States, peaks and troughs in the money series precede the corresponding peaks and troughs marking some twenty-odd cycles in economic activity, on the average by 17 months at peaks and by 13 months at troughs with, of course, much variability from cycle to cycle. A different comparison that may be more revealing for periods with sharp trends is between dates when the *level* of the monetary growth rate changes (shifting from a high level to a lower level or from a low to a higher level) and peaks and troughs in general business activity. For this comparison, the money series leads, on the average by 7.5 months at peaks and 4.5 months at troughs, again, of course, with much variability. Similar comparisons have been made for countries other than the United States. These have not been as extensive as those for the United States but the results have been much the same. A third comparison that gives about the same result as the second is between turning points in the rate of change in money and those in the rate of change in income.

These comparisons are, by themselves, not conclusive about the direction of effect. What is described above as the peak of the money series *leading* the subsequent peak of the cycle could equally be described as the peak of the money series *lagging* behind the preceding trough of the cycle. Alternatively, both the money series and economic activity could be the common result of still a third variable, but with money reacting more rapidly. These and similar possibilities have, however, been extensively explored. There is much statistical evidence suggesting that they do not, in fact, account for the observed results, and that these are more readily explained as reflecting the independent influence of monetary changes.

To summarize, cyclical studies indicate that changes in the monetary growth rate are a necessary and sufficient condition for changes in the growth of income over periods covering the different phases of the business cycle. Short-term changes in monetary growth appear to have a major impact on changes in output and only a mild impact on changes in prices. This is the opposite of the relation found for longer periods. Longer-period changes in money incomes produced by a changed secular rate of monetary growth are reflected mainly in different price behavior rather than in different rates of growth of output.

6.3 The Link between Monetary Change and Income Change

A change in the monetary growth rate creates a discrepancy between the actual money balances the community holds and the money balances it wants to hold. The actions the community takes to try to eliminate this discrepancy create the link between monetary change and income change. To explore the implications of this, it is first necessary to discuss the way people decide how much money to hold.

6.3.1

What ultimately matters to holders of money is the *real* quantity rather than the *nominal* quantity of money they hold. For the community as a whole, the real quantity of money can be expressed in terms of the number of weeks of output to which it is equal. The reciprocal of this measure of the real quantity of money is income velocity, i.e., the ratio of annual income to the quantity of money. The calculation of velocity is made at those prices prevailing at the date to which the calculation refers. These prices are the bridge between the nominal and the real quantity of money. Another way of expressing the real quantity of money is to deflate the nominal quantity by an appropriate index of prices.

It has been shown that the real quantity of money the community wants to hold is determined by two main variables: real income and the yield on assets alternative to money. The demand for money increases as real income rises, because the rise in real income makes possible larger wealth-holding and money is one form in which to hold wealth; and it falls as interest rates rise, because a rise in interest rates makes money a less attractive asset to hold relative to other assets.

There is, then, some fairly definite real quantity of money that people wish to hold under any given circumstances. Suppose that the nominal quantity of money that people hold happens to correspond at current prices to a real quantity larger than that which they want. They will, then, seek to dispose of what they regard as excess money balances. They will try to spend, lend and give in gifts more than they are currently receiving. But one man can reduce his nominal money balances only by persuading someone else to increase his. The community cannot spend more than it receives. The attempt to do so, however, will raise the volume of expenditures and receipts, leading to a bidding-up of prices and, perhaps, an increase in output. With no change in the nominal quantity of money, the initial excess of money balances will be eliminated, either by a reduction in the real quantity available to hold as a result of the price rise, or by an increase in the real quantity desired as a result of the increase in output.

In the opposite situation, if nominal balances happen to correspond to a smaller real quantity of money than people would like to hold, they will try to spend, lend and give in gifts *less* than they are receiving. As a group, they cannot do so. But their attempt will, in the process, lower expenditures and receipts, driving down prices or output. Even though there is no change in the nominal quantity of money, the initial deficiency in the amount of money balances will be eliminated, either by an increase in the real quantity available to hold as a result of the price fall, or by a decline in the real quantity desired as a result of the reduction of output.

It is clear from all this that, in principle, changes in income can be produced either by changes in the real balances that people wish to hold or by changes in the nominal balances available for them to hold. The evidence suggests that, in practice, changes in the demand for money (desired real balances) occur slowly or are the result of earlier changes in supply, whereas changes in the supply of nominal balances can occur and frequently have occurred independently of any changes in demand.

6.3.2

To describe the link between monetary change and income change does not mean that we know the process of adjustment in detail. The prevailing orthodoxy presumes that a change in the nominal quantity of money must have its impact first on the bond market, an increase in money raising the price of bonds and hence lowering interest rates, while a decrease lowers the price of bonds and hence raises interest rates. These interest rate changes are assumed to reconcile actual and desired money balances. The sequence of events is then traced from financial to non-financial markets. The change in nominal interest rates is treated as leading to a change in investment expenditures—a qualification is often added: insofar as investment expenditures are responsive to interest rate changes—and the multiplier effect of investment expenditures on income as ultimately leading to further expenditures on consumer goods and capital goods.

The prevailing view takes it for granted that changes in the nominal quantity of money are equivalent to changes in the real quantity of money, so that price changes resulting from monetary change play no part in reconciling the demand for money with the change in supply. Only changes in interest rates produce the reconciliation. The more responsive the quantity of money demanded to a given change in interest rates, the less interest rates will have to change to achieve the reconciliation. Similarly, according to the prevailing view, the interest rate is the only link between monetary change and real income. The less responsive is investment to a given change in interest rates, the less will any given change in interest rates affect real income. If, therefore, the demand for money is highly responsive to interest rate changes, while investment expenditure is unresponsive, most of the change in supply of money will be absorbed by a corresponding change in amount demanded, with little effect on real income or prices.

This was the view adopted by the *Radcliffe Report*. By implication, changes in the quantity of money are important only insofar as they lead to changes in interest rates that influence decisions to hold money or other liquid assets. Changes in market interest rates on the liquid part of total wealth relative to the real rates of return on capital in the illiquid other part of total wealth are deemed to be the channel through which changes in spending are transmitted. Hence, interest rates are viewed as essentially the only market variable that reconciles the structure of assets supplied with the structure demanded. Yet, no evidence exists showing that this approach is valid. The correlations between the level of or rates of change in interest rates, on the one hand, and rates of change in nominal income, prices, and output, on the other, are considerably worse than those between rates of change in the quantity of money and these magnitudes.

6.3.3

The alternative monetary analysis that has been replacing the Radcliffe view is based on evidence that a change in the quantity of money is followed by changes in both prices and output. The price changes are one channel of adjustment of the real quantity of money to the change in the nominal quantity. Interest rate changes and real output changes are other channels. When actual and desired money balances are in disequilibrium, flows of every conceivable sort may be affected in the process of altering stocks of financial and non-financial assets to restore equilibrium.

On this alternative view, the particular mechanical sequence from money to bonds to interest rates to investment expenditures and, thence, to income is one, but only one, possible channel of transmission of monetary change to income change. There is no reason to suppose that it is exclusive. A discrepancy between actual and desired money balances may also be eliminated by initial spending effects on all manner of goods and services. Such a discrepancy may affect expenditures on durable and non-durable consumer goods, investment in education, in financial assets of the wide variety available, including not only bonds but also equities, mortgages, life insurance, and so on, and in durable producers' goods. The effects are then further diffused as demand shifts for current output of goods and services and new sources of productive services. The precise sequence of transmission may well vary from time to time because it depends on the initial points of impact of the change in money. However, the consistency of the relation between monetary and income changes argues that the initial effects are dominated by the more general diffused effects that monetary changes set off.

To complete this account of the relation between changes in money and in money income, some discussion is required of the link between changes in money and the division of the change in incomes between price and output. The most widely held view of what determines this division is probably that it depends on the level of utilization of capacity. When there is much unemployment of men and machines, an income change will be absorbed primarily by increased output, and prices will rise little. When there is high employment and high utilization of capacity, the output change will be moderate and prices will absorb the rest of the income change. Some recent findings indicate that past price experience is at least as important as the rate of capacity utilization in influencing the rate of current price rise. A 5 percent rate of monetary growth tends to mean a more rapid rate of price rise and a lower rate of output growth if prices have been rising at 5 percent per year in the immediate past than if prices have been stable. But past price experience is itself related to earlier monetary growth rates. Hence, this explanation implicitly makes the current division of a change in money income between prices and output a function of the earlier history of monetary change. However, the precise extent of the influence of capacity utilization and that of earlier price experience is still under investigation. Indeed, this issue of the forces determining the division of a change in income between prices and output is perhaps the major gap in our present knowledge of monetary relations and effects.

6.4 The Link Between Monetary Change and Financial Markets

Monetary policy is often examined in relation to its effects on credit rather than on the quantity of money. The chief function of the central bank, on this view, is regarded as the control of commercial bank assets in the form of loans and investments, the terms of credit in the loan market and the yields on a few widely traded securities. The effect of monetary policy on the quantity of money is not given special consideration.

Yet, there are many reasons for believing that the concentration on credit aspects of central bank actions provides an unreliable indication of the thrust of monetary policy. The importance attached to asset targets of central bank operations reflects the view that the "first" round of circulation associated with asset creation by the banking system needs special attention. Spending consequences of such a first round are assumed to exhaust the monetary effects of changes in assets. Loans to the private sector are deemed to play a crucial role because it is taken for granted that the transactions velocity of such funds is markedly higher than that of swaps of bank deposits for Treasury bills or other securities held by the public. Alternatively, stress on bank loans as the main channel through which banks affect spending sometimes rests on the assumption that the market for credit is fragmented, so that borrowers denied bank loans perforce must abandon or postpone investment plans they wish to finance.

It is conceivable that the first round may exhaust the monetary effects of the change in assets. This would be the case if a change in the supply of money associated with asset creation just equalled a change in the demand for money. However, if a change in supply produces a discrepancy between the public's actual and desired money holdings, there will be future effects in subsequent rounds of circulation, which will escape the notice of a central bank whose targets are restricted to bank assets.

In any event, the link between changes in reserves over short periods and the volume of particular earning assets is quite loose. The distribution of earning assets among liquid assets, other investments and loans is, in the first instance, subject to the banks' control. Similarly, the link between changes in reserves over short periods and changes in interest rates and credit conditions is quite loose. Interest rates and credit conditions are the outcome of the interaction of demand and supply in markets in which the central bank may not participate or, if it does, may not be dominant. Bank assets in the form of loans and investments are a minor fraction of the total outstanding volume of credit. It has been shown that, in the United States, central bank action, measured by the rate of change in money, accounts only in part for the pattern of interest rates with respect to the peaks and troughs in general business, and explains only about a quarter of the cyclical variation in the movements of interest rates. Clearly, central banks exert an important influence on credit conditions, but it is far from being controlling.

Moreover, changes in the volume of particular types of credit or of total bank credit, in credit conditions, in the level of or the rate of change in interest rates provide a poor basis for interpreting the stance of monetary policy. However money is defined, the evidence is clear that it changes at very different rates than do particular types of bank credit or total bank credit. There is no unambiguous measure of credit conditions. They can be described only qualitatively in degrees of ease or tightness, and the determination of what credit conditions are "appropriate" is equally amorphous. Since interest rates tend to move within a relatively limited range, a common fallacy is to assume that the top of the range is proof of tightness, and the bottom of the range proof of ease. Yet, tightness and ease are relative, not absolute, terms. A high interest rate when demand is strong may not be restrictive, while the same rate with weak demand may be highly restrictive.

6.4.1

Recent studies have shown that, while interest rates are initially lowered by increasing the quantity of money, this action produces income and price effects which will offset the reduction within several months. Conversely for decreases in the quantity of money. That is why we observe rising interest rates during business expansions as a delayed consequence of a higher monetary growth rate and falling interest rates during business contractions as a delayed consequence of a lower monetary growth rate. The initial effects on interest rates of higher or lower monetary growth rates are temporary: they are swamped by the effects of the ensuing increase or decrease in demand for credit and the effects of price anticipations. To the extent that lenders and borrowers anticipate changes in the purchasing power of money, bond prices will tend to be lower and nominal yields higher when prices in general are rising than when prices in general are falling, since the decline (or the rise) in the real value of the principal is a deduction from (or addition to) the nominal interest paid. Hence, central banks will be misled if they regard the level of or change in interest rates as an indication of whether their own actions are expansionary or contractionary.

Though interest rates have some influence on the demand for and supply of money, and though there are undoubtedly some influences running from prices and output to changes in the nominal quantity of money, the weight of the evidence supports the proposition that the rate of growth of the quantity of money is a relatively unambiguous indicator of monetary conditions. A sustained rise in the rate of growth of money means the central bank is creating a monetary expansion on its own or acquiescing in monetary expansion set in motion by the other determinants. Likewise, a sustained decline in the rate of growth of money means the central bank is creating a monetary contraction on its own or acquiescing in monetary contraction set in motion by the other determinants.

In post-war years one target of Bank of England operations has been the clearing banks' advances to the private sector. The object has been to control private sector borrowing by restricting to a given percentage figure the increase, over some stated period, in the banks' advances, in order to hold down the demand for imports and domestic spending, both of which are assumed to be strongly associated with private borrowing. Recently, control of private advances has been exercised also as a means of curbing the quantity of money. Even if the banks hit the target—or, to use a more exact metaphor, get under the ceiling—control of advances would still be a poor way to control the money supply. The links between advances and the money supply are too loose. To curb the rate of growth of the money supply, the essential requisite is control of the monetary base. This can best be done by Bank of England actions affecting the flow of reserves to the banks.

6.5   British Monetary Experience

Reasonably accurate annual data on the quantity of money in the United Kingdom are available for 1880–1967. Comparable annual data for money income, prices and real income are available for an even longer period. An analysis of long-period movements in these series is now under way at the National Bureau of Economic Research in New York, but at this stage only the basic data in the form in which they are being studied, not the final results, can be presented. But, even from this elementary material, it can be seen that the evidence for the United Kingdom is broadly consistent with that for the United States on the relation between monetary changes and changes in other economic magnitudes.

For a study of long-period movements, it is desirable to remove from the data, so far as possible, the effects of shorter-term movements of business cycles. A standard chronology of British business cycles dating from the mid-nineteenth century until the second world war has recently been extended into the 1960s. On this basis, it is possible to convert the annual data for the United Kingdom into average values of a series over the successive phases of business cycles, the expansion phase running from a cycle trough to a cycle peak, and a contraction phase running from a cycle peak to a cycle trough. The initial phase covered by the money series is the contraction running from a peak in 1883 to a trough in 1886; for the other series, it is the proceeding contraction running from a peak in 1873 to a trough in 1879. The average values for incomes, prices and the stock of money are shown in figure 6.1 plotted in the middle of each phase.

From the chart it will be seen that there is clearly a striking similarity between the course of the lines for the quantity of money and for money income (the correlation is .972). It is, perhaps, not surprising to find the prices and the quantity of money curves moving so closely together

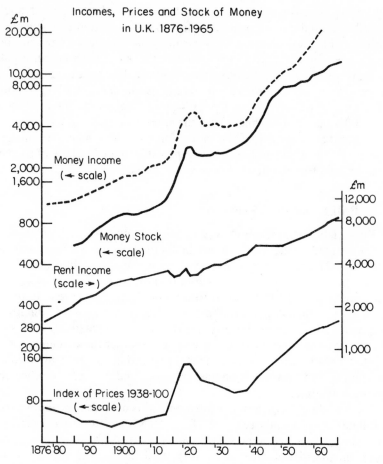

Fig. 6.1   Incomes, prices, and stock of money in the United Kingdom, 1876–1965.

(the correlation is .976). What may be surprising is that, despite the differences in long-period trends, there is an appreciable relation between the levels of money and real income (the correlation is .970).

In addition to the absolute levels of these series, it is helpful to examine their rates of change, as shown in figure 6.2. Rates of change are notoriously erratic. Yet, there is scarcely a movement of any size in the money stock line that does not have its counterpart in that of money income (the correlation is .742). The similarity between the two series does not reflect any spurious correlation arising from reliance on common data, and occurs despite independent errors of measurement in the data underlying the two series. As in figure 6.1, the cor-

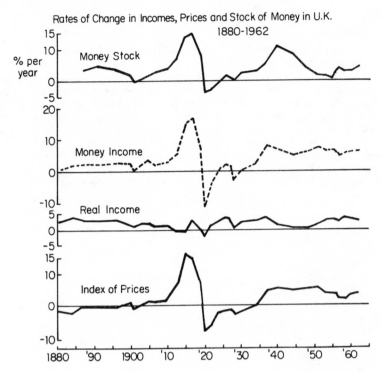

Rates of Change in Incomes, Prices and Stock of Money in U.K.
1880-1962

Fig. 6.2   Rates of change in incomes, prices, and stock of money in the United Kingdom, 1880–1962.

relation of the rates of change in money and in prices (.798) is somewhat closer than that between the rates of change in money and in money income. The two war-time peaks in the rate of change in money are reflected in the rate of change in prices. Real income possibly reproduces the first war-time peak in a muted form but not that of the second world war. Omitting the war periods, the correlation between money stock and real income growth rates (.362) is not nearly so good as that between monetary and price change.

The close connection between movements in Britain's stock of money and in money income recorded in the figures is an economic phenomenon that must be explained in economic terms. It is a relation that has persisted for as long a period as there are data to examine, for cyclical as well as longer-term movements. Study of the data for the United States has revealed that monetary influences operate in subtle ways and with long lags, but with highly regular and understandable patterns. There is no reason to believe that British monetary experience is an exception to this conclusion.

Notes

1. Because actual current tax receipts and certain government expenditures (such as unemployment compensation) reflect the level of economic activity at current tax and expenditure rates, the measure of "high-employment" government receipts and expenditures has been devised to reflect the effect of the budget independently of the reverse influence of current economic activity. This measure shows the federal government's receipts and expenditures that *would* occur if the economy were at high employment, a situation in which, but for frictions, all looking for jobs at the going wage rate would be able to obtain employment—in the United States, considered to be when 96 or 97 percent of the labor force is employed.

2. The actual figures are .70 for the U.S. and .77 for the U.K.

7 How Feasible Is a Flexible Monetary Policy?

Phillip Cagan and Anna Jacobson Schwartz

7.1 Flexibility and the Lag in Monetary Policy

The position now held by monetary policy as the main tool of short-run stabilization has yet to be reconciled with the accumulating evidence of a substantial lag in its effects on economic activity. A lag complicates the execution of policy, since it means that actions take effect well after they are initiated. Hence a policy of stabilizing short-run fluctuations in the economy implies the ability to forecast the course of economic activity and the subsequent effects of policy actions.

Twenty-five years ago Milton Friedman pointed to the problems of a flexible short-run stabilization policy.[1] Adapting the argument specifically to flexible monetary policy, he later wrote: "We seldom in fact know which way the economic wind is blowing until several months after the event, yet to be effective, we need to know which way the wind is going to be blowing when the measures we take now will be effective, itself a variable date that may be a half year or year or two years from now."[2] He concluded that countercyclical monetary policy in the United States was more often a destabilizing rather than a stabilizing influence and proposed as a policy rule a constant rate of increase in the money stock.

In recent years research on monetary policy has begun to explore the problems faced by stabilization programs with short-run objectives.[3] In this paper we bring together the results of studies that provide evidence of the lag in monetary effects. The lag patterns indicate that a change in the money stock in the current quarter induces a change in GNP not only in that quarter but also in many succeeding quarters. Thus, according to these patterns, the value of GNP in any quarter is a sum of the effects produced by money stock changes in a string of preceding quarters.

Generally speaking, given the limitations of present forecasting capabilities, the longer the lag the more impracticable a policy of short-run stabilization becomes. The flexibility allowed by the short inside lag of monetary policy—the lag between the provision of reserves to the banks by the Federal Reserve System and the change in the money stock—can be negated by a long outside lag—the lag between the change in the money stock and its effects. The studies we review suggest that the problem posed by imperfect forecasting techniques combined with long lags persists and, as Friedman pointed out, seriously limits the feasibility of flexible monetary policy.

We begin by distinguishing the short-run monetary policy actions at issue here from the day-to-day and week-to-week flexibility also advocated by the proponents of flexibility. Possible conflicts are noted between the objective of stabilizing economic activity by short-run flexible monetary policy and the objective of moderating transient money market disturbances by a policy of stabilizing interest rates (section 7.2). We then compare some estimates of lags after World War II with those for the 1920s for evidence of possible changes in the lag. We were unable to establish that such changes had occurred. Our main focus is on four versions of distributed lag patterns in regression models relating GNP to the behavior of the money stock in past quarters. All the lags cover many quarters (section 7.3). We predict GNP quarterly from M_1 data for 1921 to 1970, based on each lag pattern, and select peaks and troughs in the estimated GNP series. The timing of these turns compared with actual peaks and troughs in GNP or NBER reference dates suggests that the lag pattern itself is not fixed (section 7.4). For each of these lag patterns, we calculate the hypothetical required course of monetary growth in order to achieve a specified increase in GNP above its previous level. If the attempt were made to attain the target within a few quarters, it would require a complex path of monetary growth with the attendant possibility that the attempted policy itself, if not right on target, would become a source of instability. Neither the pattern estimated by the most sophisticated methods nor by simpler methods is favorable to a flexible monetary policy (section 7.5). The effects on GNP of seasonal or other periodic movements in monetary growth are briefly discussed in section 7.6. Section 7.7 summarizes our findings.

7.2 Kinds of Flexibility

Proponents of a flexible monetary policy often have several objectives in mind, not all of which are beset by a lag problem. Indeed, a lag in monetary effects on economic activity means that day-to-day variations in monetary growth may be smoothed over by the lag and have no long-run importance for economic activity and prices. Consequently, such day-to-day variations can be made in pursuit of a transient objective without interfering with economic stabilization goals. In appraising the flexibility of monetary policy, therefore, we should distinguish three different objectives of monetary policy according to the time span over which they apply. Spans from a day up to two or three weeks may be termed transient; the short run covers spans from a month to three or four quarters, and the long run from one to several years or longer.

On a day-to-day basis, open-market operations may be used to offset transient variations in the expansion multiplier of the banking system. Such variations originate within the monetary system and affect the growth rate of the money stock. A major part of the day-to-day activity of Federal Reserve open-market operations is devoted to offsetting such variations and is believed to be desirable to control the stock of money in the short run. It can be debated whether day-to-day variations in monetary growth are of consequence, and therefore whether it is worthwhile trying to moderate them, but in any event such policy actions to offset transient movements in financial markets, typically undertaken by Federal Reserve, have little import for economic stabilization.

For the long run, policy seeks a high level of employment and reasonable price stability. There may be disagreement at any particular time on the combination of employment and price change it is desirable to try to achieve. But, given the long-run goal, it will be consistent with a particular average rate of monetary growth. So far as the long-run goal is concerned, the monetary growth rate would not have to be adjusted except perhaps infrequently for changes in the growth trend of monetary velocity. The transient and long-run objectives of monetary policy entail no problem with lags. It is the short-run objectives which face a problem.

Proponents of a flexible monetary policy argue that all three time horizons should be the concern of monetary policy, but they put particular emphasis on the need for short-run flexibility. The purpose is to moderate cyclical fluctuations in economic activity and financial disturbances which last longer than a few weeks. These two objectives are partly related, since moderating fluctuations in financial markets may help to stabilize economic activity. This is true of shifts in preferences by the public as between money balances and other financial assets. These shifts lead to changes in interest rates that can affect aggregate demand, and an accommodating monetary policy would in this case keep both interest rates and aggregate demand on a stable course. The problem is that changes in interest rates can also reflect shifts in the demand for capital goods, and if interest rates are stabilized under these circumstances, an accommodating monetary policy will destabilize aggregate activity by feeding an inflation when interest rates rise or deepening a depression when they fall.[4] Unfortunately, there is often no clear indication of the reason for changes in interest rates at the moment they occur. To avoid the possibility of interfering with the more important long-run objective of stabilizing aggregate demand, therefore, a policy of moderating changes in interest rates has to reverse itself within a short time period so as not to veer away from the appropriate long-run rate of monetary growth.

Discussions of monetary policy have long noted this conflict between the stabilization of interest rates and of aggregate demand. But the conflict is often obscured by the altogether different question of using interest rates and general financial conditions as input data for forecasting economic activity and as indicators of whether the long-run goals are being achieved. A long-run goal for employment and prices implies some appropriate behavior of monetary growth and interest rates as well as other economic variables, and any group of these variables can in principle serve as indicators. In this way interest rates and financial conditions may certainly be relevant to policy-making, but their function as indicators does not mean that they should be stabilized as targets—that is, as the objective of policy. The proper role of financial conditions in forecasting economic activity and as indicators of policy is a technical question which we put aside here.

The frequent changes that occur in financial markets nevertheless invite short-run variations in policy both to moderate the financial disturbances and to counteract the change in economic activity which those disturbances appear to indicate is underway (assuming the two objectives are consistent). Here the flexibility of policy can come into sharp conflict with the lag in its effect. Suppose that money has been growing at a rate which was thought appropriate to achieve the desired growth in aggregate demand for several years ahead. Then some new information (financial or other) becomes available indicating that aggregate demand will be lower—though not permanently so—than the long-run goal in the next several quarters. Should monetary policy attempt to correct the shortfall? The answer depends in part upon how quickly policy actions can be expected to affect aggregate demand. A change in money balances sets in motion a chain of adjustments which ultimately produces a change in aggregate expenditures, but the adjustments are spread over a considerable period of time. Hardly anyone expects policy to have its major effect on aggregate expenditures within a couple of months. But suppose it has some partial effect within a few quarters. The question can then be reformulated to bring out the problem: Should monetary growth be sharply adjusted to produce the desired effect in a few quarters with the intention of reversing it later to avoid interfering with the long-run goal?

Whether such short-run flexibility in monetary policy accomplishes its purpose is a lively issue, because the Federal Reserve makes large and frequent changes in the rate at which it supplies reserves to the banking system, apparently for all the reasons cited above. Present monetary policy works to offset transient fluctuations in the utilization of reserves by banks and to moderate other sources of disturbance to financial markets as they occur; this is the first kind of flexibility cited above. Monetary policy also pursues the second kind of flexibility to achieve stability over the short run: it is clear from the reports of the Open Market Committee that short-run operations are based on forecasts of economic activity for several quarters ahead with a view to altering the outcome in line with employment and price-level objectives, not to mention stability of financial markets.

To what extent, then, can short-run variations in policy be successful in stabilizing economic activity and prices and, despite the lag in its effect, not be a source of instability? If the net effect of a flexible policy is to increase instability in the economy at large, it cannot be justified. We shall first examine the accumulated evidence on the lag, and then the implications for policy.

7.3 Evidence on the Monetary Lag

7.3.1 Step Dates

The first statistical evidence on the lag was presented some years ago by Clark Warburton and then by Friedman and Anna J. Schwartz.[5] Warburton's measure of the lag, based on turning points in the deviations of monetary growth from its trend, is subject to considerable error because of difficulties in determining the trend. Friedman and Schwartz measured the lag from steps in the rate of change of money to corresponding business cycle turns.[6] The step method treats the monetary lag as discrete; that is, after a delay, the impact of the change in monetary growth on activity is assumed to be concentrated at one point in time.

The lags based on these steps since 1921 are shown in table 7.1 for cyclical turns in general business activity, as given by the National Bureau chronology, and in GNP. The starting date is the earliest for which quarterly GNP is available. General business activity is the most relevant single benchmark for monetary effects. While GNP gives somewhat different results, it is also relevant because most of the statistical lag patterns to be examined were estimated for GNP.[7]

Table 7.1   **Lead (−) or Lag (+) of Steps in Monetary Growth Rate[a] Compared with Corresponding Cyclical Turns in Business Activity and GNP, 1921–1970 (Quarters)**

Date and Direction of Step Turn in Monetary Growth Rate[a]		Reference Cycles[b] (1)	GNP[c] (2)
1921 IV	up	+1	0
1922 IV	down	−2	−5
1924 I	up	−2	−2
1925 III	down	−4	−5
1926 IV	up	−4	−6
1928 I	down	−6	−6
1932 II	up	−3	−3
1936 II	down	−4	−5
1938 II	up	0	0
1945 III	down	+2	+1
1949 III	up	−1	−1
1952 IV	down	−2	−2
1954 I	up	−2	−1
1955 III	down	−8	−8
1957 IV	up	−2	−1
1959 II	down	−4	−4
1960 II	up	−3	−3
1962 I	down	none	none
1962 III	up	none	none
1966 I	down	none	−3
1966 IV	up	none	−1
1969 II	down	−2	−1
1969 IV	up	−4	−4
Median 1920–38		−3	−5
1945–70		−2	−1½

Sources: Monetary step turns, Friedman and Schwartz (unpublished manuscript), giving dates for M_1 through 1969 IV, as in Edward Gramlich, "The Usefulness of Monetary and Fiscal Policy as Discretionary Stabilization Tools," *Journal of Money, Credit, and Banking* 3 (May 1971): 506–32. Reference dates, Geoffrey H. Moore, ed., *Business Cycle Indicators* (Princeton, N.J.: Princeton University Press for NBER, 1961), 1:671, and Solomon Fabricant, "Recent Economic Changes and the Agenda of Business-Cycle Research," *National Bureau Report* 8, Supplement (May 1971):26, table 2. GNP before 1929, Harold Barger and Lawrence Klein (unpublished worksheets; thereafter, Department of Commerce).

[a]Narrow money supply, M_1.

[b]Skipped reference turns are 1945 IV (trough) and 1948 IV (peak).

[c]Nominal GNP through 1962 trough, real GNP thereafter.

The lags in column 1 of table 7.1 for business activity have an interquartile range of 1½ to 4 quarters and an overall median of 2.

7.3.2   The Step Dates before and after World War II

It is interesting that the medians shown for the two subperiods suggest that the lags after World War II are somewhat shorter than before. The growth of various money substitutes since World War II (particularly savings and loan deposits, time certificates of deposit, Treasury bills, and commercial paper) is often taken to imply just the opposite. John G. Gurley and Edward Shaw, writing of developments in the 1950s, touched off a voluminous literature on the dangers of money substitutes to the efficacy of monetary policy.[8] Their argument was that the growth of substitutes makes the demand for money balances more responsive to changes in interest rates, with the result that changes in the money stock take longer to affect aggregate expenditures. Supposedly a very elastic demand for money balances readily absorbs changes in the money stock through movements along the demand curve, thus delaying the effect on aggregate expenditures. Whatever the merits of the argument, the interest elasticity does not appear to have increased. We have estimated the short-run interest elasticity of money demand separately for the 1920s and 1953–65, using the same functional form to facilitate comparison, and find no evidence of an increase. It seems to be roughly the same or possibly lower now. Although the growth of money substitutes contributed to the long-run decline in money demand which is reflected in the postwar rise in monetary velocity, apparently it did not increase the interest elasticity of the remaining balances.[9]

7.3.3   Distributed Lags

The reduction in the average length of the lag after World War II, however, has not been great enough to counter a basic difficulty confronting a flexible monetary policy. The difficulty pertains to our imperfect knowledge of the lag in monetary effects on economic activity. The lag varies considerably over time, owing in part to errors in the data as well as the existence of other cyclical developments that reinforce or offset the monetary effects. The variation is also a reflection of the diverse channels through which monetary effects are produced, which means that the resulting changes in aggregate expenditures occur after delays of different durations. Hence, depending on the particular channels of response characterizing a cyclical episode, the average duration of the lag is likely to vary from one period to the next.

Even without changes from period to period, the various channels through which monetary effects are produced have different lag times. The differences mean that the total effects of a monetary step are distributed over time. Numerous studies have estimated the average time distribution of the lag by relating GNP to the behavior of the money stock in past quarters, taking account in some cases of other influences on GNP. The regression coefficients of past monetary changes can be interpreted as forming the weights of a distributed lag. The regression which estimates these weights has the advantage of utilizing every observation of the time series within the period examined, instead of ignoring all observations except those around the step turns. But it also has the disadvantage, which is not true of the step dates, of assuming a fixed lag distribution over the period covered and of treating every observation as equally important in estimating monetary effects.[10]

Estimates of a distributed lag were presented by Friedman and David I. Meiselman in their 1963 study,[11] and their general approach was followed in subsequent work by the research staff of the Federal Reserve Bank of St. Louis.[12] The widely discussed St. Louis equation is a relation between changes in GNP and lagged changes in the money stock, holding constant a variable representing fiscal policy (namely, changes in high-employment federal expenditures). Various versions of the lag pattern have been estimated, depending upon the period covered and the number of terms in the lag.

All versions of the St. Louis lag pattern have the same general form.[13] The weights are the largest for the current and most recent past quarters, gradually declining thereafter, and becoming negative after the fourth quarter if lag terms are included for such earlier quarters. Overshooting at the beginning is indicated when initial terms produce more than the final total effect. Negative weights at the end provide a partial offset. Such a lag pattern is theoretically appealing. It means that monetary changes induce a movement in the ratio of money to GNP initially away from its starting level because of the delayed effect on GNP, but that the ratio eventually moves back toward a long-run equilibrium level. At some point, therefore, the rate of change in GNP will have to exceed the rate of change in the money stock for a while in order that the ratio of money to GNP can move back toward its starting level. Hence we observe overshooting in which the rate of change of GNP goes past its new equilibrium for a while.[14]

We reestimated various versions of the St. Louis equation and selected one as representative.[15] Its lag pattern is presented in column 2 of table 7.2 as St. Louis A along with others to be discussed shortly. The shape of the lag pattern remains largely the same for a smaller or larger number of lag terms included in the regression equation. As usually presented, the St. Louis equation expresses the variables in dollar amounts, but here we used percentage changes. The percentage form makes the result more applicable to a variety of time periods among which the dollar levels of the variables differ considerably.

Table 7.2   **Estimates of the Distributed Lag of Monetary Effects**

Lag Period (Quarters)	Steps (1)	St. Louis A (2)	St. Louis B (3)	Silber (4)	FRB-MIT-Penn A (5)	FRB-MIT-Penn B (6)
0		.52	0	.32	.17	.13
1		.62	.96	.75	.12	.05
2		.47	.63	.68	.25	.16
3		.22	.26	.32	.10	.03
4		−.03	−.06	−.12	.21	.10
5		−.21	−.26	−.46	.00	.00
6		−.26	−.31	−.49	.12	.05
7		−.22	−.22	−.01	.02	.03
8		−.10			.02	.03
9						.11
10						.11
11						.11
12						.11
Average length of lag[a]	2.6	1.2	1.6	1.5	2.8	6.1

Note: No entry is shown in col. 1 since the step lag is not distributed. Cols. 2–4 give regression coefficients of a regression of GNP on the monetary variable. Cols. 5–6 give coefficients based on a simulation. Coefficients have been adjusted to sum to unity (see n. 25 below). Details of estimation of cols. 2–6 are as follows: (Col. 2) Percentage change in GNP regressed on percentage change in M_1, 1954 I to 1971 II. The fitting used an Almon polynomial lag, 4th degree, with zero end-point constraint at the tailend. (Col. 3) Same as col. 2, except that the monetary variable for the concurrent quarter was omitted. (Col. 4) Change in GNP regressed on change in monetary base as compiled and published by Federal Reserve Bank of St. Louis, 1953 I to 1969 I. See William L. Silber, "The St. Louis Equation: 'Democratic' and 'Republican' Versions and Other Experiments," *Review of Economics and Statistics* 53 (Nov. 1971): 372–75. (Cols. 5 and 6) Simulation of model (see note 24 below). Franco Modigliani, "Monetary Policy and Consumption: Linkages via Interest Rate and Wealth Effects in the FMP Model," in Federal Reserve Bank of Boston, *Consumer Spending and Monetary Policy: The Linkages* (Boston, 1971), pp. 9–84: figures kindly supplied by the author. Col. 5 is a simulation of a decrease in demand deposits, and col. 6, a simulation of an increase.

[a]For col. 1, mean of entries in table 7.1, col. 1. For cols. 2–6, weighted averages, each a sum of products of the lag period (through period 3 only for cols. 2–4, and full period for cols. 5–6) times the coefficients, divided by the sum of the coefficients included.

The other lag patterns represent various attempts, with only partial success, to overcome a problem of feedback for which the St. Louis equation has been criticized. This problem is the bias produced by economic influences on the money supply. An increase in GNP, for example, may induce banks to expand loans by reducing excess reserve ratios or increasing borrowings from Federal Reserve Banks. There are limits to how far this bank-generated expansion can go without an increase in nonborrowed reserves, but it may produce some concurrent correlation between changes in GNP and in the money supply which is not due to monetary effects on GNP. The lag weight at time zero may be spuriously enlarged by this feedback and make the average lag in monetary effects appear shorter than it is.

A drastic method for avoiding concurrent feedback is arbitrarily to assume that the concurrent coefficient is zero and to impose that constraint on the estimated pattern. The lag pattern shown in column 3 of table 7.2 as St. Louis *B* was derived by this method. It has a slightly longer average lag, as expected, but two obvious drawbacks. The method forces any concurrent monetary effects to be zero as well, which makes the average lag appear longer than it probably is. At the same time the method does not avoid the effect of feedback in the remaining lag terms.[16]

One method of dealing with feedback is to use the monetary base (that is, bank reserves plus currency held by the public) in place of the money supply. The effects of GNP on the expansion multiplier of the banking system are thereby omitted. As an alternative to the equation using the money supply, a version of the St. Louis equation using the monetary base was also presented.[17] The latter approach was then adopted by staff members of the Board of Governors and of the Federal Reserve Bank of New York.[18] Column 4 of table 7.2 gives a later version by William L. Silber which is preferable for our purposes because he included more terms at the far end of the lag distribution.[19] We have assumed that his estimates can be treated as pertaining to changes in the money stock.

The Silber equation has the disadvantage that it incorporates the lag time from the monetary base to the money stock as well as from money to GNP. Yet the average length of his lag pattern does not exceed most of the others, perhaps because the inside lag of the banking system is short. If we were to go further and exclude member-bank borrowing as well from the monetary variable, on the grounds that such borrowing is endogenous and not offset by Federal Reserve open-market operations, the appropriate monetary variable is nonborrowed reserved. Richard G. Davis has shown that the inside lag (from a change in nonborrowed reserves to a change in demand deposits) then appears to be longer, and Michael J. Hamburger, that the total inside and outside lag is longer.[20] We have not included such lag distributions in order to maintain the comparability of the different lag patterns analyzed here. The longer lag implied by models based on nonborrowed reserves would increase the difficulty of conducting a stabilizing monetary policy.

Although Silber's use of the monetary base avoids feedback from GNP to bank reserve ratios and currency holdings, it incorporates any feedback from GNP to the monetary base due to a systematic Federal Reserve response to economic and financial developments (as do the other equations as well as those using nonborrowed reserves). For example, if the Federal Reserve moderated movements in interest rates which accompany fluctuations in GNP, the monetary base would tend to display a positive covariation with GNP. A special econometric technique devised by Christopher A. Sims shows, however, that feedback on the money stock is not strong enough to account for the lag relationship between money and GNP, and indeed does not appear to be very important if we disregard the concurrent quarter.[21] Sim's technique does not deal with feedback in that quarter and so does not rule out an important immediate feedback from GNP to money. If it is important, however, it has the effect of raising the estimated weight of the concurrent term in the lag distribution and of making the average lag appear shorter than it is. Hence the St. Louis and Silber patterns may understate the lag and therefore the difficulties of flexible monetary policy. (The St. Louis B pattern in table 7.2 does not appear to be an adequate solution to this feedback problem, possibly because of serial correlation in the variables.)

Another estimation problem recently discussed by Levis Kochin arises from the policy control of monetary growth to stabilize the economy.[22] Insofar as monetary policy succeeds in offsetting the effects on economic activity of various nonmonetary disturbances, part of the fluctuation in monetary growth will not correspond with observed movements in GNP. In the extreme case, if monetary policy succeeded in removing all fluctuation from GNP, the correlation between GNP and money would be zero. If the stabilization policy is partially but not completely successful, the correlation will be negative, and if the stabilization policy overcorrects for nonmonetary disturbances, the correlation will be positive. Since we observe a positive correlation, monetary policy in practice overcorrects; that is, less fluctuation in monetary growth would reduce the fluctuation in GNP growth. But insofar as monetary policy is successful in offsetting the effect on GNP of some nonmonetary disturbances, the observed relationship between GNP and money does not portray the full effects of money. Moreover, in that case, it is not at all clear how the estimates of the lag distribution are affected.

In theory the solution to this estimation problem is to take account of all the effects on GNP of nonmonetary variables which monetary policy partially offsets. The estimation procedure can then allow for the interaction between monetary growth and other variables.

The intention of the large econometric models is indeed to take account of all influences on GNP. Columns 5 and 6 of table 7.2 present the lag pattern of monetary effects implied by the FRB-MIT-Penn econometric model.[23] This is a large-scale model which takes into account many relationships, including feedback from GNP to the financial system and nonmonetary influences on GNP. Despite simplifications to make the model manageable, it has the most elaborate financial sector of any econometric model so far constructed and represents the "state of the art" of model building as it exists today. Yet we are not alone in doubting seriously whether even this elaborate model deals adequately with feedback and with the more important problem just discussed of isolating the effects of stabilization policies. So far it has proved difficult to capture in an econometric model all the disturbances affecting GNP which monetary policy may try, in part successfully, to offset. We regard the lag estimates produced by the FRB-MIT-Penn model—the best of the attempts to allow for interactions—as representative of large econometric models.

The lag pattern of this model was derived by simulation.[24] The estimates represent the effect of a hypothetical $1 billion change in demand deposits on the level of GNP in 1967 I. A simulation for a decrease in demand deposits is shown as *A* in table 7.2, and one for an increase as *B*. Because monetary policy will produce changes in GNP before the full effects on the level occur, we expect the FRB-MIT-Penn lag pattern to be longer than the others. The longer average lag of the pattern may also be due to the fixed channels of monetary effects it prescribes. Changes in monetary policy in the model have the effect of changing particular interest rates and thereby various components of investment and consumption. Insofar as the actual channels are more diverse and varying than the model provides for, the effects tend to be understated and very likely tend to be faster in coming than it predicts.

The lag patterns in table 7.2 have been adjusted to sum to unity.[25] Thus each weight gives the percentage of the total effect which occurs in each quarter. Although none of the estimation procedures imposed such a condition, we made the adjustment so that they would all give the same long-run relation between GNP and the money stock. (The adjustment also converts the FRB-MIT-Penn patterns, which were estimated from variables in dollar terms, into a form applicable to variables in percentage terms.) The condition is theoretically appealing. For the levels of the variables, a sum equal to unity means that the ratio of money to GNP eventually returns to its initial level. For rates of change of the variables, it means that the growth rates of GNP and the money stock eventually become equal.[26]

The patterns shown in table 7.2 represent the best of recent research on monetary lags.[27] Each of the methods of estimation presents certain problems, as noted, and none can be clearly preferred. Hence the exact form of the pattern remains in doubt. All agree, however, in showing a distributed lag covering many quarters. On that the evidence is clear. If monetary policy is to take account of lags, it will have to reckon with the results of studies such as these.

7.4   Turning Points Implied by the Lag Patterns

Whether the lag in monetary effects implied by these patterns is biased toward the long or the short side can be tested by the turning points in business activity derived from them. This test also indicates how consistently such fixed lag patterns fit the data over a long period, and particularly whether the variability of the leads in step turns can be explained by the configuration of monetary growth surrounding the steps.

We calculated the predicted levels of GNP from 1921 to 1971 estimated by each lag pattern. As noted earlier, we used the predicted level before 1960 and the level divided by the implicit price deflator for GNP thereafter, because of the difficulty of selecting turns in the undeflated level during the second half of the 1960s. For the FRB-MIT-Penn pattern pertaining to levels, the logarithm of demand deposits was run through the lag pattern to derive an index of the level of GNP (in logarithms). Of course, this procedure gives only an approximation to a full simulation of the model. For the other patterns pertaining to rates of change, the quarterly rate of change of M_1 was run through the lag pattern to generate an estimated rate of change of GNP (with the constant term omitted). These rates of change of GNP were then used to derive an index of the level of GNP. Since the lag patterns are adjusted to sum to unity, the average rate of growth of this GNP index is the same as that of the money stock. The trend of the index and the trend of actual GNP differ by the trend in the ratio of GNP to the money stock. But these trend differences have little effect on the dates of turning points.

We selected peaks and troughs in the estimated GNP indexes. The turns not corresponding to turns in actual GNP were disregarded. The selected turns were compared with the actual peaks and troughs in National Bureau reference cycles (which sometimes differ from the turns in GNP).[28] The timing differences are presented in table 7.3, together with the average of these differences compared with the average deviation for step cycle turns.

The FRB-MIT-Penn model has the shortest leads or longest lags (because of its long pattern). It fails to register many of the turns. The turning points of the other lag patterns, which are shorter than it is, are generally close to the turns in business activity. The differences in timing among the three lag patterns excluding FRB-MIT-Penn do not appear significant. (As we shall see below, however, the differences are important for policy purposes.) On this evidence, it is hard to choose among these three. The variability in their timing is about the same. The Silber pattern has the smallest average deviation because of its bullseye at the 1957 III peak, which the St. Louis patterns miss by well over a year. Otherwise it is not more accurate.

Table 7.3   **Lead (−) or Lag (+) and Average Deviation of Estimated Turns Compared with Actual Turns in Business Activity, 1921–70 (Quarters)**

Peaks and Troughs in Business Activity[a]		Steps	St. Louis		Silber	FRB-MIT-Penn
			A	B		
1921 III	trough	+3.6	+2	+2	+2	b
1923 II	peak	+0.6	+1	+1	0	b
1924 III	trough	+0.6	−1	−1	−1	−2
1926 III	peak	−1.4	−2	−2	−2	b
1927 IV	trough	−1.4	−1	−2	−2	b
1929 III	peak	−3.4	+1	+2	+2	+1
1933 I	trough	−0.4	+1	−1	−1	+7
1937 II	peak	−1.4	−1	0	0	+2
1938 II	trough	+2.6	+1	+1	+1	b
						b
1948 IV	peak	b	−4	−3	−3	b
1949 IV	trough	+1.6	0	0	−1	b
1953 II	peak	+0.6	0	+1	−1	b
1954 III	trough	+0.6	−1	0	−1	b
1957 III	peak	−5.4	−6	−7	0	b
1958 II	trough	+0.6	−1	0	0	b
1960 II	peak	−1.4	−3	−2	−3	b
1961 I	trough	−0.4	−1	−1	−1	b
1966 IV	peak	−0.4	−1	0	−1	−1
1967 I	trough	+1.6	0	+1	+1	0
1969 IV	peak	+0.6	−1	0	−1	−2
1970 IV	trough	−1.4	−3	−2	−2	−3
Average absolute deviation[c]		1.5	1.5	1.3	1.2	2.2

Note: Entries for step turns are the deviations from the average lead of 2.6 quarters (see table 7.2). GNP, estimated from lag patterns, was deflated for 1966–70 before selecting turns. Without deflation, most of the estimates skip the turns. For FRB-MIT-Penn estimated GNP, peaks were selected from estimates based on table 7.2, col. 5, troughs from estimates based on table 7.2, col. 6.

[a]Peaks and troughs in National Bureau reference cycles (see source note to table 7.1) except for 1966–67, which is not designated a reference cycle and is based on turns in real GNP. The 1945 reference peak and trough are omitted.

[b]No matching turn.

[c]Average of leads or lags, without regard to sign, excluding 1948 peak and, for FRB-MIT-Penn, other skipped turns.

This last result deserves emphasis. If the variability in step lags were due to the assumption of a discrete rather than distributed lag, a distributed lag should give more consistent estimates of turning point dates. As measured by average deviations, the estimated lag patterns perform only a little better than the step dates. The failure of the lag distributions to give sharply better predictions is presumably due to variability in the true lag pattern over time, so that fixed patterns do not give very good estimates.

7.5   Implications of the Monetary Lag for Policy

Effects which are distributed over time create problems for policy. Granted, if the lag pattern were known with certainty, the monetary authorities could calculate a path of monetary growth to achieve the desired path of GNP. But the calculated path appears to require wide swings in monetary growth. Because of uncertainty over the effects, large swings pose the danger of adding to instability.

We can examine the problems inherent in these lag patterns by means of a simple but common situation. Suppose that the economy lies below the desired growth path of GNP and monetary policy is called upon to close the gap in one quarter and thereafter to hold GNP at the previous rate of growth. The gap between the desired and actual level of GNP is the most common criterion by which policy is judged, for this gap influences the rate of unemployment and rate of change of prices; but a more complicated assessment of policy would take the effects on these and other variables explicitly into account. For present purposes we do not distinguish between monetary effects on prices and on real output. Table 7.4 gives the required path of monetary growth for closing a gap between the desired and actual levels of GNP. It is assumed that the previous monetary growth rate, if unchanged, would keep GNP growing at the desired rate but along a trend now viewed as 2 percent too low. The figures shown for monetary growth increase GNP 2 percent above its previous level in one quarter and thereafter maintain the previous rate of growth.

The results point to two serious difficulties for policy. First, the initial increase in the monetary growth rate must be relatively large, because the concurrent effect on GNP is small. Thereafter the rate must swing up and down to offset the continuing effects of the initial and subsequent changes. For example, with the St. Louis pattern, to achieve a 2 percent increase in GNP above its previous level in one quarter, the money stock must grow in that quarter at a 15.5 percent annual rate ($2 \times 4/.52$). To offset the lagged effect of that 15.5 percent rate of monetary growth, the growth rate in the next quarter would have to drop to -18.6 at an annual rate. To offset the cumulated lagged effects of the 15.5 percent rate in the initial quarter and the -18.6 percent in the quarter after that, the monetary growth rate in the following quarter would then have to rise to 8.4 percent, and so back and forth in subsequent quarters.[29]

The lag patterns are jagged, due no doubt to errors in the estimates. The true distribution of monetary effects could theoretically have a

Table 7.4   **Monetary Growth Policy Which Achieves Target Level of GNP 2 Percent above Trend in One Quarter: Deviations from Long-run Growth (Percentage per Year)**

Quarter	St. Louis		Silber	FRB-MIT-Penn	
	A	B		A	B
0	15.5	none	25.0	46.2	63.0
1	− 18.6		− 58.6	− 30.7	− 23.8
2	8.4		84.2	− 46.4	− 100.5
3	0.0		− 97.8	49.6	40.3
4	1.5		118.4	− 5.5	31.1
5	− 0.5		− 139.7	− 4.6	− 26.8
6	0.1		159.4	9.6	− 10.5
7	0.4		− 199.7	− 42.1	− 7.3
8	− 1.1		299.8	52.6	15.9
9	1.3		− 467.2	1.7	− 18.9
10	1.4		694.8	− 62.2	− 40.5
11	− 1.9		− 991.2	59.5	58.4
12	0.7		1379.2	− 20.4	16.2
13	0.1		− 1865.9	− 12.6	− 24.0
14	0.4		2475.4	49.6	24.1

Note: Method of computation—For each quarter a change in monetary growth is calculated which will maintain GNP 2 percent above trend, given the lag pattern and past monetary growth. It is assumed that monetary growth was at the trend rate before the beginning quarter and thereafter is as calculated. Rates would be double for 4 percent increase in target, and so on.

variety of patterns, but it is more likely represented by a relatively smooth curve. The jagged estimates therefore impose jumps on the required monetary growth path here which are not in fact needed to stabilize GNP. But this source of fluctuation is probably of minor importance.

The main difficulty is that the swings become larger and larger—that is, they are explosive or close to it for all except the regular St. Louis equation (A).[30] If not explosive, the fluctuations in the monetary growth rate would converge upon the long-run equilibrium rate which, in table 7.4, is assumed to be zero (the rates are given as deviations from the long-run path). There is nothing in the property of lag distributions which requires them to have this kind of stability for policy purposes. Even in the St. Louis case, which is convergent, the changes in monetary growth have to follow a complicated back-and-forth pattern for many quarters.

A necessary requirement for stability is that the later effects and the needed offsets to them be sufficiently small relative to the initial effects. It might seem, therefore, that the overshooting produced by some patterns is beneficial to policy, since a given early effect on GNP can be produced by small increases in monetary growth. But the overshooting requires complicated offsets later as the initial increase runs through the negative part of the lag distribution.

Given the uncertainties in forecasting future GNP and our limited knowledge of the precise lag patterns, monetary policy cannot risk large swings in monetary growth. Small errors of diagnosis would reinforce rather than reduce instability in the economy. It is clear from table 7.4 that monetary growth rates appropriate for one pattern would produce considerable undesired fluctuation in GNP if one of the other patterns were in fact the correct one. Much of the literature on stabilization policies assumes that the magnitude of errors of execution is given independently of the complexity of the policies to be followed. But actually the magnitude of error is likely to increase sharply with complexity.

Based on such lag patterns as these, we conclude that stabilization goals must be content with longer time horizons than one quarter. How long? A first step toward an answer is provided by table 7.5. Here the policy goal is to achieve a 2 percent increase in GNP in two quarters rather than one. The required monetary growth in each quarter is determined by the difference between the desired and actual level of GNP and the weight of the first two terms of the lag pattern, which give the monetary effect on GNP occurring in the first two quarters.

While this policy rule reduces the fluctuation in monetary growth considerably, much still remains. The least fluctuating path is still given by the St. Louis pattern A, but its required monetary growth goes from 7 to −3 percent at an annual rate in the first three quarters and follows a convergent but still complicated course thereafter. The gain of a less fluctuating monetary growth path occurs at the expense of deviations from the GNP target. The target is never reached but only approached, since policy is continually offsetting the accumulating effects of previous monetary changes.[31] Deviations from the target are shown in table 7.6 for the St. Louis A and FRB-MIT-Penn models. The deviations are expressed as percentages of the target increase and in this form are invariant to the size of the desired target increase. For St. Louis, deviations from the target level of GNP of nearly 20 percent continue until the fifth quarter, after which the discrepancy remains between 5 and 11 percent. For FRB-MIT-Penn, the deviations continue to range up to 16 percent.

At first sight a discrepancy which after a few quarters remains below 11 or even 16 percent seems attractive. But we need only glance back at table 7.5 to realize how unattainable even this weak policy rule is. It entails extremely complicated and continuing variations in monetary growth. A realistic policy must be based on fairly modest and simple variations in monetary growth. However, as we weaken the stabili-

Table 7.5   **Monetary Growth Policy Which Aims for Target Level of GNP 2 Percent above Trend in Two Quarters: Deviations from Long-run Growth (Percentage per Year)**

Quarter	St. Louis A	St. Louis B	Silber	FRB-MIT-Penn A	FRB-MIT-Penn B
0	7.0	8.3	7.5	27.8	45.7
1	0.0	0.0	0.0	−11.1	−12.5
2	−2.9	−5.4	−4.8	−19.7	−38.1
3	−1.4	−2.2	−2.2	8.2	13.5
4	1.4	4.1	3.9	−2.9	8.4
5	2.4	5.1	6.1	8.8	−0.8
6	1.2	0.3	1.1	−0.3	−1.7
7	−0.4	−4.1	−7.2	−10.0	−12.6
8	−1.2	−3.7	−5.2	10.2	5.0
9	−0.6	2.0	5.5	−3.0	−11.6
10	0.8	5.7	10.0	−0.2	−16.2
11	1.4	2.1	0.5	3.6	20.1
12	0.5	−4.3	−11.1	−6.3	2.5
13	−0.6	−5.0	−8.2	5.8	11.8
14	−0.8	1.0	7.9	0.2	11.3

Note: Method of computation—Same as table 7.4, except that monetary growth in each quarter is determined by dividing the deviation from the target level of GNP by the fraction of monetary effects which occurs in two quarters according to the lag distribution. Thus the entry for St. Louis A in quarter 0 is 2 × 4/1.14 (sum of first two weights in table 7.2), or 7 percent per year. This yields an increase in GNP above trend in that quarter of .91 (7 × .52/4). The deviation from the target level of a 2 percent increase above trend is 1.09. This is reduced to zero in the next quarter, because the 7 percent monetary growth of the initial quarter then increases GNP by 1.09 (7 × .62/4). Hence a zero monetary growth rate in period 1 achieves the target level of an increase in GNP of 2 percent above trend. No further change would be required in period 2, but past monetary growth will generate an increase in GNP above trend of .82 (7 × .47/4), producing a deviation from the target level. A negative monetary growth rate in period 2 is therefore required: −2.9 (−.82 × 4/1.14). And so on. Monetary growth rates would be double for 4 percent increase in target, and so on.

zation target further in order to reduce the fluctuations in monetary growth, say by achieving the target in three quarters instead of two, the deviations from the target will increase. There is no smooth pattern of monetary growth which will closely approximate desired changes in GNP within a few quarters. As policy tries to reduce deviations from the target, the more complex becomes the monetary growth path.

The two-quarter rule depicted by tables 7.5 and 7.6 seems to us a reasonable way to extend the perfect but unattainable one-quarter policy depicted by table 7.4. There is a trade-off here between the size of required variations in monetary growth and that of deviations from the target level of GNP. Different rules produce different combinations of fluctuation in the two variables, and there is no clear optimum. Continuing fluctuations in monetary growth can be avoided, of course, by

Table 7.6   **Deviations of GNP from Given Target Level under a Two-quarter Policy Horizon (Percentage of Target Increase)**

Quarter	St. Louis A	FRB-MIT-Penn A	B
0	−55	−40	−27
1	0	−24	−20
2	+22	+4	+3
3	+12	−8	−5
4	−11	−3	−10
5	−19	−16	−10
6	−9	−15	−9
7	+3	−1	−1
8	+9	−16	−4
9	+5	−11	+3
10	−7	−4	+13
11	−11	−6	+0
12	−4	+9	−1
13	+5	+4	−8
14	+6	+8	−15

Note: The data shown are cumulated changes in GNP in each quarter, based on current quarter and past monetary growth rates, expressed as a percentage of target increase in table 7.5. Results are the same for any target level which is a constant percentage of the trend level.

simply making a change in one quarter and then maintaining a stable rate. Such a policy, however, does not solve the problem of lags. It merely shifts the consequences of the lag from money to GNP. We may illustrate with the lag pattern of the regular St. Louis equation (A). An initial growth rate of 7 percent achieves a 2 percent increase in GNP in the second quarter (table 7.5). No change in monetary growth from trend is required in the second quarter, but changes are required in subsequent quarters to offset the initial increase. If these subsequent changes were not made, it would greatly lessen the complexity of the policy. But the result would be to increase the subsequent fluctuations in GNP, as the initial increase in money worked through the lag pattern and no offsets were provided. The deviations from the GNP target increase are given in table 7.7. They do not fall below 40 percent of the target increase until the sixth quarter. Since the lag is eight quarters in length, GNP does not fluctuate after that, though it only attains seven-eighths of the target increase. This is the most favorable case for a one-shot change in monetary growth among these lag patterns. The other patterns produce even more fluctuation in GNP, because they require larger offsets.

Perhaps someone can offer a more appealing strategy than simply extending the two-quarter rule illustrated here to three or more quarters. A rule which is sometimes suggested is based on rates of change

Table 7.7   Deviations of GNP from Given Target Level for a One-quarter
                   Increase in Monetary Growth (Percentage of Target Increase)

Quarter	St. Louis A
0	−55
1	0
2	40
3	60
4	57
5	39
6	16
7	−3
8	−12

Note: The data shown are changes in GNP in each quarter, based on monetary growth
rate in quarter 0 only, expressed as a percentage of target increase. Results are the same
for any target level which is a constant percentage of the trend level.

in GNP rather than levels.[32] While such a rule appears to require less
volatility in monetary growth,[33] it does so only at the cost of larger
discrepancies from the target level. Unless shown otherwise, we conclude that any other rules which may be suggested for these lag patterns
will be equally unsatisfactory.

These results do not prove that policy cannot contribute at all to
short-run stability. Given reliable forecasts of GNP, small uncomplicated changes in monetary growth can be made to bring the economy
closer to the target. Because of uncertainty, however, the changes will
have to be modest if they are not frequently to be a source of instability.
But, if they are modest, the achievements will likewise be modest, so
that the risks of error do not obviously outweigh the possible gains.

7.6   Seasonal or Other Periodic Movements in Monetary Growth

If policy objectives with a short-run horizon are not feasible because
of lags, day-to-day objectives for financial markets might for that reason
seem feasible, on the grounds that the lag smooths over transient variations in monetary growth. For long, flat lag distributions, that is true.
But for lag distributions with overshooting, it is generally not true. The
consequences of periodic variations in monetary growth are shown in
table 7.8 for the two sample patterns used previously. It is assumed
that an average 4 percent per year rate of monetary growth is concentrated all in the first one, two, or three quarters of a symmetrical cycle.
The table shows the effect on GNP. As calculated, the level of GNP
starts below or even with the old trend, goes above, and then returns
to it, because monetary growth first speeds up and then is reversed.

Table 7.8   **Deviations of GNP from Trend Level Produced By 100 Percent Variations Around a Monetary Growth of 4 Percent per Year (Percentage of Trend Level)**

	Pattern of Monetary Growth and Lag Pattern					
	1Q Variation (8, 0, 8, 0, etc.)		2Q Variation (8, 8, 0, 0, etc.)		3Q Variation (8, 8, 8, 0, 0, 0, etc.)	
Quarter	St. Louis A	FRB-MIT-Penn A	St. Louis A	FRB-MIT-Penn A	St. Louis A	FRB-MIT-Penn A
1	+.17	+.54	−.24	+.04	−.97	0
2	0	0	+.35	+.08	−1.07	−.16
3	Repeats		+.59	+.04	−.03	+.23
4			0	0	+.93	+.22
5			Repeats		+1.04	+.38
6					0	0
					Repeats	

Note: It is assumed that the pattern of monetary growth has been in effect at least for the length of the lag patterns. Cumulated change in GNP in each quarter, based on alternative monetary growth patterns, is converted to a deviation from a 4 percent trend in GNP.

The lag patterns smooth the effect but not completely, and GNP fluctuates cyclically around the new growth path. Some of the fluctuations are not minor. The fluctuation for St. Louis with the two-quarter pattern is from −.24 to +.59, or an amplitude of .83 percent. In a trillion dollar economy, that is a fluctuation of $8.3 billion. For the three-quarter pattern, the fluctuation is $20 billion. For FRB-MIT-Penn, the fluctuations are narrower as a consequence of its long, flat lag pattern. Such fluctuations could well be eradicated in the data by an overly absorbent seasonal adjustment, but they remain real contributions to instability nonetheless.

7.7   Summary and Conclusions

For monetary policy to be stabilizing on net, either it must operate with a short lag in its effects, or if the lag is long, economic forecasting must be accurate far ahead so that monetary policy can take the lag in effect into account and be guided appropriately. These prerequisites are not an important obstacle to either transient or long-run objectives. Transient effects on financial markets can be produced with little carry-over to economic activity if the lag in effect on activity is long. And monetary policies designed for the long run have a long-run effect which is independent of lags. But for short-run policies—those which range from a quarter to a year—the unreliability of economic forecasting and the lag in monetary effects become important. The continued use and defense of short-run flexibility in monetary policy have yet to be reconciled with the growing evidence on the lag in its effect.

The issue has remained unsettled in large part because the exact pattern of the monetary lag has not been determined. Numerous studies of the lag give somewhat different results. We examined four of the most sophisticated estimates of the lag pattern and found that their predictive power of turning points in economic activity was only slightly better than that of the simple step method. This suggests that the lag distribution varies over time and cannot be reliably estimated by a fixed pattern.

Despite these drawbacks, the estimates all agree on a distributed lag of monetary effects which spans two years or more, with the strong possibility that the initial effects overshoot the long-run effect. In the light of this evidence, it no longer seems possible to maintain that the lag is short and uncomplicated. We pointed out that the step lag appeared to be shorter since World War II than formerly (contrary to some theoretical implications of the growth of money substitutes), but the decline, if any, was too slight to lessen materially the difficulties of short-run monetary stabilization.

We explored these difficulties by calculating the path of monetary growth required to achieve target levels of GNP. In the first set of calculations the target was an increase in the level to be achieved in one quarter and maintained thereafter. Such policies are sharply circumscribed by a long lag pattern because of its tendency to be explosive. This causes the offsets to the future effects of policies to become unmanageably large. The version of the St. Louis equation used here is not explosive, though pursuit of a flexible policy under its lag structure is still severely constrained by the practical need to avoid complicated swings in monetary growth. All the other patterns examined are explosive or close to it, especially the pattern implied by the FRB-MIT-Penn model, which, despite its limitations, many consider to be the most sophisticated representation of the economy so far constructed. These other patterns circumscribe much more severely than does the St. Louis equation the degree to which stabilizing variations in monetary growth are feasible.

We presented a second set of calculations for a weaker policy rule which aimed to achieve the target level in two quarters. Even under the weaker rule, the required path of monetary growth entails swings up and down from quarter to quarter, much too complicated, we believe, even to be approximated by the present state of the policy art. Attempts to do so, in the light of uncertainties over the exact form of the lag pattern, are likely to increase instability rather than reduce it. Given in addition the usual uncertainties over the course of economic activity, limited policies which push the economy mildly in the desired direction are the most that appear feasible.

Very short-run variations in monetary growth will not have large disruptive effects, because a long lag pattern tends to smooth out the effects of such variations in monetary growth. But we showed that periodic variations which are offset within one to three quarters do not necessarily have insignificant effects on economic activity. If such variations are intentionally introduced to offset undesired changes in economic activity, they must be timed and executed with considerable precision, else they will miss the mark and add to instability. Unless precisely executed, they are still a net detriment to economic stability. It is the basic difficulty of monetary sharpshooting, given the available evidence on the lag distribution and our meager knowledge of it, that stacks the case against the success of a flexible short-run monetary policy.

The evidence which has accumulated on monetary lags since Milton Friedman first proposed a constant rate of monetary growth as the wisest policy has by and large supported his case. The estimates of the lag reviewed here all indicate similar difficulties for policy. At the same time, estimates of the lag distribution differ sufficiently to indicate that we still lack the precise knowledge which, if it were available, might partially overcome these difficulties.

Notes

1. Friedman, "The Effects of a Full-Employment Policy on Economic Stability: A Formal Analysis," in *Essays in Positive Economics* (Chicago: University of Chicago, 1953), pp. 117–32.

2. Friedman, *A Program for Monetary Stability* (New York: Fordham University, 1960), p. 93.

3. Stanley Fischer and J. Phillip Cooper, "Stabilization Policy and Lags," *Journal of Political Economy* 81 (1973): 847–77; Edward Gramlich, "The Usefulness of Monetary and Fiscal Policy as Discretionary Stabilization Tools," *Journal of Money, Credit, and Banking* 3 (May 1971): 506–32; Michael J. Hamburger, "The Impact of Monetary Variables: A Survey of Recent Econometric Literature," in Federal Reserve Bank of New York, *Essays in Domestic and International Finance* (New York, 1969), pp. 37–49; James L. Pierce, "The Trade-Off between Short- and Long-Term Policy Goals," in Board of Governors of the Federal Reserve System, *Open Market Policies and Operating Procedures—Staff Studies* (Washington, D.C., 1971), pp. 99–105; James L. Pierce and Thomas D. Thomson, "Controlling the Money Stock" (manuscript, April 3, 1972).

4. In terms of the usual textbook analysis, changes in interest rates due to shifts in the *LM* schedule affect aggregate demand. Such shifts would be offset by stabilizing the general level of interest rates, so that the intersection point

of the *LM* and *IS* schedules would remain the same. When changes in interest rates reflect shifts in the *IS* schedule, however, a policy of keeping interest rates unchanged would amplify the change in aggregate demand. Numerous articles have made this point. See, for example, Jerome L. Stein, "A Method of Identifying Disturbances Which Produce Changes in Money National Income," *Journal of Political Economy* 68 (Feb. 1960): 1–16, and William Poole, "Rules-of-Thumb for Guiding Monetary Policy," in Board of Governors of the Federal Reserve System, *Open Market Policies*, pp. 135–89.

5. Clark Warburton, "The Theory of Turning Points in Business Fluctuations," *Quarterly Journal of Economics* 64 (Nov. 1950): 525–49; Friedman and Schwartz, "Money and Business Cycles," *Review of Economics and Statistics* 45 (Feb. 1963): 32–64.

6. The steps are successive high and low levels of the month-to-month percentage rate of change in money—a step peak corresponding to the last month of a high level of monetary change, a step trough to the last month of a low level of monetary change.

7. For the turns in the second half of the 1960s, GNP deflated for price changes is used, because the turns are difficult to identify in nominal GNP. The deflation, may, however, tend to shorten the lag.

8. Gurley and Shaw, *Money in a Theory of Finance* (Washington, D.C.: Brookings, 1960).

9. The possibility that such a leftward shift in the demand schedule for money balances need not increase the elasticity of the schedule was pointed out by Alvin L. Marty, "Gurley and Shaw on Money in a Theory of Finance," *Journal of Political Economy* 69 (Feb. 1961): 56–69.

10. However, dummy variables are sometimes used to hold constant the quarters in which strikes occurred. We may also note that spectral analysis can be used to segregate various frequency bands of movement in the variables. See Christopher A. Sims, "Money, Income, and Causality," *American Economic Review* 62 (Sept. 1972): 540–52.

11. Friedman and Meiselman, "The Relative Stability of Monetary Velocity and the Investment Multiplier in the United States, 1897–1958," in *Stabilization Policies* (Englewood Cliffs, N.J.: Prentice-Hall, for the Commission on Money and Credit, 1964), pp. 165–268.

12. Leonall C. Andersen and Keith M. Carlson, "A Monetarist Model for Economic Stabilization," Federal Reserve Bank of St. Louis, *Review* 52 (April 1970): 7–21; Leonall C. Andersen and Jerry Jordan, "Monetary and Fiscal Actions: A Test of Their Relative Importance and Economic Stabilization," ibid., 50 (Nov. 1968): 11–23; Michael W. Ketan, "Monetary and Fiscal Influences on Economic Activity—The Historical Evidence," ibid., 51 (Nov. 1969): 5–23.

13. One exception is the Laffer-Ranson model which involves no lag; see Arthur B. Laffer and R. David Ranson, "A Formal Model of the Economy," *Journal of Business* 44 (July 1971): 247–70. However, Michael J. Hamburger, "The Lag in the Effect of Monetary Policy: A Survey of Recent Literature," Federal Reserve Bank of New York, *Monthly Review* 53 (Dec. 1971): 289–98, has shown that their results depend critically on the inclusion of the years 1948–53, which other studies exclude as atypical due to the Federal Reserve's bond support program.

14. Although negative values in the lag distribution imply that the ratio of money to GNP begins to move back toward its original position after having first moved away from it, the return movement does not take the ratio all the way back unless the sum of the positive terms equals the sum of the negative terms (signs reversed). This condition is not imposed on the estimates and is

not satisfied in those reported here, presumably because long-run changes in the money-GNP ratio during a particular period are not captured by the constant term of the regression but instead affect the lag pattern. Ideally, movements which are not produced by variations in monetary growth should be absorbed by other variables and not be allowed to bias the estimates of the lag pattern. But such bias is difficult to prevent. The estimates of the lag pattern, therefore, will depend to some extent upon the particular period covered.

15. Our selected equation omits the fiscal variable. The omission makes little difference to the shape of the lag pattern. With the fiscal variable included in percentage terms, the lag coefficients are: .22, .37, .31, .16, .00, −.11, −.16, −13, −06.

16. Such feedback is possible even though GNP can only affect concurrent and later changes in the money stock. While there is no direct feedback on past changes in money, GNP can correlate with lagged money terms statistically because of autocorrelation in the variables.

17. Andersen and Carlson.

18. E. Gerald Corrigan, "The Measurement and Importance of Fiscal Policy Changes," Federal Reserve Bank of New York, *Monthly Review* 52 (June 1970): 133–43; Frank de Leeuw and John Kalchbrenner, "Monetary and Fiscal Actions: A Test of Their Relative Importance in Economic Stabilization—Comment," Federal Reserve Bank of St. Louis, *Review* 51 (April 1969): 6–11.

19. Silber, "The St. Louis Equation: 'Democratic' and 'Republican' Versions and Other Experiments," *Review of Economics and Statistics* 53 (Nov. 1971): 372–75. This particular version excludes the fiscal variable. With that variable included, the pattern is still about the same: .43, .97, .86, .36, −24, −.69, −70, .01.

20. Davis, "Estimating Monthly Changes in Deposits with Reduced-Form Equations" (manuscript, 1972); Hamburger, "Lag in the Effect of Monetary Policy."

21. See n. 10 above.

22. Kochin, "Judging Stabilization Policies" (Ph.D. dissertation, University of Chicago, 1972).

23. Franco Modigliani, "Monetary Policy and Consumption: Linkages via Interest Rate and Wealth Effects in the FMP Model," in Federal Reserve Bank of Boston, *Consumer Spending and Monetary Policy: The Linkages* (Boston, 1971), pp. 9–84.

24. In the simulation, demand deposits in one run were decreased and in another run increased from their actual level by $1 billion in each of the two successive quarters 1967 I and II. For each run the model then generated values of the level of GNP, given the actual values of all other exogenous variables (though it was not said what was done about nonborrowed reserves). The source (Modigliani) gives the resulting dollar decreases or increases in GNP in subsequent quarters. We have adjusted these figures to reflect a $1 billion change in the initial quarter only and then, as noted below, expressed each weight as its proportional part of the total effect. Some missing values of the lag pattern were interpolated.

25. This was done by dividing each term by the cumulative sum of the terms before adjustment.

26. For rates of change of the variables, a condition that the ratio of money to GNP return all the way to its starting level requires that the areas of the cumulative lag pattern above and below unity be equal.

The lag patterns as estimated did not satisfy these conditions of long-run equilibrium, because such conditions are difficult to meet by unconstrained equations fit to particular periods. However, if constrained estimates had been derived, they would no doubt differ somewhat from the adjusted lag patterns of table 7.2.

27. We have disregarded two estimates due to J. Ernest Tanner, "Lags in the Effects of Monetary Policy: A Statistical Investigation," *American Economic Review* 59 (Dec. 1969): 794–805, and "Lags in the Effects of Monetary Policy: Reply and Some Further Thoughts," ibid., 62 (March, 1972): 234–37, and Paul E. Smith, "Lags in the Effects of Monetary Policy: Comment," ibid., pp. 230–33, which give very short lag patterns, because they are so far at odds with other research and because their method of estimation is likely to bias the lag pattern toward the short side. In each case, the underlying model used Koyck lags to estimate the effect of interest rates on aggregate expenditures and the demand for money balances. Because of autocorrelation in the variables, the implied lag in the monetary effect on expenditures can be biased toward the short side. If the very short lags derived from these estimates were correct, full monetary effects would occur in one quarter, and a trial-and-error monetary policy to stabilize the economy would be feasible.

28. The NBER chooses reference turns after examining a variety of economic measures, including GNP in current and constant dollars, industrial production, employment, personal income, and business sales. It is the consensus of the turns in these measures, rather than the turn in GNP alone, that is the basis for the NBER decision on reference dates.

We prefer the reference dates to turns in GNP for present purposes because variations in monetary growth have effects on general business activity and not only on GNP, even though the lag distributions are estimated from regressions which use GNP as the dependent variable.

29. The FRB-MIT-Penn pattern pertains to levels of the money stock and GNP. The calculations were therefore applied to levels. The required levels of the money stock to achieve the target were then converted to rates of change for presentation in table 7.4.

30. This has a mathematical interpretation. For equations using rates of change of the money stock, the difference equation of the lag coefficients has an explosive solution if the largest root of the characteristic equation is greater than unity. It is not possible, however, to make revealing inferences about the stability of the difference equation from casual observation of the general shape of the lag pattern. See Robert S. Holbrook, "Optimal Economic Policy and the Problem of Instrument Instability," *American Economic Review* 62 (March 1972): 57–65.

31. The target could be achieved every second quarter if policy in the intervening quarters abstained from any correction, set monetary growth to the trend rate, and awaited the results of the previous quarter's correlation. But this would simply produce large deviations from the target in the intervening quarters, whereas the policy described in the text produces a deviation in every quarter which on the average is smaller.

32. Another possibility is a policy which diminishes in intensity as the goal is approached, with constraints on very large or very low rates of monetary growth. Such a policy strategy was investigated by William Poole, "Alternative Paths to a Stable Full Employment Economy," in *Brookings Papers on Economic Activity*, no. 3 (1971): 579–614, in simulations with the FRB-MIT-Penn model. His results are similar to ours, in that his rapid recovery option (see his fig. 4) takes three quarters to achieve most of the target and entails large swings in monetary growth.

33. J. Phillip Cooper and Stanley Fischer, "Simulations of Monetary Rules in the FRB-MIT-Penn Model," *Journal of Money, Credit, and Banking* 4 (May 1972): 384–96.

8   Has the Growth of Money Substitutes Hindered Monetary Policy?

Phillip Cagan and Anna J. Schwartz

8.1   Introduction

In the decade following World War II the efficacy of monetary policy as a tool for stabilizing the economy was widely debated. Many reasons were offered for questioning the efficacy of monetary policy, but most of them derived from the judgment that the interest elasticity of demand for money balances was or had become quite high. This was the main theme of Warren Smith's influential article "On the Effectiveness of Monetary Policy"[1] and of numerous other writings in the early post–World War II period before and after the Treasury-Federal Reserve Accord.

The emphasis on interest elasticity was inspired by the theoretical notion of a "liquidity trap," D. H. Robertson's (1940) apt phrase for the Keynesian special case of an infinitely elastic liquidity preference schedule, to which the monetary literature has obsessedly devoted so much attention.[2] A liquidity trap is clearly damaging to the efficacy of monetary policy, notwithstanding the Pigou wealth effect and the Patinkin real-balance effect. This is so because it implies that open-market purchases will lead money holders to absorb additional money balances and open-market sales will lead them to absorb bonds without any effect on aggregate spending on goods and services. To be sure, if the elasticity is anything less than infinite, open-market operations will affect such spending. The size of the operation required to produce the desired effect on spending in the short run is, nevertheless, positively related to the elasticity. If the elasticity is finite but very high, therefore, effective operations for stabilization purposes will have to be very large.

The authors are grateful for comments on an earlier draft from Karl Brunner, Franklin Edwards, Arthur Gandolfi, Benjamin Klein, James Lothian, Allan H. Meltzer, and William Silber.

Why be concerned about large operations? The resource costs of open-market operations do not rise with increases in size (money today is created at near zero marginal cost). Large operations are said to be harmful and undesirable because they have disruptive side effects on financial institutions and markets.[3] Ironically, these effects have shown up mainly in periods of severe monetary restraint (such as 1966 and 1969–70) precisely because of large changes in interest rates. For moderate changes of monetary policy in which financial effects are tolerable, large operations would be a problem only if the size of errors in the execution of policy due to faulty forecasting were positively related to the size of operations. If so (which is not at all obvious), high elasticity would mean that operations large enough to do the job exposed the economy to large errors of policy. It would then be better to rely on some other policy tool (if it exists) for which the effects of likely errors were smaller.

Seeming support for these views came from the growing complexity of financial markets and particularly from the growing importance of financial intermediaries. Goldsmith's empirical documentation of *The Share of Financial Intermediaries in National Wealth and National Assets, 1900–49* was published in 1954 and heightened the recognition of this historical development. Financial intermediaries were providing a rapidly growing quantity of deposit liabilities and other liquid assets which are close substitutes for checking account money. The widely discussed writings of Gurley and Shaw (1955, 1956, 1957) highlighted the diminished role of commercial banks in financial markets and raised doubts about the effectiveness of traditional monetary policy, since monetary authorities lacked control over a growing part of the financial system. Their conclusions were cautious, but many others extended their argument to claim that the growth of money substitutes had raised the interest elasticity of money demand and thus had reduced central bank control via open market operations. Later the Radcliffe *Report* in Great Britain (1959) viewed monetary policy as impotent, submerged in a sea of liquidity. The decline and fall of monetary policy was prematurely but widely proclaimed.

This earlier skepticism over the efficacy of monetary policy has diminished in the United States, and in recent years its powerful effects are generally acknowledged. Much controversy remains, however, particularly concerning its proper conduct and whether a flexible policy is desirable. But the objection to a flexible policy is based on lags in the effects and is different from the earlier criticism based on allegedly high cross-elasticities between money and other assets. Controversies over monetary policy are a tradition which goes back centuries; the corner of economics concerned with monetary theory would seem strangely peaceful without them. Our interest in this now-dated controversy reflects in part a desire to tidy up the history of monetary economics and, more importantly, a desire to help resolve some of the questions left open. The implications of the growth of financial intermediaries, despite the earlier misconceptions, are still important to monetary theory and policy.

The passage of time allows us to test the centerpiece of the earlier view: Has the growth of financial intermediaries and other financial instruments increased the short-run interest elasticity of demand for money balances (interpreted here as M_1)? This question summarizes the concern of most of the discussion since the 1950s. While the interest elasticity of money demand is pertinent to the effect of the growth of financial intermediaries, preoccupation with that elasticity in this paper does not imply a denial of channels of monetary effects which bypass financial markets.

An earlier view expounded by Henry Simons (1936) was that the growth of money substitutes was contributing to financial instability, which could be interpreted to mean instability of the demand function for money expressed in terms of the usual variables. We do not take up the instability argument here because it is largely neglected in the postwar literature dealing with the efficacy of monetary policy.

Three earlier studies presented estimates suggesting that the interest elasticity had *declined*. In his examination of the elasticity over a long period, Meltzer (1963) provided decade estimates which showed a decline from the 1920s to the 1950s. He was concerned with other issues, however, and did not comment on the decline. Teigen (1964), who took a two-equation approach to allow for supply effects, estimated the short-run interest elasticity of money demand to be $-.09$ from annual data for 1924–41 and $-.02$ from quarterly data for 1946.IV–1959.IV. He expressed surprise over the decline and attributed it to a reduction in the use of money as a store of wealth. Laidler (1966) reported a similar decline for first differences of annual data 1919–40 and 1946–60 but virtually no change in the elasticity for levels of the variables. Although we believe that the decline in interest elasticity that these three studies suggested was correct, their estimates of the difference between the 1920s and post–World War II must be regarded as tentative. Only short stretches of the later period were available at the time those studies were undertaken. Furthermore, except for Meltzer's, they included some data from 1942 to 1953—years that were contaminated by the Federal Reserve bond-support program.

At the time of writing (1972) the period for estimating the interest elasticity since the end of that program covered nearly twenty subsequent years. For comparison with an earlier period of similar economic conditions, we selected 1921–31. We examined a variety of alternative regressions designed to make estimates for the earlier and the later period fully comparable. Most of our estimates also show a decline in the interest elasticity. In a final section we discuss some reasons for the decline and the implications for policy. We also point out, as have previous studies, that the short-run elasticity, while lower in the post-war period, has never been very high.

8.2 Statistical Results

To test for changes in the interest elasticity of money demand, we estimated demand functions of various forms for quarterly data 1921.I–1931.IV and 1954.I–1971.IV. The first period begins on the earliest date for which quarterly GNP estimates are available. We wanted to make the earlier period as long as possible but believed that the abnormal fluctuations following Britain's suspension of gold payments should be excluded. The second period begins for obvious reasons with the actual (not official) termination of the Federal Reserve bond support program and ends with the latest data available at the time of computation. (Because of problems associated with the sharp rise in interest rates after 1965 discussed further below, we also use the truncated period 1954.I–1965.IV.) We omitted from consideration the intervening period 1932–53 because of the series of shocks due to the banking crisis, severe depression, wartime controls, and bond support program. The earlier period and the later truncated period are reasonably comparable in general economic climate (except perhaps for the business contraction of 1921, which was more severe than any contraction since World War II), but differ substantially in the relative importance of financial intermediaries. For example, the ratio of M_1/M_3 in 1924 was .49, and in 1964 was .37.[4]

In estimating the interest elasticity of demand for money balances, we are immediately faced with a choice of interest rates. Ideally, we should include the yields on all relevant substitutes for money, but multicollinearity makes a broad inclusion impractical. We have confined the statistical analysis to the average rate paid on savings deposits and to short-term rates on open-market instruments, principally commercial paper but also Treasury bills and call money. We interpret the concern in the literature over the efficacy of monetary policy to pertain to a short-run interest elasticity and, accordingly, we focus on short-term open-market rates. The particular series used were selected mainly because they are available for both periods; nevertheless, they are generally representative of short-term rates.

In examining the efficacy of monetary policy, it is important to separate the short-run from the long-run response of money demand to interest rates. Monetary policy also effects long-term rates; such effects are important, to be sure, but in the short run short-term open market rates generally display the strongest response to policy and the strongest effects on the demand for money balances.

In addition to interest rates, money demand equations contain real income or wealth. We use GNP, since it is the best of such aggregate series available quarterly for the earlier period. We use current GNP rather than, as is common, some moving average to approximate the concept of permanent income. This transformation will affect the absolute size of the interest coefficient but very likely not the comparative size between periods. We have omitted those variations in the specification of the regression equation which appear least likely to affect the comparison between periods.

8.2.1   A Standard Money Demand Equation

A standard form is

$$(1) \qquad \ln M/P = k + a \ln GNP/P + bi$$

where ln denotes natural logarithm, M/P is deflated money balances, GNP/P real gross national product, i a short-term interest rate, and k the constant intercept. k and a and b are regression coefficients to be estimated. To deflate M and GNP, we use the consumer price index for the earlier period and the GNP deflator (not available for the 1920s) for the later period. We shall refer to b, which theoretically should be negative in this form of the function, as the interest coefficient or slope of demand (not elasticity), because it is the percentage change in demand with respect to arithmetic (not percentage) changes in the interest rate (measured as percent per annum).[5] We purposely do not use the logarithm of the interest rate in the equation in order to avoid the resulting blow-up of small changes which occurs at low levels of the interest rate. Unlike M and GNP, the interest rate is not a dollar magnitude but a percentage rate, and therefore it does not require a log transformation to avoid heteroscedasticity.[6] Since the interest slope and elasticity move in the same direction, no important theoretical or policy issue is raised by our choice of form.

Regressions of the form of equation (1) are shown in table 8.1. The most appropriate interest rate available for both periods is the commercial paper rate. As a second choice, we compare the call money rate in the earlier period with the three-month Treasury bill rate in the later period; call loans played a role in the 1920s paralleling that of Treasury bills in the post–World War II money market.

We note that the interest coefficient has a larger negative value (statistically significant) in the earlier period, but we were not disposed to accept these results without further examination of some problems. For one thing, the interest coefficient for the later full period is positive (it should be negative to indicate a substitution between money and

Table 8.1   **Standard Money Demand Equation** (ln $M/P = k + a$ ln $GNP/P + bi^c$)

	Regression Coefficients (and t values)				
Period	ln GNP/P a	Commercial Paper Rate b	Call Money Rate b	Treasury Bill Rate b	Adj. R^2
1921.I–1931.IV	.49 (15.8)	−2.7 (7.2)	—	—	.89
	.57 (15.4)	—	−1.5 (4.8)	—	.85
1954.I–1965.IV	.08 (1.8)	−1.3 (2.0)	—	—	.05
	.04 (0.9)	—	—	−0.5 (0.8)	.00
1954.I–1971.IV	.17 (5.0)	+0.2 (0.4)	—	—	.59
	.16 (4.4)	—	—	+0.3 (0.6)	.59

Source: See Appendix.

Note: Signs of t values have been dropped. Units of measurement: a is an elasticity, b is the percentage change in dependent variable per arithmetic change of 1 percentage point in the interest rate. c denotes a short-term interest rate, measured as a decimal like .04. Estimate of the regression constant k is not shown.

other assets). When the years after 1965 are omitted, the coefficient reverses sign. The positive coefficients are not statistically significant and may be interpreted as essentially zero.

The later years present a problem. After 1966 the trend of the money stock relative to that of *GNP* rose, as is shown in figures 8.1 and 8.2 by the *slower* upward trend in the velocity ratio (*GNP* to the money stock) for those years. The regression associates this change in relative trends with the sharp rise in the interest rate, which tends to pull the regression coefficient for the interest rate in a positive direction and thus hides all or part of the negative substitution effect. The positive association is misleading: The change in relative trends of money and GNP after 1966 is not to be explained by the outbreak of inflation and the accompanying increase in the anticipated rate of inflation and in interest rates. The increase would, if anything, *reduce* the demand for money balances and *raise* the upward trend of velocity. It may be that the inflation increased uncertainty and for that reason increased money demand,[7] but no proxy for uncertainty has found wide use, and we have not experimented with one.

There is the additional problem that, to some extent, the positive coefficient may be indicative of an extraneous supply effect in which

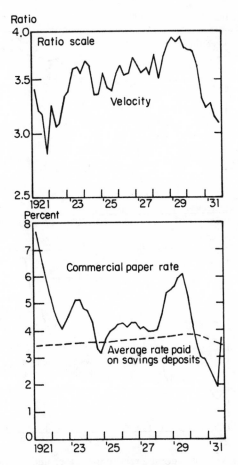

Fig. 8.1   Velocity, commercial paper rate, and average rate paid on savings deposits, quarterly, 1921–31.

rising interest rates induced an expansion of the money stock. This supply effect may have been stronger than usual during these years owing to the sharp restraints imposed by policy. We have not tried to allow econometrically for supply effects for two reasons. One is the difficulty of doing so satisfactorily. The second is that we interpret other evidence to indicate that the interest elasticity of supply is usually small and equally unimportant in both periods, except perhaps for the years after 1965.[8] This is so both with respect to the feedback on the deposit multiplier and consistency of the response of the monetary base to market rates.

For purposes of this temporal comparison we focus on the truncated period 1954–65. We give results for the full period, nevertheless, which

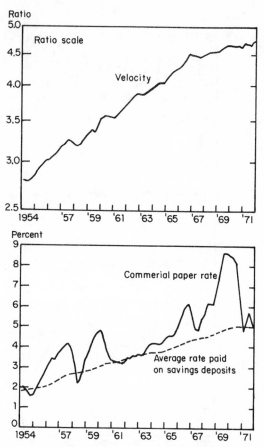

Fig. 8.2   Velocity, commercial paper rate, and average rate paid on savings deposits, quarterly, 1954–71.

do not alter our main conclusions. The unexplained change in trend is one piece of evidence of instability of the demand function, admittedly, but it does not shift the weight of the evidence on the comparison of elasticities.

A different problem of trend exists for the truncated period, because the variables all have had steeply rising trends since World War II. Upward trends in velocity since World II appear to be worldwide occurrence, which presumably reflects in large part the accompanying rise in interest rates and inflation. But any other variable with a rising trend which has influenced money demand and is omitted from the regression will be collinear with the trends in *GNP* and the interest rate and be partly represented by them. If the interest rate happens to correlate with the omitted influence, the estimate of the interest coefficient will be affected. Omitted influences which may have been important are the upward trend in the rate of interest on savings deposits, improvements in their quality (in the United States due in part to favorable terms enacted in 1950 for federal deposit insurance on savings and loan deposits), and improvements in cash management techniques and technology. Although the last two developments may have come at particular points in time, the response of money demand to them could have occurred slowly over many years and so have made their effects appear as a trend influence.

The following tables report our various attempts to allow for the trend by including other variables or short-run adjustment terms, in order to ascertain the effect, if any, on the estimates of the short-run interest elasticity. Our conclusions are presented at the end of this section.

8.2.2 Money Demand Equations with a Variable to Account for Trend

An appealing candidate for such a variable is the average rate paid on savings deposits. This is relevant to the growth of savings deposits as substitutes for demand deposits. It may be explained in part by a general rise since World War II in the interest rate paid on savings relative to a zero rate, because of the prohibition since 1933 on demand deposits. (We ignore checking charges as insignificant. The possibility that increases in services or indirect payments on demand deposits took the place of prohibited interest payments is considered later.) The effect of the rise in the interest rate on savings deposits probably occurred gradually over many years; the short-run changes in this rate were small (even though the rates paid on large denomination certificates of deposit beginning in the mid-1960s behave like commercial paper rates), and the short-run response to its changes was likely low. If we allow for the gradual effect of the savings deposit rate on money demand, the commercial paper rate is relieved from acting as proxy for the upward trend in the savings deposit rate, and the coefficient of the paper rate should then reveal the short-run response of money demand to changes in open market rates. There is sufficient dissimilarity between the movements in these two rates for the regression to distinguish their effects on money demand (see figures 8.1 and 8.2).

Table 8.2 presents these regressions. The savings deposit rate, i^s, is an annual series interpolated for quarterly values. It is an average of the rates paid on U.S. postal savings and time and savings deposits of commercial banks, mutual savings banks, and savings and loan associations (the last was omitted as relatively unimportant for the earlier period), each weighted by the relative amounts outstanding. (The call money and Treasury bill rates are not used here and subsequently,

Table 8.2   Money Demand Equation with Two Interest Rates ln $M/P = k + a \ln GNP/P + fi^s + bi^c$

| Period | Regression Coefficients (and t values) | | | |
	ln GNP/P a	Savings Deposit Rate f	Commercial Paper Rate b	Adj. R^2
1921.I–1931.IV	.45 (6.8)	+6.4 (0.8)	−2.8 (7.1)	.89
	.49 (15.8)	—	−2.7 (7.2)	.89
1954.I–1965.IV	.69 (23.7)	−11.8 (23.2)	−0.7 (4.2)	.93
1954.I–1971.IV	.73 (11.4)	−11.5 (9.3)	+0.4 (1.4)	.82

Source: See Appendix.

Note: Signs of t values have been dropped. Units of measurement: same as for table 8.1. i^s denotes the savings deposit rate and i^c a short-term interest rate. Second line is taken from table 8.1. Estimate of the regression constant k is not shown.

inasmuch as they gave essentially the same results in table 8.1 as the commercial paper rate did.)

While the savings deposit rate has the correct negative sign for the later period and helps to raise the implausibly low *GNP* elasticity as compared with table 8.1, the inclusion of this rate has no effect on the coefficient of the commercial paper rate (except to raise its statistical significance), which still appears to be lower (in absolute value) for the later periods and incorrectly positive for the later full period. The savings deposit rate has an incorrect positive sign for the earlier period, but the coefficient is not statistically significant and probably should be disregarded. The results with it omitted in that period are also shown. This rate displayed very little variation in the earlier period (the maximum range was from 3.5 to 3.8 percent per annum) and so had too little effect on money demand to be measured adequately, unlike its substantial long-run rise in the later period.

8.2.3 Velocity Equations with Trend Influences

For most of this century taken as a whole, M_1 velocity has no clear-cut trend, and estimates of the elasticity of M_1 with respect to wealth or permanent income for periods before World War II with a span of two decades or longer are around unity. (See Meltzer 1963.) Yet in tables 8.1 and 8.2 the elasticity for real *GNP* is well below unity. What is the reason? We have thought of three possibilities, the last of which may affect our estimates of the interest coefficient. First, the income elasticity of transactions velocity may in fact be below unity, as Irving Fisher believed, but the income elasticity used to be dominated by a higher income elasticity of balances held as a store of wealth. These may no longer dominate because of the availability since World War II of many good substitutes. Second, our use of current *GNP* incorporates transitory changes, which by the permanent-income theory have smaller effects on money demand than the permanent component (but see Darby 1972) and therefore pull the estimated elasticity below the long-run level of unity. Since transitory changes are a larger fraction of total variance in shorter periods, this may explain the low elasticities for the 1920s as well as post–World War II. Finally, third, there could be a statistical misattribution of trends. If the negative effect of the interest rate is suppressed for some reason and its regression coefficient becomes zero or positive, the rising trend of *GNP* relative to the money stock in the post–World War II period can be "explained" in the regression by reducing the coefficient for *GNP*. This may account for the very low estimates of the real *GNP* elasticity for the later period in table 8.1.

To test whether trend movements were improperly lowering the *GNP* elasticity and thereby introducing difficulties for the interest coefficients, we forced the *GNP* elasticity to be unity. The results, presented in table 8.3 increase the effect of the savings deposit rate and lower that of the commercial paper rate, which nonetheless was still larger for the earlier period.[9]

With monetary velocity as the dependent variable, the theoretically correct signs of the interest-rate coefficients are positive. The problem

Table 8.3   **Velocity Equation with Two Interest Rates** $\ln V = k + f i^s + b i^c$

| | Regression Coefficients (and t values) | | |
| | Savings Deposit Rate f | Commercial Paper Rate b | Adj. R^2 |
Period			
1921.I–1931.IV	50.0 (8.3)	+1.6 (2.6)	.63
1954.I–1965.IV	16.7 (43.8)	+1.2 (3.9)	.99
1954.I–1971.IV	16.4 (33.0)	−0.1 (0.3)	.98

Source: See Appendix.

Note: Signs of t values have been dropped. Units of measurement: for V, percentage change in velocity per year; for other coefficients, same as for table 8.1. V is GNP/M, i^s is savings deposit rate, and i^c is a short-term interest rate. Estimate of the regression constant k is not shown.

with the years after 1965, noted above, is exemplified here by a negative coefficient for the commercial paper rate. The reason for the wrong sign is not hard to find: The slower upward trend of velocity after 1966 is not explained by the savings deposit rate. It continues to rise despite the largely unchanged regulatory ceilings on these rates,[10] because the rates paid by many institutions were still below the ceilings and could go higher. Consequently, the regression "calls upon" the commercial paper rate, which rose sharply after 1965 as did all other open market rates, to explain this decline in trend of velocity, thus turning the coefficient of the paper rate negative—quite inappropriately. Since the outbreak of the Vietnam inflation and associated increases in interest rate would explain a *rise* in monetary velocity, the decline in trend remains a puzzle.[11] It is not readily explained by any of the other variables commonly included in the money demand function such as permanent rather than current income—which is used to distinguish between anticipated and transitory changes in income. No sharp difference in trends occurred between current and permanent income, however measured, after 1966.

Confining our attention to the top two regressions in the table, we find that the coefficient of the paper rate was lower in the later period than in the 1920s. This is also true of the savings deposit rate by a large margin. A deposit-rate coefficient of 17 for the later period does not seem too high as a reflection of the substitution between savings and demand deposits. (It means that the demand for money balances declines 17 percent for each rise in the rate of 1 percentage point.) The coefficient of 50 for the 1920s does seem too high, however, since these assets (except for postal savings) were not federally insured and for this reason, among others, were not as good substitutes for demand deposits then as they became in the 1950s.[12] As already noted, the savings deposit rate changed very little during the earlier period, and such a high coefficient suggests that it is spuriously representing other influences. If we exclude it for the earlier period, the simple regression of ln *GNP/M* on the paper rate gives a smaller coefficient of 1.4 (n. 9), which is still larger than those for the later period in table 8.2. If we force the deposit-rate coefficient to be the same in both periods by means of a pooled regression, we obtain a higher coefficient for the commercial paper rate in the earlier period, though not significantly higher.[13]

In the absence of a common proxy for trend influences on velocity in both periods, we may as an alternative employ a simple time trend like *T* in table 8.4. The results show once again that the simple correlation between velocity and the commercial paper rate in the later period (n. 9) reflects the trend in these series. The response of money demand to interest-rate deviations from the later trend gives a coeffi-

Table 8.4   **Velocity Equation with Time Trend** $\ln V = k + gT + bi^c$

	Regression Coefficients (and t values)		
Period	Linear Time Trend g	Commercial Paper Rate b	Adj. R^2
1921.I–1931.IV	1.43 (4.2)	+3.3 (3.5)	.30
1954.I–1965.IV	3.31 (55.9)	+1.2 (5.0)	.99
1954.I–1971.IV	3.07 (31.2)	+0.3 (0.9)	.98

Source: See Appendix.
Note: Signs of t values have been dropped. Units of measurement: same as for tables 8.1 and 8.3. T is a linear time trend, increasing one integer per year. Estimate of the regression constant k is not shown.

cient in table 8.4 of a little above unity (0.3 including 1966–71), only about one-third the size of the coefficient for the 1920s.

The strong upward trend in velocity since World War II can be interpreted as representing a long-run response to increases in the *total* return to money substitutes (including nonpecuniary returns from management technology and quality). Until a measure of this return is provided, we cannot estimate the corresponding demand elasticity. But, for present purposes, that is not crucial. The time trend is satisfactory as long as it correctly tracks long-run influences. Admittedly, a linear time trend may spuriously absorb some of the correlation between velocity and the paper rate, thus reducing the estimate of the short-run interest-rate effect. Although future developments will provide a test of this possibility (since these influences should gradually slacken), at present it remains unconfirmed.

As an alternative approach we may turn to adjustment equations, which are also designed to abstract from long-run influences.

8.2.4 Demand Equations with Short-Run Adjustments

A standard adjustment equation postulates that

$$(2) \qquad \Delta \ln V = e(\ln V^d - \ln V),$$

in which the change in velocity is proportional to the percentage difference between desired (V^d) and actual velocity. In discrete form,

$$(3) \qquad \ln V_t = e \ln V_t^d + (1 - e) \ln V_{t-1}$$

where

$$(4) \qquad \ln V_t^d = f i_t^s + b i_t^c + k$$

and

$$0 < e \leq 1.$$

Substituting (4) into (3) we derive

$$(5) \qquad \ln V_t = ek + ef i_t^s + eb i_t^c + (1 - e) \ln V_{t-1}$$

where ef and eb are the short-run (within one quarter) responses to changes in interest rates. Regressions of this form are presented in table 8.5.

These regressions also show the short-run interest effect to be larger in the earlier period. The estimate for the later period is held down, however, by the unusually high coefficient on the lagged dependent variable, as a result of the strong upward trend in velocity. (As noted before, this is responsible for the very high implied estimates of the long-run effects, here f and b.) To circumvent this trend bias, the third line shows the results of a regression in which the adjustment coefficient $1 - e$ is assigned the (lower) value estimated for the 1920s. As a result, the estimates of the short-run interest effect are raised, though they still lie below those for the earlier period.

The equations in Table 8.5 presuppose that money balances are adjusted to their desired level relative to *GNP*—which is to say that monetary velocity is the variable being adjusted. An alternative and

Table 8.5   **Velocity Equation with Adjustment Term** $\ln V_t = ek + ef i_t^s + eb i_t^c + (1 - e) \ln V_{t-1}$

	Regression Coefficients (and *t* values)			
Period	Savings Deposit Rate *ef*	Commercial Paper Rate *eb*	Lagged Velocity $1 - e$	Adj. R^2
1921.I–1931.IV	28.8 (2.9)	+1.2 (2.0)	0.41 (2.6)	.68
1954.I–1965.IV	3.6 (2.0)	+0.5 (2.1)	0.77 (7.4)	.99
$1 - e$ set* = .41	9.7 (33.8)	+0.8 (3.5)	—	.98
1954.I–1971.IV	−0.1 (0.1)	+0.05 (0.4)	0.99 (19.3)	.997

Source: See Appendix.

Note: Signs of *t* values have been dropped. For units of measurement and other notes: see tables 8.1 and 8.3. *e* is percentage adjustment in dependent variable per quarter. Estimate of regression constant *k* is not shown.

*Regression equation is $(\ln V_t - .41 \ln V_{t-1}) = ek + ef i_t^s + eb i_t^c$.

more common adjustment equation is based on money balances alone, where GNP helps determine the desired balances.

(6) $$\Delta \ln M_t = e(\ln M_t^d - \ln M_{t-1})$$

(7) $$\ln M_t^d = k + a \ln GNP_t + fi_t^s + bi_t^c.$$

Substituting (7) into (6) gives

(8) $$\ln M_t = ek + ea \ln GNP_t + efi_t^s + ebi_t^c + (1 - e) \ln M_{t-1}.$$

Regressions of this form are presented in table 8.6. (The savings deposit rate is not statistically significant in these equations and has little effect on the other coefficients; hence it has been omitted.) The coefficient of the commercial paper rate is very small but still double that in the later period after we assign the earlier value to the adjustment factor for the later period; otherwise it takes on a meaningless value above unity.

In adjustment equations the dependent variable is conventionally measured in *un*deflated dollars (since to measure in real terms implies an immediate adjustment of prices), and we have followed that convention in table 8.6. However, in doing so we implicitly assume that the elasticities of demand with respect to real GNP and to the price level are the same, since these two influences are combined in the GNP variable. (In equation (1), without the adjustment term, however, the elasticity with respect to the price level was unity and that of real GNP

Table 8.6   Money Demand Equation with Adjustment Term $\ln M_t = ek + ea \ln GNP_t + ebi_t^c + (1 - e) \ln M_{t-1}$

	Regression Coefficients (and t values)			
	ln GNP	Commercial Paper Rate	Lagged ln M	Adj.
Period	ea	eb	$1 - e$	R^2
1921.I–1931.IV	.21	−0.8	.61	.96
	(5.2)	(3.5)	(8.1)	
1954.I–1965.IV	−.02	−0.6	1.14	.996
	(0.9)	(6.4)	(21.3)	
$1 - e$ set* = .61	.15	−0.4	—	.93
	(19.4)	(2.6)		
1954.I–1971.IV	.02	−0.3	1.01	.999
	(2.1)	(4.2)	(52.4)	

Source: See Appendix.

Note: Signs of t values have been dropped. Units of measurement and other notes: see table 8.1. e is percentage adjustment in dependent variable per quarter. Estimate of regression constant k is not shown.

*Regression equation is $(\ln M_t - .61 \ln M_{t-1}) = ek + ea \ln GNP_t + ebi_t^c$.

was allowed to be less than unity.) We can avoid this assumption by separating *GNP* into its real component and its price component, each with its own coefficient. This is usually not done because of difficulties in measuring the elasticity of the price deflator for short periods. Alternatively, we can avoid the assumption by treating *real* balances as the adjusting variable. (See Goldfeld 1973.) This has the drawback of implying either that the price level adjusts immediately to discrepancies between actual and desired balances while real *GNP* adjusts with a lag, or that the price level is to be taken as given and not affected by the discrepancy. Either assumption seems to us theoretically untenable, though as a practical empirical question it does not appear to matter much (as Goldfeld shows), since the price level deviates very little quarter to quarter from its trend.

Table 8.7 presents regressions with real balances as the adjusting variable. These regressions are more acceptable than those of table 8.6 for the later period, in that the adjustment coefficient $1 - e$ is less than unity. It is nevertheless implausibly high, though somewhat lower when the interest rates are measured in logarithmic form (bottom panel);[14] and the savings deposit rate for the earlier period is inappropriately positive though statistically insignificant. In any event, these regressions still show the coefficient for the commercial paper rate to be larger (in absolute value) for the earlier period.

A third way to avoid the assumption that the elasticity of the price deflator is the same as that of real *GNP*, and hence that the former

Table 8.7   **Real Money Demand Equation with Adjustment Term**
$$\ln (M/P)_t = ek + ea \ln (GNP/P)_t + efi_t^s + ebi_t^c + (1 - e)\ln (M/P)_{t-1}$$

Period	Regression Coefficients (and t values)				
	ln GNP/P ea	Deposit Rate ef	Commercial Paper Rate eb	ln M/P $1 - e$	Adj. R^2
1921.I–1931.IV	.06 (1.5)	+4.04 (1.2)	−.90 (3.9)	.76 (13.0)	.98
1954.I–1971.IV	.05 (1.8)	−.05 (0.1)	−.47 (6.0	.98 (29.7)	.99
Same Equation But with Logarithm of Interest Rate					
1921.I–1931.IV	.07 (1.7)	+.16 (1.3)	−.04 (4.1)	.74 (12.0)	.98
1954.I–1971.IV	.10 (2.8)	−.02 (1.1)	−.02 (6.4)	.89 (16.5)	.99

Source: See Appendix.

Note: Signs of t values have been dropped. Units of measurement and other notes: see table 8.1. e is percentage adjustment in dependent variable per quarter. Estimate of regression constant k is not shown.

can be less than unity (implying "money illusion"), is to set both equal to unity, that is, in (8) set $a = 1$. Then

$$(9) \quad \ln M_t - \ln GNP_t = k - \ln GNP_t + e \ln GNP_t$$
$$+ efi_t^s + ebi_t^c + (1 - e)\ln M_{t-1}$$

or

$$(10) \quad \ln (M/GNP)_t = ek + efi_t^s + ebi_t^c + (1 - e)\ln (M_{t-1}/GNP_t).$$

This is the general form used in a recent version of the (then named) FRB-MIT-Penn econometric model (1971).[15]

These regressions, presented in table 8.8 are one of the only two forms in which we found a larger coefficient for the commercial paper rate in the later truncated period than in the earlier period (the other was reported in n. 9). Both coefficients, however, are extremely small, as is the difference in size which makes them practically the same. Furthermore, these regressions are also not acceptable because of the unrealistically low adjustment speed (4 to 9 percent per quarter). This may result in part from upward bias in the adjustment term $1 - e$ created by using concurrent GNP in the dependent and the lagged variable.[16]

8.2.5 Summary of Statistical Results

Despite the difficulties of fitting a satisfactory money demand equation to the post–World War II period because of unresolved questions regarding the explanation for the relative trends in the variables, we believe that we have gone far enough to establish that the coefficient

Table 8.8   **Money Demand Equation with Adjustment Term and Unitary Income Elasticity**
$\ln (M/GNP)_t = ek + ebi_t^c + (1 - e) \ln (M_{t-1}/GNP_t)$

	Regression Coefficients (and t values)		
Period	Commercial Paper Rate eb	$\ln (M_{t-1}/GNP_t)$ $1 - e$	Adj. R^2
1921.I–1931.IV	−0.4 (1.6)	.91 (25.8)	.94
1954.I–1965.IV	−0.5 (5.1)	.96 (130.8)	.999
1954.I–1971.IV	−0.2 (3.2)	.96 (135.8)	.999

Source: See Appendix.

Note: Signs of t values have been dropped. Units of measurement and other notes: See tables 8.1 and 8.3. e is percentage adjustment in M per quarter. Estimate of regression constant k is not shown.

(in absolute value) of a short-term interest rate is not higher in this period than in the 1920s and by most estimates is lower. This result does not appear to depend upon the interest-rate series used. The only regression in which the later period gave a significantly larger coefficient was for velocity on the commercial paper rate alone, with no other variable to account for the post-war upward trend in velocity. But that result clearly reflected a collinearity of trends, not the short-run variations which are relevant to the efficacy of monetary policy. The coefficient of the short-term interest rate was about the same or smaller for the later period in all the other equations which we fit to allow for trend influences on velocity: by including the savings deposit rate or a time trend, or by allowing for short-run adjustments. We interpret the results to mean that the short-run interest sensitivity of money demand has declined at least moderately since the 1920s.

Although many of the estimates of the long-run response to interest rates are sizable, the short-run response appears to be quite small in the earlier as well as the later period. Most of the short-run coefficients are less than 5 and many are around 1/2 (in absolute value). When multiplied by .04 to convert to an elasticity, this gives a range of .2 to .02. These estimates are on the low side but still within the range presented in most earlier studies.[17] These numbers imply, for example, that an increase in the annual rate of growth of the money stock by a sizable 6 percentage points *for one month* (that is, an increase in M_1 of 1/2 percent in one month) would depress short-term interest rates by 1/2 divided by coefficients ranging from 5 to 1/2. The change in short-term rates would be 0.1 to 1 percentage points, not an implausible range.

All of our equations treat the rate of return on money as constant. Charges on checking accounts we have intentionally ignored as of little importance, but deductions against fixed charges and services provided by commercial banks on these accounts could be important. Banks are able to increase the marginal return on demand deposits by raising the deduction against fixed charges on these accounts. The deduction varies with the minimum or average balance and so provides an implicit *marginal* rate of return. This rate has certainly risen over the postwar period, so that the *net* rate of return on money substitutes has risen less rapidly than gross interest rates.[18] In addition, due to the prohibition of interest payments on demand deposits in 1933, commercial banks under competition have an incentive to provide services in lieu of interest. They also have an incentive to pay interest implicitly through lower net interest charges on loans to business depositors.

Since market interest rates probably overstate the changes in the *net* return on open-market instruments relative to that on money, our regressions bias the interest coefficient downward, and perhaps more so in the later period when services and implicit interest payments were likely to be more important. We know of no satisfactory method of allowing for this bias.[19] Nevertheless, we strongly doubt its *short-run* importance. Account charges and services change very little in response to short-run changes in open market operations, which we are mainly concerned with here.

8.3 Implications for Monetary Policy

How could a *decline* in the interest sensitivity of money demand have occurred alongside the growth of money substitutes? There is an obvious reason. As Alvin Marty (1961) suggested might happen in his review of the Gurley-Shaw thesis, the growth of substitutes has shifted the money demand function to the left and in good part extinguished the holdings which were once close substitutes for savings deposits. These were balances which satisfied a "wealth" or "asset" demand for money. The remaining holdings have come to be largely "transactions" balances, and their demand is, presumably, less sensitive to changes in interest rates.[20] Our results give empirical substance to these theoretical conjectures.

Given that the response of money demand to changes in interest rates has declined, inversion of the relationship implies that a given amount of change in the money stock now produces a larger short-run effect on interest rates.[21] This increases monetary effects on interest rates and, for a given size of policy action, increases the short-run effect on that part of aggregate spending which is influenced by interest rates. These implications are the opposite of those which in the 1950s were thought to prevail because of the mistaken presumption that the interest elasticity was *increasing* with the growth of money substitutes.

The important question for monetary policy is no longer seen as *whether* open market operations affect aggregate demand but as *how* the effect is distributed over time. In the standard theory, the smaller the effect on interest rates of an open-market operation, the smaller the initial effect on aggregate expenditures (the final effect at full-employment levels remains the same). Consequently, the earlier view implied that the growth of substitutes was lengthening the lag in monetary effects. But, insofar as a given monetary policy now has greater short-run effects on the economy but the same final effect, the average lag is shorter.

The growth of money substitutes may also affect the lag in monetary policy by reducing the ratio of money to total financial wealth or *GNP*, entirely aside from any effect via the interest sensitivity of money demand. A lower ratio of money to *GNP* means that the multiplier of the final effect of monetary policy on the economy is larger, and it is possible that a larger final effect takes longer to be reached following an initial change in the money stock. We mention this possibility as relevant to the lag question without being at all sure of the answer. Discussions of money substitutes in the literature have skirted the complex question of the dynamics of monetary policy. Yet a longer lag complicates the execution of monetary stabilization policies and is at the heart of the difficulties in pursuing a flexible policy.

In an earlier paper (Cagan and Schwartz 1975) we measured the lag between step turns in monetary growth and business cycle turns before and after World War II. We found that the lag appeared to be the same or slightly shorter in the recent period than formerly. So far, therefore, the growth of money substitutes has not made the lag perceptibly longer. Perhaps the effect on the lag of a decrease in interest sensitivity and a decline in the ratio of money to GNP have offset each other. Whether future reductions in money demand, if they occur, will henceforth work to lengthen the lag remains to be seen. In any event, even at present the lag is sufficiently long and unreliable, as experience in 1966, 1969, and 1970 demonstrates, to pose formidable problems for a flexible monetary policy.

One further implication of these results concerns the effect of fiscal deficits. According to the usual formulation, the effect of a government deficit on aggregate demand increases with the interest sensitivity of money demand. This dependence pertains to the residual effect after the deficit borrowing has produced adjustments in private portfolios and crowding-out effects on private investment that partially offset the initial impact on *GNP* of the change in the government budget.(Lags probably delay this offset.) An increase in the deficit financed by Treasury borrowing which, for example, raised the commercial paper rate by 1 percentage point would by one of our results reduce money demand by 0.7 percent compared with 2.7 percent in the 1920s (table 8.2). The lower the interest sensitivity of money demand, the smaller is the effect on *GNP* of fiscal deficits.

Paradoxical as it seems at first, the growth of money substitutes has, if anything, increased the effectiveness of monetary policy and reduced the effect of fiscal policy.

Appendix
Data Sources

M_1:   Currency held by the public plus adjusted demand deposits at all commercial banks, quarterly averages of monthly figures, seasonally adjusted.
1921–31: Friedman and Schwartz (1970), table 1, col. 8.

1954–71: ibid. through 1963; thereafter, *Federal Reserve Bulletin*, Nov. 1971, p. 884, and Mar. 1972, p. A-17.

P: 1921–31: Consumer price index (1957–58 = 100). Bureau of Labor Statistics Release, *Consumer Price Index–U.S.: All Items, 1913–60, Series A,* quarterly averages of monthly figures.

1954–71: *GNP* deflator (1958 = 100), quarterly, seasonally adjusted. *The National Income and Product Accounts of the United States,* 1929–65, through 1963; thereafter, *Survey of Current Business,* July 1968 for 1964–65; July 1969 for 1965–66; July 1970 for 1966–67; July 1971 for 1967–68; July 1972 for 1968–71.

GNP: Gross national product in current prices, quarterly, seasonally adjusted at annual rates.

1921–31: Compiled by Harold Barger and Lawrence R. Klein. See *Business Cycle Indicators,* vol. 2, G. H. Moore, ed., Princeton: Princeton Univ. Press for NBER, 1961, p. 133. Series 16.1 for series in form of quarterly totals.

1954–71: Same as for *GNP* deflator, above.

i^c: Commercial paper rate, quarterly averages of monthly figures, seasonally adjusted by NBER.

1921–31: F. R. Macaulay, *The Movements of Interest Rates, Bond Yields, and Stock Prices in the United States since 1856,* New York: NBER, 1938, table 10, pp. A158–160.

1954–71: Weekly figures from Bank and Quotation Record of *Commercial and Financial Chronicle; or*

Call money rate, quarterly averages of monthly figures, seasonally adjusted by NBER through June 1931.

1921–31: Same as for commercial paper rate, above.

Treasury bill rate, market yield on 3-month bills, quarterly averages of monthly figures.

1954–71: *Supplement to Banking and Monetary Statistics,* Section 12, Board of Governors of the Federal Reserve System, 1966, for 1954–63, pp. 51–52; thereafter, *Federal Reserve Bulletin,* monthly issues.

i^s: Savings deposit rate, annual average of rates paid on U.S. postal savings and time and savings deposits of commercial banks, mutual savings banks, and savings and loan associations (omitted for 1921–31), each weighted by relative amounts outstanding, interpolated along a straight line to mid-quarter values.

1921–31: Friedman and Schwartz (1970), table 9, p. 173, extended to 1932; rate paid on member commercial bank time deposits, extrapolated before 1927 on basis of

rate on mutual savings deposits, used as proxy for all
commercial bank time deposits.
1954–71: same as for 1921–31, p. 174, extended to 1972.

Notes

1. Smith (1956), "I am arguing that the liquidity preferences of the public
are typically quite elastic, so that it is ordinarily possible for potential spenders
or their financial agents . . . to find buyers of such securities among the holders
of idle cash balances without producing a rise in interest rates large enough to
have a very great effect on expenditures" (n. 45).

2. For a claim of empirical support for the liquidity trap, see Latané (1960).
"If bonds are a good substitute for money, and other assets are relatively poor
substitutes, which seems a reasonable hypothesis, then a change in money
supply will tend to affect the bond market rather than spending on other assets.
Under these conditions the interest elasticity of demand for cash balances has
considerable influence on the effectiveness of monetary policy . . . Large differences in the logarithms of M/Y are accompanied by very small differences
in the logarithms of interest rates, thus indicating a very high interest elasticity
of demand for proportionate cash balances if the observations fall on the same
demand schedule. This would support the Keynesian 'liquidity trap' theory"
(p. 448). See also Tobin (1947).

3. It is worth remembering that Keynes became disillusioned with monetary
policy for the opposite reason, namely, that when needed, central banks failed
to conduct bold operations in long-term debt markets.

4. M_1 is currency outside banks and adjusted demand deposits. M_3 includes
also postal savings with the U.S. Post Office, time and savings deposits in
mutual savings banks, commercial banks, and savings and loan associations.
See Friedman and Schwartz (1970), table 1, cols. 8 and 13.

5. The interest rate is measured in the regressions as a decimal, such as .04.
Then $b = (d \ln M)/di = (d\ 100 \ln M)/d\ 100\ i)$, the form given in the tables,
may be referred to as the percentage change in demand with respect to arithmetic changes in the interest rate in percentage points.

6. Thus a coefficient of 1 means that a 1 percentage point increase in the
interest rate (say from 4 to 5 percent per year) raises money demand by 1
percent. To convert to an elasticity, we may express this arithmetic change in
the interest rate as a ratio or percentage change, 1/4 or 25 percent, and take
the ratio of such changes in the two variables: $(dM/M)/(di/i) = 1\%/25\% = .04$.
Hence the coefficient can be converted to an elasticity by multiplying by the
average level of the interest rate in decimal form. The average level of the
commercial paper rate in the three periods in decimal form is .044 for 1921–
31, .035 for 1954–65, and .044 for 1954–71. As a further example applicable
to all three periods, a coefficient of 5 approximates an elasticity of 5 ×
.04 = .2.

The very small size of our estimates generally agrees with the results obtained
by Teigen (1964) and Laidler (1966), both of whom also used the commercial
paper rate. Meltzer's estimates (1963) are much larger (by 5 to 25 times or so),
which can be explained by his use of Durand's series on basic corporate bond
yields. That series has appreciably less fluctuation than the paper rate and, in

consequence, tends to give a larger regression coefficient. We obtain results comparable to Meltzer's for the savings deposit rate.

Most authors have measured interest rates in logarithmic form. In particular, Goldfeld (1973) obtained good results from such a form for the postwar period, and we present a comparable equation below in table 8.7. Otherwise, we used the nonlogarithmic form of interest rates because we believe it is more appropriate.

7. Juster and Wachtel (1972) argue that inflation creates uncertainty, which is the reason for the high ratios of household saving to disposable income in the late 1960s.

8. See Rasche (1972) and Cagan (1969).

9. If we constrain the GNP elasticity to unity but do not add another variable, the estimated interest coefficient for the later truncated period is higher ($\ln V = 9.9i^c + k$, compared with 1.4 for the earlier period), but this simply reflects an incorporation into the interest-rate coefficient of the unexplained upward trend in velocity.

10. Except mainly for the increase to 6 percent in 1968 for large negotiable certificates of deposit of 3–6 month maturity, and to 6¼ percent for longer maturities, and in 1970 for savings deposits of two-year maturity.

11. For the problem of deposits held by foreigners, which apparently became relatively large during this period and may have contributed to the change in trend of measured velocity, see Burger and Balbach (1972).

Since writing this passage in 1972, we notice that velocity has been growing more rapidly again in 1973 and 1974. This may indicate that the slowing of the upward trend was confined to the period 1966–72 and reflected, perhaps, uncertainty over inflation (see n. 7) to which the public is now beginning to adjust.

Goldfeld (1973) fits a demand function to the full period 1952–1972 with reasonable success but by using a form of the equation which we find questionable. His results are discussed below.

12. Although the coefficient of 50 for the 1920s is implausibly high, we do not argue that it should necessarily be lower then than later. A wholesale shift of money balances held as a store of wealth to other more attractive assets in the early post–World War II years may have reduced the elasticity of the remaining money balances with respect to these assets. This possibility, suggested by Marty (1961) and Teigen (1964), is discussed later.

13. The regression is $\ln V = k_1 + k_2 + fi^s + b_1 i_1^c + b_2 i_2^c$, where the subscript 1 denotes the earlier period 1921–31 and 2 the later period 1954–65, and the variables are zero outside their designated periods. The estimated coefficients are $f = 18.4$, $b_1 = 1.5$, and $b_2 = 0.2$. Hence $b_1 - b_2 = 1.3$ (with a t statistic of 1.1).

14. The bottom panel regressions are in the form used by Goldfeld (1973) and differ from his only in that he used the time deposit rate instead of the average rate on time and savings deposits and he covered the longer period 1952.II–1972.IV. Goldfeld's equation (table 18, for ordinary least squares) gave:

$\ln GNP/P$	ln Time Deposit Rate	ln Commercial Paper Rate	Lagged ln M/P	R^2
.18	−.04	−.02	.75	.99
(5.4)	(4.1)	(8.2)	(13.6)	

15. In this model the money-demand equation also includes the savings deposit rate and the change in the discount rate.

16. The Durbin-Watson statistics for the adjustment equations in tables 5–8 are somewhat higher than those for the previous regressions but are still well below 2, indicating appreciable autocorrelation of the residuals. This is a deficiency of these equations which we did not believe would be properly handled by the standard assumption of a first-order linear relation between the residuals. Goldfeld does make the correction for first-order serial correlation of the residuals but also shows the results without the correction. There is virtually no difference in the regression coefficient of the commercial paper rate between his corrected and uncorrected equations (Goldfeld, 1973, table 18).

17. For some recent estimates, which fall at the lower end of the range, see Zwick (1971), Feldstein and Eckstein (1970), and Goldfeld (1973).

18. Barro and Santomero present estimates of this marginal rate based on survey data. When their estimate is subtracted from the savings deposit rate, the net rate reaches a peak in 1963 and remains practically level for the next five years. This plateau helps partially but does not by itself fully explain the slowing of the upward trend in velocity after 1966, since the breaks in trend of the two series differ in timing by several years.

19. The marginal rate compiled by Barro and Santomero (1972) is an annual series based on their survey of selected large banks. No independent data exist to indicate how representative it is of the entire banking system. Consequently, we have not used their series to derive a net interest rate.

Benjamin Klein (1973) measures the nonpecuniary yield of services on demand deposits by the open-market interest rate *times* the complement of the reserve ratio for demand deposits. The rationale is that this approximates the gross return to banks of their demand deposit liabilities, and under competition banks would use a fraction of it to attract deposits. This measure cannot be properly used in our short-run money equations for technical reasons, however, because the complement of the reserve ratio changes little in the short run. Hence this measure correlates almost perfectly with the open-market interest rate and provides no additional explanation of short-run variations in money balances.

20. Data on the ownership of demand deposits (Shapiro 1943; *Federal Reserve Bulletin*, various issues) show very little change between consumer and business sectors from 1929 to 1960. But the reduction in interest-sensitive holdings within each sector could have been substantial. Unfortunately, we have no method of measuring such holdings and must rely on our estimates of the interest sensitivity of aggregate money balances.

Nevertheless, balances held by both sectors remain high in relation to sales or income in terms of any reasonable transactions use (see Friedman and Schwartz 1970, p. 107). "Nontransactions" holdings of money have by no means disappeared.

21. This inference assumes that the short-run demand for money is always equal to actual balances held, so that any change in balances held must be accompanied by sufficiently large changes in interest rates immediately to equate the demand and supply. The adjustment equations reported above allow for a lag in response of money demand to changes in interest rates but not for the obverse lag of portfolio adjustments in response to open market operations. But undoubtedly there is such an obverse lag, and it is relevant here to the extent that it is not the same in the earlier and later periods, as the text statement assumes.

The disregard of this lag can lead to overstatement of the speed of monetary effects. Thus, if short-run money demand is always equal to the balance held, a lag in response of money demand to changes in interest rates, which as said implies large changes in interest rates as a result of portfolio adjustments to open market operations, can offset long lags in the response of investment expenditures to changes in interest rates and thus shorten the lag in effect on *GNP* (Tucker 1966). But such an offset does not necessarily occur if lags in portfolio adjustments mean as noted that short-run money demand is not immediately equated to the actual balances held.

9 Clark Warburton: Pioneer Monetarist

Michael D. Bordo and Anna J. Schwartz

9.1 Introduction

The central question debated in monetary economics for at least the past decade has been whether changes in the quantity of money are the dominant independent determinant of cyclical changes in economic activity. The challenge to the Keynesian view of business fluctuations represented by the question has been taken up by a significant number of economists. Thirty years ago by contrast a lone voice expressed reservations about Keynesian neglect of the role of monetary change in analyzing business fluctuations. The voice was that of Clark Warburton who persisted in arguing the merits of his case, undaunted by the isolation of his position. By this date, he is a patriarchal figure. A retrospective on Warburton's contribution to monetary thought is long overdue.

A salient characteristic of Warburton's work is that it was empirically oriented. His autobiographical discussion of the development of his ideas traces the shifts in emphasis they underwent as his examination of statistical data and the literature on banks and business cycles altered his perception. Antedating this examination, at the start of his career, he echoed conventional views on changes in bank reserves and the volume of bank credit as passive factors in cyclical episodes. He did not entertain these views for long, however. By the early 1940s, after studying annual tabulations for 1920–35 of bank deposits, by counties, he became convinced that the role of money "was an active factor in producing the downswing of 1930–33" and that the contraction of the stock of money that was then experienced had been avoidable. Sub-

The authors are grateful to Clark Warburton for his careful review of this paper.

sequent analysis of quarterly data that he developed for the interwar period "led to emphasis, in articles published after 1945, on an erratic money supply as the chief originating factor in business recessions and not merely an intensifying force in the case of severe depressions" (1966, Introduction, p. 9). This in turn led him to focus on the theory of the founders of the Federal Reserve System, its operating procedures, and measures to improve monetary control. In addition, he extended back to Revolutionary times observations on the quantity of money and the timing of business cycles.

The structure of ideas that emerged from the empirical work was essentially completed in the years 1945–53. Warburton, who found time for his investigations when he could be spared from more immediate problems of the Federal Deposit Insurance Corporation, where he was employed as an economist from 1934 until his retirement in 1965, suspended his independent studies in 1953. In part this action may have been dictated by the withdrawal of permission for him to engage in his research on FDIC time. In part one conjectures that Warburton may well have been disheartened by the failure of his ideas to gain adherents during the years of the ascendancy of Keynesianism. At any rate, Warburton did not resume his studies until 1962 when he was employed for three months by the House Banking and Currency Committee. Thereafter he published widely on the range of issues his earlier studies encompassed, based on a revision and extension of the interwar data to cover the period 1919–65. The resumption of Warburton's monetary studies coincided with the upsurge of interest in monetary theory and empirical research that has attracted a new generation of economists. Belatedly, he won recognition as a forerunner of ideas that became current long after he had first enunciated them.

In reviewing Warburton's contribution, it is convenient to begin with his own classification of his papers: the role of money in business fluctuations (section 9.2); the relation of the quantity and velocity of money to effective demand and the price level (section 9.3); the relation of saving, debt, and liquidity preference to monetary policy and business instability (section 9.4); central banking and monetary policy (section 9.5); improvement of monetary policy (section 9.6); and ending with an evaluation of his life work (section 9.7).

9.2 Money and Business Cycles

In his earliest writings, Warburton subscribed to a real theory of the cycle.[1] Subsequently, he linked changes in real forces to changes in debt, which led to changes in bank assets and deposits, and hence changes in the quantity of money, with changes in velocity acting as an accommodating factor. In formulating a business cycle hypothesis in 1942,[2] Warburton described money as an accentuating factor capable of converting a mild contraction into a deep recession. By 1945, he was convinced that this emphasis was in error. Study of the data impelled him to emphasize instead "an erratic money supply as the chief originating factor in business recessions and not merely an intensifying force in the case of severe depressions" (1966, Introduction, p. 9).

Once he arrived at this view, Warburton proceeded to criticize contemporary economists for failing to pay heed to the traditional theory of monetary disequilibrium.[3] Economists in the late nineteenth and twentieth centuries understood the importance of monetary disturbances, especially those occurring in the banking sector, as the key cause of business fluctuation.[4] Yet in the second quarter of the twentieth century, the role of variations in the quantity of money and its velocity of circulation, bank reserves, and monetary policy was neglected.[5] Warburton set himself the task of redressing that neglect.

Using deviations from trend of quarterly data, 1918–47, he found that negative deviations from trends in bank reserves and the quantity of money preceded turning points in the value of sales of final products, which led, first, quantities sold, then prices, and finally the circuit velocity of money.[6] Approximately twenty years later, Warburton updated his series to 1965. Using two measures of effective demand and two measures of money, all in detrended form, he found, as in his earlier work, that deviations from trend of money generally preceded turning points in business, while those of velocity generally followed.[7]

A feature of Warburton's work is his explanation for the timing of the breakdown of changes in aggregate spending into changes in prices and output. The initial impact of a decline (rise) in spending will be on output, he noted,[8] because

> we may assume that in general, market prices are stated by sellers. The decline in spending therefore may be expected to have its initial impact primarily upon the quantity of goods purchased at prevailing prices; with the reduction in prices at which goods are offered and sold occurring chiefly as a result of accumulating inventories and retardation in the receipt of new orders. [1966, ch. 8 (1948b), p. 188]

In updating his work, Warburton found that downturns in 1950–65 exhibited a decline only in output.[9] He attributed downward price rigidity to the Full Employment Act of 1946, which encouraged businessmen to believe in the inevitability of future expansionary policy, "the spread of 'target' pricing," and the "demands of organized labor" (1971, p. 129).

Warburton anticipated the Keynesian-monetarist debate of the 1960s by a decade and more. His 1951 paper *"The Misplaced Emphasis in Contemporary Business-Fluctuations Theory"* is his best known and most important contribution.[10] In it he took issue with Keynes and his followers who "have placed great emphasis upon maladjusted savings-investment relationships as a basic causal factor in business fluctuations" [1966, ch. 4 (1946c), p. 73]. He argued that

> the emphasis of contemporary economists . . . has been misplaced, because a far more potent factor of economic instability in recent years, namely, erratic variation in the quantity of money has been ignored.

Warburton compared the cyclical behavior of the Keynesian psychological factors—liquidity preference, the propensity to consume, and the prospective yield on new capital (MEC)—to that of the quantity of money over the period 1919–45. His proxy for liquidity preference was "the ratio of cash balances held by individuals and business to their expenditures for the final products of the economy" (Cambridge k).[11] Evidence that deviations of Cambridge k from its trend tend to move opposite to those of the quantity of money and to follow them led Warburton to the conclusion that:

> liquidity preference is primarily a function of deviation in the quantity of money from a normal rate of expansion and should therefore be regarded as a dependent, rather than an independent, variable in the set of equations used in the Keynesian type of analysis; and . . . changes in liquidity preference should be regarded as an accentuating, rather than an originating, factor in business depression. [1966, ch. 4 (1946c), pp. 79–80]

He also reported that "the amplitude of variation in the propensity to consume appears to have been small relative to the amplitude of variation in the quantity of money" (p. 80), and since its movements were countercyclical, it was not an important cyclical factor. As a proxy for the MEC, he examined the value of corporate security issues for productive use, which tended to lag movements in the quantity of money. He concluded that

> the expectations of business regarding the prospective yield on new capital are dominated by the experience of the recent past and should be regarded as an accentuating, rather than an originating, factor in business fluctuations. [1966, ch. 4 (1946c), p. 81]

Warburton also brought to bear historical evidence on the relation between money and business cycles. For the period 1835–85, he found that annual cycles in bank note circulation and deposits, as given in Amasa Walker's *Science of Wealth,* tended to precede changes in output, as measured by NBER reference cycle dates.[12] His evidence also suggested that changes in money, largely the result of changes in high-powered money, were independent of changes in income.

In addition, Warburton found that from the third quarter of the nineteenth century until the establishment of the Federal Reserve System in 1914, monetary disturbances produced by external forces (adherence to the international specie standard) and exacerbated by the banking system accounted for cyclical changes. However, since 1914, he argued that countercyclical monetary policy tended to worsen business fluctuations, citing as prime examples the policy mistakes which produced the great contraction of 1929–33, and the recession of 1937–38.[13]

9.3   Quantity Theory of Money

In the course of his writings, Warburton developed an empirically useful version of the quantity theory of money. He clearly distinguished between the long-run or equilibrium version of the theory and the short-run or disequilibrium version [1966, Introduction and ch. 8 (1949b)].[14] For purposes of empirical measurement of the long-run influence of the quantity of money on the level of prices, as well as the effect of short-run variations in money on aggregate spending, Warburton used an adaptation of Fisher's Equation of Exchange:[15]

$$M_t R_t = P_t Q_t,$$

where

M_t = the volume of money relative to the volume in a selected base year, with M usually defined as M_2,[16]

R_t = the rate of use of money relative to the base year,

P_t = an index of prices of final output relative to the base year,

Q_t = the quantity of output of final products relative to the base year.[17]

The quantity theory and the equation of exchange served as the framework for his analysis of (1) the secular behavior of velocity, money, and prices, (2) the Great Depression, and (3) inflation in World War II.

9.3.1   Secular Behavior of Velocity, Money and Prices

Warburton presented data by decades, 1799–1939, and annually, 1909–1947, on the long-run decline in velocity of somewhat more than 1 percent per year,[18] and on the stability of the long-run trend in the interwar period excluding 1930–35.[19] His findings indicated that even in periods of extreme monetary instability, velocity was relatively stable.

To test whether the quantity theory enabled one to explain changes in the price level in the interwar period, Warburton developed an index of "demonstrated capacity" on the argument that "productive capacity, used or unused, has more relation to the price level than the actual rate of production" [1966, ch. 6 (1945d), p. 133]. To this index, on the base 1923–28 (a period of full employment) he applied a measure of the secular increase in desired real money balances of 1.4 percent per year, which he then compared to the actual average annual quantity of money relative to the base for the period 1919–1943. The ratio of actual money to the need for money was close to the measured index of prices of final products in the majority of nonwar years. An unusual accumulation of inventories in 1920, a tendency for money balances to be stable in 1929, and special wartime developments in 1942–43 seemed to him to account for the exceptional years. Warburton concluded:

> Excluding periods of war, variation in the quantity of money, relative to the demonstrated capacity of the nation to provide goods and services and the established monetary habits of the population, is the overwhelmingly dominant factor responsible for changes in the level of prices of goods and services. [1966, ch. 6 (1945d), p. 138]

9.3.2   The Great Depression

Warburton's explanation of the Great Depression hinges on the failure of annual monetary growth to equal that required for continued full employment at stable prices. Using annual data, he estimated the required rate of monetary growth per capita as the calculated full employment growth per capita of 1.5 percent per year plus the secular growth in the demand for real money balances per capita of 1.5 percent per year. The required monetary growth rate and actual monetary growth were similar, 1923–1928, but actual growth rates began to fall significantly below the 3 percent trend in 1929, bringing the depression in its wake.

> . . . in 1929 the decline in prices normally resulting from monetary deficiency was retarded, for in that year individuals continued their normal volume of purchases by accelerating the rate of use of money and by ending the year with a substantial loss in their cash balances. This situation could not continue long, and prices of final products dropped sharply from 1930 to 1933 with the reduction in the volume of money. Monetary contraction was followed, with a year's lag, by a decline in the rate of use of money, measured by the ratio of expenditures for final products to the cash balances of individuals and business. This was a natural and inevitable effect of monetary contraction, because individuals and enterprises were faced with the necessity, as their cash balances dwindled, of attempting to conserve them by postponing as many expenditures as possible. [1966, ch. 5 (1945b, 1953a), pp. 116–117][20]

He calculated the shortfall in the rate of monetary growth in 1933 to be 57 percent of the required rate. He concluded that, had the monetary authorities maintained the 1923–1928 rate of monetary growth, instead of the Great Contraction of 1929–1933, the United States would have experienced "a moderate business depression . . . in 1930."[21]

9.3.3   Wartime Inflation

Warburton used the quantity theory framework to forecast the level of prices for years following 1943. He forecasted the increase in the quantity of money, 1943–1945, based on an assumed rate of government expenditures and the amount to be financed by bond sales to the commercial banks, which, combined with a stable trend in velocity and a decline in consumer goods production led to upward biased predictions of price rise.[22] However, with corrected estimates of government expenditures and proper allowance for wartime controls and the tendency of households to defer consumption, his model predicted inflation in the postwar period rather accurately.

In his analysis of the "inflationary gap,"[23] which he identified with excess supply of money,[24] Warburton did not develop the concept of inflation as a tax on money balances, so that holders have to replenish existing balances to maintain their real value constant. Hence he failed to note that it is the reduction in private real expenditures resulting in a transfer of real resources to the government that closes the gap.[25]

9.4   Savings, Debt, and Liquidity Preference

In a series of articles written between 1947 and 1950, Warburton expanded his criticism of Keynesian economics and effectively argued that most of the differences between Keynes and the Classics can be formulated as empirical questions. He focused his critique on (1) the notion of liquidity preference, and (2) the theory of deficit spending.

9.4.1   Liquidity Preference

Warburton disputed the relationship between money and velocity in Keynesian theory, namely, velocity and the rate of interest vary positively, while money and the rate of interest vary inversely, so that money and velocity "tend to be compensatory." In this connection, he cited the evidence he had assembled on the lag in deviations from trend of velocity with respect to deviations from trend of money and the positive correlations of the two sets of deviations.[26]

Warburton also criticized Tobin's evidence on the interest elasticity of the demand for "idle deposits," derived from the ratio of bank debits to demand deposits as a measure of velocity.[27] He argued that bank debits, largely reflecting payments for property and other technical transactions, were an unreliable measure of total payments, and that time deposits should be included in the definition of money. Conducting his own test, Warburton found little relationship between circuit velocity and short- and long-term interest rates [1966, ch. 12 (1948b), p. 271]. He concluded that Tobin had documented a relationship between the volume of security speculation and the short-term interest rate.

In addition, he denied that liquidity preference could independently produce variations in economic activity, since the lead in movements in money over those in velocity contradicted the hypothesis. The evidence that changes in velocity generally followed changes in money made it difficult to conceive of the private nonbank sector as an important independent source, through decisions to hoard, of economic instability.[28]

9.4.2 A Critique of Deficit Spending

One of Warburton's most important contributions to the monetarist position was his clear statement of the view that fiscal policy not financed by money is ineffective.[29] He argued that government expenditure financed by taxation and borrowing from the private sector other than banks affects spending only to the extent it affects velocity, which was possible in the short run [1966, ch. 11 (1945c), p. 237].[30] However, government expenditure financed by borrowing from the banking system results in monetary expansion which directly affects spending.

In contrast to well-established Keynesian doctrines, Warburton stated that deficit spending by government or the business sector, financed by nonbanking sources, could not alter the size of the income stream beyond possible effects on the velocity of use of money.[31] Only spending by government or the business sector financed by borrowing from the banking system, by enlarging the volume of money, which multiplied by velocity, constituted the income stream, provided a net increase in income. As a simple test of these propositions, Warburton compared movements in the level of income and of money adjusted for the long-term trend in velocity and the government deficit from 1919 to 1941. He concluded:[32]

> . . . changes in the size of the income stream are much more closely related to changes in the volume of money, adjusted for the trend in the volume of money held as a store of value, than to the amount of government deficit spending or to such spending plus business spending for capital purposes.

In place of fiscal policy, Warburton proposed monetary policy as "the chief key to a continuously expanding national income" and underscored neglect of the importance of monetary policy as the chief shortcoming of the writings of his Keynesian contemporaries.[33]

9.5 Monetary Policy

Throughout his work, Warburton continually stressed one overriding theme: unstable monetary growth was largely responsible for economic instability that could have been avoided had the Federal Reserve followed a monetary rule of a steady rate of monetary growth.[34] Systematically, over a period of thirty years, Warburton constructed a strong case against the use of discretionary monetary policy by examining the record of the Federal Reserve System since 1914.[35] His criticism encompassed the following points: (1) the record of unstable monetary policy; (2) the variability of lags in monetary policy; (3) the inadequacy of central banking theory; (4) money and interest rates—the confusion of credit policy with monetary policy; and (5) the inadequacy of research.

9.5.1   The Record of Unstable Monetary Policy

In Warburton's view, the record of monetary instability has been worse since the Federal Reserve System was established.[36] According to him, of the five tasks for which the System was primarily designed,[37] from 1919 to the 1950s, it paid adequate attention only to the first: providing sufficient hand-to-hand currency. Because of excessive concern over the character of bank assets, it failed to guarantee convertibility between deposits and currency during the Great Contraction without disturbing the banks' reserve position—its second task.[38] In addition, it paid insufficient attention to the control of the quantity of money, because of its emphasis on qualitative rather than quantitative guides to its actions and on loan and credit policy.[39] The doubling of reserve requirements in 1937, which led to a massive contraction of bank credit and the money supply and the ensuing business decline, was a policy mistake of the first order.[40] The mistake was a consequence of the System's lack of understanding of the precautionary character of excess reserves as well as the relationship between the New York banks and their correspondents. The System's policy of supporting the prices of government securities during World War II made monetary policy subservient to the needs of the Treasury and fueled the inflation of 1941–1948.[41] Finally, the policy in the 1950s of "leaning against the wind" aggravated fluctuations in economic activity because of the perverse timing of Federal Reserve actions.[42]

9.5.2   Variability of the Lag in Monetary Policy

Warburton provided statistical evidence on the variability of the lag by comparing the dates of cyclical peaks and troughs with the earlier peaks and troughs in member bank reserves.[43] In a more elaborate analysis,[44] he compared the lags between major policy actions, effective bank reserves, changes in the quantity of both M_1 and M_2, and finally changes in final product expenditures. He found a range of 3 to 11 quarters between monetary policy downturns and the beginning of business downswings, with shorter lags for policy expansions and business upswings. In addition, lags between changes in policy and changes in money tended to be short, about one quarter, while those between changes in money and changes in spending tended to be considerably longer.

9.5.3   Theory of Central Banking

Warburton effectively criticized the Federal Reserve System for operating on a weak and ambiguous theoretical basis. The convertibility theory of central banking, the underlying theory of the Federal Reserve Act of 1914, which took for granted that the private sector would provide adequate control of the quantity of money so long as the Federal Reserve maintained convertibility of one form of money into another, was abandoned by the late 1930s because of the evident failure of policies based upon it.[45] Yet the Federal Reserve never fully accepted the "responsibility" theory of central banking, which enjoined the monetary authority to exercise control over the quantity of money to prevent either price inflation or deflation, largely because of its belief that

> monetary policy has little influence on economic stability, and that the major cause of the inadequate use of the country's economic resources and price fluctuations is variation in the rate of use of money. [1966, ch. 14 (1946b), p. 314]

Warburton noted that this view reflected an erroneous conception of velocity behavior and the inadequacy of economic research at the Federal Reserve.[46]

9.5.4   Money and Interest Rates

An important theme in Warburton's writings is the Federal Reserve System's mistaken use of interest rates as both a guide to and technique of monetary policy.[47] He traced the System's emphasis on interest rates to its confusion of money and credit[48] and to

> the general identification of monetary policy with interest rate control or manipulation . . . implicit throughout Keynes' *General Theory* . . . [as well as] contemporary literature on business fluctuations. [1966, ch. 4 (1946c), p. 97]

With respect to the first, the emphasis on the Federal Reserve Act upon meeting loan needs indicated a confusion of the demand for loans and the demand for money, highlighted by ambiguity in usage of the words "money" and "credit," as the System's references to "the supply, availability, and cost of credit," and "supply, availability, and cost of money."[49] Warburton distinguished between the interest rate as "the rental fee for the use of money" and an incorrect interpretation as "the purchase price of money."[50] An increase in the demand for money by the public is acted upon not by requests for loans at banks but by spending a smaller fraction of its cash receipts than it formerly did.[51] The Federal Reserve, however, views interest charged by banks as a fee paid for the creation of money, not as a rental fee for the use of money, hence operates with the notion that control of the interest rate will have a significant effect on the volume of money in existence.[52]

Warburton stressed that the rate of interest is determined by the demand for and supply of loans, although excessive monetary expansion may temporarily lower the rate just as monetary contraction may temporarily raise the rate.[53] Business instability traceable to monetary instability induced interest rate fluctuations, so that manipulation of the interest rate would not eliminate the monetary instability responsible for business instability.[54] He recommended that[55]

> (1) monetary policy should be focussed directly upon the determination of the volume of money which is needed for business stability at a high level . . . and (2) the rate of interest should be left free to fluctuate according to the pressures of the market in which money is offered for rent. [1966, ch. 13 (1945a), p. 289]

9.5.5 Inadequacy of Research

An outstanding reason for faulty monetary policy, according to Warburton, was inadequate research and analysis at the Federal Reserve.[56] He cited the following examples:

> (a) lack of recognition of the need for growth in the quantity of money,[57]
> (b) use of the ratio of bank debits to average deposits as a measure of velocity, which led to the erroneous conclusion that there was little relationship between money and economic activity,[58]
> (c) neglect of research to develop guides to and techniques of monetary policy, a search for policy actions by other government agencies in explanation of economic effects attributable to the System's own operations, and emphasis on banking and credit policy irrelevant to control of the quantity of money,[59]
> (d) failure to develop statistical series required for appropriate monetary policy,[60]
> (e) faulty analysis underlying the decision to double reserve requirements in 1937,[61]
> (f) inadequate basic data as the reason monetary policy in wartime and postwar years was subservient to Treasury needs.[62]

These strictures on the System's research record were made in the 1940s and 1950s. Warburton did not temper them in his submission to the Hearings before the House Subcommittee on Domestic Finance in 1964:

> The lack of research on the relation of changes in the supply, velocity, and value of money to fluctuations in output, employment, and gross

national product becomes most evident when inquiries are made
regarding the character of the information used by the Federal Open
Market Committee in arriving at its decisions. It is not known what
quantitative guides, if any, the Committee uses in deciding what rate
of growth in money or bank reserves is needed or how much fluctuation is desirable when they adopt differing degrees of "restraint"
or "ease." The policy record of the Committee published each year
in the annual report of the Board of Governors does not provide
such information. This inadequacy in the analytical and statistical
background for formulation of monetary policy suggests that any
new legislative guidelines for Federal Reserve policy should be framed
in such a way as to foster—and in fact require—such research as a
continuing activity of the Board of Governors. (P. 1324)

9.6 Proposals for Monetary Reform

Warburton did not limit his contribution to criticism of U.S. monetary
policy. He was a forceful advocate of a number of proposals for monetary reform. These included suggestions (1) to implement a monetary
growth rule; (2) to reorganize the Federal Reserve System; (3) to improve bank supervision; (4) to coordinate monetary and fiscal policy;
(5) to include nonmember banks in the Federal Reserve System. In
addition, he argued in favor of (6) maintenance of the prohibition of
interest payments on demand deposits; and (7) international monetary
reform.

9.6.1 A Monetary Growth Rule

Warburton proposed that Congress revise the Federal Reserve Act
to include provisions for a monetary rule as a replacement for countercyclical monetary policy.[63] He would shift the duties of the Federal
Open Market Committee to the Board of Governors, and provide for
technical studies on the appropriate definition of money, the rate at
which money is needed, and the rate of growth of real national output
consistent with "maximum employment, maximum use of resources,
and maintenance of price stability."[64] As an interim rule, until the
technical studies were completed, he would instruct the governors to
provide reserves to member banks adequate to maintain a 3 percent
per year growth rate of money, for a given definition.[65]

9.6.2 Reorganization of the Federal Reserve System

A shift of the powers of the Federal Open Market Committee to the
Board of Governors has been referred to. Warburton favored this change
because he regarded the diffusion of decision-making power among the
various Reserve Banks and conflicts between the Banks and the Board
as obstacles to the formulation and execution of policy in the '20s and
'30s.[66]

9.6.3   Improvement of Bank Supervision

Warburton would relieve the Federal Reserve authorities of duties unrelated to monetary policy operations. He would lodge responsibility for bank supervision primarily with the FDIC because the soundness of individual banks has a direct effect on the Corporation's financial resources.[67]

9.6.4   Coordination of Monetary and Fiscal Policy

Warburton suggested consolidating in a new department of the executive branch of the Federal government the agencies responsible for monetary policy, bank supervisory policy, and loan policy,[68] but with strict separation of monetary policy from both fiscal and debt operations, loan policy, and bank supervision. Given such separation of monetary policy, Warburton favored consolidation as facilitating the formulation of basic government policies, reducing the number of agency heads the President confers with, and providing better means for cooperation among the banking and loan agencies.[69]

9.6.5   Nonmember Banks and the Federal Reserve System

Warburton would impose reserve requirements on nonmember banks, not because their present exemption hampers monetary policy, but because member banks may choose to give up membership in the System and nonmember banks may expand relative to country member banks.[70] His scheme to enlarge participation in the System would include making available to all banks with deposit obligations the right to borrow in case of need at Reserve Banks.[71]

9.6.6   Prohibition of Interest Payments on Demand Deposits

Warburton's argument in favor of the prohibition was based on equity: if payment of interest on demand deposits were allowed, small depositors would be discriminated against. Because charges are levied on both senders and recipients of checks, in his view, they fall more heavily in relation to the number of transfers on individuals with smaller accounts than on business firms with larger accounts.[72] Quantity discounts and the comparative bargaining power of large bank depositors thus discriminate against small account holders. Rather than removal of the prohibition of explicit interest, he would urge discontinuation of "a discriminatory and inequitable method of charging for deposit transfers."[73] Warburton thus regards the provision of bank money to be a public good[74] and would regulate the banking industry just as railroads are regulated.

9.6.7 International Monetary Reform

In 1953, Warburton proposed a modification of the role of gold in international monetary arrangements. He suggested that the world's stock of gold be an international asset, with the IMF as the world's central banker.[75] To prevent overissue, the international medium of exchange, consisting of drafts on gold accounts, would have no fiduciary element whatever. His plan involved abolition of the gold reserve requirements for Federal Reserve notes and deposits; payment of the capital subscriptions of various nations to the IMF in gold; authorization of gold loans to members by the IMF and of gold deposits by national central banks for credit to their IMF accounts; issue by the IMF of gold obligations in the form of accounts with national central banks; and the maintenance of stated rates at which central banks would buy and sell gold certificates or drafts on accounts of the Fund.[76] Warburton believed that the Fund monetary unit, and hence gold, would be a composite of the purchasing power of the currencies of the main industrialized countries, and that if U.S. monetary policy were such that U.S. price stability was maintained, that would tend to produce stability in the purchasing power of the IMF currency.[77]

9.7 An Evaluation of Warburton's Work

Warburton's chief contribution was the injection of new life into the quantity theory of money during a period when research on monetary factors was all but moribund.[78] At least six important aspects of that contribution may be noted.

First, Warburton revived monetary disequilibrium theory. His emphasis on variations in monetary growth as a key cause of business fluctuations and his systematic presentation of empirical evidence that turning points in money preceded those in economic activity paved the way for later research on money and business cycles by Friedman and Schwartz.[79] His scathing theoretical and empirical attack on the alternative Keynesian view was a forerunner of the comparison of money and autonomous expenditure by Friedman and Meiselman.[80]

Second, Warburton restated the quantity theory of money: In the long run, money and prices tend to be proportional while in the short run, exogenous changes in money, interacting with a stable velocity, produce changes in real output and prices. On the basis of the restatement he proceeded to examine systematic evidence on the stability of velocity and on the relationship between money, prices and output. His empirical work showed velocity to be relatively stable over the cycle and characterized by a long-run secular decline, anticipating later findings by Friedman.[81] In Warburton's attack on Tobin, he presented crude but effective evidence that velocity is not significantly affected by the interest rate and that causality over the business cycle runs from money to economic activity rather than the other way around, themes later stressed by Friedman.[82] He also found a close relationship between money, prices and output both in periods of deflation and inflation, again a forerunner of later research by Friedman and Schwartz, Cagan, Brunner and Meltzer, and others.

Third, Warburton challenged Keynesian orthodoxy with respect to the theory of deficit spending. He advanced the views that fiscal policy matters only to the extent that it is financed by money, that the community will discount future taxes required to pay the interest on bond finance, and that government spending will serve as a substitute for private spending. He offered evidence that variations in money are more closely related to variations in income than are variations in the deficit, a predecessor of work by Friedman, Bailey, Andersen and Jordan. Although Warburton never used regression techniques in analyzing the evidence, most of his conclusions have been substantiated by later research using such techniques.

Fourth, Warburton demonstrated the important role of monetary policy in U.S. economic history. His examination of the record of the Federal Reserve System from its founding until the Korean War established the case that poor discretionary policy was largely responsible for the great swings in economic activity. In his analysis of the Great Depression, he argued that monetary contraction was responsible for the depth and duration of the depression, and that, had the Federal Reserve not engineered the massive decline in money over the period 1929–1933, the United States and perhaps the world would have experienced only a mild recession. These views anticipated those of Friedman and Schwartz,[83] as also his evidence that the lags of monetary policy are long and variable.

Fifth, Warburton provided an analysis of the analytical errors underlying Federal Reserve operations. He attacked the inconsistency and inadequacy of the theory underlying central banking in the United States. In particular, he decried the emphasis on loan rather than monetary policy, and on the quality rather than the quantity of bank assets— a legacy of the real bills doctrine. He demonstrated that the interest rate was not useful either as a guide or a technique of monetary policy. In addition, the System's failure to base policy decisions on appropriate statistical data went a long way to explain the mistakes it made.

Sixth, convinced of the shortcomings of discretionary policy, Warburton early and strongly advocated a monetary rule of a steady growth rate of money. The magnitude of the growth rate was to be determined by the growth rate of real output, secular change in the demand for money, and the goal of price stability and full employment. His emphasis on quantitative guidelines for a monetary growth rule was seconded by Friedman and others and has apparently been adopted by policy makers in the United States and other countries.

In conclusion, Warburton's early presentation of the case that "money matters" entitles him to the designation of Pioneer Monetarist. Perhaps the chief explanation of the limited extent of his influence on his contemporaries is that, at the time Warburton began to publish, events that would call into question the prevailing Keynesian orthodoxy had not yet unfolded. Those who were not persuaded years ago by Warburton's percipient analysis have lived to see events vindicate it.

Notes

1. See Warburton (1935), where he attributed the "great plateau of 1923–29" to the expanded use in the USA of the automobile and the concomitant increase in demand for real estate. The inevitable downturn in 1929, he argued, reflected an overextension of the real estate and stock markets, the decline in bank credit acting as the accentuating force. It is interesting to note the similarity of Warburton's early views and Alvin Hansen's (1939) stagnationist thesis. Later, Warburton vigorously attacked that thesis (1948a), and [1966, ch. 3 (1950d)].

2. Warburton [1966, Introduction, 3–7].

3. Warburton [1966, ch. 1 (1950b)].

4. According to the traditional theory of monetary disequilibrium, changes in the quantity of money ultimately produce a new equilibrium price level, but that adjustment takes time, and involves changes in relative prices, profits, and output [1966, ch. 4 (1946c), p. 86]. Moreover, improvements in profit margins in the upswing (deteriorations in the downswing) tend to increase the rate of use of money (decrease in the downswing), so that movements in velocity amplify those in money (*ibid.*, 88). Finally, according to the Classical Equilibrium theory, the rate of interest (i.e., the natural rate) is determined by the forces of thrift and productivity (i.e., the demand and supply of loanable funds), but changes in the quantity of money by temporarily changing the supply of loanable funds induce interest rate adjustments to reflect changing profit opportunities (*ibid.*, 90–92).

5. Twenty-five years later, Warburton (1975, 435), again complained that:
John Maynard Keynes, and most of his contemporary economists, in seeking to understand how the resulting great depression had occurred and to devise a remedy, remembered the equilibrium theory of their nineteenth and early twentieth century predecessors, but failed to remember the concomitant theory of monetary disequilibrium; and in consequence did not even try to look carefully at the factual record with respect to the stock of money.

6. See Warburton [1966, ch. 2 (1948c), ch. 3 (1950d), and ch. 8 (1949b)].

7. Warburton (1967).

8. Elsewhere Warburton [1966, ch. 2 (1948c), 37] discussed the role of "fixed and sticky costs," narrowing profit margins, which induced firms to reduce output, as well as the effects of 'unanticipated inventory accumulation'.

9. Warburton (1971).

10. In this regard, see also Warburton's critique [1966, ch. 3 (1950d)] of Alvin Hansen (1949), in which he argued against Hansen's view that changes in the propensity to spend exert an independent effect on the level of economic activity through an effect on the quantity of money rather than the rate of use of money. Warburton noted that Hansen's view "rests on the assumption that the quantity of money is determined by the decisions of spenders; and that assumption appears to be based on a lack of understanding of the nature and behavior of banks" (ibid., 59).

11. Warburton [1966, ch. 4 (1946c), 75].

12. Warburton (1958).

13. Warburton (1962).

14. In the long run, the level of prices is determined by the quantity of money, given a stable secular trend in "circuit velocity of money," and the growth of real output, itself determined by the growth of output per capita and the growth of population [1966, ch. 8 (1949b), 186]. In the short run, it is deviations from trend in the quantity of money which induce deviations from trend in velocity, the two forces in turn producing deviations from trend in aggregate spending, which is thus broken into changes in output and prices [1966, ch. 4 (1946c)].

Throughout Warburton's work, the quantity of money is assumed to be exogenous—the quantity of money is dependent on "the policies and operations of money-issuing agencies. Under modern conditions these are dominated by central bank policies" [1966, ch. 8 (1949b), 186].

"Circuit velocity of money" is also assumed to be stable, depending "basically upon the customs and habits of users of money," which "determine the order of magnitude and the trend in monetary velocity" (ibid.).

15. Warburton [1966, ch. 5 (1945b), 105–107 and ch. 8 (1949b), 186].

16. Warburton explained his preference for M_2 over M_1 in calculating velocity as follows:

Calculations of monetary velocity made on the basis of demand deposits plus currency have been greatly affected by factors which influenced the classification of deposits without altering their use. For this reason such measures of monetary velocity are less significant for general economic analysis than measures of monetary velocity based on the total quantity of money including time deposits. [1966, ch. 9 (1949a), 206]

A further argument he offered in favor of inclusion of time deposits was that they serve as "a store of value held primarily for use at a future time as a means of payment" [1966, ch. 7 (1946a), 148].

17. Warburton's preferred measure of Q differs from GNP "by excluding changes in business inventories, net exports of goods and services, and net changes in monetary stock" [1966, ch. 5 (1945b), 105]. His adaptation of the equation of exchange also included trend-adjusted index numbers, using the concept described in recent years as potential real GNP or potential real output growth, which he referred to as "full production" or "normal production." Selecting the years 1923–28 as the closest approach to "normal production" after the establishment of the Federal Reserve System, he computed trends as a statistical framework for analysis of business fluctuations. The trend values were taken to represent equilibrium conditions. Deviations from the trends expressed as percentage ratios represented disequilibrium conditions, useful for observing coincident and lead-lag relationships.

18. Warburton [1966, ch. 9 (1949a)].

19. Warburton [1966, ch. 6 (1945d), 131].

20. Reduced expenditure led to a decline in production because of (1) "sticky costs"; (2) the decline in velocity which directly reduced the volume of sales; (3) "falling prices and reduced sales [which] reverberated upon individual incomes, inducing further reductions in sales of final products"; and (4) "the unused productive capacity accompanying the reduced demand for consumers" goods and services [which] induced a much more drastic and violent reduction in the demand for capital equipment [1966, ch. 5 (1945b) (1953a) 117].

21. Warburton [1966, ch. 5 (1945b) (1953a) 119 and ch. 8 (1949b), 180]. His results from quarterly data, a few years later, were similar. Money held by individuals declined from a peak, relative to the needed growth trends, of 100.2 in the second quarter of 1928 to a low of 58.2 in the fourth quarter of 1933.

22. Warburton (1949c).

23. Warburton (1943, 1944, 1945e).

24. ". . . (the) net change in bank loans and investments and monetary metal stocks, which, . . . , is the amount of government borrowing from banks in excess of reduction of indebtedness of other borrowers to the banks, (or alternatively as the) increase in bank deposits and currency in the hands of individuals and business" (1943, 368). This should be viewed in the context that most of Warburton's contemporaries believed that any excess of government expenditures over receipts, however financed, created the gap. See Warburton (1945e).

25. See Friedman (1953). In a private communication to us, Warburton notes that he believes the orientation of the inflation gap symposium related to a different issue than the one Friedman analyzed. For Warburton the issue was the future impact of cash balances business and individuals acquired when government spent funds borrowed from banks. The additions to cash balances were received *before* they were needed to maintain the initial real value of the holdings.

26. Warburton [1966, ch. 12 (1948b)].

27. Tobin (1947).

28. Warburton [1966, ch. 10 (1947)].

29. Warburton [1966, ch. 11 (1945c), 236]:
Fiscal policy as an instrument for increasing economic activity is a combination of (1) monetary policy, for any action increasing the volume of money or changing its rate of flow is a type of monetary policy, and (2) production policy, as expressed in the objects of governmental expenditures. Of these two aspects of fiscal policy, the monetary aspect is by far the more important with respect to the total volume of production or rate of economic activity. In fact, if fiscal policy has no effect on the volume of money or its rate of use in the purchase of products of the economy, the production policy expressed in the objects of government expenditures is a *substitution of goods and services ordered by government for goods and services which would be ordered by individuals* [emphasis added]. Except for a possible effect upon efficiency, the net effect of fiscal policy upon the total volume of economic activity or production is due solely to its monetary aspect.

30. First-round effects of tax- and bond-financed expenditures on velocity depend on factors such as: "(1) how quickly the government spends the funds after receiving them relative to the use which individuals or enterprises would have made of those funds, (2) in the case of taxation, how the taxes are collected, . . . (3) to what extent purchasers of government bonds restore the

cash balances used in making such payments or thereafter maintain smaller average cash balances.'' [1966, ch. 11 (1945c), 238]

31. In the case of government expenditure financed by borrowing, Warburton argued that the private sector would realize that such financing would entail future taxes and hence the

fiscal (revenue and expenditure) decisions of the government would be neutralized, and we would be reduced to the conclusion that the aggregate savings of individuals are dominated by business decisions respecting the funds they need for capital expansion and replacement. [1966, ch. 10 (1947), 221]

32. Warburton [1966, ch. 11 (1945c), 252].

33. *Ibid.*, 252.

34. For a clear summary of his position, see Warburton (1971, 131) and (1962, 91–92), where he states:

[T]wo centuries of American experience, with a variety of monetary standards and various criteria for the guidance of central bank operations, support the conclusion that monetary disturbances have been a basic factor in bringing about our depressions and our inflations. That experience suggests that a noncyclical monetary policy is likely to give better results than the recent countercyclical policy, and that we should experiment with central bank policies that produce a steady growth, at a reasonable rate, in the stock of money.

35. Warburton [1966, ch. 17 (1952), 368–69]:

Since the time of establishment of the Federal Reserve System, annual deviations in the quantity of money from a reasonable rate of growth have ranged from more than 30 percent excess to nearly 20 percent deficiency. There is no known need for annual variations in the quantity of money, from the estimated reasonable rate of growth, of more than 2 percent; and annual variations in the quantity of money outside this range have been invariably associated with business instability and with inflation or depression. The range of additional variation for seasonal purposes is probably not more than three percent [1966, ch. 17 (1952b), 368–69].

36. See Warburton [1966, chs. 14–19, especially ch. 14 (1946b)].

37. Warburton (1962, 83):

(1) to provide a method of issuing paper currency by the banking system free from the limitations on national bank notes and readily adjusted in quantity to the varying need for currency; (2) to provide for interconvertibility between such currency and bank deposits without disturbing the reserve position of the banks; (3) to pool a portion of bank reserves and to make them available for the relief of financial stringency in any area or locality; (4) to remove or at least reduce inappropriate seasonal variations in bank credit; and (5) to stabilize the total amount of bank credit and thus promote stability of the total circulating medium. (Warburton, 1962, 83)

38. Warburton [1966, ch. 14 (1946b), 302].

39. *Ibid.*, 301–308.

40. Warburton [1966, ch. 15 (1952a), 324–26].

41. Warburton [(1962, 89) and (1964a, 1322)].

42. *Ibid.*, (1962, 90).

43. Warburton [1966, ch. 3 (1950d), 42].

44. Warburton (1971).

45. Warburton [1966, ch. 14 (1946b), 291, 292, 316]. Like Lloyd Mints (1945), Warburton believed this view was based on the real bills doctrine (*ibid.*, ch. 14, 293).

46. Warburton [1966, ch. 14 (1946b), 316]:

The monetary theory . . . held by the Board of Governors of the Federal Reserve System is based on inadequate examination of factual data and is a barrier to development and adoption of the kind of monetary policy needed for full production without inflation. [1966, ch. 14 (1946b), 316]

47. Warburton [1966, ch. 10 (1947), 233].

48. Associated with the "convertibility theory" and the ambiguity of the criteria for policy in the Federal Reserve Act (see section 9.3, above).

49. See Warburton [1966, ch. 13 (1945a) and ch. 19 (1950c and 1951), 397].

50. Warburton [1966, ch. 13 (1945a), 282].

51. *Ibid.*, 283.

52. Here [1966, ch. 13 (1945a), 285–286], Warburton is referring to the views of the Board of Governors of the Federal Reserve System expressed in the April 1939 *Federal Reserve Bulletin,* 256, and its 1943 *Annual Report,* 10.

53. Warburton [1966, ch. 13 (1945a), 286–287].

54. *Ibid.,* 288. He argued that changes in the interest rate cannot be depended upon as a guide to monetary policy because

they must somehow be used in a manner to produce a monetary growth in accord with the need for money generated by growth of population, growth in production per capita, and increased holdings of cash reserves by individuals and business. Interest rates cannot be so used because the rate of interest must be free to respond to real changes in the demand and supply of loan funds, in order to avoid producing monetary maladjustment, and there is no method of judging accurately the "correct" level of interest rates except when monetary maladjustment is avoided. (290)

55. Also see Warburton (1964a, 1321), where he urged the Federal Reserve System to follow a neutral interest rate policy.

56. Warburton [1966, ch. 16 (1952c), 349].

57. *Ibid.,* 344. In the 1920s, Carl Snyder of the Federal Reserve Bank of New York had measured the rate of monetary growth required for price stability, but his efforts were ignored by the Federal Reserve Board.

58. Warburton [1966, ch. 19 (1950c and 1951), 399–400]. As noted in section 5.3. above, he argued that had the Federal Reserve used the ratio of final payments to money held by individuals and firms, they would have found a different result.

59. *Ibid.,* 400–401.

60. Warburton [1966, ch. 16 (1952c), 345]. In the 1920s, the New York Federal Reserve Bank had made significant progress in the development of indexes of industrial output, the overall price index, and employment. However, according to Warburton (*ibid.,* 347), the Federal Reserve Board's obsession with stock market speculation in the late 1920s led to the abandonment of whatever attention had been given to these data.

61. *Ibid.,* 347:

As a basis for its decision . . . the Board estimated that all but a very few member banks could meet this increase through use of their existing excess reserves plus a reduction of one half in correspondent balances with other banks. . . . The Board failed to take into account the impact of such a use of correspondent bank balances on the banks in the money centers, particularly in New York. . . . [They] failed to realize that the New York banks would find it necessary not only to meet the increase in their own reserve requirements but also a portion of the reserve requirements of other banks which had correspondent balances with them.

62. *Ibid.,* 348.

63. Warburton (1965, 289).

64. Warburton (1964a, 1325, 1327–1328).

65. *Ibid.*, 1328. In his earlier studies in the 1940s and 1950s, he advocated a 5 percent per year growth rate in the money stock. This reflected an adjustment for the steady secular decline in velocity of 1.5 percent. The switch to a lower growth rate incorporated the assumption that the turnaround in the trend of velocity since 1950 would continue.

66. *Ibid.*, 1323. As noted in section 9.5. above, Warburton believed that inadequate research at both the Federal Reserve banks and the Board of Governors contributed to the inadequacy of policy in the past. Recent strides in research at the Federal Reserve Bank of St. Louis under the direction of Homer Jones [see Brunner (1977)], as well as research developments at other Federal Reserve Banks and the Board of Governors, may be a response to Warburton's criticism.

67. Warburton [1966, ch. 19 (1950c and 1951), 406]. Also (1963, 355–356).

68. *Ibid.*, 411–412; also (1964a, 1319).

69. Warburton [1966, ch. 19 (1950c and 1951), 411–412].

70. Warburton (1963, 339).

71. *Ibid.*, 352.

72. Warburton (1964b, 2085).

73. Despite the payment of implicit interest on demand deposits, Warburton argued the discrimination continues (*ibid.*, 2085).

74. I.e., the deposit transfer system.

75. Warburton [1966, ch. 18 (1953a)]. According to Warburton, use of a national currency, such as sterling in the late nineteenth century, as an international reserve currency, would be acceptable provided the reserve country does not overissue. However, at the time he wrote, he argued that "there is no country which handles so large a portion of world trade and no national currency which is so universally used in international commercial contracts" (389).

76. *Ibid.*, 390.

77. *Ibid.*, 391.

78. See Friedman (1956), Patinkin (1969).

79. Friedman and Schwartz (1963a).

80. Friedman and Meiselman (1963).

81. Friedman (1959).

82. Friedman (1961).

83. Friedman and Schwartz (1963a).

10 The Importance of Stable Money: Theory and Evidence

Michael D. Bordo and Anna J. Schwartz

The importance of monetary stability derives from the significant independent influence of monetary change on the subsequent course of economic activity. If money did not matter at all or were of only secondary importance in affecting the flow of spending, income, and prices, monetary stability would be of little relevance.

Our views reflect theoretical models and the empirical evidence testing them that establish a close relation between economic stability and monetary stability, and between inflation and monetary growth in excess of the rate of real growth. Hence a stable monetary environment is crucial to achieve economic stability encompassing both stable prices and real growth immune to wide swings. The essential element required to generate a stable monetary environment is systematic policy, so as to minimize monetary shocks to the expectations of economic agents. Discretionary policy is unsystematic, hence fails this test. Increasing the variability of money growth in an attempt to fine-tune the economy will make the variance of real output greater than it would otherwise have been. An economy in which countercyclical policy is followed will end up with unstable money and unstable real output.

Postwar developments in monetary theory have shifted the issues that were the original centerpieces of analysis supporting the case for stable money. Correspondingly, the kinds of evidence suggested to test the analysis have changed to reflect the nature of the issues that are highlighted. We examine the developments in chronological order, beginning with Friedman's case for stable money, based on a theoretical argument against the pursuit of countercyclical stabilization policy (section 10.1). Section 10.2 then examines the opposing theory of economic policy associated with Theil and Tinbergen and the Phillips curve analysis. That theory holds that countercyclical policy can be employed to stabilize the economy and that stable monetary policy is not decisive for that purpose. Successful countercyclical policy would achieve a standard deviation of money growth that would precisely offset the standard deviation of real economic growth that would otherwise occur, and thereby reduce the variance of real output below that of money. The section concludes with a discussion of the natural rate hypothesis that was the culmination of the Phillips curve analysis. The latest development we cover is the rational expectations hypothesis (section 10.3). In each section we examine the implications of the theory for the stable money view and report the available evidence. In section 10.4 we summarize the case for a legislated rule and present some new evidence for a monetary growth rule. Section 10.5 concludes with a brief discussion of the role that a constant monetary growth rule plays in the views of the schools of global monetarism, of Austrian economics, and of the new monetary economics.

10.1 The Case against Discretionary Monetary Policy

The general case against discretionary monetary policy formulated by Friedman (1953) is that, to function well, stabilization policy must offset random disturbances to economic activity; that is, it should remove the variation in income due to those disturbances. To achieve such a goal, two conditions must be satisfied: one involving timing, and the other involving the magnitude of the policy action. The timing of the policy action should conform to that of the disturbance, and the size of the policy action should be congruent with the size of the disturbance. If both conditions are not satisfied, the policy response will be insufficient and may even be destabilizing.

Friedman (1948, 1953) went on to argue that the lags in the effect of discretionary monetary policy are likely to be long and variable, reflecting both an "inside lag"—the time that elapsed before the monetary authority responded to the disturbance—and an "outside lag"—the time that elapsed before changes in monetary growth affect economic activity. As a result, discretionary policy actions might exacerbate rather than mitigate cyclical disturbances. In addition, Friedman contended that there was no basis for believing that policymakers (and the economics profession) possess the detailed knowledge of the economy's complex interactions and of the lag structure requisite for the pursuit of successful countercyclical policies or for fine-tuning. Furthermore, in his view, even well-meaning monetary authorities were likely to respond to political influences. Politically advantageous, short-run actions by the authorities would ignore the long-run destabilizing consequences. The conclusion Friedman drew from this array of circumstances and from evidence to be considered in what follows was that monetary policy should be based on a legislated rule instructing the Federal Reserve to increase the quantity of money, or high-powered money, on a year-to-year basis at a steady known rate of growth.

Friedman did not allege that such a prescription would yield nirvana. He allowed for the possible accretion of knowledge of the operation of the economy once the rule was adopted that would permit improving it. Adoption of the rule would not eliminate cyclical change, but the rule would remove disturbances arising from erratic fluctuations in the supply of money. The effect would be to reduce the amplitude of the random shocks to real economic growth inherent in the operation of the economy.

Several types of evidence have been used to evaluate the case for a monetary rule, namely: the statistical record of changes in money growth rates and their relation to changes in economic activity; qualitative historical data; and simulations of the hypothetical path of economic activity under an assumed monetary growth rule, compared with the actual path. We first report the statistical and historical evidence.

One body of evidence, of which Clark Warburton was the author, predated Friedman's theoretical case against discretionary monetary policy. Warburton's writings from the early 1940s, when the Keynesian revolution was in full swing, until the end of his life in 1980, were in the quantity of money tradition and stressed the importance of monetary disequilibrium as the fundamental cause of business fluctuations. At the time that Warburton's views first appeared, attention to the role of money had all but vanished from professional work. His main evidence was based on deviations from trend of quarterly money data for the period 1918–65. He demonstrated that turning points in money preceded those in business, and concluded: "[A]n erratic money supply [was] the chief originating factor in business recessions and not merely an intensifying force in the case of severe depressions" (1966, Intro., p. 9). Warburton also cited, as prime examples of the harmful effects of discretionary policy, the mistakes of the Federal Reserve System that produced the great contraction of 1929–33 and the contraction of 1937–38:

> Since the time of the establishment of the Federal Reserve System, annual deviations in the quantity of money from a reasonable rate of growth have ranged from more than 30 percent excess to nearly 20 percent deficiency. There is no known need for annual variations in the quantity of money, from the estimated reasonable rate of growth, of more than 2 percent, and annual variations in the quantity of money outside this range have been invariably associated with business instability and with inflation or depression. The range of addi-

tional variation for seasonal purposes is probably not more than three percent. (1966, chap. 17 [1952b], pp. 368–69)

The dismal record of the Federal Reserve led Warburton to strongly favor a legislated monetary rule that would limit the growth rate of money, for a given definition, to three percent per annum.[1]

The evidence provided by Friedman and his associates also utilized statistical and qualitative historical data. Unlike Warburton, who expressed the data as deviations from trend, Friedman and Schwartz used first differences of the logarithms of the money series. They then selected turning points in the series from 1867 to 1960, and compared the peaks and troughs in the percentage rate of change of the money stock with peaks and troughs in general business as dated by the National Bureau of Economic Research reference cycle chronology. On average, of the 18 nonwar cycles since 1870, peaks in the rate of change of the stock of money preceded reference peaks by 16 months, and troughs in the rate of change of the stock of money preceded reference troughs by 12 months. On this basis, they argued strongly that: "Appreciable changes in the rate of growth of the stock of money are a necessary and sufficient condition for appreciable changes in the rate of growth of money income"; and, "this is true both for long secular changes and also for changes roughly the length of business cycles" (1963a, p. 53). Using a different methodology over the same period, William Poole (1975) found that the evidence supported the Friedman and Schwartz conclusion.

To the question whether money changes conformed positively to the business cycle with a lead or inversely with a lag, the answer Friedman and Schwartz gave was that the dispersion (measured by the standard deviation) of the leads and lags, as computed under the two interpretations, is uniformly lower when the money series is treated as conforming positively. Serial correlations, furthermore, of expansions with succeeding contractions and of contractions with succeeding expansions display the same patterns for the money change series and a proxy indicator of physical change in general business. Expansions in both series are not systematically correlated with the succeeding contractions, whereas contractions in both series are highly correlated with the succeeding expansions. This evidence supports the positive interpretation of the relation of money *changes* to the business cycle. Otherwise, if inverted conformity were the case and changes in business produced later changes in the opposite direction in money, then the correlations with the succeeding reference cycle phase for money and the physical change in general business measure should be opposite. But the pattern for business *does* reflect, with a lag, the pattern for money.

Statistical evidence provided by Friedman and Schwartz (1963b, p. 594) matched periods with a low standard deviation of year-to-year percentage changes in monetary growth with comparable periods in velocity, real income, and wholesale prices. They also matched periods with a high standard deviation of year-to-year changes in monetary growth with comparable periods in the other magnitudes. In the nine decades, 1869–1960, four periods of comparative stability in money growth were accompanied by relative stability of the rate of growth of output and the rate of change of prices: 1882–92; 1903–13: 1923–29; 1948–60. All other periods were characterized by unusually unstable money growth rates and unusually unstable rates of growth of output and rates of change of prices.

The qualitative historical evidence that Friedman and Schwartz examined also supported the conclusion that erratic money changes, as a result of discretionary actions by the authorities, were accompanied by economic changes in the same direction. Moreover, in a number of episodes when monetary changes had led changes in economic activity, the evidence that the monetary changes were independent of the changes in activity was irrefutable.

We now turn to the simulation studies that compare the hypothetical behavior of the U.S. economy under an assumed constant money growth rate rule with actual economic performance. The evidence is mixed. Friedman (1960) found that a rule would have outperformed discretionary policy in the interwar period, but that the case for the post–World War II period was less clear-cut. For the postwar period, at least until the mid-1960s, most studies (Bronfenbrenner 1961; Modigliani 1964; Argy 1971) concluded that discretionary policy outperformed a 3 or 4 percent monetary growth rule. One inference might be that the Federal Reserve had learned from its "mistakes" in the interwar period. Recently, however, Argy (1979) found that for the period from the late 1960s to the late 1970s, a simulated monetary growth rule for a sample of nine industrial countries would have reduced the variance of real growth considerably below its actual variance.

Finally, Kochin (1980) found that over much of the postwar period U.S. monetary policy was destabilizing. His study, based on an interpretation of the results of several economic models, followed Friedman's (1953) procedure for evaluating stabilization policy.

10.2 Keynesian Riposte and Return Sally

An analytical development that favored intervention along Keynesian lines was the Theil-Tinbergen theory of economic policy. That approach provided policymakers with an array of instruments—monetary, fiscal, incomes policies—to achieve multiple goals by matching instruments to goals following the principle of comparative advantage. This theory of economic policy combined with the use of optimal control procedures led to a strong case for fine-tuning. It was held that policymakers could devise feedback rules between real economic activity and monetary and fiscal policy that could be applied to offset disturbances to the private sector.

Another development that apparently advanced the case for countercyclical policy was the Phillips curve tradeoff. Phillips (1958), Samuelson and Solow (1960), and Lipsey (1960b) reported evidence of a stable inverse relationship for the U.K., the U.S., and other countries between the rate of change of money wages (alternatively, the rate of change of the price level) and the level of unemployment. The findings led to the view that policymakers could choose, based on a social preference function, between high inflation and low employment, or low inflation and high unemployment, the desired choice to be achieved by discretionary monetary and fiscal policy.

The upshot of these developments was that many economists came to believe that the economy could be stabilized at any desired level of activity. Friedman's objections to fine-tuning seemed to have been circumvented.

Friedman's response came in his 1967 presidential address to the American Economic Association. He argued that the Phillips curve tradeoff was a statistical illusion arising from the failure to account for inflationary expectations. Monetary and fiscal policy could stabilize the economy at some arbitrary level of output or employment, but only temporarily and, even then, only at the expense of accelerating inflation or deflation. Both Friedman (1968) and Phelps (1968) modified the Phillips curve approach by applying the concept of the natural rate employment—that rate consistent with the microeconomic decisions of firms and workers active in the labor force. The natural rate of employment reflects the optimal choice of workers between labor and leisure and the optimal mix of labor and other factors of production for firms in a dynamic economy. According to the "natural rate hypothesis," the natural rate of employment is determined by the intersection of the demand and supply curves for labor, given demographic factors and labor market institutions. Hence deviations of employment from the natural rate are produced only by imperfect information and the costs of acquiring information that affect job search.

One explanation given for such imperfections in information was that employers and workers have different perceptions of changes in real wage rates. It was argued that firms always have perfect information on the prices of their output so that for them actual and expected real wages are always equal. In contrast, workers base their evaluations of prospective real wage rates on their expectations of what the rate of inflation will be over the duration of their contracts. For example, suppose inflation is rising and workers' expectations do not fully reflect the higher inflation rate. Faced with lower real wage rates, firms will be willing to expand employment, which will put upward pressure on nominal wages. The result will appear as a movement along the (short-run) Phillips curve. However, once workers adjust their expectations to the higher inflation rate, they will demand higher money wages. The resultant rise in real wage rates will cause firms to reduce employment to its previous level. The economy will then return to the natural rate of unemployment consistent with labor market forces, *but at a higher rate of inflation.*

The *measured* unemployment rate is thus assumed to depend on the natural unemployment rate and the difference between the actual and expected inflation rates; that is, on the inflation forecast error, with some rate of adjustment of the unemployment rate to the forecast error. As long as the actual and expected inflation rates differ, measured unemployment can differ from the natural rate. However, in the *long run,* actual and expected inflation rates converge, and hence, measured unemployment reverts to the natural rate, though this adjustment process may be sluggish.

The theory of search is an alternative way of explaining unemployment. This theory posits that the natural rate of unemployment is determined by long-run demographic forces, but that deviations from the natural rate are caused by short-run factors affecting the costs and duration of search.

The policy implication that emerged from the natural rate hypothesis was that stabilization policies aimed at reducing unemployment below the natural rate would have only temporary success. Any attempt to achieve permanent results would produce accelerating, and ultimately runaway, inflation. In addition, policies designed to peg the unemployment rate at the natural rate could lead easily to an explosive inflation or deflation if the forces determining the natural rate were to change. Such forces include changes in the labor force skill mix and demographic determinants of the labor force. Thus, the natural rate hypothesis strengthens the case for monetary stability, since monetary instability would produce deviations between the expected and actual inflation rates, causing fluctuations in unemployment and output.

10.3   The Rational Expectations Hypothesis and the Case for Stable Money

Recent advances in the treatment of expectations supplement the case for monetary stability implied by the natural rate hypothesis. According to the rational expectations hypothesis, economic agents act rationally with respect to the gathering and processing of information, just as they do with respect to any other activity (Muth 1961). This proposition implies that agents will not make persistent forecast errors. If their forecasts turn out to be wrong, agents will learn the reason for their errors and revise their methods of forecasting accordingly. Such an approach seems more reasonable than alternative approaches commonly used to model expectations, such as static expectations that simply extrapolate existing conditions, or adaptive expectations that have the property of yielding continuous forecast errors. Additionally, in contrast to the adaptive expectations approach that uses only past values of the variable about which expectations are to be formed, the rational expectations hypothesis also uses other relevant information.

The rational expectations model assumes that private agents form expectations about the rate of inflation based on their understanding of the economic model that generates the inflation rate, as well as on the policy rule followed by the monetary authorities.

In a model based on rationally formed expectations, Sargent and Wallace (1975) demonstrated that systematic monetary policy would be completely ineffective in influencing real variables. They argued that if the monetary authorities devised a monetary feedback rule, using optimal feedback techniques, according to which the authorities systematically altered the money supply to offset disturbances in real economic activity, then private decision-makers would learn the rule and incorporate it into their rational expectations. The thrust of this model—where deviations of output from its full employment (or natural) level can only be produced by an inflation forecast error—is that if expectations are formed rationally, the forecast error cannot be manipulated by systematic (and, therefore, anticipated) monetary or fiscal policy. Indeed, the only way output or unemployment can be altered from its natural rate is by an *unexpected* shock. However, unexpected shocks—monetary or other—have the negative attribute of increasing the level of uncertainty in the economy.

If a negatively sloping Phillips curve were observed, it might result from constant price expectations in a period with *ex post* fluctuations in actual inflation due to unanticipated random shocks that are negatively correlated with *ex post* fluctuations in measured unemployment (Begg 1982, p. 141). Lucas (1973) offered a variant explanation, in a world of rational expectations, for a negatively sloped short-run Phillips curve or, alternatively, a positively sloped short-run supply curve for output, which is determined by lagged output and the discrepancy between actual and expected inflation. Lucas assumed that the economy is characterized by uncertainty, and that competitive firms cannot readily discern whether a change in the price of their output reflects a change in the price level or a change in relative prices. He then demonstrated that other things equal, the greater the variance of the aggregate price level, owing to greater monetary variability, the more likely it is that firms will mistake a price level change for a change in relative prices. Expansion of output in response to an increase in the level of prices, holding relative prices constant, will ultimately lead to accumulation of inventory, cutbacks in output, layoffs, and more inelastic supply curves and also a more inelastic aggregate supply and Phillips curve. In addition, greater price level variability will be associated with greater resource misallocation because price level variability impairs the ability to perceive the information that prices convey in a market economy.

Brunner, Cukierman, and Meltzer (1980) perceive the problem of extracting the signal from prices somewhat differently from Lucas. For them, the distinction that needs to be made is not the sorting out of aggregate from relative price changes. It is rather the distinction between transitory and permanent price changes. Firms will wait to learn whether a change is permanent before reacting to it and, with great price variability, that process is made more difficult and prolonged than would otherwise be the case.

In any event, price variability reflecting discretionary money variability clearly has negative effects on the economy and reinforces the case for monetary stability. Moreover, the entire enterprise of selecting discretionary policies by simulation of econometric models has been challenged by Lucas (1976). His critique was based on the kinds of equations that are used in econometric models. These are reduced forms of effects on the economy of existing policy arrangements that incorporate the private sector's expectations of policy effects on economic variables. Were the authorities to change the policy rule, the public would adjust its expectations accordingly. Consequently, attempts to forecast the effects of alternative policies without accounting for changes in private agents' expectations are bound to lead to inappropriate policies.

Discretionary policy (defined as policy reacting to the current situation) based on optimal control techniques has been shown by Kydland and Prescott (1977) to be suboptimal and possibly destabilizing in a world of rational expectations. The policy chosen at each point in time may be the best, given the current situation. In the authors' terminology, the policy may be consistent, but it will be suboptimal because the policymaker has failed to take into account the optimizing rules of economic agents. The decisions of agents will change as they come to recognize the change in policy. The example Kydland and Prescott cite is that agents may expect tax rates to be lowered in recessions and increased in booms and make decisions in light of those expectations.

Over successive periods, it is not optimal to continue with the initial policy because control theory is not the appropriate tool for dynamic economic planning. Current decisions of economic agents are affected by what they expect future policy to be. A government that attempted to reduce unemployment by increasing the money supply without attention to the rational inflation expectations of private agents would end up with a suboptimal mix of the natural rate of unemployment and positive inflation, despite the fact that it sought to maximize its "social welfare function" by combining the desirability of full employment and zero inflation. The authors conclude (1977, p. 487):

> The implication of this analysis is that, until we have . . . [a tested theory of economic fluctuations], active stabilization may very well be dangerous and it is best that it not be attempted. Reliance on policies such as a constant growth in the money supply and constant tax rates constitute a safe course of action. When we do have the prerequisite understanding of the business cycle, the implication of our analysis is that policymakers should follow rules rather than have discretion. The reason that they should not have discretion is not that they are stupid or evil but, rather, that discretion implies selecting the decision which is best, given the current situation. Such behavior either results in consistent but suboptimal planning or in economic instability.

Oversimplication by certain proponents of the rational expectations hypothesis should be noted. A number of factors could lead to non-neutral effects of anticipated monetary growth even in the presence of rational expectations. First, anticipated monetary growth can have effects on the natural rate of unemployment (output) through a real balance effect on the aggregate expenditure function, or by changing the steady state capital-labor ratio and thus affecting the real rate of interest (Buiter 1980).

Second, if the assumption that both government and the private sector have equal access to information is violated when there is a rule for systematic monetary policy, then it is possible for the government to change its policy after the private sector has formed its expectations and thereby affect the inflation forecast error. As a result, output and unemployment can deviate from the natural rate. Such an outcome is also possible in cases where wages are determined by multi-period overlapping contracts (Fischer 1977). In that situation, even if private agents form their expectations rationally, the government can systematically affect output and employment between contract negotiating dates. Third, if the assumption of market clearing is abandoned, yet the assumption of rational expectations is maintained, then it is possible for output to be affected by stabilization policy. Explanations for price stickiness range from the Keynesian disequilibrium approach (Buiter

1980) to price setting behavior in a world of high coordination costs (Cagan 1980).

Fourth, evidence of persistence—that unemployment does not rapidly disappear and bring the economy to full employment—or alternatively, the existence of serial correlation of output and employment over the business cycle, has been advanced as contradicting the rational expectations approach. On the other hand, McCallum (1980) explains persistence within the rational expectations context as reflecting real costs of adjusting the fixed capital stock and other factors of production. For Lucas (1975), persistence occurs because of information lags that prevent "even relevant past variables from becoming perfectly known" (p. 1114), and an accelerationist effect of physical capital. Finally, the rational expectations approach fails to explain how private agents learn from their forecast errors in forming rational expectations (De Canio 1979).

We now turn to the evidence for the rational expectations hypothesis. The evidence most generally cited is that by Barro (1977a, 1977b, 1981) and Barro and Rush (1980). Barro and Rush regressed the unemployment rate over the 1949–77 period on lagged values of a measure of unexpected monetary growth and of expected monetary growth. Expected monetary growth was estimated from a regression of current monetary growth on past monetary growth, the deviation of government spending from its trend, and past unemployment. Such a regression was designed to capture the monetary rule that economic agents perceived. The predicted values of the regression were employed to represent expected monetary growth, and the residuals, to represent unexpected monetary growth.

Barro and Rush found most of the variation in unemployment was explained by unexpected monetary growth, and that expected monetary growth was not statistically significant. They concluded that expected monetary growth is neutral and that only unsystematic elements of monetary policy affect the unemployment rate—a finding that is supportive of the rational expectations hypothesis.

The evidence that Barro has presented—that only unexpected monetary growth explains variations in unemployment—has been challenged. Cagan (1980) argued, following a more traditional approach, that most variations in output and employment can be explained by deviations in money growth from a long-run trend, without invoking rational expectations. Sargent (1976) demonstrated that it is difficult to distinguish Barro's results from those produced by a more traditional approach because of the observational equivalence of natural and unnatural rate theories. For Sargent, the only way to test a refutable hypothesis is to be able to isolate periods involving a change in clear-cut policy rules. Gordon (1976a, 1976b, 1979) argues that, unless it can be shown that the full effect of a change in nominal income is absorbed by price change, the case for the neutrality hypothesis is not confirmed. In his view, to the extent that some of the effect of expected monetary growth is absorbed by output change, scope remains for stabilization policy. Mishkin (1982) also finds that anticipated movements in monetary growth have effects on output and unemployment that are larger than those of unanticipated movements, but his evidence confirms that expectations are rational.

The rational expectations approach appears to be firmly established, despite unresolved questions including those mentioned above. A clear implication of the literature is that active monetary intervention is likely to lead to large price level changes with little favorable effect on output or employment. Unpredictable policies are likely to increase the degree of uncertainty in the economy and enlarge the fluctuations around the natural rate. The aim of policy should therefore be to establish predictable monetary rules, preferably rules that are easily understood, with full consideration of all the relevant costs and benefits.

10.4 The Case for a Legislated Rule

Modigliani's presidential address to the American Economic Association (1977) disputed monetarist views that (a) the economy is sufficiently shockproof that stabilization policies are not needed; (b) postwar fluctuations resulted from unstable monetary growth; (c) stabilization policies decreased rather than increased stability. He finds that "Up to 1974, these [stabilization] policies have helped to keep the economy reasonably stable by historical standards, even though one can certainly point to some occasional failures" (1977, p. 17). He attributes the serious deterioration in economic stability since 1973 to "the novel nature of the shocks that hit us, namely, supply shocks. Even the best possible aggregate demand management cannot offset such shocks without a lot of unemployment together with a lot of inflation. But, in addition, demand management was far from the best." The failure, he contends, was the result of ineffective use of stabilization policy "including too slavish adherence to the monetarists' constant money growth prescription."

Modigliani's defense of stabilization policies amounts to acknowledging specific failures while asserting overall success, except when exogenous supply shocks occur which "we had little experience or even an adequate conceptual framework to deal with" (1977, p. 17).

Table 10.1 shows the standard deviations of quarter-to-quarter deviations of a two-quarter moving average from a 20-quarter growth rate of M1. The standard deviations are a proxy for unexpected monetary change (shocks) that, according to both older and newer approaches,

Table 10.1   Comparative Variability of Monetary Growth and Rates of Change of Real GNP, Postwar Subperiods Quarterly, 1952I–1982III

| | Standard Deviation of Quarter-to-Quarter Percentage Changes in: | |
| | Deviations from a 20-Quarter Moving Average of M1 of a 2-Quarter Moving Average | Annualized Real Output Growth |
Period	(1)	(2)
1952I–1960IV	1.93	4.76
1961I–1971II	1.80	3.17
1961I–1973III	1.75	3.20
1971III–1982III	2.11	4.79
1973IV–1982III	2.18	4.89

Note: We are indebted to the division of research of the St. Louis Federal Reserve Bank for the data underlying col. 1.

should be associated with consequent effects on real output and, once fully anticipated, on prices. The table, therefore, also shows the standard deviations of quarter-to-quarter annualized real output growth rates for three postwar subperiods: 1952I to 1960IV; 1961I to 1971II (alternatively, 1973III); 1971III (1973IV) to 1982III.

The variability of the (unexpected) money series declined moderately during the 1960s and until the quarter preceding the Nixon price controls or, alternatively, the quarter preceding the 1973 oil price shock. Over the same subperiods, real output variability also declined, but substantially more than the decline in money variability. In the final subperiods, both money variability and real output variability rose to levels exceeding the ones prevailing in the initial subperiod.[2]

Modigliani's attribution of the serious deterioration of economic stability since 1973 to "too slavish adherence to the monetarists' constant money growth rule" is not apparent in table 10.1. The inability of stabilization policy to cope with unexpected developments *supports* monetarist views. If policymakers are thought to have an informational advantage over private agents and so able to reduce fluctuations of output around its natural rate, they must be able to make correct inferences about the precise character of current shocks. That does not seem to be the case.

Theory and evidence strongly suggest that a systematic monetary rule is superior to discretion. A fixed rule with no feedback from the current situation to policy instruments, a rule that is simple and preannounced, is the most favorable condition for stabilizing the economy. Any feedback rules that involve government manipulation of the private sector's forecast errors is doomed to failure. There is no information available to authorities that is not also available to the private sector.

A fixed, simple, preannounced rule can take a number of forms. For some who are opposed to discretionary policy, the preferred systematic rule is the gold standard rule, for others, an interest rate or price rule. We do not examine the reason such rules have won support from their adherents. The rule we favor is a constant monetary growth rule. It satisfies the requirement for a systematic preannounced policy or regime that economic agents can incorporate in their expectations. It is a rule which can easily be implemented. The case for it, as stated initially by Friedman, is that economists lack adequate knowledge to conduct discretionary policy successfully. A monetary growth rule would obviate monetary policy mistakes. When physicians take the Hippocratic oath, they pledge not to do harm to their patients. Economists should take a similar oath with respect to the instruments that they may be in a position to administer.

The development of the rational expectations approach suggests that public response to stable monetary growth would contribute to the stabilization of the economy. Constant monetary growth will not make the business cycle obsolete. But avoidance of the mistakes of discretionary monetary policy will reduce the amplitude of fluctuations inevitable in a dynamic economy.

10.5 Divergent Views on a Constant Monetary Growth Rule

Economists who accept the primacy of monetary change in producing changes in economic activity do not all agree that the policy solution is to adopt a rule for constant monetary growth. We may distinguish the views of adherents of global monetarism, Austrian economics, and the new monetary economics.

Global monetarism emphasizes that the world economy is highly integrated with respect both to commodity and capital markets, international price and interest rate arbitrage serving to coordinate national economies. The appropriate unit of analysis, therefore, is not the individual national economy but rather the world. The elements of the doctrine were constructed for a world of fixed exchange rates where the domestic rate of inflation is determined exogenously by the world rate of inflation, and the domestic money stock is determined by the rate of growth of domestic nominal income, set by the world inflation rate. For such an approach, prescribing a rule for domestic monetary growth is pointless. Under a flexible rate regime, however, domestic monetary authorities can control their money supplies *if they choose.* Regardless of the exchange rate regime, global monetarism has not supported a monetary rule for a single nation.

Austrian economics acknowledges the role of monetary policy in producing inflation, and shares the monetarist view that the result of monetary attempts to reduce unemployment below its natural level is accelerating inflation. The chief emphasis, however, is less on these propositions than on the distortions in the production process resulting from monetary expansion. Moreover, in Austrian economics, flexible exchange rates are not the path to domestic monetary control. Hayek, for example, favors fixed exchange rates as a constraint on the government's overexpansion of the domestic money supply. The preferred solution, however, is the abolition of central banks, and the establishment of a commodity money. Hayek recently has advocated the denationalization of money and giving private producers freedom to offer alternative kinds of money. The market would then choose the money that would prove to be stable. Hence no legislated rule would be required.

The new monetary economics enters under the free-market banner. In the system that we are familiar with, money is the product of pervasive government regulation. Had free-market policies prevailed for transactions services, economists of that persuasion argue, a more efficient banking system would have been created, and velocity would have been much different. The new monetary economics therefore opposes a constant monetary growth rule on the ground that macroeconomic performance, under free-market provision of money, could be much better than a rule would have produced. Different schemes have been elaborated by members of this school to replace an inefficiently regulated money stock, but as Hall (1982, p. 1555) writes: "None of them would rely on the concept of a money stock or its stability relative to total income. Whether their macroeconomic performance would equal that of a simple money growth rule is still a matter of controversy."

Proposals to change utterly root and branch the existing monetary system strike us as ignoring the enormous attachment of the private sector to arrangements that have become customary. Imposing a system that appeals to visionaries as far more satisfactory than the one markets have adjusted to, given the existing network of regulations, is not the historical way in which alterations in the monetary system have occurred. A complete breakdown in existing arrangements as a result, say, of the catastrophe of hyperinflation would be a prerequisite to adoption de novo of one of the schemes the new monetary economics espouses.

The new monetary economics, by proclaiming that results superior to those of a monetary growth rule are within reach, shares some of the confidence of interventionists. Advocates of a monetary growth rule are skeptical not only about demand management or fine-tuning by interventionists, but also about the prospects that new schemes for settling transactions can be as easily implemented as they can be devised.

Some observers predict that the deregulation process now under way will obscure the quality of moneyness of assets and hence render control by the central bank problematical. We regard this apocalyptic view as unduly alarmist. Not so long ago, it was commonly argued that payment of interest on demand deposits would mean the end of their use as transactions balances. That has not happened and we do not foresee radical changes on the horizon in the operation of the payments system. The alternatives are not the creation de novo of a set of monetary arrangements or the preservation unchanged of the existing set.

For all the talk of the adoption of monetarism by central banks, their performance gives little indication that they in fact have been influenced by the central message of the doctrine—monetary instability is a potent source of unstable economic performance. Note, for example, the wide swings that have been observed even in a smoothed two-quarter moving average of the U.S. money growth rate since 1980—1.9 percent in the second quarter, 5.8 percent in the third quarter, followed by 13.2 percent in the fourth quarter; in the four quarters of 1981, 8.1, 7.1, 4.9, 3.0 percent; and in the first three quarters of 1982, 8.3, 7.1, and 3.4 percent, with the fourth quarter figure a likely high multiple of the third quarter figure. Is this monetarism?

A legislated rule has *never* been tried. It is a modest step towards restraining monetary authorities, but both theory and evidence suggest that it could be a giant step toward achieving economic stability.

Notes

1. Warburton (1964, p. 1328). In earlier studies, in the 1940s and 1950s, Warburton advocated a 5 percent annual growth rate in the money stock, inclusive of an adjustment for a projected steady secular decline in velocity of 1.5 percent per year. The shift to a lower proposed growth rate for money incorporated the assumption that the reversal in the trend of velocity in the 1950s—from negative to positive—would continue.

2. Milton Friedman has called our attention to the similarity between the results of a table he constructed for the period 1962I through 1982IV (divided at 1971I and 1973III), and of our table. He calculated a geometric mean of 12-term moving standard deviation of growth rates of M1, M2, and real output. The increase in the variability of M1 from 1962–71 to 1971–82 of 0.26 in his table matches our finding of an increase of 0.31; the increase in the variability of real output he found of 1.61 is almost identical with the increase of 1.62 in our table. For M2, in his table, the increase in variability from the first to the second period is much sharper than for M1—1.21 compared to 0.26

11   Real and Pseudo-Financial Crises

A widely held belief in the United States and the world financial community is that the default of major debtors—whether companies or municipalities or sovereign countries—could lead to bank failures that would precipitate a financial crisis. The remedy proposed by those propagating this view is that major debtors therefore must be rescued from the threat of bankruptcy to avert the projected dire consequences for banks and for the stability of the financial system. I shall argue that (a) a debtor whose affairs have been mismanaged should be liquidated or reorganized under new management; (b) default by major debtors need not result in bank failures; (c) if defaults do result in bank failures, so long as the security of the private sector's deposits is assured, no financial crisis will ensue. The bugaboo of financial crisis has been created to divert attention from the true remedies that the present financial situation demands.

A financial crisis is fuelled by fears that means of payment will be unobtainable at any price and, in a fractional-reserve banking system, leads to a scramble for high-powered money. It is precipitated by actions of the public that suddenly squeeze the reserves of the banking system. In a futile attempt to restore reserves, the banks may call loans, refuse to roll over existing loans, or resort to selling assets. Such a sequence of events is to be distinguished from what happens during a disinflation or a deflation. A deflation or a disinflation is a consequence of restricted growth of bank reserves but it is not precipitated by the public's behavior. The essence of a financial crisis is that it is shortlived, ending with a slackening of the public's demand for additional currency. A disinflation or a deflation may be long drawn out. Nominal wealth may decline, real debts may rise, but these are not financial crises.[1]

No financial crisis has occurred in the United States since 1933, and none has occurred in the United Kingdom since 1866. All the phenomena of recent years that have been characterised as financial crisis—a decline in asset prices of equity stocks, real estate, commodities; depreciation of the exchange value of a national currency; financial distress of a large non-financial firm, a large municipality, a financial industry, or sovereign debtors—are pseudo-financial crises.[2]

A real financial crisis occurs only when institutions do not exist, when authorities are unschooled in the practices that preclude such a development, and when the private sector has reason to doubt the dependability of preventive arrangements. Institutional changes introduced since 1933 in the United States and since 1866 in the United Kingdom and the private sector's familiarity with and confidence in the responses of institutions and authorities assure that concern with financial crises is misplaced. What should be the object of concern with respect to the proposals to deal with pseudo-financial crises is the perpetuation of policies that promote inflation and waste of economic resources.

Section 11.1 reviews the last real financial crisis in England and notes developments at later dates when a financial crisis did not occur in England but did in the United States. Section 11.2 tries to account for the record in the two countries. Section 11.3 examines the link that Kindleberger (1978) attempts to establish between manias and financial crises from 1720 to 1975. Finally, section 11.4 questions the emphasis currently given to financial distress as the trigger for financial crises and shows that it is based on a misinterpretation of the development of past real financial crises. It is not financial distress that triggers a crisis. The failure of authorities or institutions to respond in a predictable way to ward off a crisis and the private sector's uncertainty about the response are the triggers of a real financial crisis.

11.1 England's Last Real Financial Crisis in 1866 and Later Dates When None Occurred There But Did Occur in the United States

I begin by reviewing the circumstances that led to a financial crisis in England in 1866 and then turn to developments in 1873, 1890, 1907, 1914, and 1931—dates when real financial crises might have but did not occur in England. I also refer to the experience of the United States at these dates leaving for the next section reference to its experience in 1884, when a financial crisis was averted and in 1893, when it was not. In that section, I try to show why the record changed after 1866 in England, and why it was variable in the United States.

11.1.1 1866

The onset of the financial crisis in 1866 may be traced to the collapse in January of a firm of contractors, Watson, Overend & Company, and two other companies, the Contract Corporation and the Joint Stock Discount Company, with which the first had ties. These three drew on paper issued to one another and discounted with Overend, Gurney & Company, among others. Overend, Gurney in earlier years had been a solid conservative partnership, one of the pillars of the City. About 1860, a younger generation then in charge of the business became less circumspect in its lending operations, accepting equity interests for unrepayable loans extended to ironworks and shipping companies. Losses led to a decision to incorporate with the possibility of turning over a new leaf. The new company was launched in 1865 just after the conclusion of the US Civil War, when there was every reason to anticipate a strong revival of demand for British exports, but the new company did not live long enough to benefit from it. The failures noted above in January 1866 were followed by additional ones in March and April, but again those were firms of marginal significance. However, when on 10 May Overend, Gurney shut down, the market was shaken. The next day panic broke loose.

11.1.2 1873

Twice during the year financial crises were said to have occurred but only the second time was the characterization accurate. The first occasion, centred on the Continent, began on 9 May with a sharp decline in prices on the Vienna Stock Exchange. The price decline spread to Germany, Switzerland, and Italy, affecting assets like real estate, building, railways, and iron and steel ventures that had been in great favour. Contraction and liquidation followed but no disruption of payments. In England, the only reflection of events abroad was a series of increases in the Bank rate over a four-week period, followed by stepwise reductions over the succeeding ten weeks.

The real financial crisis, centred on the United States, had its beginnings on 8 September when the New York Warehouse & Security Company, organized to lend on grain and produce but involved in railway loans, failed. Five days later, Kenyon, Cox & Company, a stock brokerage firm that had endorsed the paper of another railroad, also failed. A depressed railroad bond market had led these railroads to obtain temporary financing; with the loans about to fall due, neither the lenders nor borrowers were prepared to pay up. The failures were marginal firms, but on 18 and 19 September two leading firms were suspended, Jay Cooke & Company (failure followed the suspension) and Fisk & Hatch (resumed but failed in 1884). At the same time runs began on two small banks, and on 20 September, on a larger New York bank. Panic selling on the New York Stock Exchange led to the closing of the market for ten days. Currency went to a premium as the New York and interior banks restricted payment in greenbacks. By 22 October, the currency was obtainable virtually at par.

Gold was exported to the United States on 25 September by the Bank of England, exports from other central banks as well continuing until the end of October. Bank rate rose. Since investors in England and Germany were holders of American securities, the stock market crash in New York had reverberations. A sharp sell-off on the London Stock Exchange on 6 November led to a rise in Bank rate to 9 per cent the next day, but the payment system was not impaired.

11.1.3   1890

Two monetary disturbances occurred, one in New York, the other in London. Prices on the New York Stock Exchange in November had been falling, partly due to selling by English investors, in order "to carry the load of investments of a less desirable description" (Sprague 1910, p. 132) in South America. On 11 November, the failure of Decker, Howell & Company was announced, involving the Bank of North America. The next day a stock brokerage firm failed and another bank closed. On 15 November, the failure of Baring Brothers in London was cabled to New York and stock prices fell. The following week several firms failed but panic did not develop.

In England, the imminence of failure by Baring Brothers, owing to imprudent investments in the Argentine, became known to the Bank of England on 8 November. In addition to underwriting South American securities, Barings had a large short-term banking business and considerable liabilities on deposit account. The actions undertaken by the Bank of England and a syndicate of bankers, to be discussed in the following section, prevented a crisis.

11.1.4   1907

London was exposed to a series of disturbances from abroad in October, beginning with a stock market decline in New York. The London and Amsterdam stock markets registered sympathetic declines in the prices of American railway securities, but the main disturbance began during the week of 14 October when five banks that were members of the New York Clearing House and three outside banks required assistance from a group of Clearing House banks. These eight banks were controlled through stock ownership on margin by a few men of no great financial standing, who used the banks to further speculation in the stocks of copper-mining companies. A decline in the price of those stocks alarmed depositors who started runs. Order seemed to have been restored by Monday 21 October, when the Knickerbocker Trust Company, the third largest trust company in New York, began to experience unfavourable clearing balances because the president had connections with one of the men in control of the banks that were in difficulty. The former's resignation did not allay distrust. On 22 October a run on Knickerbocker forced it to suspend business. The next day, a run began on the second largest trust company, and the day following on still another trust company. Assistance was given to these two companies, but by that time alarm had spread to the rest of the country. Restriction of payments by the banks followed and currency went to a premium over deposits.

Despite the repercussions from abroad, no financial crisis developed in London. Three increases in Bank rate from 31 October to 7 November sufficed to replenish gold exported to New York during the crisis there. No bank failures occurred, although voluntary company liquidations were abnormally high in 1908, presumably because of the level interest rates reached in 1908 (Clapham 1945, II, p. 393).

11.1.5   1914

The problems that arose with heightened war fears in Europe were not dissimilar to those that characterised earlier peacetime episodes of threats to the dependability of the credit and payments system. What was different was the range of financial markets—long-term capital, short-term credit, foreign exchange, and gold markets—affected in both England and the United States.

In the summer of 1914, New York, as usual, was in debt to London on short-term account, dependent for its supply of sterling exchange on the proceeds of commercial bills accepted in London and bought on a daily basis by the London discount market. The disruption of remittances from European clients of English accepting houses to cover maturing bills led, on 27 July, to a cessation in London of discounting of foreign bills. At the same time, heavy liquidation of foreign-held securities was in process on the London and New York stock markets, the proceeds of sales in New York, on London's instructions, to be remitted abroad. New York banks without sterling exchange could remit only in gold, draining reserves. Moreover, the New York banks could not count on the proceeds of the sales to provide bank accommodation for domestic purchasers of the securities. For the London clearing banks, their main liquid assets—bills, loans to the bill market, and loans to the Stock Exchange—ceased to be liquid. Both London and New York closed the stock markets on 31 July. A countrywide panic both in England and the United States threatened.[3]

11.1.6   1931

Britain's abandonment of the gold standard on 20 September has been described as a crisis, as have all the subsequent devaluations of the pound and more recently of the dollar. The overvaluation of sterling reflected in weakness in the current account in fact was corrected by the decision to stop selling gold at a fixed price. As Moggridge has noted (1982, pp. 181–2), the many repercussions of Britain's suspension of convertibility included the decision of others to follow in her wake; elsewhere the imposition of exchange controls, tariffs, and trade controls; a traditional tightening of monetary policy in the United States in response to an external drain of gold followed by a massive wave of bank failures; and further deflation not only in the United States but in all countries that remained on gold. The so-called crisis does not refer to the situation in other countries. Indeed, there was no crisis internally, except for Bank of England, Treasury, and other officials involved in negotiating credits for the Bank before the event and scheduling meetings on what to do next as reserves dwindled. As the text of the press notice announcing the decision stated, "There will be no interruption of ordinary banking business. The banks will be open as usual for the convenience of their customers; and there is no reason why sterling transactions should be affected in any way" (Sayers 1976, 264). Schumpeter commented, "[I]n England there was neither panic nor—precisely owing to the way in which the thing had been done or, if the reader prefer, had come about—loss of 'confidence,' but rather a sigh of relief" (Schumpeter 1939, 956).

11.2 When Did a Real Financial Crisis Occur?

I begin the answer to the question by citing Bagehot's analysis with respect to 1866, the last real financial crisis in England (Bagehot 1873, repr. 1902, pp. 64–5):

And though the Bank of England certainly do make great advances in time of panic, yet as they do not do so on any distinct principle, they naturally do it hesitatingly, reluctantly, and with misgiving. In 1847, even in 1866—the latest panic, and the one in which on the whole the Bank acted the best—there was nevertheless an instant when it was believed the Bank would not advance on Consols, or at least hesitated to advance on them. The moment this was reported in the City and telegraphed to the country, it made the panic indefinitely worse. In fact, to make large advances in this faltering way is to incur the evil of making them without obtaining the advantage. What is wanted and what is necessary to stop a panic is to diffuse the impression, that though money may be dear, still money is to be had. If people could be really convinced that they could have money if they wait a day or two, and that utter ruin is not coming, most likely they would cease to run in such a mad way for money. Either shut the Bank at once, and say it will not lend more than it commonly lends, or lend freely, boldly, and so that the public may feel you mean to go on lending. To lend a great deal, and yet not give the public confidence that you will lend sufficiently and effectually, is the worst of all policies; but it is the policy now pursued.

Bagehot thus stressed the importance of predictable action by the monetary authority to prevent a panic; failing that, a bank holiday was the course to follow. In 1866, the Bank's actions were hesitant so the public was not convinced that there was no reason to panic. H. H. Gibbs, Governor of the Bank, 1875–7, referred to the 1866 crisis as "its only real blunder in his experience," because, instead of lending freely at an appropriately high rate, as Bagehot advised, "it erred in lending at too low a rate before the crisis turned into panic" (Presnell 1968, p. 188). Although in 1873, when Bagehot wrote he still regarded the Bank's behavior in 1866 as undependable, Gibbs did not blame the then Governor since "the matter was not as well understood as it is now," noting that the Bank had done the right thing in 1873, when the underlying situation was just as troublesome as in 1866.[4]

The United States, by contrast, experienced a real financial crisis in 1873 because no institutional framework was immediately available to deal with the surge of demand for high-powered money by the public and banks. Belatedly, the crisis was alleviated by the issue against collateral of clearing-house loan certificates for use in the settlement of clearing balances and by US Treasury redemption with greenbacks of outstanding government debt.[5]

During the next two decades both England and the United States were spared the experience of financial crisis in circumstances that might have been breeding grounds for it. The impact of the failure of the City of Glasgow Bank in 1878 was sufficiently great to suggest to some observers that suspension of the Act of 1844 was required (Presnell, 1968, p. 189), but it was not.[6]

In May 1884, the failure of a Wall Street brokerage firm involving a bank whose president was a partner in the brokerage firm was followed by the suspension of several other banks. However, a phenomenal rise in money market rates brought in an inflow of foreign capital and the supply of funds was further expanded by prompt issue of clearing-house loan certificates. The suspended banks were thereby enabled to resume. Sprague commented (1910, pp. 113–15):

> It will be seen that the steps taken to allay alarm were immediate and effective. . . . The success which crowned the efforts of the banks in dealing with the crisis affords convincing evidence that if clearing-house loan certificates are to be issued at all, they should be issued at the beginning of a disturbance. Local runs on the banks did not become severe, because announcement was made that assistance would be granted at the moment when the disasters which might have weakened general confidence became known to the public.[7]

The final episode of the two decades under consideration, when financial crisis did not occur either in England or the United States, was occasioned by the troubles of Baring Brothers in 1890. In the United States, Sprague noted (1910, p. 142) that it was "the prompt action taken by the clearing-house authorities," by issuing loan certificates to meet the needs of particular banks experiencing runs, that prevented "the spread of panic." Sprague summarised (p. 144) "one of two specifics for the proper treatment of a panic—the continuance of loans to solvent borrowers. A second equally important specific is the prompt payment by the banks of every demand by depositors for cash." In England, the principal device the Bank of England adopted to prevent a crisis—it also borrowed gold from France and bought it from Russia—was to advance sums to meet Barings' immediate maturing liabilities, with the guarantee of a syndicate of bankers to make good any loss sustained by the Bank in liquidiating Barings over a period of years.[8] No loss was sustained by the Bank and no call on the guarantors was needed. Presnell concludes: "The news of the guarantee allowed knowledge of Barings' troubles to spread beyond the inner circles without causing panic; indeed, anxiety lifted" (1968, p. 207).[9]

For two decades after 1873 clearing houses and the US Treasury took actions that neutralized monetary disturbances so that crisis conditions did not develop. Why did similar actions in 1893 and 1907 not have comparable effects? No simple explanation is at hand to account for the occurrence of financial crisis in the United States in 1893. It is easier to account for the crisis in 1907.

Two features of the situation in 1893 that differed from earlier experience may be noted: fears that silver advocates would succeed in forcing the country off gold first had to be put to rest, and only subsequently did the condition of the banks as a result of mercantile failures excite independent concern. At that point the clearing houses issued loan certificates. Sprague reports (1910, p. 173), "Serious strain had been met boldly and successfully," but that was not to be the end of the episode. A second wave of distrust of banks spread over the west and south with consequent withdrawals of cash reserves from New York banks. Thereupon the Erie Railroad went into receivership and the stock market suffered the worst decline of the year. Bank suspensions followed in the east as well as in the south and west. Starting with banks in New York, banks throughout the country partly restricted cash payments, sending currency to a premium. The restriction, which lasted from 3 August to 2 September, came six weeks after the issue of clearing-house loan certificates and when gold was arriving from Europe.

Why did the issue of loan certificates not cut short the episode? One suggestion is that some banks did not avail themselves of the opportunity to obtain the certificates and therefore were unable to offset the shrinkage of their reserves (Noyes 1894, p. 22). In addition, individual banks with the bulk of bankers' deposits had reserve deficiencies even though aggregate reserves of the banks were adequate. The suggestion that best conforms to the view I am presenting is that as early as July (Noyes 1894, p. 25) rumors of refusal of banks to convert deposits into cash incited the financial crisis. A misinformed public can nullify the beneficial effects of actions designed to avert panic.

In 1907, the explanation for the occurrence of crisis appears straight-forward. Assistance to troubled trust companies was granted slowly and without dramatic effect. The runs on the trust companies depleted the currency holdings of the New York Clearing House banks which were also shipping currency to interior banks and paying it out over their counters to their own frightened depositors. Although the Treasury helped by depositing currency with these banks, New York was threatened with panic, loans were obtainable only with great difficulty, and stock market prices collapsed. Sprague argued that at this point the clearing-house banks should have issued loan certificates to enable banks to extend loans more freely to borrowers and also to prevent the weakening of particular banks with unfavourable clearing-house balances. In his view, the banks did not do so due to their mistaken belief that an issue of clearing-house loan certificates would cause restriction (Sprague, pp. 257-8, 272-3). While local runs in New York subsided, alarm spread throughout the country. Loss of confidence was displayed less by the public than by country banks. They demanded currency for the funds on deposit or on call in New York. Belatedly, the New York Clearing House issued loan certificates and immediately restricted the convertibility of deposits into currency. Countrywide restriction followed. In 1907, the right actions were taken too late to be effective.[10]

The wartime features of the 1914 episode make it not wholly comparable to earlier cases of threatened crises that were averted. Yet to cope with the problems that rose in the summer of 1914, some of the methods relied on in peacetime episodes were applied. Foremost was the provision of emergency currency issues, in the United States, both clearing-house loan certificates and Aldrich-Vreeland currency (issued by groups of banks under the Act of 1908 establishing the National Monetary Commission), and in England, Treasury Currency Notes, which soon displaced gold coin. Initially, in the United States, concern was directed to limiting shipments of gold, but that became otiose: with the reopening of the sterling acceptance market in London, the belligerents' growing demand for exports, and the balance of trade turning strongly in favor of the United States. In England, initially Bank rate was lifted to 10 percent, the level at which it had stood on the suspension of the Act of 1844 on three previous dates. This time no suspension was needed, and Bank rate was lowered to 5 percent within the week to remain unchanged for the duration.

The additional measures taken to restore the channels of international and domestic financial activity were basically government subsidies (to the export trade in the United States in the form of war risk insurance) or government guarantees against loss (to the banking system in England). The guarantees in England led to the termination of an extended August Bank Holiday and of moratoria on the payment of bills making possible the renewal of availability of acceptance credits in London. A protracted closing of the stock markets in both New York and London was ultimately ended.

Britain's decision to suspend convertibility into gold in September 1931, as I noted earlier, does not qualify as a financial crisis. Real financial crises *par excellence* were experienced by the United States from 1930 to 1933. The lender-of-last-resort was responsible for a series of crises that intensified over time because it did not recognize the need to provide liquidity to the fractional reserve banking system that was confronted with surges of repeated runs. A multiple contraction of deposits was enforced by the inability of the banks to acquire adequate amounts of high-powered money. By March 1933 the entire financial system was prostrate.

The reasons may now be summarized, accounting for financial crises that did or did not occur in the past. In both cases the setting is one in which the financial distress of certain firms became known to market participants, raising alarm as creditors became concerned about the value of their claims not only on those firms but also firms previously in sound condition. Banks that were creditors of the firms in distress became targets of suspicion by their depositors. When monetary authorities failed to demonstrate readiness at the beginning of such a disturbance to meet all demands of sound debtors for loans and of depositors for cash, a financial crisis occurred. A financial crisis *per contra* could be averted by timely predictable signals to market participants of institutional readiness to make available an augmented supply of funds. The sources of the funds supplied might have been inflows from abroad—attracted by higher domestic than foreign interest rates—or emergency issues of domestic currency. The readiness was all. Knowledge of the availability of the supply was sufficient to allay alarm, so that the funds were never drawn on. In a few instances, orderly liquidation of the firms in distress, with a guarantee against loss by the liquidator, isolated the problem so that it did not spread to other firms and averted a financial crisis in this way.

A breakdown of the payments system has not occurred in the last century and more in England—ignoring the 1914 episode—and in the last half-century in the United States. The lesson has been learned that the financial distress of the few must not be permitted to become a financial crisis for all. Individual debtors fail but their difficulties do not become widespread and undermine creditors in general. Bad banks fail, or more likely are reorganized under new management or merged with a good bank, but if a run on a bank occurs—it is said to have occurred on the Banco Ambrosiano in the recent scandal in Italy—it is not permitted to cumulate into a banking panic. In the United States, federal deposit insurance attempts to remove the problem of a loss of confidence in the ability of banks to convert deposits into currency and thus to eliminate the reason for bank runs, but, as the experience of other countries proves, such insurance is not essential. Not only are authorities better educated. So also is the public. As its experience has grown with the institutional arrangements that prevent disruption of the payments system, its behavior contributes to the dependability of the system.

11.3 Manias, Panics, Crashes

The preceding sections have focused on the relation between financial distress of firms with perceived significant market presence and the historical incidence of financial crises. In this section the focus shifts to the validity of the identification of manias with financial crises (Kindleberger 1978).

For Kindleberger, manias, panics, and crashes are three phases of the same process. During manias, investors shift from money to real or financial assets. During panics, they try to shift from real or financial assets to money. Crashes are the denouement of the process, with the collapse of prices of whatever was eagerly acquired during the mania—"commodities, houses, buildings, land, stocks, bonds" (1978, p. 5). He takes for granted that manias occur during cyclical expansions and the panic phases at peaks, while disclaiming that every business expansion leads "inevitably to mania and panic. But the pattern occurs sufficiently frequently and with sufficient uniformity" (p. 5). Finally, he regards the manias, panics, and crashes that he discusses as financial crises per se.

In current economic analysis, the word "bubble" has supplanted the pejorative "mania." In the definition proposed by Flood and Garber (1982, p. 275), "The possibility of . . . a price bubble exists when the expected rate of market price change is an important factor determining current market price." No reference is made to cyclical conditions in the definition. In my view, bubbles may arise independently of the economy's cyclical stage, although business expansion may foster them. No one has systematically examined all the cases, so the ones associated with particular cycle movements have had the lion's share of attention. Kindleberger's assertion that, according to a monetarist view, "mania and panic would both be avoided if only the supply of money were stabilized at some fixed quantity, or at a regular growing level" (pp. 5–6) does not accord with my monetarist view. Bubbles, like bankruptcies, would occur even if the money stock were free of destabilising cyclical swings. The Florida land boom of 1925–6 and the gold price bubble of 1979–80 were created by opportunities those markets appeared to offer rather than the pattern of monetary growth.

A basic fact concerning bubbles is that they leave eager investors in sure-fire, get-rich schemes at the take-off considerably poorer at the landing. The loss of wealth attendant on misguided, unprofitable, voluntary investment decisions is, of course, not confined to bubbles. Bankruptcy proceedings are a daily occurrence in economic life. Willingness to spend may be reduced and previously glowing expectations may be replaced by uncertainty. But loss of wealth is not synonymous with a financial crisis.

At the stock market peak in 1929, the total value of all shares listed on the New York Stock Exchange was about $200 billion. The decline in October is estimated at nearly $15½ billion, so many investors undoubtedly were poorer. Yet no financial crisis occurred following the great crash. The reason is that prompt and effective action by the New York Federal Reserve Bank provided additional reserves to the New York banks through open market purchases. Kindleberger acknowledges that the crash did not "lead to a money market panic . . . or to runs on banks, probably because of the effective action of the New York Federal Reserve in pumping funds into the market" (p. 113), but still classifies the crash as a financial crisis apparently because it "spread liquidation to other asset markets, such as commodities, and seized up credit to strike a hard blow at output" (p. 113). Any deflation would thus qualify as a financial crisis.

In a perceptive comment on bubbles, Wood (1983) has noted that they concern markets "where quantities traded have varied little, while there have been enormous variations in price. They are interesting, but the fate of nations seldom depends on them."

Kindleberger provides a tabulation in an appendix to his book that lists some three dozen financial crisis during two and a half centuries, characterizing each one by the subject of the mania, how it was financed, dates of the peak and crash, and a final entry identifying the lender-of-last-resort. It is the final entry that motivates Kindleberger's study. He argues the importance of a lender-of-last-resort "who comes to the rescue and provides the public good of stability that the private market is unable to produce for itself" (p. 4).[11] Yet he does not discriminate between episodes in which successful action was taken to prevent the development of a crisis and episodes in which no action was taken or the action was unsuccessful.[12]

Despite his designation of all episodes as financial crises without differentiation of those where the "rescue" provided stability, even Kindleberger notes that there has been a dwindling of the number and a lessening of the severity of domestic financial crises since 1866 in Britain and since 1929 in the United States and on the Continent. He considers three possible explanations: (i) the decline of usury laws, making it possible for interest rates to be raised sufficiently to limit manias; (ii) the shunning of manias by markets that had learned from experience; (iii) the calming of anxieties owing to the known existence of a lender-of-last-resort. He dismisses the first two out of hand, but his position on the third is ambiguous. Nor is it clear why at this point he cites Minsky's reference (1977) to "near panics" in 1966, 1969–70, and 1974–5, and "incipient crises" in 1974 (p. 218).

The record on domestic financial crises may thus be reassuring to Kindleberger, but his current concern is the greater frequency now than in the nineteenth century of foreign exchange crises. The solution he suggests is an international lender-of-last resort.[13] The recent analytical literature on bubbles also encompasses runs on a currency that is fixed in price in terms of at least one other currency and runs under flexible exchange rates (Flood and Garber 1982). The underlying assumption that a run on a currency is a crisis seems to me untenable. The market will sell off an overvalued currency under fixed or floating exchange rates and will shift to an undervalued currency. If authorities resist the market's evaluation, it may be costly for them, but the problem facing the currency is more fundamental: the economic policies that are responsible for the currency's plight are the heart of the matter. If there is a crisis, it resides in the failure to adjust those policies.

I conclude that manias, panics, and crashes reduce wealth. They are not *per se* financial crises unless the shift from tangible or financial assets to money leads to a run on banks. A lender-of-last-resort can forestall such a development, so I agree with Kindleberger that there is an important role for such an entity, although I do not subscribe to the notion that only a public authority has in the past filled or can at present fill that role.

11.4 Financial Distress versus Financial Crises

In my lexicon, the events since the mid-1960s that have been termed "financial crises" or "threats of a financial crisis" have been pseudo-financial crises. Essentially the response to each of these events (to be noted in what follows) has been a form of bail-out, for which the justification was that the action averted crisis. Since no financial crisis would in fact have been experienced had a bail-out not been undertaken, the events were pseudo-financial crises. Moreover, the policies adopted were economically inefficient or inflationary in effect.

The first event to be considered here was the failure of the Penn Central Railroad in June 1970. The Federal Reserve was concerned lest the company's default on its $200 million commercial paper borrowings would jeopardize that market. The Fed assumed that lenders would not discriminate between a troubled issuer and other perfectly sound issuers. The scenario envisaged by the Fed was that the latter would need to pay off their commercial paper because of generalized distrust of the instrument. Accordingly, the banks were informed that the discount window was "wide open" (Maisel 1973, p. 9) if they needed funds to make loans to customers unable to roll over commercial paper. In addition, to enable banks to bid freely for funds in the open market, the Fed suspended interest rate ceilings on 30 to 89-day large denomination certificates of deposit—an action that was desirable in its own right. Maisel concludes that the Fed's actions averted a panic (p. 4). However, if there were commercial paper issuers that faced difficulties, as Carron notes (1982, p. 398), it was not owing to the condition of the market as such but to "conditions peculiar to those firms" (Chrysler Financial and Commercial Credit among others). The verdict of the 1971 *Economic Report of the President* (p. 69) was that no "genuine liquidity crisis existed in mid-1970."

Events in 1973–4 centred on bank failures in the United Kingdom, West Germany, the United States, and Switzerland that were thought to threaten the international financial order. Hirsch (1977, p. 248), who believes that cooperation to achieve "collective intermediate goods" of bank stability is technically easier to organize in a small group of like minded individuals and institutions than in an open group" (p. 249)—a view reminiscent of de Cecco's—describes what happened in Britain when "fringe banks," bank new-comers, experienced difficulties in December 1973. A deterioration of the market value of real estate investments of these banks led to deposit withdrawals and the switching of new deposits to established banks. To save depositors of the fringe banks from losses, the four-member oligopoly of deposit banks had to commit resources to that end. Hirsch interprets the action taken by the established banks as in their self-interest by removing a source of competition. Whatever the motivation of the established banks, their collective action bespeaks an understanding that the failure of individual banks must not be allowed to contract the aggregate money stock.

Two views have been presented with respect to the actions taken by the Federal Reserve when Franklin National Bank announced, in May 1974, that it had lost heavily in forward transactions in the foreign exchange market. The Federal Reserve initially announced that it would advance whatever funds Franklin needed, so long as it remained solvent, the loans ultimately reaching a maximum of $1.75 billion in early

October. At that point the bank was merged with another institution and the FDIC assumed the Federal Reserve's loan.

One view (Carron 1982, p. 400) is that the preconditions of a genuine financial crisis existed, as evidenced by the fact that corporations paid premiums on their borrowings that reflected risks perceived in the banking system rather than in their own positions. The preconditions were, however, mitigated both because markets remained orderly with no lack of confidence on the part of investors and the central bank intervened effectively. An opposite view is that the immediate impact of Franklin's failure was erased by a Federal Reserve bail-out that led market participants to believe that no bank failures would be tolerated and that encouraged 'banks to become more reckless than ever' (Wojnilower 1980, pp. 298–9). It was not only the losses in the foreign exchange market that the Franklin case revealed. The aftermath of its failure also disclosed the near-bankruptcy of real estate affiliates many banks owned. The affiliates had financed construction with short-term funds and invested in real estate and mortgages whose value declined when interest rates rose. Selling off real estate at distress prices further compromised the position of the affiliates, so that they experienced problems in selling their paper.

The perception of increased risk in lending to banks raised the cost of funds for them. Does this justify a bail-out or concern that a financial crisis was imminent?

Banking difficulties in Europe in 1974 that arose because of losses sustained in the foreign exchange market were apparently met without bail-outs. The Bundesbank announced the liquidation of Bankhaus I.D. Herstatt. Neither Westdeutsche Landesbank Girozentral of West Germany nor Union Bank of Switzerland was mortally wounded by its losses.

It was not banking difficulties but financial distress of two large real sector firms—Lockheed Corporation (1971) and Chrysler Corporation (1979)—and a municipality—New York City (1975)—that also provided occasions for a prognosis of a threat of financial crisis. In each case federal government legislation was enacted to guarantee private loans to these entities. The object was to avoid bankruptcy. Though Penn Central Railroad had filed for bankruptcy and subsequently restructured its operations to become an efficient firm, the view that has since come to prevail is that bankruptcy proceedings by themselves will create a financial crisis. The loan guarantees thus serve to mask the inefficient use of resources that had produced financial distress. It is true that some restructuring of claims on and operations of the entities was required as a condition of the guarantees, but it is not clear why reorganisation under bankruptcy proceedings would have precipitated a financial crisis. Again, the underlying assumptions seems to be that markets cannot discriminate between a firm or municipality in financial distress and others in sound condition. The inefficient are sustained in their misuse of resources because of the imagined hardship that would be imposed on the efficient.

Another class of events that is said to raise the prospect of domestic financial crisis is still impending—the impairment of the ability of many sovereign countries to make scheduled payments on their outstanding bank loans. Short-term loans extended to governments and to private borrowers abroad in some cases appear to be beyond their prospective capacity to repay. Acknowledgement of default on outstanding loans would require write-downs that would reduce capital of the banks involved and that would undoubtedly raise the cost to them of funds obtained in the open market. This course has been rejected on the ground that confidence in the stability of the banking system would be shaken. The alternative chosen has been the subterfuge that all the loans will be repaid, with the banks exhorted to provide an increase in lending sufficient to enable delinquent borrowers to maintain interest payments and to reschedule principal. In addition, the goal of stable non-inflationary monetary growth has been sacrificed as part of the effort to resolve the international debt problem. It is taken for granted that, if the policy of papering over the true economic prospects of the borrowing countries ultimately fails, standing in the wings will be the authorities ready to bail out the lenders. The costs of renewed inflation will then be dismissed as an unfortunate side effect.

Real financial crises need not occur because there is a well-understood solution to the problem: assure that deposits can be converted at will into currency whatever the difficulties banks encounter. The solution does not preclude failure of mismanaged banks. Recent discussion of moral hazard in relation to real financial crises would be more apt in relation to pseudo-financial crises. They provide the rationale for bailouts and shoring up inefficiency. Pseudo-financial crises in recent years have generated expectations "that no monetary authority will allow any key financial actor to fail" (Wojnilower 1980, p. 299). Political authority seems well embarked in the direction of not allowing any key non-financial actor to fail, and of encouraging inflationary actions by domestic monetary authorities and international agencies in the cause of pseudo-financial crises.

Notes

1. The example of the deflation in 1920–1 in the United States may be cited. Bank reserves declined from $2.8 billion in April 1920 to $2.4 billion in August 1921. Wholesale prices (on the base 1926) fell from a peak of 167 in May 1920

to a trough of 91 January 1922. An index of liabilities of business failures rose from a trough of 6.0 in January 1920 to a peak of 71.2 in February 1922. Although 506 banks suspended business in 1921, there was no financial crisis. The deposit-currency and the deposit-reserve ratios in August 1921 were higher than in April 1920.

2. Financial distress defines the condition of an individual, a non-financial firm or an individual bank, or an industry that has assets with realisable value in money that is less than the amount of its indebtedness.

3. De Cecco (1975) argues that no problem would have arisen, had not the joint stock banks arbitrarily begun a credit squeeze in the middle of July, recalling loans they had made to bill brokers, and refusing to finance foreign clients of the accepting houses who usually borrowed in London to meet their maturing bills that the London houses had accepted. Stock Exchange dealers who worked on loans from foreign banks dumped their stocks to be able to return borrowed money, compelling the joint stock banks to call for extra margin from customers with Lombard loans, since the value of the collateral had declined. De Cecco says that the banks assumed a crisis of confidence on the part of the public would occur but in fact it did not happen. Therefore the banks engineered a crisis of confidence by refusing to pay out gold to the public and themselves drawing on the Bank's gold. The motive for the banks' behaviour, according to de Cecco, was to "substitute themselves in lucrative international business" and "exclude traditional intermediaries from their functions," though they wanted only "to threaten them with the possibility of . . . death, in order to have them rescued *in extremis* and to paralyze their future action" (p. 149).

According to Sayers (I, p. 70), it was sales of internationally traded securities on European stock exchanges that initiated the credit squeeze in London. He also notes that the joint stock banks' refusal to pay out gold before the August Bank Holiday may be interpreted in a more favorable light than de Cecco presents (I, p. 72).

4. De Cecco (1975, pp. 80–2) dismisses Bagehot's analysis. According to de Cecco, the Bank deliberately sought the fall of Overend, Gurney because "they were encroaching upon the very branch of business on which the Bank throve: the discounting of bills from all over the country. . . . So conflict between the two giants seemed inevitable, particularly as their business had become very similar in nature" (p. 80). "The Bank watched its rival fall without making any attempt to come to its rescue; on the contrary, it implemented a six-month 'dear money' policy specifically to make Gurney's fall inevitable. Only after its rival had gone under did the Bank go to the market's rescue by extending unlimited assistance to anybody needing it, to allay the panic induced by Gurney's failure" (p. 82).

If de Cecco is right, the Bank was culpable because it deliberately ignored "what was well understood." But the evidence does not support de Cecco's opinion that by 1866 the Bank understood what needed to be done in a timely way to prevent a crisis.

5. In Austria, in 1873, the main response to the stock market decline which was followed by a large number of insolvencies and bankruptcies was the suspension of the Banking Act of 1862 to "assist the mobilization of central bank funds in case a liquidity shortage should make itself felt" (März 1982, p. 188). No shortage occurred. Six months later, a consortium of banking houses and the central bank rescued from collapse the Bodencredit-Anstalt, an issuer of mortgage bonds with credit standing abroad equal to that of Austrian treasury certificates. The firm had been involved in "risky stock-exchange operations" (p. 189).

6. *The Economist* 5 October 1878 (Gregory 1929, II, pp. 289–90), commented on the bank's failure: "There was no run, or any semblance of run; there was no local discredit. . . . The fact that the other Scottish banks are willing to take up the notes of the City of Glasgow Banks appears to support the belief that all the liabilities of the bank will be met in full. The danger of discrediting the circulation may, however, have had some influence on the other banks in determining their action in this matter."

7. Presnell (1982, p. 152) reports the actions taken in Ceylon, when the Oriental Banking Corporation, a major international bank with many branches in Southeast Asia and in Australia, collapsed in May 1884. The colony's governor guaranteed the bank's substantial note issues and the other banks imported silver rupees from India. A financial crisis was averted.

8. A similar device had apparently been used by the Bank of France in 1889. Presnell (1968, p. 205) cites a French historian as crediting France with helping England in "two ways in 1890: with gold and by her example." The example refers to the use of a collective guarantee by French banks in support of the Bank of France. A certain Comptoir d'Escompte, in 1889, experienced a run as the result of unwise loans it had made to a company that speculated in copper. The Bank provided the Comptoir with funds to reimburse its depositors and creditors and then liquidated it.

9. According to de Cecco (1975, p. 92), because of the Bank of England's rivalry with the joint stock banks, only merchant bankers were first asked to underwrite the guarantee, and the joint stock banks only later. He concludes that the Baring crisis "proved to be the swan song of the power of the Bank of England and of the merchant banks. Barings were prevented from going down and taking other houses with them; but this was made possible only by a series of expedients—all traditional instruments of policy had been abandoned" (p. 95).

Presnell deplores the device of the guarantee as "not central banking," as well as loss of the opportunity the Barings' situation created to advance reform of the Act of 1844, and more particularly the need for larger banking and larger gold reserves.

10. Bonelli's article (1982, pp. 51–65) on "The 1907 Financial Crisis in Italy" should be retitled "The 1907 Financial Crisis That Did Not Occur in Italy." He defines the crisis as a prolonged decline in prices of shares that brought one of the largest mixed banks close to suspension. It did not happen because the Banca d'Italia, the largest of the three issuing banks, initiated and coordinated "anticrisis measures" (p. 51). "It began to provide liquidity in all directions by means of discounts and advances . . . it also announced that its reserves were increasing, that it could issue money without any difficulty, and that it could even count on the government's readiness to take any extraordinary measures that might become necessary (to wit, removal of the ceiling established by law as regards the volume of circulation not enjoying full metallic coverage)" (p. 58).

11. Kindleberger cites no evidence in support of the proposition that the private market is unable to serve as the lender-of-the-last-resort. The clearing houses at times undertook that function under the National Banking System in the United States.

12. An oddity is that the tabulation includes an entry for 1819 in England. The listing for that episode is "none" under "crisis," and "none needed" under "lender-of-last-resort."

13. I share the view expressed by Griffiths (1983) that the proposal should be rejected. The grounds for rejection that he cites relate to the role of banks and international debt. They also apply to foreign exchange markets.

12   Has Government Any Role in Money?

Milton Friedman and Anna J. Schwartz

12.1 Introduction

In recent years there has been a burst of scholarly interest in various aspects of monetary reform—not the conduct of current monetary policy, which has for decades been the object of active scholarly work, but the institutional structure of the monetary system. This interest has centered on three separate but related topics: (1) competition versus government monopoly in the creation of or control over outside or high-powered money, (2) so-called free banking, and (3) the determination of the unit of account and its relation to media of exchange. The topics are related because they all deal with what role, if any, government has in the monetary system.

This burst of interest has been a response to mutually reinforcing developments, some internal to the discipline of economics; others, external.

The internal developments were threefold. One is the emergence of the theory of public choice, which has produced a large-scale shift from a public-interest to a private-interest interpretation of government activity. Instead of regarding civil servants and legislators as disinterestedly pursuing the public interest, as they judged it—in sharp contrast to the behavior we have attributed to participants in business enterprises—economists have increasingly come to regard civil servants and legislators as pursuing their private interests, treated not as narrowly pecuniary or selfish but as encompassing whatever ends enter into their utility functions, not excluding concern for the public interest. This public choice perspective is extremely attractive intellectually because it aligns our interpretations of government and private activity. It has inevitably led to extensive research on the determinants of governmental behavior as well as to renewed attention to the kinds of institutions and policies, if any, that can make each participant in government as in a free market operate as if, in Adam Smith's famous phrase, he were "led by an invisible hand to promote an end that was no part of his intention," namely, the interest of the public. Monetary policy and the monetary authorities have been obvious candidates for attention.[1]

A second internal development is the rational expectations approach, particularly its stress on the effect of the institutional structure and changes in the institutional structure on the expectations of the public. In one sense, this approach is not new. For example, the effect of the existence of central banks on the behavior of commercial banks and the public had long been explicitly recognized in the monetary literature. Yet, the coining of a new name, the application of the idea by Lucas to the validity of econometric forecasts, and the explicit modelling of the role of expectations have all had a major impact on the profession's thinking and, incidentally, have promoted greater attention to institutional structures as compared with current policy formation.

A third internal development is the renewed interest in so-called Austrian Economics, with its emphasis on invisible-hand interpretations of the origin and development of economic institutions, and its interpretation of the business cycle as largely reflecting the effect of non-neutral money. The latter in turn produced a long "Austrian" tradition of support for "hard" money and opposition to discretionary money management. Hayek's proposal (1976, 1978) for denationalizing money was especially influential in reviving this tradition.

The key external development—the ultimate consequences of which are shrouded in uncertainty—was the emergence of a world monetary system that, we believe, is unprecedented: a system in which essentially every currency in the world is, directly or indirectly, on a pure fiat standard—directly, if the exchange rate of the currency is flexible though possibly manipulated; indirectly, if the exchange rate is effectively fixed in terms of another fiat-based currency (e.g., since 1983, the Hong Kong dollar). This system emerged gradually after World War I. From then to 1971, much of the world was effectively on a dollar standard, while the U.S., though ostensibly on a gold standard (except for a brief interval in 1933–34), was actually on a fiat standard combined with a government program for pegging the price of gold. The Bretton Woods agreement in the main simply ratified that situation, despite the lip service paid to the role of gold, and the provisions for changes in exchange rates. The end of Bretton Woods in 1971 removed both the formal links to the dollar and the pretense that the U.S. was on a gold standard. The stocks of gold listed on the books of the central books of the world are a relic of a bygone era, though a slim possibility remains that they will again become more than that at some future date.

The formal ending of Bretton Woods was precipitated by an inflationary surge in the U.S. in the 1960s and in turn helped to produce a continuation and acceleration of that surge in the 1970s. The inflation and the subsequent economic instability were more directly responsible for the burst of interest in monetary reform than the momentous change in the world's monetary system of which the inflation was both a cause and a manifestation. It did so in several ways. In the first place, it brought into sharp focus the poor performance of the monetary authorities—reinforcing the conclusions about prior policy that various scholars had reached, including ourselves in our *Monetary History*. Even granted the market failures that we and many other economists had attributed to a strictly laissez-faire policy in money and banking, the course of events encouraged the view that turning to government as an alternative was a cure that was worse than the disease, at least with existing government policies and institutions. Government failure might be worse than market failure.

In the second place, the rise in nominal interest rates produced by the rise in inflation converted government control of interest rates in the U.S. via Regulation Q from a minor to a serious impediment to the effective clearing of credit markets. One response was the invention of money market mutual funds as a way to avoid Regulation Q. The money market funds performed a valuable social function. Yet, from a broader perspective, their invention constituted social waste. If either the inflation had not occurred or banks had been free to respond to market forces, there would have been no demand for the services of money market funds, and the entrepreneurial talent and other resources absorbed by the money market mutuals could have been employed in socially more productive activities. The money market funds proved an entering wedge to financial innovations that forced a relaxation and near-abandonment of control over the interest rates that banks could pay, as well as over other regulations that restricted their activities. The deregulation of banking that has occurred came too late and has been too incomplete to prevent a sharp reduction in the role of banks, as traditionally defined, in the financial system as a whole.

In Friedman's *Program for Monetary Stability,* published a quarter of a century ago, he asked the question "whether monetary and banking arrangements could be left to the market, subject only to the general rules applying to all other economic activity."

"I am by no means certain," he wrote, "that the answer is indubitably in the negative. What is clear is that monetary arrangements have seldom been left entirely to the market, even in societies following a thoroughly liberal policy in other respects, and that there are good reasons why this should have been the case" [Friedman (1959, p. 4)]. Those "good reasons" were: "[1] the resource cost of a pure commodity currency and hence its tendency to become partly fiduciary; [2] the peculiar difficulty of enforcing contracts involving promises to pay that serve as a medium of exchange and of preventing fraud in respect to them; [3] the technical monopoly character of a pure fiduciary currency which makes essential the setting of some external limit on its amount; and finally, [4] the pervasive character of money which means that the issuance of money has important effects of parties other than those directly involved and gives special importance to the preceding features. Something like a moderately stable monetary framework seems an essential prerequisite for the effective operation of a private market economy. It is dubious that the market can by itself provide such a framework. Hence, the function of providing one is an essential governmental function on a par with the provision of a stable legal framework" [Friedman (1959, p. 8), numbers added].

Of course, recognition that there are "good reasons" for government to intervene and that, as a matter of historical fact, governments, and especially modern governments, almost invariably have done so, does not mean that the actual interventions have promoted the public welfare, or that the modes of intervention have been wisely chosen. A major aim of our *Monetary History* was precisely to investigate this question for the U.S. for the period after the Civil War.

The evidence we assembled strongly suggests, indeed we believe demonstrates, that government intervention was at least as often a source of instability and inefficiency as the reverse, and that the major "reform" during the period, the establishment of the Federal Reserve System, in practice did more harm than good. Our personal conclusion, reinforced by the evidence in that work though not stated therein, is that a rigid monetary rule is preferable to discretionary monetary management by the Federal Reserve.

The aim of this paper is to consider whether the new evidence and new arguments that have emerged in recent years justify a revision of the earlier summary of "good reasons" why government has intervened, in particular of the conclusion that "the market itself cannot provide" a "stable monetary framework." In the most extreme form, does the evidence justify an unqualified affirmative rather than negative answer to the question "whether monetary and banking arrangements cannot [i.e., should not] be left to the market"?

This question in turn breaks down into three separate questions, the clear differentiation of which is one of the valuable contributions of recent writings:

(1) Can and should the determination of a unit of account linked with a medium of exchange and the provision of outside money itself be left to the market or do items [1], [3], and [4] of Friedman's

good reasons justify a government role in defining the unit of account and providing an outside money?

(2) Given a well-defined outside money involving a unit of account and a medium of exchange, can and should strict laissez-faire be the rule for banking—broadly defined to include the issuance of inside money in the form of currency as well as deposits—except only for the general rules applied to all other economic activity? This is the so-called free-banking question, which bears particularly on items [2] and [4] of Friedman's "good reasons."

In terms of institutional and legal arrangements, the major sub-issues are:

(1) Should financial intermediaries be prohibited from issuing inside money in the form of hand-to-hand currency, i.e., should hand-to-hand currency be a government monopoly?

(b) Are governmental limitations on lending and investing by financial intermediaries necessary or desirable?

(c) Is a government "lender of last resort"—a central bank—necessary or desirable?

(3) In the absence of legal obstacles, can, should, and would the unit of account be separated in practice from the medium of exchange function in the belief that financial innovation will render outside money unnecessary and obsolete? I.e., do financial innovations promise to make a 100 percent inside money the most efficient means of engaging in transactions?

It may be worth noting explicitly that the word "can" as used in these questions admits of two very different interpretations. One is narrowly economic: is a given set of arrangements internally consistent so far as narrowly economic conditions are concerned; that is, would it generate a stable equilibrium, both static and dynamic? The other is broader. Would the set of arrangements generate a stable political as well as economic equilibrium; that is, is its existence consistent with the political constitution, or would it generate political forces leading to major changes in the arrangements?

We believe that failure to distinguish between these interpretations is responsible for much of the appearance of disagreement in the discussions of monetary reform.

Of the three questions posed, we propose to discuss the first two, since the third is much less related to our earlier work, and besides, has been dealt with recently, and in our opinion correctly, by others [McCallum (1985) and White (1984b)].

The first and third questions are new in a sense in which the second is not. Essentially all participants in the nineteenth- and early twentieth-century controversies about monetary and banking matters took for granted a specie standard, in which government's role was restricted to coinage or its equivalent (i.e., provision of warehouse receipts for specie); hence they never had occasion to consider the first and third questions. Suspension of specie payments was regarded as, and in fact generally was, a temporary expedient to meet a temporary difficulty. Any government-issued money (whether notes or deposits) in excess of specie reserves was, in modern terminology, regarded as inside money, not outside money, though it clearly became the latter during periods of suspension of specie payments. This common view no doubt reflected widespread agreement that historical experience showed, as Irving Fisher put it in 1911, that "Irredeemable paper money has almost invariably proved a curse to the country employing it" [see Fisher (1929, p. 131)].

The disappearance of specie standards and the emergence of a world monetary system in which, for the first time, every country is, in Fisher's terms, on an "irredeemable paper standard" has produced two very different streams of literature: one, scientific; the other, popular. The scientific literature is that already referred to, dealing with monetary reform and the government's role in providing outside money (section 12.2 below). The popular literature is alarmist and "hard money," essentially all of it based on the proposition that Fisher's generalization will continue to hold and that the world is inevitably condemned to runaway inflation unless and until the leading nations adopt commodity standards.

There has been some, but limited, intersection between these two streams. The scientific literature has occasionally dealt with but mostly ignored the question raised by the popular literature. Have the conditions that have produced the current unprecedented monetary system also altered the likelihood that it will go the way of earlier paper standards? We consider that question in a tentative way in section 12.4 below.

By contrast with outside money, free banking was fully and exhaustively discussed in the nineteenth and early twentieth century. Recent literature has added much historical detail, discussed the arguments in terms of current monetary arrangements, and expressed old arguments in more formal and abstract terms. And we now have a much wider span of historical experience on which to base a judgment. Nonetheless, Vera Smith's 1936 *Rationale of Central Banking* provides, we believe, as accurate and complete a summary of recent theoretical arguments for and against "free banking" as it does of the earlier arguments (section 12.3).

12.2 Outside Money

Whether the government has a role in providing outside money, and what that role should be, is more basic than whether government should intervene in the provision of inside money by non-government banking institutions. Existing banking systems rest on the foundation of an outside money, and so did those "free banking" systems, such as the Scottish, Canadian and early U.S., that have recently been subjected to reexamination and offered as object lessons. Historically, a single unit of account linked to a single dominant outside money has tended to emerge, initially via a market process of transactors settling on a particular commodity, followed almost invariably by government's exercising control over one or more aspects of the issuance of outside money—typically with the ostensible purpose of standardizing the coinage and certifying its quality (purity, fineness, etc.). Occasionally, two commodities, with a flexible rate of exchange between them, have simultaneously been outside moneys, one for small transactions, the other for large, as with silver and gold in the Middle Ages, or copper and silver in China.

Insofar as governments confined themselves to producing standardized coinage, the activity was a source of revenue because of the convenience to the public of using for transaction purposes coins with a stated face value rather than bullion. The mint could make a "seignorage" charge for providing this service, and the government's visibility and authority gave it an advantage over private mints even when it did not prohibit them. However, governments have repeatedly gone farther and have used (or abused) their control over outside money to raise revenue by introducing fiat elements. Initially, this took the form of the debasement of the metallic coinage issued by the sovereign—that is, increasing the proportion of base metal in silver and gold coins, so that the stated face value of the coins exceeded the market value of the precious metal they contained. Such debasement was a source of revenue because of the lag in the adjustment of nominal prices to the lowered precious metal content of the coins. During this period, the base metal served, as it were, as inside money.

The introduction and subsequent widespread use of paper money and deposits, initially as warehouse receipts for specie, opened a broader range of possibilities, exploited both by private individuals or bankers who issued notes and deposits promising to pay specie on demand in excess of the amount of specie they held (private inside money, so long as the issuers honored the promise), and by governments that did the same (government inside money, subject to the same proviso).

As banking developed, commercial banks came to regard all non-interest bearing government issues—in the U.K., notes and deposits at the Bank of England; in the U.S., United States notes (greenbacks), national bank notes, silver certificates, Federal Reserve notes and deposits—as outside money. However, for the system as a whole, so long as convertibility into specie was maintained, only specie was in fact outside money; the excess of government issues over the government's specie holdings was government-created inside money. All such issues, however, became true outside money—pure fiat money—when convertibility was suspended, as it now has been throughout the world.

We still refer to government-issued non-interest bearing notes and deposits as government "liabilities" or "obligations," although that is not what they are, as is eminently clear in other contexts. We now take a pure fiat standard so much for granted that we no longer find any need to distinguish between the concepts of outside money relevant for the commercial banks and for the system as a whole. But that distinction remains important in judging proposals for monetary reform, and in interpreting historical experience.

That experience provides striking evidence of the value that communities attach to having a single unit of account and medium of exchange. The large revenue that governments have been able to extract by introducing fiat elements into outside money is one measure of the price that economic agents are willing to pay to preserve the unit of account and the medium of exchange to which they have become habituated. It takes truly major depreciation in the purchasing power of the dominant money before any substantial fraction of the community adopts alternatives, either with respect to the unit of account or the medium of exchange. Yet such alternatives have generally been available.

For example, students of money have repeatedly recommended what Alfred Marshall called a tabular standard, namely, the indexation of long-term contracts, so that for such contracts the unit of account becomes, to use one currency as an example, not the nominal dollar, but the real dollar, although the medium of exchange may remain the nominal dollar.[2] In most Western countries, nothing has prevented the private emergence of a tabular standard. Yet, a tabular standard has emerged on any widespread scale only in countries that have been subject to extreme movements in the price level, like some Latin American countries, Israel, etc. Indexation has been privately introduced on any substantial scale in the U.S. only with respect to labor contracts, and even there only occasionally and with respect to a minority of contracts.

Another alternative has been foreign currency, which has occasionally been resorted to both as unit of account and medium of circulation, but again only under extreme provocation.

The apparently great value to the economy of having a single unit of account linked with an (ultimate) medium of exchange does not mean that government must play any role, or that there need be a single producer of the medium of exchange. And indeed, historically, governments have entered the picture after the event, after the community had settled on a unit of account and private producers had produced media of exchange.

Two features of this history are striking. The first is that the unit of account has, invariably or nearly so, been linked to a commodity. We know of no example of an abstract unit of account—a fiduciary or fiat unit such as now prevails everywhere, having emerged spontaneously through its acceptance in private transactions. The second is how universally government has taken over, and how often it has established a monopoly in the certification or production of the outside money. In his explanation of this phenomenon, Friedman stressed considerations of economic efficiency—"can" in the narrower economic sense. But this is clearly inadequate. The theory of public choice requires attention to the political forces that have produced this result and the kind of monetary constitution, if any, that can avoid it.[3] It is not enough to document the abuses that have arisen from government control of outside money, or to demonstrate the existence of alternative arrangements that are economically more satisfactory. We shall be evading our task of explanation unless we examine the political forces that established government control under a wide range of political and economic circumstances, superseding private certification and production of outside money. And, so far as reform is concerned, we shall simply be spitting in the wind, as economists have done for 200 years with respect to tariffs, unless we explore how effective political support can be mobilized for one or another solution. We hasten to add that the latter is not the task of this paper.[4]

Item [3] of Friedman's list of "good reasons," the technical monopoly character of a *pure fiduciary* currency (italics added) has been questioned, particularly by Benjamin Klein (1974). Klein's theoretical case, resting on the necessity for a producer of money to establish confidence in his money, and the increasing capital cost of creating such confidence, is impeccable, and has received wide acceptance. Yet it is not clear that his argument can be carried over to a "pure fiduciary" currency.[5] Historically, producers of money have established confidence by promising convertibility into some dominant money, generally, specie. Many examples can be cited of fairly long-continued and successful producers of private moneys convertible into specie.[6] We do not know, however, of any example of the private production of purely inconvertible fiduciary moneys (except as temporary expedients, e.g., wooden nickels, clearing house certificates), or of the simultaneous existence in the same community of private producers of moneys convertible into different ultimate media, except for the previously mentioned case when two metals circulated simultaneously at a flexible rate of exchange, and the somewhat similar case of the greenback period (1862–1878) in the U.S. when banks had both greenback and gold deposit liabilities. Yet Klein's argument would not seem to preclude the simultaneous existence in the same community of several dominant moneys produced by different private issuers.

Hayek, in his argument for the denationalization of money, believes that such an outcome is a real possibility, if the current legal obstacles to the production of competitive moneys were removed. In particular, he believes that private issuers who produced a medium of exchange with constant purchasing power (a "real dollar") would become dominant. He recognizes that a single dominant money might tend to develop over large areas, but anticipates that different definitions of constant purchasing power would be appropriate for different areas or groups and hence that a "number of different competitive money producers would survive, with extensive overlap in border areas" [Hayek (1978, p. 112)].

Entirely aside from the question of the political forces that such arrangements would generate, we are skeptical of his conjecture, rather agreeing with Benjamin Klein's (1976, p. 514) early judgment that "I do not think that adoption of Hayek's . . . policy recommendation of complete domestic freedom of choice in currency would significantly reduce the amount of monopoly power on currency issue currently possessed by each individual European government."[7]

So far, neither Hayek's belief that privately produced constant purchasing power moneys would become dominant nor Klein's and our skepticism has any direct empirical basis, but derive rather from an interpretation of historical experience under very different monetary arrangements than those Hayek proposes. However, some direct evidence may emerge in the near future, because of developments within the present system that could facilitate the issuance of constant purchasing power money.

In the United States, the Federal Home Loan Bank Board in 1980 authorized federal savings and loan associations to make price-level-adjusted-mortgage (or PLAM) loans and, in 1982, to accept price-level-adjusted-deposits (PLAD). There seems no reason such deposits could not be readily transferable by checks or their equivalent, which would provide a medium of exchange as well as a unit of account of constant purchasing power. So far, apparently, no savings and loan has taken advantage of this possibility. However, since 1982 disinflation has been the rule, and confidence in a more stable future price level has grown rapidly. A real test will come when and if that confidence is shattered.[8]

Another U.S. development, in the course of being realized as this is written, is the introduction of futures markets in price index numbers [Friedman (1984a)]. The Coffee, Sugar & Cocoa Exchange has received permission from the Commodity Futures Trading Commission (the federal agency that regulates futures markets) to introduce a futures contract in the consumer price index. Trading in the contract began on June 21, 1985. Such futures markets would enable banks to accept deposits on a price-level adjusted basis and hedge their risk in the futures market rather than by matching price-level adjusted liabilities with price-level adjusted assets. This development seems to us the most promising of the recent innovations, in terms of its potential effect on the operation of the monetary system.

An earlier U.S. development was the removal in 1974 of the prohibition against the ownership, purchase and sale of gold by private persons. In principle, it has been possible since then for individuals in private dealings to use gold as a medium of exchange. And there have been some minor stirrings. The Gold Standard Corporation in Kansas City provides facilities for deposits denominated in gold and for the transfer of such deposits among persons by check. However, this is a warehousing operation—a 100 percent reserve bank, as it were—rather than a private currency denominated in gold and issued on a fractional reserve basis. Unfortunately, there are currently legal obstacles to any developments that would enable gold to be used not only as a store of value or part of an asset portfolio but as a unit of account or a medium of circulation. Hence, the current situation provides little evidence on what would occur if those obstacles were removed.

In the U.K., the government now issues securities that link interest and principal to a price index number. Banks could use such securities as assets to match price-level adjusted deposits.

It remains to be seen whether any of these opportunities will be exploited. Our personal view is that they will be if and only if government monetary policy produces wide fluctuations in inflation, fluctuations even wider than those that occurred in the U.S or the U.K. in recent decades. Moreover, even if they are, we conjecture that the use of a constant purchasing power of money as a unit of account and medium of circulation will be confined to large transactions involving long times delays, not to small or current transactions.

A further qualification is that the circumstance envisaged in the preceding paragraph—wide fluctuations in inflation in major countries—is not likely to prove stable and long-lasting. It is almost certain to produce political pressures for major monetary reform—in the extreme, after it has degenerated into hyperinflation; on a more hopeful note, long before.

Until recent years, true hyperinflation has occurred only in countries undergoing revolution or severe civil unrest or that have been defeated in a major war, with the possible exception of John Law's experiment of doubling the French bank-note issue in the four-year period 1716 to 1720. However, currently, several countries seem on the verge of hyperinflation under relatively peaceful circumstances—Bolivia, Argentina and Israel, to mention only the most prominent. The misfortune of these countries promises to provide us with some evidence on a so far rarely observed phenomenon.

Another recent hybrid development of considerable interest is the increased use of the ECU (European Currency Unit) in private transactions. The ECU is a composite of the separate national currencies of those Common Market countries participating in the European Monetary System—or, as it has come to be described, a basket containing specified numbers of units of each of the national currencies included in it. Its value in terms of any single national currency, including the dollar or any of the currencies composing it, is thus a weighted average of the market values in terms of that currency of the component ECU currencies. Though initially created for clearing intergovernmental balances, it has increasingly been used as a unit of account in private bond issues and other transactions [see Triffin (1984, especially pp. 150–163)], and banks in some countries have been offering ECU denominated deposits, though in others, such as Germany, they are currently not permitted to do so. So far, the ECU has been convertible into dollars and most other currencies. However, it has been in existence only since 1979, so it is still in the early stages of development. What role it will play in the future is highly uncertain.

The ECU is a governmentally created and issued currency. It is convertible only into other governmentally created and issued currencies, all of which are purely fiduciary, despite lip service still paid to gold by including gold, generally at an artificial price, as a "reserve asset" in the balance sheets of the central banks. What is unique is its composite character, resembling in this respect the fiduciary counterpart to the symmetallic proposal by Marshall and the later commodity reserve proposals.[9]

It does offer an alternative to the separate national currencies and so does enhance currency competition. However, its growth and wider use would represent joint government action in the field of money along the lines of the International Monetary Fund, rather than private action. As with national currencies, private action would take the form of producing inside money convertible into the ECU as an outside money.

Items [3] and [4] of Friedman's list of "good reasons," technical monopoly and external effects, have been questioned also by Roland Vaubel (1984) in a thoughtful article. He concludes that neither is a valid justification for a government monopoly in the production of base money.

With respect to natural monopoly, he concludes that "the only valid test of the natural monopoly argument is to abolish all barriers to entry and to admit free currency competition from private issuers on equal terms" [Vaubel (1984, p. 57)]. We agree with him entirely on this point while, as noted earlier, being highly skeptical that, given the starting point with a government currency firmly established, any private issuers would be likely to compete successfully—especially in producing a "pure fiduciary" money. As already noted, there is no historical precedent. Historical experience suggests that the only plausible alternative to a government issued fiduciary currency is a commodity currency, with private issuers producing inside money convertible into the commodity. And we believe that even that outcome is highly unlikely unless there is a major collapse of national currencies—something approximating hyperinflation on a worldwide scale.

With respect to externalities, Vaubel's negative conclusion is a quibble with respect to the basic issue of whether government has a key role to play in the monetary system. Even if there are externalities, he says, it "does not follow that government should produce money (let alone as a monopolist) rather than introduce a mandatory deposit insurance scheme or act as a lender of last resort by borrowing and lending private money" [Vaubel (1984, p. 32)]. But either of these policies would be a far cry from leaving "money and banking arrangements . . . to the market."

To summarize our answer to the first question: there is no economic reason why the determination of a unit of account linked with a medium of exchange and the provision of outside money cannot be left to the market. But history suggests both that any privately generated unit of account will be linked to a commodity and that government will not long keep aloof. Under a wide variety of economic and political circumstances, a monetary system has emerged that rests on a unit of account and on outside money at least certified, and generally more than that, by government. Such a system will not easily be dislodged or replaced by a strictly private system.

12.3 Free Banking

A number of recent authors have argued that the historical experience with "free banking" is less unfavorable than suggested by Friedman and other authors. Lawrence White has reexamined the experience in Scotland for the period up to 1845 and concluded that it supports "the case for thorough deregulation" of banking [White (1984a, p. 148)]. Rockoff (1975), Rolnick and Weber (1983) and King (1983) have reexamined the experience in the United States prior to the Civil War and come to a similar conclusion, arguing that prior studies of this period have grossly exaggerated the quantitative importance of "wildcat banking," overissue of depreciated bank notes, and the other ills generally associated with banking in that era.

The experience of Scotland, as most recently described by White, is surely the most favorable. For more than a century and a half Scotland had a system of free banking, with completely free entry and minimal governmental regulation or restraint. Scottish banks were banks of issue as well as of deposit. Their note issues circulated widely and were in practice the dominant medium of circulation. With minor exceptions the issues of different banks—numbering as many as 29 in 1826 and 19 in 1845, just before the end of the era of free banking—circulated at par with one another, thanks to an agreement among the banks to accept one another's notes [White (1984a, pp. 35, 37)]. Some banks did fail, but holders of their notes suffered negligible, if any, losses. And this system developed entirely by market forces, with government intervention consisting solely in the chartering of three of the banks.

However, before accepting the relevance of this experience to our current situation, it is important to note several special features of Scottish experience: first, it dealt only with inside money. Outside money consisted of either gold or, during the period of suspension of convertibility by the Bank of England (1797–1821), Bank of England notes. Second, as White stresses (1984a, p. 41), shareholders of banks assumed unlimited liability for the obligations of the banks.[10] As a result, bank depositors and holders of bank notes were sheltered from the failure of banks; the whole burden fell on the stockholders. Third, Scotland was an old, established community, with a relatively stable population, so that stockholders consisted in the main of persons who were well known, had considerable private wealth and valued their own reputations for probity highly enough to honor their obligations.[11] Fourth, while the only equivalent in Scotland itself of a central bank was the extent to which some of the larger banks served as bankers' banks, the Scottish banks had access to the London financial market, which performed the equivalent of some modern central bank functions for Scotland [see Goodhart (1985, sect. 5, note 3)].

For a contrast, consider the experience of the United States from, say, 1791 to 1836, the period spanning the first and second Banks of the United States. New England perhaps came closest to matching Scotland in some of its characteristics, particularly in containing substantial communities with long-settled prominent families possessing much wealth. It was taken for granted that specie was the dominant money and provided the appropriate unit of account. In the main, laissez-faire prevailed in banking, despite the existence of the two Federal banks, as Hammond (1957) calls them. There was nothing that prevented a system from developing along Scottish lines. Yet it did not. Numerous banks were established, which issued bank notes promising to pay specie on demand, yet a wide range of imaginative stratagems were adopted to postpone and impede redemption, and country bank notes circulated in Boston at varying discounts, leading Boston banks to adopt a succession of measures to enforce redemption. The end result was the famous Suffolk Bank system, which developed gradually from about 1820 on. As Hammond (1957, pp. 554, 556) remarks: "The Suffolk was in effect the central bank of New England. . . . The operators of the Suffolk Bank showed *laissez-faire* at its best." But even here, laissez-faire did not lead to unlimited liability as a rule, though there must have been private bankers who subjected themselves to unlimited liability; it did not lead to the kind of orderly, efficient, monetary system that developed in Scotland.

And the experience of the rest of the country is even less favorable to regarding the Scottish experience as highly relevant to the circumstances of the U.S. in the early decades of the nineteenth century. Various degrees of laissez-faire prevailed in the several states, but nowhere did it lead to unlimited liability, freely interconvertible bank notes, security of both note holders and depositors from loss, and the other favorable characteristics of the Scottish banking system.

Rockoff, Rolnick and Weber, and King may well be right that wildcat banking in the first half of the nineteenth century was less widespread and extensive than earlier writers made it out to be. They may also be correct that the bank failures that occurred owed far more to the legal conditions imposed on bank note issues—namely, that they be "backed" by state or U.S. bonds—and the subsequent depreciation in value of the bonds of a number of states than to irresponsible wildcat banking. Yet none of their evidence is directly relevant to the question of how banking and currency issue would have developed in the absence of state legislation.

Further, conditions have changed drastically in the past century and a half in ways that are particularly relevant to the question whether financial intermediaries should be prohibited from issuing inside money in the form of hand-to-hand currency [our point 2(a) in section 12.1]. We are no longer dealing with a sparsely settled country in which travel is slow and communication between distant points involves long delays. We now have instant communication and rapid means of transport. Book entries have replaced the physical transfer of currency or specie as the principal means of discharging monetary obligations. From being the primary medium of exchange, currency has become the counterpart of a minor fraction of aggregate transactions. Private institutions, both banks and non-banks, issue inside money in the form of traveler's checks redeemable on demand in outside money. The value of such traveler's checks outstanding is now included in the official estimates of all monetary aggregates broader than the monetary base (equal to outside money).[12] The possibility—and reality—of fraud by financial institutions remains, but under current conditions it seems unlikely to be more serious for hand-to-hand currency than for deposits.

What was a burning issue a century or two ago has therefore become a relatively minor issue today. Moreover, the arguments by Klein and

Hayek discussed in the preceding section are far more persuasive with respect to permitting the issuance of hand-to-hand inside money than with respect to the possibility that the private market might produce fiduciary outside money, i.e., a non-commodity outside money. While we therefore see no reason currently to prohibit banks from issuing hand-to-hand currency, there is no pressure by banks or other groups to gain that privilege. The question of government monopoly of hand-to-hand currency is likely to remain a largely dead issue.

The more important questions currently are the other two under this heading: namely, the restrictions, if any, that government should impose on financial intermediaries and the necessity or desirability of a "lender of last resort." Whatever conclusions one may reach about these issues, it seems to us, would currently be valid regardless of the form of the liabilities issued by the financial intermediaries.

In respect of these questions, conditions have changed much less drastically—as the recent liquidity crises arising out of the problems of Continental Illinois Bank and the failure of Home State Savings in Ohio vividly illustrate. These liquidity crises are of the same genus as those that occurred repeatedly during the nineteenth century. Their very different outcomes—no significant spread to other institutions in the Continental Illinois episode; the permanent closing of many Ohio savings and loans and temporary closing of all of them in the quantitatively far smaller Ohio episode—reflect the different way they were handled—and that too evokes historical echoes.

Governor Celeste of Ohio would have benefited greatly from reading and following Walter Bagehot's (1873) famous advice on how to handle an "internal drain": "A panic," he wrote, "in a word, is a species of neuralgia, and according to the rules of science you must not starve it. The holders of the cash reserve must be ready not only to keep it for their own liabilities, but to advance it most freely for the liabilities of others" [Bagehot (1873, p. 51)].

The run on the Ohio savings and loan associations precipitated by the failure of Home State Savings could have been promptly stemmed if Bagehot's advice had been followed. It was only necessary for Governor Celeste to arrange with the Federal Reserve Bank of Cleveland and the commercial banks of Ohio—who were apparently more than willing—to lend currency and its equivalent to the savings and loans on the collateral of their temporarily illiquid but sound assets. Once the savings and loans demonstrated their ability to meet all demands of depositors for cash, the unusual demand would have evaporated— as many historical examples demonstrate, including, most recently, the stemming of the liquidity crisis following the Continental Illinois episode.

Instead, Governor Celeste blundered by declaring a savings and loan holiday, repeating the mistaken Federal Reserve policies of 1931 to

1933, ending in the 1933 bank holiday. As in that case, the final result of not recognizing the differences between a liquidity and a solvency crisis will doubtless be the failure or liquidation of many savings and loans that would have been sound and solvent in the absence of the savings and loan holiday.

These episodes show that what used to be called "the inherent instability" of a fractional reserve banking system is, unfortunately, still alive and well. What they do not show, and what is still an open question, is whether a government "lender of last resort"—a central bank—is necessary and desirable as a cure. It did not prove to be a cure in the U.S. in the 1930s; it did in the Continental Illinois case, as well as in some earlier episodes. And, whether a satisfactory cure or not, is the emergence of a "lender of last resort" a likely or unavoidable consequence of financial development?

In a recent paper, Charles Goodhart, after surveying a wide range of historical evidence, including the studies we have referred to earlier, concludes that the emergence of "lenders of last resort" in the form of central banks was a natural and desirable development arising from the very characteristics of a fractional reserve banking system. The theoretical argument is straightforward and well-known. It rests on the distinction, already referred to, between a liquidity and solvency crisis. A bank or any other institution faces a problem of *solvency* if its liabilities exceed the value of its assets. The magnitude of the problem is measured by the difference between the two. That difference may be a small fraction of total liabilities, perhaps even less than the equity of the shareholders, so that if the assets could be liquidated in an orderly fashion the institution could pay off all other liabilities in full or for that matter continue as a going institution. The special feature of a fractional-reserve bank is that the bulk of its liabilities are payable on demand—either by contract or usage. Hence, even in the special case assumed, it will face a *liquidity* problem if its depositors demand payment. Moreover, the bank's liquidity problem will be far larger in magnitude than its solvency problem.[13] It cannot satisfy its depositors unless it can in some way convert its temporarily illiquid assets into cash.

A liquidity problem is not likely to remain confined to a single bank. The difficulty of one bank gives rise to fears about others, whose depositors, not well-informed about the banks' condition, seek to convert their deposits into cash. A full-blown liquidity crisis of major dimensions can be prevented only if depositors can somehow be reassured. An individual bank may be able to reassure its depositors by borrowing cash on the collateral of its sound assets from other banks and meeting all demands on it. But if the crisis is widespread, that recourse is not available. Some outside source of cash is necessary. A central bank with the power to create outside money is potentially such a source.

After the Federal Reserve in the early 1930s failed to perform the function for which it had been established, the U.S. enacted Federal Deposit Insurance as an alternative way to reassure depositors and thereby prevent a widespread liquidity crisis. That device worked effectively for decades, so long as banks were closely regulated—and incidentally sheltered from competition—and so long as inflation remained moderate and relatively stable. It has become less and less effective as deregulation proceeded in an environment of high and variable inflation. In the Continental Illinois case, it had to be supplemented by the Federal Reserve as "lender of last resort."

Insurance of depositors against bank insolvency is of a magnitude that is well within the capacity of private casualty insurance. It could allow for differences among banks in the riskiness of their assets much more effectively than government insurance [see Ely (1985a, b)].

A liquidity crisis, whether or not its arises out of an insolvency crisis, as it did with Continental Illinois and Home State Savings of Ohio, and whether or not it spreads to solvent banks, is a different matter. In the U.S., prior to the Federal Reserve, it was dealt with by a concerted agreement among banks to suspend convertibility of deposits into cash— to pay deposits only "through the clearing house." In some other countries, such as Canada, nationwide branch banks (subject to extensive government regulation) have preserved confidence sufficiently to avoid liquidity crises.

The U.S. has been almost unique in preserving a unit banking system with numerous independent banks. The current pressures for deregulation and the widening competition in financial intermediation is changing that situation. The barriers against interstate banking are weakening and very likely will ultimately fall completely. Such "non-banks" as Sears Roebuck, Merrill-Lynch, and so on, in most respects are the equivalent of nationwide branch banks. These developments, as they mature, will simultaneously lessen the probability of liquidity crises and increase the magnitude and severity of those that occur. It is therefore far from clear what implications they have for the "lender of last resort" function.

Vera Smith (1936, p. 148) rightly concluded: "A central bank is not a natural product of banking development. It is imposed from outside or comes into being as a result of Government favours." However, as Goodhart's (1985) exhaustive survey of the historical experience indicates, a central bank or its equivalent, once established, reluctantly assumed the responsibility of serving as a lender of last resort because of the reality or possibility of a liquidity crisis. What is impressive about his evidence is the wide range of circumstances—in respect of political and economic arrangements—and the long span of time for which that has proved the outcome.

In practice, the lender of last resort function has been combined with control over government outside money. Such a combination has obvious advantages. However, in principle the two functions could be separated, and some proposals for monetary reform would require such separation, if the government were to continue to serve as a lender of last resort.[14]

The existence of a lender of last resort has clearly enabled banks having access to the lender to operate on thinner margins of capital and cash reserves than they would otherwise have deemed prudent. This fact has been used as an argument both for and against the government assuming lender of last resort functions—for, as a way of lowering the cost of financial intermediation; against, as providing an implicit subsidy to financial intermediation. It has also led to the imposition of required reserve ratios, which has turned a subsidy into a tax by increasing the demand for non-interest bearing outside money.

Deregulation of financial intermediaries so that they are free to pay whatever interest is required to obtain funds and to offer a variety of services over broad geographical areas seems clearly desirable on grounds of market efficiency. The open question is whether that is feasible or desirable without a continued role for government in such matters as requiring registration, provision of information, and the imposition of capital or reserve requirements. Moreover, certainly during a transition period, deregulation increases the danger of liquidity crises and so may strengthen the case for a governmental "lender of last resort."[15] That role could perhaps be phased out if market developments provided protection through insurance or otherwise against the new risks that might arise in a deregulated financial system.

Goodhart's argument (1985) that such an outcome, whether desirable or not, is not achievable, can be put to the test, by enlarging the opportunities for private insurance of deposit liabilities. If such insurance became widespread, risk-adjusted premiums could render regulatory restrictions unnecessary. It is more difficult to envision the market arrangements that would eliminate the pressure for a government "lender of last resort."

12.4 The Future of Fiat Money

As noted earlier, the nations of the world are for the first time in history essentially unanimously committed to a purely fiat monetary standard. Will Fisher's (1911b) generalization that "irredeemable paper money has almost invariably proved a curse to the country employing it" hold true for the current situation? In some ways that seems to us the most interesting and important current scientific question in the monetary area. How it is answered will largely determine the relevance of the issues discussed in the preceding two sections.

We do not believe it is possible to give a confident and unambiguous answer. The experience of such countries as Argentina, Brazil, Chile, Mexico and Israel are contemporary examples of Fisher's generalization, but they are all lesser developed countries that except for chronology may have more in common with the countries Fisher had in mind than with the more advanced Western countries. The experience of those more advanced countries—Japan, the United States and the members of the Common Market—gives grounds for greater optimism. The pressures on government that led to the destruction of earlier irredeemable paper moneys are every bit as strong today in these countries than earlier—most clearly, the pressure to obtain resources for government use without levying explicit taxes. However, developments in the economy, and in financial markets in particular, have produced counter-pressures that reduce the political attractiveness of paper money inflation.

The most important such developments, we believe, are the greater sensitivity and sophistication of both the financial markets and the public at large. There has indeed been an information revolution, which has greatly reduced the cost of acquiring information and has enabled expectations to respond more rapidly and accurately to developments.

Historically, inflation has added to government resources in three ways: first, through the paper money issues themselves (i.e., the implicit inflation tax on outside money holdings); second, through the unvoted increase in explicit taxes as a result of bracket creep; third, by the reduction in the real value of outstanding debt issued at interest rates that did not include sufficient allowance for future inflation. The economic, political and financial developments of recent decades have eroded the potency of all three sources of revenue.

Though outside money remained remarkably constant at about 10 percent of national income from the middle of the past century to the Great Depression, and then rose sharply to a peak of about 25 percent in 1946, it has been on a declining trend since the end of World War II, and is currently about 7 percent of national income. However, for a modern society, with the current level of government taxes and spending, this component is perhaps the least important of the three. Even if outside money as a fraction of income did not decline as a result of inflation which it unquestionably would, a 10 percent per year increase in outside money would yield as revenue to the government only about seven-tenths of 1 percent of national income.

The second component of revenue has very likely been more important. Past rates of inflation have subjected low and moderate income persons to levels of personal income tax that could never have been voted explicitly. However, the result has been political pressure that has led to the indexation of the personal income tax schedule for inflation, which largely eliminates this source of revenue.

The third component has also been extremely important. At the end of World War II, the funded federal debt amounted to 6 percent more than a year's national income. By 1967 it was down to about 32 percent of national income despite repeated "deficits" in the official federal budget. Since then it has risen as deficits have continued and increased, but even so only to about 36 percent currently. The reason for the decline in the deficit ratio was partly real growth but mostly the reduction through inflation in the real value of debt that has been issued at interest rates that *ex post* proved negative in real terms.

The potency of this source of revenue has been sharply eroded by the developments in the financial markets referred to earlier. Market pressures have made it difficult for the government to issue long-term debt at low nominal rates. One result is that the average term to maturity of the federal debt has tended to decline. Except under wartime conditions, it is far more difficult to convert interest rates on short-term debt into *ex post* negative real rates by unanticipated inflation than to do so for long-term debt. And for both short- and long-term debt, producing unanticipated inflation of any magnitude for any substantial period has become far more difficult after several decades of historically high and variable inflation than it was even a decade or so ago, when the public's perceptions still reflected the effect of a relatively stable price level over long periods.

In the U.K., the resort to government bonds adjusted for inflation eliminates more directly the possibility that government can benefit from *ex post* negative real interest rates. There have been pressures on the U.S. Treasury to issue similar securities. Those pressures would undoubtedly intensify if the U.S. were again to experience high and variable inflation.

Perhaps if, instead, we experienced several decades of a relatively stable long-run price level, asset holders would again be lulled into regarding nominal interest rates as equivalent to real interest rates. But that is certainly not the case today.

To summarize, inflation has become far less attractive as a political option. Given a voting public very sensitive to inflation, it may currently be politically profitable to establish monetary arrangements that will make the present inconvertible paper standard an exception to Fisher's generalization.

That is a source of promise; it is far from a guarantee that Fisher's generalization is obsolete. Governments have often acted under short-run pressures in ways that have had strongly adverse long-run consequences. Israel today offers a conspicuous example. It continues to resort to inflation under conditions that make inflation a poor source of revenue, if, indeed, not itself a drain.

12.5 Conclusion

To return to where we started, Friedman's list of the "good reasons" why "monetary arrangements have seldom been left to the market," what alterations are indicated by the experience and writings of the past quarter century?

Point [1], "the resource cost of a pure commodity currency and hence its tendency to become purely fiduciary," has in one sense fully worked itself out. All money is now fiduciary. Yet the resource cost has not been eliminated; it remains present because private individuals hoard precious metals and gold and silver coins as a hedge against the inflation that they fear may result from a wholly fiduciary money. To go farther afield, a new resource cost has been added because a purely fiduciary currency reduces the long-run predictability of the price level. That cost takes the form of resources employed in futures and other financial markets to provide the additional hedging facilities demanded by individuals, business enterprises and governmental bodies. It would be a paradoxical reversal if these new forms of resource costs produced pressure for the reintroduction of commodity elements into money as a way to reduce the resource costs of the monetary system. We do not know of any study that has tried to compare the resource costs of the pre–World War I monetary system and the post-1971 monetary system. That is a challenging task for research [Friedman (1986)].

Point [2], "the peculiar difficulty of enforcing contracts involving promises to pay that serve as a medium of exchange and of preventing fraud in respect of them," remains alive and well, as the recent Continental Illinois and Ohio Savings and Loan episodes demonstrate, and, more indirectly, the much publicized failures in the government bond market. However, the character of the difficulty has changed. It no longer seems any more serious for hand-to-hand currency than for deposits or other monetary or quasi-monetary promises to pay. Moreover, it is now taken for granted that governments (i.e., taxpayers) will completely shield holders of deposit liabilities from loss, whether due to fraud or other causes. The improvements in communication and in the extent and sophistication of financial markets have in some respects increased, in others decreased, the difficulty of enforcing contracts and preventing fraud. They have certainly made it more difficult politically for governments to remain uninvolved.

Point [3], "the technical monopoly character of a pure fiduciary currency which makes essential the setting of some external limit on its amount," has been questioned, far more persuasively, we believe, for currencies convertible into a commodity, than for a pure fiduciary currency. We continue to believe that the possibility that private issuers can (in either sense of that term) provide competing, efficient and safe fiduciary currencies with no role for governmental monetary authorities remains to be demonstrated. As a result we believe that this is the most important challenge posed by the elimination of a commodity-based outside money.

Point [4], "the pervasive character of money" and the "important effects on parties other than those directly involved" in the issuance of money, has not been questioned. What has been questioned, and remains very much an open question, is what institutional arrangements would minimize those third party effects. A strong case can be made that government involvement has made matters worse rather than better both directly and indirectly because the failure of monetary authorities to pursue a stable non-inflationary policy renders performance by private intermediaries equally unstable. As yet, there has developed no consensus on desirable alternative arrangements, let alone any effective political movement to adopt alternative arrangements.

Our own conclusion—like that of Walter Bagehot and Vera Smith— is that leaving monetary and banking arrangements to the market would have produced a more satisfactory outcome than was actually achieved through governmental involvement. Nevertheless, we also believe that the same forces that prevented that outcome in the past will continue to prevent it in the future. Whether those forces produce or prevent major changes in monetary institutions will depend on developments in the monetary area in the next several decades—and that crystal ball is rendered even more murky than usual by our venture into largely unexplored monetary terrain.

The failure to recognize that we are in unexplored terrain gives an air of unreality and paradox to the whole discussion of private money and free banking. Its basis was well expressed by Walter Bagehot over a century ago, in the context of the free banking issue. Said Bagehot (1873, pp. 66–67, 68–69):

> We are so accustomed to a system of banking, dependent for its cardinal function on a single bank, that we can hardly conceive of any other. But the natural system—that which would have sprung up if Government had let banking alone—is that of many banks of equal or not altogether unequal size. . . .
>
> I shall be at once asked—Do you propose a revolution? Do you propose to abandon the one-reserve system, and create anew a many-reserve system? My plain answer is, that I do not propose it: I know it would be childish . . . [A]n immense system of credit, founded on the Bank of England as its pivot and its basis, now exists. The English

people and foreigners too, trust it implicitly . . . The whole rests on an instinctive confidence generated by use and years. . . . [I]f some calamity swept it away, generations must elapse before at all the same trust would be placed in any other equivalent. A many-reserve system, if some miracle should put it down in Lombard Street, would seem monstrous there. Nobody would understand it, or confide in it. *Credit is a power which may grow, but cannot be constructed* (italics added).

Substitute "unit of account" or "outside money" for "credit" in the italicized sentence and it is directly relevant to the outside money issue. What has happened to the role of gold since Bagehot wrote, the way in which it has been replaced by a purely fiat money, is a striking application of Bagehot's proposition. It took "generations" for confidence in gold "generated by use and years" to erode and for confidence to develop in the pieces of paper which for many years after it was meaningless continued to contain the promise that "The United States of America will pay to the bearer on demand —— dollars," or words to that effect. Now they simply state "Federal Reserve Note," "One Dollar" or "—— Dollars" plus the statement "This note is legal tender for all debts, public and private." And even now, a half-century after the effective end of the domestic convertibility of government issued money into gold, the Federal Reserve still lists the "Gold Stock," valued at an artificial "legal" price among the "Factors Supplying Reserve Funds." Like old soldiers, gold does not die; it just fades away.

Similarly, as already noted, there are no effective legal obstacles currently in the U.S. to the development of a private "real" (i.e., inflation adjusted) standard as an alternative to the paper dollar, yet, absent a major monetary catastrophe, it will take decades for such an alternative to become a serious competitor to the paper dollar, if it ever does.

The element of paradox arises particularly with respect to the views of Hayek [see especially Hayek (1979, vol. 3)]. His latest works have been devoted to explaining how gradual cultural evolution—a widespread invisible hand process—produces institutions and social arrangements that are far superior to those that are deliberately constructed by explicit human design. Yet he recommends in his recent publications on competitive currencies replacing the results of such an invisible hand process by a deliberate construct—the introduction of currency competition. This paradox affects us all. On the one hand, we are observers of the forces shaping society; on the other, we are participants and want ourselves to shape society.

If there is a resolution to this paradox, it occurs at times of crisis. Then and only then are major changes in monetary and other institutions likely or even possible. What changes then occur depend on the alternatives that are recognized as available. Decades of academic argument in favor of eliminating Regulation Q and, in a very different area, adopting flexible exchange rates had little or no impact on institutional arrangements until crises made major changes inevitable. The existence of well articulated cases for these changes made them realistic options.

Similarly, the wide-ranging discussion of possible major monetary reforms will have little effect on the course of events if the present fiat system into which the world has drifted operates in a reasonably satisfactory manner—producing neither major inflations nor major depressions. However, the possibility that it will not do so is very real—particularly that it will fall victim to Fisher's generalization and lead to major inflation. When and if it does, what happens will depend critically on the options that have been explored by the intellectual community and have become intellectually respectable. That—the widening of the range of options and keeping them available—is, we believe, the major contribution of the burst of scholarly interest in monetary reform.

Notes

1. See Acheson and Chant (1973), Brunner (1976), Buchanan (1984), Hetzel (1984) and Kane (1980).
2. In his rediscovery and advocacy of a tabular standard, R. W. R. White (1979), former governor of the Reserve Bank of New Zealand, proposed terming the corresponding unit of account, the "Real."
W. Stanley Jevons (1890, pp. 328, 331), in recommending a tabular standard of which he says "the difficulties in the way of such a scheme are not considerable," refers to a book by Joseph Lowe (*The Present State of England*) published in 1822 which contains a similar proposal.
3. See, for example, Brennan and Buchanan (1981).
4. One of us has discussed elsewhere some of the issues involved, and possible reforms for the U.S. See Friedman (1984b).
5. McCallum (1985, p. 25) also makes this point.
6. E.g., George Smith money was a widely used medium of exchange in the Middle West of the U.S. in the 1840s and 1850s. However, when George Smith retired from control of the Wisconsin Marine and Fire Insurance Company, which he created to evade the state of Wisconsin's prohibition of banks of issue, George Smith money went the way of all money. His successors could not resist the temptation of dissipating for short-term gain the "brand name capital" George Smith had built up. See Hammond (1957, p. 613). The Scottish banks discussed by White are another even more impressive example of a competitive issue of convertible money.
7. See also Martino (1984, especially p. 15).

8. See McCulloch (1980).

9. See Friedman (1951b). Interestingly, F. A. Hayek (1943) was an early supporter of such a proposal.

10. Except for the three chartered banks.

11. The extreme example was Adam Smith's patron, the Duke of Buccleigh, who was a stockholder in the ill-fated Ayr bank and suffered a major loss when it failed in 1772.

12. For banks, the Federal Reserve statistics include traveler's checks with demand deposits, so no separate estimate of their amount is available. Traveler's checks of non-bank issuers total about 3 percent of total currency, less than 1 percent of total M1.

13. For example, Continental Illinois had total deposit liabilities of close to $30 billion as of December 31, 1983, and non-performing loans of less than $2 billion. Its solvency problem was still smaller, given the presence of an equity cushion.

14. For example, the proposal to freeze the amount of high-powered money. See Friedman (1984b, pp. 48–52).

15. This point is stressed by Summers in his comment on King (1983). He contrasts the possible gain in micro-efficiency of private money with what he regards as the likely loss in macro-efficiency through increased economic instability. However, he simply takes it for granted that government control of money reduces rather than increases economic instability. That is, to put it mildly, far from clear on the basis of historical experience.

III International Monetary Arrangements

13 Reflections on the Gold Commission *Report*

13.1 Background of the Commission

13.1.1 Political Aspects

The Gold Commission was established in accordance with a provision in an Act of Congress of October 7, 1980 (P.L. 96-389), of which the main matter was enlarging the quota assigned to the United States in the International Monetary Fund. The provision, introduced as an amendment to the Senate bill by Senator Jesse Helms (Republican, North Carolina), was accepted by the leadership to obtain his acquiescence to consideration by the Senate of the IMF quota enlargement. A similar arrangement was made in the House, where the amendment to the House bill was introduced by Congressman Ron Paul (Republican, Texas).

The provision directed the secretary of the Treasury to establish and chair a commission consisting of:

1. Three members of the Board of Governors of the Federal Reserve System and two members of the Council of Economic Advisers to be designated by him
2. One majority and one minority member of the Joint Economic Committee, the Committee on Banking, Housing, and Urban Affairs of the Senate, and the Committee on Banking, Finance, and Urban Affairs of the House of Representatives, to be designated by the Speaker of the House of Representatives and the President of the Senate, respectively
3. Four distinguished private citizens with business, finance, or academic backgrounds, to be designated by the secretary of the Treasury.

The Commission was to "conduct a study to assess and make recommendations with regard to the policy of the U.S. Government concerning the role of gold in domestic and international monetary systems" and to report its findings and recommendations to the Congress no later than one year after enactment. No special budget for the Commission was provided but sums from the international operations budget of the Treasury Department were to be available to the Commission to carry out its functions.

An arrangement was reportedly made with the Carter Administration by which it would not proceed with the appointment of members of the Commission pending the November election results. If the Democrats lost, it would be left to the incoming administration to implement the provision. The new administration was slow in doing so. The names of the appointed members were not announced until June 22, 1981. The Commission's first meeting was on July 16.[1]

The law specified that the Commission have fifteen members plus a chairman. However, Henry Reuss, the chairman of the Joint Economic Committee, designated Chalmers Wylie, a close ally of his though a Republican, to represent the House side. Senator Jepsen, the vice-chairman and a Republican, designated himself to represent the Senate side. It was obviously contrary to the law to have two Republicans as the Joint Economic Committee members. Rather than withdraw Wylie's designation, Reuss named himself as the Democratic representative of the JEC from the House side. The Commission thus ended up having three, rather than two members, as prescribed by the law, representing the JEC, and with a total of sixteen members rather than fifteen members plus the chairman.

Establishment of the Gold Commission was the third piece of legislation affecting gold in which Senator Helms was a prime mover. On his initiative, the right to include gold clauses in private contracts entered into on or after October 28, 1977, was enacted (P.L. 95-147). The program of Treasury medallion sales, in accordance with the American Arts Gold Medallion Act of November 10, 1978, was a second legislative initiative of the senator (P.L. 95-630). He was unsuccessful in subsequent efforts in 1980 to suspend Treasury gold sales and to provide for restitution of IMF gold.

13.1.2 Economic Views of the Commission's Sponsors

The amendment to the IMF bill was introduced and approved in the Senate on June 16, 1980, and in the House on September 18, 1980. The year-to-year change in the consumer price index in 1980 was at a postwar peak—13.5 percent. This factor clearly motivated the sponsors of the amendment, though the Senate and House protagonists expressed rather different views of the path to follow to eliminate inflation. Here we need to limit our purview to the statements made by the sponsors of the amendment on introducing it. We can also examine differences between the two pro-gold leaders that were made clear in hearings before the Subcommittee on Mines and Mining of the Committee of Interior and Insular Affairs of the House on Feasibility of a Return to the Gold Standard.[2] The hearings were held on October 2, 1980, a few days before passage of the law enlarging the IMF quota and the provision to create the Gold Commission.

One difference between the sponsors of the amendment was revealed in their statements on introducing the amendment. In the Senate, referring to the suspension of convertibility into gold in 1971, Helms observed: "It is no coincidence that inflation of the dollar which precipitated the final break with gold, accelerated after the last vestige of gold's discipline was removed." He went on to criticize the role of the United States and the IMF in contributing to monetary instability of other nations, and to contrast the views of Keynesians and monetarists, who share skepticism about "a strong role of gold in the monetary system," with the views of classical economists who "criticize current monetary disorder and see the only proper response as reforms which take into account the changing demand for currencies, and the stability of the value of the unit of exchange." He closed with the statement, "I would expect that the commission would report to the Congress that there is little unanimity among the experts. I would expect, however, that the Keynesian view; the monetarist view; and the neoclassical view will be examined fully; the implications of each will be analyzed and recommendations will be made on the basis of the best judgment of the commission members."[3] Senator Helms referred to Arthur Laffer as one of the leaders of the neoclassical view. Congressman Paul, on the other hand, in his House Statement on the amendment expressed the hope that the commission would take into "consideration the viewpoint of the neoclassical economists better known as Austrian school economists. I would suggest their view be investigated and expressed in this commission report as well."[4]

This difference in the identification of the leadership of the neoclassical school of economics turns out to be significant for understanding the outcome of the Gold Commission performance.

At the hearings before the Subcommittee on Mines and Mining (held under the auspices of this subcommittee, as Congressman Paul noted, since "the House Banking Committee has been extremely reluctant to hold any hearings on this topic"), Paul testified on a bill he had introduced on July 30, 1980, "to repeal the privilege of banks to create money," the title, on enactment, to be the "Monetary Freedom Act." The bill outlined a plan for returning the United States to a full gold coin standard within two years of its passage. The bill provided for the repeal of legal tender laws; the redemption in gold coin or bullion in weights not less than five grams by the secretary of the Treasury 360 days after enactment of outstanding Federal Reserve notes at the mean of the spot prices of gold on the New York Commodity Exchange and the Chicago Board of Trade on five immediately preceding business days, redemption to cease after one year, and gold coin in circulation thereafter to function as the money of account, defined as the gram of gold, ninety-nine one-hundredths fine; cessation of the issue of Federal Reserve notes and United States notes on the date of enactment; free banking with a 100 percent reserve requirement effective 360 days after enactment.[5]

The argument offered for repeal of legal tender laws is that the Constitution forbids the states to make anything but gold and silver a tender in payment of debt and does not permit the federal government to make anything a legal tender. Congress passed a legal tender act for the first time in 1862 to ensure acceptance of greenbacks. Repeal of the legal tender laws would free creditors to accept in payment for debts due them only what they have contracted to accept.

The other provisions of the bill need no elaboration. They are obviously constructed from libertarian principles and a belief in the superiority of commodity money.

Senator Helms delivered a statement to the Subcommittee on Mines and Mining but did not personally appear. He submitted a bill introduced in the Senate two days earlier by him and Senators Goldwater and McClure "to provide for the reinstatement of the dollar as a gold reserve currency, to stabilize the value of the dollar, and for other purposes."[6] The bill translated into legislative language a plan that Arthur B. Laffer had published on February 29, 1980, as an economic study of A. B. Laffer Associates, "Reinstatement of the Dollar: The Blueprint."

Laffer's plan provides for an announcement by the United States of its intention to return to a convertible dollar at some prespecified time in the future, according to the bill, six months after enactment. The price of gold, designated the standard price of gold, would be fixed at the average price of gold bullion at New York for immediate delivery prevailing during the five business days preceding resumption of convertibility at the standard price. During the period before resumption, the Federal Reserve would maintain the monetary base literally unchanged and the Treasury and Federal Reserve would intervene neither in foreign exchange nor the government securities markets. Borrowings from Federal Reserve Banks would remain frozen.

On the day of resumption, the proportion of the total value of gold at the standard price of gold relative to the monetary base becomes the "target reserve quantity." Thereafter the Federal Reserve would

stand ready to sell gold at 100.7 percent of the standard price of gold
and to buy gold at 99.3 percent of the standard price, the minimum
quantity having a value of $10,000 at the standard price.

Should the gold reserve fall below 75 percent of the target reserve
quantity, no change would be permitted in the monetary base. Should
it fall below 50 percent of the target reserve quantity, the monetary
base would be decreased by 1 percent per month. Should the gold
reserve rise above 125 percent of the target reserve quantity, the monetary base would be increased by 1 percent per month. Should the gold
reserve rise above 150 percent of the target reserve quantity, the monetary base would be increased by 2 percent per month. Should the gold
reserve fall below 25 percent or rise above more than 175 percent of
the target reserve quantity, the Board of Governors of the Federal
Reserve would proclaim a gold holiday. During a gold holiday, the
standard price would cease to apply, the Federal Reserve would neither
buy nor sell gold from its reserves, and no change in the value of the
monetary base greater than 1 percent would be permitted. A new standard price of gold would be determined by the average price of gold
bullion during the five business days ending on the ninetieth day after
the proclamation.

Congressman Paul described the provision for a gold holiday as "the
weakest part" of Laffer's proposal "because it introduces the fact that
you plan not to have a stable currency and credit supply. That means
you expect and anticipate that we will continue with our Federal Reserve System, and with the Congress able to abuse the monetary system, and, therefore, you have to have a hedge, and this hedge is the
gold holiday system. This may actually be worse than what we had
before."[7]

Laffer, who was a witness at the subcommittee hearings, defended
the provision: "It is trying to protect from that situation that occurs
infrequently but every 10, 15 years when you have a brand new discovery of gold, if the quantity of gold triples, I would hate to say the
price level rises. The objective again is still maintaining price stability
of a bundle of goods and using gold as the controlling valve on the
system, but not to, per se, control the dollar price of gold but to control
the dollar price of gas [sic; goods?] and services and using as a regulator
gold. When there is a disturbance in the gold market, I don't want to
see the whole economy suffer inflation or deflation because of some
change in that market."[8]

The contrast is evident between Helms's support of Laffer's variant
of a traditional gold standard, with a fixed but adjustable price of gold,
and with some modification of the existing institutional arrangements
under the Federal Reserve System, and Paul's lack of interest in any
form of a gold standard other than a 100 percent coin standard, with

no face value for the coins, prices expressed in weights of gold, and a complete break with the existing institutional banking system.

13.2   What Purpose Was the Commission Designed to Serve?

We now turn to the question of what allies with such different gold objectives in mind hoped to achieve through the establishment of the Gold Commission.

Sponsors of a commission may have a variety of objectives. One objective may be to focus public attention on a problem that they regard as important. The sponsors may have a solution for the problem but lack the support for its implementation. One indication that the sponsors of the Commission set great store by this objective was their insistence that meetings of the Commission be open to the public. They objected strongly to the first closed meeting; thereafter, all meetings were open. Another objective may be to educate the public. Commissions can perform a genuine public service by collecting and summarizing facts and opinions on a national problem. They may make old ideas respectable, publicizing them and giving them legitimacy. Ideas that may have been limited to special groups may be given wider currency by a commission's study. Commissions may also serve to develop a consensus. The sponsors of the Gold Commission may well have had all these objectives in mind.[9]

The inclusion as members of representatives of constituencies with direct involvement in the problem under consideration—in this case, the Federal Reserve System—suggests that one purpose was to build a consensus or to develop support for a change in policy. A commission with bipartisan and bicameral balancing—as the law intended—is evidently designed to have political impact. Whatever the Commission recommended would be expected to meet the test of political acceptability.

The 1980 Republican Party platform included a paragraph on monetary reform that could be interpreted as a veiled reference to a projected return to a gold standard. The sponsors of the establishment of the Gold Commission possibly were counting on the White House to signal its interest in a strong pro-gold recommendation by the Commission. Such a signal would have influenced the designation of members. In that event, the number of members subject to White House influence would have formed a majority: four Republican Congressional members, the four public members, two members from the Council of Economic Advisers, and the chairman. No signal, however, apparently came from the White House.

As a result, the Commission came into existence with no sense of direction. The minority status of the pro-gold members of the Commission was not fully evident from the start. Whatever principled reasons the three Federal Reserve governors on the Commission (Partee, Rice, and Wallich) may have had to oppose an enlarged role for gold in the monetary system, they also had a strong self-interest in doing so, because of the implied rebuke to their conduct of monetary policy that such a recommendation would have conveyed. Their primary concern was to limit discussion touching on the performance of the Federal Reserve. Governor Wallich argued at the first meeting that the subjects of inflation and monetary policy were not a proper concern of the Commission. He was supported by the JEC House members (Reuss and Wylie), who repeatedly stressed that neither subject had been discussed in the House when the amendment to the IMF bill was introduced.

Both inflation and monetary policy, however, deeply concerned Jerry Jordan (a Council member) and Stephen Neal (the House Banking Committee majority member). The views of other congressional members (Senators Dodd and Schmitt, Senate Banking Committee minority and majority members, and Jepsen) were not initially well defined. Two Administration representatives—Murray Weidenbaum, chairman of the Council, and Secretary of the Treasury Regan—did not tip their hands until the final two meetings of the Commission. Of the four public members, one was a gold dealer (Herbert Coyne), one a businessman identified with conservative intellectual positions (Lewis Lehrman), one a California lawyer who had served in the Reagan state administration (Arthur Costamagna), one an economist, a former chairman of the Council of Economic Advisers, and a member of President Reagan's economic policy advisory board (Paul McCracken).

By the time the Commission had concluded its sessions, it was clear that the pro-gold group consisted of an awkward coalition of Congressman Paul and two of the public members, Lehrman and Costamagna. It was awkward because neither of the latter supported the conception of the monetary system that Paul advocated. Lehrman had in mind a traditional gold standard, restoring dollar convertibility into gold, although he also proposed changing Federal Reserve institutional arrangements, prohibiting open market operations and making the discount rate a penalty rate.[10] As for Costamagna, his sole concern for the present was to provide the market with U.S.-minted bullion coins.

The maximum expectations of the sponsors would have been realized if there had been White House support for a strong pro-gold recommendation by the Commission. Failing that support, the sponsors were probably content to use the Commission as a forum to promote whatever use of gold they could prevail on the Commission to accept while focusing public attention on the importance they attached to a role for gold in the monetary system.

13.3. What Did the Sponsors Gain?

13.3.1 Commission Recommendations

The *Report* of the Commission is in two volumes. Volume 1 contains what was conceived to be a report reflecting all views expressed by the members. An introductory chapter presents the Commission's recommendations on six subjects. Footnotes of dissent and qualifications of the recommendations by various members appear on nineteen of the twenty-one pages of the chapter. Four chapters follow. The first deals with the background of the establishment of the Commission; the second analyzes U.S. experience with gold since 1834; the third discusses types of monetary standards, including gold, other commodity, and paper money standards. The final chapter describes existing gold arrangements in the United States and proposals for change. An appendix on the gold market and a statistical compendium of time series relating to gold output, stocks, supply of and demand for gold, and the nominal and real price of gold complete the volume. Dissents by the Federal Reserve members, Congressmen Reuss and Wylie, and Mr. Coyne appear on various pages of these chapters.

Volume 2 of the *Report* is described as "annexes." The bulk of the volume is occupied by a minority report.

The existence of a minority report was not revealed to the Gold Commission until a few days before the final revision of the *Report* that was intended to represent all views. The minority report was prepared under the direction of Congressman Paul and mirrors his views rather than those of Lewis Lehrman who endorsed it. Arthur Costamagna gave the minority report a qualified endorsement. He proposed delay in the implementation of the program outlined therein until the Reagan Administration's fiscal and monetary programs and the recommendations of the Gold Commission were given an opportunity to prove themselves. I discuss the minority report after examining the extent to which the Commission's recommendations accomplished ends that the pro-gold minority sought.

The majority rejected the proposal that the United States should fix the price of gold and restore gold reserve requirements for the Federal Reserve. Except for Lehrman, no member of the Commission advocated such a course. They rejected a return to fixed exchange rates and endorsed a floating exchange rate system. Again, only Lehrman held a brief for fixed exchange rates.

The main substantive proposal was the recommendation that the Treasury issue gold bullion coins of specified weights, without dollar denomination or legal tender status, to be manufactured from its existing stock of gold and to be sold at a small mark-up over the market value of the gold content, the coins to be exempt from capital gains taxes and from sales taxes. This recommendation was clearly a victory for both Helms and Paul. Senator Helms had cosponsored an October 5, 1981, bill (S. 1704) that provides for the minting of gold coins exempt from U.S. and state capital gains taxes. Assigning no legal tender status to the coins was a victory for Congressman Paul.

For the pro-gold forces, introducing gold coins into circulation was a first step toward achieving their ultimate objective of linking the monetary system to gold. For them, the step represents provision of a form of currency alternative to paper dollars. They conceive that holders will engage in transactions denominated in weights of coins rather than dollars. The other members who supported the recommendation did not share that conception. They regarded such coins as alternatives to foreign bullion coins that have found a market in the United States. For them, purchase of the coins would reflect an investment, not a transactions, demand.

At least six dissents were recorded with respect to exempting the coins from capital gains taxes for the obvious reason that the exemption would provide an incentive to shift from gold bullion holdings, common stocks, or productive assets to coins.

The members would not accept, as part of the recommendation, a price or quantity limit on the minting of the coins, leaving open the possibility that the demand might exhaust the Treasury's gold stock. Those who conceived of the demand for the coins as a transactions demand were opposed to a limit on the minting of the coins. A large-scale demand for coins would, according to them, indicate dissatisfaction with the management of the dollar money supply and lead to the de facto establishment of a gold coin standard. On this view, establishment of an arbitrary quantity limit or a high seignorage fee would interfere with the expression of public preferences. Those who believed that the demand for coins would be an investment demand assumed that it would not be quantitatively significant, and on this ground neither opposed nor supported a legislated limit. Underlying this view is the assumption that only U.S. residents would acquire the coins in small quantities. It is conceivable, however, that domestic or foreign buyers would order large quantities on a given day. Such an order, if placed in the gold market, would raise the price. That consequence would not follow at the Treasury sales window.

Another aspect of the recommendation that official gold bullion coins be minted is the exclusion of private mints from the operation. Only the Treasury is accorded the right to mint such coins. Congressman Paul did not object to the restriction of the coinage to Treasury issues in the *Report,* volume 1. He did so in the minority report.

One other substantive recommendation of the Commission was that "the Congress and the Federal Reserve study the merits of establishing a rule specifying that the growth of the nation's money supply be maintained at a steady rate which insures long-run price stability." In a redundant sentence that is part of the same recommendation, the Commission added that "the Congress and the Federal Reserve should study ways to improve the conduct of monetary policy, including such alternatives as adopting a monetary rule." The recommendation was vehemently opposed by the three Federal Reserve Board governors and Congressmen Reuss and Wylie. The gold supporters voted for it.[11] Congressman Neal offered a stronger resolution that the Commission recommend that "the Congress by legislation establish a rule specifying that the growth of the nation's money supply be maintained at a steady rate which insures long-run price stability." The members were evenly split on the vote for the resolution. Congressman Neal went on record with the statement that "by recommending more study rather than outright enactment of a monetary rule, we missed a golden opportunity to help secure long-term price stability, low interest rates, and high employment. I intend to continue my efforts to enact a monetary rule through legislation."

13.3.2   Commission Hearings

Two meetings of the Commission were devoted to hearings on the role of gold in domestic and international monetary systems. Twenty-three witnesses testified. In addition, forty-seven individuals submitted written statements of their views.

The hearings validated Senator Helms's expectation that "there is little unanimity among the experts." The hearings provided an opportunity for views of Keynesians, monetarists, and neoclassical economists, as defined by Helms and Paul, to be heard. Of the twenty-three witnesses, only two forthrightly supported a return to a traditional gold standard. Two advocated nontraditional forms of a gold standard; one urged that gold be part of the solution to current problems, but prescribed no specific model. Two attorneys attacked the present monetary system as unconstitutional. The remaining witnesses were about evenly divided in ruling out any role for gold at the present or any time or in suggesting ways, short of a gold standard, to provide uses for gold, either as coin, cover for Treasury bond issues, market sales of gold to finance federal budget deficits, or to settle international payments imbalances.

The choice of witnesses was based on the rule the Treasury adopted that at least two members had to suggest the same individual. Some gold supporters apparently were disappointed that more witnesses supporting a traditional gold standard were not heard from.[12]

13.3.3   Minority Report

The minority report includes seven chapters. The first chapter deals with the present monetary crisis, which it dates from the closing of the gold window on August 15, 1971. Persistent inflation, high interest rates, a weak economy, and high unemployment are attributed to that event. The chapter focuses on monetarism as not an answer to the problem. "The monetarists share our view that the Federal Reserve's discretionary policy of the last several decades has been the cause of our inflation. However, we are confident that the monetarist solution is unworkable." The reason is that monetarism cannot be followed, that governments and the people in charge will "always abuse the 'right' to create money if it is granted to them." Moreover, "monetarism is similar to a discretionary inflationary policy in that the government remains as the monopolist fully in charge. In contrast, with a fully convertible gold standard, the people are in charge and can call the government's bluff anytime they choose by turning in their paper certificates for gold."

Before laying out the minority plans for a sound monetary system, the report presents two lengthy chapters, generally at a high level of scholarship, on U.S. money and banking history in the nineteenth and twentieth centuries. The conclusion is that that experience "illustrates the overwhelmingly superior caes for the gold standard as against any form of paper standard." The solution is to adopt a "modern gold standard" in two steps: first to tie the dollar to gold at a fixed weight and, after the public becomes accustomed to this concept, the currency unit will *become* that fixed weight. In addition, the central government's monopoly of the minting business must be abolished. It is the intervention of government that created problems under the historical gold standard. Laissez-faire must be applied to banking. "The historical evidence shows that monetary freedom does not fail, intervention by the government does."

The report then presents two chapters dealing with the case for monetary freedom and the case for the gold standard. The case for the gold standard is based on historical, theoretical, economic, and moral grounds.

The penultimate chapter deals with "the transition to monetary freedom." It outlines three possible ways of reaching monetary freedom. One is government action to create the new system, but the danger is that it will result in a pseudo- rather than a real gold standard.[13] A second way, in the absence of government action, is bottom-up reform—presumably voluntary actions by the public to use gold in ordinary transactions. A third way is for government to clear the obstacles now impeding reform from the bottom up. The immediate need under this option is for Congress to repeal the legal tender laws and the authority of the Federal Reserve to conduct open market operations. Failure to act will lead to the collapse of the official money and the official economy.

Four specific reforms are then outlined to roll back government and once again confine it within the limits of the Constitution. The monetary reforms include some already noted earlier: abolishing legal tender laws, defining the dollar as a weight of gold (the weight is not specified in the report), issuing gold coins to serve as an alternative monetary system to the present "paper money monopoly," permitting private mints to issue their own coins under their own trademarks, unrestricted money issues by competing issuers, retiring Federal Reserve notes and replacing them by notes redeemable in gold, silver, or some other commodity, 100 percent reserves to replace fractional reserve banking. Other reforms affect fiscal policy and are directed at a balanced budget, a reduction in both spending and taxes ("honest money and limited government are equally necessary in order to end our present economic crisis"), and the confining of government payments to gold or gold denominated accounts. Eventually also the government would accept gold as payment for all taxes, duties, and dues. Deregulation of banking and free entry would complete the reform program.

The chapter on transition concludes with one marked difference from the views Congressman Paul expressed in the hearings before the Subcommittee on Mines and Mining. There he stated, "If we proceed to a gold standard in an orderly fashion, such as I have proposed, then there will be no depression."[14] In the minority report, by contrast, we read: "The transition from the present monetary system to a sound system will probably not be painless, as some have suggested. Whenever the increase in the supply of money slows, there are always recessions. . . . In any transition to a sound monetary system there will, of necessity, have to be readjustments made in various sectors of the economy. Such readjustments will temporarily hurt certain individuals and enterprises." Six sectors that will suffer transitional difficulties are examined: real estate, agriculture, heavy industry, small business, exports, banking.

The prediction in the final chapter is that the "gold standard recession" will be short and mild. It is estimated that the transition will be accomplished in three years, the resulting recession lasting about a year. Thereafter ten years of prosperity will follow, with inflation, the business cycle, and high interest rates things of the past.

13.3.4   Conclusion

The creation of the Gold Commission served one paramount objective of its sponsors. It promoted discussion of gold in the media, on television, and among a lay public committed to the view expressed in the minority report that only gold is "honest" money. The minority report itself is a rallying call for the faithful. Both Helms and Paul were committed to the immediate objective of the minting of gold bullion coins by the Treasury. As the minority report noted: "We are extremely pleased that the Gold Commission has recommended to the Congress a new gold coinage. It has been almost fifty years since the last United States gold coins were struck, and renewing this Constitutional function would indeed be a cause for celebration and jubilee."[15] Short of the appointment of a Commission committed to restoring the gold standard, the sponsors probably view the limited results attained as a gain in achieving their ultimate objectives.[16]

The ultimate objectives of Helms and Paul differ but they may not part company in the interim. Like Lehrman, who did not want to distance himself from Paul and therefore endorsed the minority report, Helms may choose to support the more radical, populist posture that Paul supports than the more conventional one that he on his own might choose.[17] The desire not to split the pro-gold forces was recently also made evident by Paul. He circulated a petition entitled "Economists for Gold" among economics departments of various universities. The gold standard described in the petition did not make clear that the gold standard Paul sought was not the traditional one.

On two issues, Paul found no support in the Gold Commission. He regards the present ten-year audit of the gold inventory as totally inadequate and proposed annual audits. As had Helms independently, he also sought restitution of IMF gold to member countries.

13.4 Likely Impact of the Commission *Report*

The commission reported on March 31, 1982. It is likely that in the months ahead reviews of the *Report* will appear in the economic journals and that its contents will be examined by public discussion panels. It will be judged on its adequacy in answering the questions directed to the Commission by the law that established it. Whatever the verdict will be on the quality of the *Report,* the pro-gold group will probably find satisfaction in the very fact that it provides an establishment discussion of gold. As an April 14 editorial of the *Wall Street Journal* expressed this view, "The Gold Commission . . . has performed the very valuable service of reclaiming gold from the gold bugs."[18]

But the pro-gold group was not the only group that derived satisfaction from the outcome. So also did many economists and commentators who do not favor an expanded role for gold, among whom I include myself. Some had initially feared a Commission dominated by "gold bugs" and were pleased to find that in the Commission as in the economics profession and in the informed public, the supporters of an enlarged role for gold were in a small minority.

It also remains to be seen whether the Congress will act on the recommendations of the Commission. Even before the *Report* was submitted to the Congress, the House Banking Committee issued a statement (signed by thirty members of the Committee, not including Congressman Neal) opposing the Commission's recommendation, adopted at its meeting on February 12, that the Treasury issue gold bullion coins. According to the statement, issue of coins, without legal tender status, would create monetary confusion; the capital gains tax exemption would damage the already weakened security markets; and the sales tax exemption would deprive the states of revenues needed to cover their enhanced obligations. The statement also objected to recommendations referring "to such matters as monetary growth rules and the system of floating as compared with fixed exchange rates. The Commission was not authorized to discuss these matters, was not constituted with a view to providing a balanced and professional perspective on them, did not discuss them adequately at its meetings, and should not have mentioned them in its *Report*."[19] Congressman Reuss led the opposition to the contents of the *Report* referred to in the Banking Committee's statement. Since he is retiring from the Congress at the end of the present session, there is a possibility that the new Congress may respond more positively to the recommendations.

What is undeniable is that continued monetary instability and high and variable inflation and interest rates are the breeding ground for support for a restoration of a monetary role for gold. It may be one of the ironies of history that the Commission was established when the inflation rate was slowing and therefore undercutting some of the rationale and urgency for a return to a gold standard expressed by its adherents. The pro-gold forces, however, predict that the recent slowing of inflation is temporary and that the battle against it will be won only on their terms.[20]

Notes

1. The date for the report of the Commission, according to the law establishing it, was October 7, 1981. Due to the delay in appointment of the members, legislation was introduced in the Congress and enacted as P.L. 97-47 on September 30, 1981, to change the report date to March 31, 1982. *Report to the Congress of the Commission on the Role of Gold in the Domestic and International Monetary Systems,* 2 vols. (Washington, D.C.: Government Printing Office, March 1982). Pro-gold members would have preferred to extend the life of the Commission until June 30. Those opposed to a role for gold (in

particular, Congressman Reuss, at the Commission's first meeting) would have retained the original deadline.

2. Hereafter, cited as *Feasibility;* 96th Cong., 2nd sess., Serial No. 96-40 (Washington, D.C.: Government Printing Office, 1980).

3. U.S., Congress, Senate, *Congressional Record,* June 16, 1980, pp. S 7071–72.

4. U.S., Congress, House, *Congressional Record,* September 18, 1980, pp. H 9136–37.

5. *Feasibility,* pp. 73–89. Quotation from p. 73.

6. Ibid., pp. 51–72.

7. Ibid., p. 47.

8. Ibid., p. 48.

9. On the functions of commissions, see Frank Popper, *The President's Commissions* (New York: Twentieth Century Fund, 1970); Charles J. Hanser, *Guide to Decision: The Royal Commission* (Totowa, N.J.: Bedminster Press, 1965).

10. See his *Monetary Policy, the Federal Reserve System, and Gold,* January 25, 1980, circulated by Barton M. Biggs of Morgan Stanley Investment Research, January 29, 1980.

11. In a news release dated March 31, 1982, Senator Helms commented: "The conclusion of the Gold Commission was predictable considering the preconceived notions of the majority of the members. It was obvious from the outset that the stand-pat paper money advocates dominated the Commission, and that there was little likelihood that they would address the disastrous record of the past decade—the ten years the U.S. has been off a gold standard."

"If the U.S. does not move to adopt a gold standard, one day, historians will note that the nation's leadership failed to face the reality that the inflation and high interest rates are a result of not having a monetary standard. The closest the Commission came was to propose a study of a supply rule for money growth. Well, the Federal Reserve has tried a monetarist supply rule for the past two years, and what happened? We've had higher interest rates and more erratic money supply growth than ever before in the past."

12. In the news release referred to in the preceding note, Senator Helms complains about the inadequacy of the number of witnesses advocating "that the U.S. move swiftly to a gold standard. In all of the past six months of meetings, not one Commission member advocated replacing our present monetary disaster with a gold standard that would make the dollar convertible into gold at a fixed rate."

13. Paul has been influenced by Milton Friedman's article on "Real and Pseudo Gold Standards," *Journal of Law and Economics,* 4 (October, 1961), 66–79, reprinted in his *Dollars and Deficits* (Englewood Cliffs, N.J.: Prentice-Hall, 1968), pp. 247–65. Friedman described the post–World War I standard as a pseudo gold standard because it was not automatic but discretionary.

14. *Feasibility,* p. 7.

15. *Report to the Congress of the Commission on the Role of Gold in the Domestic and International Monetary Systems,* vol. 2, p. 269. The change in Congressman Paul's view on the subject may have evolved from his exposure to monetarist views expressed by Commission members. At the final meeting, Paul observed: "I would like to also state that even though my views are certainly not the majority views of this Commission, I think I have come to respect the views of others, especially those who recognize, as I do, that limiting the supply of money is a very important issue. I think that I have learned to understand that viewpoint, even though they would not make the use of gold as I would. I think that I understand that view better. I appreciate

the information that I have gained from the Commission. I think this has been an important thing for me and I hope some others have benefited by this." Transcript of Seventh Meeting of the Gold Commission, United States Department of the Treasury, March 8, 1982, pp. 71–72.

16. *Report*, vol. 2, p. 260.

17. Senator Helms concludes in his news release of March 31: "The Commission did accomplish one goal—it brought to the public some information about the possibility—and I stress the word, possibility—of a new gold standard. And the public responded. The overwhelming majority of mail received by the Commission members, and the majority of material submitted by the public to the Commission, favored a new gold standard.

"The Commission's work, viewed in that light, could be another step toward a new monetary standard, which the economy desperately needs. The American people want one. We shall see if political leadership will get around to providing one."

I have the impression from the mail that I received on the subject of gold that the writers were not new converts. Much of it seemed to be inspired by a coordinating source with whom the writers were in touch.

18. In a letter to the *Wall Street Journal*, April 22, 1982, Senator Helms, commenting on the April 14 editorial in the paper, wrote: "I was saddened that members of the Commission focused their discussions almost entirely upon alleged inadequacies of past gold standards—with scarcely a mention of the gross inadequacy of the existing monetary fiasco."

19. *Report*, vol. 2, pp. 305–7.

20. In recent weeks the pro-gold group has been advocating a program of stabilization of the price of gold by Federal Reserve intervention. Open market purchases of government securities when the price of gold falls and sales when the price of gold rises have been recommended in articles by Jude Wanniski in the *Wall Street Journal*, by the April 14 editorial in the paper, and in a TV program by Arthur Laffer. The assumption underlying the recommendation is that any change in the price of gold is a response to monetary forces. The evidence of disturbances in demand and supply in the gold market unrelated to monetary forces is ignored by the proponents.

14 The Postwar Institutional Evolution of the International Monetary System

The international monetary system that was designed at the Bretton Woods Conference in 1944 reflected professional views on the defects of the arrangements that had prevailed in the 1930s. Protectionist trade policies, exchange controls, and competitive currency depreciations[1] of the pre–World War II period were the cautionary experiences to be avoided by the postwar world. Removal of controls on trade and payments under a system of fixed exchange rates, with adjustment of parities limited to "fundamental" disequilibrium in the balance of payments, accordingly were the goals of the system created by the delegates to the conference. Exchange rates were to be pegged within narrow margins to the dollar. Countries would buy or sell dollars in the foreign exchange market to keep their currencies from appreciating or depreciating more than 1% from parity. The United States in turn would undertake to convert dollars into gold or the reverse at a fixed price of $35 an ounce. The International Monetary Fund, to which each member subscribed 25% of its quota in gold or 10% of its net official reserves of gold and dollars, whichever was smaller, was established by the terms of the Bretton Woods charter. It was expected that lending facilities of the Fund would be available to supplement the members' gold and foreign exchange reserves to provide them liquidity when their balances-of-payments were temporarily in deficit on current account.

The establishment of par values for currencies was an important item on the Fund's agenda. Of our sample of countries, Canada, France, the Netherlands, the United Kingdom, and the United States declared their par values in December 1946, Germany and Japan in 1953, and Italy not until 1960. Some of these parities were short-lived. An abortive attempt at convertibility of sterling in 1947 ended in September

1949, when the pound was devalued. The Netherlands thereupon devalued the guilder, and France, which had had separate rates for financial and commercial transactions, unified them, depreciating the franc vis-à-vis sterling.

The pegged exchange-rate system that was created collapsed in 1971.[2] Following futile efforts to restore it, in 1973 governments reluctantly turned to managed floating exchange rates. In both regimes, the United States served as the reserve-currency country, other countries primarily holding dollar assets among their international reserves.

Discussion of the institutions of the international monetary system is instructive for all the theoretical channels of international transmission of price change. One of these is completely monetary in nature and is therefore directly affected by the character of the international monetary system; the other three are nonmonetary, or in one instance only partially monetary, and hence may be only indirectly affected. The four channels are (1) international money flows as a result of international payments imbalances that affect the growth of national money supplies and eventually rates of price change; (2) direct effects on national prices and interest rates through international arbitrage of prices of goods and services or of interest rates as a result either of changes in the world quantity of money and prices or of cost factors independent of monetary conditions; (3) shifts in foreign demand for a country's output that affect its prices; (4) effects on prices of changes in international basic commodity supplies. Some comments on each of the channels follow.

1. The money-flow channel was undoubtedly available during the postwar period. For the moment consider only the non-reserve-currency countries in the international monetary system.

Under a pegged exchange-rate system, central banks must buy from or sell to their nationals foreign exchange, according as countries face a surplus or a deficit in the balance of payments. Central banks may also choose to do so under a managed floating exchange-rate regime. Whenever a central bank buys foreign exchange, it issues newly created high-powered money—usable as reserves by banks or currency by the public—just as if it had purchased government securities in an open market operation or bankers' promissory notes through discounting. Conversely, a sale of foreign exchange destroys high-powered money just as does a reduction in the central bank's portfolio of securities or discounts. For this reason, a balance-of-payments surplus is a source of increase, a balance-of-payments deficit a source of decrease in high-powered money in a strictly arithmetic, or accounting, sense. If, however, the central bank offsets (sterilizes) the effect of a balance-of-payments surplus by reducing its portfolio of domestic securities and discounts, or increasing it less than it otherwise would, there is no effect on the growth rate of high-powered money. The sources of growth in high-powered money then are flows of international reserves and domestic credit creation by the central bank. It was thus possible for a non-reserve-currency country either to accept imported inflation or deflation, or for a time to resist such an outcome by sterilizing under pegged exchange rates.[3] Under floating rates, the country had the additional option of varying its exchange rate to protect its price level.

For the U.S., the reserve-currency country, the effect of deficits in its balance of payments had no necessary contractionary effect on Federal Reserve policies under either exchange system. The acquisition of dollars by foreign central banks did not reduce U.S. high-powered money. Dollars were either credited to the balance of those banks at Federal Reserve banks or else committed to the purchase of U.S. Treasury debt. Until March 1968, the gold requirement to which Federal Reserve notes were subject may have served as a constraint, but once abolished there was no legal limitation on the creation of high-powered money or money-supply growth, even after the 1970s, when the Federal Reserve system began specifying targets for growth rates of money.

Until U.S. monetary policy shifted to an inflationary course in the mid-1960s, deficits in the U.S. balance of payments provided the rest of the world with desired dollars. After the shift occurred, the defense of sterilizing undesired additions to dollar holdings as the U.S. balance of payments deteriorated was eventually overwhelmed by the magnitude of the required operation. Given the commitment to pegged exchange rates that surplus countries were reluctant to break by revaluing, dollars increased their high-powered money stocks and inflation rates. In the absence of such a commitment and the adoption of flexible exchange rates, short-run independence of national high-powered money stocks is increased.[4]

2. The operation of the arbitrage channels of transmission requires a high degree of, and in the extreme perfect, substitutability of goods and financial assets among countries.[5] Applied to the goods markets, the perfect-substitutability view is usually described as the "law of one price level." Another approach stresses the effects of changes in wages, external prices, and productivity on the two sectors of tradable versus nontradable goods which characterize open economies. The law of one price level, or the "goods arbitrage approach," emphasizes the impact of world monetary growth on the rise in prices; the second approach emphasizes "sructural" factors that allow no such role for monetary conditions. Restrictions on international trade and capital flows obviously block the operation of this channel, which denies the degree of autonomy to individual countries attributed to them by the first channel under fixed exchange rates. Even if international equalizing of tradable goods prices is assumed, inflation rates can differ between

countries if relative prices of traded and nontraded goods vary. Under flexible exchange rates, transmission of a different sort may occur because an immediate change in the foreign exchange value of domestic money, as a result of expectations of future domestic monetary policy, will affect domestic money prices of imports and tradable goods and thus the domestic inflation rate.[6] For the alternative approach, exchange-rate changes may provide a signal to price and wage setters of changes in economic conditions.

3. Monetary growth plays no direct role in the operation of this or the following channel. Downward shifts in foreign demand for a country's output lead to declines in prices, output, and incomes, through a contractionary multiplier effect; upwards shifts, to increases in prices, output, and incomes, through an expansionary multiplier effect.[7] This channel may be important under fixed exchange rates for particular countries, for example, the effects of U.S. real income changes on the demand for Canadian exports, or of German real income changes on the demand for Austrian exports, but not necessarily so for the transmission from the U.S. to European countries. Floating exchange rates may decrease the magnitude of the effects through this channel.

4. Transmission through this channel occurs because the rise in prices of basic commodities is viewed as entering either as supply components of products initially unaffected and raising their prices also or by pulling up the prices of substitute domestic inputs. Prices in all countries are affected, the effect depending on the input weights of these commodities in each economy. Some proponents of the importance of this channel also view exchange-rate changes as affecting export and import prices of basic commodities.

Although thus far only the pegged and managed floating exchange-rate regimes have been mentioned, it is useful to distinguish four subperiods in the evolution of the international monetary system from 1955 to date: (1) the preconvertibility phase for nondollar currencies, 1955–58; (2) the heyday of the Bretton Woods dollar-exchange standard, 1959–67; (3) the weakening and ensuing collapse of the Bretton Woods arrangements, 1968–73; (4) the managed floating exchange-rate phase, 1973 to date.

For each of the subperiods we shall summarize developments that relate to the channels of international transmission of price change.

14.1 Preconvertibility, 1955–58

In 1955, when our data begin, postwar recovery in Europe was well under way. Wartime destruction and disruption in Europe and Asia left the countries there with limited productive capacity and swelled the immediate postwar demand for U.S. exports. Restrictions against dollar transactions were widespread, and multiple exchange rates were not unusual. In the postwar years before 1955, important steps had been taken to develop a system of multilateral trade and payments for Western European countries. Of these, the most significant was the establishment in the summer of 1950, with U.S. support, of the European Payments Union (EPU). Before 1950, the conduct of trade and payments among members of the EPU as well as with non-European countries was on a bilateral basis. By contrast, under the EPU, every month the multilateral net debtor-creditor position of each member with respect to other members was determined. The dollar served as the unit of account, and each European currency was pegged at a fixed dollar parity with no band of admissible variation. Receipts and payments were expressed as claims against the clearing union, debtors paying a gradually increasing fraction of their deficits in gold or dollars, with creditor countries extending the balance as a loan to the EPU. Maximum credit lines for debtor countries were imposed, so that creditor countries were assured of eventual payment in gold or dollars.

Paralleling the adoption of the clearing union, a trade liberalization program among members advanced. In trade with the United States, however, European countries applied discriminatory tariff and quota restrictions, which the United States did not protest, in order to enable them to accumulate gold and dollar assets. It was expected that the dollar gap problem, which in 1955 was widely regarded as a long-term one, would thereby be mitigated.

In private gold markets until 1953, the price of gold was at a premium, but the IMF required monetary authorities to refrain from selling gold at premium prices. In March 1954, several months after the premium had been eliminated, reflecting balance of supply and demand, the London gold market reopened. For the rest of the decade the price of gold in private markets remained at $35 an ounce.

Faced with deficits in its current account in 1957–58, France imposed import restrictions, devalued at the end of 1958, and borrowed mainly from the United States, supplemented by EPU and IMF credits, which were conditioned on a ceiling on public expenditures and the budget deficit, as well as restrictive monetary policy by the Banque de France.

Until 1958, all foreign exchange transactions required the approval of central banks, which were the agents under the EPU for arranging settlements. They were thus well positioned to maintain exchange controls and payments restrictions. With the dissolution of the EPU on 24 December 1958, fifteen Western European countries (including the five in our sample) made their currencies convertible for current transactions. It was not until 1961, however, that restrictions against U.S. exports were removed. Most countries maintained strict controls against capital outflows. Only Germany in 1957 authorized its residents to export capital in any form anywhere in the world and permitted non-residents to convert the proceeds of capital transactions in D-marks into any other currency.

Japan's recovery from the war was less rapid than that of the Western European countries. Its current account remained in deficit until the mid-1960s, and it continued exchange and capital flow restrictions until 1964.

Canada enjoyed special status in the international system. Although the IMF, in line with the prevailing U.S. view, set fixed exchange rates as the monetary regime par excellence, it tolerated the decision made by Canada in 1950 to float its dollar. Canada did not revert to a fixed rate until 1962. The reason for floating was to resist the inflationary effects that U.S. capital inflows produced under fixed exchange rates.[8]

14.2   The Heyday of the Bretton Woods Dollar-Exchange Standard, 1959–67

With the return of many European currencies to convertibility in 1958, the achievement of the Bretton Woods conception of international monetary normalcy seemed only a matter of time. The outflow of dollars in U.S. official aid, military spending, and private investment, and economic recovery in Europe and Japan had enabled foreigners to add to their holdings of dollars and gold. Apart from the 1950–51 Korean War upsurge, U.S. prices were generally stable until the middle of the 1960s, and their rate of rise generally lower than in the rest of the world (table 14.1). Money supplies in the rest of the world (except in the U.K.) grew at a faster rate than in the U.S. (table 14.2).

Part of the difference between this generally faster monetary growth in the rest of the world than in the United States was not reflected in a difference in inflation rates. Real income growth in general was much more rapid in Europe and Japan, which were still recovering from the war. Furthermore in some of these countries at least the income elas-

Table 14.1   **Quarterly Rates of Change of Consumer Prices at Annual Rates (percent per year)**

Period[a]	CA[b]	FR	GE	IT	JA	NE	UK	US
1955I–58IV	2.02	5.37	2.05	2.01	0.88	3.32	3.75	2.04
1958IV–67IV	2.07	3.54	2.41	3.61	4.99	3.32	2.86	1.73
1967IV–73I	4.13	5.57	4.45	4.58	5.87	6.17	6.86	4.58
1973I–76IV	8.85	10.68	4.89	16.09	13.19	8.92	16.36	7.95

[a]All rates are computed from the first quarter of each period to the quarter which ends the period. Periods mark changes in international monetary institutions.

[b]Throughout this volume the following country mnemonics are used: CA, Canada; FR, France; GE, Germany; IT, Italy; JA, Japan; NE, Netherlands; UK, United Kingdom; US, United States.

Table 14.2   **Quarterly Rates of Change of Money[a] at Annual Rates (percent per year)**

Period[b]	CA	FR	GE	IT	JA	NE	UK	US
1955I–58IV	5.67	8.74	10.52	11.96	17.11	5.27	−0.46	3.34
1958IV–67IV	6.79	12.15	8.01	13.26	17.41	7.90	6.00	5.83
1967IV–73I	10.97	9.40	12.75	14.02	18.11	11.98	11.09	8.09
1973I–76IV	16.21	12.99	5.07	19.29	13.16	15.01	11.52	8.62

[a]Money is defined as currency plus adjusted demand and time deposits held by the public.
[b]All rates of change computed from the first quarter of each subperiod to the quarter which ends the subperiod.

ticity of demand for money was higher than in the U.S. (See Gandolfi and Lothian, 1983, for estimates.) That some difference in inflation was actually maintained over long periods without devaluations may be due to changes in the relative prices of tradable to nontradable goods in these more rapidly growing economies. Differences over shorter periods, particularly during the early 1970s, are explainable in terms of lags in the operation of U.S. reserve flows on monetary growth in the nonreserve countries.

The dollar's status as the reserve currency of the international economy seemed impregnable during these years. Commercial banks and private firms could make foreign payments in their convertible currencies without the approval of central banks. Tariff and quota restrictions on commodity trade among the industrialized countries were eased, and foreign trade grew at a rapid rate during the period. International transfers of capital grew, with New York at the center of the flows and the dollar as the vehicle currency in which the borrowers obtained capital and the investors lent their savings.

The successful operation of the system depended on foreign central banks intervening with their own currencies against the dollar to maintain par values and the United States standing ready to buy or sell gold at $35 per ounce in transactions with foreign monetary authorities. The U.S. balance of payments accordingly was determined by the exchange parities other countries established. In general, other countries desired surpluses that would add to their dollar reserves, and the system tended to produce a steadily weakening U.S. balance of payments and growing doubts about the sustainability of the U.S. gold convertibility commitment.

14.2.1 Gold and the Dollar

A portent of the troubled future of the system was that 1960 was the first year in which U.S. gold reserves declined below the level of its total liquid liabilities to all foreign holders of assets denominated in dollars (table 14.3).

Until March 1961, the U.S. intervened to maintain the price of gold by selling and buying dollars. Concern over the continuing conversion of dollars in gold led the Treasury to activate the Exchange Stabilization Fund. In its initial operations on 13 March 1961, acting through the Federal Reserve Bank of New York as its agent, the Fund sold forward D-marks to reduce the premium on that currency.[9] On 13 February 1962 the bank was also authorized to buy or sell foreign currencies on behalf of the Federal Open Market Committee in both spot and forward markets. For this purpose a stock of foreign currencies in addition to those acquired from the Stabilization Fund was needed. The Federal Reserve therefore negotiated a network of swap facilities with the central banks of other countries. The swap provided a specified amount of foreign currency in exchange for an equivalent dollar credit for the foreign central bank, with each party protected against loss from a change in the par value of the other party's currency. Invested balances of both parties earned the same rate of interest, foreign balances in special U.S. Treasury certificates, Federal Reserve balances in interest-earning deposits abroad. Balances were available for payments to the other party or for foreign exchange market transactions. The swap was a credit line, usually for three-month periods, renewable at maturity. By drawing on the credit, both parties initially raised their gross reserves. The Federal Reserve normally used the proceeds of a swap to absorb foreign official dollar holdings; these transactions in effect provided forward cover to foreign official dollarholders, reducing their incentive to convert dollars into gold.

Repayments of short-term swap credits meant a corresponding decline in gross reserves. For the U.S. this could entail a loss of gold. To deter this eventuality, the U.S. began issuing nonmarketable bonds, with maturities of fifteen months to two years, denominated in the holder's currency, to fund outstanding swap debt. The bonds were, however, convertible into Treasury bills on demand.[10]

A further indication of U.S. concern about gold was the prohibition after mid-1961 on the holding of gold outside the U.S. by U.S. firms and households, and on 3 March 1965 the abolition of gold reserve requirements against Federal Reserve deposits.

A focus of pressure on the U.S. dollar was the London gold market. In March 1960, the price rose above $35 an ounce, as European central banks and private investors bought gold for dollars. The Bank of England sold gold to stabilize the price, but the U.S. Treasury initially was not willing to restore the bank's holdings. Hence, when a rise in the price of gold occurred in October, the bank did not intervene. On 27 October, with the price reaching $40 an ounce, the Treasury agreed

Table 14.3   **United States Monetary Gold Stock and Liquid Liabilities to Foreigners (millions of dollars)**

End of Year (1)	Total Monetary Gold Stock[a] (2)	Total Liquid Liabilities to All Foreigners[b] (3)
1954	21,793	12,454
1955	21,753	13,524
1956	22,058	15,291
1957	22,857	15,825
1958	20,582	16,845
1959	19,507	19,428
1960	17,804	⌈ 20,994 ⌊ 21,027
1961	16,947	⌈ 22,853 ⌊ 22,936
1962	16,057	24,068
1963	15,596	⌈ 26,361 ⌊ 26,322
1964	15,471	⌈ 28,951 ⌊ 29,002
1965	13,806[c]	29,115
1966	13,235	⌈ 29,904 ⌊ 29,779
1967	12,065	⌈ 33,271 ⌊ 33,119
1968	10,892	⌈ 33,828 ⌊ 33,614
1969	11,859	⌈ 41,735 ⌊ 41,894
1970	11,072	⌈ 43,291 ⌊ 43,242
1971	10,206	⌈ 64,166 ⌊ 64,223
1972	10,487[d]	78,680
1973	11,652[e]	87,620
1974	11,652	120,325[f]
1975	11,599	127,432[f]
1976	11,598	152,468[f]

Sources:
   Col. (2), *Treasury Bulletin,* December 1965, IFS-1; July 1975, IFS-1; February 1982, IFS-1.
   Col. (3), *Treasury Bulletin,* July 1975, IFS-2; February 1982, IFS-2.

[a]The stock includes gold sold to the U.S. by the IMF with the right of repurchase, and gold deposited by the IMF to mitigate the impact on the U.S. of foreign purchases for the purpose of making gold subscriptions to the IMF under quota increases.

[b]The total includes small amounts due to the IMF arising from gold transactions, amounts due to official institutions, commercial banks abroad, to other foreigners, and to non-monetary and regional organizations. Nonliquid liabilities to official institutions included in the source beginning 1962 through 1973 have been deducted. Years for which two entries are shown show differences because of changes in reporting coverage. Figures

Table 14.3   (continued)

on the first line are comparable to figures for preceding dates; figures on the second line are comparable to those for the following dates.
cThe figure excludes $259 million gold subscription to the IMF in June 1965 for a U.S. quota increase that became effective 23 February 1966.
dChange in par value of dollar on 8 May 1972 increased the value of the total gold stock by $822 million.
eChange in par value of dollar on 18 October 1973 increased the value of the gold stock by $1,165 million.
fIncludes categories of liabilities previously classified as nonliquid.

to sell gold to the bank, reserving for the bank the decision on intervention in the market. European central banks soon after agreed to refrain from buying gold in the London market for monetary purposes whenever the price rose above $35.20, the U.S. price plus shipping costs. When the price fell below that level in 1961, the central banks returned to the market. However, in October 1961, when the price again was reacting to heightened demand, an agreement to create a "gold pool" was reached among the U.S. and seven European governments. Each member undertook to supply an agreed portion of net gold sales to stabilize the market, as the Bank of England as agent of the group determined to be appropriate. The members of the pool subsequently agreed not to buy gold individually on the market, but to give the Bank of England the right to buy on their joint account when gold supply exceeded demand, the amount purchased to be distributed in proportion to each country's contribution to the pool. The pool functioned until the end of 1967, when a surge of buying led to the suspension of the agreement in March 1968. During the period of the pool's operation, the participants sold a net of $2.5 billion of gold on the London market, of which $1.6 billion was provided by the United States.

14.2.2   The Dollar's Performance

A key development for the international monetary system that was not perceived as such at the time was the acceleration of the U.S. monetary growth rate and the subsequent acceleration of the U.S. inflation rate in the final years of this subperiod. What was perceived was the cumulative growth of deficits in the U.S. balance of payments. Assets denominated in dollars grew in excess of the demand for them by the rest of the world. Their conversion into gold, by shrinking U.S. gold reserves, threatened one of the basic underpinnings of the Bretton Woods structure, namely, convertibility of dollars into gold.

One measure the U.S. authorities might have taken was a raise in the dollar price of gold, thus increasing the value of the stock and the flow of reserve assets. If other countries did not follow suit by adopting a proportional increase in the price of gold in their currencies, the U.S. in this way might have obtained a devaluation of the dollar that the Bretton Woods system otherwise ruled out. Had the price of gold risen, the gold demands of other countries might have been satisfied without the rundown in U.S. reserve assets. Some countries might also have revalued because of the inflationary consequences of their payments surplus, given the gold-based increase in their asset holdings.

The U.S., however, resolutely opposed a change in the monetary price of gold. Such action would have required an Act of Congress which would have produced a long and unsettling debate in the two Houses, during which time the foreign exchange markets would have been disturbed. Moreover, there was no assurance that other countries would not make corresponding changes in their own par values, and it was feared that confidence in the stability of the monetary system would be seriously impaired by a change in the official dollar price of gold. Given the fixed price of gold when national price levels were rising, gold became an undervalued asset with a resulting gold shortage.

The Bretton Woods system might have been able to survive an end of gold convertibility. It could not survive inflationary monetary policy in the center country that characterized the decade from the mid-1960s on. Crisis management by the IMF and the central banks of the leading industrialized countries became the hallmark of the international monetary system during the heyday of Bretton Woods.[11] The chief currency under pressure, apart from the dollar, was sterling. Persistent or recurring U.K. balance-of-payments deficits impaired the credibility of sterling's external value, already insecure by reason of the size of sterling balances held worldwide relative to U.K. gold and foreign exchange reserves. Private agents displayed lack of confidence in the dollar and sterling by shifting to currencies whose external values were regarded as stable or likely to appreciate (during this period, the D-mark and guilder). Repeated rescue operations to support the exchange value of sterling were overwhelmed in November 1967. Sterling, however, was a sideshow. The main act was the dollar's performance.

A variety of measures, adopted in countries with over- or undervalued currencies to stave off devaluation or revaluation, affected the channels of international transmission of price change.[12] Surplus countries tried to avoid price increases, deficit countries price declines, both as external consequences of their balance-of-payments positions. Intermittently, depending on cyclical conditions, countries in both categories took steps to right payments imbalances.

14.2.3   Growth of World Foreign Reserves

Since palliatives to improve the balance of payments proved ineffective, deficits had to be financed either by drawing down reserves or seeking external credit or borrowing facilities, while surpluses obviously increased net reserve accumulations. During the heyday of the Bretton Woods system, despite the growth of dollar assets, the adequacy of international liquidity, in the sense of the quantity of international monetary reserves, was widely debated. Discussions during this period growing out of misplaced concern for the supply of reserves ultimately led to the creation of SDRs by the IMF, but that development belongs in the account of the breakdown of the system.[13] Until the end of 1967, international reserves were limited to gold, convertible foreign exchange, and reserve positions in the IMF.

Contrary to the design of Bretton Woods, financing of payments imbalances for the most part was arranged through credits governments extended on a bilateral basis and through international borrowing and lending activities of commercial banks. Thus, to restore depleted reserves of countries with persistent deficits, facilities for borrowing were created in addition to drawings from the IMF.

Official dollar reserves of the surplus countries were augmented at times by actions those countries took in the Eurodollar market. Dollars acquired by their central banks and deposited in the Eurodollar market either directly or through the Bank for International Settlements would usually be re-lent to private borrowers who could resell the dollars to the central banks.

With the exception of the U.K. and the U.S., all the countries in our sample increased their holdings of international reserves. In sum, world reserves grew during the period, leaving greater scope for the direct monetary channel of transmission of inflation to operate (table 14.4).

14.3   Weakening and Collapse of Bretton Woods, 1968–73

The devaluation of sterling in November 1967 was not regarded as the prelude to changes in the par values of other currencies, the devaluation of the dollar in terms of gold, the realignment of exchange-rate relations among the major currencies, and the substitution of a short-lived regime of central rates for the par value system—all of which took place between November 1967 and December 1971. Instead, it was hoped that balance in the U.S. and U.K. external payments was finally on the point of achievement, and that the creation of a special drawing rights facility in the IMF would replace reserve assets that dollar and sterling deficits had provided.

The hope was belied. The pattern of deficits and surpluses persisted and worsened in 1970 and 1971. The U.S. current account surplus dwindled, and the U.S. capital account deficit grew dramatically, producing current account surpluses and capital inflows in other countries. The activation of SDRs in 1970–72 provided additions to already massive acquisitions of dollar reserve assets.[14]

Table 14.4 Average Quarterly Change at Annual Rates and Variance in the Level of International Reserves (millions of U.S. dollars)

	CA	FR	GE	IT	JA	NE	UK	US
1953–58IV	8	−301	797	307	−45	56	163	−297
	(9)	(824)	(831)	(126)	(238)	(92)	(522)	(1,879)
1958IV–67IV	40	766	219	199	102	90	−26	−694
	(325)	(265)	(1,471)	(364)	(118)	(76)	(936)	(1,100)
1967IV–73I	477	619	4,504	323	3,059	538	366	−339
	(1,026)	(11,638)	(68,212)	(1,359)	(22,856)	(826)	(4,642)	(13,719)
1973I–76IV	−248	−563	195	1,202	−664	406	118	537
	(638)	(20,341)	(152,624)	(44,234)	(2,005)	(743)	(3,647)	(1,523)

Note: Variances are shown in parentheses beneath the change figures.

As in the heyday of the Bretton Woods system, disbelief of market participants in the pegged external values of currencies precipitated eruptions of turbulence in foreign exchange and gold markets, but the heart of the problem affecting the international monetary system was the performance of the dollar. The failure of the U.S. to maintain price stability led to institutional change in 1968, repegging in 1971, and finally the total collapse of fixed exchange-rate parities in 1973.

14.3.1   Foreign Exchange Turbulence

In May 1968, student riots in France touched off strikes and lockouts throughout the country. The settlement raised hourly wage rates by 11%, shortened the work week, and provoked a flight of capital, primarily into D-marks but also into gold. Rumors of a revaluation of the mark encouraged further shifts of funds. France imposed tighter price controls, restricted imports and some external payments, introduced subsidies for exports, and imposed exchange controls. These measures were revoked in September, and credit restrictions substituted. In November, the flight from francs to marks intensified, and on 20 November, major European exchange markets were shut down. Between April and November 1968, official French foreign exchange reserves declined by $2.9 billion. France resisted advice to devalue, Germany advice to revalue. Germany imposed a temporary export tax and an import subsidy, and in December a 100% reserve requirement on increases in nonresident deposits in German banks, but almost immediately relaxed the measure as funds flowed out. France in turn restored exchange and credit controls, the former having only been fully relaxed a year earlier, cut public spending and increased indirect taxes, and imposed ceilings on commercial bank lending and raised interest rates.

The deficit in the French current account grew in the first two quarters of 1969, and capital that flowed to Germany not only from France but also from the U.K. and other countries totaled $4.4 billion in May. Again, Germany adopted measures to deter the inflow: a 50% reserve requirement for nonresident deposits received before 15 April and 15% on resident deposits. The French tightened restrictions on bank credit and raised minimum requirements for hire purchase. In July funds for public investment programs were frozen. When the drain on French reserves continued and short-term debts of $2.3 billion had been incurred, France finally gave in and devalued by 11.11% as of 10 August. Currencies linked to the French franc followed suit.

Thanks to increased monetary growth in the U.S. and the resultant higher balance-of-payments deficit, France rapidly moved from $1.7 billion deficit on current account in 1969 to a small surplus in 1970, an overall balance-of-payments surplus of $2 billion in that year and of $3.4 billion in 1971. Official reserves grew correspondingly.

The perception that the D-mark was undervalued in relation to the dollar, now that the French franc had been devalued, led to a further flow of funds to Germany. A few days before German elections in October 1969, the Bundesbank closed the exchange market, and a day after reopening it, permitted the D-mark to float. The spot rate against the dollar appreciated, and on 26 October, a revaluation of 9.29% was announced. Although there was a capital outflow in the last quarter of 1969, by 1970 there were large inflows of foreign funds and official reserves increased substantially. Domestic inflation in Germany was thereby eventually worsened.

The persistent outflow of funds from the U.S. overwhelmed foreign exchange markets in the first few days of May 1971. On 5 May seven European countries closed their foreign exchange markets, and five other countries on several continents withdrew their support for the dollar and suspended dealings in D-marks, guilders, and Swiss francs. On 9 May, both Germany and the Netherlands announced that their currencies would float, since they could not maintain exchange rates within the established margins.

14.3.2   Gold and the Dollar

The gold market was the second market in which participants expressed lack of confidence in the dollar-based international monetary system. After the devaluation of sterling in November 1967, the vulnerability of the dollar took center stage. In the winter of 1967–68, a surge of demand for gold threatened both the London Gold Pool and the statutory backing for Federal Reserve notes that then amounted to $10 billion. On 12 March 1968 the U.S. gold reserve requirement was abolished. Ostensibly, the gold stock was then available for conversion of dollars held by foreign central banks. On 17 March, however, the London gold market was closed to avoid further U.S. gold losses. The members of the gold pool announced that they would no longer supply gold to the London or any other gold market or buy gold from the market. Official transactions between central banks were to be conducted at the unchanged official price of $35 an ounce, but the gold price for private transactions was to be determined in the market. Central banks were still free de jure to buy U.S. Treasury gold for dollars but in fact refrained from doing so. Germany had explicitly forsworn converting its dollar holdings into gold in May 1967.

In March 1971, before the panic of the foreign exchange market, there was a request from several European countries for conversion of officially held dollars into gold to enable them to pay for an increase in their IMF quotas. The payout reduced the U.S. gold stock to the lowest level since 1936. The dollar outflow meanwhile accelerated, leading, as noted, to the floating of European currencies. The devaluation of the dollar vis-à-vis the D-mark as the result of the float left unsolved the dollar's exchange rate vis-à-vis the yen. Japan's capital controls were proof against the dollar flows that inundated European foreign exchange markets, but not against the large deficit in U.S. trade with Japan. That bilateral trade imbalance was a provocation, over and above the imbalance between U.S. reserves and outstanding dollar liabilities, for the changes the U.S. introduced on 15 August 1971 to achieve a dollar devaluation. Chief among them (besides a price and wage freeze, tax increases, and federal government spending cuts) was a 10% import surcharge on 50% of total U.S. imports. The convertibility of the dollar into gold was formally suspended, as was the use of the swap network through which dollars could be exchanged with central banks for other currencies. The effect was to oblige other countries to hold dollars or to trade them for a price determined in the market and so to revalue their currencies. Foreign exchange markets abroad, except in Japan, shut down. The Japanese initial attempt to maintain the pegged rate of the yen compelled them to purchase $4 billion in the two weeks after 15 August. The yen was then freed to float upward; other currencies floated when exchange markets were reopened on 23 August. France introduced a dual exchange market, with trade and government exchange dealings based on the par value, financial exchange dealings at a floating rate. Restoration of a repegged system of exchange rates, however, remained the goal of the U.S. and its partners.

After much negotiation, a readjustment of currency parities was arranged at a meeting at the Smithsonian Institution in Washington on 17–18 December 1971. In return the U.S. agreed to withdraw the import surcharge. The currencies of six of the countries in our sample (plus those of nonsample ones) were revalued by percentages ranging from 2¾% (the Netherlands) to 7.7% (Japan) with the proviso that 2¼% margins of fluctuation (replacing the former 1% margin) above and below the so-called central exchange rates were permissible. The Canadian dollar continued to float. The Smithsonian agreement also specified that the official dollar price of gold would henceforth be $38, a concession by the U.S. for appearance' sake only, since the dollar remained inconvertible. The new price of gold implied a depreciation of 7.9% of the gold value of the dollar rather than an appreciation of the dollar value of other currencies.

14.3.3 European Economic Community Snake

The notion of a European monetary union had been the subject of discussion for years. Implementing the notion had been scheduled for a start in June 1971. The floating of the D-mark in May delayed the introduction of the plan to keep fluctuations between EEC–country currencies within narrower limits than those vis-à-vis the dollar. The activation of the snake came in April 1972 in response to the 2¼% margin above and below the central rate that the Smithsonian agreement set. In relation to the dollar a European currency could fluctuate by 4½% from floor to ceiling, but in relation to another European currency the relative fluctuation could be as much as 9% if one rose from floor to ceiling and the other fell from ceiling to floor. The motivation for the snake was to narrow margins of fluctuation between EEC currencies by a convergence of economic and monetary policies so that exchange parities among them would be fixed.

Operationally, if an EEC currency premium over its central rate plus the discount on the central rate of another EEC currency reached 2¼% (half the amount permitted by the Smithsonian agreement), the weak currency was to be bought by the strong currency. The purchase could be made by the weak-currency country, by the strong-currency country, or by both. A monthly settlement was provided, so the creditor country could exchange the weak currency acquired for a desired reserve asset and obtain repayment for its short-term credit facility if it had lent its currency to the debtor. Debtors were to make settlement in a prescribed mix of reserve assets.

Six countries (France, Germany, Italy, Belgium, Luxemburg, the Netherlands) originally joined the snake; three others joined in May 1972 but left in June (U.K., Denmark, Eire). Denmark rejoined in October 1972, Italy left in December 1972. France left in January 1974, rejoined in July 1975, and left again in March 1976. Sweden and Norway, non–EEC countries, joined in May 1972. Sweden left in August 1977.[15]

The feasibility of the snake was dubious in the absence of consensus by the national governments to yield to the union direct monetary autonomy and control over exchange-rate changes, and to seek convergence of economic policies.

14.3.4   The End of the Sterling Area

Within weeks after joining the snake, sterling came under pressure in foreign exchange markets. The central banks of the EEC countries supported sterling, but on the next settlement day the U.K. would have had to repay them. On 22 June 1972 the bank rate was raised by 1%, and on the following day the exchange rate was floated. The float marked the end of the sterling area. Capital flows to overseas sterling areas were made subject to the same exchange controls as other areas, and Bank of England approval was required for official foreign exchange for direct investment in the overseas sterling area. Only a few small countries of the sixty-five that had formerly pegged their currencies on sterling continued to do so after sterling floated.

14.3.5 The End of the Convertible Dollar Standard

The central rates established at the Smithsonian meeting crumbled during the nine months following the floating of sterling. Once again, the disbelief of market participants in those rates was revealed in the gold and foreign exchange markets. The London free market price of gold rose with few reversals. Money growth and inflation rates continued to rise in the U.S., and both the balance of trade and the U.S. balance-of-payments deficit soared, with a corresponding surge in dollar holdings of the industrialized European countries and Japan. Capital controls were imposed in 1972 by the Netherlands and Japan before sterling was floated, and Germany followed suit afterward. On 10 February 1973 Japan closed its foreign exchange market and suspended support of the dollar. New central values were set in a hurried round of negotiations, although the lira, yen, Canadian dollar, U.K. and Irish pounds, and Swiss franc all floated. Again, the official price of gold was raised (this time to $42.22), leaving unchanged the gold value of other currencies. The new central rates did not staunch the flow of dollars abroad, and a further crisis erupted in March 1973. This time the major industrial countries discontinued pegging their exchange rates to the dollar. The EEC countries in the snake plus Sweden and Norway agreed to a joint float, with Germany revaluing by 3% (in terms of SDRs) in relation to the other members. Canada, Japan, and Switzerland floated individually, as did a handful of other countries. Though a large group of nonindustrialized countries pegged to the dollar, the dollar currency area worldwide contracted; smaller groups of countries pegged to the French franc or to the pound.

Market forces had triumphed.

14.4 Managed Floating Exchange Rates

When pegged rates were abandoned in March 1973, it was initially assumed that floating was a temporary expedient to be succeeded by a reformed par value system. The U.S. took the lead in opposing the return to such a system. The dispersion of inflation rates among the industrialized countries and the higher variability of rates of inflation since the late 1960s enforced more frequent changes of exchange rates. Under the earlier system, changes in par values were delayed until foreign exchange market crises were provoked. The lesson since the shift in March 1973 was that floating provided more flexibility. The U.S. view prevailed. With the suspension of official gold convertibility, and widespread departures from the IMF's par value provisions, negotiations were held to codify, in the form of amendments to the IMF Articles, the international monetary arrangements that had evolved in practice.

Under the amendments to the IMF Articles agreed on in early 1976 and implemented in April 1978, gold was formally removed from its previous central role in the IMF and IMF par value obligations were eliminated. The official IMF gold price was abolished, as were also gold convertibility and maintenance of gold value obligations. Gold was eliminated as a significant instrument in IMF transactions with members, and the IMF was empowered to dispose of its large gold holdings. Although the amended IMF Articles provide for the future possibility of establishing a system of stable but adjustable par values, such a decision by the Fund would require an 85% affirmative vote by the members, thus giving the United States an effective veto. The provisions in the amended IMF Articles relating to the establishment of par values specify that the common denominator of the system shall not be gold or a currency.

It is useful to examine the manner in which various aspects of the international monetary system have been affected by the shift from the pegged to the managed floating exchange-rate system. These aspects include (a) the role of reserve assets and of dollar assets; (b) the role of gold; (c) the role of central bank intervention in foreign exchange markets; (d) the variability of exchange rates; (e) the role of monetary policy.

14.4.1   Role of Reserve Assets and of Dollar Assets

It was widely believed that the stock of reserve assets would contract in a world of floating exchange rates compared to a world of pegged rates. In fact, (nominal) official holdings of reserve assets have increased every year since the float. From 1950 to 1969, on average, world reserves including gold rose by less than 3% per year, the foreign exchange component by 5% per year. From the end of 1969 to the end of 1972, the average annual rate of increase of foreign currency reserves was 43%. Since 1973, the average annual rate of increase has been 15%. The main source of growth of foreign currency reserves since 1973, as in earlier years, has been in the form of dollars.[16] The demand for reserves has increased even under floating rates because the system is substantially managed.[17]

A significant change in the distribution of foreign exchange reserves has occurred since October 1973 as a result of the rise in the price of oil. Total foreign exchange reserves of industrial oil-importing countries have increased at a slightly slower pace than reserves of all countries, which sextupled since 1970, but the major oil-exporting countries, which in 1970 held only about 8% of total world foreign exchange reserves, by the end of the decade held about one-quarter of the total. The motivations of oil-exporting countries for holding foreign-currency denominated assets are, however, clearly quite different from those of industrial countries.

Although other currencies have increased their role as reserve currencies in recent years, the dollar has continued to serve as the main reserve currency, accounting for about 80% of the world's official foreign exchange reserves. To the extent of intervention, as under pegged rates, the U.S. has settled its payments deficits in dollars, which foreigners willingly add to their asset holdings and use in payments to other countries. The dollar also remains the main official intervention currency in foreign exchange markets and serves as a common vehicle currency in the interbank market for foreign exchange. In effect, the world has adopted an inconvertible dollar standard.

One change in the international reserve profile was the creation on 13 March 1979 of the European Monetary System—replacing the "smaller" size European joint float—by nine European countries (Belgium, Denmark, France, Germany, Eire, Italy, Luxembourg, and the Netherlands; the U.K. is a member but does not participate in intervention arrangements). The center of the system is the European Currency Unit (a basket of all nine currencies), issued by the European Monetary Cooperation Fund in an amount equal to a deposit of 20% of gold and dollar reserves of participating countries, to be used for settlement of intervention debts (see below). ECUs now included in foreign exchange holdings of the participating countries, except for revaluation changes, do not increase world monetary reserves.[18]

With gold valued at market price, gold reserves at the end of 1979 were larger than foreign exchange reserves. The U.S., however, values its own gold assets at the official price of $42.22 per ounce, despite the abolition of an official IMF price for gold.

If a high rate of growth of world foreign exchange reserves provides evidence of an international transmission process at work, it is apparent that no change in behavior in the aggregate has occurred in that regard since 1973.

14.4.2 The Role of Gold

After the float, the U.S. took the position that gold should be demonetized. An opposing view was promoted principally by France. Developments reflect the extent to which one or the other dominated international decisions. At issue was the use of gold in official transactions at the free market price, and the substitution of gold for the dollar in inter–central bank settlements at a fixed but higher official price.

The prescription against official transactions in the gold market that had been adopted in March 1968 was terminated in November 1973, but the official price of $42.22 posted in February 1973 was so far below the private market price that central banks were unwilling to buy and sell gold among themselves at the official price. The central banks were equally reluctant to sell gold on the private market in view of the possible depressive effect of sales on the market price or in anticipation of the opportunity to sell in the future at a higher price. In December 1973 the IMF terminated arrangements made four years earlier, under which it had been prepared to purchase gold from South Africa.

In June 1974 countries in the Group of Ten (the U.S., the U.K., Germany, France, Italy, Japan, Canada, the Netherlands, Belgium, and Sweden) agreed that gold could be used as collateral for intercentral bank loans at a price other than the official gold price, and in September Italy obtained a loan from Germany on the pledge of Italian gold valued at a mutually agreed price. In December the U.S. and France agreed that central banks were at liberty in valuing gold holdings for balance sheet purposes to use the market price, which the Bank of France proceeded to do.

Early in 1975 the countries in the Group of Ten and Switzerland agreed for a two-year period not to increase the sum of their and the IMF's gold holdings and to contribute no support to the price of gold in the free market. In August 1975 agreement was reached by an IMF committee that[19]

the official price of gold would be abolished;

members would not be obliged to use gold in transactions with the Fund;

a part of the Fund's gold holdings would be sold at auction for the benefit of developing countries, and another part would be returned to member countries in proportion to their quotas.

The first public auction of part of the Fund's gold holdings was held in June 1976. A four-year sales program was scheduled. In the first two years, sixteen auctions were held approximately every six weeks, with aggregate sales of 12.5 million ounces. The balance of 12.5 million ounces was sold mainly in twenty-four auction lots through May 1980, and a small amount in noncompetitive sales. Restitution of 25 million ounces to member countries over a four-year period was completed in December 1979/January 1980.

The U.S. repealed the prohibition against gold holding by U.S. residents as of 31 December 1974 and empowered the Treasury to offset any increase in market price as a result of this increment to private demand by offering gold at auction. The first auctions were held in January and June 1975, when the Treasury disposed of 13 million ounces. No auctions were held in 1976 and 1977. They were resumed in 1978 and 1979, when the Treasury sold 4.0 and 11.8 million ounces, respectively, motivated both by the desire to reduce the U.S. balance-of-payments deficit on current account and by the belief "that neither gold nor any other commodity provides a suitable base for monetary arrangements."[20] Since 1979 the Treasury has sold no gold bullion.[21]

Members no longer define the exchange value of their currency in terms of gold and trade in and account for gold at any price consistent with their domestic laws. Gold is no longer the *numéraire* of the international monetary system. The introduction of SDRs (valued in terms of a basket of national currencies, as of July 1974, rather than in terms of gold) was intended to replace both the dollar and gold in the international monetary system.

The market price of gold has increased more rapidly since the float than the prices of most other durable assets.[22] The future role of gold in the international monetary system as a reserve asset and as a determinant of the world's price level may depend on the performance of the dollar. If the performance of the dollar improves, gold may be dethroned even if its use as a reserve asset continues. Failure of the dollar to perform in a stable fashion in the future leaves open the possibility of a restoration of a significant role for gold.

14.4.3   Role of Central Bank Intervention

Direct official intervention to maintain the open market price of currencies within narrow limits has not lessened under floating rates compared with the pegged parity system. Intervention in some countries is assigned to nationalized industries that borrow foreign currency in order to buy their own currency on the foreign exchange market, in Italy and the U.K. with government provision of insurance against foreign exchange loss, in France with no such provision. In Japan and sometimes in France, dollar deposits held by the government at commercial banks are used for intervention. Italian and French commercial banks intervene at the government's behest. Central bank intervention may thus be conducted by a variety of institutions at the direction of the monetary authorities.

The pattern of intervention since the float by the U.S. and its trading partners is to buy dollars both when the dollar depreciates relative to a particular foreign currency and when one foreign currency appreciates relative to another. Countries with weak currencies sell dollars. When the supply of dollars increases in foreign exchange markets, managed floaters may buy up some of the additional dollars or may permit the price of dollars to fall in terms of their own currencies. Buying up dollars has negative consequences for domestic monetary control; permitting the price of dollars to rise can have negative consequences for oil-importing countries.

There was apparently little intervention during the four months following the float in February 1973. The progressive decline in the weighted exchange rate of the dollar between February and July 1973 vis-à-vis a group of major currencies led to a decision by the governors of the central banks of the Group of Ten to support the dollar. In July 1973 the Federal Reserve Bank of New York began to intervene in the New York spot exchange market to avoid "disorderly market conditions." Intervention was effected with the Federal Reserve's own small holdings of foreign currency or by activating the much larger total of foreign currency loans through swap agreements.

Concerted exchange intervention was agreed to by the Federal Reserve, the Bundesbank, and the Swiss National Bank in May 1974, after several months of dollar depreciation. The dollar strengthened until September, when renewed weakness developed through March 1975. The explanation given by the Board of Governors was:[23]

> Contributing to this decline in the dollar's exchange value was the asymmetry in intervention policies between countries with weaker currencies and those with strengthening currencies. Intervention sales of dollars by countries supporting weaker currencies exceeded purchases of dollars by countries resisting the appreciation of their currencies. The net effect of these operations was to add to the market supply of dollars, depressing the dollar's average exchange rate.

Explicit approval of management of floating exchange rates was expressed by the IMF in six guidelines it issued in June 1974.[24] Acceptance of intervention as desirable policy was reiterated in a November 1975 meeting that preceded the revision of the IMF's Articles of Agreement in 1976.

The dollar showed little weakness in 1976, and the Federal Reserve intervened to sell dollars on behalf of other currencies. In January the Italian lira came under pressure. The decline in its exchange value weakened the French franc within the European currency snake, leading to substantial French intervention. Massive intervention to support sterling, which declined from $2.00 in March to $1.77 in mid-September, was provided by a $5.3 billion stand-by credit arranged by the Group of Ten countries, Switzerland, and the Bank for International Settlements. Sterling's further decline later in the year led to an IMF drawing, further borrowing, and a facility to reduce official sterling balances. Interventions were also engaged in to moderate appreciations of the D-mark, the Swiss franc, and the yen.

Renewed weakness of the dollar in early 1977 was masked by large intervention purchases of dollars by the Bank of England and the Bank of Italy undertaken to limit the appreciation of their currencies and to rebuild their reserve positions. The Federal Reserve intervened only occasionally during the first three quarters. When the Bank of England ended its large purchases of dollars, the dollar dropped sharply. The Federal Reserve increased the scale of intervention and in January 1978 was joined by the U.S. Treasury Exchange Stabilization Fund, which negotiated a new swap facility with the Bundesbank.

The decline in the weighted average exchange value of the dollar accelerated in 1978 through the end of October.[25] An anti-inflation program announced on 24 October (contractionary fiscal and monetary policy, voluntary wage and price standards, and a reduction in the cost of regulatory actions) had no effect on the exchange market. On 1 November, the administration and the Federal Reserve took further action. A $30 billion intervention package was arranged with Germany, Japan, and Switzerland. The Federal Reserve raised the discount rate from 8½% to 9½% and imposed a 2% supplementary reserve requirement on large time deposits. During the last two months of 1978, U.S. support operations for the dollar totaled $6.7 billion, including sales of Treasury securities denominated in foreign currencies and significant purchases of dollars by Germany, Japan, and Switzerland. By June 1979 the dollar's value (measured on a trade-weighted basis) had risen from its 1978 low by about 10%, and U.S. authorities had repurchased a greater sum of foreign currency than had been sold in the last two months of 1978. The dollar then began to weaken, and U.S. intervention sales of foreign currencies, chiefly D-marks, resumed. Gross sales amounted to $9½ billion equivalent between mid-June and early October. In addition, the Federal Reserve raised the discount rate to 11% in September.

On 6 October 1979 the Federal Reserve announced a wide-ranging set of measures to tighten monetary control (a shift in operating procedures to place less emphasis upon control of the Federal Funds rate and more emphasis upon control of bank reserves; an increase in the discount rate to 12%; a marginal reserve requirement on banks' managed liabilities), and the dollar began to appreciate. After April 1980, however, the dollar began to decline, a movement that was reversed in September. From October 1979 on, the U.S. intervened frequently, operating on both sides of the market. When the dollar was in demand, it acquired foreign currencies in the market and from correspondents to repay earlier debt and to build up balances. The Federal Reserve was a buyer from February to March. From late March to early April and beyond, it sold D-marks, Swiss francs, and French francs. By the end of July, the U.S. was again accumulating currencies. Both the Treasury and the Federal Reserve Trading Desk made net purchases of D-marks and lesser amounts of Swiss francs and French francs on days when the dollar was strong, selling on days when the dollar weakened. By the end of 1980, the U.S. was intervening in the foreign exchange markets virtually on a day-to-day basis. For 1980 as a whole, U.S. authorities were net buyers of foreign currencies in an amount of $8.7 billion equivalent.

The Reagan administration soon after taking office announced its intention to reduce the scale of intervention, to discontinue the policy of building up currency reserves, and to cut back its short-term swap arrangements with foreign countries. The reason for the shift in policy is the administration's view that intervention is both costly and ineffectual and that the way to restore exchange-rate stability is by the creation of more stable domestic economic conditions. Many foreign central banks do not share the Reagan administration's views and continue to intervene to affect the exchange value of their currencies. This raises a question whether the degree of control U.S. authorities can exercise over the effective exchange rate for the dollar under a floating rate system is any greater than under a pegged exchange-rate system.

The rationale for central bank intervention under floating rates is that the market does not move exchange rates smoothly to equilibrium levels, produces "disorderly conditions," and sets rates at variance with underlying economic conditions. It is assumed that central banks can determine better than markets the correct level of exchange rates and the proper degree of variability. A policy of leaning against the wind is justified by advocates of intervention as slowing the movement of exchange rates in either direction.

To stabilize foreign exchange markets central banks should buy their currencies when prices are low to drive them up and sell their currencies when prices are high to drive them down. Such operations should net the central banks a profit. Buying at high but falling prices and selling at low but rising prices are defended as needed to achieve "orderly" markets. By resisting a gradual movement in exchange rates, central banks lose reserves and money until they abandon the support operation, with a resulting sudden large movement in exchange rates.

If the purpose of intervention were to reduce deviations of the market exchange rate from the equilibrium exchange rate, central bank operations would net profits but might not reduce the variance of exchange-rate movements. If the equilibrium exchange rate shifts as a result of an economic shock, leaning against the wind may lower the variance of the exchange rate but will increase the size of the deviation of the exchange rate from its equilibrium level. In addition, the central bank will lose money on the operation. If there is no intervention, the variance will be larger, the central bank will not lose money, and the exchange rate will reflect the new equilibrium value sooner, thus allowing the rate to transmit undistorted information.

The central banks as a group have not been conducting a profitable exercise by intervening in foreign exchange markets. An estimate for nine countries puts the loss for central bank intervention since the beginning of the float at $10 to $12 billion, far in excess of losses sustained by nationalized industries although for selected time periods a country may record a profit.[26] The evidence is that central banks have been suffering from an anachronistic behavior, resisting exchange-rate changes under nominally floating rates much as they did under pegged rates. Central banks have no way of knowing when there is a change in the fundamental equilibrium level of exchange rates.[27] By assuming the absence of a change in the equilibrium exchange rate and intervening to hold the exchange rate, they lose substantial amounts of money and ultimately have no choice but to permit the exchange rate to move.

14.4.4   Variability of Exchange Rates

One major change since the float has been the increased variability of exchange rates of the major industrial countries (table 14.5). Critics of the floating regime argue that the variability has been excessive. Much of the movement, it is said, is unrelated to underlying economic and financial conditions which are not themselves likely to undergo rapid changes. Injury to international trade through exchange-rate fluctuation is claimed. The exchange rate is regarded as contributing to inflation, strong currencies not experiencing a reduction in exports as a result of appreciation, and weak currencies not experiencing a reduction in imports as a result of depreciation. The widening of bid-ask spreads or increase of transactions costs and the failure of forward rates to predict future spot prices as well in the 1970s as in the 1960s are offered as evidence that speculators destabilize foreign exchange markets. The impact of floating rates is said to increase uncertainty.

The negative assessment of the behavior of exchange rates since the float omits a crucial factor: the market's expectations with respect to inflation rates, monetary and fiscal policy, and general economic conditions. Unstable domestic policies contribute to unstable exchange rates.[28] Exchange-rate changes are dominated by speculation about these underlying economic factors. If, despite appreciation, strong-currency countries experience growth in exports and, despite depreciation, weak-currency countries experience growth in imports, the explanation is that costs of production in the former remain favorable if policies in the latter permit inflationary expansion of demand, wage hikes, and increase in strike activity. It is uncertainty about domestic policies that produces higher transactions costs in foreign exchange markets. With respect to the failure of forward rates to predict future spot rates, the predictions have not been biased. Despite the volatility of exchange rates, no major disruptions to trade and capital flows have occurred since the float. In fact, floating exchange rates permitted the elimination of some capital controls. Capital controls introduced since the float are associated with the snake, where rates of exchange among the bloc were relatively fixed and moved in relation to one another

Table 14.5   **Average Quarterly Change at Annual Rates and the Variance of the Exchange Rate**

	CA	FR	GE	IT	JA	NE	UK
1955I–58IV	-.21	6.30	-.14	-.01	0	-.19	-.16
	(1.58)	(2.27)	(.39)	(.001)	(0)	(1.68)	(1.82)
1958IV–67IV	1.18	1.12	-.54	-.03	.07	-.51	1.12
	(1.31)	(.46)	(9.18)	(0.27)	(1.42)	(7.58)	(39.26)
1967IV–73I	-1.45	-.43	-6.54	-.144	-4.96	-3.17	.66
	(16.41)	(121.49)	(161.53)	(13.90)	(89.18)	(55.04)	(87.44)
1973I–76IV	-.13	1.05	-4.53	10.69	1.40	-5.15	10.59
	(33.)	(499.)	(560.)	(413)	(141)	(403)	(401)

Note: The table understates the variability of exchange rates for individual countries before 1973I. For a correct measure for the individual countries, the subperiods would be chosen for each country to correspond with dates for stable or changing exchange rates. Variances are shown in parentheses beneath the change figures.

only within relatively narrow bands.[29] The balance-of-payments motive for tariffs is also defused by floating rates. If protectionism is perceived as on the rise since the float, it is related to stagflation rather than exchange-rate developments.

A final point with respect to exchange rates relates to experience within the European Monetary System. The initial year after the activation of the exchange-rate mechanism of the European Monetary System in 1979 reduced the range of movements of the participant currencies against the D-mark compared to the range in the preceding year. Nevertheless, two realignments of exchange rates were required as a result of divergencies in economic performance and in inflation experience (Germany, September 1979; Denmark, November 1979). Large-scale interventions were undertaken to preserve the former exchange rates but to no avail. The continued existence of large inflation differentials among the countries in the EMS suggests the fragility of the arrangement is not less than it was for the predecessor snake. Countries that inflate at a faster rate than their trading partners cannot avoid depreciation of their currencies. As markets have become more insistent on allowing for expected future price movements in setting nominal interest rates, wider swings in interest-rate differentials among countries are also likely to contribute to exchange-rate instability.

14.4.5 Role of Monetary Policy

The Bretton Woods system broke down essentially because non-reserve-currency countries were unwilling as a group to adopt the policy of inflationary monetary growth the reserve-currency country was pursuing. To achieve independent monetary policy, the only workable exchange-rate system was floating. It was hoped that flexible exchange rates would permit a country to choose its desired long-run trend rate of monetary growth and of inflation, independent of other countries' choices.

Even when autonomy exists, monetary policy may perform badly. It is in this context that the movement in a number of countries during the 1970s toward the improvement of monetary control must be viewed.

Central banks have typically used short-term interest rates as the instruments to control monetary growth. Under noninflationary conditions, this conduct produced a procyclical movement in monetary growth. Under the gathering inflationary conditions since the mid-1960s, the inflation premium that became embedded in interest rates made the instrument unreliable as an indicator of restriction or ease. Reliance on it contributed to a secular rise in the rate of monetary growth. Central banks in a number of countries, some more willingly than others, in the 1970s adopted targets for monetary growth without necessarily abandoning their desire to hold down interest rates or exchange rates, so that successful targeting has not invariably been the result. If it was hoped that public announcement of targets for monetary growth would itself reduce expectations of inflation, the failure time after time to achieve the targets has diluted any possible effect on the formation of expectations.

14.5 Summary

By the end of 1958, the idealized Bretton Woods regime of exchange rates pegged within relatively narrow bounds seemed on the point of achievement. Problems arose in the 1960s when individual countries resorted to restrictions on trade and commodities in order to contain balance-of-payments deficits which would have otherwise required lower rates of monetary growth and inflation. The United States, the reserve-currency country, was the prime destabilizer of the system. Because countries were unwilling to subordinate domestic monetary policies to the requirements of a fixed exchange-rate system, recurring financial crises led to occasionally large devaluations and to some revaluations of individual currencies. In the end, the system broke down and countries were free after 1973 to float their currencies or to adopt regional pegged currency schemes that floated against the dollar. Since the float has been a managed system, with substantial official intervention to prevent or slow exchange-rate movements, countries have continued to hold foreign exchange reserves and internal monetary policy independence has not invariably produced noninflationary monetary growth.

Notes

1. We share the view of Harry G. Johnson (1978) expressed in *Exchange Rate Flexibility:* "It is not clear, actually, that there was much competitive devaluation even in the 1930's."

2. Foreshadowing that breakdown were the revaluations of the deutsche mark in October 1969 and the return to floating, albeit of a heavily manged sort, of the Canadian dollar in May 1970.

3. Laskar in chapter 11 of Darby et al. (1983) provides a particularly thorough econometric investigation of this sterilization question. Cassese and Lothian in chapter 4 and Darby and Stockman in chapter 6 of the same volume also present evidence relevant to this issue.

4. Some, however, view currency substitution and asset substitution as limiting national monetary independence even under floating exchange rates. See, for instance, Miles (1978) and Brittain (1981). The Darby and Stockman investigation of this question in chapter 6, however, lends considerably less support to these propositions.

5. See section 17.2 of Darby et al. (1983, pp. 498–505) for a summary of the evidence on the arbitrage channel contained in various papers in that volume.

6. Frenkel and Mussa (1981) discuss this and other channels.

7. The deterioration in the U.S. current account in 1971 has been identified by Harry G. Johnson (1972) as a source of increased demand by U.S. residents for foreign goods and services that raised their prices.

8. See Paul Wonnacott (1965) for a discussion of the Canadian float during this period.

9. See "Treasury and Federal Reserve Foreign Exchange Operations," in the September 1962 *Federal Reserve Bulletin* (pp. 1138–53), for a discussion of the system's role in the gold market during this period.

10. In addition, the United States issued nonmarketable bonds, starting in 1963.

11. Margaret de Vries (1976).

12. For a description of the controls that were imposed, see the various editions of the IMF *Annual Report on Exchange Restrictions*.

13. Underlying the emphasis upon international liquidity during this period and the subsequent introduction of SDRs, as Lance Girton (1974) has pointed out, was the real-bills doctrine, in this instance applied to the international realm rather than to its preferred habitat, the domestic.

14. By the end of the fourth quarter of 1972, the value of SDRs was slightly over $9.4 billion, or 6% of total world international reserves as reported by the IMF (*International Financial Statistics*, July 1974).

15. Many changes in exchange rates within the snake were made. On four occasions between March 1973 and October 1978, the mark was revalued within the system. The guilder and the Norwegian krone were each revalued once. Countries other than Germany devalued in October 1976. The Swedish krona was subsequently devalued again, as was the Danish krone, and the Norwegian krone several times. For a table on these changes, see Major (1979, pp. 212–13).

16. Although in December 1978 the IMF resumed the allocation of SDRs to member countries at a rate of 4 billion SDR per year (to be continued for a period of three years), the action had no immediate effect on the growth of reserves. The reason is that an increase in quotas, of which one-fourth was payable in SDRs, took effect in 1979. Accordingly, about 5 billion SDRs reverted to the IMF in that year.

17. Frenkel (1978), using time series of cross section data, provides evidence of substantial similarities in the demand for international reserves between exchange-rate regimes.

18. The ECUs issued value gold on the basis of either the average market price of the six preceding months or the average market price on the day before issue, whichever was lower.

19. IMF *Annual Report*, 1975, p. 44.

20. See *Annual Report of the Secretary of the Treasury on the State of the Finances,* 1979, p. 491, Exhibit 60, a press release on the increase in the amount of gold sales, announced 22 August 1978 ("The sales will make an important contribution toward reducing the U.S. balance of payments deficit on current account"), and Exhibit 61, a statement by Assistant Secretary Bergsten before the Senate Committee on Banking, Housing, and Urban Affairs, in which the quotation in the text appears.

21. The Reagan administration announced that its position on the proper role of gold in the international monetary system would not be formulated until the congressionally mandated gold commission issued its report in March 1982.

Testimony of Beryl W. Sprinkel, under secretary for monetary affairs, Treasury Department, at hearings of the Joint Economic Committee, 4 May 1981.

22. The price of gold from the end of 1973 to the end of 1980 increased at an average annual rate of 20.7%. By comparison the total returns on common stock and on long-term government bonds (computed according to Ibbotson and Sinquefield 1977) increased at average annual rates of 7.2% and 4.0%, respectively. The U.S. CPI over this period increased at a rate of 7.8% per year on average, and the *London Economist's* world commodity price index in dollars at a 9.5% rate.

23. Board of Governors of the Federal Reserve System, *61st Annual Report*, 1974, pp. 65–66.

24. The first guideline stated: "A member with a floating exchange rate should intervene on the foreign exchange market as necessary to prevent or moderate sharp and disruptive fluctuations from day to day and from week to week in the exchange value of the currency." A second guideline encouraged intervention to moderate movements from month to month and quarter to quarter "where factors recognized to be temporary are at work." A third guideline suggested consultation with the Fund if a country sought to move its exchange rate "to some target zone of rates." A fourth guideline dealt with the size of a country's reserve relative to planned intervention; a fifth, with avoiding restrictions for balance-of-payments purposes; a sixth, with the interests of other countries than the intervening one. IMF *Annual Report*, 1974, pp. 112–16.

25. The index of weighted average exchange values of the dollar against the Group of Ten countries plus Switzerland (March 1973 = 100) declined at an average annual rate of 9.3% between January and November 1978. From January 1976 to January 1978 it had declined at a 3.3% annual rate.

26. For the source of the estimate on losses and an illuminating discussion of intervention, see Taylor (1982).

27. Darby et al. (1983, chap. 15) presents evidence relevant to this issue. He shows that growth rates of the dollar exchange rates of the countries in our sample tend on average to a purchasing-power parity relation but that the levels of exchange rates become unpredictable.

28. Frenkel and Mussa (1980) present a particularly concise statement of this position.

29. The D-mark was revalued by 5½% relative to other snake currencies on 20 June 1973, and simultaneously controls on capital inflow were tightened to defend the new rate.

15   Alternative Monetary Regimes: The Gold Standard

The gold standard has recently been the subject of much discussion. The discussion is largely attributable to dissatisfaction with the high and variable rates of inflation and interest rates, the low productivity growth, and the turbulence in foreign exchange markets since 1970. These undesired developments are associated with the existing discretionary fiat money regime, and they have encouraged examination of a monetary regime linked to gold, the vestiges of which the world abandoned early in the 1970s.

The desirability of a return to the gold standard is a controversial issue. Informed judgment of this issue requires an understanding of past experience. In addition, examination of the operation of the historical gold standard has intellectual interest. Scholars differ in their explanations of the functioning of the gold standard and in their assessments of its performance.

The historical gold standard evolved over centuries. It was a regime in which a particular weight of gold served as the supreme type of money with which all lesser types of money—government fiduciary issues, bank notes, and deposits—were interconvertible. During the gold standard era, the institutions and practices related to payments for the settlement of debts underwent evolutionary change.

In this chapter, we analyze the historical gold standard and its relevance to the solution of current economic problems. The first section surveys the evolution of the historical gold standard from the final decades of the nineteenth century to the collapse of the Bretton Woods system in the early 1970s. Section 15.2 presents the evidence on the performance of the gold standard as viewed by its advocates and opponents. Section 15.3 examines the necessary conditions for the restoration of the gold standard. Conclusions are summarized in section 15.4.

15.1 Evolution of the Gold Standard

Gold standards have varied historically depending on the presence or absence of the following elements:

1. a national money unit
2. nongold national money issued by either the government or by a fractional-reserve commercial banking system
3. a central bank
   a. with gold reserves only
   b. with mainly foreign exchange reserves
4. convertibility of nongold money into gold coin or gold bars
5. classes of holders for whom nongold money is convertible

15.1.1   National Money Units

Although a gold standard without national money units is conceivable—coins would circulate by weight with no price in a national money unit attached and prices would be expressed in weights of gold—the countries that adopted the gold standard before 1914 defined their national money units as a specific weight of gold. This set the price of an ounce of gold in terms of that unit. In 1879, for example, when the United States restored the link between the dollar and gold, after a 17-year interruption, the dollar was defined as 23.22 grains of fine gold. There are 480 grains of gold in a fine troy ounce. Thus the price of a fine troy ounce of gold was $20.67 (480 ÷ 23.22 = 20.67). In all countries with a gold standard, prices of gold were set in terms of the country's national money unit—dollars, pounds, marks, francs, and other monetary units. Each government was committed to buying gold from the public at its fixed price and to converting the gold into coin. Each government was also committed to selling gold to the public at a slightly higher price. The difference between the purchase and sale prices is called *brassage,* the government's fee for manufacturing coins.

The external value of a national currency under the gold standard was determined by comparing it with another widely used currency. For instance, the pound sterling was worth $4.8665 before World War I and from 1925 to 1931. Since the dollar was defined as 23.22 grains of fine gold and a pound sterling as 113.0016 grains of fine gold, a pound sterling had 4.8665 as much gold by weight as a U.S. dollar. The exchange rate between these two currencies was a fixed rate because the gold weight of each currency did not vary (or, equivalently, the price of gold per ounce in terms of each currency did not change).

Varying the weights of gold represented by a currency would have meant changes in the price of gold in that country.

The link between currencies was gold at a fixed price. Imbalances in international payments might be settled by claims in the form of bills of exchange in national currencies of other countries that had fixed gold equivalents. (A bill of exchange on a British firm, for example, is an order on the firm to pay a certain amount of British pounds to the exporter on a certain date. American exporters typically drew up such bills of exchange when they sold goods to foreign firms.) If the demand for and supply of a national currency did not balance, gold flows would be activated.

Thus, whenever the dollar price of a British pound at the official exchange rate of $4.86 deviated by more than 1 or 2 percent above or below the official rate (these limits were referred to as the gold points and represented the cost of packing, insuring, and shipping gold between the two countries), it paid either to convert U.S. dollars into gold and transfer it abroad, or else to convert British pounds into gold and transfer it here. If U.S. demand for cheaper British goods increased, for example, this raised the dollar price of bills of exchange denominated in pounds. Once the dollar price of the pound reached $4.92, the U.S. gold export point, it paid importers to convert U.S. dollars into gold, ship the gold to England, and purchase pounds at $4.86. Conversely, at the U.S. gold import point, which might have been as low as $4.83, it paid exporters to convert pounds sterling into gold, ship the gold to the United States, and purchase dollars. Gold shipments in either direction would thus restore the price of foreign exchange to parity.

Therefore, not only new gold output but inflows or outflows related to movements in the balance of payments affected the size of the domestic money supply. A reduction in a country's money supply and ultimately in its price level enhanced the country's appeal as a source of goods and services to foreigners and reduced the domestic demand for foreign goods and services. An increase in a country's money supply and ultimately in its price level diminished that country's appeal as a source of goods and services to foreigners and increased the domestic demand for foreign goods and services. Because of this automatic adjustment process, the duration and size of imbalances of international payments tended to be self-limiting. Gold flows served to equalize price movements across countries.

Economists debate the details of this process. Some argue that the gold flows before 1914 were minimal and that prices worldwide adjusted rapidly. There was one world price level, and the external adjustment process posed no greater problem than interregional adjustment of prices within a country. These refinements need not detain us.

15.1.2   Nongold National Money

As the gold standard evolved, substitutes for gold were developed. The motive for substitution was a reduction in the real resources employed in mining gold. Paper money substitutes may be produced with much smaller real resources. The substitutes included fiat currency issued by governments and commercial bank notes and deposits, with gold reserves of the government and the banks equal to a fraction of their monetary liabilities. The incentive to limit the size of the fraction of gold reserves was strengthened during trend periods when the supply of gold did not keep pace with the demand for it for both monetary and nonmonetary uses.

Fractional gold reserves were held as evidence of the issuers' readiness to convert nongold money into gold at the pleasure of the holder, at a fixed price of gold, not a changing market price of gold. In this system, domestic disturbances, such as banking panics, could affect the size of a country's gold reserves. Public alarm about the adequacy of the gold reserve ratio could trigger an internal drain of gold when holders of bank notes and bank deposits chose to shift to gold. The aftermath of such episodes was that the government and the banks subsequently took action to contract their monetary liabilities, and this resulted in an increase in their gold reserve ratios.

A fractional-reserve gold standard accentuated the effects of gold flows on the quantity of money. A $1 gold inflow, depending on the size of the reserve ratio, might increase the quantity of money as much as $8 or $10; a $1 gold outflow might reduce the quantity of money by as much as $8 or $10, with parallel effects on domestic spending and prices.

International capital flows, however, alleviated to some extent either the size of gold flows or their consequences. Short-term capital flows served to reduce and smooth the immediate flows of gold that would otherwise have been required to settle payments imbalances. Long-term capital flows enabled developing countries to borrow real resources from developed countries by running a persistent excess of imports of goods and services over exports of goods and services without entailing gold flows. In the event of a rise in the domestic quantity of money, in the short run, interest rates would tend to decline, inducing investors to shift funds to foreign money markets. The size of the change in export prices relative to import prices that would otherwise have occurred would be reduced by the resulting capital outflow.

In a fractional-reserve banking system combined with a gold standard, domestic and international convertibility of claims on the monetary authorities was the mechanism to ensure that the growth of the money supply was held in check.

15.1.3   Central Banks with Gold Reserves

Central banks in Europe predated the gold standard. After the gold standard was adopted, their behavior did not always exemplify the discipline a true gold standard imposes. They did not necessarily respond to a loss of gold due to balance of payments deficits by actions to reduce the quantity of money, or to a gain of gold due to balance of payments surpluses by actions to increase the quantity of money.

Scholars continue to debate the extent to which such behavior by the Bank of England and other central banks characterized the period before 1914. After World War I, the issue is not in doubt: central banks, including the Federal Reserve System, frequently chose not to permit gold flows either to expand or contract the quantity of money, or to do so to a lesser degree than full adjustment would have required. The gold standard was not automatic but became managed.

15.1.4   Central Banks with Foreign Exchange Reserves

Central banks also learned to economize on gold holdings by using other currencies as reserve assets, principally sterling before 1914, increasingly dollars thereafter. A central bank that held all or a large part of its international reserves in foreign exchange of a country that was on a gold standard was said to be on a gold exchange standard. The gold exchange standard was preferred because foreign exchange, in the form of deposits at foreign banks or foreign treasury bills, was earning assets, but gold holdings were not. A disadvantage of holding reserves in assets denominated in a foreign currency was that a central bank would incur losses when that currency was devalued.

The gold standard before World War I was often described as a sterling-gold exchange system and, under the Bretton Woods system after World War II, as a dollar-gold exchange system. Although both were fixed exchange rate systems in conception, the Bretton Woods system became a fixed but adjustable exchange rate system.

Under the Bretton Woods system, the par value of each national currency was established in agreement with the International Monetary Fund and was expressed either in terms of gold or in terms of U.S. dollars valued at 13.71 grains of fine gold. (The dollar of 23.22 grains of fine gold had been devalued by the United States under authority of the Gold Reserve Act of January 31, 1934, to 13.71 grains of fine gold—equivalent to $35 an ounce.) Members of the International Monetary Fund were responsible for maintaining the par value of their currencies, with the United States alone undertaking the free purchase and sale of gold at the fixed price of $35 per ounce. Other countries bought and sold their currencies for dollars to maintain their par values within the agreed limits. Settlement of international payments imbalances took place mainly by transfers of reserve assets in the major money markets.

Convertibility of many European currencies was first achieved under the Bretton Woods system in 1958. The system performed fairly effectively for only a few years. From the mid-1960s on, the Bretton Woods system was characterized by repeated foreign exchange crises. Periodically market participants anticipated that the existing par values were unsustainable and would shift funds from a weak currency to a strong currency, exacerbating the external position for both currencies. Countries with undervalued currencies resisted revaluation and countries with overvalued currencies resisted devaluation.

The system of fixed but adjustable exchange rates collapsed under the pressure of persistent balance of payments problems: deficits in the United States, the reserve center, and surpluses (and undervalued currencies) in some countries such as West Germany. The money supply in the United States grew at rates independent of the country's balance of payments position. This was contrary to the way the money supply would have behaved under an international gold standard. Unless dollar inflows were sterilized by their monetary authorities, surplus countries accumulated dollar reserves that expanded their monetary base. According to the surplus countries, the United States exported inflation through its balance of payments deficits.

15.1.5 Convertibility of Nongold Money into Gold

A gold coin standard with nongold substitutes existed in a number of countries before 1914. Gold coin circulated but was only a small part of the total money supply, and nongold money was redeemable in gold coin. As a way of economizing on the use of gold, many countries ceased to coin gold after 1914 (the United States, not until 1933). This terminated free coinage, the circulation of gold coins, and the legal tender status of gold coins. The objective was to concentrate all of a country's gold holdings into international reserves available for international payments. Nongold money became convertible into heavy gold bars. Such a gold standard is known as a *gold bullion standard*.

15.1.6 Classes of Holders

Under a gold coin standard with nongold substitutes, all holders— domestic and foreign—of nongold money could convert it into gold coin. Under a gold bullion standard, convertibility existed for both types of holders. Under the Bretton Woods dollar-gold exchange standard, the right of convertibility in the United States was limited to foreign official institutions. Foreign official institutions held dollars for the purpose of intervention in foreign exchange markets so long as they were confident that they could obtain gold from the United States for dollars at their initiative. For a time, a gentleman's agreement among central banks in certain industrial countries not to present dollar balances for convertibility into gold staved off the denouement. The chronic deficits in the U.S. balance of payments and the unwanted accumulation of dollars by foreigners that threatened a drain of all U.S. gold finally led in 1971 to formal inconvertibility for all holders.

Initially, the United States and its trading partners made several attempts to restore a system of fixed exchange rates. After much negotiation, a readjustment of currency parities was arranged at a meeting at the Smithsonian Institution in Washington on December 17–18, 1971. Wider margins of fluctuations above and below the new so-called central exchange rates were permitted. The official dollar price of gold would henceforth be $38, a devaluation of the dollar of 7.9 percent. While the dollar remained inconvertible, the new official dollar price of gold implied a depreciation of the gold value of the dollar rather than an appreciation of the gold value of other currencies. The central exchange rates established at the Smithsonian meeting lasted only a short time as market participants expressed disbelief in them.

In February 1973, new central rates were set in a hurried round of negotiations. The official dollar price of gold was raised further to $42.22, leaving unchanged the gold value of other currencies. The new central rates did not staunch the flow of dollars abroad, and another crisis erupted in March 1973. As a result of this crisis, exchange rates pegged to the dollar were abandoned by the major industrialized countries. Amendments to the Articles of Agreement of the International Monetary Fund formally removed gold from its previous central role in international monetary arrangements. The International Monetary Fund's official gold price was abolished, as were par values, gold convertibility, and maintenance of gold value obligations.

15.1.7   Arguments for a Gold Standard

Supporters of the gold standard have several basic arguments in favor of a gold standard of whatever variant. The first argument is that gold has intrinsic value and therefore serves as a standard of value for all other goods. In addition, supporters view gold as a desirable store of value because new production adds only a small fraction to the accumulated stock. Because of this, prices denominated in gold do not vary greatly from year to year. Even if other forms of money such as government-issued or bank-issued paper currency and bank deposits exist, convertibility into gold at a fixed price would compel the monetary authorities to avoid inflationary policies.

An inflationary increase in government paper currency, for example, would tend to raise prices of goods and services in terms of paper currency, and induce money holders to convert their paper dollars to gold, putting pressure on the government's gold holdings. At the same time, with gold as a country's international reserve asset, adjustment to balance of payments deficits and surpluses would be automatic. An increase in the money supply by ultimately raising the price level would raise the price of exports relative to the price of imports, leading to a balance of payments deficit and a gold outflow. In addition, the increase in the money supply would lower domestic interest rates relative to those abroad, inducing a capital outflow and a further gold outflow. In such a monetary system, political manipulation of the money supply would be avoided.

Another argument in favor of the gold standard is that the rate of increase in the gold money supply would vary automatically with the profitability of producing gold and would assure a stable money supply and stable prices in the long run. A rapid increase in the output of gold due to gold discoveries or technological improvements in gold mining, for example, would raise the prices of all other goods in terms of gold, making them more profitable to produce than gold and ultimately leading to a reduction in gold output. The reduction in the purchasing power of gold, moreover, would lead to a shift in the demand for gold from monetary to nonmonetary uses, thus reinforcing the output effects. Conversely, a decline in prices of goods and services, due to technological improvements in the nongold sector, would increase the profitability of gold production, encouraging increased gold output, which would ultimately tend to raise the price level. The initial increase in the purchasing power of gold would also lead to a shift in the demand for gold from nonmonetary to monetary uses, thus reinforcing the output effects. Long-run price stability would be the result.

In the following section, we evaluate the evidence for these arguments.

15.2   Evidence on the Performance of the Gold Standard

Assessment of the performance of the historical gold standard is based on the following issues:

1. What was the behavior of prices under the gold standard? Price behavior can be analyzed from three perspectives:
   a. long-run price predictability—the ultimate return of the price level to its initial value
   b. long-run price stability—the price level neither rising nor falling over substantial periods
   c. short-run price stability
2. What was the behavior of short-run real output under the gold standard?
3. In the world's markets, did the gold standard transmit foreign shocks both of a monetary and nonmonetary character?

4. How great was the magnitude of resource costs associated with maintaining the gold standard?
5. Was the gold standard free from political manipulation?

Economists differ in their assessment of these issues. The gold standard is often described as a rule that governs monetary policy. The rule is that the domestic money supply must rise and fall in line with the rise and fall of gold reserves. Adhering to the gold standard rule is described as a form of precommitment by monetary authorities. As explained in chapter 1 of Campbell and Dougan (1986), one respect in which economists differ in assessing the gold standard is in their judgment of the advantage of precommitment to a rule versus the advantage of discretionary actions by monetary authorities. As explained in chapter 4 of Campbell and Dougan, even those who favor precommitment are not unanimous in supporting the gold standard. Some prefer an alternative rule such as stable monetary growth. We now review the evidence concerning the five issues listed above.

15.2.1   Behavior of Prices under the Gold Standard

Table 15.1, row 1, shows that in both the United States and the United Kingdom the average annual rates of change in wholesale prices during the pre–World War I period were much lower than in the post–World War II period. Table 15.2 compares the negative average rates of change in the implicit price deflator in the United States and the United Kingdom from the 1870s to the 1890s with the average rates of inflation from the 1890s to World War I. Although the contrast in table 15.1 between the close to zero rates of change of prices in the gold standard period from the 1870s to World War I compared with the inflation in the period from 1946 to 1979 has been interpreted by some (Bordo 1981; Cagan 1984) as demonstrating near-stability of prices under the gold standard, Cooper (1982) and Dornbusch (Report 1982, pp. 414–15) have pointed out that this conclusion is not supported by the standard deviation of price changes shown in table 15.1, row 2.

Moreover, the latter argue that the very wide fluctuations in the wholesale price index from 1816 to 1913 shown in table 15.3 in the United States, United Kingdom, Germany, and France are hardly a pattern of long-term stability. (A problem with table 15.3 is that it includes dates for the four countries when they were not on the gold standard—1816 for the United Kingdom, 1873 for the United States, and the initial dates for both Germany and France.) Cagan (1984) has replied that although there was indeed a substantial decline in wholesale prices before 1896 followed by an even greater increase before 1914, during the post–World War II period, in which there was a loose or

Table 15.1   **A Comparison of Selected Economic Variables from the 1870s to World War I under the Gold Standard and from 1946 to 1979, United States and United Kingdom**

Measure	United Kingdom Gold Standard, 1870–1913	United Kingdom Postwar, 1946–1979	United States Gold Standard, 1879–1913	United States Postwar, 1946–1979
1. Average annual change in wholesale prices (percentage)[a]	−0.7	5.6	0.1	2.8
2. Standard deviation of price change (percentage)[b]	4.6	6.2[c]	5.4	4.8[c]
3. Average annual growth in real per capita income (percentage)	1.4	2.4	1.9	2.1
4. Coefficient of variation of annual percentage changes in real per capita income (ratio)[d]	2.5	1.4	3.5	1.6
5. Average unemployment rate (percentage)	4.3[e]	2.5	6.8[f]	5.0
6. Average annual growth in the money supply (percentage)[a]	1.5	5.9	6.1	5.7
7. Coefficient of variation of the growth in the money supply (ratio)[d]	1.6	1.0	0.8	0.5

Sources: Richard N. Cooper, "The Gold Standard: Historical Facts and Future Prospects," *Brookings Papers on Economic Activity* 13 (1982), 5. The table is drawn from Michael D. Bordo, "The Classical Gold Standard: Some Lessons for Today," Federal Reserve Bank of St. Louis *Review* 63 (May 1981), 14, and calculations from George F. Warren and Frank A. Pearson, *Gold and Prices* (New York: John Wiley & Sons, Inc., 1932), pp. 13–14, 87; Brian R. Mitchell, *Abstract of British Historical Statistics* (London: Cambridge University Press, 1962), pp. 367–68; Council of Economic Advisers, *Economic Report of the President, January 1982* (Washington, D.C.: Government Printing Office, 1982); and International Monetary Fund, *International Financial Statistics* (Washington, D.C.: IMF), various issues.

[a]Calculated as the time coefficient from a regression of the log of the variable on a time trend.

[b]Calculated as the standard error of estimate of the fitted equation $\ln P_t = a \ln P_{t-1}$, where P_t is the wholesale price index in year t.

[c]1949–79.

[d]Calculated as the ratio of the standard deviation of annual percentage changes to their mean.

[e]1888–1913.

[f]1890–1913.

Table 15.2   Rate of Change in Prices and Real Income between Cycle Phases,[a] 1873–1914, United States and United Kingdom

	Percentage Change per Year		
	Implicit Price Deflator (1)	Real Income (2)	Real Income per Capita (3)
United States			
Deflation:			
From the 1873–78 contraction to the 1895–96 contraction	−1.5	3.6	1.4
From the 1878–82 expansion to the 1895–96 contraction	−1.3	2.5	0.3
Inflation:			
From the 1895–96 contraction to the 1913–14 contraction	1.9	3.8	1.9
United Kingdom			
Deflation:			
From the 1874–79 contraction to the 1893–1900 expansion	−0.6	2.3	1.4
Inflation:			
From the 1893–1900 expansion to the 1913–14 contraction	0.8	1.6	0.8

Sources: Phillip Cagan, "The Report of the Gold Commission (1982)," in *Monetary and Fiscal Policies and Their Application,* Karl Brunner and Allan H. Meltzer, Ed., Carnegie-Rochester Conference Series on Public Policy, vol. 20 (Amsterdam: North-Holland, 1984), pp. 247–67; Milton Friedman and Anna J. Schwartz, *Monetary Trends in the United States and the United Kingdom* (Chicago: University of Chicago, Press, 1982), based on tables 5.7 and 5.8.

[a]The cycle phases are from the National Bureau of Economic Research reference cycles. See U.S. Department of Commerce, *Business Conditions Digest* (February 1984), p. 104.

nonexistent tie to gold, wholesale prices quadrupled the rise under the gold standard.

Although the decline and rise in prices between the 1870s and World War I nearly canceled each other, that reversal is dismissed by gold opponents as accidental. Contemporaries, it is contended, could hardly have known that the price level following a period of decline would be restored by a period of price increase. Even if it were in part accidental, the tendency for declines or increases in prices to be reversed after a long lag is a basic characteristic of a commodity standard, as Cagan (1984) notes. Although the gold standard did not provide short-term or long-term price stability, it did provide long-term price predictability— the price level returned to its initial level.

Table 15.3   Level and Percentage Change of Wholesale Price Indexes for the
                United States, United Kingdom, Germany, and France, Selected
                Years, 1816–1913

	United States	United Kingdom	Germany	France
Year:		(1913 = 100)		
1816	150	147	94	143
1849	82	86	67	94
1873	137	130	114	122
1896	64	72	69	69
1913	100	100	100	100
Period:		Percentage Change		
1816–49	−45	−41	−29	−33
1849–73	67	51	70	30
1873–96	−53	−45	−40	−45
1896–1913	56	39	45	45

Sources: Richard N. Cooper; "The Gold Standard: Historical Facts and Future Prospects," *Brookings Papers on Economic Activity* 13 (1982), 9. Data for the United States and the United Kingdom are from George F. Warren and Frank A. Pearson, *Gold and Prices* (New York: John Wiley & Sons, Inc., 1955), pp. 87–88; data for Germany and France are from Brian R. Mitchell, *European Historical Statistics, 1750–1970* (New York: Columbia University Press, 1975), pp. 736–39.

The use of the wholesale price index to measure price trends has been criticized by Reynolds (1983), a proponent of the gold standard. He claims that because the wholesale price index was dominated by farm commodity prices, it did not reflect changes in the purchasing power of gold; the decline in 1894–96 was only an "apparent" deflation. This criticism is not supported by other information about prices. The implicit price deflator paralleled the wholesale price index, and accounts of the period leave no doubt that the price movements as measured by the wholesale price index were not merely statistical artifacts.

The concept of the gold standard as a guarantor of price stability was criticized by prominent contemporaries. What occasioned the criticism was precisely the long-term secular price movements—the rise in prices associated with the mid–nineteenth-century gold discoveries and the decline in prices that began in the 1870s under an expanding international gold standard. In his (1863) pamphlet, "A Serious Fall in the Value of Gold Ascertained, and Its Social Effects Set Forth" (1884), William Stanley Jevons estimated that between 1848 and 1860 the value of gold fell 9 percent. In 1875 he questioned the use of metallic standards of value in view of the extreme changes in their values and urged as a reform a tabular standard of value, to be based on an index number.

In 1887 Alfred Marshall (1925, pp. 189, 192) discussed "the evils of a fluctuating standard of value" and concluded that "the precious metals cannot afford a good standard of value." He dismissed bimetallism as flawed and proposed as remedies for the fluctuating standard of value either symmetallism or a tabular standard. With the reversal of the secular price movement after 1896, concern shifted to the inflationary fluctuation of the standard. In 1913 the remedy that Irving Fisher (1913) proposed was the "compensated dollar," raising the gold content of the dollar (lowering the price of gold) to offset inflation, lowering the gold content of the dollar (raising the price of gold) to offset deflation.

It has been suggested by Cagan (1984) that the problem created by the tendency of gold (or any commodity) to drift in terms of its purchasing power, due to changes in the relative demands for and supplies of gold (or any commodity), is not serious since it can be solved by periodically adjusting the gold content of the dollar in line with Fisher's proposal. If the price index rose 2 percent, for example, the gold content of the dollar would be increased 2 percent. The reduced price of gold would reduce the value of the gold reserve and discourage inflows both from domestic and foreign gold holdings. This would reduce the growth rate of the money supply. Downward pressure on prices would eventually stabilize the price index and a long-run drift of prices would be avoided.

Implementing this proposal might have several undesirable effects: speculative buying and selling of gold, international complications if prices moved idiosyncratically in one country, and overshooting because of lags in the response of prices to changes in the money stock. Despite these problems, the main contention of the proponents of this proposal is that since there is a solution to the problem of long-run drift, drift cannot be a serious objection to the gold standard.

However imperfect the record of price behavior under the gold standard, the main argument in its favor is that inflation rates were never as high and variable as in the post–World War II period. Moreover, because the gold standard promoted long-term domestic and international price predictability, it provided incentives to private market agents to make long-term contracts, which are vital for the efficient operation of a market economy. In the inflationary environment since the mid-1960s, markets have increasingly shunned long-term contracts with a consequent loss of economic efficiency.

15.2.2 Behavior of Short-run Real Output

Table 15.1, rows 3 and 4, shows that the average annual growth in real per capita income was higher from 1946 to 1979 in both the United States and the United Kingdom than from the 1870s to World War I. Also, this table shows that the variability (coefficient of variation of annual percentage changes in real per capita income) was smaller from 1946 to 1979 than in the earlier period. Table 15.2, columns 2 and 3, shows that real output in the United Kingdom rose more rapidly during deflation than during inflation in the period from the 1870s to World War I; in the United States real output grew more rapidly during periods of inflation than in periods of deflation. Again, as in the case of price behavior, conflicting assessments have been made of these data on output behavior. Opponents of the gold standard interpret this evidence as showing both lower annual average growth in real per capita income and greater instabilty of the growth rate under the gold standard than during the post–World War II period. They also cite higher unemployment rates under the gold standard than during the later period (table 15.1, row 5).

Proponents of the gold standard question the reliability of the estimates of national income and of unemployment in years past. Also, they cite the slowdown in real per capita income growth in 1979–82 as reversing the favorable comparison of the post–World War II period relative to gold standard years. In addition, they believe that the high unemployment in the 1890s may have resulted from the surge in immigration despite growing employment.

Banking panics were frequent under the gold standard, and sharp monetary contractions that produced output instability occurred in 1884, 1890, 1893, 1907, and 1914 (see table 15.4). The issue is whether greater stability of monetary growth in the post–World War II period (table 15.1, lines 6–7) is explainable by the shift from the gold standard. The improvement may instead reflect the establishment of the Federal Deposit Insurance Corporation, which stabilized money growth relative to growth of the monetary base (Barro 1984). If similar structural changes

Table 15.4   **A Comparison of U.S. Business Cycles in 1879–1897 (Period of Deflation) and 1897–1914 (Period of Inflation)**

Years	Duration in Months		Average Change in Economic Activity (percentage)	
	Expansions	Contractions	Expansions	Contractions
1879–1897	123 (56%)[a]	96 (44%)	21.7	−22.2
1897–1914	109 (52%)	101 (48%)	20.0	−18.7

Sources: Phillip Cagan, "The Report of the Gold Commission (1982)," in *Monetary and Fiscal Policies and Their Application,* Karl Brunner and Allan H. Meltzer, eds., Carnegie-Rochester Conference Series on Public Policy, vol. 20 (Amsterdam: North-Holland, 1984), pp. 247–67. Based on Geoffrey H. Moore, ed., *Business Cycle Indicators,* vol. I (Princeton: Princeton University Press for National Bureau of Economic Research, 1961), pp. 104, 671.

[a]Percentage of total period is in parentheses.

had been introduced under the gold standard, the low year-to-year variability in the world's monetary gold stock might have resulted in greater relative stability of money growth and of real variables.

The behavior of real output under the gold standard was not exemplary, but if allowance is made for factors unrelated to the gold standard that may account for the deficiencies, the record is respectable.

15.2.3 Monetary and Nonmonetary Foreign Shocks

Gold proponents extol the fixed exchange rates under the gold standard for the efficiencies resulting from a stable international money that integrated the world's commodity and capital markets.

To opponents of the gold standard, a disadvantage of these fixed exchange rates is that they transmitted monetary and nonmonetary disturbances to other countries. Before World War I, such disturbances typically were related to shifts in capital exports by Great Britain from one part of the world to another, for example, the shift from investment in U.S. railways to South American projects in the late 1880s or the significant decline in aggregate British capital exports to all countries in the 1890s. Also, business cycles tended to be synchronized under the gold standard. A boom in one country would lead to an increase in demand by its residents for goods and services in the rest of the world. The opposite happened when there was a recession. To preserve fixed exchange rates, gold flows required actions by monetary authorities or the banking system.

Changes in U.S. tariffs were a type of nonmonetary disturbance that was transmitted to the rest of the world. The Dingley Tariff of 1897 imposed the highest import duties in history to that date, and the Smoot-Hawley Tariff of 1930 raised tariff rates on imported commodities, notably agricultural imports, well above postwar levels. Since the United States was a relatively closed economy, keeping imports out of the United States injured its trading partners more than it did the United States. Smoot-Hawley not only reduced the exports of our trading partners and aggravated the decline in their terms of trade but also led to the eventual default of their foreign debts. The gold standard required short-term domestic adjustments to correct balance of payments disequilibria that arose from policies transmitted by fixed exchange rates from other countries.

An additional problem under the gold standard was that capital movements were sometimes uncontrollable and aggravated the underlying situation that generated the capital flows. Raising the discount rate at the beginning of the Great Depression did not stop the capital flight but intensified that flight and was interpreted as a signal that further flight would lead to devaluation. At the same time, the discount-rate rise served to heighten deflationary pressures on the domestic economy.

The gold standard was thus charged with having contributed to the instability of the world economic system after 1929.

Professional support of a paper standard to replace the gold standard gained ground in the 1930s. This support, however, was tempered by the belief that unrestrained, a paper standard would encourage beggar-thy-neighbor policies. The Bretton Woods system embodied the views and experience of the 1930s. It was widely believed that pegged exchange rates were essential to prevent chaos in international financial and trade transactions, but national economies should be free to restrict capital flows and to devalue the international value of their currency whenever necessary. This would make it possible to avoid deflating domestic prices when there was a balance of payments deficit in current account. Under the Bretton Woods system, the objectionable feature of pegged rates that forced governments to implement monetary changes that conflicted with goals of full employment or price stability would be removed, and at the same time stable conditions in foreign exchange markets would be assured.

15.2.4 Resource Costs Associated with Maintaining the Gold Standard

For prices to remain stable under a gold standard, the monetary gold stock must increase at the same rate as the demand for money rises in response to real income growth plus or minus any change in the ratio of GNP to the money stock (a change in velocity). A well-known estimate for the United States by Milton Friedman (1951b, p. 210) was that something over a 4 percent per year increase in the monetary gold stock would have been required to maintain price stability under a gold standard from 1900 to 1950. "Something over 4 percent" was derived as the sum of an average rate of growth of real income of 3 percent per year plus an average decline in velocity of 1 percent per year. With the money stock about half the size of national income, neglecting the change in velocity, about 1.5 percent of the national income would have to be devoted to the increase in monetary gold in order to maintain stable prices.

The world's monetary gold stock before 1929 did not grow at a constant 4 percent annual rate of increase. It grew by much smaller amounts (1 percent in the 1880s, 3 percent in the 1890s, 3.8 percent in the 1900s, 3 percent in the 1910s, 2 percent in the 1920s). In these decades, nongold money substitutes, however, increased at a rate far exceeding the rate of increase in monetary gold.

The resource cost of a gold standard has not played a significant role in current discussions (Cagan 1984). The issue has either been ignored or dismissed except by gold standard proponents. To them, high re-source costs are a positive value of the gold standard since gold is regarded as having intrinsic value. It is difficult to reconcile this argument with the historical trend toward increasing use of substitutes for gold in circulation and in reserves. The market appears to seek means to achieve lower resources costs.

15.2.5 Political Manipulation

Under a fully functioning gold standard, government intervention in the determination of the price level and the overall level of economic activity is limited. How closely did the historical gold standard approximate the ideal?

There were two kinds of intervention: in the gold mining industry and in the required short-term adjustments of prices and incomes to maintain fixed exchanges rates.

Since the demand for gold was perfectly elastic with respect to its nominal price under the historical gold standard, government actions to stimulate gold mining during periods of falling prices and low real output would be stabilizing (Rockoff 1984). It is possible to interpret the legalization of hydraulic mining in California in 1893 in this light. Farmers had earlier succeeded in closing down hydraulic mines because debris from the mines ruined farmland downstream. The act authorizing the restoration of such mining was intended to stimulate a depressed industry as well as to expand the money supply. Possibly the extension of the railroad network into gold mining areas in the United States and Mexico also represented government support for the industry. There is also evidence of government regulation of the gold mining industry by means of direct and indirect taxation, as in South Africa.

Government intervention in gold mining, however, was not necessarily stabilizing. Profits in gold mining decline when prices in general (costs) rise. Government aid to the industry at times of inflation would inhibit an equilibrating decline in gold output. Recent actions by the Soviet Union and South Africa apparently to take advantage of the strategic role of gold have disregarded possibly destabilizing consequences.

Political conflict has obviously played a part in affecting the world's gold supply. Gold production declined during the Latin American wars of independence in 1815 and in the twentieth century during the Mexican and Russian revolutions. However, most gold output under the historic gold standard came from politically stable parts of the world, so wars and revolutions did not significantly affect world production. For example, although the Boer War interrupted gold production in South Africa, the effect on the total supply of gold in the world was limited.

There is disagreement about the amount of intervention by monetary authorities before 1914 in the operation of the gold standard. Some scholars deny that intervention was possible or that authorities ever exercised such an option; they believe international arbitrage in the commodity and capital markets operated quickly to equalize prices and interest rates worldwide without the need or opportunity for intervention by monetary authorities. Others interpret selected actions by monetary authorities as discretionary and interventionist. However, the gold standard could function effectively even if the kind of response by monetary authorities required by the gold standard was delayed. Though there was leeway in reducing monetary growth when gold or capital movements were decreasing the domestic monetary base, ultimately, given fixed exchange rates, monetary growth had to be reduced. Also, though there was leeway in accelerating monetary growth, if such action was not ultimately taken, the system would be undermined by maldistribution of gold and unequal burdens of adjustment across countries.

In the post–World War I period, intervention was indeed exercised by the monetary authorities. For example, from 1923 to 1929 the Federal Reserve System offset inflows of gold by open market sales of government securities and outflows by open market purchases. Federal Reserve credit moved inversely with movements in the gold stock. France also did not permit gold inflows to affect its money stock and prices after returning to the gold standard in 1928 at a parity that undervalued the franc. Similarly, gold standard requirements were ignored by the Federal Reserve System in 1929–31, when gold inflows were not matched by an expansion of the U.S. money stock and the quantity of money was even permitted to decline. After 1934, both inflows and outflows of gold were not permitted to affect monetary growth and the performance of the economy. When gold reserve ratios applicable to Federal Reserve deposits and notes approached the minimum legal requirement, the minimum was lowered and eventually abolished. Gold became a symbol rather than an effective constraint on the monetary authorities.

The Bretton Woods system had no provision requiring the internal supply of a country's currency to be governed by its gold holdings, as was the case before 1914, nor was there a requirement that a country had to undergo deflation or inflation to balance its external accounts. Although fixed exchange rates carried over to the post–World War II world, they were fundamentally divorced from gold standard restraints. The monetary system was fully subject to political control.

15.3   Conditions for the Restoration of the Gold Standard

A variety of proposals exists to restore the use of gold in some form in monetary arrangements. Here we limit consideration to two proposals: that the United States should unilaterally return to a domestic gold standard or alternatively that the industrialized countries should collectively agree to establish an international gold standard.

To achieve long-run price stability, advocates of a restoration of a domestic gold standard recommend that the government establish a new official fixed price of gold (by defining the dollar by its weight in gold) and maintain this price by buying and selling gold freely. The government would also maintain a ratio, possibly with upper and lower bounds, of the stock of gold to the total amount of Federal Reserve notes in circulation (or the monetary base); the Federal Reserve System would be required to reduce its monetary liabilities consisting of Federal Reserve notes (or the monetary base) when the reserve ratio declined and expand them when it rose. Legal tender gold coins, denominated in dollars, would be issued to serve both as hand-to-hand currency and as legal reserves for commercial and other bank deposits. No restrictions would apply to ownership of gold coin or bullion. Nongold currency would be convertible into gold on demand.

Under the alternative proposal for an international gold standard, the United States would fix the price of gold and then maintain fixed exchange rates with other countries after they defined the amount of gold in their monetary unit. Such a standard could be achieved either by international agreement or by evolution—the United States could be the first to reinstitute the fixed price of gold and other countries would follow suit. International payments imbalances would be settled by gold flows or by flows of dollars or dollar assets convertible into gold at the fixed price. The monetary base and the money supply would vary with gold flows.

To implement a restoration of either a domestic or international gold standard in the United States requires the solution of a series of interlocking problems.

15.3.1 Choosing the Price of Gold

A basic problem is called the *reentry problem:* how to determine the right fixed price at which to resume the convertibility of the dollar into gold. In the past, when a country reinstituted the gold standard, there was an old official price that was once again restored or that served as the base for revaluation or devaluation. The last official price of an ounce of gold, $42.22, is so out of line with current market prices of gold that it provides no guidance. The risk involved in choosing the wrong price is great. An incorrect price might lead to a huge inflow of gold and inflation if it were too high, or a huge outflow and economic contraction if it were too low.

There are three principal proposals to solve the reentry problem:

1. Arthur Laffer (1980) proposes that an announcement be made by the government that at a date some months hence a dollar unit of the

monetary base of the Federal Reserve System would be linked to a fixed quantity of gold at that day's average transaction price in the London gold market. That would become the official price of gold in terms of dollars henceforth. If the price were too high or too low, the proposal recommends suspension of convertibility. The procedure would then be repeated, with a new announcement that convertibility would be reinstated at a future date at the price then prevailing in the market. Unfortunately, the proposal could result in instability in the price of gold as speculators bid up the price before the end of the first announcement period. Then if convertibility were suspended because the price was too high, speculators would unload gold and the price of gold would probably fall very low before the end of the second announcement period. Prospects for suspension of convertibility would be destabilizing and would probably undermine confidence in the system.

2. Another way to arrive at an equilibrium price of gold is to follow the approach of Robert Aliber (1982). He takes the price of $35 per ounce in 1961, a year when the United States had virtual price stability, as an initial equilibrium price. Assuming no other factors have affected the real price of gold, since 1961 the nominal price should have increased to the same extent as the U.S. price level plus a return equal to the real rate of interest. The U.S. consumer price index tripled between 1961 and 1980; hence for that reason alone the nominal price of gold should have been $105 in 1980. With the change in the world consumer price index, the price should have been $155.

Other factors have affected the real price of gold in addition to the increase in the general price level. If world real income elasticity of industrial demand for gold is assumed to be 1.85 (based on econometric results for 1950–80), and the increase in world income is approximately 83 percent (based on an index of world real GNP), the demand for gold would have increased 154 percent (83 percent of 185) from 1961 to 1980. During the same period, the total world gold stock increased 35 percent. Thus the excess demand for gold amounted to about 120 percent (154 − 35 = 119). The real price would also have increased about 120 percent if we assume that the price elasticity of industrial demand for gold is −1 (that is, the percentage increase in the quantity demanded is just equal to the percentage decrease in the price) and that the price elasticity of supply is close to zero. Based on this estimate, the equilibrium price of gold in 1980 would have been between $230 and $340 (105 × 2.2 = 231 and 155 × 2.2 = 341). This calculation assumes that factors affecting the net asset demand for gold are transitory and would vanish once price stability under a gold standard is restored.

Assume that a gold standard is restored with the price per ounce of gold set within the calculated range of $230 to $340. In the current free market, a monetary demand essentially does not exist. Under a reinstituted gold standard, a monetary demand for gold would recur because the government must satisfy all demands for gold at that price. Only after the monetary demand for gold had been accommodated would the nonmonetary demand for gold be satisfied. Thus econometric results for the asset demand relationship for 1969–80 of a 1 to 2 percent real income elasticity would no longer be relevant. The supply equation, however, would presumably be unaffected by a return to the gold standard. The question then resolves itself into the adequacy of the supply relative to the prospective monetary and nonmonetary demand for gold.

3. A third approach to the problem of the price at which to reinstitute the gold standard seizes on the opportunity the selection offers to adopt simultaneously a 100 percent gold reserve against the money supply. The price of an ounce of gold is to be determined, under this scheme, by dividing a money aggregate, such as the M1 measure of the U.S. money supply, by the number of ounces of gold held by the Treasury. One such calculation yielded a price of $1,500 per ounce. A variant of this approach divides the world dollar GNP by the world stock of monetary gold, yielding a price of $3,500 per ounce. Under either variant, a massive inflation would probably result. Because of the increase in the price of gold, production of gold would be very profitable, and the output of gold would be increased. This would increase the supply of money and the prices of goods and services until prices rose sufficiently to bring an end to the exceptional profits from gold mining.

15.3.2 Profits of Gold Devaluation

When the price of gold is raised, one dollar is equal to a smaller quantity of gold. This is called *gold devaluation*. All holders of gold profit when the price is raised. Assuming that the profits received by the Federal Reserve banks or the U.S. Treasury from a rise in the price of gold (gold devaluation) were sterilized in some fashion, would other central banks in the rest of the world also sterilize the gold devaluation? If not, the United States would be open to the transmission of inflation from foreign economies that chose to monetize the profits of revaluation. The reserve deposits of commercial banks at a foreign central bank that did not sterilize the gold devaluation would increase, and this would increase the money supply and prices in that country.

15.3.3 Pegging the Gold Price

Once a presumably correct price of gold had been determined, the principal central banks would then have to peg it. To prevent a rise in the price of gold, central banks would have to sell gold from existing stocks. To support the price, central banks would have to engage in open market purchases, with possible inflationary consequences. The pegging operation might conceivably be successful; responsibility for intervention in the gold market might be managed as it was under the Gold Pool of 1961 when the Bank of England acted as agent for the members of the pool. To be successful, all countries would have to support the effort, and there must be no changes in the exchange rate of any country. If a country changed its exchange rate, this would constitute a change in the price of gold in that country. Changes in the price of gold would encourage speculation in gold markets.

15.3.4 Linking the Domestic Money Supply to Gold Reserves

Once a pegged price of gold was established, a next step for reinstatement of the gold standard would be to link the domestic money supply to the country's gold reserves. The immediate problem would be to determine the conditions for convertibility of paper currency into gold.

Under a limited U.S. gold standard with convertibility between gold and the dollar available only to residents of the United States, the problem of how to enforce the limitation of convertibility appears intractable. Residents might be required to declare under oath that they were acting for themselves or for other residents, but not for foreigners, when demanding gold or supplying gold at the gold window. Alternatively, gold imports and exports might be embargoed. Opportunities for profitable violation would arise whenever there were discrepancies between the U.S. fixed price and the world market price of gold.

Restoring an international gold standard would involve restoring convertibility to dollar claims of foreign governments and central banks, not to mention private institutions and individuals in foreign countries. Such claims could affect the monetary base and thus the money supply in the United States, regardless of payments flows.

If we assume that convertibility can be arranged without creating serious problems, countries would then be required to give up the discretion that they currently exercise in determining the level and growth rate of their domestic money supplies; under a gold standard, they must accept the effects on their money supply that changing gold reserves would dictate. This is the key issue raised by the proposal to return to the gold standard.

15.3.5 Adequacy of Gold Output

It is arguable that if velocity were to increase at a rate of 3 to 4 percent per year, as was true of the ratio of GNP to the sum of currency plus demand deposits from 1960 to 1980, and real output growth were to remain on average at 3 percent per year, a constant money supply would be optimal. No increase in the monetary gold stock to support a growing demand for money balances would be needed since the upward trend in velocity would accomplish an equivalent expansion of the use of money in economic activity. Under such conditions, a return to the gold standard would involve no resource cost in mining gold for monetary use. An implicit stock resource cost, however, would still exist. Countries maintaining gold reserves could avoid this resource cost by selling their gold for nonmonetary use and putting the proceeds in earning assets.

If velocity failed to grow at a rate matching real income growth, returning to a gold standard would require a policy to assure adequate monetary growth. That would involve an adequate increase in the supply of gold. World gold reserves above and below ground may seem more than adequate when quoted in billions of ounces, but gold production responds sluggishly to changes in market price and since the 1960s has responded perversely. The trend of gold output, holding the real price of gold constant, has declined, generally 1 to 2 percent per year. Forecasts of gold output for the rest of the century in the market economies with known gold reserves are pessimistic. The inadequacy of the projected increase in supply might be offset by discovery of new mines or mining processes, changing patterns of industrial demand for gold, or shifts from current investment stocks. Reinstatement of the gold standard nevertheless poses a risk of long-run deflation of the economy. The political unrest in the United States during the deflation before 1896 was halted only by the upturn in prices when gold in ample quantities became available. Because of the change in social climate and the more activist role of government, a long and uncertain lag in the response of the gold supply to the changing demand for money would probably create greater problems today than in the nineteenth century.

The fact that the bulk of current world output of gold is from South Africa and the Soviet Union adds to the uncertainty of future gold supplies. Shocks in the gold market at home or abroad might also arise from changes in the demand for gold for investment and, on the supply side, from gold discoveries. Such shocks would make it difficult for one country alone to return to the gold standard because it would bear unilaterally the adjustment costs—inflation or deflation—imposed by the shocks.

15.3.6 Fixing Exchange Rates

The objective of a unilateral return to a gold standard by the United States would be to preserve flexible exchange rates and yet constrain domestic monetary growth by having a gold reserve requirement. Under such an arrangement, however, a shift from a foreign currency into gold by an American investor would impose the whole burden of adjustment on the exchange rate between the foreign currency and the dollar since the dollar price of gold would not change. A shift to gold from the pound, for example, would tend to lower the price of the pound in terms of dollars. If there were significant portfolio shifts by Americans between foreign currencies and gold, exchange rates would tend (all other things equal) to become more variable than they are under the present floating system. A major question is how such gold transactions (or possible purchases or sales of gold by other countries) would affect domestic monetary policy.

If all industrial countries returned to the gold standard, each country would adopt par rates of exchange for its currency relative to the dollar or other currencies. Under the pre-1914 gold standard, the official rate of exchange expressed an equilibrium that had gradually evolved among national price levels. At the present time, par rates of exchange would have to be arbitrarily chosen. The mistakes made in the choice of exchange rates when European countries resumed the gold standard in the 1920s and again under the Bretton Woods arrangements are not reassuring.

In 1925, for example, Great Britain returned to the gold standard at an unrealistically high gold price for the pound. In 1947, it repeated that mistake. In the first attempt, it struggled for six years in a vain attempt to deflate the economy to make the gold price viable in the face of gold outflows. The pound was then freed to float. In the second attempt, after two years the pound was devalued. In 1928, France returned to the gold standard at an unrealistically low gold price for the franc. Gold inflows into France (and U.S. sterilization of its gold inflow) destabilized the system.

A multilateral return to the gold standard would require international agreement and amendment of the International Monetary Fund rules. Yet there is no evidence that other countries are interested in reinstating the gold standard. The views they have expressed, in fact, are negative with respect to the desirability or feasibility of a return to the gold standard.

15.4 Summary

The historical gold standard before 1914 was a monetary regime in which there was a commitment by governments to buy and sell gold at a fixed price; there were fixed gold requirements for the issue of national currencies that were convertible into gold. Governments were restrained from issuing unlimited amounts of their national currencies by the obligation to pay gold on demand. Fixed exchange rates between different national currencies, each linked to gold, united countries in an international system.

These features of the gold standard were not set in concrete. They varied over space and time, particularly after 1914. Some central banks substituted for gold holdings interest-earning assets denominated in other national currencies and did not invariably respond promptly to increases or decreases in reserves by expanding or contracting the domestic money supply. Progressively, convertibility of nongold money into gold coin was withdrawn and replaced by convertibility into much heavier minimum weight units of gold bars, a right that was in turn withdrawn from domestic moneyholders and restricted to official institutions. The gold restraint on national money issues was ended with the abandonment of gold reserve requirements. The link was broken between alterations of a country's domestic money supply and deficits or surpluses in its international payments account. Fixed exchange rates under the Bretton Woods system evolved into adjustable pegged exchange rates. The system collapsed in the early 1970s, when confidence eroded in the gold convertibility of the U.S. dollar, the dominant reserve currency. Thereafter no significant role for gold remained in domestic and international monetary systems.

How satisfactory was the historical gold standard as a monetary regime? The key virtue that advocates claim for the gold standard is that it provided price stability. Yet price movements before World War I and during the interwar period were characterized by short-term variability and trends. The main benefit of the gold standard was long-term price predictability. Market participants undertook long-term contracts acting on the tendency for the price level ultimately to revert to its initial level. Although output growth was not smooth under the gold standard, cyclical changes may have reflected instability in money growth associated with the peculiarities of the U.S. banking system rather than with the character of the gold standard.

However, to the extent that cyclical changes occurred because of foreign monetary and nonmonetary disturbances that were transmitted by fixed exchange rates, fluctuations in output indeed were related to the monetary regime. Maintaining the gold standard also imposed resource costs on the economy. The stock of monetary gold could have been used for nonmonetary purposes and so deprived the economy of the yield from that alternative use. Furthermore, the costs of mining additions to the monetary gold stock to match increases in demand must be taken into account. Resource costs are acceptable to gold standard advocates but not to its detractors. Finally, although a fully functioning gold standard would be free of political intervention, increasingly governments and monetary authorities intervened to avoid the discipline the gold standard was designed to achieve.

Having given up the discipline of the gold standard, the world turned to a discretionary fiat money regime with managed flexible exchange rates. The record under the present regime has been one of high and variable inflation and interest rates, low productivity growth, and unstable foreign exchange rates, so the subject has been opened up of returning to the gold standard as a way of improving the record. Is it currently feasible to restore the gold standard regime? Serious technical problems would be encountered in an attempt to restore the gold standard. These include choosing the right price of gold, deciding what to do with the profits of gold devaluation, arranging for the pegging of the new gold price, linking the domestic money supply to gold reserves, assuring the adequacy of gold output, and fixing sustainable foreign exchange rates. These are technical issues. The solution to the difficulties each of these requirements poses would still not guarantee that the restored gold standard would provide a viable monetary regime. For that outcome, more than the solution of technical difficulties is required. Essentially, there must be precommitment by governments and their constituencies to the gold standard.

The gold standard can survive in a world in which countries allow gold to move freely; gold does not accumulate in any country, and gold does not drain away from any country without being allowed to exercise an expansionary or contractionary effect, respectively, on the level of prices; major disequilibria in price levels and financial conditions among countries are not endured. The forces that caused the breakdown of the Bretton Woods system were unleashed by actions of countries with a persistent deficit or surplus in their balance of payments. Those actions were taken to delay or resist changes in prices and costs expressed in national currencies. Under fixed exchange rates, convergence of national economic policies is essential for the system to be viable. The European Monetary System presupposes such behavior. Yet since 1979, when the system was established, member countries have repeatedly preferred to alter the relation between national price and cost levels by exchange-rate changes. This is not a good augury for restoration of an international gold standard.

Under the pre–World War I gold standard, governments in peacetime did not undertake expenditures that were financed by the printing press. (The gold standard collapsed when countries were engulfed by war or revolution.) In some gold standard countries, government was not divorced from business, and social insurance was accepted policy. Government participation in economic activity, however, was restrained by concern to preserve the integrity of the national currency and to maintain its domestic and external value. These concerns receded after 1929 as governments extended their activities to finance stabilization policies in response to interest groups wielding political influence.

The question then arises whether governments will reverse their course, returning to a more limited role, as in the pre–World War I era.[1] Of course, a limited role of the state is not in itself a guarantee of a viable international monetary system since in earlier eras international monetary affairs were often in disarray, even with limited states (Dam 1982, p. 38). The fundamental hurdle to a successful return to the gold standard is the resistance of political authorities and of modern democracies to precommitment and to forswearing of discretion. That hurdle is also a problem for a fiat money regime governed by a rule.[2]

The gold standard flourished before World War I possibly because of the special position of sterling and London. That position was threatened even before World War I when Paris and Berlin became important rivals of London. Thereafter, London's predominance was never reestablished. Under the Bretton Woods system, the dollar and the United States were in a special position. As the convertibility of the U.S. dollar into gold crumbled, the system collapsed. An important aspect of the successful operation of a gold-centered monetary system is an unshakable confidence that the reserve currency of a dominant country will always be converted into gold on demand. What country is willing to be the candidate for such a role in a future gold standard? The failure of the U.S. Gold Commission in 1982 to endorse a larger, if not central, role for gold in monetary arrangements bespeaks the absence of the necessary commitment to adherence to gold standard rules in the United States.

Notes

1. Schumpeter's (1950, p. 451) verdict, referring to post–World War I developments, was that "no return to prewar policies proved possible even where it was attempted. This has been strikingly verified by England's gold policy and its ultimate failure. In a world that was no longer the world of free enterprise, the gold standard—the naughty child that keeps on telling unpleasant truths—ceased to work."

2. Compare this conclusion with that in the recent study of the gold standard by Flood and Garber (1984, p. 90): "Even a well-designed commodity money scheme is a foolproof inflation guard only when the scheme's permanence is guaranteed. Permanence may possibly be guaranteed by an underlying political economy that abhors inflation, but merely enactment of a new ephemeral rule does not ensure permanence."

16 Lessons of the Gold Standard Era and the Bretton Woods System for the Prospects of an International Monetary System Constitution

The pre–World War I gold standard and the Bretton Woods system are the closest approximations to a constitution for the international monetary system that the world has experienced. By a constitution I mean established rules, whether or not a written instrument embodies the rules. No such written instrument embodied the gold standard rules. Individual countries determined at discrete times that their national interest would be served by assuming the obligation to live by the rules imposed by adherence to the gold standard. The international gold standard evolved gradually as an organic development during roughly three decades before World War I without any overall design coordinated by a supranational agency.

Rules were embodied in a formal constitution for Bretton Woods. Although membership in the Bretton Woods system was voluntary, there were compelling inducements, to be discussed at a later point, for countries to participate in a consciously planned arrangement for the international monetary system that was to last for a quarter of a century. The impersonality of rules without a formal constitution contrasts with the role of bureaucrats interpreting the rules of a formal constitution.

Currently two views have been advanced concerning the way to achieve a constitution for the international monetary system. One view is that stable international arrangements can only develop as individual countries adopt appropriate monetary and fiscal policies that stabilize their own economies. The alternative view is that rules governing international monetary behavior must first be agreed upon by key countries and that adherence to those rules by the contracting parties and additional countries will in turn produce national monetary stability. The gold standard appears to conform to the first view, the Bretton Woods system to the second view.

The pre–World War I gold standard and the Bretton Woods system are only two of many international monetary arrangements that were proposed over the past century and either implemented or not implemented. Earlier proposals include:

1) the attempt to institute a form of international bimetallism during the secular deflation of the last quarter of the nineteenth century;

2) the proposals the British delegation presented to the Genoa Conference that met between April 10 and May 19, 1922, with the participation of thirty-three governments, the United States present unofficially;

3) circumscribed monetary arrangements such as the Latin Monetary Union of 1866–78, the Scandinavian Monetary Union of 1873–1914, the Tripartite Monetary Agreement of September 25, 1936, among six participating countries, and the creation on March 13, 1979, of the European Monetary System—replacing the "snake," the European joint float.

It is instructive to review the past record. What light does it shed on the prospects for implementation of the crop of proposals that are currently advocated to reform international monetary arrangements? These range from variants of a gold standard to consolidating the money supplies of the United States, Japan, and West Germany (McKinnon 1984), to the creation of a common currency for all the industrial democracies with a common monetary policy and a joint Bank of Issue (Cooper 1984), to the issue of a new international monetary unit by private money producers (Hayek 1984).

To determine why certain international monetary arrangements were adopted and others not, section 16.1 assesses the costs and benefits of those international monetary proposals that were implemented in the past, and section 16.2 of those that were never implemented. Section 16.3 applies the lessons that emerge from the past to current proposals for international monetary reform. Which, if any, are likely to be adopted? Section 16.4 gives a summary that appraises the two views on how to achieve international monetary reform.

16.1   Why Were Certain International Monetary Proposals Implemented?

In the century before World War I the international monetary system was simply the aggregation of monetary preferences of individual countries. Most countries chose a bimetallic monetary system before they shifted to the gold standard during the final decades of the nineteenth century, although in some cases fiat money episodes punctuated their adherence to a commodity standard. Commodity standards imposed rules requiring each government to define its monetary unit as a specified weight of gold or silver, or of gold and silver, leaving banks free to produce money convertible into central bank money or government money issues that were in turn convertible into the standard metal or metals.

The chief benefit for countries that adopted the gold standard at the close of the nineteenth century was access to capital markets, centered in London, Paris, or Berlin. That benefit was invaluable for developing countries, which was the stage of economic maturity of most countries at the time. The chief cost, as viewed at the time, was the need to acquire a gold reserve. Except for Germany, which obtained it as the war indemnity from France in 1870–71, countries borrowed at home and abroad to get the funds with which to buy gold. The standing as a debtor the country achieved by embracing the gold standard far outweighed the interest cost of such borrowing.

With that choice made, governments did not have to coordinate policies they adopted explicitly, in pursuit of their national economic interest. Coordination was achieved by the maintenance of convertibility, which fixed exchange rates between national monetary units within narrow limits, with no external agency guiding the result. National price levels moved in close harmony. It was no myth of the gold standard world, as some latter-day critics describe it, that people, goods, capital, and money moved with reasonable freedom across national boundaries. International monetary arrangements reflected the independent choices of countries linked by market forces.

That world came to an end in World War I. I now turn to the cost–benefit reasons that account for the adoption of the Bretton Woods international monetary system.

The international monetary system that was designed at the Bretton Woods Conference in 1944 reflected professional views on the defects of the arrangements that had prevailed in the 1930s. The aim was to avoid in the postwar world protectionist trade policies, exchange controls, and competitive currency depreciation that had infected the pre–World War II period. The goals of the system created by the delegates to the conference accordingly were the removal of controls on trade and payments under a system of fixed exchange rates, with adjustment of parities limited to "fundamental disequilibrium" in the balance of payments. The lending facilities of the International Monetary Fund were to be available to supplement IMF members' gold and foreign exchange reserves in order to provide liquidity to overcome temporary balance of payments deficits.

The system was designed to operate with the United States as the reserve currency country. Other countries would peg their currencies to the dollar. Stable economic policy in the United States would assure stable economic policy worldwide.

The Bretton Woods system initially conferred many benefits and imposed few costs on IMF members. The attitude of the United States was paternalistic. Wartime destruction and disruption had left countries in Europe and Asia with limited productive capacity and swelled the immediate postwar demand for U.S. exports. To promote economic recovery in the rest of the world, the United States encouraged an outflow of dollars by official U.S. aid, military spending, and private investment. The United States did not protest discriminatory tariff and quota restrictions that Western European countries applied. As Europe and Japan recovered, the U.S. balance of payments turned negative. The United States resorted to capital controls and restrictions on domestic gold convertibility but still regarded the deficit in its balance of payments as a contribution to international liquidity. The overvaluation of the dollar and the decline in the competitiveness of U.S. exports came to be regarded as an intolerable cost only at a later stage in the evolution of the Bretton Woods system.

For the nonreserve currency countries, the benefits were the obverse of the costs from the perspective of the United States. A weakening of the U.S. balance of payments was acceptable to other countries as long as they desired surpluses in their balance of payments in order to add to their dollar reserves. Once assets denominated in dollars grew in excess of the demand for them by the rest of the world, nonreserve-currency countries insisted on action by the United States to right its balance of payments. They held that accelerating inflation in the United States from the mid-1960s on undermined price stability in their economies. The system collapsed amid growing doubts that the United States would be able to maintain external gold convertibility.

Although nonreserve-currency countries were unwilling as a group to adopt the inflationary policies the United States was pursuing, the dispersion of inflation rates among them enforced more frequent changes of exchange rates. Yet countries with strong exports and weak imports resisted revaluation of their currencies, and other countries with weak exports and excessive imports delayed changes in par values until a foreign exchange crisis developed. Parity changes were basically unilateral decisions. This latitude for national discretion initially made the system acceptable but ultimately eroded its vitality.

Having considered the two global approaches to an international monetary constitution, I now turn to the reasons more circumscribed collaborative monetary arrangements have been implemented. Here the limited objectives are usually spelled out, and the advantages to the participating countries are clear. The currency areas involved are optimum in the limited sense of the goals sought.

One example is the Latin Monetary Union, effective August 1866, that was formed by France, Belgium, Switzerland, and Italy, and subsequently gained additional members. The union achieved its limited objective to standardize the fineness of currencies of five-franc pieces that were then issued by each of the countries on the bimetallic standard. The coins in various other denominations as well were to circulate freely throughout the union. However, a fall in the price of silver led to the reduced coinage of standard silver pieces in 1874 and its discontinuation in 1878. Bimetallism's sun set, but the union was not formally dissolved until 1925.

A gold-based monetary union to replace the silver standard was created by Denmark and Sweden in May 1873 and joined by Norway in October 1875. The Scandinavian Monetary Union established a common currency unit, the Scandinavian krona. The monetary agreement among the three participants provided that gold coins, as well as common subsidiary silver and copper coins, were legal tender in all of them, no matter in which country the coins were minted. The three central banks accepted each other's notes at par and settled balances through a clearing system. It has been noted that no closer monetary cooperation was achieved by the union than would have been the case had each country independently adopted the gold standard (Jonung 1984). This conclusion holds if the only consideration is the fixed exchange rates the gold standard sets. However, the monetary union contributed the additional feature of eliminating national currency distinctions. The union was dissolved by World War I.

Another example of a limited international monetary constitution is the Tripartite Monetary Agreement of 1936. The initial French proposal including fixed parities and eventual return to gold convertibility was turned down by the United States and Britain as limiting their freedom to manage exchange rates. Instead, an agreement of lesser scope emerged. Following the French devaluation in September, the chief participants used their exchange stabilization funds to manage fluctuations in the exchange rates rather than permitting market forces to determine exchange rates. To prevent management at cross purposes, with risk of exchange losses from independent management tactics, the three initial participants—France, Great Britain, and the United States—signed a Gold Agreement on October 12–13. It provided that each country would cable the other two the price of its own currency at which it would buy and sell gold, and the three exchange funds would decide on a common currency to be bought for gold or sold and converted into gold at the specified price at the close of the business day. The quotations were valid for twenty-four hours, so there was no risk of exchange loss during the interval. Belgium, Holland, and Switzerland subsequently subscribed to the agreement. Not permitting market forces to determine exchange rates left intervention open to exchange losses. Agreement to convert currencies into gold without limit at an agreed but changeable price eliminated exchange risk for the authorities without sacrificing exchange rate flexibility. A student of the agreement concludes, "In 1936, each country's interests, as interpreted by the government in power, was virtually the sole criterion for public policy" (Clark 1977, p. 57). In particular, the French Popular Front found the agreement useful as a coverup for elusive economic recovery and the need for franc devaluation. For all the governments, the agreement provided "exchange market management with autonomy of national policy" (Eichengreen 1985, p. 171).

The final example of a limited international monetary constitution is the ongoing effort to achieve European monetary union. When convertibility of the dollar was formally suspended in August 1971, EEC countries sought to narrow fluctuations among their currencies vis-à-vis the devalued dollar, and again, after the Smithsonian Agreement of December 1971, against the dollar and other non-European currencies. The so-called snake was intended to achieve fixed exchange parities among the EEC countries by a convergence of economic and monetary policies. The snake was not viable because the national governments were not willing to yield to the union direct monetary autonomy and control over exchange rates changes or, alternatively, to achieve close convergence of economic policies. The snake was succeeded by the European Monetary System in March 1979. The center of the system is the European Currency Unit, a basket of nine currencies, issued by the European Monetary Cooperation Fund in an amount equal to a deposit of 20% of each participating country's gold and dollar reserves to be used in settlement of international debts. Two groups of countries are allied in the EMS—Denmark, Belgium, Germany, and the Netherlands in the low-inflation group, and France and Italy in the high-inflation group—with the remaining countries in between. Both sets of countries profit from the alliance. In the EMS no currency can reach the top of the permitted range without some other currency at the bottom, so Germany, for example, would not be forced to inflate because the DM was strong, without pressure on France, say, because the franc was weak to limit its inflation. The high-inflation countries periodically must devalue but limit the extent of their currency change by the revaluation of the low-inflation countries. Similarly, the extent of the revaluation by the low-inflation countries is limited, so the effect on their export growth is smaller than might otherwise be the case. It is a strength of the system that it imposes parity changes on both weak and strong currencies but does not free the weak ones from the need to adjust internal prices and costs.

A less sanguine view of the operation of the EMS has been advanced (Shafer 1985, pp. 362–65). The critic questions its contribution to macroeconomic stability and sees little indication that what he regards as the "fundamental agenda" behind the EMS—"momentum towards greater political and economic unification in the community"—has been fostered by the system. He finds little evidence that collaboration is growing and cites capital controls and intra-EEC trade restrictions as holding the system together. The presence of such influences on the willingness of member countries to remain within the EMS would not contradict the theme of self-interest of my approach.

International monetary arrangements are implemented, the preceding global examples suggest, only when national economic interests are not subordinated. Even U.S. paternalism at the genesis of the Bretton Woods arrangements was not fundamentally altruistic. The United States intended to establish world economic relations according to its lights for a brave new monetary order.

Limited international monetary agreements are adopted when the commitments by the participants are in their short-term interest. The proposals that were implemented did not encroach on the independence of participating governments to formulate domestic policies. Individual governments retained freedom of action, constrained only by the commitment each had made with respect to a well-defined external monetary arrangement.

16.2 Why Were Selected International Monetary Proposals Not Implemented?

One failed attempt to design a constitution for the international monetary system was the campaign to institute a form of international bimetallism during the last quarter of the nineteenth century. International conferences in 1878, 1881, and 1892, the Gold and Silver Commission in England in 1886, and a Silver Commission in Germany were organized by proponents of bimetallism who touted the system for its virtue, compared to a monometallic system, in reducing commodity price fluctuations. The attempt to induce nations to give up the gold standard for a bimetallic standard offered that benefit, but the proponents could not effectively counter the arguments of the opponents. The countries of the world that had recently demonetized silver in response to enormous increases in the supply of silver were unconvinced by the intellectual demonstration that substitution between monetary and nonmonetary uses of gold and silver would bring the market ratio of gold to silver into equilibrium with the mint ratio. Actual experience instead indicated that a bimetallic standard alternated between a monometallic gold standard and a monometallic silver standard. Advocates of bimetallism, who included silver mine owners, debtors, farmers, and politicians representing these constituents, were regarded as inflationists rather than as seeking a stable price level. Their influence in the United States was potent enough to increase the deflationary pressure on the economy. No other country was subject to equal agitation to force restoration of a monetary role to silver. In the event, the enormous increase in gold output that began in the 1890s ultimately produced a 40% increase in prices between 1896 and 1913 and doomed the bimetallism initiative.

The other failed attempt to restructure the international monetary system that merits comment was the set of proposals that the British delegation presented to the 1922 Genoa Conference of thirty-three governments (*Federal Reserve Bulletin,* 1922). The objective of the proposals was to restore the international monetary system that had existed before the war, with London at the center, and nonreserve center countries authorized to hold their reserves partly in foreign exchange. A global approach to the international monetary system was rejected by the conference, mainly owing to U.S. opposition expressed by Benjamin Strong, the key figure at the time in U.S. international as well as domestic monetary affairs. One of his objections centered on the conflict between the Genoa proposal that monetary policy should attempt to limit fluctuations in the purchasing power of gold and a central bank's duty to maintain domestic monetary stability. He noted that "the regulation of credit for the purpose of maintaining the purchasing power of gold or the parity of currencies would imply that the nation which had a discount on its currency should undertake, through its bank of issue, to bring about a contraction of credit and currency; or, as in the present case, the United States with its currency at a premium the world over, should undertake, through the Reserve Banks, to regulate credit policies as to expand credit and currency to a point where the value of our currency would decline and consequently other currencies would approach the value of ours" (quoted in Clarke 1967, p. 37). The proposal had "an ominous sound to" Strong. In addition, he wanted assurance that the conference would not place the United States in the position of "handing a blank check" to impoverished countries or their banks of issues or governments with disordered finances. It was clear to Strong that the policies of central banks would "be dictated by the interests of their respective governments rather than by purely monetary considerations" (Clarke 1967, p. 40). As a result, under Strong the United States dealt with monetary stabilization problems only on a country-by-country basis.

One conclusion that emerges from investigating the fate of defeated international monetary proposals is that they were judged not to serve national interests. The intellectual case supporting a proposal may not be convincing, as happened to the proposal to restore bimetallism. The existing deflationary experience would have had to be far worse and the resurgence of gold output much more delayed for bimetallism to have won the day. The Genoa proposals got nowhere because the United States perceived them as undermining its independence to formulate domestic policy.

As already noted, international proposals that have been implemented have not encroached on national sovereignty in fiscal and monetary matters. Bretton Woods mustered support, given the kinds of inducements to countries to participate that that system created, while imposing few restrictions on the freedom of action of member governments. Modest international monetary proposals that demand surrender of only limited sovereignty, as in the Latin Monetary Union and the Tripartite Agreement, are also workable. Whether the EMS is the harbinger of a far-reaching integration of national economic policies remains to be seen.

16.3 Prospects for Implementing Current International Monetary Proposals

Padoa Schioppa has contrasted the shift in the 1970s to emphasis on rules for domestic macroeconomic policy—targeting money aggregates rather than fine-tuning money growth, and pressure for a constitutional amendment to achieve a balanced fiscal budget—and the shift to emphasis on discretion for international macroeconomic policy, particularly the conduct of exchange rate policy (Padoa Schioppa 1985, pp. 332–34). In the international sphere, however, the shift is not unambiguously a movement from rules to discretion. Had a shift from fixed exchange rates to pure floating occurred, it would not have been accurately characterized as a movement from rules to discretion but rather from one rule to another. It is the shift to discretionary management of the floating system that is the true contrast with the tendencies to introduce rules in the domestic sphere.

Critics of the managed floating exchange rate system include both those who favor and those who do not favor rules to correct what are perceived to be imperfections of the system. The latter endorse more discretionary intervention than has been practiced. The indictment of the existing system is threefold: allegedly it has produced large and prolonged misalignments of exchange rates, the prime example being the dollar's rise from 1980 to 1985, which, it is claimed, has misdirected trade, direct investment, and international capital flows; has led to the accumulation of balance-of-payments deficits by the United States with unfortunate repercussions on the rest of the world; and fostered increased volatility of exchange rates under floating that has encouraged speculation, though research fails to show that it has hampered trade.

Those who argue for more discretionary intervention applaud the September meeting in New York at which officials representing the

Group of Five committed themselves to greater cooperation to drive down the external value of the dollar, as if market forces were not already producing that result. A favorite extension of the interventionist approach is the establishment by the authorities of target or reference zones that would define the range of parities that ought to exist (Williamson 1983; Roosa 1984). When nominal market exchange rates deviate from the target zones that are themselves alterable, the authorities would decide on intervention moves. I exclude this type of proposal from consideration here. Discretion has a large role in this approach. I limit my discussion to proposals that would impose some type of rule on international monetary behavior. Nor am I concerned with the validity of the criticisms of the managed floating exchange rate system as it exists. My interest is only in the probability that governments will agree to live by the rules that would be established by the sample of current proposals that I have chosen—by Hall, McKinnon, Cooper, and Hayek.

Various proposals exist (Laffer 1980; Paul and Lehrman 1982; Mundell 1981) to return to a conventional gold standard or Bretton Woods System—the dollar would be defined as a specified weight in gold, and the United States would announce the price at which it would buy and sell gold. Presumably an international gold standard could be created if other governments adopted one of these proposals along with the United States. The proposals differ mainly in the choice of the price of gold to be announced. The costs and benefits of adopting the gold standard that prevailed at the close of the nineteenth century are today irrelevant. Neither the costs of accumulating a gold reserve nor the benefits of capital market access dominate the debate about the merits of restoring the gold standard. The issues today center on the stability of the purchasing power of gold, the adequacy of additions to the monetary gold stock in the context of a duopoly of gold producers of uncertain political reliability, a host of technical difficulties in selecting the price of gold to be pegged, determining exchange rates, and linking domestic money supplies to gold. The ultimate hurdle, however, to a return to an enduring and effective gold standard is the resistance of political authorities and of modern democracies to precommitment and to forswearing of discretion. No country has expressed an interest in returning to a conventional gold standard.

Less conventional proposals for a gold standard also have been suggested. One would eliminate national monetary units. Each country would issue coins of different gold weights, and prices would be quoted in weights of gold. In Hall's proposal, national monetary units would continue to exist, but the promise to pay, say dollars, would be a promise to pay gold or something of equal purchasing power. Under this proposal presumably someone who borrowed $100 in 1896 would have been required to repay $140 in 1913.

Hall describes his variant as a free market gold standard but dismisses it as no less flawed than the conventional variants. Although systematic adjustment of the gold content of the dollar could remedy the instability of the purchasing power of gold, the necessity for that adjustment detracts from the virtue of the gold standard as an automatic stabilizer of the economy. Hall also faults the gold standard for creating an inefficient demand for precautionary balances in gold by banks and other financial institutions. He associates pressures to suspend the gold standard in the short run and abandon it in the long run with runs on reserves. An international monetary system clearly could be organized on gold standard lines if countries regarded the benefits of such a system as worth the loss of national monetary independence.

McKinnon envisions a new international monetary standard. During a transition period the United States, Germany, and Japan would each choose a domestic money supply growth rate to stabilize nominal exchange rates vis-à-vis the other two currencies. The three countries would then jointly target world money growth at a rate that would be determined by estimated future GNP growth, trend velocity, and the price trend of nontradables in each. Consequently, a weighted sum of the money stocks of the three countries would grow at a noninflationary rate. If exchange rates for a given country appreciated, that would indicate the need for that country to expand money growth, compensated for by a contraction of money growth in the other two countries. World money stock would grow at the predetermined target rate, and the world price level would be stabilized.

At a subsequent stage, the world would return to pegged exchange rates, and the weighted sum of the money stocks of the three countries would grow at a constant rate.

The basic notion of a collective monetary rule underlying the transition phase of McKinnon's proposal is hard to credit. It reflects his acceptance of two propositions for which empirical evidence is far from robust: inflation is the product of world, rather than domestic, money growth; and the demand for domestic currencies has been destabilized by shifts in demand for foreign currencies. Could the United States, Germany, and Japan—a trio without common cultural or political ties (unlike EMS constituents)—agree on a target rate for monetary growth of a combined aggregate? Would each country agree to alter its monetary growth rate to offset the opposite changes in money growth rates of the other two countries, particularly if the alteration conflicted with domestic goals? Since U.S. money growth would have the greatest weight, it would require a 1.3 percentage point decline in German and a 2.5 percentage point decline in Japanese money growth to offset a 1 percentage point increase in U.S. money growth. Policymakers are likely to respond as Benjamin Strong did to the Genoa proposals. They may find disturbing simulations of the second stage of the McKinnon rule based on equations for the internal macroeconomic structure of the United States, Japan, and the rest of the OECD region (McKibbin and Sachs 1986). The reported results include standard deviations of output, inflation, the current account, and the fiscal deficit, given shocks to aggregate demand, prices, velocity. Unless the shocks across countries were negatively correlated, the simulations indicate destabilizing effects for the countries whose money stocks decline in response to expansions elsewhere.

Nothing in the historical record or in current developments suggests that policymakers in individual countries will take actions in line with some blueprint that sacrifices apparent independent national interests. Currently the United States is exerting pressure on Germany and Japan to push for higher growth as a way of increasing their imports and shrinking their trade surpluses. Both countries are resisting for fear of a resurgence of inflation and loss of their export markets. If agreement is not at hand in this instance, would not rules that enforce such action be rejected?

McKinnon does not date the time for realizing the second stage of his proposal. Cooper dates his proposal as a possibility for 2010. He visualizes a world monetary union by that time with a single central bank, the rule governing member nations the simple one that they forswear independent monetary policy.

Cooper believes that one-world money is the answer to the inevitable decline in the role of the dollar as the U.S. role in the world shrinks. In addition, national monetary policies will be undermined as improvements in telecommunications speed capital and even goods flows across national borders. Fiscal policy would be set independently by each country in the new regime, but deficits would have to be financed, beyond a prorated share of the world central bank's open market purchases, by borrowing on the world capital market in the one common money. World monetary policy would be set by the board of governors of the world central bank—probably finance ministers—but would not be responsible to any one legislature.

Cooper advocates two transitional steps on the path to the one-money regime. One is to enhance the usefulness of SDRs so that they might eventually become the one-world money. The way to do so would be to give SDRs a role as a private transaction money. The other transitional step Cooper advocates is to enhance the importance of exchange rates in setting monetary policy. The target zone arrangement meets with his approval. In the one-money regime balance-of-payments adjustments would be no more difficult than regional adjustments in the United States at present.

The analogy to monetary union that the United States represents would apply to the world if, like the U.S. federal government, there were a comparable world federal government. In the absence of such a central political unit or any provision for the emergence of such a unit as a precondition for monetary unification, it is hard to conceive of the impetus for the creation of a one-money world. No one would dispute the argument that a single money issuer for the world, provided that it maintained a stable, noninflationary money stock, would improve the efficiency of money. Cooper's vision does not extend to the need for a rule binding the world monetary authority. Would a single monopolistic monetary authority possess the information to govern the provision of the appropriate supply of money without a rule? As Cooper himself acknowledges, unlike McKinnon, he is not concerned to assure behavior by monetary authorities either in a nonunified world or in his projected unified world to provide steady, noninflationary money growth. His main concern is to limit movements of real exchange rates in the existing world economy, and discretionary actions by authorities to achieve that goal are quite acceptable to him pending the arrival of his utopia.

Hayek's proposal to restructure the international monetary system is that governments refrain from issuing and regulating money. Instead, competitive private firms would be free to issue money convertible on demand in whatever amounts of competing moneys would buy, at market prices, collections of internationally traded commodities whose values they would pledge to stabilize. Each issuer would undertake to stabilize the value of his money unit in terms of the particular collection of raw materials defining the standard unit. Arbitrage would serve to eliminate any difference in value between the monetary unit and the standard unit. During a transition period, privately issued money units would be introduced as transferable deposits redeemable in government currency until such time as holders of money abandoned that currency and private issuers were allowed to provide currency.

In a world with competing private issuers, the money units would not be identified with particular geographical areas. In this world, as in Cooper's, balance-of-payments problems would not exist. Regional differences in distributions of relative and absolute quantities of money would arise but would not cause any more difficulties than do similar redistributions within a given territory.

In Hayek's scheme money producers find it in their self-interest to offer stable money with a sphere of circulation encompassing the globe. Different monetary units would circulate only so long as they successfully maintained their value in purchasing power. If a money depreciated, courts would determine the amount of some other currency to which holders were entitled and oblige the unsuccessful money producer to discharge his debt to them. Even if holders of a particular money were not compensated for the shrinkage of the value of their holdings, the damage would not extend to the rest of the community. Hayek thus sees the supply of money as market regulated.

Many questions arise in connection with Hayek's scheme. Wouldn't the information costs for agents confronting a variety of competitive moneys based on a variety of units of account be an overwhelming objection? It is not clear what fixes the price level in the competitive money order if money producers promise only to stabilize the price level of alternative collections of commodities. Money producers would presumably hold precautionary reserves, but Hayek does not say in what form. What assets would money producers hold as the counterpart of their liabilities that would enable them to meet their commitments? But these questions do not touch the essential objection to his scheme, which is, What would induce governments and their policymakers to give up a right that they have claimed and exercised for centuries? Hayek counts on the market to eliminate governments if their money issues cannot compete in providing purchasing power equal in stability to what he expects private money producers to provide. Since not even the catastrophe of hyperinflation has hitherto led governments to yield to the private sector their power to determine money growth, or the private sector to demand such abnegation by governments, in what circumstances would such a revolutionary change be conceivable?

The four proposals for restructuring the international monetary system based on the conventional or Hall gold standard rule, the McKinnon rule of a collective monetary growth rate, the Cooper rule of a one-money world subject to the decisions of a supranational board of governors, or a Hayek rule of no government involvement in money creation are all far removed from the kinds of historical rule-based global or limited international monetary agreements reviewed here. The proposals do not deal with the self-interest of policymakers and governments to preserve existing power over the choice of domestic objectives, or over which policies to adopt to achieve those objectives. If policymakers believed that monetary policy had no effect on employment in the short run or prices in the long run, then they might agree to give up control over monetary policy. But even then, they clearly believe that monetary policy has importance in managing interest and exchange rates. There is no indication currently or in the past, except possibly during the heyday of the Radcliffe view, that governments and their policymakers are not or have not been jealous of their power to determine national monetary policy.

Political unification would have to be well advanced for governments and their policymakers to be willing to yield monetary sovereignty to gold, a coalition of countries, a world central bank, or private money producers. The benefits are of the pie-in-the-sky genre. The costs are down-to-earth. I conclude that the prospects for implementing the current proposals for a rule-based international monetary system are dim.

16.4 How to Achieve an International Monetary System Constitution

The literature on international macropolicy coordination and cooperation has been growing apace. It is not primarily directed to the notion of a rule-based international monetary system. It rather embraces the view that international macropolicy coordination is justified on grounds analogous to market failures—the existence of public goods, externalities from the action of one government to the environment of another, monopoly power of certain governments—and lags in reaching equilibrium that could be shortened by coordination (Cooper 1985). The types of studies reported in the literature include the case for coordination given a positive—rather than negative—pattern of international transmission, game and control theoretical models of interaction among countries, dynamic versus static models of coordination. A sour view of these studies is that their results are either "rather obvious or rather obvious nonsense" (Marris 1985, p. 380).

Essentially the studies bear on the question whether cooperation between governments would result in higher real output and lower inflation worldwide than would independent policies of governments to achieve those goals. The authors of the studies tend to believe that representatives of the industrialized democracies working in tandem can nudge monetary growth rates, interest rates, exchange rates, and fiscal budgets in directions that would improve macroeconomic performance for all of them over what it would otherwise be. In their view, only the obduracy of short-sighted politicians prevents them from responding to the demands of their peers to reshape their national policies.

Even if the authors of those studies possessed the requisite information about the structure of markets in the different countries, knew the quantitative magnitude of key structural parameters, and could factor in differences in economic outlook of each country, there would still be a case against proceeding directly to coordinating policy. Divergent inflation rates, real growth rates, and unemployment rates among the industrialized democracies suggest that coordination would be facilitated if each country initially concentrated on narrowing the divergences.

In the EMS, it is true, divergences have not destroyed the monetary union, but there is otherwise greater homogeneity among the members and willingness to accept West Germany as the dominant country that characterizes the Summit group of countries.

The literature on coordination therefore leads me to the conclusion that the way to achieve an international monetary constitution is first to persuade individual countries to accept such a constitution. If persuasion fails on the individual basis, a constitution for the international monetary system is illusory.

Appendix: Publications of Anna J. Schwartz

1940 "British Share Prices, 1811–1850." *Review of Economics and Statistics* (May): 78–93.

1947 *Currency Held by the Public, the Banks, and the Treasury, Monthly, December 1917–December 1944*. Technical Paper 4. National Bureau of Economic Research. (With E. Oliver)

"The Beginning of Competitive Banking in Philadelphia, 1782–1809." *Journal of Political Economy* (October): 417–31.

"An Attempt at Synthesis in American Banking History." *Journal of Economic History* (November): 208–16.

1953 *The Growth and Fluctuation of the British Economy, 1790–1850.* 2 vols. Oxford: Clarendon Press. 2d ed.: Sussex, Harvester Press, 1975. (With A. D. Gayer and W. W. Rostow)

1960 "Gross Dividend and Interest Payments by Corporations at Selected Dates in the 19th Century." In *Trends in the American Economy in the Nineteenth Century.* Studies in Income and Wealth 24. New York: National Bureau of Economic Research. Pp. 407–45.

1963 "Money and Business Cycles." *Review of Economics and Statistics* supp. (February): 32–64. (With Milton Friedman)

A Monetary History of the United States, 1867–1960. Princeton, N.J.: Princeton University Press. (With Milton Friedman)

1969 "The Definition of Money." *Journal of Money, Credit, and Banking* (February): 1–4. (With Milton Friedman)

"Short-Term Targets of Some Foreign Central Banks." In K. Brunner, ed., *Targets and Indicators of Monetary Policy.* San

Francisco: Chandler. Pp. 27–65.

"Why Money Matters." *Lloyds Bank Review* (October): 1–16.

1970 *Monetary Statistics of the United States.* New York: Columbia University Press. (With Milton Friedman)

1972 "The Aliber, Dewald, and Gordon Papers: A Comment." *Journal of Money, Credit, and Banking* (November): 978–84.

1973 "Secular Price Change in Historical Perspective," pt. 2. *Journal of Money, Credit, and Banking* (February): 243–69.

1975 "How Feasible Is a Flexible Monetary Policy?" In R. T. Selden, ed., *Capitalism and Freedom, Problems and Prospects.* University Press of Virginia. Pp. 262–93. (With Phillip Cagan)

"Has the Growth of Money Substitutes Hindered Monetary Policy?" *Journal of Money, Credit, and Banking* (May): 137–59. (With Phillip Cagan)

"Monetary Trends in the United States and the United Kingdom, 1878–1970: Selected Findings." *Journal of Economic History* (March): 138–59.

1976 "Comments." In Jerome Stein, ed., *Conference on Monetarism.* The Haig: North-Holland. Pp. 43–49.

"Comments." In William L. Silber, ed., *Financial Innovation.* Lexington, Mass.: Heath. Pp. 45–51.

1977 "Issues in Monetary Economics and Their Impact on Research in Economic History." In R. E. Gallman, ed., *Research in Economic History.* Greenwich, Conn.: Johnson Associates. Pp. 81–129. (With M. D. Bordo)

"Policies for Research in Monetary Economics." In M. Perlman, ed., *The Organization and Retrieval of Economic Knowledge.* New York: Macmillan. Pp. 281–93.

1978 "Comments on Papers by Fourcans, Fratianni, and Korteweg." In K. Brunner and A. H. Meltzer, eds., *Carnegie-Rochester Conference Series on Public Policy.* Vol. 7. The Haig: North-Holland. Pp. 193–201.

1979 "The Banking Reforms of the 1930's." In Gary M. Walton, ed., *Regulatory Change in an Atmosphere of Crisis: The Current-day Implications of the Roosevelt years.* New York: Academic Press. Pp. 93–99.

"Clark Warburton: Pioneer Monetarist." *Journal of Monetary Economics* (January): 43–65. (With M. D. Bordo)

1980 "Money and Prices in the Nineteenth Century: An Old Debate Rejoined." *Journal of Economic History* (March): 61–67. (With M. D. Bordo)

1981 "Understanding 1929–1933." In Karl Brunner, ed., *The Great Depression Revisited*. Boston: Martinus Nyhoff. Pp. 5–48.

"A Century of British Market Interest Rates, 1974–1975." The Henry Thornton Lecture, The City University, Centre for Banking and International Finance, London. (January)

"Money and Prices in the Nineteenth Century: Was Thomas Tooke Right?" *Explorations in Economics History* 18:97–127. (With M. D. Bordo)

1982 "The Effect of the Term Structure of Interest Rates on the Demand for Money in the United States." *Journal of Political Economy* (February): 201–12. (With Milton Friedman)

"Interrelations Between the United States and the United Kingdom, 1873–1975." *Journal of International Money and Finance* 1 (April): 3–19. (With Milton Friedman)

Monetary Trends in the United States and the United Kingdom: Their Relation to Income, Prices, and Interest Rates, 1867–1975. Chicago: University of Chicago Press. (With Milton Friedman)

Report to the Congress of the Commission on the Role of Gold in the Domestic and International Monetary Systems. Vol. 1. (March).

"Reflections on the Gold Commission *Report*," pt. 1. *Journal of Money, Credit, and Banking* (November): 538–51.

1983 "International Debt, Insolvency, and Illiquidity." *Journal of Economic Affairs* (April). (With K. Brunner et al.)

"The Importance of Stable Money: Theory and Evidence." *Cato Journal* 3 (May): 63–82. (With M. D. Bordo)

The International Transmission of Inflation. Chicago: University of Chicago Press. (With M. R. Darby et al.)

1984 "Introduction." In M. D. Bordo and A. J. Schwartz, eds., *A Retrospective on the Classical Gold Standard, 1821–1931*. Chicago: University of Chicago Press.

"Comments on the paper by Alan Budd, Sean Holly, Andrew Longbottom and David Smith." In Brian Griffiths and Geoffrey E. Woods, eds., *Monetarism in the U.K.* New York: Macmillan. Pp. 129–36.

"International Lending and the Economic Environment." *Cato Journal* 4 (September).

"Currents and Countercurrents in Political and Economic Thought: A Comment on the Fellner Paper." In K. Brunner and A. H. Meltzer, eds., *Carnegie-Rochester Conference Series on Public Policy*. Vol. 21, pp. 253–57.

1986   "Real and Pseudo-Financial Crises." In Geoffrey E. Wood, ed., *Financial Crises and the World Banking System*. New York: Macmillan.

"Comments on 'The Open Economy: Implications for Monetary and Fiscal Policy' by Dornbusch and Fischer." In R. J. Gordon, ed., *Business Cycles*. Chicago: University of Chicago Press.

"Has Government Any Role in Money?" *Journal of Monetary Economics* (January): 37–62. (With Milton Friedman)

" 'The Failure of the Bank of the United States: A Reappraisal': A Reply." *Explorations in Economic History* (April): 199–204. (With Milton Friedman)

"Alternative Monetary Regimes: The Gold Standard." In C. Campbell and W. Dougan, eds., *Alternative Monetary Regimes*. Baltimore: Johns Hopkins University Press.

"Sustained Recovery and Trade Liberalization: How the Transfer Problem can be Solved." In H. Giersch, ed., *The International Debt Problem—Lessons for the Future*. Pp. 133–44. J. C. B. Mohr (Paul Siebeck) for Institute für Weltwirtschaft des Universität Kiel.

1987   "The Behavior of Money Stock under Interest Rate Control: Some Evidence for Canada." *Journal of Money, Credit, and Banking* 19, no. 2 (May). (With M. D. Bordo and E. U. Choudhri)

The Search for Stable Money: Essays on Monetary Reform. Edited by J. A. Dorn and A. J. Schwartz. Chicago: University of Chicago Press (forthcoming).

Book Reviews

English Bank Note Circulation 1694–1954, by Emmanuel Coppieters. Review, *Journal of Political Economy* (August 1956): 353–54.

The Origins of Hamilton's Fiscal Policies, by Donald F. Swanson. Review, *Kyklos* 18 (1964): fasc. 3, pp. 517–19.

The Greenback Era, by Irwin Unger. Review, *Political Science Quarterly* (December 1965): 625–27.

Commercial Bank Behavior and Economic Activity, by Stephen M. Goldfield. Review, *Kyklos* 20 (1967): fasc. 2, pp. 539–40.

Commercial Bank Cooperation: 1924–31, by Stephen V. O. Clarke. Review, *Kyklos* 21 (1968): fasc. 1, pp. 161–63.

Statistics of the British Economy, by F. M. M. Lewis. Review, *Kyklos* 21 (1968): fasc. 2, pp. 392–94.

The Jacksonian Economy, by Peter Temin. Review, *Journal of Economic History* (June 1970): 476–79.

Sovereignty and an Empty Purse: Banks and Politics in the Civil War, by Bray Hammond. Review, *Journal of Economic Literature* (March 1972): 74–75.

The International Economy and Monetary Movements in France, 1493–1725, by Frank C. Spooner. Review, *Journal of European Economic History* (Spring 1974): 252–55.

The Banking Crisis of 1933, by Susan E. Kennedy. Review, *Journal of Monetary Economics* (January 1975): 129–30.

The World in Depression, 1929–1939, by Charles P. Kindleberger. Review, *Journal of Political Economy* (February 1975): 231–37.

Domestic Monetary Management in Britain, 1919–38, by Susan Howson. Review, *Journal of European Economic History* 5, no. 2 (1976): 500–503.

Money and Empire, by Marcello de Cecco. Review, *Journal of Modern History* (September 1977): 490–91.

The Bank of England, 1891–1944, by R. S. Sayers. Review, *Journal of Economic Literature* (September 1977): 945–47.

The Golden Constant: The English and American Experience, 1560–1976, by Roy W. Jastram. Review, *Journal of Economic History* (September 1978): 784–86.

Growth and Fluctuations, 1870–1913, by W. Arthur Lewis. Review, *Journal of European Economic History* 8 (1979): 504–6.

The Collected Writings of John Maynard Keynes. Vol. 21. *Activities 1932–1939: World Crisis and Policies in Britain and America,* edited by Donald Moggridge. Review, *Journal of Economic Literature* (September 1983): 12–14.

The Floating Pound and the Sterling Area, 1931–1939, by Ian Drummond. Review, *Journal of European Economic History* 13 (1984): 668–70.

The Development and Operation of Monetary Policy, 1960–1983, a selection of material from the *Quarterly Bulletin* of the Bank of England. Review, *The Banker* (February 1985): 100–101.

The Gold Standard in Theory and History, edited by Barry Eichengreen. Review, *Journal of Economic History* (December 1986).

A Financial History of Western Europe, by Charles P. Kindleberger. Review, *Journal of European Economic History* (forthcoming).

World Inflation since 1950: An International Comparative Study, by A. J. Brown. Review, *Economic History Review* (forthcoming).

References

Abramovitz, M. 1977. "Determinants of Nominal-Income and Money-Stock Growth and the Level of the Balance of Payments: Two-Country Models under a Specie Standard." Stanford University. Unpublished.

————. N.D. "The Monetary Side of Long Swings in U.S. Economic Growth." Memorandum no. 146. Stanford University Center for Research in Economic Growth.

Acheson, K., and Chant, J. 1973. "Bureaucratic Theory and the Choice of Central Bank Goals: The Case of the Bank of Canada." *Journal of Money, Credit, and Banking* 5:637–55.

Aliber, Robert Z. 1982. "Inflationary Expectations and the Price of Gold." In Alberto Quadrio-Curzio, ed., *The Gold Problem: Economic Perspectives.* Oxford: Oxford University Press for the Banca Nationale del Lavoro and Nomisma. Pp. 151–61.

Argy, Victor. 1971. "Rules, Discretion in Monetary Management and Short-term Stability." *Journal of Money, Credit, and Banking* 3 (February): 102–22.

————. 1979. "Monetary Stabilization and the Stabilization of Output in Selected Industrial Countries." Banca Nazionale del Lavoro. *Quarterly Review* 129 (June): 155–66.

Arndt, H. W. 1944. *The Economic Lessons of the Nineteen-Thirties.* London: Oxford University Press.

Ashburton, Alexander B. 1808. *An Inquiry into the Causes and Consequences of the Orders in Council.* 2d ed. London: J. M. Richardson.

Ashton, T. S. 1959. *Economic Fluctuations in England, 1700–1800.* Oxford.

————. 1960. Review of *British Monetary Experiments, 1650–1710*, by J. K. Horsefield. *Economic History Review,* 2d series, no. 1, pp. 119–22.

Bagehot, W. 1873. *Lombard Street* (London: P. S. King).

Barber, C. L. 1978. "On the Origins of the Great Depression." *Southern Economic Journal* 44:432–56.

Barro, Robert J. 1977a. "Unanticipated Money Growth and Unemployment in the United States." *American Economic Review* 67 (March): 101–15.

————. 1977b. "Long-term Contracting, Sticky Prices, and Monetary Policy." *Journal of Monetary Economics* 3 (July): 305–16.

————. 1981. "The Equilibrium Approach to Business Cycles." In R. J. Barro, *Expectations and Business Cycles*. New York: Academic Press.

————. 1984. "Comment." In Michael D. Bordo and Anna J. Schwartz, eds., *A Retrospective on the Classical Gold Standard, 1821–1931*. Chicago: University of Chicago Press.

Barro, Robert J., and Rush, M. 1980. "Unanticipated Money and Economic Activity." In Stanley Fisher, ed., *Rational Expectations and Economic Policy*. Chicago: University of Chicago Press.

Barro, R. J., and Santomero, A. M. 1972. "Household Money Holdings and the Demand Deposit Rate." *Journal of Money, Credit, and Banking* 4 (May): 397–413.

Beckhart, B. H. 1932. *The New York Money Market*. Vol. 3. New York: Columbia University Press.

Beckhart, B. H.; Smith, J. G.; and Brown, W. A. 1932. *The New York Money Market*. Vol. 4. New York: Columbia University Press.

Begg, David K. H. 1982. *The Rational Expectations Revolution in Macroeconomics: Theories and Evidence*. Oxford: Philip Allan.

Bezanson, A. 1951. *Prices and Inflation during the American Revolution: Pennsylvania, 1770–1790*. Philadelphia.

Board of Governors of the Federal Reserve System. 1974. *Annual Report*.

————. 1976–80. *Federal Reserve Bulletin*.

Bonelli, F. 1982. "The 1907 Financial Crisis in Italy: A Peculiar Case of the Lender of Last Resort in Action." In C. P. Kindleberger, ed., *Financial Crises: Theory, History, Policy*. Cambridge: Cambridge University Press.

Bordo, Michael D. 1981. "The Classical Gold Standard: Some Lessons for Today." Federal Reserve Bank of St. Louis *Review* 63:1–17.

Brennan, G., and Buchanan, J. M. 1981. *Monopoly in Money and Inflation*. London: Institute of Economic Affairs.

Brenner, Y. S. 1961. "The Inflation of Prices in Early Sixteenth Century England." *Economic History Review*, 2d series (December): 225–39.

————. 1962. "The Inflation of Prices in England, 1551–1650." *Economic History Review*, 2d series (December): 266–84.

Brittain, B. 1981. "International Currency Substitution and the Apparent Instability of Velocity in Some Western European Economies and in the United States." *Journal of Money, Credit, and Banking* 13, no. 2 (May): 135–55.

Bronfenbrenner, Martin. 1961. "Statistical Tests of Rival Monetary Rules: Quarterly Data Supplement." *Journal of Political Economy* 69 (December): 621–15.

Brown, E. H. Phelps, and Browne, M. H. 1968. *A Century of Pay*. New York.

Brown, E. H. Phelps, and Hopkins, S. V. 1950. "The Course of Wage-Rates in Five Countries, 1860–1939." *Oxford Economic Papers* (June): 226–96.

————. 1956. "Seven Centuries of the Prices of Consumables, Compared with Builders' Wage-Rates." *Economica* (November): 296–314.

————. 1957. "Wage-Rates and Prices: Evidence for Population Pressure in the Sixteenth Century." *Economica* (November): 289–306.

Brown, E. H. Phelps, and Ozga, S. A. 1955. "Economic Growth and the Price Level." *Economic Journal* (March): 1–18.

Brown, M. L. 1927. "William Bingham, Eighteenth Century Magnate." *Pennsylvania Magazine of History and Biography*, 51:405.

Brunner, K. 1976. "Programmatic Suggestions for a 'Political Economy of Inflation,' in Comment." *Journal of Law and Economics* 18:851–57.

————. 1977. Contributions in Honor of Homer Jones. Foreward, *Journal of Monetary Economics* 2:431–32.

Brunner, Karl; Cukierman, Alex; and Meltzer, Allan H. 1980. "Stagflation, Persistent Unemployment and the Permanence of Economic Shocks." *Journal of Monetary Economics* 6 (October): 467–92.

Brunner, K., and Meltzer, A. H. 1968. "What Did We Learn from the Monetary Experience of the United States in the Great Depression?" *Canadian Journal of Economics* 1:334–48.

Bry, G. 1960. *Wages in Germany, 1871–1945*. New York: National Bureau of Economic Research.

Bryan, S. C. 1899. *History of State Banking in Maryland*. Baltimore: Johns Hopkins University Press.

Buchanan, J. M. 1984. "Can Policy Activism Succeed? A Public Choice Perspective." Paper presented at Federal Reserve Bank of St. Louis Conference on the Monetary versus Fiscal Policy Debate.

Buiter, Willem H. 1980. "Real Effects on Anticipated and Unanticipated Money: Some Problems of Estimation and Hypothesis Testing." *Working Paper* 601. National Bureau of Economic Research.

Bullock, C. J.; Williams, J. H.; and Tucker, R. S. 1919. "The Balance of Trade of the United States. *Review of Economic Statistics* 1.

Burger, A. E., and Balbach, A. 1972. "A Measurement of the Domestic Money Stock." Federal Reserve Bank of St. Louis Review 54 (May): 10–23.

Cagan, P. 1965. *Determinants and Effects of Changes in the Stock of Money, 1875–1960*. New York: Columbia University Press, for the National Bureau of Economic Research.

——. 1969. "Interest Rates and Bank Reserves—a Reinterpretation of the Statistical Association." In J. Guttentag and P. Cagan, eds., *Essays on Interest Rates*. Vol. 1. New York: National Bureau of Economic Research.

——. 1980. "Reflections on Rational Expectations." *Journal of Money, Credit, and Banking* 12 (November): 826–32.

——. 1984. "On the Report of the Gold Commission (1982)." *Carnegie Rochester Conference on Public Policy* 20 (Spring).

Cagan, P., and Schwartz, A. 1975. "Is a Flexible Monetary Policy Feasible." In R. T. Selden, ed., *Capitalism and Freedom: Problems and Prospects*. Charlottesville: University of Virginia.

Campbell, C., and Dougan, W., eds. 1986. *Alternative Monetary Regimes*. Baltimore: Johns Hopkins University Press.

Carron, A. S. 1982. "Financial Crises: Recent Experience in US and International Markets." *Brookings Papers on Economic Activity* 2:395–422.

Cassese, Anthony, and Lothian, James R. 1983. "The Timing of Monetary and Price Changes and the International Transmission of Inflation." In Michael R. Darby et al., *The International Transmission of Inflation*. Chicago: University of Chicago Press. Chap. 4.

Chandler, L. V. 1970. *American's Greatest Depression, 1919–1941*. New York: Harper & Row.

Choudhri, E., and Kochin, L. 1977. "International Transmission of Business Cycle Disturbances under Fixed and Flexible Exchange Rates: Some Evidence from the Great Depression." Carleton University and University of Washington. Unpublished.

Clapham, Sir. 1945. *The Bank of England: A History*. Vol 2. *1797–1914*. New York: Macmillan.

Clark, C. 1977. "The 'Golden' Age of the Great Economists: Keynes, Robbins et al. in 1930." *Encounter* 49:80–90.

Clarke, Stephen V. O. 1967. *Central Bank Cooperation, 1924–31*. Federal Reserve Bank of New York.

Clarke, Stephen V. O. 1977. *Exchange-Rate Stabilization in the Mid-1930s: Negotiating the Tripartite Agreement*. Princeton Studies in International Finance no. 41.

Conway, M. D. 1894–96. *The Writings of Thomas Paine*. Vol. 2. New York: Putnams.

Cook, Joel. 1903. *The Philadelphia National Bank: A Century's Record, 1803–1903 by a Stockholder*. Philadelphia: W. H. Fell.

Cooper, Richard N. 1982. "The Gold Standard: Historical Facts and Future Prospects. *Brookings Papers on Economic Activity* 13:1–45.

———. 1984. "Is There a Need for Reform." In *The International Monetary System Forty Years after Bretton Woods*. Conference Series no. 28. Federal Reserve Bank of Boston.

———. 1985. "Panel Discussion: The Prospects for International Economic Policy Coordination." In W. H. Buiter and R. C. Marston, eds., *International Economic Policy Coordination*. Cambridge: Cambridge University Press.

Currie, L. 1935. *The Supply and Control of Money in the United States*. Cambridge, Mass.: Harvard University Press.

Dam, Kenneth W. 1982. *The Rules of the Game*. Chicago: University of Chicago Press.

Darby, Michael R. 1972. "The Allocation of Transitory Income among Consumers' Assets." *American Economic Review* 62 (December): 928–41.

———. 1976. "Three-and-a-Half Million U.S. Employees Have Been Mislaid; or, an Explanation of Unemployment, 1934–41." *Journal of Political Economy* 84:1–16.

———. 1983. "Movements in Purchasing Power Parity: The Short and Long Runs." Chapter 15 in Michael R. Darby et al., *The International Transmission of Inflation*. Chicago: University of Chicago Press.

Darby, Michael R.; Lothian, James R.; Gandolfi, Arthur E.; Schwartz, Anna J.; and Stockman, Alan C. 1983. *The International Transmission of Inflation*. Chicago: University of Chicago Press.

Darby, Michael R., and Stockman, Alan C. 1983. "The Mark III International Transmission Model: Estimates." Chapter 6 in Michael R. Darby et al., *The International Transmission of Inflation*. Chicago: University of Chicago.

De Canio, Stephen J. 1979. "Rational Expectations and Learning from Experience." *Quarterly Journal of Economics* 93 (February): 47–57.

de Cecco, M. 1975. *Money and Empire: The International Gold Standard, 1890–1914*. Totowa, N.J.: Rowman and Littlefield.

de Vries, M. G. 1976. *The International Monetary Fund, 1966–71: The System Under Stress*. Vol. 1. Washington: International Monetary Fund.

Domett, H. W. 1884. *A History of the Bank of New York*. New York: G. P. Putnam's Sons.

Dornbusch, Rudiger. 1982. *"Testimony" Report to Congress on the Role of Gold in the Domestic and International Monetary Systems*. Vol. 2. Washington, D.C.: Secretary of the Treasury. Pp. 414–15.

Economic Report of the President. 1971. Washington, D.C.: Government Printing Office.

Eichengreen, Barry. 1985. "International Policy Coordination in Historical Perspective: A View from the Interwar Years." In W. H. Buiter and R. C. Marston, eds., *International Economic Policy Coordination*. Cambridge: Cambridge University Press.

Ely, B. 1985a. "No Deposit Reform, No Return to Stable Banking." *Wall Street Journal*, 5 March.

————. 1985b. "Yes—Private Sector Deposit Protection Is a Viable Alternative to Federal Deposit Insurance." Paper presented at Conference on Bank Structure and Competition, Chicago, Illinois, May 2–3.

Fand, D. 1967. "Some Implications of Money Supply Analysis." *American Economic Review* 57:380–400.

Federal Reserve Bulletin. 1922. "Genoa Financial Commission Report." Vol. 8:678–80.

Federal Reserve Bulletin. 1962. "Treasury and Federal Reserve Foreign Exchange Operations." (September): 1138–53.

Feldstein, M., and Eckstein, O. 1970. "The Fundamental Determinants of the Interest Rate." *Review of Economics and Statistics* 52 (November): 363–75.

Fischer, Stanley. 1977. "Long-Term Contracts, Rational Expectations and the Optimum Money Supply." *Journal of Political Economy* 85 (February): 191–205.

Fisher, I. 1911a. "Recent Changes in Price Levels and Their Causes." American Economic Association, *Papers and Proceedings* (April): 37–45.

————. 1911b. *The Purchasing Power of Money.* New York.

————. 1913. "A Compensated Dollar." *Quarterly Journal of Economics* 27 (February): 213–35, 385–97.

————. 1929. *The Purchasing Power of Money.* New ed. New York: Macmillan.

Flood, R. P., and Garber, P. M. 1982. "Bubbles, Runs, and Gold Monetization." In P. Wachtel, ed., *Crises in the Economic and Financial Structure.* Lexington, Mass.: Heath.

————. 1984. "Gold Monetization and Gold Discipline. *Journal of Political Economy* 92 (February): 90–107.

FRB-MIT-Penn Model Coding. July 13, 1971.

Frenkel, J. A. 1978. "International Reserves: Pegged Exchange Rates and Managed Float." In K. Brunner and A. H. Meltzer, eds., *Public Policies in Open Economies.* Vol. 9. Carnegie-Rochester Conference Series on Public Policy, and supplementary series to the *Journal of Monetary Economics,* 111–40.

Frenkel, J. A., and Mussa, M. L. 1980. "The Efficiency of Foreign Exchange Markets and Measures of Turbulence." *American Economic Review* 70 (May): 374–81.

————. 1981. "Monetary and Fiscal Policies in an Open Economy." *American Economic Review* 71 (May): 253–58.

Freund, W. C. 1962. "Financial Intermediaries and Federal Reserve Controls over the Business Cycle." *Quarterly Review of Economics and Business* 2 (February): 21–29.

Friedman, Milton. 1948. "A Monetary and Fiscal Framework for Economic Stability.' *American Economic Review* 38 (June): 245–64. Reprinted in *Essays in Positive Economics.* Chicago: University of Chicago Press, 1953.

————. 1951a. "The Effects of a Full Employment Policy on Economic Stability: A Formal Analysis." Reprinted in *Essays in Positive Economics.* Chicago: University of Chicago Press, 1953.

————. 1951b. "Commodity-Reserve Currency." *Journal of Political Economy* 59, 203–232. Reprinted in M. Friedman, *Essays in Positive Economics.* Chicago: University of Chicago Press, 1953. Pp. 204–50.

————. 1952. "Price, Income, and Monetary Changes in Three Wartime Periods." *American Economic Review* (May).

————. 1953. "Discussion of the Inflationary Gap." In *Essays in Positive Economics.* Chicago: University of Chicago Press. Pp. 251–62.

————. 1956. "The Quantity Theory of Money: A Restatement." In M. Friedman, ed., *Studies in the Quantity Theory of Money.* Chicago: University of Chicago Press. Pp. 3–21.

————. 1959. "The Demand for Money: Some Theoretical and Empirical Results." *Journal of Political Economy* 67:327–51.

————. 1960. *A Program for Monetary Stability.* New York: Fordham University Press.

————. 1961. "The Lag in the Effect of Monetary Policy." *Journal of Political Economy* 69:447–66.

————. 1968. "The Role of Monetary Policy." *American Economic Review* 58 (March): 1–17.

————. 1984a. "Financial Futures Markets and Tabular Standards." *Journal of Political Economy* 91:165–67.

————. 1984b. "Monetary Policy for the 1980s." In J. H. Moore, ed., *To Promote Prosperity: U.S. Domestic Policy in the Mid-1980s.* Stanford, Calif.: Hoover Institution Press. Pp. 40–54.

————. 1986. "The Resource Cost of Irredeemable Paper Money." *Journal of Political Economy* 94:642–47.

Friedman, M., and Mieselman, D. 1963. "The Relative Stability of Monetary Velocity and the Investment Multiplier in the United States, 1897–1958." In *Stabilization Policies.* Englewood Cliffs, N.J.: Prentice-Hall. Pp. 167–268.

Friedman, M., and Schwartz, A. J. 1963a. *A Monetary History of the United States, 1867–1960.* Princeton, N.J.: Princeton University Press, for the National Bureau of Economic Research.

————. 1963b. "Money and Business Cycles." *Review of Economics and Statistics* 45:32–78.

————. 1970. *Monetary Statistics of the United States.* New York: Columbia University Press, for the National Bureau of Economic Research.

Gandolfi, A. E. 1974. "Stability of the Demand for Money during the Great Contraction—1919–1922." *Journal of Political Economy* 82:969–83.

Gandolfi, A. E., and Lothian, J. R. 1976. "The Demand for Money from the Great Depression to the Present." *American Economic Review* 66:45–51.

————. 1977. "Review of 'Did Monetary Forces Cause the Great Depression?' " *Journal of Money, Credit, and Banking* 9:679–91.

————. 1983. "International Price Behavior and the Demand for Money." In Michael R. Darby et al., eds., *The International Transmission of Inflation.* Chicago: University of Chicago Press. Pp. 421–61.

Garvy. G. 1959. *Debits and Clearings Statistics and Their Use.* Rev. ed. Washington, D.C.: Board of Governors of the Federal Reserve System.

Girton, L. 1974. "SDR Creation and the Real-Bills Doctrine." *Southern Economic Journal* 43 (January): 57–61.

Glotz, G. 1926. *Ancient Greece at Work.* New York.

Goldfeld, S. M. 1973. "The Demand for Money Revisited." *Brookings Papers on Economic Activity,* no. 3:577–646.

Goodhart, C. A. E. 1985. "The Evolution of Central Banks: A Natural Development?" *Working Paper.* London: London School of Economics.

Gordon, Robert J. 1976a. "Recent Developments in the Theory of Inflation and Unemployment." *Journal of Monetary Economics* 2 (April): 185–219.

————. 1976b. "Can Econometric Policy Evaluation Be Salvaged?—a Comment." In Karl Brunner and Allan H. Meltzer, eds., *The Phillips Curve and Labor Markets.* Supplement 1 to the *Journal of Monetary Economics* 1:47–58.

―――. 1979. "New Evidence That Full Anticipated Monetary Changes Influence Real Output after All." *Working Paper* 361. New York: National Bureau of Economic Research.

Gordon, R. J., and Wilcox, J. A. 1981. "Monetarist Interpretations of the Great Depression: An Evaluation and Critique." In Karl Brunner, ed., *The Great Depression Revisited*. Boston: Martinus Nijhoff.

Gouge, W. M. 1833. *A Short History of Paper Money and Banking in the United States*. Philadelphia: T. W. Ustick.

Gould, J. D. 1964. "The Price Revolution Reconsidered." *Economic History Review*, 2d series (December): 249–66.

―――. 1970. *The Great Debasement*. Oxford.

Granger, C. W. J. 1969. "Investigating Causal Relations by Econometric Models and Cross-Spectral Methods." *Econometrica* 37:424–38.

Grauman, J. V. 1968. "Population Growth." In *International Encyclopedia of the Social Sciences* 12:376–81.

Gregory, T. E., ed. 1929. *Select Statutes, Documents and Reports Relating to British Banking, 1832–1928*. Vol. 2. *1847–1928*. London: Humphrey Milford.

Griffiths, B. 1983. "Banking in Crisis." *Policy Review* 25 (Summer): 515–38.

Gurley, J., and Shaw, E. 1955. "Financial Aspects of Economic Development." *American Economic Review* 45 (September): 515–38.

―――. 1956. "Financial Intermediaries and the Saving-Investment Process." *Journal of Finance* 11 (March): 257–76.

―――. 1957. "The Growth of Debt and Money in the United States 1800–1950: A Suggested Interpretation." *Review of Economics and Statistics* 39 (August): 250–62.

Haberler, G. 1976. *The World Economy, Money and the Great Depression, 1919–1939*. Washington, D.C.: American Enterprise Institute for Public Policy Research.

Hadsworth, J. T. 1910. *The First Bank of the United States*. Washington, D.C.: Government Printing Office.

Hall, Robert E. 1982. "Three Views of Friedman and Schwartz *Monetary Trends:* A Neo-Chicagoan View." *Journal of Economic Literature* 20 (December): 1551–56.

―――. 1984. "A Free Market Policy to Stabilize the Purchasing Power of the Dollar." In B. N. Siegel, ed., *Money in Crisis*. Cambridge: Ballinger.

Hamilton, E. J. 1929. "American Treasure and the Rise of Capitalism (1500–1700)." *Economica* (November): 338–57.

―――. 1934. *American Treasure and the Price Revolution in Spain, 1501–1650*. Cambridge, Mass.

―――. 1936a. *Money, Prices, and Wages in Valencia, Aragon, and Navarre, 1351–1500*. Cambridge, Mass.

―――. 1936b. "Prices and Wages at Paris Under John Law's System," *Quarterly Journal of Economics* (November): 42–70.

―――. 1947. *War and Prices in Spain, 1651–1800*. Cambridge, Mass.

Hamilton, J. C., ed. 1950–51. *The Works of Alexander Hamilton*. Vol. 1. New York: J. C. Trow. P. 417.

Hammarström, I. 1957. "The Price Revolution of the Sixteenth Century: Some Swedish Evidence." *Scandinavian Economic History Review*, pp. 118–54.

Hammond, B. 1957. *Banks and Politics in America*. Princeton, N.J.: Princeton University Press.

Hansen, A. H. 1939. "Economic Progress and Declining Population Growth." *American Economic Review* 29:1–15.

———. 1949. *Monetary Theory and Fiscal Policy*. New York: McGraw-Hill.

Harris, S. 1930. *The Assignats*. Cambridge, Mass.

Hayek, F. 1943. "A Commodity Reserve Currency." *Economic Journal* 53:176–84.

———. 1976. *Denationalization of Money, 1978*. 2d extended ed. London: Institute of Economic Affairs.

———. 1979. *Law, Legislation and Liberty, especially Vol. 3: The Political Order of A Free People*. Chicago: University of Chicago Press.

———. 1978. *Denationalization of Money*. London: Institute of Economic Affairs.

———. 1984. "The Future Monetary Unit of Value." In B. N. Siegel, ed., *Money in Crisis*. Cambridge: Ballinger.

Heichelheim, F. M. 1935. "New Light on Currency and Inflation in Hellenistic-Roman Times from Inscriptions and Papyri." *Economic History* (February): 1–11.

Hetzel, R. L. 1984. "The Formulation of Monetary Policy." *Working Paper*. Federal Reserve Bank of Richmond, Va.

Higonnet, R. P. 1957. "Bank Deposits in the United Kingdom, 1870–1914." *Quarterly Journal of Economics* (August): 329–67.

Hirsch, F. 1977. "The Bagehot Problem," *The Manchester School of Economic and Social Studies* 46 (September): 241–55.

Hoffmann, W. G. 1965. *Das Wachstum der Deutschen Wirtschaft seit der mitte des 19. Jahrhunderts*. Berlin.

Homer, S. A. 1963. *A History of Interest Rates*. New Brunswick, N.J.

Horsefield, J. K. 1960. *British Monetary Experiments, 1650–1710*. Cambridge, Mass.

Ibbotson, R. G., and R. A. Sinquefield. 1977. *Stocks, Bonds, Bills and Inflation: The Past (1926–1976) and the Future (1977–2000)*. Charlottesville, Va.: Financial Analysts Research Foundation.

International Monetary Fund, 1974–75. *Annual report*.

———. 1970–80. *Annual Report on Exchange Restrictions*.

Jacobs, A., and Richter, T. 1935. "Die Grosshandelspreise in Deutschland von 1792 bis 1934." Deutsche Institut für Wirtschaftsforschung, *Sonderhefte*, pp. 82–83.

Jevons, William Stanley. [1863] 1884. "A Serious Fall in the Value of Gold Ascertained and Its Social Effects Set Forth." In H. S. Foxwell, ed., *Investigations in Currency and Finance*. London: Macmillan.

———. [1875] 1884. "An Ideally Perfect System of Currency." In H. S. Foxwell, ed., *Investigations in Currency and Finance*. London: Macmillan.

———. 1890. *Money and the Mechanism of Exchange*. 9th ed. London: Kegan Paul.

Johnson, H. G. 1972. "The Bretton Woods System, Key Currencies, and the Dollar Crisis of 1971." *Three Banks Review*, 17–18 June.

———. 1978. "Commentaries: Evaluation of the Performance of the Floating Exchange Rate Regime." In J. S. Dreyer, G. Haberler, and T. D. Willet, eds., *Exchange Rate Flexibility*. Washington: American Enterprise Institute for Public Policy Research.

Jones, A. H. M. 1953. "Inflation under the Roman Empire." *Economy History Review*, 2d series, no. 3:293–318.

Jonung, Lars. 1984. "Swedish Experience under the Classical Gold Standard, 1873–1914." In M. D. Bordo and A. J. Schwartz, eds., *A Retrospective on the Classical Gold Standard, 1821–1931*. Chicago: University of Chicago Press.

Juster, F. T., and Wachtel, P. 1972. "Inflation and the Consumer." *Brookings Papers on Economic Activity*, no. 1:71–121.

Kane, E. J. 1980. "Politics and Fed Policymaking." *Journal of Monetary Economics* 6:199–211.

Kessell, R. A., and Alchian, A. A. 1960. "The Meaning and Validity of the Inflation-induced Lag of Wages behind Prices." *American Economic Review* (March): 43–66.

Kindleberger, C. P. 1973. *The World in Depression, 1929–1939*. Berkeley, Calif.: University of California Press.

———. 1978. *Manias, Panics, and Crashes: A History of Financial Crises*. New York: Basic Books.

King, R. G. 1983. "On the Economics of Private Money." *Journal of Monetary Economics* 12:127–58.

Klein, B. 1973. "Income Velocity, Interest Rates, and the Money Supply Multiplier." *Journal of Money, Credit, and Banking* 5 (May): 656–68.

———. 1974. "The Competitive Supply of Money." *Journal of Money, Credit, and Banking* 6:423–53.

———. 1976. "Competing Monies." *Journal of Money, Credit, and Banking* 8:513–19.

Kochin, Levis. 1980. "Judging Monetary Policy." *Proceedings of Second West Coast Academic/Federal Reserve Economic Research Seminar*. Federal Reserve Bank of San Francisco.

Kuznets, Simon. 1946. *National Product since 1869*. New York: National Bureau of Economic Research.

———. 1961. *Capital in the American Economy: Its Formation and Financing*. Princeton, N.J.: Princeton University Press, for the National Bureau of Economic Research.

Kydland, Finn E., and Prescott, Edward C. 1977. "Rules Rather Than Discretion: The Inconsistency of Optimal Plans." *Journal of Political Economy* 85 (June): 473–91.

Laffer, Arthur B. 1980. *Reinstatement of the Dollar: The Blueprint*. Rolling Hills Estates, Calif.: A. B. Laffer Associates (29 February).

Laidler, D. 1966. "The Rate of Interest and the Demand for Money—Some Empirical Evidence." *Journal of Political Economy* 74 (December): 543–55.

Laskar, Daniel M. 1983. "Short-Run Independence of Monetary Policy under a Pegged Exchange-Rates System: An Econometric Approach." In Michael R. Darby et al., *The International Transmission of Inflation*. Chicago: University of Chicago Press. Chap. 11.

Latané, H. A. 1960. "Income Velocity and Interest Rates: A Pragmatic Approach." *Review of Economics and Statistics* 42 (November): 448.

Laughlin, J. L. 1909. "Gold and Prices, 1890–1907." *Journal of Political Economy* (May): 257–71.

———. 1911. "Causes of the Changes in Prices since 1896." American Economic Association, *Papers and Proceedings* (April): 26–36.

League of Nations. 1929–33. *Monthly Bulletin of Statistics*. Vols. 10–14. Geneva: Financial and Economic Intelligence Service.

———. 1932. *Report of the Gold Delegation of the Financial Committee*. Document C.502, M. 343. Geneva.

Letwin, W. 1964. *The Origin of Scientific Economics*. Garden City, New York.

Lewis, Lawrence, Jr. 1882. *A History of the Bank of North America*. Philadelphia: Lippincott.

Librarie de Recueil Sirey. 1937. *L'Evolution de l'economie francaise, 1910–1937*. Paris.

Lindert, P. 1981. "Comments on 'Understanding 1929–1933.' " In Karl Brunner, ed., *The Great Depression Revisited*. Boston: Martinus Nijhoff. Pp. 125–33.

Lipsey, R. G. 1960b. "Does Money Always Depreciate." *Lloyds Bank Review* (October): 1–13.

———. 1960b. "The Relation between Unemployment and the Rate of Change of Money Wage Rates in the United Kingdom, 1862–1957: A Further Analysis." *Economica* 27 (February): 1–31.

Louis, P. 1927. *Ancient Rome at Work*. London.

Lucas, Robert E. 1973. "Some International Evidence on Output-Inflation Tradeoffs." *American Economic Review* 68 (June): 326–34.

———. 1975. "An Equilibrium Model of the Business Cycle." *Journal of Political Economy* 83 (December): 1113–44.

———. 1976. "Econometric Policy Evaluation: A Critique." In Karl Brunner and Allan H. Meltzer, eds., *The Phillips Curve and Labor Markets*. Supplement 1 to the *Journal of Monetary Economics* 1:19–46.

McCallum, Bennett T. 1980. "Rational Expectations and Macroeconomics Stabilization Policy." *Journal of Money, Credit, and Banking* 12 (November): 716–46.

———. 1985. "Bank Deregulation, Accounting Systems of Exchange and the Unit of Account: A Critical Review." *Working Paper*. New York: National Bureau of Economic Research.

McCulloch, J. H. 1980. "The Ban on Indexed Bonds, 1973–77." *American Economic Review* 70:1018–21.

McKibbin, Warwick J., and Sachs, Jeffrey D. 1986. "Coordination of Monetary and Fiscal Policies in the OECD." *Working Paper* no. 1800. New York: National Bureau of Economic Research.

McKinnon, Ronald I. 1984. *An International Standard for Monetary Stabilization*. Washington, D.C.: Institute for International Economics.

Maclay, E. S., ed. 1927. *The Journal of Maclay*. New York: A. & C. Boni.

Maisel, S. J. 1973. *Managing the Dollar*. New York: Norton.

Major, R., ed. 1979. *Britain's Trade and Exchange Rate Policy*. NIESR Economic Policy Papers 3. London: Heinemann Educational Books.

Marris, Stephen. 1984. *Managing the World Economy: Will We Ever Learn?* Essays in International Finance no. 155. Princeton University.

Marshall, Alfred. [1887] 1925. *Memorials of Alfred Marshall*. Edited by A. C. Pigou. London: Macmillan.

Martino, A. 1984. "Toward Monetary Stability?" *Economia Internazionale* 37:1–16.

Marty, A. L. 1961. "Gurley and Shaw on Money in a Theory of Finance." *Journal of Political Economy* 69:56–62.

März, E. 1982. "Comment." In C. P. Kindleberger, ed., *Financial Crises, Theory, History, Policy*. Cambridge: Cambridge University Press.

Mattingly, H. 1928. *Roman Coins from the Earliest Times to the Fall of the Western Empire*. London.

Mayer, T. 1978a. "Consumption in the Great Depression." *Journal of Political Economy* 86:139–45.

———. 1978b. "Money and the Great Depression: Some Reflections on Professor Temin's Recent Book." *Explorations in Economic History* 14:137–45.

Meltzer, A. 1963. "The Demand for Money: The Evidence from the Time Series." *Journal of Political Economy* 71 (June): 219–46.

———. 1976. "Monetary and Other Explanations of the Start of the Great Depression." *Journal of Monetary Economics* 2:455–71.

Michell, H. 1946. "The Impact of Sudden Accessions of Treasure Upon Prices and Real Wages." *Canadian Journal of Economics* (February): 1–9.

———. 1947. "The Edict of Diocletian: A Study of Price Fixing in the Roman Empire." *Canadian Journal of Economics* (February): 1–12.

Miles, M. A. 1978. "A Theory of Systematic Fragility." In E. I. Altman and A. W. Sametz, eds., *Financial Crises: Institutions and Markets in a Fragile Financial Environment.* New York: Wiley.

Minsky, H. P. 1977. "A Theory of Systematic Fragility." In E. I. Altman and A. W. Sametz, eds., *Financial Crises: Institutions and Markets in a Fragile Financial Environment.* Wiley: New York.

Mints, L. W. 1945. *A History of Banking Theory.* Chicago: University of Chicago Press.

Mishkin, Frederic S. 1982. "Does Anticipated Monetary Policy Matter? An Econometric Investigation." *Journal of Political Economy* 90, no. 1 (February): 22–51.

Miskimin, H. A. 1963. *Money, Prices, and Foreign Exchange in the Fourteenth Century France.* New Haven, Conn.

Mitchell, B. R., and Deane P. 1962. *Abstract of British Historical Statistics.* Cambridge.

Mitchell, W. C. 1977. *Business Cycles: The Problem and Its Setting.* New York: National Bureau of Economic Research.

Mitchell, W. C., and Burns, A. F. 1936. *Production during the American Business Cycle 1917–1933.* Bulletin 61. New York: National Bureau of Economic Research.

Modigliani, Franco. 1964. "Some Empirical Tests of Monetary Management and Rules versus Discretion." *Journal of Political Economy* 72 (June): 211–45.

———. 1977. "The Monetarist Controversy or, Should We Forsake Stabilization Policies?" *American Economic Review* 67 (March): 1–19.

Moggridge, D. E. 1982. "Policy in the Crises of 1920 and 1929." In C. P. Kindleberger, ed., *Financial Crises: Theory, History, Policy.* Cambridge: Cambridge University Press.

Moore, G. H., ed. 1961. *Business Cycle Indicators.* 2 vols. Princeton, N.J.: Princeton University Press, for the National Bureau of Economic Research.

Mundell, Robert. 1981. "Gold Would Serve into the 21st Century." *Wall Street Journal,* 30 September.

Muth, John F. 1961. "Rational Expectations and the Theory of Price Movements." *Econometrica* 29 (July): 315–35.

Nef, J. U. 1941. "Silver Production in Central Europe, 1450–1618." *Journal of Political Economy* (August): 575–91.

Noyes, A. D. 1894. "The Banks and the Panic of 1893." *Political Science Quarterly* 9 (March): 12–30.

Padoa Schioppa, Tommaso. 1985. "Policy Cooperation and EMS Experience." In W. H. Buiter and R. C. Marston, eds., *International Economic Policy Coordination.* Cambridge: Cambridge University Press.

Patinkin, D. 1969. "The Chicago Tradition, the Quantity Theory, and Friedman." *Journal of Money, Credit, and Banking* 1:46–70.

Paul, Ron, and Lehrman, Lewis. 1982. *The Case for Gold.* Washington, D.C.: Cato Institute.

Phelps, Edmund S. 1968. "Money-Wage Dynamics and Labor Market Equilibrium." *Journal of Political Economy* 78 (July/August): 678–711.

Phillips, A. W. 1958. "The Relation between Unemployment and the Rate of Change of Money Wage Rates in the United Kingdom, 1861–1957." *Econometrica* 25 (November): 283–99.

Poole, William. 1975. "The Relationship of Monetary Decelerations to Business Cycle peaks: Another Look at the Evidence." *Journal of Finance* 30 (June): 697–712.

Presnell, L. S. 1968. "Gold Reserves, Banking Reserves, and the Baring Crisis of 1890." In C. R. Whittlesey, and J. S. G. Wilson, eds., *Essays in Money and Banking in Honour of R. S. Sayers*. Oxford: Clarendon Press.

———. 1982. "The Sterling System and Financial Crises before 1914." In C. P. Kindleberger, ed., *Financial Crises: Theory, History, Policy*. Cambridge: Cambridge University Press.

Radcliffe Committee on the Working of the Monetary System. 1959. *Report* 827, London: H.M.S.O. (August).

Rasche, R. H. 1972. "A Review of Empirical Studies of the Money Supply Mechanism." Federal Reserve Bank of St. Louis *Review* 54:11–19.

Report to the Congress of the Commission on the Role of Gold in the Domestic and International Monetary Systems. 1982. Washington, D.C.: Government Printing Office.

Reynolds, Alan. 1983. "Why Gold" *Cato Journal* 3, no. 1:211–38.

Robertson, D. H. 1940. "Mr. Keynes and the Rate of Interest." In *Essays in Monetary Theory*. London: King. (Lecture given in 1939.)

Rockoff, H. 1975. *The Free Banking Era: A Re-examination*. New York: Arno Press.

———. 1984. Some Evidence on the Real Price of Gold, Its Cost of Production, and Commodity Prices." In M. D. Bordo and A. J. Schwartz, eds., *A Retrospective on the Classical Gold Standard, 1821–1931*. Chicago: University of Chicago Press.

Rolnick, A. J., and Weber, W. E. 1983. "New Evidence on the Free Banking Era." *American Economic Review* 73:1080–91.

Roosa, Robert V. 1984. "Exchange Rate Arrangements in the Eighties." In *The International Monetary System Forty Years after Bretton Woods*. Federal Reserve Bank of Boston Conference series no. 28.

Samuelson, Paul A., and Solow, Robert M. 1960. "Analytical Aspects of Anti-Inflation Policy." *American Economic Review* 50 (May): 177–94.

Sargent, Thomas. 1976. "The Observational Equivalence of Natural and Unnatural Rate Theories of Macroeconomics." *Journal of Political Economy* 84 (August): 631–40.

Sargent, Thomas, and Wallace, Neil. 1975. "Rational Expectations and the Theory of Economic Policy." *Journal of Monetary Economics* 2 (April): 169–83.

Sayers, R. S. 1976. *The Bank of England, 1891–1944*. 3 Vols. Cambridge: Cambridge University Press.

Schumpeter, J. A. 1939. *Business Cycles*. 2 Vols. New York: McGraw-Hill.

———. 1950. "The March into Socialism." *American Economic Review* 40 (May):446–56.

Selden, R. T. 1963. *Trends and Cycles in the Commercial Paper Market*. Occasional Paper 85. New York: National Bureau of Economic Research.

Seybert, Adam. 1818. *Statistical Annals*. Philadelphia: T. Dobson & Son.

Shafer, Jeffrey R. 1985. "Comment." In W. H. Buiter and R. C. Marston, eds., *International Economic Policy Coordination*. Cambridge: Cambridge University Press.

Shapiro, S. 1943. "The Distribution of Deposits and Currency in the United States 1919–39." *Journal of the American Statistical Association* 38 (December): 438–44; table 3, p. 442.

Simons, H. 1936. "Rules versus Authorities in Monetary Policy." *Journal of Political Economy* 44 (February): 1–30.

Sims, C. A. 1972. "Money and Causality." *American Economic Review* 62:540–51.

———. 1977a. "Comment on D. A. Pierce, Relationships—and the Lack Thereof—between Economic Time Series, with Special Reference to Money and Interest Rates." *Journal of American Statistical Association* 72:23–24.

———. 1977b. "Macroeconomics and Reality." Discussion Paper 77-91. Department of Economics, University of Minnesota.

Sirkin, G. 1975. "The Stock Market of 1929 Revisited. A Note." *Business History Review* 49:223–31.

Smith, V. C. 1936. *The Rationale of Central Banking*. London: P. S. King.

Smith, W. L. 1956. "On the Effectiveness of Monetary Policy." *American Economic Review* 46 (September): 588–606.

Sparks, Jared, ed. 1830. *The Diplomatic Correspondence of the American Revolution*. Vol. 12. Boston: Nathan Hall and Gray & Bowen.

Sprague, O. M. W. 1910. *History of Crises under the National Banking System*. National Monetary Commission. Washington, D.C.: Government Printing Office.

Sprinkel, B. W. 1981. Testimony at Hearings of the Joint Economic Committee, 4 May.

Spufford, B. 1965. "Coinage and Currency." In Postan, Rich, and Miller, eds., *The Cambridge Economic History of Europe*. Vol. 3. Cambridge. Pp. 576–602.

Summers, L. H. 1983. "Comments." *Journal of Monetary Economics* 12:159–162.

Sumner, W. G. 1892. *The Financier and the Finances of the American Revolution*. Vol. 1. New York: Dodd, Mead. Pp. 99–100.

Svenilson, I. 1954. *Growth and Stagnation in the European Economy*. Geneva: United Nations, Economic Commission for Europe.

Taylor, D. 1982. "Official Intervention in the Foreign Exchange Market or Bet against the Central Bank. *Journal of Political Economy* 90 (April): 356–68.

Teigen, R. L. 1964. "Demand and Supply Functions for Money in the United States: Some Structural Estimates." *Econometrica* 32 (October): 476–509.

Temin, P. 1976. Did Monetary Forces Cause the Great Depression? New York: W. W. Norton.

———. 1981. "Notes on the Causes of the Great Depression." In Karl Brunner, ed., *The Great Depressions Revisited*. Boston: Martinus Nijhoff.

Thornton, Henry. 1802. *An Enquiry into the Nature and Effects of the Paper Credit of Great Britain*. London: Library of Economics Reprints, 1939.

Tobin, J. 1947. "Liquidity Preference and Monetary Policy." *Review of Economics and Statistics* 29:124–31.

Triffin, R. 1984. "The European Monetary System: Tombstone or Cornerstone?" In *The International Monetary System: Forty Years after Bretton Woods*. Conference Series no. 28:127–173. Federal Reserve Bank of Boston.

Troy, L. 1965. *Trade Union Membership, 1897–1962*. New York: National Bureau of Economic Research, O.P. 92.

Tucker, D. P. 1966. "Dynamic Income Adjustment to Money-Supply Changes." *American Economic Review* 56 (June): 433–49.

U.S. Board of Governors of the Federal Reserve System. 1943. *Banking and Monetary Statistics*. Washington, D.C.: National Capital Press.

U.S. Bureau of the Census. 1949. *Historical Statistics of the United States*. Washington, D.C.: Government Printing Office.

———. 1960. *Historical Statistics of the United States, Colonial Times to 1957*. Washington, D.C. Pp. 773–74.

————. 1975. *Historical Statistics of the United States, Colonial Times to 1970.* Bicentennial ed., pt. 1, Washington, D.C.: Government Printing Office.

U.S. Treasury Department. 1929–31. *Statement of the Public Debt.* Washington, D.C.: Government Printing Office. (Monthly)

————. 1979. *Annual Report of the Secretary of the Treasury on the Finances.*

Vaubel, R. 1984. "The Government's Money Monopoly: Externalities or Natural Monopoly?" *Kylos* 37:27–58.

Warburton, Clark. 1935. "Plateaus of Prosperity and Plains of Depressions." In *Economic Essays in Honor of Wesley Clair Mitchell.* New York: Columbia University Press. Pp. 497–516.

————. 1943. "Measuring the Inflationary Gap." *American Economic Review* 33:365–69.

————. 1944. "Monetary Expansion and the Inflationary Gap." *American Economic Review* 34:303–27.

————. 1945a. "Business Stability and Regulation of the Cost of Money." *American Journal of Economics and Sociology* 4:175–84. Reprinted in Warburton 1966, chap. 13.

————. 1945b. "Monetary Theory, Full Production, and the Great Depression." *Econometrica* 13:114–128. Reprinted in Warburton 1966, chap. 5.

————. 1945c. "The Monetary Theory of Deficit Spending." *Review of Economics and Statistics* 27:74–84. Reprinted in Warburton 1966, chap. 11.

————. 1945d. "The Volume of Money and the Price Level between the World Wars." *Journal of Political Economy* 53:150–163. Reprinted in Warburton 1966, chap. 6.

————. 1945e. "Messrs. Mosak and Salant on Wartime Inflation: A Rejoinder." *American Economic Review* 35:658–60.

————. 1945f. "Normal Production, Income, and Employment 1945 to 1965." *Southern Economic Journal* 11:219–45.

————. 1946a. "Quantity and Frequency of Use of Money in the United States, 1919–45." *Journal of Political Economy* 54:436–50. Reprinted in Warburton 1966, chap. 7.

————. 1946b. "Monetary Control under the Federal Reserve Act." *Political Science Quarterly* 61:503–34. Reprinted in Warburton 1966, chap. 14.

————. 1946c. "The Misplaced Emphasis in Contemporary Business-Fluctuations Theory." *Journal of Business* 19:199–220. Reprinted in Warburton 1966, chap. 4.

————. 1947. "Volume of Savings, Quantity of Money, and Business Instability." *Journal of Political Economy* 55:222–33. Reprinted in Warburton 1966, chap. 10.

————. 1948a. "Hansen and Fellner on Full Employment Policies." *American Economic Review* 38:128–34.

————. 1948b. "Monetary Velocity and Monetary Policy." *Review of Economics and Statistics* 30:304–14. Reprinted in Warburton 1966, chap. 12.

————. 1948c. "Bank Reserves and Business Fluctuations." *Journal of the American Statistical Association* 43:547–58. Reprinted in Warburton 1966, chap. 2.

————. 1949a. "The Secular Trend in Monetary Velocity." *Quarterly Journal of Economics* 63:68–91. Reprinted in Warburton 1966, chap. 9.

————. 1949b. "[Abstract of] Index Numbers of the Elements of the Equation of Exchange." *Econometrica* 17:176. Complete paper in Warburton 1966, chap. 8.

————. 1949c. "Monetary Policy and Business Forecasting, Parts I–II." *Journal of Business* 22:71–82, 178–87.

————. 1950a. "Monetary Velocity and the Rate of Interest." *Review of Economics and Statistics* 32:256–57. Reprinted in Warburton 1966, chap. 12.

————. 1950b. "The Monetary Disequilibrium Hypothesis." *American Journal of Economics and Sociology* 10:1–11. Reprinted in Warburton 1966, chap. 1.

————. 1950c. "Co-ordination of Monetary, Bank Supervisory and Loan Agencies of the Federal Government." *Journal of Finance* 5:148–69. Reprinted in Warburton 1966, chap. 19.

————. 1950d. "The Theory of Turning Points in Business Fluctuations." *Quarterly Journal of Economics* 64:525–49. Reprinted in Warburton 1966, chap. 3.

————. 1951. "An Additional Note on Co-ordination of Banking and Monetary Agencies." *Journal of Finance* 6:338–40.

————. 1952a. "Has Bank Supervision Been in Conflict with Monetary Policy?" *Review of Economics and Statistics* 34:69–74. Reprinted in Warburton 1966, chap. 15.

————. 1952b. "How Much Variation in the Quantity of Money Is Needed?" *Southern Economic Journal* 18:495–509. Reprinted in Warburton 1966, chap. 17.

————. 1952c. "Monetary Difficulties and the Structure of the Monetary System." *Journal of Finance* 7:523–45. Reprinted in Warburton 1966, chap. 16.

————. 1953a. "Rules and Implements for Monetary Policy." *Journal of Finance* 8:1–21. Reprinted in Warburton 1966, chap. 18.

————. 1953b. "Elementary Algebra and the Equation of Exchange." *American Economic Review* 43:358–61.

————. 1958. "Variations in Economic Growth and Banking Developments in the United States from 1835 to 1885. *Journal of Economic History* 18:283–97.

————. 1962. "Monetary Disturbances and Business Fluctuations in Two Centuries of American History." In L. Yeager, ed., *In Search of a Monetary Constitution*. Cambridge, Mass.: Harvard University Press.

————. 1963. "Nonmember Banks and the Effectiveness of Monetary Policy." In *Monetary Management*. Englewood Cliffs, N.J.: Prentice-Hall. Pp. 317–59.

————. 1964a. *Four Statements, in: The Federal Reserve System after Fifty Years*. (Hearings before the Subcommittee on Domestic Finance of the Committee on Banking and Currency, House of Representatives. 88th Cong., 2d sess.) Vol. 2. Washington, D.C.: Government Printing Office. Pp. 1314–42.

————. 1964b. *Prohibition of Interest on Demand Deposits, in: The Federal Reserve System after Fifty Years*. (Hearings before the Subcommittee on Domestic Finance of the Committee on Banking and Currency, House of Representatives, 88th Cong., 2d sess.) Vol. 3. Washington, D.C.: Government Printing Office. Pp. 2080–92.

————. 1965. "Maintaining Prosperity and Achieving Its Equitable Distribution." *Southern Economic Journal* 31:289–97.

————. 1966. "Depression, Inflation and Monetary Policy." *Selected Papers 1945–54*. Baltimore: Johns Hopkins University Press.

————. 1967. "Cyclical Fluctuations in the Stock of Money and in Effective Demand 1919–1965." *Southern Journal of Business* 2:140–45.

————. 1971. "Variability of the Lag in the Effect of Monetary Policy." *Western Economic Journal* 9:115–33.

————. 1975. "Taxonomy and the Effects of Fiscal and Monetary Policy." *Economic Inquiry* 13:432–36.

Warren, G. F., and Pearson, F. A. 1932. *Wholesale Prices for 213 Years, 1720–1932*. Ithaca, New York.

———. 1933. *Prices*. New York.

Webster, Pelatiah. 1791. *Political Essays*. Philadelphia: Joseph Crukshank.

Weiss, R. W. 1970. "The Issue of Paper Money in the American Colonies, 1720–1774." *Journal of Economic History* (December): 778–79.

West, L. C. 1951. "The Coinage of Diocletian and the Edict on Prices." In P. R. Coleman-Norton, ed., *Studies in Roman Economic and Social History in Honor of Allan Chester Johnson*. Princeton, N.J.: Princeton University Press.

Wetterau, J. O. "Letters from Two Business Men to Alexander Hamilton on Federal Fiscal Policy, November 1789." *Journal of Economic and Business History* 3:681–82.

White, L. H. 1984a. "Competitive Payment Systems and the Unit of Account." *American Economic Review* 74:699–712.

———. 1984b. *Free Banking in Britain: Theory, Experience, and Debate, 1800–1845*. New York: Cambridge University Press.

White, R. W. R. 1979. "Money and the New Zealand Economy." Reserve Bank of New Zealand *Bulletin,* 371–74.

Wicker, E. R. 1966. *Federal Reserve Monetary Policy, 1917–1933*. New York: Random House.

Williamson, John. 1983. *The Exchange Rate System.* Washington, D.C.: Institute for International Economics.

Wilson, James. 1785. *Considerations on the Bank of North America*. Philadelphia: Hall & Sellers.

Winslow, Stephen N. 1864. *Biographies of Successful Philadelphia Merchants*. Philadelphia: James K. Simon.

Wojnilower, A. M. 1980. "The Central Role of Credit Crunches in Recent Financial History. *Brookings Papers on Economic Activity,* no. 2:277–326.

Wonnacott, P. 1965. *The Canadian Dollar, 1948–1962*. Toronto: University of Toronto Press.

Wood, G. E. 1983. Review of *Crises in the Economic and Financial Structure. The Banker* (June):266–67.

Zwick, B. 1971. "The Adjustment of the Economy to Monetary Changes." *Journal of Political Economy* 79 (January/February): 77–97.

Index